2017 EDITION

Greenberg's GUIDES®

LIONEL® TRAINS

POCKET PRICE GUIDE

Edited by Roger Carp

KALMBACH BOOKS

WAUKESHA, WI

Kalmbach Books
21027 Crossroads Circle
Waukesha, Wisconsin 53186
www.Kalmbach.com/Books

Published in 2016
Thirty-seventh Edition

Manufactured in the United States of America

ISBN: 978-1-62700-287-5

Front cover photo: 2368 B&O F3 Diesel A Unit,
model courtesy Joe Algozzini

Back cover photo: 3666 Minuteman Boxcar with cannon

We constantly strive to improve Greenberg's Pocket Price Guides. If
you find missing items or detect misinformation, please contact us.
Send your comments, new information, or corrections via e-mail
to books@kalmbach.com or by mail to Lionel Pocket Price Guide
Editor at the address above.

Library of Congress Control Number: 2016931490

CONTENTS

INTRODUCTION

Whether you are a longtime Lionel enthusiast or a
newcomer to the toy train hobby, this guide contains the
information you need to identify and evaluate thousands of
items made by Lionel since 1901. Most of all, you'll have at
your fingertips the most up-to-date prices for locomotives,
freight cars, passenger cars, stations, tunnels, signals, track
sections, transformers, and other items.

What is listed

Almost every Lionel O gauge toy train produced over the
years is listed in the pages that follow.

This edition of the *Lionel Pocket Price Guide* contains
information about new additions to the product line as
described in Lionel catalogs, press releases, and other
sources. Any additions that Lionel makes to its line after
this book is printed will be reported in the next edition.

In addition, the *Lionel Pocket Price Guide* provides
information about items associated with Lionel yet
not mentioned in its catalogs. These uncataloged or
promotional items include unique models and specially
decorated locomotives and cars that Lionel produces for
national and regional toy train collecting and operating
groups, museums, local railroad clubs, and other
customers.

When to consult this guide

Many readers of the *Lionel Pocket Price Guide* use it after
the fact. They already have some trains and accessories
and now want to identify and evaluate those items.
Maybe someone lucked upon a bridge at a garage sale
and wants to know whether it's a 300 Hellgate or a
314 deck girder type. Somebody else needs to provide his
or her insurance agent with a complete list of O gauge
locomotives that includes their conditions and current
values. This guide contains the information needed to
identify that bridge as well as determining present values
for that engine roster.

In addition, the *Lionel Pocket Price Guide* can help
you think about what to acquire in the future. That's
really when the fun begins! You just have to spend some
time considering how you want to approach the hobby.
Collect, operate, or both? Prewar, postwar, or modern?
Particular types of locomotives or cars? Favorite railroads?
Promotional items?

Once you have a general idea of how to enjoy this
hobby, you can make informed decisions about which
trains you want.

UNDERSTANDING VALUES

The values presented here are an averaged reflection of prices for items bought and sold across the country during the year prior to the publication of this edition. These values are offered as guidelines and should be viewed as starting points that buyers and sellers can use to begin informed and reasonable negotiations.

In a listing for a steam locomotive, the value includes a tender, even if the tender is not listed in the description. The value of steam locomotives, particularly prewar items, may be affected significantly by the type of tender included.

Values for individual items may differ from what is listed in this price guide due to a few key factors. Where collectible trains are scarce and demand outruns supply, actual values may exceed what is shown. Values may also rise where certain items are especially popular, often because of their road names. And as with all collectibles, national and local economic conditions will impact values, which tend to drop when times are tough and demand falls.

Original packaging

Items in Like New or better condition require their original packaging to maintain their high level of value. The values given for items in Good and Excellent condition are not based on the expectation that a box and other associated items are present.

Items that do have their original packaging, especially if it is complete and undamaged, command a premium among collectors of prewar and postwar trains. No hard-and-fast rules can be stated as to how much higher their value is over the same items in Excellent condition. Generally speaking, though, boxed items in Like New condition are valued about 50 percent above the same item without a box.

Using the values

The values listed are what a consumer would pay—more or less—to get a particular item in a specific condition. One collector selling that item to another would probably ask the stated value and expect to get something close to it.

However, someone selling that same item to a person or business that intends to resell it (a train dealer) is unlikely to receive the stated value. Experience shows that sellers get about half the amount. Dealers offer less so they can earn a profit when reselling an item.

When buying or selling a toy train, you should learn more about it. Start by consulting this price guide and then look for more about it in a reference guide or website on toy trains. You can also ask more experienced hobbyists for their opinion about the item's condition and value.

FINDING A PRODUCT

The *Lionel Pocket Price Guide* has been divided into seven major sections.

Section 1: Prewar 1901–1942

Section 1 of the *Lionel Pocket Price Guide* is devoted to the prewar period. The entries cover just about every train, accessory, and transformer associated with Lionel's line during its first 42 years.

The only outfits (sets) listed are those of articulated streamlined trains that consist of a powered unit and attached unpowered cars.

In an item's listing, the basic description specifies its gauge (the distance between the inside of the outermost rails). During this time, Lionel catalogued models in four sizes. It is noted in parentheses whether an item is 2⅞-inch, Standard (2⅛ inches), O (1¼ inches), or OO (¾ inches). O gauge models intended to run on tighter 27-inch-diameter track belong to Lionel's O27 gauge line and are identified as such.

Transformers, rheostats, and many accessories were not limited to a single gauge, so their descriptions do not specify a gauge.

Section 2: Postwar 1945–1969

Section 2 concentrates on the postwar period. Nearly every train and accessory (except outfits) that Lionel cataloged between 1945 and 1969 has its own listing. By this time, Lionel no longer made trains in 2⅞-inch, Standard, or OO gauge. Instead, it offered trains that ran on track that had a diameter of either 31 inches (O gauge) or 27 inches (O27 gauge). However, the entries in this section do not distinguish between O and O27 since only a handful of locomotives and cars could operate solely on the wider curves.

Section 3: Modern Era 1970–2017

Section 3 shows the trains, accessories, transformers, and other items that Lionel has cataloged since 1970. The modern era encompasses the products of three companies: Model Products Corp. (MPC, a division of General Mills), 1970–85; Lionel Trains Inc. (LTI), 1986–95; and Lionel LLC (LLC), 1996–2017.

These incarnations of Lionel are responsible for an enormous inventory of trains, rolling stock, transformers, and accessories. Cataloged and uncataloged O gauge items (ranging from the near-scale Standard O to the toy-like O27) can be found within the pages of this section.

All items in Section 3 are arranged according to their Lionel catalog number (omitting the numeral 6 used as a prefix). The descriptions of products made during the modern era may include information that relates to where in the product line a particular item belongs. Models derived from MPC designs have been described as *traditional*. Rolling stock whose dimensions and features approach scale realism may be designated as Standard O (abbreviated as std O). Locomotives equipped with TrainMaster Command Control or its successor, Legacy, are identified with the abbreviation CC.

Section 4: Lionel Corporation Tinplate

Section 4 features 700 products developed jointly by Lionel and MTH Electric Trains since 2009. These Lionel Corporation trains and accessories are reproductions of Lionel (and some American Flyer) tinplate items from the prewar era. You'll find trains here that operate as tinplate trains did prior to 1942 as well as others that have been updated with modern features and technology, such as Proto-Sound. The retail prices are listed for these products.

Section 5: Club Cars and Special Production

Section 5 gathers the various items, principally locomotives and rolling stock, that Lionel has made or sponsored for different hobby organizations, museums, and businesses since the 1970s. These uncataloged club cars and special production items are arranged according to the groups that offered them for sale. Those groups are listed alphabetically; regional divisions of national organizations follow the parent organization's listing. Within each subordinate section, items are listed in a numerical (not chronological) order, with a basic description similar to that used for cataloged entries.

Section 6: Boxes

Over the past 20 years, original boxes and other forms of packaging have assumed significance for some collectors. These hobbyists insist that the trains they buy come in the boxes and have the paperwork and ancillary pieces (inserts, instruction sheets, and envelopes) that the manufacturer packed with them before offering them for sale.

Cardboard boxes, inserts, and assorted sheets of paper are more fragile than die-cast metal or plastic trains. They were also deemed to be less important to the children playing with toy trains long ago and so were not treated with the same care. Instruction sheets were lost, and boxes were discarded. As a result, fewer boxes and instruction sheets have survived than have the trains and accessories that went with them. In some cases, the box that a particular locomotive, car, or even set came in is now valued more than the item itself.

Boxes are evaluated according to standards and conditions established by the Train Collectors Association, similar to those developed for toy trains and accessories:

P-10 Mint: Brand new, complete, all original as manufactured, and unused. Flaps appear to never have been opened, and edges are crisp. No tears, fading, or wear marks. Contains original contents and all applicable sealing tape, wrap, and staples.

P-9 Store New: Complete, all original, and unused. Box may have merchant additions such as store stamps and price tags. Must have appropriate inner liners.

P-8 Like New: Complete and all original. There is evidence of light use and aging. Box may have notations (discrete) added since leaving the manufacturer.

P-7 Excellent: Complete and all original. Box shows moderate signs of being opened and closed including edge and corner wear. All flaps must be intact.

P-6 Very Good: Complete and all original. Box shows signs of usage such as minor abrasions, small tears, color changes, and minor soiling. Inner liners may be missing, and inner flaps may require strengthening. The box can still safely store its original contents.

P-5 Good: Box shows substantial wear, and edges may be damaged. Box may have extensive color fading but no evident water damage or cardboard deterioration. Exterior flaps are present, but their connection to the box may require repair. Inner liners may be missing. With care, the box can still store contents. (Any box that has been repaired cannot be graded above P-5.)

P-4 Fair: Box shows heavy damage and may have been repaired. Inner flaps may be missing. Box cannot store its original contents. Water damage may be present.

Values for postwar boxes in this section are shown for Good (P-5) and Excellent (P-7) conditions.

Lionel used these box types during the postwar years:

Art Deco: Original postwar box with bold orange and blue design and lettering. It was used in 1946 and 1947.

Classic: More understated design than Art Deco. It was the main component box from 1948 through 1958. Boxes can be divided into Early (1948–49), Middle (1949–55), and Late (1956–58) Classic designs, which are marked by minor lettering changes.

Orange Perforated: This was a significant change from the Classic design. The solid orange box features white lettering and a tear-out perforated front panel. It was used in 1959 and 1960.

Orange Picture: Instead of a perforated panel, this version of the Orange Perforated box features an illustration of a steam locomotive and an F3 diesel on the front. It was used from 1961 to 1964.

Hillside Orange Picture: Similar to an Orange Picture box, it is labeled with Hillside, N.J., where Lionel's plant was located. It was used in 1965.

Cellophane: Used in 1966, this box features a clear cellophane window on the front.

Hagerstown Checkerboard: It has a Lionel checkerboard pattern and Hagerstown, Maryland, printed on end flap bottoms. The box was used in 1968.

Hillside Checkerboard: This 1969 box is the same as the Hagerstown Checkerboard box, but with Hillside, New Jersey, printed on it.

Lionel also used brown corrugated and plain white boxes.

Section 7: Sets

This section lists boxed train sets catalogued by Lionel during the postwar years, 1945–1969. When collecting sets, it is important that the sets, or outfits, contain all the items, including ancillary ones, that Lionel packed with them. These items include the locomotive (and tender if a steam engine) rolling stock, any accessories, track, transformer, instructions and other paper pieces, component boxes, and the set box.

The listings include the set's catalog number, a short description, and product numbers for the locomotives, rolling stock, and any major accessories. Sets came with O27 gauge, O gauge, or Super O track. O27 and Super O track are listed in the set's description. If no track is listed, the set came with O gauge.

Set values are listed for Excellent (C-7) condition. The presence and condition of original component boxes, set boxes, inserts and other packaging materials can have a significant effect on a set's value. The values reflect the inclusion of these materials. Values of individual set and component boxes can be found in Section 6.

Due to space constraints, not every item found in a set is listed in the description. You can find more complete information on a set's contents on various websites and in *Greenberg's Guide to Lionel Trains 1945–1969 Volume III: Catalogued Sets* by Paul Ambrose. (Although the book is out of print, it is available from booksellers on the Internet.)

USING THE GUIDE

Number	Description	Condition ——Good	Exc	Cond/$
2561	Vista Valley Observation Car, *59–61* *	90	250	___
X6454	NYC Boxcar, *48*			
	(A) Brown body	15	40	___
	(B) Orange body	60	140	___
	(C) Tan body	20	70	___
6475	Libby's Crushed Pineapple Vat Car, *63 u*	35	90	___

Identifying a catalog number

A Lionel catalog number is usually stamped, printed, or painted on an item. However, some products do not contain a catalog number. In these cases, you can match the product with its catalog number using a comprehensive reference book or website, including Lionel.com, which contains past and current catalogs.

Two-, three-, and four-digit numbers predominated during the prewar (1901–42) and postwar (1945–69) periods. Four- and five-digit numbers have been most common during the modern era (1970–2017).

On the models, catalog numbers often double as road numbers, although sometimes separate road numbers were added.

Locating an item

Sections are arranged in numerical order of catalog numbers. Items having one or more zeroes as placeholders are listed before those without placeholders. For example, a 004 4-6-4 Locomotive is listed before a 4 Electric Locomotive.

In the prewar and postwar sections, some items such as transformers and track pieces, are identified by a letter. These products follow the numbered items.

Reading an entry

Every entry begins with the product's catalog number assigned by Lionel. (Club and special production cars may have numbers that were assigned by the group.)

A basic description of the model follows. It gives the type of product, lists the name of any railroad identified with it, and includes identifying characteristics, such as color or lettering. If the item has a road number that differs from its catalog number, that number is shown in quotation marks. (Most of these are seen in Section 3). Abbreviations used in the descriptions, including those of railroad names, are listed at the back of the price guide.

Next, you'll find the year or years during which that item was part of Lionel's cataloged product line. The years are shown in italics. If a year is followed by a *u*, this item is considered to be uncataloged. It was not part of the cataloged line but a promotional item that Lionel made or sponsored for an outside business or group.

Entries that show an asterisk (*) after the year have had one or more reissues of the item made.

Many entries feature variations, each indicated by a separate letter (A, B, and so forth). Variations amount to slight yet noteworthy differences in appearance that distinguish models that otherwise seem identical. These differences can relate to color, lettering, and details that were added or deleted. For items having many variations, an entry may not include every variation.

An entry concludes with an indication of the value of the item for several common conditions.

Condition

Lionel enthusiasts should be familiar with the condition and grading standards established by the Train Collectors Association, which are used as the basis for evaluating the condition of toy trains and accessories:

C-10 **Mint:** Brand new—all original, unused, and unblemished.

C-9 **Factory New:** Same condition as Mint but with evidence of factory rubs or slight signs of handling, shipping, and being test run at the factory.

C-8 **Like New:** Complete and all original with no rust or no missing parts; may show effects of being displayed or signs of age and may have been run.

C-7 **Excellent:** All original and may have minute scratches and paint nicks; no rust, no missing parts, and no distortion of component parts.

C-6 **Very Good:** Has minor scratches, paint nicks, or minor spots of surface rust; is free of dents and may have minor parts replaced.

C-5 **Good:** Shows evidence of heavy use and signs of play wear—small dents, scratches, minor paint loss, and minor surface rust.

C-4 **Fair:** Shows evidence of heavy use—scratches and dents, moderate paint loss, missing parts, and surface rust.

C-3 **Poor:** Requires major body repair and is a candidate for restoration; major rust, missing parts, and heavily scratched.

C-2 **Restoration:** Needs to be restored.

C-1 **Junk:** Parts value only.

Values are listed for prewar and postwar trains in Good (C-5) and Excellent (C-7) conditions. For modern-era trains, including special production and club cars, the values for Excellent (C-7) and Mint (C-10) are shown.

You may also see NRS listed as a value. NRS (No Reported Sales) refers to an item with limited pricing data since only a handful of these scarce items may have been reported.

Determining a model's condition

Look over a model carefully to see whether it has suffered serious damage, including warping and breaking. Then note whether any parts are missing. Feel for dents in metal and cracks in plastic. Check for areas marred by rust, mildew, or chipped paint.

The TCA condition standards will assist you in evaluating your model, such as deciding whether a prewar or postwar model falls below Good or above Excellent.

The assessment of a toy train's value is based on the expectations that it has not been modified and that all parts are present and original to it. Repainting or relettering a model seriously undermines a train's value, regardless of how beat-up and scratched it may have been before undergoing modification. Any model that has been altered should be labeled as a restoration; potential buyers deserve to be informed about how it has been modified, so they do not mistake it for an original.

A model that is missing some parts should be sold *as is* or have those parts replaced by identical originals. A tank car cataloged in 1935 that needs a brake wheel must have a part from 1935 put on it to be considered a true original. Adding a brake wheel from 1936 undermines the car's legitimacy as much as adding one from 2016 does.

The same rule applies to the ancillary items that came with various models. The value of a flatcar may depend largely on the miniature airplane or rocket packed with it; therefore, having a load that is a genuine original is essential to maintaining the value of that flatcar. Similarly, freight loaders must have whatever cargo came with them (coal, logs, trailers, and so forth). Reproductions should be identified as such.

Section 1
PREWAR 1901–1942

		Good	Exc	
001	4-6-4 Locomotive (OO), *38–42*	195	360	____
1	Bild-A-Motor (O), *28–31*	60	140	____
1	Trolley (std), *06–14*			
	(A) Cream body, orange band and roof	1900	4750	____
	(B) White body, blue band and roof	1750	4750	____
	(C) Cream body, blue band and roof	1300	3150	____
	(D) Cream body, blue band and roof, Curtis Bay	2150	5550	____
	(E) Blue, cream band, blue roof	1450	3150	____
1/111	Trolley Trailer (std), *06–14*	1000	2700	____
002	4-6-4 Locomotive (OO), *39–42*	160	285	____
2	Bild-A-Motor (std), *28–31*	100	180	____
2	Trolley (std), *06–16**			
	(A) Yellow, red band	1200	3575	____
	(B) Red, yellow band	1200	2250	____
2/200	Trolley Trailer (std), *06–16*	1000	1800	____
003	4-6-4 Locomotive (OO), *39–42*			
	(A) 003W whistling Tender	190	395	____
	(B) 003T nonwhistling Tender	175	355	____
3	Trolley (std), *06–13*			
	(A) Cream, orange band	1400	3100	____
	(B) Cream, dark olive green band	1400	3100	____
	(C) Orange, dark olive green band	1400	3100	____
	(D) Dark green, cream windows	1400	3100	____
	(E) Green, cream windows, Bay Shore	1650	3700	____
3/300	Trolley Trailer (std), *06–13*	1500	3500	____
004	4-6-4 Locomotive (OO), *39–42*			
	(A) 004W whistling Tender	210	350	____
	(B) 004T nonwhistling Tender	190	310	____
4	Electric Locomotive 0-4-0 (O), *28–32**			
	(A) Orange, black frame	550	875	____
	(B) Gray, apple green stripe	580	1050	____
4	Trolley (std), *06–12*			
	(A) Cream, dark olive green band	3000	4950	____
	(B) Green or olive green, cream roof	3000	4950	____
4U	No. 4 Kit Form (O), *28–29*	1150	1600	____
5	0-4-0 Locomotive, no tender, early (std), *06–07*			
	(A) NYC & HRR	1000	1450	____
	(B) Pennsylvania	1400	2300	____
	(C) NYC & HRRR (3 Rs)	1250	2050	____
	(D) B&O RR	1500	2400	____
5	0-4-0 Locomotive, tender, early Special (std), *06–09*	980	1300	____

			Good	Exc
____	5	0-4-0 Locomotive, no tender, later (std), *10–11*	750	1150
____	5	0-4-0 Locomotive, tender, later Special (std), *10–11*	920	1200
____	5/51	0-4-0 Locomotive, tender, latest (std), *12–23*	800	1100
____	6	4-4-0 Locomotive (std), *06–23*	860	1250
____	6	0-4-0 Locomotive Special (std), *08–09*	2050	2950
____	7	Steam 4-4-0 Locomotive (std), *10–23**	1850	2300
	8	Electric Locomotive 0-4-0 (std), *25–32*		
____		(A) Maroon or mojave, brass windows and trim	130	250
____		(B) Olive green, brass windows	155	205
____		(C) Red, brass or cream windows	195	250
____		(D) Peacock, orange windows	520	750
	8	Trolley (std), *08–14**		
____		(A) Cream, orange band and roof	3000	5400
____		(B) Dark green, cream windows	3000	5400
	8E	Electric Locomotive 0-4-0 (std), *26–32*		
____		(A) Mojave, brass windows and trim	175	250
____		(B) Red, brass or cream windows	150	225
____		(C) Peacock, orange windows	370	590
____		(D) Pea green, cream stripe	465	670
____	9	Electric Locomotive 0-4-0 (std), *29**	1200	2150
____	9	Motor Car (std), *09–12*		NRS
____	9	Trolley (std), *09*	3000	5400
	9E	Electric Locomotive (std), *28–35**		
____		(A) 0-4-0, orange	700	1250
____		(B) 2-4-2, two-tone green	880	1600
____		(C) 2-4-2, gunmetal gray	860	1100
____	9U	Electric Locomotive 0-4-0 Kit (std), *28–29*	1050	1750
	10	Electric Locomotive 0-4-0 (std), *25–29**		
____		(A) Mojave, brass trim	150	215
____		(B) Gray, brass trim	125	205
____		(C) Peacock, brass inserts	145	205
____		(D) Red, cream stripe	580	880
	10	Interurban (std), *10–16*		
____		(A) Maroon	3000	5750
____		(B) Dark olive green	1200	2150
	10E	Electric Locomotive 0-4-0 (std), *26–30*		
____		(A) Olive green, black frame		NRS
____		(B) Peacock, dark green or black frame	245	400
____		(C) State brown, dark green frame	435	630
____		(D) Gray, black frame	165	220
____		(E) Red, cream stripe	620	890
____	011	Switches, pair (O), *33–37*	15	35
____	11	Flatcar, early (std), *06–08*	150	360
____	11	Flatcar, later (std), *09–15*	50	90

		Good	Exc	
11	Flatcar, latest (std), *16–18*	50	90	___
11	Flatcar, Lionel Corp. (std), *18–26*	50	80	___
012	Switches, pair (O), *27–33*	20	40	___
12	Gondola, early (std), *06–08*	150	360	___
12	Gondola, later (std), *09–15*	50	100	___
12	Gondola, latest (std), *16–18*	45	70	___
12	Gondola, Lionel Corp. (std), *18–26*	50	70	___
013	012 Switches and 439 panel board, *27–33*	120	190	___
13	Cattle Car, early (std), *06–08*	300	450	___
13	Cattle Car, later (std), *09–15*	150	225	___
13	Cattle Car, latest (std), *16–18*	65	115	___
13	Cattle Car, Lionel Corp. (std), *18–26*	65	115	___
0014	Boxcar (OO), *38–42*			
	(A) Yellow, Lionel Lines	80	155	___
	(B) Tuscan, Pennsylvania	50	75	___
14	Boxcar, early (std), *06–08*	195	435	___
14	Boxcar, later (std), *09–15*	80	105	___
14	Boxcar, latest (std), *16–18*	80	105	___
14	Boxcar, Lionel Corp. (std), *18–26*	80	105	___
0015	Tank Car (OO), *38–42*			
	(A) Silver, Sun Oil	40	90	___
	(B) Black, Shell	40	75	___
15	Oil Car, early (std), *06–08*	200	360	___
15	Oil Car, later (std), *09–15*	75	115	___
15	Oil Car, latest (std), *16–18*	75	115	___
15	Oil Car, Lionel Corp. (std), *18–26*	75	115	___
0016	Hopper Car (OO), *38–42*			
	(A) Gray	75	160	___
	(B) Black	75	115	___
16	Ballast Dump Car, early (std), *06–11*	400	700	___
16	Ballast Dump Car, later (std), *09–15*	95	175	___
16	Ballast Dump Car, latest (std), *16–18*	95	175	___
16	Ballast Dump Car, Lionel Corp. (std), *18–26*	95	175	___
0017	Caboose (OO), *38–42*	50	90	___
17	Caboose, early (std), *06–08*	220	440	___
17	Caboose, later (std), *09–15*	70	135	___
17	Caboose, latest (std), *16–18*	75	135	___
17	Caboose, Lionel Corp. (std), *18–26*	50	90	___
18	Pullman Car (std), *08*			
	(A) Dark olive green, nonremovable roof	700	2150	___
	(B) Dark olive green, removable roof	105	215	___
	(C) Yellow-orange, removable roof	315	870	___
	(D) Orange, removable roof	90	205	___
	(E) Mojave, removable roof	305	890	___
18	Pullman Car (std), *11–13*	600	900	___

			Good	Exc
____	18	Pullman Car (std), *13–15*	150	270
____	18	Pullman Car (std), *15–18*	150	270
____	18	Pullman Car (std), *18–22*	90	155
____	18	Pullman Car (std), *23–26*	270	530
	19	Combine Car (std), *08*		
____		(A) Dark olive green, nonremovable roof	1100	2600
____		(B) Dark olive green, removable roof	90	145
____		(C) Yellow-orange, removable roof	260	430
____		(D) Orange, removable roof	115	205
____		(E) Mojave, removable roof	305	890
____	19	Combine Car (std), *11–13*	600	900
____	19	Combine Car (std), *13–15*	200	270
____	19	Combine Car (std), *15–18*	200	270
____	19	Combine Car (std), *18–22*	90	155
____	19	Combine Car (std), *23–26*	265	520
____	020	90-degree Crossover (O), *15–42*	2	5
____	020X	45-degree Crossover (O), *17–42*	3	10
____	20	90-degree Crossover (std), *09–32*	4	10
____	20	Direct Current Reducer, *06*	95	195
____	20X	45-degree Crossover (std), *28–32*	5	10
____	021	Switches, pair (O), *15–37*	20	50
____	21	90-degree Crossover (std), *06*	10	20
____	21	Switches, pair (std), *15–25*	40	70
____	022	Remote Control Switches, pair (O), *38–42*	40	70
____	22	Manual Switches, pair (std), *06–25*	45	75
____	023	Bumper (O), *15–33*	15	35
____	23	Bumper (std), *06–23*	15	40
____	0024	Pennsylvania Boxcar (OO), *39–42*	45	75
____	24	Railway Station (std), *06*		NRS
____	025	Bumper (O), *28–42*	20	40
	0025	Tank Car (OO), *39–42*		
____		(A) Black, Shell	40	90
____		(B) Silver, Sunoco	40	80
____	25	Open Station (std), *06*		NRS
____	25	Bumper (std), *27–42*	30	45
____	26	Passenger Bridge (std), *06*	15	40
____	0027	Caboose (OO), *39–42*	40	70
____	27	Lighting Set, *11–23*	15	40
____	27	Station (std), *09–12*		NRS
____	28	Double Station with dome, *09–12*		NRS

		Good	Exc	
29	Day Coach (std), *07–22*			
	(A) Dark olive green, 9 windows	1500	3000	____
	(B) Maroon, 10 windows	1200	1500	____
	(C) Dark green, 10 windows	3000	4500	____
	(D) Dark olive green, 10 windows	680	1000	____
	(E) Dark green, 10 windows	500	900	____
0031	2-rail 13" Curve Track (OO), *39–42*	5	10	____
31	Combine Car (std), *21–25*			
	(A) Maroon	70	90	____
	(B) Orange	125	195	____
	(C) Dark olive green	70	90	____
	(D) Brown	75	95	____
0032	2-rail 12" Straight Track (OO), *39–42*	10	15	____
32	Mail Car (std), *21–25*			
	(A) Maroon	85	125	____
	(B) Orange	120	185	____
	(C) Dark olive green	65	85	____
	(D) Brown	70	90	____
32	Miniature Figures, *09–18*	95	250	____
33	Electric Locomotive 0-6-0, early (std), *13*			
	(A) Dark olive green, NYC in oval	90	175	____
	(B) Black, NYC	440	950	____
	(C) Dark olive green, NYC	440	950	____
	(D) Pennsylvania RR	580	1250	____
33	Electric Locomotive 0-4-0, later (std), *13–24*			
	(A) Dark olive green or black, NYC	105	170	____
	(B) Black, lettered C&O	395	720	____
	(C) Maroon, red, or peacock	340	620	____
0034	2-rail 13" Curve Track, electrical connectors (OO), *39–42*	10	15	____
34	Electric Locomotive 0-6-0, early (std), *12*	520	860	____
34	Electric Locomotive 0-4-0 (std), *13*	200	385	____
35	Pullman Car (std), *12–13*			
	(A) Dark blue	470	900	____
	(B) Dark olive green	170	235	____
35	Pullman Car (std), *14–16*			
	(A) Dark olive green, maroon windows	40	70	____
	(B) Maroon, green windows	75	105	____
	(C) Orange, maroon windows	125	195	____
35	Pullman Car (std), *15–18*	40	70	____

			Good	Exc
35		Pullman Car (std), *18–23*		
___		(A) Dark olive green, maroon windows	30	50
___		(B) Maroon, green windows	25	45
___		(C) Orange, maroon windows	120	210
___		(D) Brown, green windows	30	50
___	**35**	Boulevard Street Lamp, 6⅛" high, *40–42*	25	50
___	**35**	Pullman Car (std), *24*	40	55
___	**35**	Pullman Car (std), *25–26*	40	55
	36	Observation Car (std), *12–13*		
___		(A) Dark blue	315	810
___		(B) Dark olive green	145	205
	36	Observation Car (std), *14–16*		
___		(A) Dark olive green, maroon windows	60	95
___		(B) Maroon, green windows	50	70
___		(C) Orange, maroon windows	180	290
___		(D) Brown, green windows	50	75
___	**36**	Observation Car (std), *15–18*	60	80
	36	Observation Car (std), *18–23*		
___		(A) Dark olive green, maroon windows	40	55
___		(B) Maroon, green windows	40	55
___		(C) Orange, maroon windows	130	215
___		(D) Brown, green windows	40	55
___	**36**	Observation Car (std), *24*	40	55
___	**36**	Observation Car (std), *25–26*	40	55
	38	Electric Locomotive 0-4-0 (std), *13–24*		
___		(A) Black	100	135
___		(B) Red	475	680
___		(C) Mojave or pea green	405	540
___		(D) Dark green	270	360
___		(E) Brown	270	315
___		(F) Red, cream trim	405	540
___		(G) Maroon	170	270
___		(H) Gray	70	125
___	**41**	Accessory Contactor, *37–42*	3	7
___	**042**	Switches, pair (O), *38–42*	15	40
___	**42**	Electric Locomotive 0-4-4-0, square hood, early (std), *12**	760	1650
	42	Electric Locomotive 0-4-4-0, round hood, later (std), *13–23*		
___		(A) Black or gray	300	510
___		(B) Maroon	1250	2050
___		(C) Dark gray	375	600
___		(D) Dark green or mojave	500	800
___		(E) Peacock	1100	1800
___		(F) Olive or dark olive green	750	1200

		Good	Exc	
043/43	Bild-A-Motor Gear Set, *29*	40	85	____
0044	Boxcar (OO), *39–42*	40	80	____
0044K	Boxcar Kit (OO), *39–42*	75	120	____
0045	Tank Car (OO), *39–42*			
	(A) Black, Shell	40	95	____
	(B) Silver, Sunoco	40	80	____
0045K	Tank Car Kit (OO), *39–42*	75	120	____
45N	Automatic Gateman (std O), *37–42*	40	85	____
0046	Hopper Car (OO), *39–42*	50	90	____
0046K	Hopper Car Kit (OO), *39–42*			
	(A) Southern Pacific	75	135	____
	(B) Reading		NRS	____
46	Crossing Gate, *39–42*	75	120	____
0047	Caboose (OO), *39–42*	30	60	____
0047K	Caboose Kit (OO), *39–42*	75	135	____
47	Crossing Gate, *39–42*	70	140	____
48W	Whistle Station, *37–42*	20	65	____
50	Electric Locomotive 0-4-0 (std), *24*			
	(A) Dark green or dark gray	145	250	____
	(B) Maroon	315	600	____
	(C) Mojave	175	345	____
50	Cardboard Train, Cars, Accessory (O), *43**	200	360	____
0051	7" Curve Track (OO), *39–42*	5	15	____
51	0-4-0 Locomotive, late, 8-wheel (std), *12–23*	800	1150	____
0052	7" Straight Track (OO), *39–42*	10	15	____
52	Lamp Post, *33–41*	45	95	____
53	Electric Locomotive 0-4-4-0, early (std), *12–14*	1200	2450	____
53	Electric Locomotive 0-4-0, later (std), *15–19*			
	(A) Maroon	550	950	____
	(B) Mojave	670	1350	____
	(C) Dark olive green	560	1150	____
53	Electric Locomotive 0-4-0, latest (std), *20–21*	200	450	____
53	Electric Locomotive 0-6-6-0, early (std), *11*		NRS	____
53	Lamp Post, *31–42*	30	50	____
0054	7" Curve Track, electrical connectors (OO), *39–42*	10	15	____
54	Electric Locomotive 0-4-4-0, early (std), *12**	2500	4050	____
54	Electric Locomotive 0-4-4-0, late (std), *13–23*	1800	2700	____
54	Lamp Post, *29–35*	60	130	____

			Good	Exc
56		Lamp Post, removable lens and cap, *24–42*		
____		(A) Mojave	85	185
____		(B) Dark gray	50	110
____		(C) 45N green	25	45
____		(D) Pea green	30	50
____		(E) Aluminum	30	45
____		(F) Copper	60	160
____		(G) Dark green	30	40
57		Lamp Post with street names, *22–42*		
____		(A) Orange post, Main St. & Broadway	35	55
____		(B) Orange post, Fifth Ave. & 42nd St.	40	100
____		(C) Orange post, Broadway & 21st St.	50	90
____		(D) Orange post, Broadway, 42nd St., Fifth Ave. & 21st St.	70	120
____		(E) Yellow post, Main St. & Broadway	35	65
58		Lamp Post, 7⅜" high, *22–42*		
____		(A) Cream	30	60
____		(B) Peacock	30	60
____		(C) Silver	30	60
____		(D) Maroon	30	85
____		(E) Dark green	30	50
____		(F) Orange	30	60
____	**59**	Lamp Post, 8¾" high, *20–36*	40	100
____	**060**	Telegraph Post (O), *29–42*	10	25
____	**60**	Telegraph Post (std), *20–28*	10	25
	60	Electric Locomotive 0-4-0, FAO Schwartz (std), *15 u*		
____				NRS
____	**0061**	7" Curve Track, tubular (OO), *38*	3	10
____	**61**	Lamp Post, one globe, *14–36*	40	65
	61	Electric Locomotive 0-4-4-0, FAO Schwartz (std), *15 u*		
____				NRS
____	**0062**	7" Straight Track, tubular (OO), *38*	5	10
____	**62**	Semaphore, *20–32*	30	50
	62	Electric Locomotive 0-4-0, FAO Schwartz (std), *24–32 u*		
____				NRS
____	**0063**	Half Curve Track, tubular (OO), *38–42*	8	15
____	**63**	Semaphore, single arm, *15–21*	25	50
____	**63**	Lamp Post, two globes, *33–42*	135	265
____	**0064**	7" Curve Track, tubular, electrical connectors (OO), *38*	8	15
____	**64**	Lamp Post, *40–42*	35	70
____	**64**	Semaphore, double arm, *15–21*	30	60
____	**0065**	Half Straight Track, tubular (OO), *38–42*	10	15
____	**65**	Semaphore, one-arm, *15–26*	30	60
____	**65**	Whistle Controller, *35*	5	10
____	**0066**	5⅝" Straight Track (OO), *38–42*	10	15

|---|---|---|---|
66	Semaphore, two-arm, *15–26*	35	70 ____
66	Whistle Controller, *36–39*	5	10 ____
67	Lamp Post, *15–32*	85	145 ____
67	Whistle Controller, *36–39*	4	10 ____
068	Warning Signal (0), *25–42*	10	25 ____
69N	Electric Warning Signal (std 0), *36–42*	35	70 ____
0070	90-degree Crossing, *38–42*	5	10 ____
70	Outfit: 62 (2), 59 (1), 68 (1), *21–32*	60	130 ____
071	060 Telegraph Poles, 6 pieces (std), *24–42*	70	160 ____
71	60 Telegraph Post Set, 6 pieces, *21–31*	70	160 ____
0072	Remote Control Switches, pair (00), *38–42*	175	290 ____
0072L	Remote Control Switch, left hand (00), *38–42*	50	95 ____
0072R	Remote Control Switch, right hand (00)	50	95 ____
0074	Boxcar (00), *39–42*	35	85 ____
0075	Tank Car (00), *39–42*	50	145 ____
076	Block Signal (0), *23–28*	35	105 ____
76	Warning Bell and Shack, *39–42*	65	180 ____
0077	Caboose (00), *39–42*	30	60 ____
77/077	Automatic Crossing Gate, *23–35*	25	50 ____
78/078	Train Signal, *24–32*	40	100 ____
79	Flashing Signal, *28–42*	90	150 ____
80/080	Semaphore, *26–35*	50	120 ____
81	Controlling Rheostat, *27–33*	2	6 ____
82/082	Semaphore, *27–35*	50	120 ____
83	Flashing Traffic Signal, *27–42*	65	195 ____
084	Semaphore, *28–32*	60	100 ____
84	Semaphore, *27–32*	55	85 ____
85	Telegraph Pole (std), *29–42*	15	30 ____
86	Telegraph Poles, 6 pieces, *29–42*	60	120 ____
87	Flashing Crossing Signal, *27–42*	85	300 ____
88	Rheostat, *15–27*	3	10 ____
88	Direction Controller, *33–42*	4	10 ____
89	Flagpole, *23–34*	40	75 ____
90	Flagpole, *27–42*	40	95 ____
91	Circuit Breaker, *30–42*	30	50 ____
092	Signal Tower, *23–27*	85	190 ____
92	Floodlight Tower, *31–42**	150	215 ____
93	Water Tower, *31–42*	60	110 ____
94	High Tension Tower, *32–42**	150	290 ____
95	Controlling Rheostat, *34–42*	2	10 ____
96	Coal Elevator, manual, *38–40*	165	220 ____
097	Telegraph Set (0)	50	75 ____
97	Coal Elevator, *38–42*	125	240 ____
98	Coal Bunker, *38–40*	160	320 ____
99N	Train Control Block Signal, *36–42*	45	180 ____

			Good	Exc
___	**100**	Wooden Gondola (2⅞"), *01*		NRS
___	**100**	Bridge Approaches, 2 ramps (std), *20–31*	20	40
___	**100**	Electric Locomotive (2⅞"), *03–05**	2900	5200
	100	Trolley (std), *10–16*		
___		(A) Blue, white windows	1300	2700
___		(B) Blue, cream windows	1850	3600
___		(C) Red, cream windows	1300	2700
___	**101**	Bridge, span (104) and 2 approaches (100), *20–31*	65	120
___	**101**	Summer Trolley (std), *10–13*	1300	2700
___	**102**	Bridge, 2 spans (104) and 2 approaches (100), *20–31*	70	175
___	**103**	Bridge (std), *13–16*	40	75
___	**103**	Bridge, 3 spans (104) and 2 approaches (100), *20–31*	60	145
___	**104**	Bridge Center Span (std), *20–31*	20	45
___	**104**	Tunnel, papier mache (std), *09–14*	50	135
___	**105**	Bridge (std), *11–14*	40	70
___	**105**	Bridge Approaches, 2 ramps (O), *20–31*	50	70
___	**106**	Bridge, span (110) and 2 approaches (105), *20–31*	30	65
___	**106**	Rheostat, *11–14*	3	10
___	**107**	DC Reducer, 110V, *23–32*		NRS
___	**108**	Bridge, 2 spans (110) and 2 approaches (105), *20–31*	50	90
___	**109**	Bridge, 3 spans, (110) and 2 approaches (105), *20–32*	50	115
___	**109**	Tunnel, papier mache (std), *13–14*	30	70
___	**110**	Bridge Center Span (O), *20–31*	10	25
___	**111**	Box of 50 Bulbs, *20–31*	55	105
___	**112**	Gondola, early (std), *10–12*	225	400
___	**112**	Gondola, later (std), *12–16*	40	65
___	**112**	Gondola, latest (std), *16–18*	40	65
___	**112**	Gondola, Lionel Corp. (std), *18–26*	40	65
___	**112**	Station, *31–35*	145	270
___	**113**	Cattle Car, later (std), *12–16*	50	70
___	**113**	Cattle Car, latest (std), *16–18*	50	70
___	**113**	Cattle Car, Lionel Corp. (std), *18–26*	30	55
___	**113**	Station with light fixtures, *31–34*	150	310
___	**114**	Boxcar, later (std), *12–16*	50	90
___	**114**	Boxcar, latest (std), *16–18*	40	70
___	**114**	Boxcar, Lionel Corp. (std), *18–26*	40	70
___	**114**	Station with light fixtures, *31–34*	530	1200
___	**115**	Station with train control, *35–42**	185	370
___	**116**	Ballast Car, early and later (std), *10–16*	85	115
___	**116**	Ballast Car, latest (std), *16–18*	65	105

		Good	Exc	
116	Ballast Car, Lionel Corp. (std), *18–26*	55	95	____
116	Station with train control, *35–42**	640	920	____
117	Caboose, early (std), *12*	40	75	____
117	Caboose, later (std), *12–16*	40	75	____
117	Caboose, latest (std), *16–18*	40	75	____
117	Caboose, Lionel Corp. (std), *18–26*	30	60	____
117	Station, *36–42*	125	235	____
118	Tunnel, metal, 8" long (O), *20–32*	20	60	____
118L	Tunnel, metal, lighted, 8" long, *27*	20	55	____
119	Tunnel, metal, 12" long, *20–42*	25	60	____
119L	Tunnel, metal, lighted, 12" long, *27–33*	20	55	____
120	Tunnel, metal, 17" long, *22–27*	30	75	____
120L	Tunnel, metal, lighted, 17" long, *27–42*	75	140	____
121	Station, lighted (std), *09–16*			
	(A) 14" x 10" x 9"		NRS	____
	(B) 13" x 9" x 13"	150	300	____
121	Station (std), *20–26*	75	165	____
121X	Station (std), *17–19*	110	255	____
122	Station (std), *20–30*	80	190	____
123	Station (std), *20–23*	75	210	____
123	Tunnel, paperboard base, 18½" long (O), *33–42*	105	235	____
124	Lionel City Station, *20–36**			
	(A) Tan or gray base, pea green roof	90	240	____
	(B) Pea green base, red roof	200	360	____
125	Lionelville Station, *23–25*	80	185	____
125	Track Template, *38*	1	5	____
126	Lionelville Station, *23–36*	95	205	____
127	Lionel Town Station, *23–36*	80	160	____
128	115 Station and 129 Terrace, *35–42**	900	1900	____
128	124 Station and 129 Terrace, *31–34**	900	1900	____
129	Terrace, *28–42**	600	1100	____
130	Tunnel, 26" long (O), *20–36*	100	450	____
130L	Tunnel, lighted, 26" long, *27–33*	150	450	____
131	Corner Display, *24–28*	125	295	____
132	Corner Grass Plot, *24–28*	125	295	____
133	Heart-shaped Plot, *24–28*	125	295	____
134	Lionel City Station with stop, *37–42*	230	445	____
134	Oval-shaped Plot, *24–28*	125	300	____
135	Circular Plot, *24–28*	125	295	____
136	Large Elevation, *24–28*		NRS	____
136	Lionelville Station with stop, *37–42*	85	180	____
137	Station with stop, *37–42*	85	160	____
140L	Tunnel, lighted, 37" long, *27–32*	460	1050	____
150	Electric Locomotive 0-4-0, early (O), *17*	90	160	____

			Good	Exc
150		Electric Locomotive 0-4-0, late (O), *18–25*		
____		(A) Brown, brown or olive windows	95	150
____		(B) Maroon, dark olive windows	90	135
152		Electric Locomotive 0-4-0 (O), *17–27*		
____		(A) Dark green	90	135
____		(B) Gray	100	160
____		(C) Mojave	340	680
____		(D) Peacock	340	680
____	**152**	Crossing Gate, *40–42*	20	40
____	**153**	Block Signal, *40–42*	25	45
153		Electric Locomotive 0-4-0 (O), *24–25*		
____		(A) Dark green	100	160
____		(B) Gray	100	160
____		(C) Mojave	100	160
____	**154**	Electric Locomotive 0-4-0 (O), *17–23*	100	180
154		Highway Signal, *40–42*		
____		(A) Black base	25	50
____		(B) Orange base	90	185
155		Freight Shed, *30–42**		
____		(A) Cream base, terra cotta floor	180	320
____		(B) Ivory base, red floor	240	400
____	**156**	Electric Locomotive 0-4-0 (O), *17–23*	400	720
____	**156**	Station Platform, *39–42*	85	115
156		Electric Locomotive 4-4-4 (O), *17–23*		
____		(A) Dark green	475	810
____		(B) Maroon	540	890
____		(C) Olive green	600	1050
____		(D) Gray	670	1200
156X		Electric Locomotive 0-4-0 (O), *23–24*		
____		(A) Maroon	380	495
____		(B) Olive green	200	400
____		(C) Gray	530	710
____		(D) Brown	470	600
____	**157**	Hand Truck, *30–32*	20	40
158		Electric Locomotive 0-4-0 (O), *19–23*		
____		(A) Gray or red windows	75	205
____		(B) Black	95	250
158		Station Set: 136 Station and 2 platforms (156), *40–42*		
____			120	280
____	**159**	Block Actuator, *40*	10	30
____	**161**	Baggage Truck, *30–32**	40	80
____	**162**	Dump Truck, *30–32**	40	80
163		Freight Station Set: 2 hand trucks (157), baggage truck (161), and dump truck (162), *30–42**		
____			220	360
____	**164**	Log Loader, *40–42*	160	225

		Good	Exc	
165	Magnetic Crane, *40–42*	175	340	____
165-22	Scrap Steel with bag, *40–42*	50	125	____
165-83	Steel Blanks with bag, *40–42*	50	110	____
166	Whistle Controller, *40–42*	3	10	____
167	Whistle Controller, *40–42*	8	25	____
167X	Whistle Controller (OO), *40–42*	5	15	____
168	Magic Electrol Controller, *40–42*	25	50	____
169	Controller, *40–42*	4	18	____
170	DC Reducer, 220V, *14–38*	5	10	____
171	DC to AC Inverter, 110V, *36–42*	5	15	____
172	DC to AC Inverter, 229V, *39–42*	3	7	____
180	Pullman Car (std), *11–13*			
	(A) Maroon body and roof	145	205	____
	(B) Brown body and roof	145	255	____
180	Pullman Car (std), *13–15*	80	160	____
180	Pullman Car (std), *15–18*	80	160	____
180	Pullman Car (std), *18–22*	80	135	____
181	Combine Car (std), *11–13*			
	(A) Maroon, dark olive doors	145	205	____
	(B) Brown, dark olive doors	145	205	____
	(C) Yellow-orange, orange doors	350	495	____
181	Combine Car (std), *13–15*	80	160	____
181	Combine Car (std), *15–18*	80	160	____
181	Combine Car (std), *18–22*	80	135	____
182	Observation Car (std), *11–13*			
	(A) Maroon, dark olive doors	145	205	____
	(B) Brown, dark olive doors	145	205	____
	(C) Yellow-orange, orange doors	300	495	____
182	Observation Car (std), *13–15*	80	160	____
182	Observation Car (std), *15–18*	80	160	____
182	Observation Car (std), *18–22*	80	135	____
184	Bungalow, illuminated, *23–32**	65	85	____
185	Bungalow, *23–24*	50	115	____
186	184 Bungalows, set of 5, *23–32*	195	610	____
186	Log Loader Outfit, *40–41*	130	340	____
187	185 Bungalows, set of 5, *23–24*	170	590	____
188	Elevator and Car Set, *38–41*	115	370	____
189	Villa, illuminated, *23–32**	133	225	____
190	Observation Car (std), *08*			
	(A) Dark olive green, nonremovable roof	1150	2600	____
	(B) Dark olive green, removable roof	115	205	____
	(C) Yellow-orange, removable roof	320	620	____
	(D) Orange, removable roof	115	205	____
	(E) Mojave, removable roof	345	870	____

			Good	Exc
____	**190**	Observation Car (std), *11–13*	600	900
____	**190**	Observation Car (std), *13–15*	200	295
____	**190**	Observation Car (std), *15–18*	200	295
____	**190**	Observation Car (std), *18–22*	80	135
____	**190**	Observation Car (std), *23–26*	230	475
____	**191**	Villa, illuminated, *23–32**	125	325
____	**192**	Illuminated Villa Set: 189, 191, 184 (2), *27–32*	400	800
____	**193**	Automatic Accessory Set (O), *27–29*	150	325
____	**194**	Automatic Accessory Set (std), *27–29*	100	325
____	**195**	Terrace, *27–30*	350	740
____	**196**	Accessory Set, *27*	200	335
____	**200**	Electric Express (2⅞"), *03–05**	4000	6300
____	**200**	Trailer, matches No. 2 Trolley (std), *11–16*	1200	2400
____	**200**	Turntable (std), *28–33**	85	190
	201	0-6-0 Locomotive (O), *40–42*		
____		(A) 2201B Tender, bell	375	760
____		(B) 2201T Tender, no bell	345	690
	202	Summer Trolley (std), *10–13*		
____		(A) Electric Rapid Transit	1300	2700
____		(B) Preston St.	3250	4500
____	**203**	Armored 0-4-0 (O), *17–21*	1100	1800
	203	0-6-0 Locomotive (O), *40–42*		
____		(A) 2203B Tender, bell	400	495
____		(B) 2203T Tender, no bell	375	550
	204	2-4-2 Locomotive (O), *40–42 u*		
____		(A) Black	55	105
____		(B) Gunmetal gray	80	165
____	**205**	Merchandise Containers, 3 pieces, *30–38**	130	320
____	**206**	Sack of Coal, *38–42*	5	20
____	**208**	Tool Set: 6 assorted tools, *34–42**	65	150
	0209	Barrels, wooden, 6 pieces (O), *34–42*		
____		(A) Solid barrels	10	25
____		(B) 2-piece barrels	53	135
____	**209**	Barrels, wooden, 4 pieces (std), *34–42*	10	25
____	**210**	Switches, pair (std), *26, 34–42*	40	75
____	**211**	Flatcar (std), *26–40**	125	195
	212	Gondola (std), *26–40**		
____		(A) Gray or light green	100	205
____		(B) Maroon	75	135
	213	Cattle Car (std), *26–40**		
____		(A) Mojave, maroon roof	160	365
____		(B) Terra-cotta, pea green roof	130	290
____		(C) Cream, maroon roof	300	650

		Good	Exc	
214	Boxcar (std), *26–40**			
	(A) Terra-cotta, dark green roof	195	390	___
	(B) Cream body, orange roof	150	270	___
	(C) Yellow, brown roof	300	495	___
214R	Refrigerator Car (std), *29–40**			
	(A) Ivory or white, peacock roof	325	495	___
	(B) White, light blue roof	435	790	___
215	Tank Car (std), *26–40**			
	(A) Pea green	150	215	___
	(B) Ivory	220	360	___
	(C) Aluminum	315	720	___
216	Hopper Car (std), *26–38**			
	(A) Dark green, brass plates	195	335	___
	(B) Dark green, nickel plates	445	1100	___
217	Caboose (std), *26–40**			
	(A) Orange, maroon roof	250	510	___
	(B) Red, peacock roof	120	235	___
	(C) Red body and roof, ivory doors	150	320	___
217	Lighting Set, *14–23*		NRS	___
218	Dump Car (std), *26–38**	220	365	___
219	Crane Car (std), *26–40**			
	(A) Peacock, red boom	135	255	___
	(B) Yellow, light green or red boom	270	440	___
	(C) Ivory, light green boom	270	520	___
220	Floodlight Car (std), *31–40**			
	(A) Terra-cotta base	225	385	___
	(B) Green base	340	485	___
220	Switches, pair (std), *26**	25	90	___
222	Switches, pair (std), *26–32*	40	100	___
223	Switches, pair (std), *32–42*	35	120	___
224/224E	2-6-2 Locomotive (O), *38–42*			
	(A) Black, die-cast 2224 Tender	155	255	___
	(B) Black, plastic 2224 Tender	110	195	___
	(C) Gunmetal, die-cast 2224 Tender	385	950	___
	(D) Gunmetal, sheet-metal 2689 Tender	120	210	___
225	222 Switches and 439 Panel, *29–32*	115	260	___
225/225E	2-6-2 Locomotive (O), *38–42*			
	(A) Black, 2235 or 2245 Tender	210	370	___
	(B) Black, 2235 plastic Tender	185	320	___
	(C) Gunmetal, 2225 or 2265 Tender	210	360	___
	(D) Gunmetal, 2235 die-cast Tender	285	730	___
226/226E	2-6-4 Locomotive (O), *38–41*	275	630	___
227	0-6-0 Locomotive (O), *39–42*			
	(A) 2227B Tender, bell	600	1250	___
	(B) 2227T Tender, no bell	600	1150	___

			Good	Exc
	228	0-6-0 Locomotive (O), *39–42*		
____		(A) 2228B Tender, bell	600	1250
____		(B) 2228T Tender, no bell	600	1150
	229	2-4-2 Locomotive (O), *39–42*		
____		(A) Black or gunmetal, 2689W Tender	155	240
____		(B) Black or gunmetal, 2689T Tender	120	200
____		(C) Black, 2666W whistle Tender	155	280
____		(D) Black, 2666T nonwhistling Tender	120	200
____	**230**	0-6-0 Locomotive (O), *39–42*	1100	2050
____	**231**	0-6-0 Locomotive (O), *39*	1000	1800
____	**232**	0-6-0 Locomotive (O), *40–42*	1000	1800
____	**233**	0-6-0 Locomotive (O), *40–42*	1000	1800
____	**238**	4-4-2 Locomotive (O), *39–40 u*	430	710
	238E	4-4-2 Locomotive (O), *36–38*		
____		(A) 265W or 2225W whistle Tender	280	345
____		(B) 265 or 2225T nonwhistling Tender	275	360
____	**248**	Electric Locomotive 0-4-0 (O), *27–32*	150	240
	249/249E	2-4-2 Locomotive (O), *36–39*		
____		(A) Gunmetal, 265T or 265W Tender	100	270
____		(B) Black, 265W Tender	110	210
____	**250**	Electric Locomotive 0-4-0, early (O), *26*	125	220
	250	Electric Locomotive 0-4-0, late (O), *34*		
____		(A) Yellow-orange body, terra-cotta frame	145	245
____		(B) Terra-cotta body, maroon frame	160	270
____	**250E**	4-4-2 Hiawatha Locomotive (O), *35–42**	400	1100
____	**250W**	Hiawatha Tender (O), *35–42**	125	250
	251	Electric Locomotive 0-4-0 (O), *25–32*		
____		(A) Gray body, red windows	190	340
____		(B) Red body, ivory stripe	215	410
____		(C) Red body, no ivory stripe	200	380
	251E	Electric Locomotive 0-4-0 (O), *27–32*		
____		(A) Red body, ivory stripe	225	425
____		(B) Red body, no ivory stripe	215	395
____		(C) Gray, red trim	195	350
	252	Electric Locomotive 0-4-0 (O), *26–32*		
____		(A) Peacock or olive green	85	130
____		(B) Terra-cotta or yellow-orange	125	220
	252E	Electric Locomotive 0-4-0 (O), *33–35*		
____		(A) Terra-cotta	145	250
____		(B) Yellow-orange	125	205

		Good	Exc	
253	Electric Locomotive 0-4-0 (O), *24–32*			
	(A) Maroon	180	430	____
	(B) Dark green	105	250	____
	(C) Mojave	105	235	____
	(D) Terra-cotta	180	430	____
	(E) Peacock	95	195	____
	(F) Red	210	475	____
253E	Electric Locomotive 0-4-0 (O), *31–36*			
	(A) Green	150	205	____
	(B) Terra-cotta	190	305	____
254	Electric Locomotive 0-4-0 (O), *24–32*	240	340	____
254E	Electric Locomotive 0-4-0 (O), *27–34*	180	270	____
255E	2-4-2 Locomotive (O), *35–36*	485	1000	____
256	Electric Locomotive 0-4-4-0 (O), *24–30**			
	(A) Rubber-stamped lettering	470	1175	____
	(B) no outline around Lionel	425	770	____
	(C) Lionel Lines and No. 256 on brass	450	1050	____
257	2-4-0 Locomotive (O), *30–35 u*			
	(A) Black tender	145	300	____
	(B) Black crackle-finish tender	240	435	____
258	2-4-0 Locomotive, early (O), *30–35 u*			
	(A) 4-wheel 257 Tender	85	170	____
	(B) 8-wheel 258 Tender	100	195	____
258	2-4-2 Locomotive, late (O), *41 u*			
	(A) Black	60	100	____
	(B) Gunmetal	85	135	____
259	2-4-2 Locomotive (O), *32*	70	135	____
259E	2-4-2 Locomotive (O), *33–42*	80	165	____
259T	Tender	15	30	____
260E	2-4-2 Locomotive (O), *30–35**			
	(A) Black body, green or black frame	385	475	____
	(B) Dark gunmetal body and frame	440	640	____
261	2-4-2 Locomotive (O), *31*	125	210	____
261E	2-4-2 Locomotive (O), *35*	190	285	____
262	2-4-2 Locomotive (O), *31–32*	210	320	____
262E	2-4-2 Locomotive (O), *33–36*			
	(A) Gloss black, copper and brass trim	100	210	____
	(B) Satin black, nickel trim	125	260	____
263E	2-4-2 Locomotive (O), *36–39**			
	(A) Gunmetal gray	315	610	____
	(B) 2-tone blue, from Blue Comet	415	950	____
263W	Tender, gunmetal	90	200	____

			Good	Exc
264E		2-4-2 Locomotive (0), *35–36*		
____		(A) Red, Red Comet	135	295
____		(B) Black	220	380
265E		2-4-2 Locomotive (0), *35–40*		
____		(A) Black or gunmetal	170	330
____		(B) Light blue, Blue Streak	460	800
____		(B) Tender	30	55
____	**267E/W**	Set: 616, 617 (2), 618, *35–41*	275	560
____	**270**	Bridge, 10" long (0), *31–42*	20	50
____	**270**	Lighting Set, *15–23*		NRS
____	**271**	270 Bridges, set of 2, *31–33, 35–40*	65	150
____	**271**	Lighting Set, *15–23*		NRS
____	**272**	270 Bridges, set of 3, *31–33, 35–40*	60	165
____	**280**	Bridge, 14" long (std), *31–42*	50	115
____	**281**	280 Bridges, set of 2, *31–33, 35–40*	90	205
____	**282**	280 Bridges, set of 3, *31–33, 35–40*	105	265
____	**289E**	2-4-2 Locomotive (0), *37 u*	120	305
____	**300**	Electric Trolley Car (2⅞"), *01–05*	2000	3600
	300	Hellgate Bridge (std), *28–42**		
____		(A) Cream towers, green truss	800	1350
____		(B) Ivory towers, aluminum truss	765	1600
____	**303**	Summer Trolley, *10–13*	1500	3150
____	**308**	Signs, set of 5 (0), *40–42*	30	70
____	**309**	Electric Trolley Trailer (2⅞"), *01–05*	2500	4050
	309	Pullman Car (std), *26–39*		
____		(A) Maroon body and roof, mojave windows	100	160
____		(B) Mojave body and roof, maroon windows	100	160
____		(C) Light brown body, dark brown roof	120	190
____		(D) Medium blue body, dark blue roof	170	280
____		(E) Apple green body, dark green roof	170	280
____		(F) Pale blue body, silver roof	100	185
____		(G) Maroon body, terra-cotta roof	130	195
____	**310**	Rails and Ties, complete section (2⅞"), *01–02*	5	15
	310	Baggage Car (std), *26–39*		
____		(A) Maroon body and roof, mojave windows	100	160
____		(B) Mojave body and roof, maroon windows	85	160
____		(C) Light brown body, dark brown roof	115	185
____		(D) Medium blue body, dark blue roof	170	280
____		(E) Apple green body, dark green roof	170	280
____		(F) Pale blue body, silver roof	100	175

		Good	Exc	
312	Observation Car (std), *24–39*			
	(A) Maroon body and roof, mojave windows	100	160	____
	(B) Mojave body and roof, maroon windows	85	160	____
	(C) Light brown body, dark brown roof	120	185	____
	(D) Medium blue body, dark blue roof	170	280	____
	(E) Apple green body, dark green roof	170	280	____
	(F) Pale blue body, silver roof	100	175	____
	(G) Maroon body, terra-cotta roof	130	195	____
313	Bascule Bridge (O), *40–42*			
	(A) Silver bridge	235	500	____
	(B) Gray bridge	250	590	____
314	Girder Bridge (O), *40–42*	20	40	____
315	Illuminated Trestle Bridge (O), *40–42*	30	80	____
316	Trestle Bridge (O), *40–42*	25	50	____
318	Electric Locomotive 0-4-0 (std), *24–32*			
	(A) Gray, dark gray, or mojave	150	250	____
	(B) Pea green	150	250	____
	(C) State brown	250	395	____
318E	Electric Locomotive 0-4-0, *26–35*			
	(A) Gray, mojave, or pea green	150	250	____
	(B) State brown	275	440	____
	(C) Black	550	1275	____
319	Pullman Car (std), *24–27*	105	175	____
320	Baggage Car (std), *25–27*	100	175	____
320	Switch and Signal (2⅞"), *02–05*		NRS	____
322	Observation Car (std), *24–27, 29–30 u*	100	175	____
330	90-degree Crossing (2⅞"), *02–05*		NRS	____
332	Baggage Car (std), *26–33*			
	(A) Red body and roof, cream doors	80	120	____
	(B) Peacock body and roof, orange doors	75	115	____
	(C) Gray body and roof, maroon doors	75	115	____
	(D) Olive green body and roof, red doors	90	145	____
	(E) State brown body, dark brown roof	190	430	____
337	Pullman Car (std), *25–32*			
	(A) Red body and roof, cream doors	95	190	____
	(B) Mojave body and roof, maroon doors	95	190	____
	(C) Olive green body and roof, red doors	105	225	____
	(D) Olive green body and roof, maroon doors	95	190	____
	(E) Pea green body and roof, cream doors	210	500	____
338	Observation Car (std), *25–32*			
	(A) Red body and roof, cream doors	95	190	____
	(B) Mojave body and roof, maroon doors	95	190	____
	(C) Olive green body and roof, red doors	105	225	____
	(D) Olive green body and roof, maroon doors	95	190	____

			Good	Exc
	339	Pullman Car (std), *25–33*		
___		(A) Peacock body and roof, orange doors	55	90
___		(B) Gray body and roof, maroon doors	55	100
___		(C) State brown body, dark brown roof	135	380
___		(D) Peacock body, dark green roof	75	130
___		(E) Mojave body, maroon roof and doors	145	230
___	**340**	Suspension Bridge (2⅞"), *02–05**		NRS
	341	Observation Car (std), *25–33*		
___		(A) Peacock body and roof, orange doors	50	70
___		(B) Gray body and roof, maroon doors	50	70
___		(C) State brown body, dark brown roof	75	160
___		(D) Peacock body, dark green roof	65	95
___		(E) Mojave body, maroon roof and doors	135	165
___	**350**	Track Bumper (2⅞"), *02–05*	225	550
___	**380**	Elevated Pillars (2⅞"), *04–05**	30	70
___	**380**	Electric Locomotive 0-4-0 (std), *23–27*	310	440
	380E	Electric Locomotive 0-4-0 (std), *26–29*		
___		(A) Mojave	445	630
___		(B) Maroon	295	400
___		(C) Dark green	370	460
___	**381**	Electric Locomotive 4-4-4 (std), *28–29**	1600	2100
	381E	Electric Locomotive 4-4-4 (std), *28–36**		
___		(A) State green, apple green subframe	1500	2500
___		(B) State green, red subframe	1900	3250
___	**381U**	Electric Locomotive 4-4-4 Kit (std), *28–29*	1600	4100
___	**384**	2-4-0 Locomotive (std), *30–32**	415	730
___	**384E**	2-4-0 Locomotive (std), *30–32**	425	650
___	**385E**	2-4-2 Locomotive (std), *33–39**	370	670
___	**390**	2-4-2 Locomotive (std), *29**	460	820
	390E	2-4-2 Locomotive (std), *29–31**		
___		(A) Black, with or without orange stripe	460	690
___		(B) 2-tone blue, cream-orange stripe	650	1050
___		(C) 2-tone green, orange or green stripe	990	2050
	392E	4-4-2 Locomotive (std), *32–39**		
___		(A) Black, 384 Tender	750	1250
___		(B) Black, large 12-wheel tender	1050	1850
___		(C) Gunmetal gray	1000	1800
___	**400**	Express Trail Car (2⅞"), *03–05**	3500	5850
	400E	4-4-4 Locomotive (std), *31–39**		
___		(A) Black	1400	2150
___		(B) Blue	1550	2350
___		(C) Gunmetal or light blue	1650	2800
___		(D) Black crackle finish	1600	3500

		Good	Exc	
402	Electric Locomotive 0-4-4-0 (std), *23–27*	365	570	____
402E	Electric Locomotive 0-4-4-0 (std), *26–29*	345	550	____
404	Summer Trolley (std), *10*		NRS	____
408E	Electric Locomotive 0-4-4-0 (std), *27–36**			
	(A) Apple green or mojave, red pilots	770	980	____
	(B) State brown, brown pilots	2000	3000	____
	(C) State green, red pilots	2000	3800	____
412	California Pullman Car (std), *29–35**			
	(A) Light green body, dark green roof	590	1750	____
	(B) Light brown body, dark brown roof	620	2100	____
413	Colorado Pullman Car (std), *29–35**			
	(A) Light green body, dark green roof	590	1750	____
	(B) Light brown body, dark brown roof	620	2100	____
414	Illinois Pullman Car (std), *29–35**			
	(A) Light green body, dark green roof	590	1750	____
	(B) Light brown body, dark brown roof	620	2050	____
416	New York Observation Car (std), *29–35**			
	(A) Light green body, dark green roof	590	1750	____
	(B) Light brown body, dark brown roof	620	2100	____
418	Pullman Car (std), *23–32**	225	320	____
419	Combination (std), *23–32**	190	280	____
420	Faye Pullman Car (std), *30–40**			
	(A) Brass trim	485	900	____
	(B) Nickel trim	500	1200	____
421	Westphal Pullman Car (std), *30–40**			
	(A) Brass trim	500	900	____
	(B) Nickel trim	500	1200	____
422	Tempel Observation Car (std), *30–40**			
	(A) Brass trim	485	900	____
	(B) Nickel trim	500	1200	____
424	Liberty Bell Pullman Car (std), *31–40**			
	(A) Brass trim	350	530	____
	(B) Nickel trim	385	650	____
425	Stephen Girard Pullman Car (std), *31–40**			
	(A) Brass trim	350	530	____
	(B) Nickel trim	385	650	____
426	Coral Isle Observation Car (std), *31–40**			
	(A) Brass trim	350	530	____
	(B) Nickel trim	385	650	____
428	Pullman Car (std), *26–30**			
	(A) Dark green body and roof	250	385	____
	(B) Orange body and roof, apple green windows	390	890	____

		Good	Exc
429	Combine Car (std), *26–30**		
___	(A) Dark green body and roof	250	385
___	(B) Orange body and roof, apple green windows	390	890
430	Observation Car (std), *26–30**		
___	(A) Dark green body and roof	250	385
___	(B) Orange body and roof, apple green windows	390	890
431	Diner (std), *27–32**		
___	(A) Mojave body, screw-mounted roof	350	540
___	(B) Mojave body, hinged roof	465	720
___	(C) Dark green body, orange windows	410	720
___	(D) Orange body, apple green windows	410	720
___	(E) Apple green body, red windows	410	720
___ **435**	Power Station, *26–38**	215	400
436	Power Station, *26–37**		
___	(A) Power Station plate	135	265
___	(B) Edison Service plate	270	610
___ **437**	Switch Signal Tower, *26–37**	190	430
438	Signal Tower, *27–39**		
___	(A) Mojave base, orange house	185	325
___	(B) Black base, white house	325	640
___ **439**	Panel Board, *28–42**	85	145
___ **440/0440**	Signal Bridge, *32–35**	180	470
___ **440C**	Panel Board, *32–42*	90	145
___ **441**	Weighing Station (std), *32–36*	495	1325
___ **442**	Landscaped Diner, *38–42*	120	215
___ **444**	Roundhouse (std), *32–35**	1350	2850
___ **444-18**	Roundhouse Clip, *33*		NRS
450	Electric Locomotive 0-4-0, Macy's (O), *30 u*		
___	(A) Red, black frame	295	700
___	(B) Apple green, dark green frame	415	880
___ **450**	Set: 450, matching 605, 606 (2), *30 u*	750	1800
___ **490**	Observation Car (std), *23–32**	190	255
___ **500**	Electric Derrick Car (2⅞"), *03–04**	5000	6750
511	Flatcar (std), *27–40*		
___	(A) Dark green	65	95
___	(B) Medium green	75	165
512	Gondola (std), *27–39*		
___	(A) Peacock	35	60
___	(B) Light green	50	95
513	Cattle Car (std), *27–38*		
___	(A) Olive green, orange roof	70	165
___	(B) Orange, pea green roof	60	110
___	(C) Cream, maroon roof	90	250

		Good	Exc	
514	Boxcar (std), *29–40*			
	(A) Cream, orange roof	90	155	____
	(B) Yellow, brown roof	115	285	____
514	Refrigerator Car, ivory or white, peacock roof, (std), *27–28*	240	400	____
514R	Refrigerator Car (std), *29–40*			
	(A) Ivory, peacock roof	140	190	____
	(B) White, light blue roof	350	540	____
515	Tank Car (std), *27–40*			
	(A) Terra-cotta	90	145	____
	(B) Ivory	105	185	____
	(C) Aluminum	90	175	____
	(D) Orange, red Shell decal	340	750	____
516	Hopper Car (std), *28–40*			
	(A) Red	170	240	____
	(B) Red, rubber-stamped data	200	300	____
	(C) Light red, nickel trim	200	325	____
517	Caboose (std), *27–40*			
	(A) Pea green body, red roof	50	85	____
	(B) Red body and roof	105	155	____
	(C) Red body, black roof, orange windows	355	640	____
520	Floodlight Car (std), *31–40*			
	(A) Terra-cotta base	110	210	____
	(B) Green base	110	240	____
529	Pullman Car (O), *26–32*			
	(A) Olive green body and roof	25	45	____
	(B) Terra-cotta body and roof	25	60	____
530	Observation Car (O), *26–32*			
	(A) Olive green body and roof	25	45	____
	(B) Terra-cotta body and roof	25	60	____
550	Miniature Figures, boxed (std), *32–36**	175	455	____
551	Engineer (std), *32*	25	45	____
552	Conductor (std), *32*	20	40	____
553	Porter with stool (std), *32*	25	50	____
554	Male Passenger (std), *32*	25	45	____
555	Female Passenger (std), *32*	25	45	____
556	Red Cap with suitcase (std), *32*	25	65	____
600	Derrick Trailer (2⅞"), *03–04**	5000	8550	____
600	Pullman Car, early (O), *15–23*			
	(A) Dark green	65	170	____
	(B) Maroon or brown	45	85	____
600	Pullman Car, late (O), *33–42*			
	(A) Light red or gray, red roof	50	90	____
	(B) Light blue, aluminum roof	70	120	____

			Good	Exc
	601	Observation Car, late (O), *33–42*		
____		(A) Light red body and roof	50	85
____		(B) Light gray, red roof	50	90
____		(C) Light blue body, aluminum roof	70	120
____	**601**	Pullman Car, early (O), *15–23*	50	70
	602	Lionel Lines Baggage Car, late (O), *33–42*		
____		(A) Light red or gray, red roof	60	110
____		(B) Light blue, aluminum roof	90	150
____	**602**	NYC Baggage Car (O), *15–23*	30	45
____	**602**	Observation Car (O), *22 u*	30	45
____	**603**	Pullman Car, early (O), *22 u*	40	70
____	**603**	Pullman Car, later (O), *20–25*	20	45
	603	Pullman Car, latest (O), *31–36*		
____		(A) Light red body and roof	45	85
____		(B) Red body, black roof	35	60
____		(C) Stephen Girard green body, dark green roof	35	60
____		(D) Maroon body and roof, Macy Special	60	125
____	**604**	Observation Car, later (O), *20–25*	35	60
	604	Observation Car, latest (O), *31–36*		
____		(A) Light red body and roof	45	85
____		(B) Red body, black roof	35	60
____		(C) Yellow-orange body, terra-cotta roof	35	60
____		(D) Stephen Girard green body, dark green roof	35	60
____		(E) Maroon body and roof	70	150
	605	Pullman Car (O), *25–32*		
____		(A) Gray, Lionel Lines	85	170
____		(B) Gray, Illinois Central	85	170
____		(C) Red, Lionel Lines	170	255
____		(D) Red, Illinois Central	255	340
____		(E) Orange, Lionel Lines	170	255
____		(F) Orange, Illinois Central	300	430
____		(G) Olive green, Lionel Lines	255	340
	606	Observation Car (O), *25–32*		
____		(A) Gray, Lionel Lines	130	215
____		(B) Gray, Illinois Central	90	170
____		(C) Red, Lionel Lines	170	255
____		(D) Red, Illinois Central	255	340
____		(E) Orange, Lionel Lines	170	255
____		(F) Orange, Illinois Central	170	255
____		(G) Olive green, Lionel Lines	255	340

		Good	Exc	
607	Pullman Car (0), *26–27*			
	(A) Peacock, Lionel Lines	50	70	____
	(B) Peacock, Illinois Central	75	115	____
	(C) 2-tone green, Lionel Lines	50	75	____
	(D) Red, Lionel Lines	75	110	____
608	Observation Car (0), *26–37*			
	(A) Peacock, Lionel Lines	50	70	____
	(B) Peacock, Illinois Central	75	115	____
	(C) 2-tone green, Lionel Lines	50	75	____
	(D) Red, Lionel Lines	75	110	____
609	Pullman Car (0), *37*	60	85	____
610	Pullman Car, early (0), *15–25*			
	(A) Dark green body and roof	50	65	____
	(B) Maroon body and roof	60	95	____
	(C) Mojave body and roof	60	95	____
610	Pullman Car, late (0), *26–30*			
	(A) Olive green body and roof	65	80	____
	(B) Mojave body and roof	55	80	____
	(C) Terra-cotta body, maroon roof	100	155	____
	(D) Pea green body and roof	70	115	____
	(E) Light blue body, aluminum roof	130	260	____
	(F) Light red body, aluminum-painted roof	100	155	____
611	Observation Car (0), *37*	55	80	____
612	Observation Car, early (0), *15–25*			
	(A) Dark green body and roof	40	60	____
	(B) Maroon body and roof	70	90	____
	(C) Mojave body and roof	70	90	____
612	Observation Car, late (0), *26–30*			
	(A) Olive green body and roof	55	80	____
	(B) Mojave body and roof	55	80	____
	(C) Terra-cotta body, maroon roof	100	155	____
	(D) Pea green body and roof	70	115	____
	(E) Light blue body, aluminum roof	130	260	____
	(F) Light red body, aluminum-painted roof	100	155	____
613	Pullman Car (0), *31–40**			
	(A) Terra-cotta body, maroon/terra-cotta roof	85	195	____
	(B) Light red body, light red/aluminum roof	175	350	____
	(C) Blue, two-tone blue roof	115	225	____
614	Observation Car (0), *31–40**			
	(A) Terra-cotta body, maroon/terra-cotta roof	100	190	____
	(B) Light red body, light red/aluminum roof	175	350	____
	(C) Blue, two-tone blue roof	115	225	____
615	Baggage Car (0), *33–40**	150	260	____
616E/W	Diesel only (0), *35–41*	90	215	____

			Good	Exc
____ **616E/W**	Set: 616, 617 (2), 618		225	570
617	Coach (0), *35–41*			
____	(A) Blue and white		55	85
____	(B) Chrome, gunmetal skirts		55	85
____	(C) Chrome, chrome skirts		55	85
____	(D) Silver-painted		55	85
618	Observation Car (0), *35–41*			
____	(A) Blue and white		55	85
____	(B) Chrome, gunmetal skirts		55	85
____	(C) Chrome, chrome skirts		55	85
____	(D) Silver-painted		55	85
619	Combine Car (0), *36–38*			
____	(A) Blue, white windows band		100	205
____	(B) Chrome, chrome skirts		100	205
____ **620**	Floodlight Car (0), *37–42*		50	85
629	Pullman Car (0), *24–32*			
____	(A) Dark green body and roof		25	40
____	(B) Orange body and roof		25	40
____	(C) Red body and roof		20	35
____	(D) Light red body and roof		30	55
630	Observation Car, *24–32*			
____	(A) Dark green body and roof		25	40
____	(B) Orange body and roof		25	40
____	(C) Red body and roof		20	35
____	(D) Light red body and roof		30	55
____ **636W**	Diesel only (0), *36–39*		90	175
____ **636W**	Set: 636W, 637 (2), 638, *36–39*		375	640
____ **637**	Coach (0), *36–39*		70	105
____ **638**	Observation Car (0), *36–39*		70	105
____ **651**	Flatcar (0), *35–40*		30	65
____ **652**	Gondola (0), *35–40*		30	55
____ **653**	Hopper Car (0), *34–40*		35	65
654	Tank Car (0), *34–42*			
____	(A) Orange or aluminum		35	60
____	(B) Gray		40	75
655	Boxcar (0), *34–42*			
____	(A) Cream, maroon roof		35	60
____	(B) Cream, tuscan roof		45	75
656	Cattle Car (0), *35–40*			
____	(A) Light gray, vermilion roof		40	100
____	(B) Burnt orange, tuscan roof		70	125
657	Caboose (0), *34–42*			
____	(A) Red body and roof		20	35
____	(B) Red body, tuscan roof		25	40

		Good	Exc	
659	Dump Car (O), *35–42*	40	90	____
700	Electric Locomotive 0-4-0 (O), *15–16*	360	690	____
700E	4-6-4 NYC Hudson "5344," scale (O), *37–42**	1400	2950	____
700K	4-6-4 Locomotive, unbuilt gray primer (O), *38–42*	4400	5950	____
701	0-6-0 PRR Locomotive "8976," *41*	900	2100	____
701	Electric Locomotive 0-4-0 (O), *15–16*	390	660	____
702	Baggage Car (O), *17–21*	115	305	____
703	Electric Locomotive 4-4-4 (O), *15–16*	1400	2350	____
706	Electric Locomotive 0-4-0 (O), *15–16*	375	630	____
708	0-6-0 PRR Locomotive "8976" (O), *39–42**	1450	2850	____
710	Pullman Car (O), *24–34*			
	(A) Red, Lionel Lines	200	300	____
	(B) Orange, Lionel Lines	150	225	____
	(C) Orange, New York Central	175	225	____
	(D) Orange, Illinois Central	300	450	____
	(E) 2-tone blue, Lionel Lines	300	415	____
	(F) Orange, New York Central	200	260	____
711	Remote Control Switches, pair (O72), *35–42*	80	190	____
712	Observation Car (O), *24–34*			
	(A) Red, Lionel Lines	185	355	____
	(B) Orange, Lionel Lines	140	265	____
	(C) Orange, New York Central	160	310	____
	(D) Orange, Illinois Central	280	530	____
	(E) 2-tone blue, Lionel Lines	280	485	____
714	Boxcar (O), *40–42**	350	610	____
714K	Boxcar, unbuilt (O), *40–42*	220	480	____
715	Tank Car (O), *40–42**			
	(A) SEPS 8124 decal	340	610	____
	(B) SUNX 715 decal	435	880	____
715K	Tank Car, unbuilt (O), *40–42*	250	530	____
716	Hopper Car (O), *40–42**	290	400	____
716K	Hopper Car, unbuilt (O), *40–42*	350	730	____
717	Caboose (O), *40–42**	340	510	____
717K	Caboose, unbuilt (O), *40–42*	275	590	____
720	90-degree Crossing (O72), *35–42*	20	40	____
721	Manual Switches, pair (O72), *35–42*	50	105	____
730	90-degree Crossing (O72), *35–42*	20	40	____
731	Remote Control Switches, pair, T-rail (O72), *35–42*	80	135	____
751E/W	Set: 752, 753 (2), 754 (O), *34–41**	640	1050	____
752E	Diesel only (O), *34–41**			
	(A) Yellow and brown	170	355	____
	(B) Aluminum	145	340	____

			Good	Exc
	753	Coach (O), *36–41*		
___		(A) Yellow and brown	85	185
___		(B) Aluminum	75	180
	754	Observation Car (O), *36–41*		
___		(A) Yellow and brown	80	185
___		(B) Aluminum	75	180
___	**760**	Curved Track, 16 pieces, (O72), *35–42*	40	80
___	**761**	Curved Track (O72), *34–42*	1	2
___	**762**	Straight Track (O72), *34–42*	1	2
___	**762S**	Insulated Straight Track (O72), *34–42*	2	5
	763E	4-6-4 Locomotive (O), *37–42*		
___		(A) Gunmetal, 263 or 2263W Tender	1000	2125
___		(B) Gunmetal, 2226X or 2226WX Tender	1150	2950
___		(C) Black, 2226WX Tender	965	2650
___	**771**	Curved Track, T-rail (O72), *35–42*	3	10
___	**772**	Straight Track, T-rail (O72), *35–42*	5	20
___	**772S**	Insulated Straight Track, T-rail (O72), *35–42*	15	30
___	**773**	Fishplate Set, 50 plates (O72), *36–42*	15	30
___	**782**	Hiawatha Combine Car (O), *35–41**	230	380
___	**783**	Hiawatha Coach (O), *35–41**	140	290
___	**784**	Hiawatha Observation Car (O), *35–41**	205	445
___	**792**	Rail Chief Combine Car (O), *37–41**	215	580
___	**793**	Rail Chief Coach (O), *37–41**	290	800
___	**794**	Rail Chief Observation Car (O), *37–41**	250	800
___	**800**	Boxcar (2⅞"), *04–05**	2500	4050
	800	Boxcar (O), *15–26*		
___		(A) Light orange body, brown-maroon roof	45	70
___		(B) Orange body and roof, PRR	25	45
___	**801**	Caboose (O), *15–26*	30	50
___	**802**	Stock Car (O), *15–26*	40	60
___	**803**	Hopper Car, early (O), *23–28*	25	55
___	**803**	Hopper Car, late (O), *29–34*	30	55
___	**804**	Tank Car (O), *23–28*	20	45
	805	Boxcar (O), *27–34*		
___		(A) Pea green, terra-cotta roof	35	55
___		(B) Pea green, maroon roof	45	115
___		(C) Orange, maroon roof	45	95
	806	Stock Car (O), *27–34*		
___		(A) Pea green, terra-cotta roof	40	75
___		(B) Orange, various color roofs	35	50
	807	Caboose (O), *27–40*		
___		(A) Peacock body, dark green roof	20	35
___		(B) Red body, peacock roof	20	40
___		(C) Light red body and roof	20	40

		Good	Exc	
809	Dump Car (0), *31–41*			
	(A) Orange bin	40	55	___
	(B) Green bin	40	85	___
810	Crane Car (0), *30–42*			
	(A) Terra-cotta cab, maroon roof	170	270	___
	(B) Cream cab, vermilion roof	130	205	___
811	Flatcar (0), *26–40*			
	(A) Maroon	40	70	___
	(B) Aluminum	50	100	___
812	Gondola (0), *26–42*	40	70	___
812T	Tool Set: pick, shovel, spade, *30–41*	40	95	___
813	Stock Car (0), *26–42*			
	(A) Orange body, pea green roof	65	145	___
	(B) Orange body, maroon roof	55	135	___
	(C) Cream body, maroon roof	100	225	___
	(D) Tuscan body and roof	800	1600	___
814	Boxcar (0), *26–42*			
	(A) Cream, orange roof	50	145	___
	(B) Cream, maroon roof	115	140	___
	(C) Yellow, brown roof	110	120	___
814R	Refrigerator Car (0), *29–42*			
	(A) Ivory, peacock roof	100	200	___
	(B) White, light blue roof	120	265	___
	(C) Flat white, brown roof	600	900	___
815	Tank Car (0), *26–42*			
	(A) Pea green, maroon frame	250	510	___
	(B) Pea green, black frame	70	155	___
	(C) Aluminum, black frame	50	100	___
	(D) Orange-yellow, black frame	150	255	___
816	Hopper Car (0), *27–42*			
	(A) Olive green	85	155	___
	(B) Red body	65	140	___
	(C) Black body	370	680	___
817	Caboose (0), *26–42*			
	(A) Peacock body, dark green roof	45	70	___
	(B) Red body, peacock roof	45	80	___
	(C) Light red body and roof	45	80	___
820	Boxcar (0), *15–26*			
	(A) Orange, Illinois Central	40	80	___
	(B) Orange, Union Pacific	50	105	___
820	Floodlight Car (0), *31–42*			
	(A) Terra-cotta	100	180	___
	(B) Green	100	175	___
	(C) Light green	105	180	___
821	Stock Car (0), *15–16, 25–26*	45	85	___

			Good	Exc
____	822	Caboose (O), *15–26*	35	65
____	831	Flatcar (O), *27–34*	20	45
____	840	Industrial Power Station, *28–40**	1200	3050
____	900	Ammunition Car (O), *17–21*	120	340
____	900	Box Trail Car (2⅞"), *04–05**	2000	3600
____	901	Gondola (O), *19–27*	25	50
____	902	Gondola (O), *27–34*	25	45
____	910	Grove of Trees, *32–42*	70	155
____	911	Country Estate, *32–42*	195	440
____	912	Suburban Home	300	620
____	913	Landscaped Bungalow, *40–42*	140	285
____	914	Park Landscape, *32–35*	90	205
____	915	Tunnel, 65" or 60" long, *32–33, 35*	160	435
____	916	Tunnel, 29" long, *35*	95	180
____	917	Scenic Hillside, 34" x 15", *32–36*	90	205
____	918	Scenic Hillside, 30" x 10", *32–36*	90	205
____	919	Park Grass, cloth bag, *32–42*	10	20
____	920	Village, *32–33*	600	1600
____	921	Scenic Park, 3 pieces, *32–33*	980	2600
____	921C	Park Center, *32–33*	400	1050
____	922	Terrace, *32–36*	90	255
____	923	Tunnel, 40" long, *33–42*	125	225
____	924	Tunnel, 30" long (072), *35–42*	50	135
____	925	Lubricant, *35–42*	25	120
____	927	Flag Plot, *37–42*	70	135
____	1000	Passenger Car (2⅞"), *05**	4500	6750
____	1000	Trolley Trailer (std), *10–16*	1400	2250
____	1010	Electric Locomotive 0-4-0, Winner Lines (O), *31–32*	90	160
____	1010	Interurban Trailer (std), *10–16*	1000	1800
____	1011	Pullman Car, Winner Lines (O), *31–32*	45	75
____	1012	Station, *32*	40	70
____	1015	0-4-0 Locomotive (O), *31–32*	100	205
____	1017	Winner Station, *33*	25	70
____	1019	Observation Car (O), *31–32*	50	70
____	1020	Baggage Car (O), *31–32*	65	110
____	1021	90-degree Crossover (027), *32–42*	1	5
____	1022	Tunnel, 18" long (O), *35–42*	15	30
____	1023	Tunnel, 19" long, *34–42*	20	40
____	1024	Switches, pair (027), *37–42*	5	15
____	1025	Bumper (027), *40–42*	15	25
____	1027	Transformer Station, *34*	50	115
____	1028	Transformer, 40 watts, *39*	3	10
____	1029	Transformer, 25 watts, *36*	5	20

No.	Description	Good	Exc	
1030	Electric Locomotive 0-4-0 (O), 32	75	135	___
1030	Transformer, 40 watts, 35–38	6	25	___
1035	0-4-0 Locomotive (O), 32	75	115	___
1037	Transformer, 40 watts, 40–42	7	25	___
1038	Transformer, 30 watts, 40	2	5	___
1039	Transformer, 35 watts, 37–40	7	20	___
1040	Transformer, 60 watts, 37–39	10	30	___
1041	Transformer, 60 watts, 39–42	15	30	___
1045	Watchman, 38–42	30	65	___
1050	Passenger Car Trailer (2⅞"), 05*	5000	7200	___
1100	Summer Trolley Trailer (std), 10–13		NRS	___
1100	Mickey Mouse Handcar, 35–37*			
	(A) Red base	405	640	___
	(B) Apple green base, orange shoes	500	880	___
	(C) Orange base	600	1225	___
1103	Peter Rabbit Handcar (O), 35–37*	330	820	___
1105	Santa Claus Handcar (O), 35–35*			
	(A) Red base	660	1050	___
	(B) Green base	720	1200	___
1107	Transformer Station, 33	25	70	___
1107	Donald Duck Handcar (O), 36–37*			
	(A) White dog house, red roof	475	1200	___
	(B) White dog house, green roof	450	1100	___
	(C) Orange dog house, green roof	640	1850	___
1121	Switches, pair (027), 37–42	15	35	___
1506L	0-4-0 Locomotive (O), 33–34	95	125	___
1506M	0-4-0 Locomotive (O), 35	250	430	___
1508	0-4-0 Commodore Vanderbilt with 1509 Mickey Mouse stoker Tender, 35	420	690	___
1511	0-4-0 Locomotive (O), 36–37	110	160	___
1512	Gondola (O), 31–33, 36–37	25	50	___
1514	Boxcar (O), 31–37	25	40	___
1515	Tank Car (O), 33–37	25	40	___
1517	Caboose (O), 31–37	25	40	___
1518	Mickey Mouse Circus Dining Car (O), 35	120	260	___
1519	Mickey Mouse Band Car (O), 35	120	260	___
1520	Mickey Mouse Circus Car (O), 35	120	260	___
1536	Mickey Mouse Circus Set: 1508, 1509, 1518, 1519, 1520, 35	770	1350	___
1550	Switches, for windup trains, pair, 33–37	2	5	___
1555	90-degree Crossover, for windup trains, 33–37	1	2	___
1560	Station, 33–37	15	35	___
1569	Accessory Set, 8 pieces, 33–37	35	70	___
1588	0-4-0 Locomotive (O), 36–37	150	250	___

			Good	Exc
	1630	Pullman Car (0), *38–42*		
____		(A) Aluminum windows	35	70
____		(B) Light gray windows	45	80
	1631	Observation Car (0), *38–42*		
____		(A) Aluminum windows	35	70
____		(B) Light gray windows	45	80
____	**1651E**	Electric Locomotive 0-4-0 (0), *33*	130	240
____	**1661E**	2-4-0 Locomotive (0), *33*	75	160
____	**1662**	0-4-0 Locomotive (027), *40–42*	218	420
____	**1663**	0-4-0 Locomotive (027), *40–42*	200	385
	1664/E	2-4-2 Locomotive (027), *38–42*		
____		(A) Gunmetal	60	100
____		(B) Black	60	95
	1666/E	2-6-2 Locomotive (027), *38–42*		
____		(A) Gunmetal	115	170
____		(B) Black	95	145
	1668/E	2-6-2 Locomotive (027), *37–41*		
____		(A) Gunmetal	75	115
____		(B) Black	75	130
	1673	Coach (0), *36–37*		
____		(A) Aluminum windows	35	75
____		(B) Light gray windows	45	90
____	**1674**	Pullman Car (0), *36–37*	35	75
____	**1675**	Observation Car (0), *36–37*	30	70
	1677	Gondola (0), *33–35, 39–42*		
____		(A) Light blue, Ives	40	60
____		(B) Blue or red, Lionel	20	40
	1679	Boxcar (0), *33–42*		
____		(A) Cream, Ives	25	40
____		(B) Cream, Lionel	25	40
____		(C) Cream or yellow, Baby Ruth	20	40
	1680	Tank Car (0), *33–42*		
____		(A) Aluminum, Ives Tank Lines	60	95
____		(B) Aluminum, no Ives lettering	20	35
____		(C) Orange, Shell Oil	15	30
	1681	2-4-0 Locomotive (0), *34–35*		
____		(A) Black, red frame	55	120
____		(B) Red, red frame	110	145
	1681E	2-4-0 Locomotive (0), *34–35*		
____		(A) Black, red frame	65	130
____		(B) Red, red frame	130	165
	1682	Caboose (0), *33–42*		
____		(A) Vermilion, Ives	35	70
____		(B) Red or tuscan, Lionel	20	40

		Good	Exc	
1684	2-4-2 Locomotive (027), *41–42*			
	(A) Black	45	70	____
	(B) Gunmetal	45	70	____
1685	Coach (0), *33–37 u*			
	(A) Gray, maroon roof	240	495	____
	(B) Red, maroon roof	170	335	____
	(C) Blue, silver roof	170	315	____
1686	Baggage Car (0), *33–37 u*			
	(A) Gray, maroon roof	240	495	____
	(B) Red, maroon roof	170	335	____
	(C) Blue, silver roof	170	315	____
1687	Observation Car (0), *33–37 u*			
	(A) Gray, maroon roof	170	315	____
	(B) Red, maroon roof	180	315	____
	(C) Blue, silver roof	170	315	____
1688/E	2-4-2 Locomotive (027), *36–46*	50	125	____
1689E	2-4-2 Locomotive (027), *36–37*			
	(A) Gunmetal	75	115	____
	(B) Black	60	100	____
1689T	Tender, black	15	30	____
1690	Pullman Car (0), *33–40*	35	60	____
1691	Observation Car (0), *33–40*	35	60	____
1692	Pullman Car (027), *39 u*	45	70	____
1693	Observation Car (027), *39 u*	45	70	____
1700E	Diesel, power unit only (027), *35–37*	45	70	____
1700E	Set: 1700, 1701 (2), 1702, *35–37 u*			
	(A) Aluminum and light red	140	250	____
	(B) Chrome and light red	140	250	____
	(C) Orange and gray	155	285	____
1701	Coach (027), *35–37*			
	(A) Chrome sides and roof	20	45	____
	(B) Silver sides and roof	30	55	____
	(C) Orange and gray	75	150	____
1702	Observation Car (027), *35–37*			
	(A) Chrome sides and roof	20	45	____
	(B) Silver sides and roof	30	55	____
	(C) Orange and gray	75	150	____
1703	Observation Car, hooked coupler, *35–37 u*	50	110	____
1717	Gondola (0), *33–40 u*	30	50	____
1717X	Gondola (0), *40 u*	25	50	____
1719	Boxcar (0), *33–40 u*	30	50	____
1719X	Boxcar (0), *41–42 u*	30	50	____
1722	Caboose (0), *33–42 u*	25	50	____
1722X	Caboose (0), *39–40 u*	25	40	____

			Good	Exc
	1766	Pullman Car (std), *34–40**		
____		(A) Terra-cotta, maroon roof, brass trim	300	650
____		(B) Red, maroon roof, nickel trim	300	540
	1767	Baggage Car (std), *34–40**		
____		(A) Terra-cotta, maroon roof, brass trim	295	850
____		(B) Red, maroon roof, nickel trim	295	700
	1768	Observation Car (std), *34–40**		
____		(A) Terra-cotta, maroon roof, brass trim	300	650
____		(B) Red, maroon roof, nickel trim	300	540
____	1811	Pullman Car (O), *33–37*	35	70
____	1812	Observation Car (O), *33–37*	30	65
____	1813	Baggage Car (O), *33–37*	60	135
____	1816/W	Diesel (O), *35–37*	100	240
____	1817	Coach (O), *35–37*	25	50
____	1818	Observation Car (O), *35–37*	25	50
____	1835E	2-4-2 Locomotive (std), *34–39*	470	730
____	1910	Electric Locomotive 0-6-0, early (std), *10–11*	920	1550
____	1910	Electric Locomotive 0-6-0, late (std), *12*	550	1350
____	1910	Pullman Car (std), *09–10 u*	860	1800
____	1911	Electric Locomotive 0-4-0, early (std), *10–12*	860	1700
____	1911	Electric Locomotive 0-4-0, late (std), *13*	700	1100
	1911	Electric Locomotive 0-4-4-0 Special (std), *11–12*	860	2500
	1912	Electric Locomotive 0-4-4-0 (std), *10–12**		
____		(A) New York, New Haven & Hartford	1550	3200
____		(B) New York Central Lines	1300	2700
____	1912	Electric Locomotive 0-4-4-0 Special (std), *11**	2500	4500
____	2200	Summer Trolley Trailer (std), *10–13*	1100	2250
____	2203B	Tender	40	80
____	2224W	Tender	55	115
____	2225W	Tender	30	60
____	2228B	Tender	140	280
____	2235W	Tender	25	50
____	2600	Pullman Car (O), *38–42*	80	155
____	2601	Observation Car (O), *38–42*	60	115
____	2602	Baggage Car (O), *38–42*	90	185
	2613	Pullman Car (O), *38–42**		
____		(A) Blue, 2-tone blue roof	100	300
____		(B) State green, 2-tone green roof	200	440
	2614	Observation Car (O), *38–42**		
____		(A) Blue, 2-tone blue roof	100	300
____		(B) State green, 2-tone green roof	200	440
	2615	Baggage Car (O), *38–42**		
____		(A) Blue, 2-tone blue roof	115	300
____		(B) State green, 2-tone green roof	200	420

	Good	Exc
2620	Floodlight Car (O), *38–42*	65	100 ___
2623	Pullman Car (O), *41–42*			
	(A) Irvington	175	335 ___
	(B) Manhattan	165	310 ___
2624	Pullman Car (O), *41–42*	750	1700 ___
2630	Pullman Car (O), *38–42*	30	70 ___
2631	Observation Car (O), *38–42*	30	70 ___
2640	Pullman Car, illuminated (O), *38–42*			
	(A) Light blue, aluminum roof	30	70 ___
	(B) State green, dark green roof	30	70 ___
2641	Observation Car, illuminated (O), *38–42*			
	(A) Light blue, aluminum roof	30	70 ___
	(B) State green, dark green roof	30	70 ___
2642	Pullman Car (O), *41–42*	30	70 ___
2643	Observation Car (O), *41–42*	30	65 ___
2651	Flatcar (O), *38–42*	30	50 ___
2652	Gondola (O), *38–41*	25	65 ___
2653	Hopper Car (O), *38–42*			
	(A) Stephen Girard green	35	70 ___
	(B) Black	60	130 ___
2654	Tank Car (O), *38–42*			
	(A) Aluminum, Sunoco	35	60 ___
	(B) Orange, Shell	35	60 ___
	(C) Light gray, Sunoco	40	70 ___
2655	Boxcar (O), *38–42*			
	(A) Cream, maroon roof	35	65 ___
	(B) Cream, tuscan roof	40	70 ___
2656	Stock Car (O), *38–41*			
	(A) Light gray, red roof	45	75 ___
	(B) Burnt orange, tuscan roof	75	115 ___
2657	Caboose (O), *40–41*	30	45 ___
2657X	Caboose (O), *40–41*	25	40 ___
2659	Dump Car (O), *38–41*	40	70 ___
2660	Crane Car (O), *38–42*	85	165 ___
2672	Caboose (027), *41–42*	20	50 ___
2677	Gondola (027), *39–41*	25	40 ___
2679	Boxcar (027), *38–42*	15	30 ___
2680	Tank Car (027), *38–42*			
	(A) Aluminum, Sunoco	15	40 ___
	(B) Orange, Shell	15	40 ___
2682	Caboose (027), *38–42*	15	30 ___
2682X	Caboose (027), *38–42*	20	35 ___
2689T	Tender	15	25 ___
2689W	Tender	35	50 ___
2717	Gondola (O), *38–42 u*	20	40 ___

			Good	Exc
____	2719	Boxcar (O), *38–42 u*	30	50
____	2722	Caboose (O), *38–42 u*	25	50
____	2755	Tank Car (O), *41–42*	70	130
____	2757	Caboose (O), *41–42*	25	45
____	2757X	Caboose (O), *41–42*	25	40
____	2758	Automobile Boxcar (O), *41–42*	35	60
____	2810	Crane Car (O), *38–42*	145	210
____	2811	Flatcar (O), *38–42*	65	95
	2812	Gondola (O), *38–42*		
____		(A) Green	40	85
____		(B) Dark orange	45	95
____	2813	Stock Car (O), *38–42*	120	225
	2814	Boxcar (O), *38–42*		
____		(A) Cream, maroon roof	85	150
____		(B) Orange, brown roof, rubber-stamped lettering	200	700
	2814R	Refrigerator Car (O), *38–42*		
____		(A) White, light blue roof, nickel plates	150	260
____		(B) White, brown roof, no plates	375	660
	2815	Tank Car (O), *38–42*		
____		(A) Aluminum	85	165
____		(B) Orange	135	215
	2816	Hopper Car (O), *35–42*		
____		(A) Red	100	190
____		(B) Black	110	220
	2817	Caboose (O), *36–42*		
____		(A) Light red body and roof	90	140
____		(B) Flat red body, tuscan roof	140	180
	2820	Floodlight Car (O), *38–42*		
____		(A) Stamped nickel searchlights	110	205
____		(B) Gray die-cast searchlights	120	260
____	2954	Boxcar (O), *40–42**	145	350
	2955	Sunoco Tank Car (O), *40–42**		
____		(A) Shell decal	225	500
____		(B) Sunoco decal	340	690
____	2956	Hopper Car (O), *40–42**	160	400
____	2957	Caboose (O), *40–42**	70	310
____	3300	Summer Trolley Trailer (std), *10–13*	1400	2250
____	3651	Operating Lumber Car (O), *39–42*	25	55
____	3652	Operating Gondola (O), *39–42*	35	75
____	3659	Operating Dump Car (O), *39–42*	20	40
____	3811	Operating Lumber Car (O), *39–42*	35	100
____	3814	Operating Merchandise Car (O), *39–42*	90	195
____	3859	Operating Dump Car (O), *38–42*	45	90

Other Transformers and Motors

		Good	Exc	
A	Miniature Motor, *04*	50	95	____
A	Transformer, 40, 60 watts, *21–37*	8	25	____
B	New Departure Motor, *06–16*	75	135	____
B	Transformer, 50, 75 watts, *16–38*	8	25	____
C	New Departure Motor, *06–16*	100	180	____
D	New Departure Motor, *06–14*	100	180	____
E	New Departure Motor, *06–14*	100	180	____
F	New Departure Motor, *06–14*	100	180	____
G	Fan Motor, battery-operated, *06–14*	100	180	____
K	Transformer, 150, 200 watts, *13–38*	20	95	____
L	Transformer, 50, 75 watts, *13–16, 33–38*	8	25	____
M	Peerless Motor, battery-operated, *15–20*	30	80	____
N	Transformer, 50 watts, *41–42*	8	25	____
Q	Transformer, 50 watts, *14–15*	15	30	____
Q	Transformer, 75 watts, *38–42*	15	40	____
R	Peerless Motor, battery-operated, reversing, *15–20*	30	75	____
R	Transformer, 100 watts, *38–42*	25	60	____
S	Transformer, 50 watts, *14–17*	20	40	____
T	Transformer, 75, 100, 150 watts, *14–28*	10	30	____
U	Transformer, Aladdin, *32–33*	5	15	____
V	Transformer, 150 watts, *39–42*	55	95	____
W	Transformer, 75 watts, *32–33*	10	35	____
Y	Peerless Motor, battery-operated, 3-speed, *15–20*	40	80	____
Z	Transformer, 250 watts, *39–42*	110	170	____

Track, Lockons, and Contactors

	Good	Exc	
0 Straight		1	____
0 Curve		1	____
072 Straight	1	2	____
072 Curve	1	2	____
027 Straight		1	____
027 Curve		1	____
Standard Straight	1	3	____
Standard Curve	1	2	____
Standard Insulated Straight, *33–42*	2	4	____
Standard Insulated Curve, *33–42*	1	2	____
0 Gauge Lockon		1	____
Standard Gauge Lockon		1	____
UTC Lockon		1	____
145C Contactor	3	10	____
153C Contactor	3	7	____
Track Clips, dozen (0), *37*	5	10	____

		Good	Exc
_____ 5C	Test Set	700	1325
_____ 5E	Electronic Set Tester, *46–49*	1000	3000
_____ 5F	Test Set	700	1360
_____ 011-11	Fiber Pins, dozen (0), *46–50*	1	3
_____ 011-43	Insulating Pins, dozen (0), *61*	1	2
_____ 020	90-degree Crossover (0), *45–61*	3	6
_____ 020X	45-degree Crossover (0), *46–59*	4	9
_____ 022	Remote Control Switches, pair (0), *45–69*	20	45
_____ 022-500	Adapter Set (0), *57–61*	1	6
_____ 022A	Remote Control Switches, pair (0), *47*	28	102
_____ 022C-1	Switch Controller	6	15
_____ 25	Bumper (0), *46–47*	5	16
26	Bumper, *48–50*		
_____	(A) Red, *49–50*	6	14
_____	(B) Gray, *48*	18	52
_____ 027C-1	Track Clips, box of 12 (027), *47, 49*	4	17
_____ 027C-1	Track Clips, box of 50 (027)	30	90
_____ 30	Water Tower, *47–50*	23	80
_____ 31	Curved Track (Super 0), *57–66*	1	3
_____ 31-7	Power Blade Connection, dozen (Super 0), *57–60*		12
_____ 31-15	Ground Rail Pin, dozen (Super 0), *57–66*		5
_____ 31-45	Power Blade Connection, dozen (Super 0), *61–66*		12
_____ 32	Straight Track (Super 0), *57–66*	2	4
_____ 32-10	Insulating Pin, dozen (Super 0), *57–60*		12
_____ 32-20	Power Blade Insulator, dozen (Super 0), *57–60*		4
_____ 32-25	Insulating Pin (Super 0), *57–61*		1
_____ 32-30	Ground Pin (Super 0), *57–61*		1
_____ 32-31	Power Pin (Super 0), *57–61*		1
_____ 32-32	Insulating Pin (Super 0), *57–61*		1
_____ 32-33	Ground Pin (Super 0), *57–61*		1
_____ 32-34	Power Pin (Super 0), *57–61*		1
_____ 32-35	Insulating Pin, dozen (Super 0 to 027), *57–61*		3
_____ 32-45	Power Blade Insulators, dozen (Super 0), *61–66*	3	8
_____ 32-55	Insulating Pins, dozen (Super 0), *61–66*	3	8
_____ 33	Half Curved Track (Super 0), *57–66*	1	3
_____ 34	Half Straight Track (Super 0), *57–66*	2	4
_____ 35	Boulevard Lamp, *45–49*	10	40
_____ 36	Operating Car Remote Control Set (Super 0), *57–66*	10	20
_____ 37	Uncoupling Track Set (Super 0), *57–66*	8	20
_____ 38	Accessory Adapter Tracks, pair (Super 0), *57–61*	6	15

		Good	Exc
38	Operating Water Tower, *46–47*	110	307 ____
39	Operating Set (Super O), *57*	4	8 ____
39-5	Operating Set (Super O), *57–58*	4	8 ____
39-6	Operating Set (Super O), *57–58*	4	13 ____
39-10	Operating Set (Super O), *58*	4	8 ____
39-15	Operating Set with blade (Super O), *57–58*	4	8 ____
39-20	Operating Set (Super O), *57–58*	4	8 ____
39-25	Operating Set (Super O), *61–66*	8	23 ____
39-35	Operating Set (Super O), *59*	8	23 ____
40	Hookup Wire, *50–51, 53–63*		
	(A) Single reel, orange or gray, with tape	6	33 ____
	(B) 8 sealed reels in dealer box	115	410 ____
40-25	Conductor Wire with envelope, *56–59*	10	38 ____
40-50	Cable Reel with envelope, *60–61*	10	35 ____
41	Contactor (Super O)	1	2 ____
41	U.S. Army Switcher, *55–57*		
	(A) Unpainted black body	71	100 ____
	(B) Black-painted body	200	900 ____
042/42	Manual Switches, pair (O), *46–59*	10	25 ____
42	Picatinny Arsenal Switcher, *57*	100	277 ____
43	Power Track (Super O), *59–66*	4	16 ____
44	U.S. Army Mobile Launcher, *59–62*	62	185 ____
44-80	Missiles, *59–60*	10	25 ____
45	U.S. Marines Mobile Launcher, *60–62*	90	255 ____
45	Automatic Gateman, *46–49*	15	45 ____
45N	Automatic Gateman, *45*	20	50 ____
48	Insulated Straight Track (Super O), *57–66*	4	10 ____
49	Insulated Curved Track (Super O), *57–66*	4	10 ____
50	Section Gang Car, *54–64*		
	(A) Gray bumpers, rotating blue man and fixed olive men, center horn, *54*	265	724 ____
	(B) Blue bumpers, rotating olive man and fixed blue men, center horn	32	61 ____
	(C) Blue bumpers, rotating olive man and fixed blue men, off-center horn	25	43 ____
51	Navy Yard Switcher, *56–57*	70	175 ____
52	Fire Car, *58–61*	68	185 ____
53	Rio Grande Snowplow, *57–60*		
	(A) Backwards "a" in Rio Grande	68	210 ____
	(B) Correctly printed "a"	150	580 ____
54	Ballast Tamper, *58–61, 66, 68–69*	75	170 ____
55	PRR Tie-Jector Car, *57–61*		
	(A) Ventilation slot behind motorman	52	165 ____
	(B) No slot behind motorman	45	105 ____
55-150	Ties, 24 pieces, *57–60*	13	30 ____
56	Lamp Post, *46–49*	23	45 ____
56	M&StL Mine Transport, *58*	165	370 ____

		Good	Exc
____57	AEC Switcher, *59–60*	152	522
____58	GN Snowplow, *59–61*	175	410
____58	Lamp Post, *46–50*	17	43
____59	Minuteman Switcher, *62–63*	185	453
60	Lionelville Rapid Transit Trolley, *55–58*		
____	(A) Metal motorman silhouettes	112	258
____	(B) No motorman silhouettes	53	100
____61	Ground Lockon (Super O), *57–66*	2	5
61-25	Super O Ground clips, dozen, with dealer envelope		
____		5	18
____62	Power Lockon (Super O), *57–66*	1	4
____64	Street Lamp, *45–49*	15	40
65	Handcar, *62–66*		
____	(A) Light yellow	80	270
____	(B) Dark yellow	70	240
____68	Executive Inspection Car, *58–61*	77	165
____69	Maintenance Car, *60–62*	85	215
____70	Yard Light, *49–50*	13	30
____71	Lamp Post, *49–59*	9	13
____75	Goose Neck Lamps, set of 2, *61–63*	10	20
76	Boulevard Street Lamps, set of 3, *59–66, 68–69*		
____		15	30
____88	Controller, *46–60*	9	15
____89	Flagpole, *56–58*	15	50
90	Controller, *55–66*		
____	(A) Metal clip	6	11
____	(B) No metal clip	5	8
____91	Circuit Breaker, *57–60*	10	23
____92	Circuit Breaker, *59–66, 68–69*	6	13
____93	Water Tower, *46–49*	18	48
____96C	Controller, *45–54*	3	9
____97	Coal Elevator, *46–50*	65	163
____108	Trestle Set, 12 black piers	10	25
____109	Partial Trestle Set, *61*	5	17
____110	Graduated Trestle Set, 22 or 24 piers, *55–69*	8	18
____110-75	Graduated Trestle Set with 110-78 envelope	10	35
____111	Elevated Trestle Set, 10 A piers, *56–69*	7	13
____111-100	Elevated Trestle Piers, set of 2, *60–63*	15	45
____112	Remote Control Switches, pair (Super O), *57–66*	50	90
____114	Newsstand with horn, *57–59*	38	85
____115	Passenger Station, *46–49*	130	270
____118	Newsstand with whistle, *57–58*	40	90
____119	Landscaped Tunnel, *57–58*	200	400
____120	90-degree Crossing (Super O), *57–66*	7	15
____121	Landscaped Tunnel, *59–66*		NRS
____122	Lamp Assortment, *48–52*	30	210
____123	Lamp Assortment, *55–59*	70	175

		Good	Exc	
123-60	Lamp Assortment, *60–63*	25	180	___
125	Whistle Shack, *50–55*			
	(A) Gray base	10	40	___
	(B) Green base	20	50	___
128	Animated Newsstand, *57–60*	68	113	___
130	60-degree Crossing (Super O), *57–66*	8	13	___
131	Curved Tunnel, *59–66*		NRS	___
132	Passenger Station, *49–55*	38	73	___
133	Passenger Station, *57, 61–62, 66*	20	50	___
138	Water Tower, *53–57*	25	68	___
140	Automatic Banjo Signal, *54–66*	15	30	___
142	Manual Switches, pair (Super O), *57–66*	30	61	___
145	Automatic Gateman, *50–66*			
	(A) Red roof	13	40	___
	(B) Maroon roof	10	35	___
145C	Contactor, *50–60*	3	9	___
147	Whistle Controller, *61–66*	2	6	___
148	Dwarf Trackside Signal, *57–60*	25	55	___
148-100	Controller (SPDT switch), *57–60*	7	18	___
150	Telegraph Pole Set, *47–50*	30	55	___
151	Automatic Semaphore, *47–69*			
	(A) Green base, yellow blade, *47*	20	60	___
	(B) Black base, yellow blade, *47*	15	25	___
	(C) Black base, red blade, *47*	165	398	___
	(D) Green base, yellow blade with raised lenses	20	88	___
152	Automatic Crossing Gate, *45–49*	8	18	___
153	Automatic Block Control Signal, *45–59*	15	25	___
153C	Contactor	3	8	___
154	Automatic Highway Signal, *45–69*	15	25	___
154C	Contactor	4	10	___
155	Blinking Light Signal with bell, *55–57*	20	50	___
156	Station Platform, *46–49*	33	85	___
156-5	Station Platform Fence with envelope	30	68	___
157	Station Platform, *52–59*			
	(A) Maroon base	15	38	___
	(B) Red base	25	75	___
157-23	Station Platform Fence with envelope	13	60	___
160	Unloading Bin, *52–57*			
	(A) Black plastic, long	3	11	___
	(B) Black metal, short	34	70	___
	(C) Multicolor Bakelite, short	7	26	___
	(D) Black Bakelite, short	4	14	___
161	Mail Pickup Set, *61–63*	20	58	___
163	Single Target Block Signal, *61–69*	15	30	___
164	Log Loader, *46–50*	73	175	___
164-64	Log Set, 5 pieces, *52–58*	35	70	___

			Good	Exc
____**167**	Whistle Controller, *45–46*		3	11
____**175**	Rocket Launcher, *58–60*		58	158
____**175-50**	Extra Rocket, *59–60*		10	25
____**182**	Magnetic Crane, *46–49*		108	250
____**182-22**	Steel Scrap with bag, *46–49*		48	132
____**192**	Operating Control Tower, *59–60*		115	248
193	Industrial Water Tower, *53–55*			
____	(A) Red		50	85
____	(B) Black, *53*		90	180
195	Floodlight Tower, *57–69*			
____	(A) Medium tan base, rubber-stamped lettering		25	70
____	(B) All other variations		23	55
____**195-75**	Floodlight Extension, 8-bulb (with box), *58–60*		30	92
____**196**	Smoke Pellets, *46–47*		35	125
197	Rotating Radar Antenna, *57–59*			
____	(A) Orange platform		40	103
____	(B) Gray platform		30	75
____**197-75**	Separate Sale Radar Head with box		48	175
____**199**	Microwave Relay Tower, *58–59*		30	75
____**202**	UP Alco Diesel A Unit, *57*		35	80
____**204**	Santa Fe Alco Diesel AA Units, *57*		75	220
205	Missouri Pacific Alco Diesel AA Units, *57–58*			
____	(A) Pilot without support		45	130
____	(B) Pilot with painted metal support		70	175
____**206**	Artificial Coal, large bag, *46–68*		13	23
____**207**	Artificial Coal, small bag, *46–48*		7	15
____**208**	Santa Fe Alco Diesel AA Units, *58–59*		58	235
____**209**	New Haven Alco Diesel AA Units, *58*		225	685
____**209**	Wooden Barrels, set of 6, *46–50*		10	17
____**210**	Texas Special Alco Diesel AA Units, *58*		50	135
____**211**	Texas Special Alco Diesel AA Units, *62–66*		60	138
____**212**	Santa Fe Alco Diesel AA Units, *64–66*		65	165
____**212**	USMC Alco Diesel A Unit, *58–59*		65	150
____**212T**	USMC Diesel Dummy A Unit, *58 u*		285	975
____**213**	M&StL Alco Diesel AA Units, *64*		75	225
____**214**	Plate Girder Bridge, *53–69*		7	17
215	Santa Fe Alco Diesel Units, *65 u*			
____	(A) AB Units		60	130
____	(B) AA Units		75	150
____**216**	Burlington Alco Diesel A Unit, *58*		105	360
216	M&StL Alco Diesel AA Units (213T dummy			
____	A unit), *64 u*		63	240
____**217**	B&M Alco Diesel AB Units, *59*		90	225
____**217C**	B&M Alco Diesel B Unit, *59*		30	75

		Good	Exc
218	Santa Fe Alco Diesel Units, *59–63*		
	(A) AA Units	70	165____
	(B) AB Units	65	155____
	(C) AA Units, solid nose decal	70	233____
218C	Santa Fe Alco B Unit, *61–63*	45	95____
219	Missouri Pacific Alco Diesel AA Units, *59 u*	75	165____
220	Santa Fe Alco Diesel Units, *60–61*		
	(A) A Unit	40	110____
	(B) AA Units	65	195____
221	2-6-4 Locomotive, 221W Tender, *46–47*		
	(A) Gray body, black drivers	60	155____
	(B) Black body, nickel-rimmed black drivers, *47*	70	170____
	(C) Gray body, cast-aluminum drivers, *46*	110	255____
221	Rio Grande Alco Diesel A Unit, *63–64*	30	65____
221	Santa Fe Alco Diesel A Unit, *63–64 u*	173	675____
221	U.S. Marine Corps Alco Diesel A Unit, *63–64 u*	180	550____
221T	Tender		
	(A) Gray	15	40____
	(B) Black	15	45____
221W	Whistle Tender	28	60____
222	Rio Grande Alco Diesel A Unit, *62*	25	60____
223	Santa Fe Alco Diesel AB Units, *63*	73	198____
224	2-6-2 Locomotive, 2466W or 2466WX Tender, *45–46*		
	(A) Blackened handrails, *45*	125	245____
	(B) Silver handrails	85	165____
224	U.S. Navy Alco Diesel AB Units, *60*	120	260____
225	C&O Alco Diesel A Unit, *60*	45	85____
226	B&M Alco Diesel AB Units, *60 u*	75	168____
226C	B&M Alco Diesel B Unit, *60 u*	40	90____
227	CN Alco Diesel A Unit, *60 u*	75	145____
228	CN Alco Diesel A Unit, *61 u*	75	145____
229	M&StL Alco Diesel Units, *61–62*		
	(A) A Unit, *61*	65	113____
	(B) AB Units, *62*	80	185____
230	C&O Alco Diesel A Unit, *61*	55	110____
231	Rock Island Alco Diesel A Unit, *61–63*		
	(A) With red stripe	53	113____
	(B) Without red stripe	152	438____
232	New Haven Alco Diesel A Unit, *62*	53	133____
233	2-4-2 Scout Locomotive, 233W Tender, *61–62*	30	70____
233W	Whistle Tender	20	43____
234T	Lionel Lines Tender	5	25____
234T	Pennsylvania Tender	13	62____
234W	Lionel Whistle Tender	23	48____
234W	Pennsylvania Whistle Tender	25	125____

		Good	Exc
235	2-4-2 Scout Locomotive, 1130T or 1060T Tender, *60 u*	75	243
236	2-4-2 Scout Locomotive, *61–62*		
	(A) 1050T slope-back Tender	20	45
	(B) 1130T Tender	20	45
237	2-4-2 Scout Locomotive, *63–66*		
	(A) 1060T Tender	35	65
	(B) 234W Tender	48	90
238	2-4-2 Scout Locomotive, stripe on running board, 234W Tender, *63–64*	65	163
239	2-4-2 Scout Locomotive, 234W Tender, *65–66*	55	90
240	2-4-2 Scout Locomotive, 242T Tender, *64 u*	115	280
241	2-4-2 Scout Locomotive, *65 u*		
	(A) Narrow stripe, 234W Tender	35	110
	(B) Wide stripe, 1130T Tender	30	78
242	2-4-2 Scout Locomotive, 1060T or 1062T Tender, *62–66*	20	40
243	2-4-2 Scout Locomotive, 243W Tender, *60*	40	95
243W	Whistle Tender	15	50
244	2-4-2 Scout Locomotive, 244T or 1130T Tender, *60–61*	25	43
244T	Tender	5	20
245	2-4-2 Scout Locomotive, 1130T Tender, *59 u*	30	70
246	2-4-2 Scout Locomotive, 244T or 1130T Tender, *59–61*	15	25
247	2-4-2 Scout Locomotive, 247T Tender, *59*	30	70
247T	B&O Tender	15	30
248	2-4-2 Scout Locomotive, 1130T Tender, *58*	30	75
249	2-4-2 Scout Locomotive, 250T Tender, *58*	25	60
250	2-4-2 Scout Locomotive, 250T Tender, *57*	25	60
250T	Tender	10	28
251	2-4-2 Scout Locomotive, *66 u*		
	(A) 1062T slope-back Tender	93	223
	(B) 250T-type Tender	93	223
252	Crossing Gate, *50–62*	13	25
253	Block Control Signal, *56–59*	15	30
256	Illuminated Freight Station, *50–53*		
	(A) Standard	25	45
	(B) Light green roof	60	140
257	Freight Station with diesel horn, *56–57*		
	(A) Maroon base	30	85
	(B) Brown base	40	120
	(C) Maroon or brown base, light green roof	70	165
260	Bumper, *51–69*		
	(A) Die-cast	7	15
	(B) Black plastic	15	42
262	Highway Crossing Gate, *62–69*	15	45

		Good	Exc	
264	Operating Forklift Platform, *57–60*	120	235	___
282	Portal Gantry Crane, *54–57*	100	170	___
282R	Portal Gantry Crane, *56–57*	80	155	___
299	Code Transmitter Beacon Set, *61–63*	45	127	___
308	Railroad Sign Set, die-cast, *45–49*	23	40	___
309	Yard Sign Set, plastic, *50–59*	10	23	___
310	Billboard Set, *50–68*	10	20	___
313	Bascule Bridge, *46–49*	115	360	___
313-82	Fiber Pins, dozen, *46–60*	1	2	___
313-121	Fiber Pins, dozen, *61*	1	2	___
314	Scale Model Girder Bridge, *45–50*	10	38	___
315	Illuminated Trestle Bridge, *46–48*	33	88	___
316	Trestle Bridge, *49*	18	38	___
317	Trestle Bridge, *50–56*	18	33	___
321	Trestle Bridge, *58–64*	15	35	___
321-100	Trestle Bridge	20	78	___
332	Arch-Under Trestle Bridge, *59–66*	20	38	___
334	Operating Dispatching Board, *57–60*	83	208	___
342	Culvert Loader, *56–58*	55	195	___
345	Culvert Unloader, *57–59*	60	200	___
346	Culvert Unloader, manual, *65 u*	55	140	___
347	Cannon Firing Range Set, *64 u*	228	820	___
348	Culvert Unloader, manual, *66–69*	75	160	___
350	Engine Transfer Table, *57–60*	125	275	___
350-50	Transfer Table Extension, *57–60*	85	168	___
352	Ice Depot with 6352 Ice Car, *55–57*	55	143	___
353	Trackside Control Signal, *60–61*	15	35	___
356	Operating Freight Station, *52–57*			
	(A) Dark green roof, *52–57*	45	95	___
	(B) Light green roof, *57*	70	190	___
362	Barrel Loader, *52–57*			
	(A) Gold lettering	28	73	___
	(B) Red lettering	103	395	___
362-78	Wooden Barrels, 6 pieces, *52–57*			
	(A) Brown	7	20	___
	(B) Red	85	340	___
364	Conveyor Lumber Loader, *48–57*	30	80	___
364C	On/Off Switch, *48–64*	6	12	___
365	Dispatching Station, *58–59*	65	125	___
375	Turntable, *62–64*	85	183	___
390C	Switch, double-pole, double-throw, *60–64*	6	16	___
394	Rotary Beacon, *49–53*			
	(A) Steel tower, red platform	20	45	___
	(B) Steel tower, green platform	35	86	___
	(C) Aluminum tower, platform, and base	18	34	___
	(D) Aluminum tower, red steel base	30	63	___
	(E) Steel tower, red platform, stick-on nameplate	28	80	___

		Good	Exc
395	Floodlight Tower, *49–56*		
____	(A) Light green, silver, or unpainted aluminum	23	50
____	(B) Red	35	113
____	(C) Dark green	98	324
____	(D) Yellow	53	140
397	Operating Coal Loader, *48–57*		
____	(A) Yellow generator, *48*	148	358
____	(B) Blue generator, *49–57*	40	93
____**400**	B&O Passenger Rail Diesel Car, *56–58*	80	168
____**404**	B&O Baggage-Mail Rail Diesel Car, *57–58*	145	313
____**410**	Billboard Blinker, *56–58*	25	45
____**413**	Countdown Control Panel, *62*	22	62
____**415**	Diesel Fueling Station, *55–57*	60	130
____**419**	Heliport Control Tower, *62*	175	395
443	Missile Launching Platform with ammo dump, *60–62*	25	60
____**445**	Switch Tower, lighted, *52–57*	25	50
____**448**	Missile Firing Range Set, *61–63*	53	160
____**450**	Operating Signal Bridge, *52–58*	28	50
____**450L**	Signal Light Head, *52–58*	14	28
____**452**	Overhead Gantry Signal, *61–63*	40	105
455	Operating Oil Derrick, *50–54*		
____	(A) Dark green tower, green top	50	128
____	(B) Dark green tower, red top	58	182
____	(C) Apple green tower, red top	95	390
456	Coal Ramp with 3456 Hopper, *50–55*		
____	(A) Light gray ramp	60	150
____	(B) Dark gray ramp	80	170
____**456C**	Coal Ramp Controller	5	35
460	Piggyback Transportation Set, *55–57*		
____	(A) Metal stick-on signs on lift truck	53	120
____	(B) Rubber-stamped lettering on lift truck	75	163
____**460P**	Piggyback Platform, *55–57*	20	65
____**461**	Platform with truck and trailer, *66*	80	175
____**462**	Derrick Platform Set, *61–62*	125	310
____**464**	Lumber Mill, *56–60*	48	125
____**465**	Sound Dispatching Station, *56–57*	48	95
470	Missile Launching Platform with target car, *59–62*	62	108
____**479-1**	Truck for 6362 Truck Car with envelope, *55–56*	25	100
____**480-25**	Conversion Magnetic Coupler, *50–60*	1	5
____**480-32**	Conversion Magnetic Coupler, *61–69*	1	5
494	Rotary Beacon, *54–66*		
____	(A) Painted steel	23	45
____	(B) Unpainted aluminum	23	66
____**497**	Coaling Station, *53–58*	65	143

		Good	Exc
520	LL Boxcab Electric Locomotive, *56–57*		
	(A) Black pantograph	30	80____
	(B) Copper-colored pantograph	40	110____
600	MKT NW2 Switcher, *55*		
	(A) Black frame, black end rails	75	120____
	(B) Gray frame, yellow or black end rails	115	212____
601	Seaboard NW2 Switcher, *56*		
	(A) Red stripes with square ends	88	203____
	(B) Red stripes with round ends	100	163____
602	Seaboard NW2 Switcher, *57–58*	88	165____
610	Erie NW2 Switcher, *55*		
	(A) Black frame	73	125____
	(B) Yellow frame	128	397____
	(C) Replacement body with nameplates	90	294____
611	Jersey Central NW2 Switcher, *57–58*	75	155____
613	UP NW2 Switcher, *58*	90	235____
614	Alaska NW2 Switcher, *59–60*		
	(A) Plastic bell, no brake	115	205____
	(B) No bell, yellow brake	112	242____
	(C) "Built by Lionel" outlined in yellow near nose	190	345____
616	Santa Fe NW2 Switcher, *61–62*		
	(A) Open E-unit slot and bell/horn slots	105	190____
	(B) Plugged E-unit slot and open bell/horn slots	92	273____
	(C) Plugged E-unit slot and bell/horn slots	95	290____
617	Santa Fe NW2 Switcher, *63*	115	258____
621	Jersey Central NW2 Switcher, *56–57*	75	153____
622	Santa Fe NW2 Switcher, *49–50*		
	(A) Large GM decal on cab	175	290____
	(B) Small GM decal on side	105	235____
623	Santa Fe NW2 Switcher, *52–54*	90	138____
624	C&O NW2 Switcher, *52–54*	90	185____
625	LV GE 44-ton Switcher, *57–58*	50	98____
626	B&O GE 44-ton Switcher, *56–57, 59*	120	310____
627	LV GE 44-ton Switcher, *56–57*	40	75____
628	NP GE 44-ton Switcher, *56–57*	58	110____
629	Burlington GE 44-ton Switcher, *56*	173	330____
633	Santa Fe NW2 Switcher, *62*	80	130____
634	Santa Fe NW2 Switcher, *63, 65–66*		
	(A) Safety stripes	85	145____
	(B) No safety stripes	50	110____
635	UP NW2 Switcher, *65 u*	60	114____
637	2-6-4 Locomotive, 2046 736W Tender, *59–63*		
	(A) 2046W Lionel Lines Tender	55	150____
	(B) 736W Pennsylvania Tender	70	170____
638-2361	Van Camp's Pork & Beans Boxcar, *62 u*	20	40____

		Good	Exc
____**645**	Union Pacific NW2 Switcher, *69*	60	138
____**646**	4-6-4 Locomotive, 2046W Tender, *54–58*	115	235
665 ____	4-6-4 Locomotive, 2046W, 6026W, or 736W Tender, *54–59, 66*	95	253
671 ____	6-8-6 Steam Turbine Locomotive, smoke bulb, *46*	115	208
671	6-8-6 Steam Turbine Locomotive, *47–49*		
____	(A) 671W Tender	75	190
____	(B) 2671W Tender, backup lights	122	403
____	(C) 2671W Tender, no backup lights	143	243
____**671-75**	Smoke Lamp, 12 volt, *46*	10	18
671R ____	6-8-6 Steam Turbine Locomotive, 4424W or 4671 Tender, *46–49*	165	303
671RR ____	6-8-6 Steam Turbine Locomotive, 2046W-50 Tender, *52*	90	195
____**671S**	Smoke Conversion Kit	20	135
____**671W**	Whistle Tender, *46–48*	30	60
675	2-6-2 Locomotive, 2466WX or 6466WX Tender, *47–49*		
____	(A) Aluminum smokestack, *47*	85	220
____	(B) Black smokestack, *48–49*	85	180
____**675**	2-6-4 Locomotive, 2046W Tender, *52*	80	190
681 ____	6-8-6 Steam Turbine Locomotive, 2046W-50 or 2671W Tender, *50–51, 53*	118	195
682 ____	6-8-6 Steam Turbine Locomotive, 2046W-50 Tender, *54–55*	165	330
____**685**	4-6-4 Hudson Locomotive, 6026W Tender, *53*	97	224
____**703-10**	Smoke Lamp, 18 volt, *46*	8	25
726	2-8-4 Berkshire, *46–49*		
____	(A) 2426W Tender, smoke lamp, *46*	300	545
____	(B) 2426W Tender, *47–49*	240	470
____**726RR**	2-8-4 Berkshire Locomotive, 2046W Tender, *52*	140	265
____**726S**	Smoke Conversion Kit	40	145
736 ____	2-8-4 Berkshire Locomotive, 2671WX, 2046W, or 736W Tender, *50–66*	188	305
____**736W**	Whistle Tender	18	65
746	N&W 4-8-4 Class J Northern, *57–60*		
____	(A) Tender with long stripe	520	983
____	(B) Tender with short stripe	300	770
____**746W**	Tender, short stripe	30	115
____**760**	Curved Track, 16 sections (072), *54–57*	18	62
____**773**	4-6-4 Hudson Locomotive, 2426W Tender, *50*	662	1462
773	4-6-4 Hudson Locomotive, *64–66*		
____	(A) 773W NYC Tender	703	1133
____	(B) 736W PRR Tender	520	910
____**773T**	NYC Tender	70	150
____**902**	Elevated Trestle Set, *60*	25	115

		Good	Exc
909	Smoke Fluid, large or small bottle, *57–66, 68–69*		
	(A) ½ ounce bottle	8	20____
	(B) 2 ounce bottle	8	40____
B909	Smoke Capsules, pack of three, *57–66, 68–69*	5	30____
919	Artificial Grass, *46–64*	5	15____
920	Scenic Display Set, *57–58*	55	66____
920-2	Tunnel Portals, pair, *58–59*	15	30____
920-3	Green Grass, *57*	3	13____
920-4	Yellow Grass, *57*	5	16____
920-5	Artificial Rock, *57–58*	3	11____
920-6	Dry Glue, *57–58*	3	10____
920-8	Dyed Lichen, *57–58*	3	15____
925	Lubricant, 2 ounce tube, *46–69*	3	14____
925-1	Lubricant, 1 ounce tube, *50–69*	1	5____
926	Lubricant, ½ ounce tube, *55*	2	3____
926-5	Instruction Booklet, *46–48*	1	5____
927	Lubricating Kit, *50–59*	10	26____
928	Maintenance and Lubricating Kit, *60–63*	25	60____
943	Ammo Dump, *59–61*	16	38____
950	U.S. Railroad Map, *58–66*	20	48____
951	Farm Set, 13 pieces, *58*	50	140____
952	Figure Set, 30 pieces, *58*	34	65____
953	Figure Set, 32 pieces, *59–62*	40	63____
954	Swimming Pool and Playground Set, 30 pieces, *59*	40	70____
955	Highway Set, 22 pieces, *58*	30	70____
956	Stockyard Set, 18 pieces, *59*	40	100____
957	Farm Building and Animal Set, 35 pieces, *58*	60	135____
958	Vehicle Set, 24 pieces, *58*	45	85____
959	Barn Set, 23 pieces, *58*	38	86____
960	Barnyard Set, 29 pieces, *59–61*	46	156____
961	School Set, 36 pieces, *59*	40	135____
962	Turnpike Set, 24 pieces, *58*	60	125____
963	Frontier Set, 18 pieces, *59–60*	60	148____
964	Factory Site Set, 18 pieces, *59*	65	245____
965	Farm Set, 36 pieces, *59*	55	125____
966	Firehouse Set, 45 pieces, *58*	70	190____
967	Post Office Set, 25 pieces, *58*	50	127____
968	TV Transmitter Set, 28 pieces, *58*	55	125____
969	Construction Set, 23 pieces, *60*	65	123____
970	Ticket Booth, *58–60*	40	125____
971	Lichen with box, *60–64*	40	89____
972	Landscape Tree Assortment, *61–64*	25	95____
973	Complete Landscaping Set, *60–64*	45	153____
974	Scenery Set, *58*	70	260____
980	Ranch Set, 14 pieces, *60*	50	150____

			Good	Exc
____**981**	Freight Yard Set, 10 pieces, *60*		55	170
____**982**	Suburban Split Level Set, 18 pieces, *60*		35	256
____**983**	Farm Set, 7 pieces, *60–61*		35	85
____**984**	Railroad Set, 22 pieces, *61–62*		35	150
____**985**	Freight Area Set, 32 pieces, *61*		35	165
____**986**	Farm Set, 20 pieces, *62*		45	230
____**987**	Town Set, 24 pieces, *62*		35	65
____**988**	Railroad Structure Set, 16 pieces, *62*		40	100
1001	2-4-2 Scout Locomotive, plastic body, 1001T Tender, *48*			
____	(A) Silver rubber-stamped cab number		30	80
____	(B) White heat-stamped cab number		15	40
____**1001T**	Tender		8	18
1002	Gondola, *48–52*			
____	(A) Black, white lettering		4	8
____	(B) Blue, white lettering		5	10
____	(C) Silver, black lettering		125	475
____	(D) Yellow, black lettering		120	460
____	(E) Red, white lettering		120	460
____**X1004**	PRR Baby Ruth Boxcar, *48–52*		5	10
____**1005**	Sunoco 1-D Tank Car, *48–50*		7	11
1007	LL SP-type Caboose, *48–52*			
____	(A) Red body		3	11
____	(B) Red body, raised board on catwalk		10	35
____	(C) Tuscan body		200	950
____**1008**	Uncoupling Unit (027), *57–62*		3	7
____**1008-50**	Uncoupling Track Section (027), *57–62*		4	8
____**1009**	Manumatic Track Section (027), *48–52*		6	12
____**1010**	Transformer, 35 watts, *61–66*		7	11
____**1011**	Transformer, 25 watts, *48–49*		4	9
____**1012**	Transformer, 35 watts, *50–54*		5	11
____**1013**	Curved Track (027), *45–69*			1
____**1013-17**	Steel Pins, dozen (027), *46–60*			1
____**1013-42**	Steel Pins, dozen (027), *61–68*			2
____**1014**	Transformer, 40 watts, *55*		5	11
____**1015**	Transformer, 45 watts, *56–60*		9	11
____**1016**	Transformer, 35 watts, *59–60*		7	11
____**1018**	Half Straight Track (027), *55–69*			1
____**1018**	Straight Track (027), *45–69*			1
____**1019**	Remote Control Track Set (027), *46–48*		4	8
____**1020**	90-degree Crossing (027), *55–69*		2	5
____**1021**	90-degree Crossing (027), *45–54*		2	4
____**1022**	Manual Switches, pair (027), *53–69*		7	15
____**1023**	45-degree Crossing (027), *56–69*		3	5
____**1024**	Manual Switches, pair (027), *46–52*		7	14
____**1025**	Illuminated Bumper (027), *46–47*		10	18

		Good	Exc
1025	Transformer, 45 watts, *61–69*	6	13____
1026	Transformer, 25 watts, *61–64*	3	6____
1032	Transformer, 75 watts, *48*	15	30____
1033	Transformer, 90 watts, *48–56*	20	35____
1034	Transformer, 75 watts, *48–54*	15	23____
1035	Transformer, 60 watts, *47*	10	20____
1037	Transformer, 40 watts, *46–47*	6	12____
1041	Transformer, 60 watts, *45–46*	13	27____
1042	Transformer, 75 watts, *47–48*	15	30____
1043	Transformer, 50 watts, *53–57*	6	12____
1043-500	Transformer, 60 watts, ivory, *57–58*	82	149____
1044	Transformer, 90 watts, *57–69*	25	45____
1045	Operating Watchman, *46–50*	20	49____
1045C	Contactor	4	14____
1047	Operating Switchman, *59–61*	32	136____
1050	0-4-0 Scout Locomotive, 1050T Tender, *59 u*	50	170____
1050T	Tender	5	20____
1053	Transformer, 60 watts, *56–60*	10	20____
1055	Texas Special Alco Diesel A Unit, *59–60*	25	65____
1060	2-4-2 Locomotive, 1050T or 1060T Tender, *60–62*	15	30____
1060T	Lionel Lines Tender	10	20____
1060T-50	Southern Pacific Tender	12	28____
1061	0-4-0 or 2–4–2 Scout Locomotive, 1061T Tender, *64, 69*		
	(A) Slope-back Lionel Lines tender	15	35____
	(B) Paper number labels	43	230____
	(C) No number stamped on cab	35	95____
1061T	Tender	4	17____
1062	0-4-0 or 2-4-2 Scout Locomotive, *63–64*		
	(A) Streamlined Southern Pacific Tender	20	45____
	(B) Other tenders	18	33____
1063	Transformer, 75 watts, *60–64*	15	30____
1065	Union Pacific Alco Diesel A Unit, *61*	30	70____
1066	Union Pacific Alco Diesel A Unit, *64 u*	35	80____
1073	Transformer, 60 watts, *61–66*	13	25____
1101	Transformer, 25 watts, *48*	4	8____
1101	2-4-2 Scout Locomotive, 1001T Tender, *48 u*		
	(A) Cab correctly marked "1101"	20	40____
	(B) Cab marked "1001"	145	325____
1110	2-4-2 Locomotive, 1001T Tender, *49, 51–52*	15	25____
1120	2-4-2 Scout Locomotive, 1001T Tender, *50*	20	35____
1121	Remote Control Switches, pair (027), *46–51*	15	28____
1122	Remote Control Switches, pair (027), *52–53*	15	28____
1122-34	Remote Control Switches, pair, *52–53*	15	25____
1122-500	Gauge Adapter (027), *57–66*	4	10____
1122E	Remote Control Switches, pair (027), *53–69*	15	30____

		Good	Exc
1130	2-4-2 Locomotive, 6066T or 1130T Tender, *53–54*		
___	(A) Plastic body	20	35
___	(B) Die-cast body	35	125
1130T	Tender		
___	(A) Black-painted shell	33	113
___	(B) Black plastic shell	8	25
___**1130T-500**	Tender, pink, from Girls Set	83	175
___**1144**	Transformer, 75 watts, *61–66*	10	23
___**1232**	Transformer, 75 watts, made for export, *48*	15	45
1615	0-4-0 Locomotive, 1615T Tender, *55–57*		
___	(A) No grab irons	75	150
___	(B) Grab irons on locomotive and tender	145	265
___**1615T**	Tender	13	23
___**1625**	0-4-0 Locomotive, 1625T Tender, *58*	165	350
___**1625T**	Tender	23	43
___**1640-100**	Presidential Kit, *60*	60	161
___**1654**	2-4-2 Locomotive, 1654W Tender, *46–47*	35	78
___**1654T**	Tender	10	20
___**1654W**	Whistling Tender	13	30
___**1655**	2-4-2 Locomotive, 6654W Tender, *48–49*	43	73
1656	0-4-0 Locomotive, 6403B Tender, *48–49*		
___	(A) Large silver cab number	120	245
___	(B) Small silver cab number	130	263
___**1665**	0-4-0 Locomotive, 2403B Tender, *46*	190	360
1666	2-6-2 Locomotive, 2466W or 2466WX Tender, *46–47*		
___	(A) Number plate and two-piece bell	55	135
___	(B) Rubber-stamped number and one-piece bell	60	150
___**1666T**	Tender	10	25
1862	4-4-0 Civil War General, 1862T Tender, *59–62*		
___	(A) Gray smokestack	85	180
___	(B) Black smokestack	90	200
___**1862T**	Tender	25	38
___**1865**	Western & Atlantic Coach, *59–62*	25	45
___**1866**	Western & Atlantic Mail-Baggage Car, *59–62*	30	48
___**1872**	4-4-0 Civil War General, 1872T Tender, *59–62*	105	270
___**1872T**	Tender	25	40
___**1875**	Western & Atlantic Coach, *59–62*	85	258
___**1875W**	Western & Atlantic Coach, whistle, *59–62*	55	150
___**1876**	Western & Atlantic Baggage Car, *59–62*	35	85
___**1877**	Flatcar with fence and horses, *59–62*	45	100
___**1882**	4-4-0 Civil War General, 1882T Tender, *60 u*	193	400
___**1882T**	Tender, *60 u*	30	65
___**1885**	Western & Atlantic Coach, *60 u*	105	283
___**1887**	Flatcar with fences and horses, *60 u*	70	175
___**2001**	Track Make-up Kit (027), *63*	300	750

		Good	Exc
2002	Track Make-up Kit (027), *63*	500	1300 ___
2003	Track Make-up Kit (027), *63*	600	1900 ___
2016	2-6-4 Locomotive, 6026W Tender, *55–56*	55	100 ___
2018	2-6-4 Locomotive, *56–59, 61*		
	(A) 6026T Tender	35	70 ___
	(B) 6026W Tender	60	110 ___
	(C) 1130T Tender	35	65 ___
2020	6-8-6 Steam Turbine Locomotive, 2020W or 2466WX Tender, smoke lamp, *46*	90	195 ___
2020	6-8-6 Steam Turbine Locomotive, 2020W or 6020W Tender, *47–49*	70	175 ___
2020W	Whistling Tender	35	60 ___
2023	Union Pacific Alco Diesel AA Units, *50–51*		
	(A) Yellow body	112	225 ___
	(B) Gray nose and side frames	1080	3265 ___
	(C) Silver body	70	210 ___
2024	C&O Alco Diesel A Unit, *69*	30	74 ___
2025	2-6-2 Locomotive, 2466WX or 6466WX Tender, *47–49*		
	(A) Black smokestack, *48–49*	80	175 ___
	(B) Aluminum smokestack, *47*	95	200 ___
2025	2-6-4 Locomotive, 6466W Tender, *52*	82	165 ___
2026	2-6-2 Locomotive, 6466WX Tender, *48–49*	65	100 ___
2026	2-6-4 Locomotive, 6466W, 6466T, or 6066T Tender, *51–53*	40	95 ___
2028	Pennsylvania GP7 Diesel, *55*		
	(A) Gold lettering	150	275 ___
	(B) Yellow lettering	115	245 ___
	(C) Tan frame	245	605 ___
2029	2-6-4 Locomotive, *64–69*		
	(A) 234W Lionel Lines Tender	58	120 ___
	(B) LL Tender with "Hagerstown" on bottom	65	135 ___
	(C) 234W Pennsylvania Tender	120	205 ___
2031	Rock Island Alco Diesel AA Units, *52–54*	75	233 ___
2032	Erie Alco Diesel AA Units, *52–54*	115	185 ___
2033	Union Pacific Alco Diesel AA Units, *52–54*	90	210 ___
2034	2-4-2 Scout Locomotive, 6066T Tender, *52*	28	65 ___
2035	2-6-4 Locomotive, 6466W Tender, *50–51*	65	158 ___
2036	2-6-4 Locomotive, 6466W Tender, *50*	60	115 ___
2037	2-6-4 Locomotive, *54–55, 57–63*		
	(A) 6026T or 1130T Tender	48	93 ___
	(B) 6026W, 233W, or 234W whistle Tender	70	125 ___
2037-500	2-6-4 Locomotive, pink, 1130T-500 Tender, *57–58*	310	995 ___
2041	Rock Island Alco Diesel AA Units, *69*	70	150 ___
2046	4-6-4 Locomotive, 2046W Tender, *50–51, 53*	95	180 ___
2046T	Tender, for export	70	248 ___

		Good	Exc
___**2046W**	Whistle Tender	33	60
___**2046W-50**	PRR Whistle Tender	38	67
2055	4-6-4 Locomotive, 2046W or 6026W Tender, *53–55*		
___		80	160
___**2056**	4-6-4 Locomotive, 2046W Tender, *52*	80	212
2065	4-6-4 Locomotive, 2046W or 6026W Tender, *54–56*		
___		95	171
___**2203B**	Tender	58	120
___**2224W**	Whistle Tender	23	95
___**2240**	Wabash F3 AB Units, *56*	225	595
___**2242**	New Haven F3 AB Units, *58–59*	190	668
___**2242C**	New Haven F3 B Unit, *58–59*	50	175
2243	Santa Fe F3 AB Units, *55–57*		
___	(A) Gray body mold, raised molded cab door ladder	123	297
___	(B) Typical molded cab door ladder	110	242
___**2243C**	Santa Fe F3 B Unit, *55–57*	65	160
2245	Texas Special F3 AB Units, *54–55*		
___	(A) B Unit with portholes, *54*	220	440
___	(B) B Unit without portholes, *55*	283	683
2257	SP-type caboose, *47*		
___	(A) Red body, no smokestack	7	15
___	(B) Tuscan body and smokestack	85	315
___	(C) Red body and smokestack	120	428
2321	Lackawanna FM Train Master Diesel, *54–56*		
___	(A) Gray roof	210	316
___	(B) Maroon roof	190	448
2322	Virginian FM Train Master Diesel, *65–66*		
___	(A) Unpainted blue body, yellow stripes	265	498
___	(B) Blue or black body, painted blue and yellow stripes	335	635
___**2328**	Burlington GP7 Diesel, *55–56*	105	245
2329	Virginian GE E-33 or EL-C Electric Locomotive, *58–59*		
___		178	517
2330	Pennsylvania GG1 Electric Locomotive, green, *50*		
___		360	1190
2331	Virginian FM Train Master Diesel, *55–58*		
___	(A) Black and yellow stripes, gray mold, *55*	340	710
___	(B) Yellow stripes, blue mold, *56–58*	245	640
___	(C) Blue and yellow stripes, gray mold	605	1215
2332	Pennsylvania GG1 Electric Locomotive, *47–49*		
___	(A) Black	585	1335
___	(B) Dark green	205	480
2333	NYC F3 Diesel AA Units, *48–49*		
___	(A) Rubber-stamped lettering	280	670
___	(B) Heat-stamped lettering	225	512
___**2333**	Santa Fe F3 Diesel AA Units, *48–49*	215	445
___**2337**	Wabash GP7 Diesel, *58*	120	250

		Good	Exc	
2338	Milwaukee Road GP7 Diesel, *55–56*			
	(A) Orange band around shell	435	1193	___
	(B) Interrupted orange band	80	183	___
2339	Wabash GP7 Diesel, *57*	125	270	___
2340	Pennsylvania GG1 Electric Locomotive, *55*			
	(A) Tuscan	455	1255	___
	(B) Dark green	335	775	___
2341	Jersey Central FM Train Master Diesel, *56*			
	(A) High-gloss orange	980	2175	___
	(B) Dull orange	900	1985	___
2343	Santa Fe F3 Diesel AA Units, *50–52*	175	445	___
2343C	Santa Fe F3 B Unit, *50–55*			
	(A) Screen roof vents	110	268	___
	(B) Louver roof vents	95	193	___
2344	NYC F3 Diesel AA Units, *50–52*	195	490	___
2344C	NYC F3 B Unit, *50–55*	126	235	___
2345	Western Pacific F3 Diesel AA Units, *52*	478	1020	___
2346	B&M GP9 Diesel, *65–66*	160	345	___
2347	C&O GP7 Diesel, *65 u*	1590	4050	___
2348	M&StL GP9 Diesel, *58–59*	154	320	___
2349	Northern Pacific GP9 Diesel, *59–60*	165	358	___
2350	New Haven EP-5 Electric Locomotive, *56–58*			
	(A) Painted nose trim, white N and orange H	231	583	___
	(B) Decaled nose trim, white N and orange H	160	300	___
	(C) Painted nose trim, orange N and black H	860	1600	___
	(D) Decaled nose trim, orange N and black H	418	885	___
	(E) Orange and white stripes go through doorjambs	345	1005	___
2351	Milwaukee Road EP-5 Electric Locomotive, *57–58*	175	440	___
2352	Pennsylvania EP-5 Electric Locomotive, *58–59*			
	(A) Tuscan body	201	342	___
	(B) Chocolate brown body	188	360	___
2353	Santa Fe F3 Diesel AA Units, *53–55*	220	432	___
2354	NYC F3 Diesel AA Units, *53–55*	285	460	___
2355	Western Pacific F3 Diesel AA Units, *53*	445	940	___
2356	Southern F3 Diesel AA Units, *54–56*	358	660	___
2356C	Southern F3 B Unit, *54–56*	157	262	___
2357	SP-type Caboose, *47–48*			
	(A) Red body and smokestack	148	560	___
	(B) Tuscan body and smokestack	15	35	___
	(C) Tile red, no smokestack, "6357" stamped on bottom	85	250	___
2358	Great Northern EP-5 Electric Locomotive, *59–60*	239	625	___
2359	Boston & Maine GP9 Diesel, *61–62*	125	260	___

			Good	Exc
2360		Pennsylvania GG1 Electric Locomotive, *56–58, 61–63*		
____		(A) Tuscan, 5 gold stripes	570	1358
____		(B) Dark green, 5 gold stripes	408	870
____		(C) Tuscan, gold stripe, heat-stamped letters	420	795
____		(D) Tuscan, gold stripe, decaled lettering	400	700
2363		Illinois Central F3 Diesel AB Units, *55–56*		
____		(A) Black lettering	340	740
		(B) Brown lettering	385	860
____	**2365**	C&O GP7 Diesel, *62–63*	115	260
____	**2367**	Wabash F3 Diesel AB Units, *55*	320	690
____	**2368**	B&O F3 Diesel AB Units, *56*	445	1423
____	**2373**	CP F3 Diesel AA Units, *57*	675	1770
	2378	Milwaukee Road F3 Diesel AB Units, *56*		
____		(A) Yellow roof line stripes	585	1340
____		(B) No roof line stripes	545	1150
	2378C	Milwaukee Road F3 Diesel B Unit, yellow roof line stripe, *56*		
____			300	560
____	**2379**	Rio Grande F3 Diesel AB Units, *57–58*	375	780
____	**2383**	Santa Fe F3 Diesel AA Units, *58–66*	220	425
____	**2400**	Maplewood Pullman Car, green, *48–49*	48	125
____	**2401**	Hillside Observation Car, green, *48–49*	38	110
____	**2402**	Chatham Pullman Car, green, *48–49*	45	117
____	**2404**	Santa Fe Vista Dome Car, *64–65*	35	75
____	**2405**	Santa Fe Pullman Car, *64–65*	35	75
____	**2406**	Santa Fe Observation Car, *64–65*	33	70
____	**2408**	Santa Fe Vista Dome Car, *66*	45	80
____	**2409**	Santa Fe Pullman Car, *66*	40	80
____	**2410**	Santa Fe Observation Car, *66*	35	75
	2411	Lionel Lines Flatcar, *46–48*		
____		(A) With pipes, *46*	38	78
____		(B) With logs, *47–48*	15	35
____	**2412**	Santa Fe Vista Dome Car, *59–63*	35	80
____	**2414**	Santa Fe Pullman Car, *59–63*	35	83
____	**2416**	Santa Fe Observation Car, *59–63*	25	70
____	**2419**	DL&W Work Caboose, *46–47*	20	53
	2420	DL&W Work Caboose with searchlight, *46–48*		
____		(A) Light or dark gray, heat-stamped lettering	45	95
____		(B) Light or dark gray, rubber-stamped lettering	75	160
	2421	Maplewood Pullman Car, *50–53*		
____		(A) Gray roof	30	70
____		(B) Silver roof	25	50
	2422	Chatham Pullman Car, *50–53*		
____		(A) Gray roof	33	70
____		(B) Silver roof	25	53
	2423	Hillside Observation Car, *50–53*		
____		(A) Gray roof	28	68
____		(B) Silver roof	23	48

		Good	Exc
2426W	Whistle Tender, *50*	155	225 ___
2429	Livingston Pullman Car, *52–53*	50	90 ___
2430	Pullman Car, blue, *46–47*	30	95 ___
2431	Observation Car, blue, *46–47*	25	90 ___
2432	Clifton Vista Dome Car, *54–58*	38	80 ___
2434	Newark Pullman Car, *54–58*	35	80 ___
2435	Elizabeth Pullman Car, *54–58*	40	120 ___
2436	Mooseheart Observation Car, *57–58*	30	75 ___
2436	Summit Observation Car, *54–56*	30	55 ___
2440	Pullman Car, green, *46–47*		
	(A) Silver lettering	45	75 ___
	(B) White lettering	33	65 ___
2441	Observation Car, green, *46–47*		
	(A) Silver lettering	45	75 ___
	(B) White lettering	28	60 ___
2442	Clifton Vista Dome Car, *56*	50	105 ___
2442	Pullman Car, brown, *46–48*		
	(A) Silver lettering	43	78 ___
	(B) White lettering	30	65 ___
2443	Observation Car, brown, *46–48*		
	(A) Silver lettering	40	75 ___
	(B) White lettering	30	65 ___
2444	Newark Pullman Car, *56*	45	105 ___
2445	Elizabeth Pullman Car, *56*	95	223 ___
2446	Summit Observation Car, *56*	45	103 ___
2452	Pennsylvania Gondola, *45–47*		
	(A) Whirly wheels, *45*	20	45 ___
	(B) Regular wheels	9	20 ___
	(C) Early flying shoe trucks, two holes in floor, *45*	33	138 ___
2452X	Pennsylvania Gondola, *46–47*	9	18 ___
X2454	Baby Ruth Boxcar, PRR logo, *46–47*	20	40 ___
X2454	Pennsylvania Boxcar, *46*		
	(A) Brown door	68	203 ___
	(B) Orange door	122	409 ___
2456	Lehigh Valley Hopper, *48*		
	(A) Flat black, 2 lines of data, *48*	10	40 ___
	(B) Flat black, 3 lines of data, *48*	95	265 ___
2457	PRR N5-type Caboose "477618," tintype, *45–47*		
	(A) Red, white lettering	20	45 ___
	(B) Brown, offset white lettering	168	603 ___
	(C) Brown, centered white lettering	30	100 ___
X2458	PRR Automobile Boxcar, *46–48*	25	45 ___
2460	Bucyrus Erie Crane Car, 12-wheel, *46–50*		
	(A) Gray cab	90	255 ___
	(B) Black cab	45	87 ___

			Good	Exc
2461		Transformer Car, die-cast, *47–48*		
____		(A) Red transformer	28	95
____		(B) Black transformer	30	75
____		(C) Red transformer, number rubber-stamped on bottom	35	175
2465		Sunoco 2-D Tank Car, *46–48*		
____		(A) "Gas, Sunoco, and Oils" in diamond, centered	135	395
____		(B) "Sunoco" in diamond	8	18
____		(C) "Sunoco" extends beyond diamond	8	17
____	**2466T**	Tender	15	43
____	**2466WX**	Whistle Tender, *45–48*	30	65
____	**2472**	PRR N5-type Caboose, tintype, *46–47*	15	30
____	**2481**	Plainfield Pullman Car, yellow, *50*	107	259
____	**2482**	Westfield Pullman Car, yellow, *50*	115	256
____	**2483**	Livingston Observation Car, yellow, *50*	92	240
____	**2521**	President McKinley Observation Car, *62–66*	75	160
____	**2522**	President Harrison Vista Dome Car, *62–66*	80	170
____	**2523**	President Garfield Pullman Car, *62–66*	75	160
2530		REA Baggage Car, *54–60*		
____		(A) Large doors	210	433
____		(B) Small doors	57	147
2531		Silver Dawn Observation Car, *52–60*		
____		(A) Ribbed channels, round rivets	38	100
____		(B) Ribbed channels, hex rivets	48	113
____		(C) Ribbed channels, hex rivets, red center taillight	58	163
____		(D) Flat channels, glued nameplates	57	148
2532		Silver Range Vista Dome Car, *52–60*		
____		(A) Ribbed channels, round rivets	38	107
____		(B) Flat channels, glued nameplates	30	160
2533		Silver Cloud Pullman Car, *52–59*		
____		(A) Ribbed channels, round rivets	43	100
____		(B) Flat channels, glued nameplates	30	160
2534		Silver Bluff Pullman Car, *52–59*		
____		(A) Ribbed channels, round rivets	53	120
____		(B) Flat channels, glued nameplates	30	160
____	**2541**	Alexander Hamilton Observation Car, *55–56**	58	160
____	**2542**	Betsy Ross Vista Dome Car, *55–56**	58	160
____	**2543**	William Penn Pullman Car, *55–56**	60	165
____	**2544**	Molly Pitcher Pullman Car, *55–56**	60	165
____	**2550**	B&O Baggage-Mail Rail Diesel Car, *57–58*	183	407
____	**2551**	Banff Park Observation Car, *57**	135	260
____	**2552**	Skyline 500 Vista Dome Car, *57**	160	270
____	**2553**	Blair Manor Pullman Car, *57**	220	440
____	**2554**	Craig Manor Pullman Car, *57**	210	440
____	**2555**	Sunoco 1-D Tank Car, *46–48*	25	65

		Good	Exc
2559	B&O Passenger Rail Diesel Car, *57–58*	140	285 ____
2560	Lionel Lines Crane Car, 8-wheel, *46–47*		
	(A) Black boom	23	77 ____
	(B) Brown boom	28	80 ____
	(C) Green boom	35	97 ____
2561	Vista Valley Observation Car, *59–61**	88	253 ____
2562	Regal Pass Vista Dome Car, *59–61**	100	280 ____
2563	Indian Falls Pullman Car, *59–61**	110	290 ____
2625	Irvington Pullman Car, *46–50**		
	(A) No silhouettes	75	155 ____
	(B) Silhouettes	105	275 ____
2625	Madison Pullman Car, *46–47**	95	180 ____
2625	Manhattan Pullman Car, *46–47**	95	180 ____
2627	Madison Pullman Car, *48–50**		
	(A) No silhouettes	75	170 ____
	(B) Silhouettes	110	265 ____
2628	Manhattan Pullman Car, *48–50**		
	(A) No silhouettes	78	170 ____
	(B) Silhouettes	113	268 ____
2671T	PRR Tender, for export	40	125 ____
2671W	Whistle Tender	45	85 ____
2671WX	Whistle Tender	47	79 ____
2755	Sunoco 1-D Tank Car, *45*	30	75 ____
X2758	PRR Automobile Boxcar, *45–46*	28	65 ____
2855	Sunoco 1-D Tank Car, *46–47*		
	(A) Black	85	255 ____
	(B) Black, decal without "Gas" and "Oils"	70	205 ____
	(C) Gray	45	175 ____
3309	Turbo Missile Launch Car, red body, *63–64*	25	50 ____
3309-50	Turbo Missile Launch Car, olive body, *63–64*	165	667 ____
3330	Flatcar with submarine kit, *60–62*	60	165 ____
3330-100	Operating Submarine Kit with box, *60–61*	110	364 ____
3349	Turbo Missile Launch Car, red body, *62–65*	13	45 ____
3356	Operating Horse Car and Corral Set, *56–60, 64–66*	60	125 ____
3356	Operating Horse Car only, *56–60, 64–66*		
	(A) Built date, bar-end trucks, *56–60*	30	73 ____
	(B) No built date, AAR trucks, *64–66*	50	135 ____
3356-100	Black Horses, 9 pieces, *56–59*	15	30 ____
3356-150	Horse Car Corral, *57–60*	27	57 ____
3357	Hydraulic Maintenance Car, *62–64*	25	65 ____
3357-27	Trestle Components for Cop and Hobo Car, *62*	23	55 ____
3359	Lionel Lines Twin-bin Coal Dump Car, *55–58*	25	40 ____
3360	Operating Burro Crane, self-propelled, *56–57*	76	200 ____
3361	Operating Log Dump Car, *55–58*	15	38 ____
3362	Helium Tank Unloading Car, *61–63, 69*	20	45 ____

			Good	Exc
____	3364	Operating Dump Car with 3 logs, *65–66, 68*	15	33
____	3366	Circus Car Corral Set, *59–62*	120	260
____	3366	Circus Car only, *59–62*	70	133
____	3366-100	White Horses, 9 pieces, *59–62*	33	58
	3370	W&A Sheriff and Outlaw Car, *61–64*		
____		(A) AAR trucks	15	50
____		(B) Archbar trucks	25	65
	3376	Bronx Zoo Car, *60–66, 69*		
____		(A) Blue, white lettering	20	62
____		(B) Green, yellow lettering	35	85
____		(C) Blue, yellow lettering	105	331
____	3386	Bronx Zoo Car, *60*	25	65
____	3409	Helicopter Car, *61*	33	120
	3410	Helicopter Car, *61–63*		
____		(A) 2 operating couplers, gray Navy helicopter	30	90
____		(B) Single operating coupler, yellow helicopter, *63*	65	173
____	3413	Mercury Capsule Car, *62–64*	45	165
____	3419	Helicopter Car, *59–65*	35	80
____	3424	Wabash Operating Boxcar, *56–58*	27	60
____	3424-75	Low Bridge Signal, *56–57*	80	220
____	3424-100	Low Bridge Signal Set, *56–58*	20	45
____	3428	U.S. Mail Operating Boxcar, *59–60*	40	75
____	3429	USMC Helicopter Car, *60*	155	492
	3434	Poultry Dispatch Car, *59–60, 64–66*		
____		(A) Gray man	55	100
____		(B) Blue man	60	125
	3435	Traveling Aquarium Car, *59–62*		
____		(A) Gold lettering, tank designations, and circle around L	425	1050
____		(B) Gold lettering, tank designations, no circle around L	268	680
____		(C) Gold lettering, no tank designations, no circle around L	130	250
____		(D) Yellow lettering, no tank designations, no circle around L	50	142
____	3444	Erie Operating Gondola, *57–59*	35	60
	3451	Operating Log Dump Car, *46–48*		
____		(A) Heat-stamped lettering	15	40
____		(B) Rubber-stamped lettering	25	65
	3454	PRR Operating Merchandise Car, *46–47*		
____		(A) Red lettering	990	4130
____		(B) Blue lettering	39	138
____	3456	N&W Operating Hopper, *50–55*	20	55
	3459	LL Operating Coal Dump Car, *46–48*		
____		(A) Aluminum bin	85	250
____		(B) Black bin	15	52
____		(C) Green bin	26	79

		Good	Exc
3460	Flatcar with trailers, *55–57*	30	75 ____
3461	LL Operating Log Car, *49–55*		
	(A) Black car, heat-stamped lettering	23	35 ____
	(B) Black car, rubber-stamped lettering	158	383 ____
3461-25	LL Operating Log Car, green	25	55 ____
3462	Automatic Milk Car, *47–48*		
	(A) Flat white or cream, steel base mechanism	15	60 ____
	(B) Flat white or cream, brass base mechanism	25	70 ____
	(C) Glossy cream	70	275 ____
3462-70	Magnetic Milk Cans, *52–59*	9	18 ____
3462P	Milk Car Platform, *47–48*	8	17 ____
X3464	ATSF Operating Boxcar, *49–52*		
	(A) Orange body	8	22 ____
	(B) Tan body	400	1200 ____
X3464	NYC Operating Boxcar, *49–52*	10	23 ____
3469	LL Operating Coal Dump Car, *49–55*	20	45 ____
3470	Target Launching Car, dark blue, *62–64*	30	65 ____
3470-100	Target Launching Car, light blue, *63*	60	230 ____
3472	Automatic Milk Car, *49–53*	28	55 ____
3474	Western Pacific Operating Boxcar, *52–53*	25	65 ____
3482	Automatic Milk Car, *54–55*		
	(A) "RT3472" on right	32	92 ____
	(B) "RT3482" on right	22	65 ____
3484	Pennsylvania Operating Boxcar, *53*	22	55 ____
3484-25	ATSF Operating Boxcar, *54*		
	(A) White lettering	25	70 ____
	(B) Black lettering	320	1140 ____
3494-1	NYC Operating Boxcar, *55*	40	115 ____
3494-150	MP Operating Boxcar, *56*	65	138 ____
3494-275	State of Maine Operating Boxcar, *56–58*		
	(A) "3494275" on side	40	105 ____
	(B) No number on side	67	178 ____
3494-550	Monon Operating Boxcar, *57–58*	200	379 ____
3494-625	Soo Operating Boxcar, *57–58*	213	463 ____
3509	Satellite Launching Car, *61*		
	(A) Chrome satellite cover	25	70 ____
	(B) Gray satellite cover	75	292 ____
3510	Satellite Launching Car, *62*	43	107 ____
3512	Fireman and Ladder Car, *59–61*		
	(A) Black extension ladder	60	128 ____
	(B) Silver extension ladder	80	205 ____
3519	Satellite Launching Car, *61–64*	20	60 ____
3520	Searchlight Car, *52–53*		
	(A) Serif lettering	23	57 ____
	(B) Sans serif lettering	20	35 ____

		Good	Exc
3530	GM Generator Car, *56–58*		
_____	(A) Blue fuel tank	60	130
_____	(B) Black fuel tank	55	115
_____	(C) 3530 underscored	415	2000
_____**3530-50**	Searchlight with pole and base, *56–56*	15	63
_____**3535**	Security Car with searchlight, *60–61*	40	105
_____**3540**	Operating Radar Car, *59–60*	40	103
_____**3545**	Operating TV Monitor Car, *61–62*	58	167
3559	Operating Coal Dump Car, *46–48*		
_____	(A) Black coil housing	15	48
_____	(B) Brown coil housing	40	132
3562-1	ATSF Operating Barrel Car, *54*		
_____	(A) Black, black unloading trough	68	195
_____	(B) Black, yellow unloading trough	68	190
_____	(C) Gray, red lettering	800	2970
3562-25	ATSF Operating Barrel Car, gray, *54*		
_____	(A) Red lettering, no bracket tab	195	470
_____	(B) Blue lettering, no bracket tab	20	52
_____	(C) Blue lettering, bracket tab	16	75
3562-50	ATSF Operating Barrel Car, yellow, *55–56*		
_____	(A) Painted	45	101
_____	(B) Unpainted	25	60
_____**3562-75**	ATSF Operating Barrel Car, orange, *57–58*	35	83
3619	Helicopter Reconnaissance Car, *62–64*		
_____	(A) Light yellow	40	120
_____	(B) Dark yellow	65	213
3620	Searchlight Car, orange generator, *54–56*		
_____	(A) Unpainted gray plastic searchlight	22	40
_____	(B) Gray-painted gray plastic searchlight	30	45
_____	(C) Unpainted orange plastic searchlight	53	125
_____	(D) Gray-painted orange plastic searchlight	65	200
3650	Extension Searchlight Car, *56–59*		
_____	(A) Light gray	40	75
_____	(B) Dark gray	65	135
_____	(C) Olive gray	115	265
3656	Armour Operating Cattle Car, some with an open coil, *49–55*		
_____	(A) Black letters, Armour sticker	105	245
_____	(B) White letters, Armour sticker	30	63
_____	(C) Black letters, no Armour sticker	58	190
_____	(D) White letters, no Armour sticker	25	62
_____**3656**	Stockyard with cattle, *49–55*	28	70
3656-34	Cattle, black, 9 pieces, *49–58*		
_____	(A) Rounded ridge on base, *49*	60	117
_____	(B) Plain base	15	50
_____**3656-150**	Corral Platform, yellow tray	215	505

		Good	Exc
3662	Automatic Milk Car, *55–60, 64–66*	48	75____
3662-79	Nonmagnetic Milk Cans, 7 pieces, white envelope	18	54____
3662-80	Nonmagnetic Milk Cans, 7 pieces, manila envelope	17	48____
3665	Minuteman Operating Car, *61–64*		
	(A) Medium blue roof	80	190____
	(B) Dark blue roof	54	98____
3666	Minuteman Boxcar with cannon, *64 u*	200	513____
3672	Bosco Operating Milk Car, *59–60*		
	(A) Unpainted yellow body	85	185____
	(B) Painted yellow body	145	290____
3672-79	Bosco Can Set, 7 pieces, *59–60*	25	102____
3820	USMC Operating Submarine Car, *60–62*	120	215____
3830	Operating Submarine Car, *60–63*	40	93____
3854	Automatic Merchandise Car, *46–47*	205	520____
3927	Lionel Lines Track Cleaning Car, *56–60*	28	48____
3927-38	Track Cleaning Fluid Bottle	9	18____
3927-50	Track Wiping Cylinders, 25 pieces, *57–60*	10	30____
3927-75	Track-Clean Detergent, can, *56–69*	5	18____
4357	SP-type Caboose, electronic, die-cast stack, *48–49*		
	(A) Die-cast metal smokestack	75	200____
	(B) Matching plastic smokestack	115	265____
	(C) Matching plastic smokestack, raised board on catwalk	110	255____
4452	PRR Gondola, electronic, *46–49*	50	125____
4454	Baby Ruth PRR Boxcar, electronic, *46–49*	60	180____
4457	PRR N5-type Caboose, tintype, electronic, *46–47*	55	150____
4671W	Whistle Tender	80	178____
5159-50	Maintenance and Lube Kit, *66–69*	30	80____
5459	LL Coal Dump Car, electronic, *46–49*	55	140____
6001T	Tender	9	18____
6002	NYC Gondola, *50*	4	9____
X6004	Baby Ruth PRR Boxcar, *50*	4	7____
6007	Lionel Lines SP-type Caboose, *50*	3	7____
6009	Remote Control Uncoupling Track, *53–54*	2	8____
6012	Gondola, *51–56*	2	6____
6014	Bosco PRR Boxcar, *58*		
	(A) White body	23	45____
	(B) Red body	4	8____
	(C) Orange body	4	7____
6014	Chun King Boxcar, *57 u*	60	138____

			Good	Exc
6014	Frisco Boxcar, *57, 63–69*			
_____	(A) White body		5	11
_____	(B) Red body		4	7
_____	(C) White body, coin slot		22	45
_____	(D) Orange body, *57*		18	63
_____	(E) Orange body, *69*		10	25
X6014	Baby Ruth PRR Boxcar, *51–56*			
_____	(A) White body		5	9
_____	(B) Red body		5	11
_____**6014-100**	Airex Boxcar, *60 u*		20	40
_____**6014-150**	Wix Boxcar, *59 u*		93	185
6015	Sunoco 1-D Tank Car, *54–55*			
_____	(A) Painted tank		80	320
_____	(B) Unpainted tank		4	12
6017	Lionel Lines SP-type Caboose, *51–62*			
_____	(A) Glossy tuscan-painted orange mold		25	85
_____	(B) Semigloss tuscan-painted, orange mold		13	38
_____	(C) Tile red-painted, blue mold		13	38
_____	(D) Common red, tuscan, and brown bodies		4	10
_____	(E) Bright red, black mold, *62*		50	250
_____**6017**	SP-type Caboose, maroon, "Lionel" only, *56*		15	35
_____**6017-50**	U.S. Marine Corps SP-type Caboose, *58*		30	70
_____**6017-85**	LL SP-type Caboose, gray, *58*		25	70
6017-100	B&M SP-type Caboose, *59, 62, 65–66*			
_____	(A) Purple-blue		155	430
_____	(B) Medium or light blue		15	53
_____**6017-185**	ATSF SP-type Caboose, *59–60*		15	35
_____**6017-200**	U.S. Navy SP-type Caboose, *60*		50	155
_____**6017-225**	ATSF SP-type Caboose, *61–62*		15	50
_____**6017-235**	ATSF SP-type Caboose, *62*		15	50
_____**6019**	Remote Control Track (027), *48–66*		2	10
_____**6020W**	Whistle Tender		28	70
_____**6024**	Nabisco Shredded Wheat Boxcar, *57*		15	30
_____**6024**	RCA Whirlpool Boxcar, *57 u*		30	60
6025	Gulf 1-D Tank Car, *56–58*			
_____	(A) Gray body, blue lettering		5	12
_____	(B) Orange body, blue lettering		6	17
_____	(C) Black body, red-orange Gulf emblem		5	18
_____**6026T**	Tender		11	30
_____**6026W**	Whistle Tender		25	61
_____**6027**	Alaska SP-type Caboose, *59*		31	65
_____**6029**	Remote Control Uncoupling Track, *55–63*		2	8
_____**6032**	Short Gondola, black (027), *52–54*		2	7
X6034	Baby Ruth PRR Boxcar, *53–54*			
_____	(A) Orange, blue lettering		5	10
_____	(B) Orange, black lettering		5	11

		Good	Exc
6035	Sunoco 1-D Tank Car, *52–53*	3	8 ____
6037	Lionel Lines SP-type Caboose, *52–54*		
	(A) Tuscan	3	6 ____
	(B) Red	5	11 ____
6042	Short Gondola, *59–61, 62–64 u*	3	11 ____
6044	Airex Boxcar, orange lettering, *59–60 u*		
	(A) Medium blue	10	20 ____
	(B) Teal blue	30	65 ____
	(C) Purple-blue	83	303 ____
6044-1X	Nestles/McCall's Boxcar, *62–63 u*	300	1700 ____
6045	Lionel Lines 2-D Tank Car, *59–64*		
	(A) Gray	10	20 ____
	(B) Orange	15	35 ____
	(C) Beige	10	30 ____
6045	Cities Service 2-D Tank, *60 u*	15	35 ____
6047	Lionel Lines SP-type Caboose, *62*		
	(A) Unpainted, medium red	2	5 ____
	(B) Painted, brown	80	265 ____
	(C) Unpainted, coral pink	15	70 ____
6050	Lionel Savings Bank Boxcar, *61*		
	(A) Blt by Lionel	20	50 ____
	(B) Built by Lionel	55	160 ____
6050-110	Swift Boxcar, *62–63*		
	(A) Red body	10	25 ____
	(B) Dark red body, 2 open holes in roof walk	45	160 ____
6050-175	Libby's Tomato Juice Boxcar, *63 u*		
	(A) Green stems on tomatoes	20	40 ____
	(B) Green stems missing	23	50 ____
	(C) No white lines between glass and tomatoes	30	90 ____
6057	LL SP-type Caboose, *59–62*		
	(A) Unpainted red plastic	3	7 ____
	(B) Red-painted	35	105 ____
	(C) Unpainted coral pink plastic	20	65 ____
6057-50	LL SP-type Caboose, orange, *62*	20	59 ____
6058	C&O SP-type Caboose, *61*		
	(A) Blue lettering	20	50 ____
	(B) Black lettering	35	80 ____
6059	M&StL SP-type Caboose, *61–69*		
	(A) Painted, red	15	38 ____
	(B) Unpainted, red	4	11 ____
	(C) Unpainted, maroon	9	13 ____
6062	NYC Gondola with 3 cable reels, *59–62*		
	(A) No metal undercarriage	10	28 ____
	(B) Metal undercarriage	25	69 ____
	(C) No metal undercarriage, no paint on bottom	55	80 ____
6062-50	NYC Gondola with 2 canisters, *69*	6	17 ____

		Good	Exc
___6066T	Tender	10	20
6067	SP-type Caboose, unmarked, *61–62*		
___	(A) Red	3	8
___	(B) Yellow	6	14
___	(C) Brown	9	18
___6076	ATSF Hopper, *63 u*	10	30
6076	Lehigh Valley Hopper, short, *63*		
___	(A) Gray body	8	14
___	(B) Black body	7	13
___	(C) Red body	8	13
___	(D) Yellow body, painted	350	1333
___6076-100	Hopper, gray, unmarked, *63*	10	25
___6110	2-4-2 Locomotive, 6001T Tender, *50–51*	15	35
6111	Flatcar with logs, *55–57*		
___	(A) Yellow with black lettering	10	35
___	(B) Yellow with white lettering	111	460
6112	Short Gondola with 4 canisters, *56–58*		
___	(A) Black body	7	15
___	(B) Blue body	7	15
___	(C) White body	18	40
6112-5	Canister, *56–58*		
___	(A) Red or white	1	3
___	(B) Red with black letters	18	60
6112-25	Canister Set, 4 pieces, red or white, with box, *56–58*	30	65
___6119	DL&W Work Caboose, red, *55–56*	13	25
___6119-25	DL&W Work Caboose, orange, *56–59*	15	35
___6119-50	DL&W Work Caboose, brown, *56*	20	55
6119-75	DL&W Work Caboose, *57*		
___	(A) Heat-stamped letters on frame	15	35
___	(B) Closely spaced rubber-stamped letters on frame	60	263
___	(C) Widely spaced rubber-stamped letters on frame	53	223
6119-100	DL&W Work Caboose, red cab, gray tool tray, *57–66, 69*		
___	(A) Black frame, white letters	10	25
___	(B) "Built By Lionel" builders plate, *66*	20	103
___	(C) Black frame, red-painted cab	60	223
___	(D) Santa Fe cab, gray tool box	10	35
___6119-125	Rescue Caboose, olive, black frame, *64*	85	180
___6120	Work Caboose, yellow, unmarked, *61–62*	5	14
6121	Flatcar with pipes, *56–57*		
___	(A) Yellow, red, or gray	10	35
___	(B) Maroon	15	60

		Good	Exc
6130	ATSF Work Caboose, *61, 65–69*		
	(A) Red painted, no builders plate	13	35 ___
	(B) Red unpainted, builders plate	10	30 ___
	(C) Red painted, builders plate	62	255 ___
6139	Remote Control Uncoupling Track (O27), *63*	1	4 ___
6142	Short Gondola, green, blue, or black, with 2 canisters, *63–66, 69*	6	13 ___
6142-175	Short Gondola, olive drab, with 2 canisters	40	145 ___
6149	Remote Control Uncoupling Track (O27), *64–69*	1	4 ___
6151	Flatcar with patrol truck, *58*		
	(A) Yellow frame	35	90 ___
	(B) Orange frame	25	75 ___
	(C) Cream frame	35	83 ___
6162	NYC Gondola with 3 white canisters, *59–68*		
	(A) Blue body	8	25 ___
	(B) Red body	73	274 ___
6162-60	Alaska Gondola with 3 red canisters, *59*	38	85 ___
6167	LL SP-type Caboose, red, *63–64*		
	(A) Unpainted	3	9 ___
	(B) Painted	35	155 ___
6167	SP-type Caboose, unmarked, no end rails, *63–64*		
	(A) Red body	3	9 ___
	(B) Brown body	8	23 ___
6167-50	SP-type Caboose, unmarked, yellow	5	23 ___
6167-85	Union Pacific SP-type Caboose, *69*	10	35 ___
6167-175	SP-type Caboose, unmarked, olive	80	390 ___
6175	Flatcar with rocket, *58–61*		
	(A) Black frame	35	68 ___
	(B) Red frame	35	65 ___
6176	Hopper, unmarked, *63–69*		
	(A) Dark yellow	10	38 ___
	(B) Gray	8	14 ___
	(C) Red	10	25 ___
	(D) Bright yellow	25	70 ___
6176	Lehigh Valley Hopper, *64–66, 69*		
	(A) Dark yellow	6	9 ___
	(B) Gray	7	11 ___
	(C) Black	3	8 ___
	(D) Red	14	33 ___
	(E) Bright yellow	25	55 ___
6176-100	Olive Drab Hopper, unmarked	35	117 ___
6219	C&O Work Caboose, *60*	20	45 ___
6220	Santa Fe NW2 Switcher, *49–50*		
	(A) Large GM decal on cab	130	270 ___
	(B) Small GM decal on side	105	215 ___

			Good	Exc
6250		Seaboard NW2 Switcher, *54–55*		
____		(A) Seaboard decal	110	235
____		(B) Widely spaced rubber-stamped letters	132	250
____		(C) Closely spaced rubber-stamped letters	165	464
6257		SP-type Caboose, *48–52*		
____		(A) Dark red, matching plastic smokestack	175	463
____		(B) All other variations	5	15
6257-25		SP-type Caboose, circled-L logo, *53–55*		
____		(A) Red painted	7	19
____		(B) Unpainted red plastic	4	11
____	**6257-50**	SP-type Caboose, *56*	4	12
	6257-100	Lionel Lines SP-type Caboose, smokestack, *63–64*		
____			10	25
____	**6257X**	SP-type Caboose, red, 2 couplers, with box, *48*	23	50
6262		Flatcar with wheel load, *56–57*		
____		(A) Black frame, *56–57*	30	65
____		(B) Red frame, *56*	319	768
6264		Flatcar with lumber for 264 Fork Lift Platform, *57–60*		
____		(A) Bar-end trucks	28	60
____		(B) Plastic trucks	30	70
____		(C) Separate-sale box and envelope	100	236
____	**6311**	Flatcar with 3 pipes, *55*	20	48
6315		Gulf 1-D Chemical Tank Car, *56–59, 68–69*		
____		(A) Early, painted	40	80
____		(B) Late, unpainted	30	55
____		(C) Late, unpainted, built date	50	125
6315		Lionel Lines 1-D Tank Car, *63–66*		
____		(A) Unpainted orange body	15	25
____		(B) Painted orange body	115	330
6342		NYC Gondola with culvert channel and 7 pipes, *56–58, 64–66*		
____			15	38
____	**6343**	Barrel Ramp Car with 6 barrels, *61–62*	20	38
____	**6346**	Alcoa Quad Hopper, *56*	30	65
6352-1		PFE Ice Car from 352 Ice Depot, *55–57*		
____		(A) 3 lines of data	70	127
____		(B) 4 lines of data	50	105
____		(C) Separate-sale box	1000	3750
6356		NYC Stock Car, 2-level, *54–55*		
____		(A) Heat-stamped lettering	25	40
____		(B) Rubber-stamped lettering	40	85
6357		SP-type Caboose, SP logo, *48–53*		
____		(A) Tile red, tuscan, or maroon	15	35
____		(B) Tile red, extra board on catwalk	165	567
6357		SP-type Caboose, no logo, *57–61*		
____		(A) Number to left	10	30
____		(B) Number to right	17	53

		Good	Exc
6357-25	SP-type Caboose, circle L logo, *53–56*		
	(A) Maroon or tuscan body, black metal smokestack	10	25____
	(B) Maroon body, maroon metal smokestack	115	475____
6357-50	ATSF SP-type Caboose, lighted, *60*	315	937____
6361	Timber Transport Car, *60–61, 64–69*		
	(A) White lettering	25	73____
	(B) No lettering	75	150____
6362	Truck Car with 3 trucks, *55–56*		
	(A) Shiny orange	25	48____
	(B) Dull orange	43	98____
6376	LL Circus Stock Car, *56–57*	35	63____
6401	Flatcar, no load, gray, *60*	4	12____
6401-25	Gray flatcar with load, *64–67*		
	(A) Jeep and cannon	115	275____
	(B) Tank	80	175____
	(C) Payton automobile	25	50____
	(D) Logs	13	27____
6402	Flatcar with orange or gray reels, *62, 64–66*	10	25____
6402	Flatcar with blue boat, *69*	33	60____
6402-150	Maroon Flatcar with white trailer	10	35____
6403B	Tender	35	80____
6404	Black Flatcar with auto, *60*		
	(A) Red auto	30	80____
	(B) Yellow auto	40	125____
	(C) Brown auto	75	213____
	(D) Green auto	80	243____
6405	Flatcar with piggyback van, *61*	15	50____
6406	Flatcar with auto, *61*		
	(A) Maroon frame, red auto	25	65____
	(B) Maroon frame, yellow auto	55	143____
	(C) Gray frame, dark brown auto	80	198____
	(D) Gray frame, green auto	90	228____
	(E) Gray frame, yellow auto	50	100____
6407	Flatcar with rocket, *63*	95	420____
6408	Flatcar with pipes, *63*	15	43____
6408	Flatcar with 2 orange cable reels, *67*	15	45____
6409-25	Flatcar with pipes, *63*	15	43____
6410-25	Flatcar with 2 automobiles, *63*		
	(A) Yellow autos	115	460____
	(B) Brown autos	150	560____
6411	Flatcar with logs, *48–50*	15	38____
6413	Mercury Capsule Carrying Car, *62–63*		
	(A) Medium blue frame	67	143____
	(B) Aquamarine frame	90	210____
	(C) Teal frame	90	258____

		Good	Exc
6414	Evans Auto Loader with 4 cars, *55–66*		
	(A) Premium cars (chrome bumpers, windows, rubber wheels): red, yellow, blue-green, and white	60	108
	(B) Cheapie cars (no wheels): 2 red and 2 yellow	180	308
	(C) Red cars with gray bumpers	70	160
	(D) Yellow cars with gray bumpers	160	395
	(E) Brown cars with gray bumpers	340	860
	(F) Green cars with gray bumpers	549	893
	(G) Metal trucks, number right of Lionel, premium cars	55	123
6415	Sunoco 3-D Tank Car, *53–55, 64–66, 69*	18	30
6416	Boat Transport Car, 4 boats, *61–63*	120	260
6417	PRR N5c Porthole Caboose, *53–57*		
	(A) New York Zone	15	35
	(B) Without New York Zone	106	226
6417-25	Lionel Lines N5c Porthole Caboose, *54*	15	35
6417-50	LV N5c Porthole Caboose, *54*		
	(A) Tuscan	398	1350
	(B) Gray	60	140
6418	Machinery Car with 2 steel girders, *55–57*		
	(A) Black girders, "Lionel" in raised letters	70	130
	(B) Orange girders, "Lionel" in raised letters	60	100
	(C) Pinkish orange girders, U.S. Steel	70	120
	(D) Black girders, U.S. Steel	70	120
6419	DL&W Work Caboose, *48–50, 52–55*	20	40
6419-25	DL&W Work Caboose, one coupler, *54–55*	15	35
6419-50	DL&W Work Caboose, short smokestack, *56–57*	15	43
6419-75	DL&W Work Caboose, one coupler, *56–57*	15	40
6419-100	N&W Work Caboose, *57–58*	45	109
6420	DL&W Work Caboose with searchlight, *48–50*		
	(A) Heat-stamped serif lettering	40	80
	(B) Rubber-stamped sans serif lettering	70	170
6424	Twin Auto Flatcar, *56–59*		
	(A) Black frame, premium cars	18	60
	(B) 6805 slots, no rail stops	55	140
	(C) AAR trucks, number on right	28	83
6424-110	Twin Auto Flatcar, 6805 slots and rail stops, *58–59*	85	184
6425	Gulf 3-D Tank Car, *56–58*	15	35
6427	Lionel Lines N5c Porthole Caboose, *54–60*	15	35
6427-60	Virginian N5c Porthole Caboose, *58*	185	437
6427-500	PRR N5c Porthole Caboose, sky blue, from Girls Set, *57–58**	163	335
6428	U.S. Mail Boxcar, *60–61, 65–66*	20	48
6429	DL&W Work Caboose, AAR trucks, *63*	130	265

		Good	Exc
6430	Flatcar with 2 trailers, *56–58*		
	(A) Gray Cooper-Jarrett trailers	30	58____
	(B) White Cooper-Jarrett trailers	30	73____
	(C) Green Fruehauf trailers	25	58____
	(D) Gray Cooper-Jarrett trailers with Fruehauf stickers	35	90____
6431	Flatcar with 2 yellow or white vans and Midgetoy tractor, *66*	65	232____
6434	Poultry Dispatch Stock Car, *58–59*	33	70____
6436-1	LV Open Quad Hopper, black, *55*		
	(A) Spreader brace with holes	15	35____
	(B) No spreader brace holes	45	185____
6436-25	LV Open Quad Hopper, maroon, *55–57*		
	(A) Spreader brace with holes	20	45____
	(B) No spreader brace holes	180	563____
6436-110	LV Quad Hopper, red, *63–68*		
	(A) No built date	20	40____
	(B) Built date "New 3-55"	37	115____
6436-500	LV Open Quad Hopper, lilac, from Girls Set, *57–58**		
	(A) Spreader brace with holes	70	310____
	(B) No spreader brace holes	98	425____
6437	PRR N5c Porthole Caboose, *61–68*	15	38____
6440	Flatcar with gray vans, *61–63*	35	80____
6440	Green Pullman Car, *48–49*	35	90____
6441	Green Observation Car, *48–49*	30	80____
6442	Brown Pullman Car, *49*	40	83____
6443	Brown Observation Car, *49*	38	75____
6445	Fort Knox Gold Reserve Boxcar with coin slot, *61–63*	45	103____
6446	N&W Covered Quad Hopper, black or gray, *54–55*	25	55____
6446-25	N&W Covered Quad Hopper, *55–57*		
	(A) Black, white lettering	25	70____
	(B) Gray, black lettering	33	70____
	(C) Gray, plastic trucks, spreader brace holes	67	183____
6446-60	LV Covered Quad Hopper, *63*	95	240____
6447	PRR N5c Porthole Caboose, *63*	93	325____
6448	Exploding Target Range Boxcar, *61–64*		
	(A) Red sides, white roof and ends	23	40____
	(B) White sides, red roof and ends	25	40____
6452	Pennsylvania Gondola, black, *48–49*		
	(A) Numbered "6462," *48*	25	55____
	(B) Numbered "6452," *49*	10	25____
X6454	Baby Ruth PRR Boxcar, *48*	65	263____
X6454	Santa Fe Boxcar, *48*	10	30____

			Good	Exc
X6454		NYC Boxcar, *48*		
____		(A) Brown body	15	38
____		(B) Orange body	60	140
____		(C) Tan body	20	70
____ **X6454**		Erie Boxcar, *49–52*	20	40
____ **X6454**		PRR Boxcar, *49–52*	25	45
X6454		SP Boxcar, *49–52*		
____		(A) Break in herald circle between R and N, *49*	24	88
____		(B) Complete herald circle	20	48
6456		Lehigh Valley Short Hopper, *48–55*		
____		(A) Black	10	25
____		(B) Maroon	8	20
____ **6456-25**		Lehigh Valley Short Hopper, gray, *54–55*	20	40
6456-50		Lehigh Valley Short Hopper, enamel red, white lettering, *54*	261	623
6456-75		Lehigh Valley Short Hopper, enamel red, yellow lettering, *54*	65	130
____ **6457**		SP-type Caboose, *49–52*	15	25
6460		Bucyrus Erie Crane Car, black cab, 8-wheel, *52–54*	20	45
____ **6460-25**		Bucyrus Erie Crane Car, red cab, 8-wheel, *54*	40	110
____ **6461**		Transformer Car, *49–50*	35	70
____ **6462**		NYC Gondola, black, with 6 barrels, *49–54*	11	20
6462-25		NYC Gondola, green, with 6 barrels, *54–57*		
____		(A) N in second panel, 2 lines of data	10	35
____		(B) N in third panel, 3 lines of data	15	50
6462-75		NYC Gondola, red-painted, with 6 barrels, *52–55*	10	30
____ **6462-125**		NYC Gondola, red plastic, with 6 barrels, *55–57*	10	23
6462-500		NYC Gondola, pink, from Girls Set, with 4 canisters, *57–58**	75	175
____ **6463**		Rocket Fuel 2-D Tank Car, *62–63*	20	63
6464-1		WP Boxcar, *53–54*		
____		(A) Blue lettering	30	55
____		(B) Red lettering	425	1220
____ **6464-25**		GN Boxcar, *53–54*	31	85
____ **6464-50**		M&StL Boxcar, *53–56*	20	75
6464-75		RI Boxcar, green, *53–54, 69*		
____		(A) Built date, *53–54*	30	60
____		(B) No built date, *69*	40	90
6464-100		Western Pacific Boxcar, *54–55*		
____		(A) Silver body, yellow feather	35	135
____		(B) Orange body, blue feather	263	855
____ **6464-125**		NYC Pacemaker Boxcar, *54–56*	45	83
____ **6464-150**		MP Boxcar, *54–55, 57*	45	118
6464-175		Rock Island Boxcar, *54–55*		
____		(A) Blue lettering	40	120
____		(B) Black lettering	375	1033

	Good	Exc

6464-200 Pennsylvania Boxcar, *54–55, 69* — 84, 144 _____

6464-225 SP Boxcar, *54–56* — 55, 120 _____

6464-250 WP Boxcar, *66* — 75, 230 _____

6464-275 State of Maine Boxcar, *55, 57–59*
  (A) Striped doors — 35, 75 _____
  (B) Solid doors — 55, 133 _____

6464-300 Rutland Boxcar, *55–56*
  (A) Rubber-stamped lettering — 45, 85 _____
  (B) Split door with bottom painted green — 270, 420 _____
  (C) Rubber-stamped lettering with solid shield — 1575, 4225 _____
  (D) Heat-stamped lettering — 75, 165 _____
  (E) Painted yellow body — 300, 870 _____

6464-325 B&O Sentinel Boxcar, *56* — 183, 413 _____

6464-350 MKT Boxcar, *56* — 95, 325 _____

6464-375 Central of Georgia Boxcar, *56–57, 66*
  (A) Unpainted maroon body — 40, 75 _____
  (B) Painted red body — 775, 3878 _____

6464-400 B&O Time-Saver Boxcar, *56–57, 69*
  (A) BLT 5-54 — 40, 90 _____
  (B) BLT 2-56 — 98, 264 _____
  (C) No built date — 35, 95 _____

6464-425 New Haven Boxcar, *56–58* — 30, 60 _____

6464-450 Great Northern Boxcar, *56–57, 66* — 70, 135 _____

6464-475 B&M Boxcar, *57–60, 65–66, 68*
  (A) Medium blue-painted or unpainted plastic — 38, 75 _____
  (B) Dark purple-painted, gray or blue mold — 68, 275 _____
  (C) Dark blue-painted, yellow mold — 140, 483 _____

6464-500 Timken Boxcar, white side band and charcoal lettering, *57–59, 69*
  (A) Unpainted yellow body — 55, 135 _____
  (B) Painted yellow body, Type IV — 70, 135 _____
  (C) Painted yellow body, Type II — 180, 450 _____

6464-510 NYC Pacemaker Boxcar, *57–58* — 260, 675 _____

6464-515 MKT Boxcar, *57–58* — 260, 668 _____

6464-525 M&StL Boxcar, *57–58, 64–66*
  (A) Red, white lettering — 38, 75 _____
  (B) Maroon, white lettering — 115, 505 _____

6464-650 D&RGW Boxcar, *57–58, 66*
  (A) Yellow body, silver roof, black stripe — 65, 135 _____
  (B) Yellow body, silver roof, no black stripe — 95, 248 _____
  (C) Painted yellow body and yellow roof — 500, 2380 _____

6464-700 Santa Fe Boxcar, *61, 66* — 55, 145 _____

6464-725 New Haven Boxcar, *62–66, 68*
  (A) Orange body — 25, 50 _____
  (B) Black body — 75, 215 _____

6464-825 Alaska Boxcar, *59–60* — 118, 315 _____

		Good	Exc
___**6464-900**	NYC Boxcar, *60–66*	37	92
6465	Sunoco 2-D Tank Car, *48–56*		
___	(A) Silver tank, rubber-stamped "6465"	6	12
___	(B) Silver tank, rubber-stamped "6455"	20	75
___	(C) Silver tank, no number on frame	7	20
___	(D) Glossy gray tank	10	40
___**6465-60**	Gulf 2-D Tank Car, *58*		
___	(A) Black tank	23	53
___	(B) Gray tank	10	35
___**6465-85**	LL 2-D Tank Car, black, *59*	20	60
___**6465-110**	Cities Service 2-D Tank, *60–62*	23	63
___**6465-160**	LL 2-D Tank Car, orange with black ends, *63–64*	13	25
___**6466T**	Tender, *49–53*	13	30
___**6466W**	Whistle Tender, *49–53*	20	45
___**6466WX**	Whistle Tender, *49–53*	20	50
___**6467**	Miscellaneous Car, *56*	25	55
___**6468**	B&O Auto Boxcar, blue, *53–55*	20	42
___**6468X**	B&O Auto Boxcar, tuscan, *53–55*	128	312
6468-25	NH Auto Boxcar, *56–58*		
___	(A) Black N over white H, black doors	25	75
___	(B) White N over black H, black doors	68	249
___	(C) Black N over white H, painted Tuscan doors	28	89
___**6469**	Liquified Gas Tank Car, *63*	48	125
___**6470**	Explosives Boxcar, *59–60*	15	38
___**6472**	Refrigerator Car, *50–53*	13	25
___**6473**	Horse Transport Car, *62–69*	15	25
___**6475**	Libby's Crushed Pineapple Vat Car, *63 u*	35	90
___**6475**	Pickles Vat Car, *60–62*	25	102
6476	LV Short Hopper, *57–63*		
___	(A) Red body	7	18
___	(B) Gray body	10	20
___	(C) Black body	7	18
___**6476-75**	LV Short Hopper, black, Type VI body, *63*	10	20
___**6476-135**	LV Short Hopper, yellow, *64–66, 68*	7	18
___**6476-160**	LV Short Hopper, black, *69*	7	16
___**6476-185**	LV Short Hopper, yellow, *69*	7	18
___**6477**	Miscellaneous Car with pipes, *57–58*	25	65
___**6480**	Explosives Boxcar, red, *61*	23	45
___**6482**	Refrigerator Car, *57*	18	40
6500	Flatcar with Bonanza airplane, *62, 65*		
___	(A) Plane, red top and wings	358	680
___	(B) Plane, white top and wings	385	825
___**6501**	Flatcar with jet boat, *62–63*	70	155
6502	Flat Car with Girder, *62*		
___	(A) Black flatcar	17	76
___	(B) Red flatcar	35	118

		Good	Exc
6502-50	Flatcar, blue or teal, no lettering, with bridge girder, *62*	11	35 ____
6511	Flatcar with pipes, *53–56*		
	(A) Die-cast truck plates, *53*	20	55 ____
	(B) Stamped metal truck plates	13	40 ____
6511-24	Set of 6 pipes with box, *55–58*	35	150 ____
6512	Cherry Picker Car, *62–63*	35	85 ____
6517	LL Bay Window Caboose, *55–59*		
	(A) Built date underscored	25	75 ____
	(B) Built date not underscored	25	50 ____
	(C) Built date not underscored, lettering higher	15	50 ____
6517-75	Erie Bay Window Caboose, *66*	155	477 ____
6518	Transformer Car, *56–58*	30	68 ____
6519	Allis-Chalmers Flatcar, *58–61*		
	(A) Dark or medium orange base	35	70 ____
	(B) Dull light orange base	42	130 ____
6520	Searchlight Car, *49–51*		
	(A) Tan generator	550	1415 ____
	(B) Green generator	115	280 ____
	(C) Maroon generator	22	50 ____
	(D) Orange generator	15	40 ____
	(E) Green generator, black searchlight housing	65	325 ____
6530	Firefighting Instruction Car, *60–61*		
	(A) Red body, white lettering	35	83 ____
	(B) Black body, white lettering	105	415 ____
6536	M&StL Open Quad Hopper, *58–59, 63*	30	75 ____
6544	Missile Firing Car, 4 missiles, *60–64*		
	(A) White-lettered console	55	168 ____
	(B) Black-lettered console	110	340 ____
6555	Sunoco 1-D Tank Car, *49–50*	20	65 ____
6556	MKT Stock Car, *58*	100	355 ____
6557	SP-type Smoking Caboose, *58–59*		
	(A) Tuscan, with non-reverse lettering	105	205 ____
	(B) Brown, with reverse lettering	600	1350 ____
6560	Bucyrus Erie Crane Car, smokestack, *55–58, 68–69*		
	(A) Black frame, red-orange cab	48	110 ____
	(B) Black frame, gray cab	35	75 ____
	(C) Black frame, red cab	25	40 ____
	(D) Dark blue frame, red cab	40	90 ____
	(E) Black frame, red cab, rubber-stamped "6560"	66	316 ____
	(F) Black frame, black cab	30	150 ____
6560-25	Bucyrus Erie Crane Car, 8-wheel, *56*	40	85 ____
6561	Cable Car, 2 reels, *53–56*		
	(A) Orange reels	25	60 ____
	(B) Gray reels	30	153 ____

		Good	Exc
6562	NYC Gondola with 4 red canisters, *56–58*		
____	(A) Gray body, *56*	20	45
____	(B) Red body, *56, 58*	15	30
____	(C) Black body, *57*	10	25
6572	REA Refrigerator Car, *58–59, 63*		
____	(A) Passenger trucks	65	245
____	(B) Bar-end trucks	40	105
____	(C) AAR trucks, *63*	35	73
6630	Missile Launching Car, *61*	25	76
6636	Alaska Open Quad Hopper, *59–60*	45	95
6640	USMC Missile Launching Car, *60*	100	220
6646	Lionel Lines Stock Car, *57*	20	43
6650	IRBM Rocket Launcher, *59–63*		
____	(A) "6650" stamped on left	25	50
____	(B) "6650" stamped on right	90	260
6650-80	Missile, *60*	4	10
6651	USMC Cannon Car, *64 u*	90	228
6654W	Whistle Tender	18	40
6656	Lionel Lines Stock Car, *49–55*		
____	(A) Brown Armour decal	23	70
____	(B) No decal	10	25
6657	Rio Grande SP-type Caboose, *57–58*		
____	(A) With ladder slots	75	170
____	(B) Without ladder slots	180	430
6660	Boom Car, *58*	30	80
6670	Derrick Car, *59–60*		
____	(A) "6670" stamped on left	25	60
____	(B) "6670" stamped on right	60	205
6672	Santa Fe Refrigerator Car, *54–56*		
____	(A) Blue lettering, 2 lines of data	25	38
____	(B) Black lettering, 2 lines of data	23	65
____	(C) Blue lettering, 3 lines of data	92	348
6736	Detroit & Mackinac Open Quad Hopper, *60–62*	20	40
6800	Flatcar with airplane, *57–60*		
____	(A) Plane, black top and wings	40	90
____	(B) Plane, yellow top and wings	45	115
6800-60	Airplane, *57–58*	40	243
6801	Flatcar with boat, white hull, brown deck, *57*	40	70
6801-50	Flatcar with boat, yellow hull, white deck, *58–60*	45	85
6801-60	Boat, *57–58*	20	110
6801-75	Flatcar with boat, blue hull, white deck, *58–60*	45	90
6802	Flatcar with 2 U.S. Steel girders, *58–59*	15	35
6803	Flatcar with USMC tank and sound truck, *58–59*	118	222
6804	Flatcar with USMC antiaircraft and sound trucks, *58–59*	85	206

		Good	Exc	
6805	Atomic Energy Disposal Flatcar, *58–59*	40	206	____
6806	Flatcar with USMC radar and medical trucks, *58–59*	105	202	____
6807	Flatcar with amphibious vehicle, *58–59*	63	142	____
6808	Flatcar with USMC tank and searchlight truck, *58–59*	103	222	____
6809	Flatcar with USMC antiaircraft and medical trucks, *58–59*	103	208	____
6810	Flatcar with trailer, *58*	25	50	____
6812	Track Maintenance Car, *59*			
	(A) Dark yellow superstructure	20	63	____
	(B) Black base, gray platform and crank handle	20	70	____
	(C) Gray base, black platform and crank handle	20	67	____
	(D) Cream superstructure	40	198	____
	(E) Light yellow superstructure	25	80	____
6814	Rescue Caboose, *59–61*	40	110	____
6816	Flatcar with Allis-Chalmers bulldozer, *59–60*			
	(A) Red car	205	445	____
	(B) Black car	500	1100	____
6816-100	Allis-Chalmers Bulldozer, *59–60*			
	(A) No box	85	270	____
	(B) Separate-sale box	243	763	____
6817	Flatcar with Allis-Chalmers motor scraper, *59–60*			
	(A) Red car	210	485	____
	(B) Black car	490	1205	____
6817-100	Allis-Chalmers Motor Scraper, *59–60*			
	(A) No box	125	280	____
	(B) Separate-sale box	245	755	____
6818	Flatcar with transformer, *58*	15	35	____
6819	Flatcar with helicopter, *59–60*	20	60	____
6820	Aerial Missile Transport Car with helicopter, *60–61*			
	(A) Light blue frame	105	230	____
	(B) Medium blue frame	80	190	____
6821	Flatcar with crates, *59–60*	20	40	____
6822	Searchlight Car, *61–69*			
	(A) Black base, gray light	15	38	____
	(B) Gray base, black light	25	48	____
6823	Flatcar with 2 IRBM missiles, *59–60*	35	65	____
6824	USMC Work Caboose, *60*	80	268	____
6824-50	Rescue Caboose, white, *64*	40	115	____
6825	Flatcar with arch trestle bridge, *59–62*	25	40	____
6826	Flatcar with Christmas trees, *59–60*	28	92	____
6827	Flatcar with Harnischfeger power shovel, *60–63*	70	215	____
6827-100	Harnischfeger Power Shovel, *60*			
	(A) No box	55	105	____
	(B) Separate-sale box	115	253	____

		Good	Exc
6828	Flatcar with Harnischfeger crane, *60–63, 66*		
_____	(A) Black flatcar, light yellow crane cab	73	230
_____	(B) Black flatcar, dark yellow crane cab	75	255
_____	(C) Red flatcar, dark yellow crane cab	270	1185
6828-100	Harnischfeger Construction Crane, *60*		
_____	(A) No box	35	105
_____	(B) Separate-sale box	90	258
_____**6830**	Flatcar with submarine, *60–61*	60	145
6844	Missile Carrying Car, 6 missiles, *59–60*		
_____	(A) Black frame	30	85
_____	(B) Red frame	345	1150

Other Track, Transformers, and Assorted Items

		Good	Exc
_____**A**	Transformer, 90 watts, *47–48*	20	50
_____**CO-1**	Track Clips, dozen, with envelope (O), *49*	5	12
_____**CO-1**	Track Clips, box of 100 (O), *49*	40	150
_____**CTC**	Lockon (O and O27), *47–69*	1	2
_____**CTC-14**	Lockons, dozen, with envelope	15	50
_____**ECU-1**	Electronic Control Unit, *46*	30	80
_____**KW**	Transformer, 190 watts, *50–65*	40	83
_____**LTC**	Lockon (O and O27), *50–69*	2	9
_____**LW**	Transformer, 125 watts, *55–56*	33	72
_____**OC**	Curved Track (O), *45–61*	0	1
_____**OC½**	Half Section Curved Track (O), *45–66*	0	1
_____**OCS**	Curved Insulated Track (O), *46–50*	10	20
_____**OS**	Straight Track (O), *45–61*	0	2
_____**OSS**	Straight Insulated Track, *46–50*	5	18
_____**OTC**	Lockon Track (O and O27)	2	5
_____**Q**	Transformer, 75 watts, *46*	15	30
_____**R**	Transformer, 110 watts, *46–47*	20	40
_____**RCS**	Remote Control Track (O), *45–48*	4	10
_____**RW**	Transformer, 110 watts, *48–54*	10	28
_____**RX**	Transformer, 100 watts, *47–48*	10	33
_____**S**	Transformer, 80 watts, *47*	15	30
SP	Smoke Pellets, bottle, *48–69*		
_____	(A) Tall, light amber bottle	15	55
_____	(B) Tall, dark amber bottle	10	60
_____	(C) Short, light amber bottle	13	58
_____	(D) All other bottles	5	14
_____	(E) Bottle on blister pack, *65*	20	58
_____**SP-12**	Dealer Display Box with 12 full smoke bottles	115	345
_____**ST-300**	Nut Driver Set with holder, service station item	485	1000
_____**ST-303**	E Unit Spreader, service station item	22	88
_____**ST-311**	Wheel Puller, service station item	73	132
_____**ST-320**	Phillips Screwdriver, service station item	160	280
_____**ST-322**	Flathead Screwdriver, service station item	40	150

		Good	Exc	
ST-325	Screwdriver Set, service station item	400	900	___
ST-342	Track Pliers, service station item	75	165	___
ST-343	O Gauge Track Pliers, service station item	450	1000	___
ST-350	Rivet Press, service station item	470	945	___
ST-350-5	Rivet Press Tool Block with tools, service station item	300	500	___
ST-350-17	Sliding Shoe Anvil, service station item	4	16	___
ST-375	Wheel Cup Tool Set, service station item	400	900	___
ST-378	E Unit Vice, service station item	133	272	___
ST-384	Track Pliers, service station item	125	250	___
SW	Transformer, 130 watts, *61–66*	35	65	___
TW	Transformer, 175 watts, *53–60*	50	80	___
TOC	Curved Track (O), *62–66, 68–69*		1	___
TOC½	Half Section Straight Track (O), *62–66*		1	___
TOS	Straight Track (O), *62–69*		1	___
UCS	Remote Control Track (O), *45–69*	5	12	___
UTC	Lockon (O, 027, Standard), *45*		2	___
V	Transformer, 150 watts, *46–47*	50	95	___
VW	Transformer, 150 watts, *48–49*	45	90	___
Z	Transformer, 250 watts, *45–47*	70	120	___
ZW	Transformer, 250 watts, *48–49*	50	110	___
ZW	Transformer, 275 watts, *50–56*	60	155	___
ZW	Transformer, 275 watts, R type, *57–66*	93	170	___

		Exc	Mint
366	Menards C&NW 4-4-2 Locomotive with tender, 09	45	75
____**400**	Menards C&NW Chicago Combine Car, 09	25	40
403	Menards C&NW Lake Superior Observation Car, 09	25	40
____**410**	Menards C&NW Lake Michigan Coach, 09	40	65
____**0512**	Toy Fair Reefer, 81 u	60	70
____**550C**	31" Diameter Curved Track (O), 70	1	2
____**550S**	Straight Track (O), 70	1	2
____**665E**	Johnny Cash Blue Train 4-6-4 Locomotive, 71 u		NRS
____**1050**	New Englander Set, 80–81	155	205
____**1052**	Chesapeake Flyer Set, 80	140	150
____**1053**	James Gang Set, 80–82	155	195
____**1070**	Royal Limited Set, 80	285	350
____**1071**	Mid Atlantic Limited Set, 80	225	230
____**1072**	Cross Country Express Set, 80–81	240	385
____**1081**	Wabash Cannonball Set, 70–72	105	120
____**1082**	Yard Boss Set, 70	120	165
____**1083**	Pacemaker Set, 70	105	120
____**1084**	Grand Trunk Western Freight Set, 70	120	140
____**1085**	Santa Fe Express Diesel Freight Set, 70	175	190
____**1091**	Sears Special Steam Freight Set, 70 u	150	165
____**1092**	Sears GTW Steam Freight Set, 70 u	150	165
____**1100**	Happy Huff n' Puff, 74–75 u	55	70
____**1150**	L.A.S.E.R. Train Set, 81–82	155	195
____**1151**	Union Pacific Thunder Freight Set, 81–82	150	175
____**1153**	JCPenney Thunderball Freight Set, 81 u	165	180
____**1154**	Reading Yard King Set, 81–82	170	190
____**1155**	Cannonball Freight Set, 82	75	85
____**1157**	Lionel Leisure Wabash Cannonball Set, 81 u		250
____**1158**	Maple Leaf Limited Set, 81	405	435
____**1159**	Toys "R" Us Midnight Flyer Set, 81 u	130	140
____**1160**	Great Lakes Limited Set, 81	280	330
____**T-1171**	CN Locomotive Set, 71 u	240	275
____**T-1172**	Yardmaster Set, 71 u		200
____**T-1173**	Grand Trunk Western Freight Set, 71–73 u	175	195
____**T-1174**	Canadian National Set, 71–73 u	265	300
____**1182**	Yardmaster Set, 71–72	85	105
____**1183**	Silver Star Set, 71–72	65	80
____**1184**	Allegheny Set, 71	120	150
____**1186**	Cross Country Express Set, 71–72	210	260
____**1187**	Illinois Central Set (SSS), 71	400	485
____**1190**	Sears Special #1 Set, 71 u	85	100
____**1195**	JCPenney Special Set, 71 u	150	165
____**1198**	Unnamed Set, 71 u		175
____**1199**	Ford-Autolite Allegheny Set, 71 u	187	207
____**1200**	Gravel Gus, 75 u	75	100
____**1250**	New York Central Set (SSS), 72	315	380
____**1252**	Heavy Iron Set, 82–83	90	130
____**1253**	Quicksilver Express Set, 82–83	265	340

Exc Mint

		Exc	Mint	
1254	Black Cave Flyer Set, *82*	75	105	___
1260	Continental Limited Set, *82*	290	385	___
1261	Sears Black Cave Flyer Set, *82 u*	165	195	___
1262	Toys "R" Us Heavy Iron Set, *82 u*	150	165	___
1263	JCPenney Overland Freight Set, *82 u*	150	165	___
1264	Nibco Express Set, *82 u*	190	195	___
1265	Tappan Special Set, *82 u*	130	155	___
T-1272	Yardmaster Set, *72–73 u*	150	165	___
T-1273	Silver Star Set, *72–73 u*	90	115	___
1280	Kickapoo Valley & Northern Set, *72*	60	75	___
1284	Allegheny Set, *72*	140	165	___
1285	Santa Fe Twin Diesel Set, *72*	95	140	___
1287	Pioneer Dockside Switcher Set, *72*	95	100	___
1290	Sears Steam Freight Set, *72 u*	150	165	___
1291	Sears Steam Freight Set, *72 u*	150	165	___
1300	Gravel Gus Junior, *75 u*	70	90	___
1350	Canadian Pacific Set (SSS), *73*	460	620	___
1351	Baltimore & Ohio Set, *83–84*	205	280	___
1352	Rocky Mountain Freight Set, *83–84*	75	95	___
1353	Southern Streak Set, *83–85*	75	95	___
1354	Northern Freight Flyer Set, *83–85*	230	280	___
1355	Commando Assault Train, *83–84*	175	248	___
1359	Display Case for Set 1355, *83 u*	75	95	___
1361	Gold Coast Limited Set, *83*	390	400	___
1362	Lionel Leisure BN Express Set, *83 u*	200	300	___
1380	U.S. Steel Industrial Switcher Set, *73–75*	60	75	___
1381	Cannonball Set, *73–75*	70	75	___
1382	Yardmaster Set, *73–74*	110	135	___
1383	Santa Fe Freight Set, *73–75*	100	125	___
1384	Southern Express Set, *73–76*	75	120	___
1385	Blue Streak Freight Set, *73–74*	100	120	___
1386	Rock Island Express Set, *73–74*	120	140	___
1387	Milwaukee Road Special Set, *73*	185	285	___
1388	Golden State Arrow Set, *73–75*	215	240	___
1390	Sears 7-unit Steam Freight Set, *73 u*	170	190	___
1392	Sears 8-unit Steam Freight Set, *73 u*	150	165	___
1393	Sears 6-unit Diesel Freight Set, *73 u*	150	165	___
1395	JCPenney Set, *73 u*	150	165	___
1400	Happy Huff n' Puff Junior, *75 u*	130	140	___
1402	Chessie System Set, *84–85*	125	150	___
1403	Redwood Valley Express Set, *84–85*	170	205	___
1450	D&RGW Set (SSS), *74*	335	415	___
1451	Erie-Lackawanna Limited Set, *84*	415	465	___
1460	Grand National Set, *74*	300	330	___
1461	Black Diamond Set, *74 u, 75*	100	120	___
1463	Coca-Cola Special Set, *74 u, 75*	211	260	___
1487	Broadway Limited Set, *74–75*	160	255	___
1489	Santa Fe Double Diesel Set, *74–76*	140	165	___
1492	Sears 7-unit Steam Freight Set, *74 u*	150	165	___
1493	Sears 7-unit Steam Freight Set, *74 u*	150	165	___
1499	JCPenney Great Express Set, *74 u*	150	165	___
1501	Midland Freight Set, *85–86*	75	95	___

		Exc	Mint
____**1502**	Yard Chief Set, *85–86*	205	230
____**1506**	Sears Centennial Chessie System Set, *85 u*	165	195
____**1512**	JCPenney Midland Freight Set, *85 u*	90	115
____**1549**	Toys "R" Us Heavy Iron Set, *85–89 u*	180	215
____**1552**	Burlington Northern Limited Set, *85*	500	570
____**1560**	North American Express Set, *75*	275	365
____**1562**	Fast Freight Flyer Set, *85 u*	120	140
____**1577**	Liberty Special Set, *75 u*	224	232
____**1579**	Milwaukee Road Set (SSS), *75*	325	410
____**99000**	Keebler Elf Express Steam Freight Set, *99 u*		1100
____**1581**	Thunderball Freight Set, *75–76*	90	100
____**1582**	Yard Chief Set, *75–76*	115	155
____**1584**	N&W "Spirit of America" Set, *75*	160	180
____**1585**	75th Anniversary Special Set, *75–77*	212	226
____**1586**	Chesapeake Flyer Set, *75–77*	160	190
____**1587**	Capitol Limited Set, *75*	270	300
____**1593**	Sears Set, *75 u*		100
____**1595**	Sears 6-unit Diesel Freight Set, *75 u*	150	165
____**1602**	Nickel Plate Special Set, *86–91*	120	125
____**1606**	Sears Centennial Nickel Plate Set, *86 u*	165	195
____**1608**	American Express General Set, *86 u*	205	320
____**1615**	Cannonball Express Set, *86–90*	65	75
____**1632**	Santa Fe Work Train (SSS), *86*	220	255
____**1652**	B&O Freight Set, *86*	140	185
____**1658**	Town House TV and Appliances Set, *86 u*	80	95
____**1660**	Yard Boss Set, *76*	100	115
____**1661**	Rock Island Line Set, *76–77*	80	100
____**1662**	Black River Freight Set, *76–78*	75	95
____**1663**	Amtrak Lake Shore Limited Set, *76–77*	215	265
____**1664**	Illinois Central Freight Set, *76–77*	265	355
____**1665**	NYC Empire State Express Set, *76*	310	435
____**1672**	Northern Pacific Set (SSS), *76*	215	280
____**1685**	True Value Freight Flyer Set, *86–87 u*	60	75
____**1686**	Kay Bee Toys Freight Flyer Set, *86 u*	150	165
____**1687**	Freight Flyer Set, *87–90*	39	47
____**1693**	Toys "R" Us Rock Island Line Set, *76 u*	110	130
____**1694**	Toys "R" Us Black River Freight Set, *76 u*	110	130
____**1696**	Sears Steam Freight Set, *76 u*	110	130
____**1698**	True Value Rock Island Line Set, *76 u*	125	145
____**1760**	Trains n' Truckin' Steel Hauler Set, *77–78*	105	110
____**1761**	Trains n' Truckin' Cargo King Set, *77–78*	95	165
____**1762**	Wabash Cannonball Set, *77*	135	190
____**1764**	Heartland Express Set, *77*	185	240
____**1765**	Rocky Mountain Special Set, *77*	210	315
____**1766**	B&O Budd Car Set (SSS), *77*	335	390
____**1776**	Seaboard U36B Diesel, *74–76*	88	140
____**1790**	Lionel Leisure Steel Hauler Set, *77 u*	150	200
____**1791**	Toys "R" Us Steel Hauler Set, *77 u*	130	175
____**1792**	True Value Rock Island Line Set, *77 u*	100	135
____**1793**	Toys "R" Us Black River Freight Set, *77 u*	120	155
____**1796**	JCPenney Cargo Master Set, *77 u*		200
____**1860**	"Workin' on the Railroad" Timberline Set, *78*	65	85

No.	Description	Exc	Mint
1862	"Workin' on the Railroad" Logging Empire Set, *78*	85	110
1864	Santa Fe Double Diesel Set, *78–79*	155	190
1865	Chesapeake Flyer Set, *78–79*	155	180
1866	Great Plains Express Set, *78–79*	195	285
1867	Milwaukee Road Limited Set, *78*	230	275
1868	M&StL Set (SSS), *78*	215	255
1892	JCPenney Logging Empire Set, *78 u*	95	125
1893	Toys "R" Us Logging Empire Set, *78 u*	175	225
1960	Midnight Flyer Set, *79–81*	55	75
1962	Wabash Cannonball Set, *79*	90	105
1963	Black River Freight Set, *79–81*	75	85
1965	Smokey Mountain Line Set, *79*	65	85
1970	Southern Pacific Limited Set, *79 u*	340	365
1971	Quaker City Limited Set, *79*	315	335
1990	Mystery Glow Midnight Flyer Set, *79 u*	75	90
1991	JCPenney Wabash Cannonball Deluxe Express Set, *79 u*	150	165
1993	Toys "R" Us Midnight Flyer Set, *79 u*	110	130
2110	Graduated Trestle Set, 22 pieces, *70–88*	9	13
2111	Elevated Trestle Set, 10 pieces, *70–88*	8	11
2113	Tunnel Portals, pair, *84–87*	11	16
2115	Dwarf Signal, *84–87*	9	13
2117	Block Target Signal, *84–87*	23	29
2122	Extension Bridge, rock piers, *76–87*	24	34
2125	Whistling Freight Shed, *71*	36	43
2126	Whistling Freight Shed, *76–87*	18	26
2127	Diesel Horn Shed, *76–87*	25	30
2128	Operating Switchman, *83–86*	26	29
2129	Illuminated Freight Station, *83–86*	30	33
2133	Lighted Freight Station, *72–78, 80–84*	34	38
2140	Automatic Banjo Signal, *70–84*	17	21
2145	Automatic Gateman, *72–84*	31	47
2151	Operating Semaphore, *78–82*	15	19
2152	Automatic Crossing Gate, *70–84*	21	25
2154	Automatic Highway Flasher, *70–87*	19	24
2156	Illuminated Station Platform, *70–71*	26	34
2162	Automatic Crossing Gate and Signal "262," *70–87, 94, 96–98, 05*	16	27
2163	Block Target Signal, *70–78*	14	19
2170	Street Lamps, set of 3, *70–87*	13	19
2171	Gooseneck Street Lamps, set of 2, *80–81, 83–84*	15	18
2175	"Sandy Andy" Gravel Loader Kit, *76–79*	34	55
2180	Road Signs, 16 pieces, *77–98*		6
2181	Telephone Pole Set "150," *77–98*		5
2195	Floodlight Tower, *70–71*	38	50
2199	Microwave Tower, *72–75*	30	39
2214	Girder Bridge, *70–71, 72 u, 73–87*	5	9
2256	Station Platform, *73–81*	17	18
2260	Illuminated Bumper, *70–71, 72 u, 73*	23	35
2280	Nonilluminated Bumpers, set of 3, *73–84*	2	4
2282	Die-cast Bumpers, pair, *83 u*	12	18
2283	Die-cast Illuminated Bumpers "260," *84–99*	10	16
2290	Illuminated Bumpers, pair, *75 u, 76–86*	7	11

		Exc	Mint
2292	Station Platform, *85–87*	5	9
2300	Operating Oil Drum Loader, *83–87*	80	90
2301	Operating Sawmill, *80–84*	60	65
2302	Union Pacific Manual Gantry Crane, *80–82*	24	31
2303	Santa Fe Manual Gantry Crane, *80–81, 83 u*	17	21
2305	Getty Operating Oil Derrick, *81–84*	105	115
2306	Operating Ice Station with 6700 Ice Car, *82–83*	90	105
2307	Lighted Billboard, *82–86*	12	13
2308	Animated Newsstand, *82–83*	105	120
2309	Mechanical Crossing Gate, *82–92*	4	7
2310	Mechanical Crossing Gate, *73–77*	2	4
2311	Mechanical Semaphore, *82–92*	4	7
2312	Mechanical Semaphore, *73–77*	2	4
2313	Floodlight Tower, *75–86*	22	27
2314	Searchlight Tower, *75–84*	22	27
2315	Operating Coaling Station, *83–84*	80	83
2316	N&W Operating Gantry Crane, *83–84*	90	125
2317	Operating Drawbridge, *75 u, 76–81*	100	130
2318	Operating Control Tower, *83–86*	40	50
2319	Illuminated Watchtower, *75–78, 80*	29	56
2320	Flagpole Kit, *83–87*	10	14
2321	Operating Sawmill, *84, 86–87*	115	133
2323	Operating Freight Station, *84–87*	43	47
2324	Operating Switch Tower, *84–87*	60	65
2390	Lionel Mirror, *82 u*	80	115
2494	Rotary Beacon, *72–74*	37	44
2709	Rico Station Kit, *81–98*		42
2710	Billboards, set of 5, *70–84*	4	10
2714	Tunnel, *75 u, 76–77*	36	43
2716	Short Extension Bridge, *88–98*	3	8
2717	Short Extension Bridge, *77–87*	2	4
2718	Barrel Platform Kit, *77–84*	3	5
2719	Watchman's Shanty Kit, *77–87*	3	5
2720	Lumber Shed Kit, *77–84, 87*	3	5
2721	Operating Log Mill Kit, *78*	2	4
2722	Barrel Loader Kit, *78*	2	4
2783	Freight Station Kit, *84*	6	10
2784	Freight Platform Kit, *81–90*	5	8
2785	Engine House Kit, *73–77*	31	39
2786	Freight Platform Kit, *73–77*	4	6
2787	Freight Station Kit, *73–77, 83*	7	10
2788	Coal Station Kit, *75 u, 76–77*	18	30
2789	Water Tower Kit, *75–77, 80*	19	24
2791	Cross Country Set, *70–71*	22	30
2792	Whistle Stop Set, *70–71*	24	34
2792	Layout Starter Pack, *80–84*	9	21
2793	Alamo Junction Set, *70–71*	22	30
2796	Grain Elevator Kit, *76 u, 77*	43	47
2797	Rico Station Kit, *76–77*	23	37
2900	Lockon, *70–98*		1
2901	Track Clips, dozen (027), *71–98*		6
2905	Lockon and Wire, *74–00*		3

		Exc	Mint
2909	Smoke Fluid, *70–98*		4____
2910	OTC Contactor, *84–86, 88*	4	7____
2911	Smoke Pellets, *70–73*	18	35____
2925	Lubricant, *70–71, 72 u, 73–75*		2____
2927	Maintenance Kit, *70, 78–98*		11____
2928	Oil, *71*		2____
2951	Track Layout Book, *70–86*	1	2____
2952	Train and Accessory Manual, *70–74*	1	2____
2953	Train and Accessory Manual, *75–86*	1	2____
2960	Lionel 75th Anniversary Book, *75 u, 76*	14	26____
2980	Magnetic Conversion Coupler, *70–71*	1	2____
2985	The Lionel Train Book, *86–98*		11____
3100	Great Northern 4-8-4 (FARR 3), *81*	335	388____
4044	Transformer, 45-watt, *70–71*	2	7____
4045	Safety Transformer, *70–71*	2	3____
4050	Safety Transformer, *72–79*	2	3____
4060	Power Master Transformer, *80–93*		13____
4090	Power Master Transformer, *70–84*	47	65____
4125	Transformer, 25-watt, *72*	2	3____
4150	Trainmaster Transformer, *72–73, 75–77*	6	15____
4250	Trainmaster Transformer, *74*	5	10____
4651	Trainmaster Transformer, *78–79*	1	2____
4690	MW Transformer, *86–89*	60	80____
4851	AC Transformer, red or black, *85–91, 94–96*	5	10____
5012	27" Diameter Curved Track, card of 4 (027), *70–96*		17____
5013	27" Diameter Curved Track (027), *70–78*		1____
5014	Half Curved Track (027), *70–98*		1____
5016	36" Straight Track (027), *87–88*	1	2____
5017	Straight Track, card of 4 (027), *70–96*		4____
5018	Straight Track (027), *70–78*		1____
5019	Half-Straight Track (027), *70–98*		1____
5020	90-degree Crossover (027), *70–98*		7____
5021	27" Manual Switch, left hand (027), *70–98*		15____
5022	27" Manual Switch, right hand (027), *70–98*		15____
5023	45-degree Crossover (027), *70–98*		6____
5024	35" Straight Track (027), *88–98, 05*		3____
5025	Manumatic Uncoupler, *71–72*	1	2____
5027	27" Manual Switches, pair (027), *74–84*	13	21____
5030	Track Expander Set (027), *71–84*	18	26____
5031	Ford-Autolite Layout Expander Set, *71 u*	50	65____
5033	27" Diameter Curved Track (027), *79–98*		1____
5038	Straight Track (027), *79–98*		1____
5041	Insulator Pins, dozen (027), *70–98*		1____
5042	Steel Pins, dozen (027), *70–98*		1____
5045	54" Diameter Curved Track Ballast (027), *87–88*	1	2____
5046	27" Diameter Curved Track Ballast (027), *87–88*	1	2____
5047	Straight Track Ballast (027), *87–88*	1	2____
5049	42" Diameter Curved Track (027), *88–98*	1	2____
5090	27" Manual Switches, 3 pair (027), *78–84*	55	70____
5113	54" Diameter Curved Track (027), *79–98*	1	2____
5121	27" Remote Switch, left hand (027), *70–98*	18	22____

			Exc	Mint
____	5122	27" Remote Switch, right hand (027), *70–98*	20	22
____	5125	27" Remote Switches, pair (027), *71–83*	20	30
____	5132	31" Remote Switch, right hand (0), *80–94*	29	30
____	5133	31" Remote Switch, left hand (0), *80–94*	22	30
____	5149	Remote Uncoupling Section (027), *70–98*		15
____	5165	72" Remote Switch, right hand (0), *87–98*	23	65
____	5166	72" Remote Switch, left hand (0), *87–98*	23	75
____	5167	42" Remote Switch, right hand (027), *88–98*	25	37
____	5168	42" Remote Switch, left hand (027), *88–98*	25	37
____	5193	27" Remote Switches, 3 pair (027), *78–83*	80	95
____	5500	10" Straight Track (0), *71–98*		1
____	5501	31" Diameter Curved Track (0), *71–98*		1
____	5502	Remote Uncoupling Section (0), *71–72*	7	9
____	5504	Half Curved Track (0), *83–98*		1
____	5505	Half Straight Track (0), *83–98*		1
____	5520	90-degree Crossover (0), *71–72*	6	9
____	5522	36" Straight, *87–88*		3
____	5523	40" Straight Track (0), *88–98*		4
____	5530	Remote Uncoupling Section (0), *81–98*	10	19
____	5540	90-degree Crossover (0), *81–98*		10
____	5543	Insulator Pins, dozen (0), *70–98*		1
____	5545	45-degree Crossover (0), *83–98*		11
____	5551	Steel Pins, dozen (0), *70–98*		1
____	5554	54" Diameter Curved Track (0), *90–98*		2
____	5560	72" Diameter Curved Track Ballast (0), *87–88*	1	2
____	5561	31" Diameter Curved Track Ballast (0), *87–88*	1	2
____	5562	Straight Track Ballast (0), *87–88*	1	2
____	5572	72" Diameter Curved Track (0), *79–98*	2	3
____	5600	Curved Track (Trutrack), *73–74*	1	2
____	5601	Curved Track, card of 4 (Trutrack), *73–74*	6	10
____	5602	Curved Track Ballast, card of 4 (Trutrack), *73–74*	5	9
____	5605	Straight Track (Trutrack), *73–74*	1	2
____	5606	Straight Track, card of 4 (Trutrack), *73–74*	5	9
____	5607	Straight Track Ballast, card of 4 (Trutrack), *73–74*	5	9
____	5620	Manual Switch, left hand (Trutrack), *73–74*	4	13
____	5625	Remote Switch, left hand (Trutrack), *73–74*	9	17
____	5630	Manual Switch, right hand (Trutrack), *73–74*	4	13
____	5635	Remote Switch, right hand (Trutrack), *73–74*	9	17
____	5640	Left Switch Ballast, card of 2 (Trutrack), *73–74*	5	9
____	5650	Right Switch Ballast, card of 2 (Trutrack), *73–74*	5	9
____	5655	Lockon (Trutrack), *73–74*	1	2
____	5660	Terminal Track with lockon (Trutrack), *74*	1	3
____	5700	Oppenheimer Reefer, *81*	30	38
____	5701	Dairymen's League Reefer, *81*	21	23
____	5702	National Dairy Despatch Reefer, *81*	16	21
____	5703	North American Despatch Reefer, *81*	22	26
____	5704	Budweiser Reefer, *81–82*	64	70
____	5705	Ball Glass Jars Reefer, *81–82*	30	35
____	5706	Lindsay Brothers Reefer, *81–82*	18	27
____	5707	American Refrigerator Transit Reefer, *81–82*	17	20
____	5708	Armour Reefer, *82–83*	16	21
____	5709	REA Reefer, *82–83*	22	26

		Exc	Mint	
5710	Canadian Pacific Reefer, *82–83*	22	25	____
5711	Commercial Express Reefer, *82–83*	13	15	____
5712	Lionel Lines Reefer, *82 u*	58	94	____
5713	Cotton Belt Reefer, *83–84*	19	22	____
5714	Michigan Central Reefer, *83–84*	17	24	____
5715	Santa Fe Reefer, *83–84*	19	26	____
5716	Vermont Central Reefer, *83–84*	20	23	____
5717	Santa Fe Bunk Car, *83*	22	30	____
5719	Canadian National Reefer, *84*	10	16	____
5720	Great Northern Reefer, *84*	75	90	____
5721	Soo Line Reefer, *84*	21	23	____
5722	NKP Reefer, *84*	16	18	____
5724	PRR Bunk Car, *84*	15	23	____
5726	Southern Bunk Car, *84 u*	22	27	____
5727	USMC Bunk Car, *84–85*	25	30	____
5728	Canadian Pacific Bunk Car, *86*	18	23	____
5730	Strasburg Reefer, *85–86*	20	27	____
5731	L&N Reefer, *85–86*	19	24	____
5732	Jersey Central Reefer, *85–86*		24	____
5733	Lionel Lines Bunk Car, *86 u*	18	24	____
5735	NYC Bunk Car, *85–86*	33	35	____
5739	B&O Tool Car, *86*	32	37	____
5745	Santa Fe Bunk Car (SSS), *86*	39	45	____
5760	Santa Fe Tool Car (SSS), *86*	30	35	____
5900	AC/DC Converter, *79–83*	3	10	____
6076	LV Hopper (027), *70 u*	17	21	____
6100	Ontario Northland Covered Quad Hopper, *81–82*	30	34	____
6101	BN Covered Quad Hopper, *81–82*	17	31	____
6102	GN Covered Quad Hopper (FARR 3), *81*	26	28	____
6103	Canadian National Covered Quad Hopper, *81*	35	38	____
6104	Southern Quad Hopper with coal (FARR 4), *83*	50	60	____
6105	Reading Operating Hopper, *82*	34	39	____
6106	N&W Covered Quad Hopper, *82*	30	40	____
6107	Shell Covered Quad Hopper, *82*	22	26	____
6109	C&O Operating Hopper, *83*	29	41	____
6110	MP Covered Quad Hopper, *83–84*	17	27	____
6111	L&N Covered Quad Hopper, *83–84*	13	20	____
6113	Illinois Central Hopper (027), *83–85*	15	25	____
6114	C&NW Covered Quad Hopper, *83*	63	80	____
6115	Southern Hopper (027), *83–86*	15	19	____
6116	Soo Line Ore Car, *84*	21	27	____
6117	Erie Operating Hopper, *84*	29	39	____
6118	Erie Quad Hopper, *84*	31	45	____
6122	Penn Central Ore Car, *84*	20	25	____
6123	PRR Covered Quad Hopper (FARR 5), *84–85*	55	105	____
6124	D&H Covered Quad Hopper, *84*	19	32	____
6126	Canadian National Ore Car, *86*	18	24	____
6127	Northern Pacific Ore Car, *86*	20	24	____
6131	Illinois Terminal Covered Quad Hopper, *85–86*	15	21	____
6134	BN 2-bay ACF Hopper (std O), *86 u*	95	115	____
6135	C&NW 2-bay ACF Hopper (std O), *86 u*	65	80	____
6137	NKP Hopper (027), *86–91*	13	17	____

		Exc	Mint
____**6138**	B&O Quad Hopper with coal, *86*	21	28
____**6142**	Gondola, black, *70*	20	33
____**6150**	Santa Fe Hopper (027), *85–86, 92 u*	10	15
____**6177**	Reading Hopper (027), *86–90*	14	19
____**6200**	FEC Gondola with canisters, *81–82*	13	24
____**6201**	Union Pacific Animated Gondola, *82–83*	19	25
____**6202**	WM Gondola with coal, *82*	34	36
____**6203**	Black Cave Gondola (027), *82*	2	4
____**6205**	CP Gondola with canisters, *83*	18	26
____**6206**	C&IM Gondola with canisters, *83–85*	18	26
____**6207**	Southern Gondola with canisters (027), *83–85*	6	8
____**6208**	Chessie System Gondola with canisters, *83 u*	21	24
____**6209**	NYC Gondola with coal (std O), *84–85*	42	46
____**6210**	Erie-Lackawanna Gondola with canisters, *84*	21	30
____**6211**	C&O Gondola with canisters, *84–85*		10
____**6214**	Lionel Lines Gondola with canisters, *84 u*	38	45
____**6230**	Erie-Lackawanna Reefer (std O), *86 u*	95	120
____**6231**	Railgon Gondola with coal (std O), *86 u*	66	76
____**6232**	Illinois Central Boxcar (std O), *86 u*	65	80
____**6233**	CP Flatcar with stakes (std O), *86 u*	47	50
____**6234**	Burlington Northern Boxcar (std O), *85*	55	75
____**6235**	Burlington Northern Boxcar (std O), *85*	33	43
____**6236**	Burlington Northern Boxcar (std O), *85*	33	43
____**6237**	Burlington Northern Boxcar (std O), *85*	32	47
____**6238**	Burlington Northern Boxcar (std O), *85*	33	43
____**6239**	Burlington Northern Boxcar (std O), *86 u*	37	55
____**6251**	NYC Coal Dump Car, *85*	25	42
____**6254**	NKP Gondola with canisters, *86–91*	6	11
6258	Santa Fe Gondola with canisters (027), *85–86, 92 u*		3
____**X6260**	NYC Gondola with canisters, *85–86*	13	15
____**6272**	Santa Fe Gondola with cable reels (SSS), *86*	20	25
____**6300**	Corn Products 3-D Tank Car, *81–82*	19	25
____**6301**	Gulf 1-D Tank Car, *81*	20	26
____**6302**	Quaker State 3-D Tank Car, *81*	42	46
____**6304**	GN 1-D Tank Car (FARR 3), *81*	44	55
____**6305**	British Columbia 1-D Tank Car, *81*	55	76
____**6306**	Southern 1-D Tank Car (FARR 4), *83*	45	50
____**6307**	PRR 1-D Tank Car (FARR 5), *84–85*	70	75
____**6308**	Alaska 1-D Tank Car (027), *82–83*	27	35
____**6310**	Shell 2-D Tank Car (027), *83–84*	19	24
____**6312**	C&O 2-D Tank Car (027), *84–85*	18	26
____**6313**	Lionel Lines 1-D Tank Car, *84 u*	43	50
____**6314**	B&O 3-D Tank Car, *86*	31	38
____**6317**	Gulf 2-D Tank Car (027), *84–85*	18	22
____**6357**	Frisco 1-D Tank Car, *83*	42	50
____**6401**	Virginian Bay Window Caboose, *81*	37	47
____**6403**	Amtrak Vista Dome Car (027), *76–77*	24	31
____**6404**	Amtrak Passenger Coach (027), *76–77*	24	31
____**6405**	Amtrak Passenger Coach (027), *76–77*	24	31
____**6406**	Amtrak Observation Car (027), *76–77*	22	29
____**6410**	Amtrak Passenger Coach (027), *77*	28	48

		Exc	Mint
6411	Amtrak Passenger Coach (027), *77*	24	35____
6412	Amtrak Vista Dome Car (027), *77*	22	33____
6420	Reading Transfer Caboose, *81–82*	20	28____
6421	Joshua L. Cowen Bay Window Caboose, *82*	34	40____
6422	DM&IR Bay Window Caboose, *81*	32	38____
6425	Erie-Lackawanna Bay Window Caboose, *83–84*	35	43____
6426	Reading Transfer Caboose, *82–83*	14	24____
6427	BN Transfer Caboose, *83–84*	12	21____
6428	C&NW Transfer Caboose, *83–85*	22	25____
6430	Santa Fe SP-type Caboose, *83–89*	4	14____
6431	Southern Bay Window Caboose (FARR 4), *83*	42	55____
6432	Union Pacific SP-type Caboose, *81–82*	6	10____
6433	Canadian Pacific Bay Window Caboose, *81*	60	70____
6435	U.S. Marines Transfer Caboose, *83–84*	9	17____
6438	GN Bay Window Caboose (FARR 3), *81*	48	65____
6439	Reading Bay Window Caboose, *84–85*	22	30____
6441	Alaska Bay Window Caboose, *82–83*	45	50____
6446-25	N&W Covered Quad Hopper, *70 u*	203	290____
6449	Wendy's N5c Caboose, *81–82*	64	74____
6464-500	Timken Boxcar, orange, *70 u*	208	290____
6464-500	Timken Boxcar, yellow, *70 u*	210	350____
6476-135	LV Hopper "25000" (027), *70–71 u*	6	11____
6478	Black Cave SP-type Caboose, *82*	5	9____
6482	Nibco Express SP-type Caboose, *82 u*	26	34____
6485	Chessie System SP-type Caboose, *84–85*	6	10____
6486	Southern SP-type Caboose, *83–85*	5	7____
6490	NKP N5c Caboose, *84 u*		NRS____
6491	Erie-Lackawanna Transfer Caboose, *85–86*	9	17____
6493	L&C Bay Window Caboose, *86–87*	21	36____
6494	Santa Fe Bobber Caboose, *85–86*	7	9____
6496	Santa Fe Work Caboose (SSS), *86*	21	29____
6504	L.A.S.E.R. Flatcar with helicopter (027), *81–82*	18	26____
6505	L.A.S.E.R. Radar Car, *81–82*	17	25____
6506	L.A.S.E.R. Security Car, *81–82*	18	26____
6507	L.A.S.E.R. Flatcar with cruise missile, *81–82*	21	30____
6508	Canadian Pacific Crane Car, *81*	50	70____
6509	Depressed Center Flatcar with girders, *81*	60	85____
6510	Union Pacific Crane Car, *82*	55	60____
6515	Union Pacific Flatcar (027), *83–84, 86*	5	9____
6521	NYC Flatcar with stakes (std 0), *84–85*	29	35____
6522	C&NW Searchlight Car, *83–85*	27	30____
6524	Erie Crane Car, *84*	55	60____
6526	Searchlight Car, *84–85*	23	25____
6529	NYC Searchlight Car, *85–86*	21	27____
6531	Express Mail Flatcar with trailers, *85–86*	23	32____
6560	Bucyrus Erie Crane Car, *71*	100	130____
6561	Flatcar with cruise missile (027), *83–84*	13	26____
6562	Flatcar with fences (027), *83–84*	13	21____
6564	U.S. Marines Flatcar with 2 tanks (027), *83–84*	13	21____
6573	Redwood Valley Express Log Dump Car (027), *84–85*	8	13____
6574	Redwood Valley Express Crane Car (027), *84–85*	7	13____

		Exc	Mint
6575	Redwood Valley Express Flatcar with fences (027), *84–85*	7	13
6576	Santa Fe Crane Car (027), *85–86, 92 u*	7	10
6579	NYC Crane Car, *85–86*	36	44
6585	PRR Flatcar with fences (027), *86–90*	5	9
6587	W&ARR Flatcar with horses, *86 u*	18	26
6593	Santa Fe Crane Car (SSS), *86*	41	48
6700	PFE Ice Car, *82–83*		70
6900	N&W Extended Vision Caboose, *82*	60	65
6901	Ontario Northland Extended Vision Caboose, *82 u*	44	55
6903	Santa Fe Extended Vision Caboose, *83*	80	95
6904	Union Pacific Extended Vision Caboose, *83*	115	135
6905	NKP Extended Vision Caboose, *83 u*	50	65
6906	Erie-Lack. Extended Vision Caboose, *84*	75	90
6907	NYC Wood-sided Caboose (std O), *86 u*	90	92
6908	PRR N5c Caboose (FARR 5), *84–85*	43	47
6910	NYC Extended Vision Caboose, *84 u*	55	60
6912	Redwood Valley Express SP-type Caboose, *84–85*	9	16
6913	Burlington Northern Extended Vision Caboose, *85*	70	90
6916	NYC Work Caboose, *85–86*	16	22
6917	Jersey Central Extended Vision Caboose, *86*	36	50
6918	B&O SP-type Caboose, *86*	10	15
6919	Nickel Plate Road SP-type Caboose, *86–91*	5	9
6920	B&A Wood-sided Caboose (std O), *86 u*	65	80
6921	PRR SP-type Caboose, *86–90*	5	9
7200	Quicksilver Passenger Coach (027), *82–83*	26	34
7201	Quicksilver Passenger Coach (027), *82–83*	26	34
7202	Quicksilver Observation Car (027), *82–83*	26	34
7203	N&W Diner "491," *82 u*	130	180
7204	Southern Pacific Diner, *82 u*	190	235
7207	NYC Diner, *83 u*	70	140
7208	PRR Diner, *83 u*	80	90
7210	Union Pacific Diner, *84*	85	110
7211	Southern Pacific Vista Dome Car, *83 u*	145	185
7215	B&O Passenger Coach, *83–84*	43	50
7216	B&O Passenger Coach, *83–84*	43	50
7217	B&O Baggage Car, *83–84*	43	50
7220	Illinois Central Baggage Car, *85, 87*	105	135
7221	Illinois Central Combination Car, *85, 87*	85	105
7222	Illinois Central Passenger Coach, *85, 87*	85	105
7223	Illinois Central Passenger Coach, *85, 87*	85	105
7224	Illinois Central Diner, *85, 87*	75	90
7225	Illinois Central Observation Car, *85, 87*	95	115
7227	Wabash Diner (FF 1), *86–87*	115	130
7228	Wabash Baggage Car (FF 1), *86–87*	90	100
7229	Wabash Combination Car (FF 1), *86–87*	90	100
7230	Wabash Passenger Coach (FF 1), *86–87*	90	100
7231	Wabash Passenger Coach (FF 1), *86–87*	90	100
7232	Wabash Observation Car (FF 1), *86–87*	85	95
7241	W&ARR Passenger Coach, *86 u*	43	50
7242	W&ARR Baggage Car, *86 u*	43	50
7301	Norfolk & Western Stock Car, *82*	34	45

		Exc	Mint
7302	Texas & Pacific Stock Car (027), *83–84*	11	14
7303	Erie Stock Car, *84*	41	50
7304	Southern Stock Car (FARR 4), *83 u*	41	45
7309	Southern Stock Car (027), *85–86*	12	16
7312	W&ARR Stock Car (027), *86 u*	25	30
7401	Chessie System Stock Car (027), *84–85*	13	17
7404	Jersey Central Boxcar, *86*	26	40
7500	Lionel 75th Anniversary U36B Diesel, *75–77*	124	144
7501	Lionel 75th Anniversary Boxcar, *75–77*	24	34
7502	Lionel 75th Anniversary Reefer, *75–77*	27	36
7503	Lionel 75th Anniversary Reefer, *75–77*	29	40
7504	Lionel 75th Anniversary Covered Quad Hopper, *75–77*	28	40
7505	Lionel 75th Anniversary Boxcar, *75–77*	29	41
7506	Lionel 75th Anniversary Boxcar, *75–77*	16	21
7507	Lionel 75th Anniversary Reefer, *75–77*	27	39
7508	Lionel 75th Anniversary N5c Caboose, *75–77*	24	29
7509	Kentucky Fried Chicken Reefer, *81–82*	67	77
7510	Red Lobster Reefer, *81–82*	62	68
7511	Pizza Hut Reefer, *81–82*	62	68
7512	Arthur Treacher's Reefer, *82*	58	63
7513	Bonanza Reefer, *82*	61	67
7514	Taco Bell Reefer, *82*	63	82
7515	Denver Mint Car, *81*	64	81
7517	Philadelphia Mint Car, *82*	38	39
7518	Carson City Mint Car, *83*	34	43
7519	Toy Fair Reefer, *82 u*	35	42
7520	Nibco Express Boxcar, *82 u*	265	440
7521	Toy Fair Reefer, *83 u*	50	65
7522	New Orleans Mint Car, *84 u*	33	38
7523	Toy Fair Reefer, *84 u*	44	49
7524	Toy Fair Reefer, *85 u*	55	60
7525	Toy Fair Boxcar, *86 u*	65	80
7530	Dahlonega Mint Car, *86 u*	37	48
7600	Frisco "Spirit of '76" N5c Caboose, *74–76*	33	39
7601	Delaware Boxcar, *74–76*	16	19
7602	Pennsylvania Boxcar, *74–76*	24	27
7603	New Jersey Boxcar, *74–76*	17	24
7604	Georgia Boxcar, *74 u, 75–76*	22	26
7605	Connecticut Boxcar, *74 u, 75–76*	22	32
7606	Massachusetts Boxcar, *74 u, 75–76*	25	29
7607	Maryland Boxcar, *74 u, 75–76*	22	34
7608	South Carolina Boxcar, *75 u, 76*	38	50
7609	New Hampshire Boxcar, *75 u, 76*	38	46
7610	Virginia Boxcar, *75 u, 76*	155	200
7611	New York Boxcar, *75 u, 76*	50	65
7612	North Carolina Boxcar, *75 u, 76*	35	60
7613	Rhode Island Boxcar, *75 u, 76*	36	50
7700	Uncle Sam Boxcar, *75 u*	44	51
7701	Camel Boxcar, *76–77*	60	70
7702	Prince Albert Boxcar, *76–77*	62	78
7703	Beechnut Boxcar, *76–77*	33	51

			Exc	Mint
____	7704	Toy Fair Boxcar, *76 u*	110	120
____	7705	Canadian Toy Fair Boxcar, *76 u*	130	145
____	7706	Sir Walter Raleigh Boxcar, *77–78*	60	68
____	7707	White Owl Boxcar, *77–78*	60	68
____	7708	Winston Boxcar, *77–78*	58	73
____	7709	Salem Boxcar, *78*	58	68
____	7710	Mail Pouch Boxcar, *78*	59	70
____	7711	El Producto Boxcar, *78*	52	68
____	7712	Santa Fe Boxcar (FARR 1), *79*	25	44
____	7800	Pepsi Boxcar, *76 u, 77*	74	82
____	7801	A&W Boxcar, *76 u, 77*	48	62
____	7802	Canada Dry Boxcar, *76 u, 77*	44	57
____	7803	Trains n' Truckin' Boxcar, *77 u*	20	26
____	7806	Season's Greetings Boxcar, *76 u*	70	95
____	7807	Toy Fair Boxcar, *77 u*	70	95
____	7808	Northern Pacific Stock Car, *77*	37	44
____	7809	Vernors Boxcar, *77 u, 78*	50	65
____	7810	Orange Crush Boxcar, *77 u, 78*	40	55
____	7811	Dr Pepper Boxcar, *77 u, 78*	48	63
____	7813	"Season's Greetings" Boxcar, *77 u*	65	90
____	7814	"Season's Greetings" Boxcar, *78 u*	70	95
____	7815	Toy Fair Boxcar, *78 u*	65	85
____	7816	Toy Fair Boxcar, *79 u*	65	85
____	7817	Toy Fair Boxcar, *80 u*	95	105
____	7900	D&RGW Operating Cowboy Car (027), *82–83*	22	26
____	7901	LL Cop and Hobo Car (027), *82–83*	24	27
____	7902	Santa Fe Boxcar (027), *82–85*	5	9
____	7903	Rock Island Boxcar (027), *83*	8	13
____	7904	San Diego Zoo Giraffe Car (027), *83–84*	44	55
____	7905	Black Cave Boxcar (027), *82*	6	9
____	7908	Tappan Boxcar (027), *82 u*	39	55
____	7909	L&N Boxcar (027), *83–84*	40	49
____	7910	Chessie System Boxcar (027), *84–85*	18	23
____	7912	Toys "R" Us Giraffe Car (027), *82–84 u*	70	80
____	7913	Turtleback Zoo Giraffe Car (027), *85–86*	50	60
____	7914	Toys "R" Us Giraffe Car (027), *85–89 u*	70	90
____	7920	Sears Centennial Boxcar (027), *85–86 u*	39	44
____	7925	Erie-Lackawanna Boxcar (027), *86–90*	10	18
____	7926	NKP Boxcar (027), *86–91*	8	10
____	7930	True Value Boxcar (027), *86–87 u*	34	50
	7931	Town House TV and Appliances Boxcar (027), *86 u*	31	39
____	7932	Kay Bee Toys Boxcar (027), *86–87 u*	40	49
____	8001	NKP 2-6-4 Locomotive, *80 u*	55	65
____	8002	Union Pacific 2-8-4 Locomotive (FARR 2), *80*	310	345
____	8003	Chessie System 2-8-4 Locomotive, *80*	360	540
____	8004	Rock Island 4-4-0 Locomotive, *80–82*	190	220
____	8005	Santa Fe 4-4-0 Locomotive, *80–82*	65	75
____	8006	ACL 4-6-4 Locomotive, *80 u*	245	340
____	8007	NYNH&H 2-6-4 Locomotive, *80–81*	65	75
____	8008	Chessie System 4-4-2 Locomotive, *80*	65	75
____	8010	Santa Fe NW2 Switcher, *70, 71 u*	50	83

		Exc	Mint	
8020	Santa Fe Alco Diesel A Unit, *70–72, 74–76*	65	85	____
8020	Santa Fe Alco Diesel A Unit, dummy, *70*	45	60	____
8021	Santa Fe Alco Diesel B Unit, *71–72, 74–76*	47	70	____
8022	Santa Fe Alco Diesel A Unit, *71 u*	80	105	____
8025	CN Alco Diesel A Unit, *71–73 u*	85	105	____
8025	CN Alco Diesel A Unit, dummy, *71–73 u*	45	65	____
8030	Illinois Central GP9 Diesel, *70–72*	103	140	____
8031	Canadian National GP7 Diesel, *71–73 u*	80	150	____
8031	Illinois Central GP9 Diesel Dummy Unit, *70*		NRS	____
8040	Canadian National 2-4-2 Locomotive, *71 u*	43	85	____
8040	NKP 2-4-2 Locomotive, *70–72*	26	34	____
8041	NYC 2-4-2 Locomotive, *70*	55	65	____
8041	PRR 2-4-2 Locomotive, *71 u*	55	65	____
8042	GTW 2-4-2 Locomotive, *70, 71–73 u*	26	34	____
8043	NKP 2-4-2 Locomotive, *70 u*	45	65	____
8050	D&H U36C Diesel, *80*	105	220	____
8051	D&H U36C Diesel Dummy Unit, *80*	95	115	____
8054/55	Burlington F3 Diesel AA Set, *80*	360	385	____
8056	C&NW FM Train Master Diesel, *80*	175	225	____
8057	Burlington NW2 Switcher, *80*	100	115	____
8059	Pennsylvania F3 Diesel B Unit, *80 u*	190	290	____
8060	Pennsylvania F3 Diesel B Unit, *80 u*	335	420	____
8061	Chessie System U36C Diesel, *80*	110	140	____
8062	Burlington F3 Diesel B Unit, *80 u*	205	255	____
8063	Seaboard SD9 Diesel, *80*	80	100	____
8064	Florida East Coast GP9 Diesel, *80*	150	200	____
8065	Florida East Coast GP9 Diesel Dummy Unit, *80*	95	120	____
8066	TP&W GP20 Diesel, *80–81, 83 u*	65	80	____
8071	Virginian SD18 Diesel, *80 u*	135	155	____
8072	Virginian SD18 Diesel Dummy Unit, *80 u*	75	110	____
8100	Norfolk & Western 4-8-4 "611," *81*	360	402	____
8101	Chicago & Alton 4-6-4 Locomotive "659," *81*	275	445	____
8102	Union Pacific 4-4-2 Locomotive, *81–82*	49	65	____
8104	Union Pacific 4-4-0 Locomotive "3," *81 u*	180	235	____
8111	DT&I NW2 Switcher, *71–74*	55	65	____
8140	Southern 2-4-0 Locomotive, *71 u*	22	30	____
8141	PRR 2-4-2 Locomotive, *71–72*	41	43	____
8142	C&O 4-4-2 Locomotive, *71–72*		55	____
8150	PRR GG1 Electric Locomotive "4935," *81*	330	395	____
8151	Burlington SD28 Diesel, *81*	120	145	____
8152	Canadian Pacific SD24 Diesel, *81*	170	180	____
8153	Reading NW2 Switcher, *81–82*	100	155	____
8154	Alaska NW2 Switcher, *81–82*	120	160	____
8155	Monon U36B Diesel, *81–82*	110	135	____
8156	Monon U36B Diesel Dummy Unit, *81–82*		65	____
8157	Santa Fe FM Train Master, *81*	280	325	____
8158	DM&IR GP35 Diesel, *81–82*	90	150	____
8159	DM&IR GP35 Diesel Dummy Unit, *81–82*	55	75	____
8160	Burger King GP20 Diesel, *81–82*	101	125	____
8161	L.A.S.E.R. Switcher, *81–82*	23	55	____
8162	Ontario Northland SD18 Diesel, *81 u*	150	210	____
8163	Ontario Northland SD18 Diesel Dummy Unit, *81 u*	95	140	____

		Exc	Mint
___8164	Pennsylvania F3 Diesel B Unit, *81 u*	340	370
___8182	Nibco Express NW2 Switcher, *82 u*	90	130
___8190	Diesel Horn Kit, *81 u*		30
___8200	Kickapoo Dockside 0-4-0T, *72*	28	39
___8203	PRR 2-4-2 Locomotive, *72, 74 u, 75*	26	34
___8204	C&O 4-4-2 Locomotive, *72*	55	60
___8206	NYC 4-6-4 Locomotive, *72–75*	140	155
___8209	Pioneer Dockside 0-4-0T with tender, *72*	45	65
___8209	Pioneer Dockside 0-4-0T, no tender, *73–76*	42	55
___8210	Joshua L. Cowen 4-6-4 Locomotive, *82*	245	350
___8212	Black Cave 0-4-0 Locomotive, *82*	30	49
___8213	D&RGW 2-4-2 Locomotive, *82–83, 84–91 u*	65	70
___8214	Pennsylvania 2-4-2 Locomotive, *82–83*	55	65
___8215	Nickel Plate Road 2-8-4 Locomotive "779," *82 u*	245	285
___8250	Santa Fe GP9 Diesel, *72, 74–75*	120	145
___8251-50	Horn/Whistle Controller, *72–74*	1	2
___8252	D&H Alco Diesel A Unit, *72*	85	125
___8253	D&H Alco Diesel B Unit, *72*	50	70
___8254	Illinois Central GP9 Diesel Dummy Unit, *72*	60	65
___8255	Santa Fe GP9 Diesel Dummy Unit, *72*	60	65
___8258	Canadian National GP7 Diesel Dummy Unit, *72–73 u*	65	85
___8260/62	Southern Pacific F3 Diesel AA Set, *82*	490	520
___8261	Southern Pacific F3 Diesel B Unit, *82 u*	435	445
___8263	Santa Fe GP7 Diesel, *82*	65	80
___8264	CP Vulcan Switcher Snowplow, *82*	80	100
___8265	Santa Fe SD40 Diesel, *82*	205	225
___8266	Norfolk & Western SD24 Diesel, *82*	150	225
___8268	Quicksilver Alco Diesel A Unit, *82–83*	85	105
___8269	Quicksilver Alco Diesel A Unit, dummy, *82–83*	55	65
___8272	Pennsylvania EP-5 Electric Locomotive, *82 u*	205	265
___8300	Santa Fe 2-4-0 Locomotive, *73–74*	22	25
___8302	Southern 2-4-0 Locomotive, *73–76*	29	30
___8303	Jersey Central 2-4-2 Locomotive, *73–74*	55	59
___8304	B&O 4-4-2 Locomotive, *75*	75	105
___8304	C&O 4-4-2 Locomotive, *75–77*	75	105
___8304	Pennsylvania 4-4-2 Locomotive, *74–75*	75	105
___8304	Rock Island 4-4-2 Locomotive, *73–75*	85	105
___8305	Milwaukee Road 4-4-2 Locomotive, *73*	95	120
___8307	Southern Pacific 4-8-4 Locomotive "4449," *83*	490	560
___8308	Jersey Central 2-4-2 Locomotive, *73–74 u*	36	43
___8309	Southern 2-8-2 Locomotive "4501" (FARR 4), *83*	385	495
___8310	Jersey Central 2-4-0 Locomotive, *74–75 u*	26	50
___8310	Nickel Plate Road 2-4-0 Locomotive, *73 u*	26	50
___8310	Santa Fe 2-4-0 Locomotive, *74–75 u*	26	34
___8311	Southern 0-4-0 Locomotive, *73 u*	26	34
___8313	Santa Fe 0-4-0 Locomotive, *83–84*	13	17
___8314	Southern 2-4-0 Locomotive, *83–85*	17	21
___8315	B&O 4-4-0 Locomotive, *83–84*	85	120
___8341	ACL SP-type Caboose, *86 u, 87–90*	6	8
___8350	U.S. Steel Switcher, *73–75*	18	26
___8351	Santa Fe Alco Diesel A Unit, *73–75*	60	65

		Exc	Mint	
8352	Santa Fe GP20 Diesel, *73–75*	65	105	____
8353	Grand Trunk Western GP7 Diesel, *73–75*	90	120	____
8354	Erie NW2 Switcher, *73, 75*	80	105	____
8355	Santa Fe GP20 Diesel Dummy Unit, *73–74*	65	90	____
8356	Grand Trunk Western GP7 Diesel Dummy Unit, *73–75*	65	75	____
8357	PRR GP9 Diesel, *73–75*	100	120	____
8358	PRR GP9 Diesel Dummy Unit, *73–75*	55	100	____
8359	Chessie System GP7 Diesel "GM50," *73*	95	120	____
8360	Long Island GP20 Diesel, *73–74*	70	105	____
8361	Western Pacific Alco Diesel A Unit, *73–75*	50	70	____
8362	Western Pacific Alco Diesel B Unit, *73–75*	45	65	____
8363	B&O F3 Diesel A Unit, *73–75*	280	310	____
8364	B&O F3 Diesel A Unit, dummy, *73–75*	120	160	____
8365/66	CP F3 Diesel AA Set (SSS), *73*	355	405	____
8367	Long Island GP20 Diesel Dummy Unit, *73–75*	80	100	____
8368	Alaska Vulcan Switcher, *83*	120	129	____
8369	Erie-Lackawanna GP20 Diesel, *83–85*	125	140	____
8370/72	NYC F3 Diesel AA Set, *83*	330	435	____
8371	NYC F3 Diesel B Unit, *83*	105	150	____
8374	Burlington Northern NW2 Switcher, *83–85*	105	110	____
8375	C&NW GP7 Diesel, *83–85*	135	165	____
8376	Union Pacific SD40 Diesel, *83*	175	200	____
8377	U.S. Marines Switcher, *83–84*	55	65	____
8378	Wabash FM Train Master Diesel "550," *83 u*	500	690	____
8379	PRR Fire Car, *83 u*	80	100	____
8380	Lionel Lines SD28 Diesel, *83 u*	235	315	____
8402	Reading 4-4-2 Locomotive, *84–85*	47	55	____
8403	Chessie System 4-4-2 Locomotive, *84–85*	55	65	____
8404	PRR 6-8-6 "6200" (FARR 5), *84–85*	360	460	____
8406	NYC 4-6-4 Locomotive "783," *84*	445	571	____
8410	Redwood Valley Express 4-4-0 Locomotive, *84–85*	34	50	____
8452	Erie Alco Diesel A Unit, *74–75*	75	95	____
8453	Erie Alco Diesel B Unit, *74–75*	55	75	____
8454	D&RGW GP7 Diesel, *74–75*	80	110	____
8455	D&RGW GP7 Diesel Dummy Unit, *74–75*	50	85	____
8458	Erie-Lackawanna SD40 Diesel, *84*	160	190	____
8459	D&RGW Vulcan Rotary Snowplow, *84*	125	146	____
8460	MKT NW2 Switcher, *74–75*	45	65	____
8463	Chessie System GP20 Diesel, *74 u*	130	190	____
8464/65	D&RGW F3 Diesel AA Set (SSS), *74*	220	325	____
8466	Amtrak F3 Diesel A Unit, *74–76*	225	250	____
8467	Amtrak F3 Diesel A Unit, dummy, *74–76*	80	90	____
8468	B&O F3 Diesel B Unit, *74–75*	95	100	____
8469	CP F3 Diesel B Unit (SSS), *74*	85	110	____
8470	Chessie System U36B Diesel, *74*	80	110	____
8471	Pennsylvania NW2 Switcher, *74–76*	170	195	____
8473	Coca-Cola NW2 Switcher, *74 u, 75*	109	128	____
8474	D&RGW F3 Diesel B Unit (SSS), *74*	95	110	____
8475	Amtrak F3 Diesel B Unit, *74*	85	105	____
8477	NYC GP9 Diesel, *84 u*	150	205	____
8480/82	Union Pacific F3 Diesel AA Set, *84*	280	365	____

		Exc	Mint
____8481	Union Pacific F3 Diesel B Unit, *84*	150	155
____8485	USMC NW2 Switcher, *84–85*	105	135
____8500	Pennsylvania 2-4-0 Locomotive, *75–76*	17	21
____8502	Santa Fe 2-4-0 Locomotive, *75*	17	21
____8506	PRR 0-4-0 Locomotive, *75–77*	75	90
____8507	Santa Fe 2-4-0 Locomotive, *75 u*	25	30
____8512	Santa Fe 0-4-0T Locomotive, *85–86*	22	30
____8516	NYC 0-4-0 Locomotive, *85–86*	115	140
____8550	Jersey Central GP9 Diesel, *75–76*	120	155
____8551	Pennsylvania EP-5 Electric Locomotive, *75–76*	115	120
____8552/53/54	SP Alco Diesel ABA Set, *75–76*	200	245
____8555/57	Milwaukee Road F3 Diesel AA Set (SSS), *75*	240	315
____8556	Chessie System NW2 Switcher, *75–76*	160	200
____8558	Milwaukee Road EP-5 Electric Locomotive, *76–77*	160	195
____8559	N&W GP9 Diesel "1776," *75*	115	145
____8560	Chessie System U36B Diesel Dummy Unit, *75*	85	130
____8561	Jersey Central GP9 Diesel Dummy Unit, *75–76*	70	95
____8562	Missouri Pacific GP20 Diesel, *75–76*	130	145
____8563	Rock Island Alco Diesel A Unit, *75–76 u*	65	90
____8564	Union Pacific U36B Diesel, *75*	110	155
____8565	Missouri Pacific GP20 Diesel Dummy Unit, *75–76*	55	70
____8566	Southern F3 Diesel A Unit, *75–77*	220	370
____8567	Southern F3 Diesel A Unit, dummy, *75–77*	105	135
____8568	Preamble Express F3 Diesel A Unit, *75 u*	90	115
____8569	Soo Line NW2 Switcher, *75–77*	60	65
____8570	Liberty Special Alco Diesel A Unit, *75 u*	75	90
____8571	Frisco U36B Diesel, *75–76*	75	95
____8572	Frisco U36B Diesel Dummy Unit, *75–76*		55
____8573	Union Pacific U36B Diesel Dummy Unit, *75 u*	145	190
____8575	Milwaukee Road F3 Diesel B Unit (SSS), *75*	105	160
____8576	Penn Central GP7 Diesel, *75 u, 76–77*	90	120
____8578	NYC Ballast Tamper, *85, 87*	85	90
____8580/82	Illinois Central F3 Diesel AA Set, *85, 87*	420	485
____8581	Illinois Central F3 Diesel B Unit, *85, 87*	130	155
____8585	Burlington Northern SD40 Diesel, *85*	355	385
____8587	Wabash GP9 Diesel "484," *85 u*	250	280
____8600	NYC 4-6-4 Locomotive, *76*	175	195
____8601	Rock Island 0-4-0 Locomotive, *76–77*	17	21
____8602	D&RGW 2-4-0 Locomotive, *76–78*	22	26
____8603	C&O 4-6-4 Locomotive, *76–77*	135	190
____8604	Jersey Central 2-4-2 Locomotive, *76 u*	39	44
____8606	B&A 4-6-4 Locomotive "784," *86 u*	720	760
____8610	Wabash 4-6-2 "672" (FF 1), *86–87*	435	610
____8615	L&N 2-8-4 Locomotive "1970," *86 u*	540	630
____8616	Santa Fe 4-4-2 Locomotive, *86*	60	65
____8617	Nickel Plate Road 4-4-2 Locomotive, *86–91*	60	65
____8625	Pennsylvania 2-4-0 Locomotive, *86–90*	21	34
____8630	W&ARR 4-4-0 Locomotive "3," *86 u*	125	150
____8635	Santa Fe 0-4-0 (SSS), *86*	80	100
____8650	Burlington Northern U36B Diesel, *76–77*	120	170
____8651	Burlington Northern U36B Diesel Dummy Unit, *76–77*	70	90

8652	Santa Fe F3 Diesel A Unit, *76–77*	260	510____
8653	Santa Fe F3 Diesel A Unit, dummy, *76–77*	135	160____
8654	Boston & Maine GP9 Diesel, *76–77*	155	195____
8655	Boston & Maine GP9 Diesel Dummy Unit, *76–77*	90	110____
8656	Canadian National Alco Diesel A Unit, *76*	150	195____
8657	Canadian National Alco Diesel B Unit, *76*	60	75____
8658	CN Alco Diesel A Unit, dummy, *76*	85	170____
8659	Virginian Electric Locomotive, *76–77*	125	137____
8660	CP Rail NW2 Switcher, *76–77*	100	135____
8661	Southern F3 Diesel B Unit, *76*	165	170____
8662	B&O GP7 Diesel, *86*	120	130____
8664	Amtrak Alco Diesel A Unit, *76–77*	85	120____
8665	BAR Jeremiah O'Brien GP9 Diesel "1776," *76 u*	100	170____
8666	Northern Pacific GP9 Diesel (SSS), *76*	125	175____
8667	Amtrak Alco Diesel B Unit, *76–77*	60	80____
8668	Northern Pacific GP9 Diesel Dummy Unit (SSS), *76*	100	130____
8669	Illinois Central Gulf U36B Diesel, *76–77*	125	165____
8670	Chessie System Switcher, *76*	30	55____
8679	Northern Pacific GP20 Diesel, *86*	90	105____
8687	Jersey Central FM Train Master Diesel, *86*	198	276____
8690	Lionel Lines Trolley, *86*	105	115____
8701	W&ARR 4-4-0 Locomotive "3," *77–79*	163	219____
8702	Southern 4-6-4 Locomotive, *77–78*	280	398____
8703	Wabash 2-4-2 Locomotive, *77*	22	30____
8750	Rock Island GP7 Diesel, *77–78*	110	125____
8751	Rock Island GP7 Diesel Dummy Unit, *77–78*	50	70____
8753	Pennsylvania GG1 Electric Locomotive, *77 u*	290	315____
8754	New Haven Electric Locomotive, *77–78*	100	115____
8755	Santa Fe U36B Diesel, *77–78*	130	150____
8756	Santa Fe U36B Diesel Dummy Unit, *77–78*	75	95____
8757	Conrail GP9 Diesel, *76 u, 77–78*	110	140____
8758	Southern GP7 Diesel Dummy Unit, *77 u, 78*	75	95____
8759	Erie-Lackawanna GP9 Diesel, *77–79*	115	175____
8760	Erie-Lackawanna GP9 Diesel Dummy Unit, *77–79*	95	115____
8761	GTW NW2 Switcher, *77–78*	95	130____
8762	Great Northern EP-5 Electric Locomotive, *77–78*	130	140____
8763	Norfolk & Western GP9 Diesel, *76 u, 77–78*	110	120____
8764	B&O Budd RDC Passenger (SSS), *77*	110	135____
8765	B&O Budd RDC Baggage Dummy Unit (SSS), *77*	80	100____
8766	B&O Budd RDC Baggage (SSS), *77*		310____
8767	B&O Budd RDC Passenger Dummy Unit (SSS), *77*	85	105____
8768	B&O Budd RDC Passenger Dummy Unit (SSS), *77*	85	105____
8769	Republic Steel Switcher, *77–78*	22	39____
8770	NW2 Switcher, *77–78*		65____
8771	Great Northern U36B Diesel, *77*	110	140____
8772	GM&O GP20 Diesel, *77*	85	95____
8773	Mickey Mouse U36B Diesel, *77–78*	493	645____
8774	Southern GP7 Diesel, *77 u, 78*	110	135____
8775	Lehigh Valley GP9 Diesel, *77 u, 78*	85	105____
8776	C&NW GP20 Diesel, *77 u, 78*	87	129____
8777	Santa Fe F3 Diesel B Unit (SSS), *77*	160	175____

		Exc	Mint
____8778	Lehigh Valley GP9 Diesel Dummy Unit, *77 u, 78*	90	110
____8779	C&NW GP20 Diesel Dummy Unit, *77 u, 78*	73	109
____8800	Lionel Lines 4-4-2 Locomotive, *78–81*	75	105
____8801	Blue Comet 4-6-4 Locomotive, *78–80*	380	500
____8803	Santa Fe 0-4-0 Locomotive, *78*	14	24
____8850	Penn Central GG1 Electric Locomotive, *78 u, 79*	250	305
____8851/52	New Haven F3 Diesel AA Set, *78 u, 79*	320	430
____8854	CP Rail GP9 Diesel, *78–79*	100	120
____8855	Milwaukee Road SD18 Diesel, *78*		115
____8857	Northern Pacific U36B Diesel, *78–80*	140	180
____8858	Northern Pacific U36B Diesel Dummy Unit, *78–80*	55	85
____8859	Conrail Electric Locomotive, *78–82*	105	150
____8860	Rock Island NW2 Switcher, *78–79*	85	100
____8861	Santa Fe Alco Diesel A Unit, *78–79*	65	85
____8862	Santa Fe Alco Diesel B Unit, *78–79*	36	43
____8864	New Haven F3 Diesel B Unit, *78*	85	105
____8866	M&StL GP9 Diesel (SSS), *78*	85	120
____8867	M&StL GP9 Diesel Dummy Unit (SSS), *78*	65	95
____8868	Amtrak Budd RDC Baggage, *78, 80*	195	235
____8869	Amtrak Budd RDC Passenger Dummy Unit, *78, 80*	75	95
____8870	Amtrak Budd RDC Passenger Dummy Unit, *78, 80*	85	115
____8871	Amtrak Budd RDC Baggage Dummy Unit, *78, 80*	85	105
____8872	Santa Fe SD18 Diesel, *78 u*	125	155
____8873	Santa Fe SD18 Diesel Dummy Unit, *78 u*	60	85
____8900	Santa Fe 4-6-4 Locomotive (FARR 1), *79*	270	310
____8902	ACL 2-4-0 Locomotive, *79–82, 86 u, 87–90*	13	17
____8903	D&RGW 2-4-2 Locomotive, *79–81*	17	21
____8904	Wabash 2-4-2 Locomotive, *79, 81 u*	30	34
____8905	Smokey Mountain Dockside 0-4-0T Locomotive, *79*	9	17
____8950	Virginian FM Train Master Diesel, *79*	230	285
____8951	Southern Pacific FM Train Master Diesel, *79*	237	335
____8952/53	PRR F3 Diesel AA Set, *79*	350	500
____8955	Southern U36B Diesel, *79*	120	195
____8956	Southern U36B Diesel Dummy Unit, *79*	80	125
____8957	Burlington Northern GP20 Diesel, *79*	120	150
____8958	Burlington Northern GP20 Diesel Dummy Unit, *79*	85	90
____8960	Southern Pacific U36C Diesel, *79 u*	130	180
____8961	Southern Pacific U36C Diesel Dummy Unit, *79 u*	70	80
____8962	Reading U36B Diesel, *79*	115	130
____8970/71	PRR F3 Diesel AA Set, *79 u, 80*	330	425
____9001	Conrail Boxcar (027), *86–87 u, 88–90*	5	10
____9010	GN Hopper (027), *70–71*	6	8
____9011	GN Hopper (027), *70 u, 75–76, 78–83*	8	10
____9012	TA&G Hopper (027), *71–72*	7	8
____9013	Canadian National Hopper (027), *72–76*	5	8
____9015	Reading Hopper (027), *73–75*	17	21
____9016	Chessie System Hopper (027), *75–79, 87–88, 89 u*	4	6
____9017	Wabash Gondola with canisters (027), *78–82*	3	5
____9018	DT&I Hopper (027), *78–79, 81–82*	6	7
____9019	Flatcar (027), *78*	2	3
____9020	Union Pacific Flatcar (027), *70–78*	3	5

		Exc	Mint	
9021	Santa Fe Work Caboose, *70–71, 73–75*	9	13	___
9022	Santa Fe Bulkhead Flatcar (027), *70–72, 75–79*	7	13	___
9023	MKT Bulkhead Flatcar (027), *73–74*	7	10	___
9024	C&O Flatcar (027), *73–75*	3	6	___
9025	DT&I Work Caboose, *71–74, 77–78*	8	10	___
9026	Republic Steel Flatcar (027), *75–82*	5	7	___
9027	Soo Line Work Caboose, *75–76*	7	9	___
9030	Kickapoo Gondola (027), *72, 79*	5	9	___
9031	NKP Gondola with canisters (027), *73–75, 82–83, 84–91 u*	4	8	___
9032	SP Gondola with canisters (027), *75–78*		3	___
9033	PC Gondola with canisters (027), *76–78, 82, 86 u, 87–90, 92 u*		3	___
9034	Lionel Leisure Hopper (027), *77 u*	30	34	___
9035	Conrail Boxcar (027), *78–82*	5	9	___
9036	Mobilgas 1-D Tank Car (027), *78–82*	7	19	___
9037	Conrail Boxcar (027), *78 u, 80*	7	10	___
9038	Chessie System Hopper (027), *78 u, 80*	15	19	___
9039	Mobilgas 1-D Tank Car (027), *78 u, 80*	10	15	___
9040	General Mills Wheaties Boxcar (027), *70–72*	9	13	___
9041	Hershey's Boxcar (027), *70–71, 73–76*	16	25	___
9042	Ford-Autolite Boxcar (027), *71 u, 72 74–76*	13	21	___
9043	Erie-Lackawanna Boxcar (027), *73–75*	13	20	___
9044	D&RGW Boxcar (027), *75–76*	5	8	___
9045	Toys "R" Us Boxcar (027), *75 u*	35	42	___
9046	True Value Boxcar (027), *76 u*	26	34	___
9047	Toys "R" Us Boxcar (027), *76 u*	40	43	___
9048	Toys "R" Us Boxcar (027), *76 u*	33	41	___
9049	Toys "R" Us Boxcar (027), *78 u*		NRS	___
9050	Sunoco 1-D Tank Car (027), *70–71*	17	23	___
9051	Firestone 1-D Tank Car (027), *74–75, 78*	15	19	___
9052	Toys "R" Us Boxcar (027), *77 u*	26	34	___
9053	True Value Boxcar (027), *77 u*	28	40	___
9054	JCPenney Boxcar (027), *77 u*	14	19	___
9055	Republic Steel Gondola with canisters, *78 u*	9	10	___
9057	CP Rail SP-type Caboose, *78–79*	10	15	___
9058	Lionel Lines SP-type Caboose, *78–79, 83*	5	7	___
9059	Lionel Lines SP-type Caboose, *79 u, 81 u*	7	9	___
9060	Nickel Plate Road SP-type Caboose, *70–72*	5	7	___
9061	Santa Fe SP-type Caboose, *70–76*	5	8	___
9062	Penn Central SP-type Caboose, *70–72, 74–76*	7	9	___
9063	GTW SP-type Caboose, *70, 71–73 u*	15	19	___
9064	C&O SP-type Caboose, *71–72, 75–77*	7	10	___
9065	Canadian National SP-type Caboose, *71–73 u*	19	24	___
9066	Southern SP-type Caboose, *73–76*	7	9	___
9067	Kickapoo Valley Bobber Caboose, *72*	6	9	___
9068	Reading Bobber Caboose, *73–76*	5	7	___
9069	Jersey Central SP-type Caboose, *73–74, 75–76 u*	5	8	___
9070	Rock Island SP-type Caboose, *73–74*	13	17	___
9071	Santa Fe Bobber Caboose, *74 u, 77–78*	7	9	___
9073	Coca-Cola SP-type Caboose, *74 u, 75*	27	32	___
9075	Rock Island SP-type Caboose, *75–76 u*	13	17	___
9076	"We The People" SP-type Caboose, *75 u*	19	28	___

			Exc	Mint
____	**9077**	D&RGW SP-type Caboose, *76–83, 84–91 u*	7	8
____	**9078**	Rock Island Bobber Caboose, *76–77*	5	7
____	**9079**	GTW Hopper (O27), *77*	28	32
____	**9080**	Wabash SP-type Caboose, *77*	9	10
____	**9085**	Santa Fe Work Caboose, *79–82*	4	5
____	**9090**	General Mills Mini-Max Car, *71*	27	32
____	**9106**	Miller Vat Car, *84–85*	33	52
____	**9107**	Dr Pepper Vat Car, *86–87*	30	36
____	**9110**	B&O Quad Hopper, *71*	25	30
____	**9111**	N&W Quad Hopper, *72–75*	15	20
____	**9112**	D&RGW Covered Quad Hopper, *73–75*	20	23
____	**9113**	Norfolk & Western Quad Hopper (SSS), *73*	27	32
____	**9114**	Morton Salt Covered Quad Hopper, *74–76*	18	27
____	**9115**	Planter's Covered Quad Hopper, *74–76*	21	33
____	**9116**	Domino Sugar Covered Quad Hopper, *74–76*	22	29
____	**9117**	Alaska Covered Quad Hopper (SSS), *74–76*	29	33
____	**9119**	Detroit & Mackinac Covered Hopper, *75 u*		20
____	**9120**	Northern Pacific Flatcar with trailers, *70–71*	33	38
____	**9121**	L&N Flatcar with bulldozer and scraper, *71–79*	47	54
____	**9122**	Northern Pacific Flatcar with trailers, *72–75*	19	32
____	**9123**	C&O Auto Carrier, 3-tier, *72 u, 73–74*	18	27
____	**9124**	P&LE Flatcar with logs, *73–74*	18	25
____	**9125**	Norfolk & Western Auto Carrier, 2-tier, *73–77*	23	28
____	**9126**	C&O Auto Carrier, 3-tier, *73–75*	23	34
____	**9128**	Heinz Vat Car, *74–76*	25	34
____	**9129**	N&W Auto Carrier, 3-tier, *75–76*	17	19
____	**9130**	B&O Quad Hopper, *70*	23	24
____	**9131**	D&RGW Gondola with canisters, *73–77*	5	8
____	**9132**	Libby's Vat Car (SSS), *75–77*	16	23
____	**9133**	BN Flatcar with trailers, *76–77, 80*	20	28
____	**9134**	Virginian Covered Quad Hopper, *76–77*		32
____	**9135**	N&W Covered Quad Hopper, *70 u, 71, 75*	19	27
____	**9136**	Republic Steel Gondola with canisters, *72–76, 79*	9	11
____	**9138**	Sunoco 3-D Tank Car (SSS), *78*	33	37
____	**9139**	PC Auto Carrier, 3-tier, *76–77*	21	29
	9140	Burlington Gondola with canisters, *70, 73–82, 87–89*	7	9
____	**9141**	BN Gondola with canisters, *70–72*	8	10
____	**9143**	CN Gondola with canisters, *71–73 u*	30	34
____	**9144**	D&RGW Gondola with canisters (SSS), *74–76*	9	13
____	**9145**	ICG Auto Carrier, 3-tier, *77–80*	21	29
____	**9146**	Mogen David Vat Car, *77–81*	21	26
____	**9147**	Texaco 1-D Tank Car, *77–78*	43	60
____	**9148**	Du Pont 3-D Tank Car, *77–81*	25	28
____	**9149**	CP Rail Flatcar with trailers, *77–78*	22	35
____	**9150**	Gulf 1-D Tank Car, *70 u, 71*	22	28
____	**9151**	Shell 1-D Tank Car, *72*	27	31
____	**9152**	Shell 1-D Tank Car, *73–76*	25	34
____	**9153**	Chevron 1-D Tank Car, *74–76*	28	35
____	**9154**	Borden 1-D Tank Car, *75–76*	33	47
____	**9156**	Mobilgas 1-D Tank Car, *76–77*	30	40
____	**9157**	C&O Crane Car, *76–78, 81–82*	35	44

Exc Mint

		Exc	Mint	
9158	PC Flatcar with shovel, *76–77, 80*	40	55	___
9159	Sunoco 1-D Tank Car, *76*	35	50	___
9160	Illinois Central N5c Caboose, *70–72*	17	23	___
9161	CN N5c Caboose, *72–74*	14	25	___
9162	PRR N5c Caboose, *72–76*	25	30	___
9163	Santa Fe N5c Caboose, *73–76*	17	24	___
9165	Canadian Pacific N5c Caboose (SSS), *73*	21	30	___
9166	D&RGW SP-type Caboose (SSS), *74–75*	20	25	___
9167	Chessie System N5c Caboose, *74–76*	24	31	___
9168	Union Pacific N5c Caboose, *75–77*	17	19	___
9169	Milwaukee Road SP-type Caboose (SSS), *75*	16	19	___
9170	N&W N5c Caboose "1776," *75*	27	30	___
9171	MP SP-type Caboose, *75 u, 76–77*	19	20	___
9172	Penn Central SP-type Caboose, *75 u, 76–77*	23	31	___
9173	Jersey Central SP-type Caboose, *75 u, 76–77*	22	33	___
9174	NYC (P&E) Bay Window Caboose, *76*	65	70	___
9175	Virginian N5c Caboose, *76–77*	24	26	___
9176	BAR N5c Caboose, *76 u*	18	30	___
9177	Northern Pacific Bay Window Caboose (SSS), *76*	25	35	___
9178	ICG SP-type Caboose, *76–77*	19	24	___
9179	Chessie System Bobber Caboose, *76*	7	11	___
9180	Rock Island N5c Caboose, *77–78*	12	23	___
9181	B&M N5c Caboose, *76 u, 77*	39	49	___
9182	N&W N5c Caboose, *76 u, 77–80*	20	26	___
9183	Mickey Mouse N5c Caboose, *77–78*	32	50	___
9184	Erie Bay Window Caboose, *77–78*	24	30	___
9185	GTW N5c Caboose, *77*	21	28	___
9186	Conrail N5c Caboose, *76 u, 77–78*	27	29	___
9187	Gulf, Mobile & Ohio SP-type Caboose, *77*	10	16	___
9188	GN Bay Window Caboose, *77*	22	27	___
9189	Gulf 1-D Tank Car, *77*	40	60	___
9193	Budweiser Vat Car, *83–84*	92	121	___
9200	Illinois Central Boxcar, *70–71*	19	25	___
9201	Penn Central Boxcar, *70*	17	25	___
9202	Santa Fe Boxcar, *70*	20	24	___
9203	Union Pacific Boxcar, *70*		21	___
9204	Northern Pacific Boxcar, *70*		21	___
9205	Norfolk & Western Boxcar, *70*	22	25	___
9206	Great Northern Boxcar, *70–71*		20	___
9207	Soo Line Boxcar, *71*	11	18	___
9208	CP Rail Boxcar, *71*	21	23	___
9209	Burlington Northern Boxcar, *71–72*	16	21	___
9210	B&O DD Boxcar, *71*	16	20	___
9211	Penn Central Boxcar, *71*	17	28	___
9213	M&StL Covered Quad Hopper (SSS), *78*	20	29	___
9214	Northern Pacific Boxcar, *71–72*	16	21	___
9215	Norfolk & Western Boxcar, *71*	19	24	___
9216	Great Northern Auto Carrier, 3-tier, *78*	25	39	___
9217	Soo Line Operating Boxcar, *82–84*	29	36	___
9218	Monon Operating Boxcar, *81*	25	30	___
9219	Missouri Pacific Operating Boxcar, *83*	27	33	___
9220	Borden Operating Milk Car, *83–86*	95	113	___

		Exc	Mint
____9221	Poultry Dispatch Operating Chicken Car, *83–85*	45	50
____9222	L&N Flatcar with trailers, *83–84*	38	60
____9223	Reading Operating Boxcar, *84*	33	40
____9224	Churchill Downs Operating Horse Car, *84–86*	85	110
____9225	Conrail Operating Barrel Car, *84*	42	55
____9226	Delaware & Hudson Flatcar with trailers, *84–85*	31	34
____9228	Canadian Pacific Operating Boxcar, *86*	24	37
____9229	Express Mail Operating Boxcar, *85–86*	21	27
____9230	Monon Boxcar (SSS), *71, 72 u*	17	24
____9231	Reading Bay Window Caboose, *79*	24	32
____9232	Allis-Chalmers Condenser Car, *80–81, 83 u*	42	50
____9233	Depressed Center Flatcar with transformer, *80*	55	65
____9234	Radioactive Waste Car, *80*	53	78
____9235	Union Pacific Derrick Car, *83–84*	16	22
____9236	C&NW Derrick Car, *83–85*	22	30
____9238	Northern Pacific Log Dump Car, *84*	16	24
____9239	Lionel Lines N5c Caboose, *83 u*	50	60
____9240	NYC Hopper (O27), *87 u*	20	29
____9240	NYC Operating Hopper, *86*	32	39
____9241	PRR Log Dump Car, *85–86*	21	27
____9250	WaterPoxy 3-D Tank Car, *70–71*	23	34
9260	Reynolds Aluminum Covered Quad Hopper, *75–77*	19	22
____9261	Sun-Maid Raisins Covered Quad Hopper, *75 u, 76*	21	27
____9262	Ralston Purina Covered Quad Hopper, *75 u, 76*	36	58
____9263	PRR Covered Quad Hopper, *75 u, 76–77*	23	30
9264	Illinois Central Covered Quad Hopper, *75 u, 76–77*	28	39
9265	Chessie System Covered Quad Hopper, *75 u, 76–77*	21	27
____9266	Southern "Big John" Covered Quad Hopper, *76*	46	65
____9267	Alcoa Covered Quad Hopper (SSS), *76*	20	25
____9268	Northern Pacific Bay Window Caboose, *77 u*	33	40
____9269	Milwaukee Road Bay Window Caboose, *78*	34	47
____9270	Northern Pacific N5c Caboose, *78*	14	27
____9271	M&StL Bay Window Caboose (SSS), *78–79*	18	30
____9272	New Haven Bay Window Caboose, *78–80*	20	34
____9273	Southern Bay Window Caboose, *78 u*	36	45
____9274	Santa Fe Bay Window Caboose, *78 u*	40	47
____9276	Peabody Quad Hopper, *78*	19	28
____9277	Cities Service 1-D Tank Car, *78*	41	45
____9278	Life Savers 1-D Tank Car, *78–79*	112	152
____9279	Magnolia 3-D Tank Car, *78, 79 u*	13	19
____9280	Santa Fe Operating Stock Car (O27), *77–81*	20	24
____9281	Santa Fe Auto Carrier, 3-tier, *78–80*	21	27
____9282	GN Flatcar with trailers, *78–79, 81–82*	22	28
____9283	Union Pacific Gondola with canisters, *77*	15	21
____9284	Santa Fe Gondola with canisters, *77*	16	27
____9285	ICG Flatcar with trailers, *77*	47	48
____9286	B&LE Covered Quad Hopper, *77*	14	26
____9287	Southern N5c Caboose, *77 u, 78*	18	30
____9288	Lehigh Valley N5c Caboose, *77 u, 78, 80*	25	31
____9289	C&NW N5c Caboose, *77 u, 78, 80*	25	36

		Exc	Mint
9290	Union Pacific Operating Barrel Car, *83*	65	75____
9300	PC Log Dump Car, *70–75, 77*	18	24____
9301	U.S. Mail Operating Boxcar, *73–84*	32	42____
9302	L&N Searchlight Car, *72 u, 73–78*	21	24____
9303	Union Pacific Log Dump Car, *74–78, 80*	17	22____
9304	C&O Coal Dump Car, *74–78*	11	23____
9305	Santa Fe Operating Cowboy Car (O27), *80–82*	16	23____
9306	Santa Fe Flatcar with horses, *80–82*	18	26____
9307	Erie Animated Gondola, *80–84*	55	70____
9308	Aquarium Car, *81–84*	125	129____
9309	TP&W Bay Window Caboose, *80–81, 83 u*	19	25____
9310	Santa Fe Log Dump Car, *78 u, 79–83*	13	24____
9311	Union Pacific Coal Dump Car, *78 u, 79–82*	13	24____
9312	Conrail Searchlight Car, *78 u, 79–83*	18	27____
9313	Gulf 3-D Tank Car, *79 u*	43	50____
9315	Southern Pacific Gondola with canisters, *79 u*	16	23____
9316	Southern Pacific Bay Window Caboose, *79 u*	47	50____
9317	Santa Fe Bay Window Caboose, *79*	21	36____
9320	Fort Knox Mint Car, *79 u*	110	135____
9321	Santa Fe 1-D Tank Car (FARR 1), *79*	25	31____
9322	Santa Fe Covered Quad Hopper (FARR 1), *79*	30	38____
9323	Santa Fe Bay Window Caboose (FARR 1), *79*	39	49____
9324	Tootsie Roll 1-D Tank Car, *79–81*	67	96____
9325	Norfolk & Western Flatcar with fences, *79–81 u*	6	10____
9326	Burlington Northern Bay Window Caboose, *79–80*	34	44____
9327	Bakelite 3-D Tank Car, *80*	19	29____
9328	Chessie System Bay Window Caboose, *80*	33	42____
9329	Chessie System Crane Car, *80*	40	47____
9330	Kickapoo Dump Car, *72, 79*	3	7____
9331	Union 76 1-D Tank Car, *79*	39	44____
9332	Reading Crane Car, *79*	37	50____
9333	Southern Pacific Flatcar with trailers, *79–80*	33	47____
9334	Humble 1-D Tank Car, *79*	21	26____
9335	B&O Log Dump Car, *86*	16	22____
9336	CP Rail Gondola with canisters, *79*	20	29____
9338	Pennsylvania Power & Light Quad Hopper, *79*	60	75____
9339	GN Boxcar (O27), *79–83, 85 u, 86*	7	10____
9340	Illinois Central Gondola with canisters (O27), *79–81, 82 u, 83*	5	9____
9341	ACL SP-type Caboose, *79–82, 86 u 87–90*	6	8____
9344	Citgo 3-D Tank Car, *80*	23	38____
9345	Reading Searchlight Car, *84–85*	20	25____
9346	Wabash SP-type Caboose, *79*	6	10____
9348	Santa Fe Crane Car (FARR 1), *79 u*	60	70____
9349	San Francisco Mint Car, *80*	55	70____
9351	PRR Auto Carrier, 3-tier, *80*	23	40____
9352	Trailer Train Flatcar with C&NW trailers, *80*	29	55____
9353	Crystal Line 3-D Tank Car, *80*	18	26____
9354	Pennzoil 1-D Tank Car, *80, 81 u*	60	85____
9355	Delaware & Hudson Bay Window Caboose, *80*	37	45____
9357	Smokey Mountain Bobber Caboose, *79*	8	10____
9359	National Basketball Association Boxcar (O27), *79–80 u*	19	24____

			Exc	Mint
____	9360	National Hockey League Boxcar (027), *79–80 u*	21	26
____	9361	C&NW Bay Window Caboose, *80*	47	50
____	9362	Major League Baseball Boxcar (027), *79–80 u*	17	21
____	9363	N&W Log Dump Car "9325" (027), *79*	4	7
____	9364	N&W Crane Car "9325" (027), *79*	7	9
____	9365	Toys "R" Us Boxcar (027), *79 u*	30	37
____	9366	UP Covered Quad Hopper (FARR 2), *80*	19	23
____	9367	Union Pacific 1-D Tank Car (FARR 2), *80*	21	30
____	9368	Union Pacific Bay Window Caboose (FARR 2), *80*	30	36
____	9369	Sinclair 1-D Tank Car, *80*	60	85
____	9370	Seaboard Gondola with canisters, *80*	19	21
____	9371	Atlantic Sugar Covered Quad Hopper, *80*	19	22
____	9372	Seaboard Bay Window Caboose, *80*	30	41
____	9373	Getty 1-D Tank Car, *80–81, 83 u*	31	42
____	9374	Reading Covered Quad Hopper, *80–81, 83 u*	39	40
____	9376	Soo Line Boxcar (027), *81 u*	40	50
____	9378	Derrick Car, *80–82*	18	22
____	9379	Santa Fe Gondola with canisters, *80–81, 83 u*	22	30
____	9380	NYNH&H SP-type Caboose, *80–81*	7	10
____	9381	Chessie System SP-type Caboose, *80*	7	9
____	9382	Florida East Coast Bay Window Caboose, *80*	34	48
____	9383	UP Flatcar with trailers (FARR 2), *80 u*	27	34
____	9384	Great Northern Operating Hopper, *81*	50	55
____	9385	Alaska Gondola with canisters, *81*	27	34
____	9386	Pure Oil 1-D Tank Car, *81*	38	50
____	9387	Burlington Bay Window Caboose, *81*	46	52
____	9388	Toys "R" Us Boxcar (027), *81 u*	38	45
____	9389	Radioactive Waste Car, *81–82*	63	78
____	9398	PRR Coal Dump Car, *83–84*	28	38
____	9399	C&NW Coal Dump Car, *83–85*	17	22
____	9400	Conrail Boxcar, *78*	14	20
____	9401	Great Northern Boxcar, *78*	18	23
____	9402	Susquehanna Boxcar, *78*	30	33
____	9403	Seaboard Coast Line Boxcar, *78*	12	17
____	9404	NKP Boxcar, *78*	19	21
____	9405	Chattahoochee Boxcar, *78*	14	19
____	9406	D&RGW Boxcar, *78–79*	17	21
____	9407	Union Pacific Stock Car, *78*	18	25
____	9408	Lionel Lines Circus Stock Car (SSS), *78*	31	40
____	9411	Lackawanna Phoebe Snow Boxcar, *78*	35	43
____	9412	RF&P Boxcar, *79*	21	27
____	9413	Napierville Junction Boxcar, *79*	18	24
____	9414	Cotton Belt Boxcar, *79*	19	23
____	9415	Providence & Worcester Boxcar, *79*	17	25
____	9416	MD&W Boxcar, *79, 81*	13	19
____	9417	CP Rail Boxcar, *79*	45	50
____	9418	FARR Boxcar, *79 u*	50	60
____	9419	Union Pacific Boxcar (FARR 2), *80*	10	17
____	9420	B&O Sentinel Boxcar, *80*	21	26
____	9421	Maine Central Boxcar, *80*	10	17
____	9422	EJ&E Boxcar, *80*	12	20
____	9423	NYNH&H Boxcar, *80*	14	22

		Exc	Mint
9424	TP&W Boxcar, *80*	17	21___
9425	British Columbia DD Boxcar, *80*	27	35___
9426	Chesapeake & Ohio Boxcar, *80*	19	30___
9427	Bay Line Boxcar, *80–81*	12	17___
9428	TP&W Boxcar, *80–81, 83 u*		23___
9429	"The Early Years" Boxcar, *80*	20	27___
9430	"The Standard Gauge Years" Boxcar, *80*	22	25___
9431	"The Prewar Years" Boxcar, *80*	20	25___
9432	"The Postwar Years" Boxcar, *80*	50	55___
9433	"The Golden Years" Boxcar, *80*	33	43___
9434	Joshua Lionel Cowen "The Man" Boxcar, *80 u*	29	37___
9436	Burlington Boxcar, *81*	25	30___
9437	Northern Pacific Stock Car, *81*	22	36___
9438	Ontario Northland Boxcar, *81*	25	31___
9439	Ashley Drew & Northern Boxcar, *81*	11	19___
9440	Reading Boxcar, *81*	50	65___
9441	Pennsylvania Boxcar, *81*	32	42___
9442	Canadian Pacific Boxcar, *81*	13	21___
9443	Florida East Coast Boxcar, *81*	19	24___
9444	Louisiana Midland Boxcar, *81*	14	18___
9445	Vermont Northern Boxcar, *81*	14	17___
9446	Sabine River & Northern Boxcar, *81*	15	21___
9447	Pullman Standard Boxcar, *81*	16	21___
9448	Santa Fe Stock Car, *81–82*	34	40___
9449	Great Northern Boxcar (FARR 3), *81*	27	31___
9450	Great Northern Stock Car (FARR 3), *81 u*	50	60___
9451	Southern Boxcar (FARR 4), *83*	26	32___
9452	Western Pacific Boxcar, *82–83*	12	16___
9453	MPA Boxcar, *82–83*	14	19___
9454	New Hope & Ivyland Boxcar, *82–83*	21	27___
9455	Milwaukee Road Boxcar, *82–83*	15	19___
9456	PRR DD Boxcar (FARR 5), *84–85*	24	30___
9461	Norfolk & Southern Boxcar, *82*	25	43___
9462	Southern Pacific Boxcar, *83–84*	18	23___
9463	Texas & Pacific Boxcar, *83–84*	15	19___
9464	NC&StL Boxcar, *83–84*	16	22___
9465	Santa Fe Boxcar, *83–84*	12	19___
9466	Wanamaker Boxcar, *82 u*	60	70___
9467	Tennessee World's Fair Boxcar, *82 u*	26	31___
9468	Union Pacific DD Boxcar, *83*	31	34___
9469	NYC Pacemaker Boxcar (std 0), *84–85*	37	53___
9470	Chicago Beltline Boxcar, *84*	15	20___
9471	Atlantic Coast Line Boxcar, *84*	13	20___
9472	Detroit & Mackinac Boxcar, *84*	22	26___
9473	Lehigh Valley Boxcar, *84*	24	28___
9474	Erie-Lackawanna Boxcar, *84*	31	35___
9475	D&H "I Love NY" Boxcar, *84 u*	28	37___
9476	PRR Boxcar (FARR 5), *84–85*	27	36___
9480	MN&S Boxcar, *85–86*	15	18___
9481	Seaboard System Boxcar, *85–86*	15	18___
9482	Norfolk & Southern Boxcar, *85–86*	13	17___
9483	Manufacturers Railway Boxcar, *85–86*	14	19___

		Exc	Mint
____9484	Lionel 85th Anniversary Boxcar, *85*	22	26
____9486	GTW "I Love Michigan" Boxcar, *86*	23	34
____9490	Christmas Boxcar for Lionel Employees, *85 u*		1800
____9491	Christmas Boxcar, *86 u*	26	37
____9492	Lionel Lines Boxcar, *86*	23	29
____9500	Milwaukee Road Passenger Coach, *73*	28	75
____9501	Milwaukee Road Passenger Coach, *73 u, 74–76*	33	37
____9502	Milwaukee Road Observation Car, *73*	30	48
____9503	Milwaukee Road Passenger Coach, *73*	33	48
____9504	Milwaukee Road Passenger Coach, *73 u, 74–76*	33	37
____9505	Milwaukee Road Passenger Coach, *73 u, 74–76*	35	38
____9506	Milwaukee Road Combination Car, *74 u, 75–76*	32	37
____9507	PRR Passenger Coach, *74–75*	34	55
____9508	PRR Passenger Coach, *74–75*	32	50
____9509	PRR Observation Car, *74–75*	41	60
____9510	PRR Combination Car, *74 u, 75–76*	30	47
____9511	Milwaukee Road Passenger Coach, *74 u*	33	48
____9513	PRR Passenger Coach, *75–76*	25	44
____9514	PRR Passenger Coach, *75–76*	23	36
____9515	PRR Passenger Coach, *75–76*	22	34
____9516	B&O Passenger Coach, *76*	27	42
____9517	B&O Passenger Coach, *75*	45	65
____9518	B&O Observation Car, *75*	45	65
____9519	B&O Combination Car, *75*	55	85
____9521	PRR Baggage Car, *75 u, 76*	65	95
____9522	Milwaukee Road Baggage Car, *75 u, 76*	65	80
____9523	B&O Baggage Car, *75 u, 76*	60	70
____9524	B&O Passenger Coach, *76*	27	37
____9525	B&O Passenger Coach, *76*	30	43
____9527	Milwaukee Road Campaign Observation Car, *76 u*	38	60
____9528	PRR Campaign Observation Car, *76 u*	48	75
____9529	B&O Campaign Observation Car, *76 u*	35	59
____9530	Southern Baggage Car, *77–78*	45	65
____9531	Southern Combination Car, *77–78*	29	37
____9532	Southern Passenger Coach, *77–78*	33	47
____9533	Southern Passenger Coach, *77–78*	27	38
____9534	Southern Observation Car, *77–78*	31	47
____9536	Blue Comet Baggage Car, *78–80*	39	55
____9537	Blue Comet Combination Car, *78–80*	35	50
____9538	Blue Comet Passenger Coach, *78–80*	35	47
____9539	Blue Comet Passenger Coach, *78–80*	35	48
____9540	Blue Comet Observation Car, *78–80*	27	40
____9541	Santa Fe Baggage Car, *80–82*	21	30
____9545	Union Pacific Baggage Car, *84*	135	200
____9546	Union Pacific Combination Car, *84*	85	105
____9547	Union Pacific Observation Car, *84*	85	105
____9548	UP Placid Bay Passenger Coach, *84*	90	110
____9549	UP Ocean Sunset Passenger Coach, *84*	85	105
____9551	W&ARR Baggage Car, *77 u, 78–80*	36	48
____9552	W&ARR Passenger Coach, *77 u, 78–80*	46	60
____9553	W&ARR Flatcar with horses, *77 u, 78–80*	32	50
____9554	Chicago & Alton Baggage Car, *81*	55	85

		Exc	Mint	
9555	Chicago & Alton Combination Car, *81*	50	75	___
9556	Chicago & Alton Wilson Passenger Coach, *81*	50	75	___
9557	Chicago & Alton Webster Groves Passenger Coach, *81*	45	65	___
9558	Chicago & Alton Observation Car, *81*	50	75	___
9559	Rock Island Baggage Car, *81–82*	42	65	___
9560	Rock Island Passenger Coach, *81–82*	43	65	___
9561	Rock Island Passenger Coach, *81–82*	42	65	___
9562	N&W Baggage Car "577," *81*	80	110	___
9563	N&W Combination Car "578," *81*	80	105	___
9564	N&W Passenger Coach "579," *81*	90	100	___
9565	N&W Passenger Coach "580," *81*	85	100	___
9566	N&W Observation Car "581," *81*	90	95	___
9567	N&W Vista Dome Car "582," *81 u*	160	255	___
9569	PRR Combination Car, *81 u*	115	160	___
9570	PRR Baggage Car, *79*	85	115	___
9571	PRR Passenger Coach, *79*	125	145	___
9572	PRR Passenger Coach, *79*	110	125	___
9573	PRR Vista Dome Car, *79*	95	120	___
9574	PRR Observation Car, *79*	75	100	___
9575	PRR Passenger Coach, *79–80 u*	100	135	___
9576	Burlington Baggage Car, *80*	145	175	___
9577	Burlington Passenger Coach, *80*	95	105	___
9578	Burlington Passenger Coach, *80*	105	110	___
9579	Burlington Vista Dome Car, *80*	95	110	___
9580	Burlington Observation Car, *80*	95	110	___
9581	Chessie System Baggage Car, *80*	55	62	___
9582	Chessie System Combination Car, *80*	47	55	___
9583	Chessie System Passenger Coach, *80*	40	47	___
9584	Chessie System Passenger Coach, *80*	31	37	___
9585	Chessie System Observation Car, *80*	55	65	___
9586	Chessie System Diner, *86 u*	85	90	___
9588	Burlington Vista Dome Car, *80 u*	110	120	___
9589	Southern Pacific Baggage Car, *82–83*	110	135	___
9590	Southern Pacific Combination Car, *82–83*	90	105	___
9591	Southern Pacific Pullman Passenger Coach, *82–83*	85	105	___
9592	Southern Pacific Pullman Passenger Coach, *82–83*	85	105	___
9593	Southern Pacific Observation Car, *82–83*	100	130	___
9594	NYC Baggage Car, *83–84*	105	130	___
9595	NYC Combination Car, *83–84*	75	85	___
9596	NYC Wayne County Passenger Coach, *83–84*	80	95	___
9597	NYC Hudson River Passenger Coach, *83–84*	70	85	___
9598	NYC Observation Car, *83–84*	75	85	___
9599	Chicago & Alton Diner, *86 u*	80	90	___
9600	Chessie System Hi-Cube Boxcar, *75 u, 76–77*	19	25	___
9601	ICG Hi-Cube Boxcar, *75 u, 76–77*	20	21	___
9602	Santa Fe Hi-Cube Boxcar, *75 u, 76–77*	17	20	___
9603	Penn Central Hi-Cube Boxcar, *76–77*	12	18	___
9604	Norfolk & Western Hi-Cube Boxcar, *76–77*	23	26	___
9605	NH Hi-Cube Boxcar, *76–77*	17	21	___
9606	Union Pacific Hi-Cube Boxcar, *76 u, 77*	10	17	___

		Exc	Mint
____**9607**	Southern Pacific Hi-Cube Boxcar, *76 u, 77*	12	15
____**9608**	Burlington Northern Hi-Cube Boxcar, *76 u, 77*	21	23
____**9610**	Frisco Hi-Cube Boxcar, *77*	25	34
____**9620**	NHL Wales Boxcar, *80*	27	35
____**9621**	NHL Campbell Boxcar, *80*	27	34
____**9622**	NBA Western Boxcar, *80*	24	30
____**9623**	NBA Eastern Boxcar, *80*	26	34
____**9624**	National League Baseball Boxcar, *80*	27	34
____**9625**	American League Baseball Boxcar, *80*	27	35
____**9626**	Santa Fe Hi-Cube Boxcar, *82–84*	10	14
____**9627**	Union Pacific Hi-Cube Boxcar, *82–83*	15	21
____**9628**	Burlington Northern Hi-Cube Boxcar, *82–84*	14	19
____**9629**	Chessie System Hi-Cube Boxcar, *83–84*	23	34
____**9660**	Mickey Mouse Hi-Cube Boxcar, *77–78*	32	43
____**9661**	Goofy Hi-Cube Boxcar, *77–78*	53	61
____**9662**	Donald Duck Hi-Cube Boxcar, *77–78*	38	49
____**9663**	Dumbo Hi-Cube Boxcar, *77 u, 78*	43	58
____**9664**	Cinderella Hi-Cube Boxcar, *77 u, 78*	56	86
____**9665**	Peter Pan Hi-Cube Boxcar, *77 u, 78*	49	77
____**9666**	Pinocchio Hi-Cube Boxcar, *78*	113	161
____**9667**	Snow White Hi-Cube Boxcar, *78*	354	466
____**9668**	Pluto Hi-Cube Boxcar, *78*	149	193
____**9669**	Bambi Hi-Cube Boxcar, *78 u*	67	105
____**9670**	Alice In Wonderland Hi-Cube Boxcar, *78 u*	61	91
____**9671**	Fantasia Hi-Cube Boxcar, *78 u*	56	91
9672 ____	Mickey Mouse 50th Anniversary Hi-Cube Boxcar, *78 u*	366	436
____**9700**	Southern Boxcar, *72–73*	22	30
____**9701**	B&O DD Boxcar, *72*	14	19
____**9702**	Soo Line Boxcar, *72–73*	15	21
____**9703**	CP Rail Boxcar, *72*	34	44
____**9704**	Norfolk & Western Boxcar, *72*	10	17
____**9705**	D&RGW Boxcar, *72*	13	20
____**9706**	C&O Boxcar, *72*	17	19
____**9707**	MKT Stock Car, *72–75*	14	22
____**9708**	U.S. Mail Boxcar, *72–75*	18	23
____**9708**	U.S. Mail Toy Fair Boxcar, *73 u*	85	95
____**9709**	BAR State of Maine Boxcar (SSS), *72–74*	29	32
____**9710**	Rutland Boxcar (SSS), *72–74*	24	28
____**9711**	Southern Boxcar, *74–75*	19	25
____**9712**	B&O DD Boxcar, *73–74*	31	34
____**9713**	CP Rail Boxcar, *73–74*	24	30
____**9713**	CP Rail "Season's Greetings" Boxcar, *74 u*	95	120
____**9714**	D&RGW Boxcar, *73–74*	16	20
____**9715**	C&O Boxcar, *73–74*	17	22
____**9716**	Penn Central Boxcar, *73–74*	15	20
____**9717**	Union Pacific Boxcar, *73–74*	21	25
____**9718**	Canadian National Boxcar, *73–74*	23	31
____**9719**	New Haven DD Boxcar, *73 u*	23	32
____**9723**	Western Pacific Boxcar (SSS), *73–74*	27	29
____**9723**	Western Pacific Toy Fair Boxcar, *74 u*	20	60
____**9724**	Missouri Pacific Boxcar (SSS), *73–74*	21	24

		Exc	Mint
9725	MKT Stock Car (SSS), *73–75*	15	18___
9726	Erie-Lackawanna Boxcar (SSS), *78*	25	30___
9729	CP Rail Boxcar, *78*		34___
9730	CP Rail Boxcar, *74–75*	23	27___
9731	Milwaukee Road Boxcar, *74–75*	16	21___
9732	Southern Pacific Boxcar, *79 u*	24	31___
9734	Bangor & Aroostook Boxcar, *79*	30	38___
9735	Grand Trunk Western Boxcar, *74–75*	15	21___
9737	Vermont Central Boxcar, *74–76*	27	34___
9738	Illinois Terminal Boxcar, *82*	33	45___
9739	D&RGW Boxcar (SSS), *74–76*	17	25___
9740	Chessie System Boxcar, *74–75*	15	19___
9742	M&StL Boxcar, *73 u*	12	19___
9742	M&StL "Season's Greetings" Boxcar, *73 u*	85	105___
9743	Sprite Boxcar, *74 u, 75*	19	27___
9744	Tab Boxcar, *74 u, 75*	17	24___
9745	Fanta Boxcar, *74 u, 75*	19	29___
9747	Chessie System DD Boxcar, *75–76*	24	28___
9748	CP Rail Boxcar, *75–76*	16	20___
9749	Penn Central Boxcar, *75–76*	16	21___
9750	DT&I Boxcar, *75–76*	13	20___
9751	Frisco Boxcar, *75–76*	21	23___
9752	L&N Boxcar, *75–76*	20	23___
9753	Maine Central Boxcar, *75–76*	16	22___
9754	NYC Pacemaker Boxcar (SSS), *75–77*	20	30___
9755	Union Pacific Boxcar, *75–76*	20	24___
9757	Central of Georgia Boxcar, *74 u*	16	17___
9758	Alaska Boxcar (SSS), *75–77*	24	31___
9759	Paul Revere Boxcar, *75 u*	36	43___
9760	Liberty Bell Boxcar, *75 u*	30	40___
9761	George Washington Boxcar, *75 u*	36	43___
9762	Toy Fair Boxcar, *75 u*	125	170___
9763	D&RGW Stock Car, *76–77*	15	20___
9764	GTW DD Boxcar, *76–77*	40	55___
9767	Railbox Boxcar, *76–77*	15	20___
9768	B&M Boxcar, *76–77*	18	27___
9769	B&LE Boxcar, *76–77*	17	21___
9770	Northern Pacific Boxcar, *76–77*	14	18___
9771	Norfolk & Western Boxcar, *76–77*	16	24___
9772	Great Northern Boxcar, *76*	60	85___
9773	NYC Stock Car, *76*	32	39___
9775	M&StL Boxcar (SSS), *76*	19	23___
9776	SP Overnight Boxcar (SSS), *76*	32	34___
9777	Virginian Boxcar, *76–77*	22	25___
9778	"Season's Greetings" Boxcar, *75 u*	165	185___
9780	Johnny Cash Boxcar, *76 u*	47	58___
9781	Delaware & Hudson Boxcar, *77–78*	19	23___
9782	Rock Island Boxcar, *77–78*	14	17___
9783	B&O Time-Saver Boxcar, *77–78*	18	27___
9784	Santa Fe Boxcar, *77–78*	13	17___
9785	Conrail Boxcar, *77–78*	20	23___
9786	C&NW Boxcar, *77–79*	18	27___

			Exc	Mint
____	9787	Jersey Central Boxcar, *77–79*	12	19
____	9788	Lehigh Valley Boxcar, *77–79*	17	21
____	9789	Pickens Boxcar, *77*	25	33
____	9801	B&O Sentinel Boxcar (std 0), *73–75*	18	26
____	9802	Miller High Life Reefer (std 0), *73–75*	28	33
____	9803	Johnson Wax Boxcar (std 0), *73–75*	27	33
____	9805	Grand Trunk Western Reefer (std 0), *73–75*	20	31
____	9806	Rock Island Boxcar (std 0), *74–75*	38	46
____	9807	Stroh's Beer Reefer (std 0), *74–76*	67	79
____	9808	Union Pacific Boxcar (std 0), *75–76*	36	50
____	9809	Clark Reefer (std 0), *75–76*	33	41
____	9811	Pacific Fruit Express Reefer (FARR 2), *80*	26	33
____	9812	Arm & Hammer Reefer, *80*	24	30
____	9813	Ruffles Reefer, *80*	18	26
____	9814	Perrier Reefer, *80*	21	30
____	9815	NYC "Early Bird" Reefer (std 0), *84–85*	34	40
____	9816	Brach's Candy Reefer, *80*	21	26
____	9817	Bazooka Bubble Gum Reefer, *80*	24	31
____	9818	Western Maryland Reefer, *80*	18	23
____	9819	Western Fruit Express Reefer (FARR 3), *81*	22	29
____	9820	Wabash Gondola with coal (std 0), *73–74*	24	38
____	9821	SP Gondola with coal (std 0), *73–75*	28	32
____	9822	GTW Gondola with coal (std 0), *74–75*	24	29
____	9823	Santa Fe Flatcar with crates (std 0), *75–76*	34	44
____	9824	NYC Gondola with coal (std 0), *75–76*	41	56
____	9825	Schaefer Reefer (std 0), *76–77*	45	60
____	9826	P&LE Boxcar (std 0), *76–77*	34	39
____	9827	Cutty Sark Reefer, *84*	34	44
____	9828	J&B Reefer, *84*	31	44
____	9829	Dewar's White Label Reefer, *84*	37	45
____	9830	Johnnie Walker Red Label Reefer, *84*	27	45
____	9831	Pepsi Cola Reefer, *82*	77	88
____	9832	Cheerios Reefer, *82*	157	181
____	9833	Vlasic Pickles Reefer, *82*	23	29
____	9834	Southern Comfort Reefer, *83–84*	34	47
____	9835	Jim Beam Reefer, *83–84*	41	58
____	9836	Old Grand-Dad Reefer, *83–84*	35	48
____	9837	Wild Turkey Reefer, *83–84*	63	93
____	9840	Fleischmann's Gin Reefer, *85*	38	43
____	9841	Calvert Gin Reefer, *85*	35	41
____	9842	Seagram's Gin Reefer, *85*	38	43
____	9843	Tanqueray Gin Reefer, *85*	41	44
____	9844	Sambuca Reefer, *86*	37	49
____	9845	Baileys Irish Cream Reefer, *86*	58	87
____	9846	Seagram's Vodka Reefer, *86*	37	43
____	9847	Wolfschmidt Vodka Reefer, *86*	34	39
____	9849	Lionel Lines Reefer, *83 u*	20	32
____	9850	Budweiser Reefer, *72 u, 73–75*	52	62
____	9851	Schlitz Reefer, *72 u, 73–75*	29	35
____	9852	Miller Reefer, *72 u, 73–77*	32	38
	9853	Cracker Jack Reefer, *72 u, 73–75*		
____		(A) Caramel-colored body	29	34
____		(B) White body, black logo border	23	28

		Exc	Mint
9854	Baby Ruth Reefer, *72 u, 73–76*	22	26____
9855	Swift Reefer, *72 u, 73–77*	23	28____
9856	Old Milwaukee Reefer, *75–76*	33	40____
9858	Butterfinger Reefer, *73 u, 74–76*	22	28____
9859	Pabst Reefer, *73 u, 74–75*	38	45____
9860	Gold Medal Reefer, *73 u, 74–76*	12	21____
9861	Tropicana Reefer, *75–77*	23	35____
9862	Hamm's Reefer, *75–76*	35	42____
9863	REA Reefer (SSS), *74–76*	24	28____
9866	Coors Reefer, *76–77*	41	56____
9867	Hershey's Reefer, *76–77*	71	81____
9869	Santa Fe Reefer (SSS), *76*	32	37____
9870	Old Dutch Cleanser Reefer, *77–78, 80*	15	21____
9871	Carling Black Label Reefer, *77–78, 80*	33	45____
9872	Pacific Fruit Express Reefer, *77–79*	24	28____
9873	Ralston Purina Reefer, *78*	25	38____
9874	Miller Lite Beer Reefer, *78–79*	52	59____
9875	A&P Reefer, *78–79*	23	31____
9876	Vermont Central Reefer, *78*	26	31____
9877	Gerber Reefer, *79–80*	68	78____
9878	Good and Plenty Reefer, *79*	24	31____
9879	Hills Bros. Reefer, *79–80*	23	29____
9880	Santa Fe Reefer (FARR 1), *79*	27	31____
9881	Rath Packing Reefer, *79 u*	23	31____
9882	NYC "Early Bird" Reefer, *79*	25	29____
9883	Nabisco Oreo Reefer, *79*	83	88____
9884	Fritos Reefer, *81–82*	26	34____
9885	Lipton Tea Reefer, *81–82*	30	38____
9886	Mounds Reefer, *81–82*	24	30____
9887	Fruit Growers Express Reefer (FARR 4), *83*	29	38____
9888	Green Bay & Western Reefer, *83*	42	49____
11000	Holiday Express Freight Set, *08*		280____
11004	NASCAR Diesel Freight Set, *06–07*		300____
11005	Dale Earnhardt Jr. Diesel Freight Set, *06–07*		240____
11006	Kasey Kahne Expansion Pack, *06–07*		130____
11006	Lionel Lion Set, *03 u*		230____
11007	Dale Earnhardt Sr. Expansion Pack, *06–07*		130____
11008	Dale Earnhardt Jr. Expansion Pack, *06–07*		130____
11009	Tony Stewart Expansion Pack, *06–07*		130____
11010	Jimmie Johnson Expansion Pack, *06–07*		130____
11011	Jeff Gordon Expansion Pack, *06–07*		130____
11020	Harry Potter Hogwarts Express Steam Passenger Set, *08–13*		330____
11025	Jimmie Johnson 2006 Champion Boxcar, *07*		45____
11038	Snow-covered Straight Track 4-pack, *08*		14____
11041	Holiday Calliope Car, *08*		45____
11067	Lionel Bear, *08*		25____
11077	Harry Potter Figures, *08*		27____
11096	Engineer Hat, *08*		18____
11098	Holiday Toy Soldier Car, *08*		50____
11100	PRR 2-8-2 Mikado Locomotive "9631," CC, *07*		370____
11101	LL 2-8-4 Berkshire Locomotive "737," CC, *06*		350____

		Exc	Mint
11103	Southern PS-4 4-6-2 Pacific Locomotive "1403," CC, *06*		1000
11104	UP Big Boy Locomotive "4014," CC, *06*		1700
11105	NYC L-2A 4-8-2 Mohawk Locomotive "2770," CC, *06*		1100
11107	LionMaster SP Cab Forward Locomotive "4276," RailSounds, *06–07*		850
11108	C&O F-19 4-6-2 Pacific Locomotive "494," CC, *06–07*		1160
11109	C&O 0-8-0 Locomotive "79," TrainSounds, *06*		420
11110	NYC 0-8-0 Locomotive "7805," TrainSounds, *06*		420
11116	UP 4-8-4 FEF-3 Locomotive "844," gray, CC, *08–09*		1160
11117	Santa Fe E6 4-4-2 Atlantic Locomotive "1484," CC, *07–09*		600
11119	Southern 0-8-0 Locomotive "6535," TrainSounds, *07*		420
11122	UP Big Boy Locomotive "4024," CC, *06*		1700
11123	UP Big Boy Locomotive "4023," CC, *06*		1700
11126	UP Big Boy Locomotive "4012," CC, *06*		1700
11127	SP GS-4 4-8-4 Northern Locomotive "4436," CC, *07–09*		1200
11128	C&O F-19 4-6-2 Pacific Locomotive "490," CC, *07*		1160
11131	UP 4-8-4 FEF-3 Locomotive "844," black, CC, *08–09*		1160
11132	Reading 2-8-0 Consolidation Locomotive "1914," RailSounds, *08*		450
11133	NYC 2-8-0 Consolidation Locomotive "1149," RailSounds, *08*		450
11134	WM 2-8-0 Consolidation Locomotive "729," RailSounds, *08*		450
11135	B&O 2-8-0 Consolidation Locomotive "2784," RailSounds, *08*		450
11136	WP 2-8-2 Mikado Locomotive "322," CC, *08*		800
11137	UP 2-8-2 Mikado Locomotive "1925," CC, *08*		800
11138	ATSF 2-8-2 Mikado Locomotive "3156," CC, *08*		800
11139	MILW 2-8-2 Mikado Locomotive "462," CC, *08*		800
11140	Cass Scenic Shay Locomotive "7," CC, *07*		800
11141	Birch Valley Lumber Shay Locomotive "5," CC, *07*		800
11142	Hogwarts Express Add-on 2-pack, *09–10*		120
11143	SP AC-4 Cab Forward Locomotive "4100," CC, *08*		1670
11146	Pere Marquette 2-8-4 Berkshire Locomotive "1225," CC, *08*		1290
11147	PRR 4-8-2 Mib Locomotive "6750," CC, *08*		1290
11148	NYC Dreyfuss J-3a 4-6-4 Hudson Locomotive "5448," CC, *08*		1130
11149	LionMaster UP Big Boy 4-8-8-4 Locomotive "4006," CC, *08*		860
11150	NYC F-12e 4-6-0 10-wheel Locomotive "827," CC, *08*		700
11151	Polar Express Tender, RailSounds, *08–10*		440
11152	D&RGW LionMaster 4-6-6-4 Challenger Locomotive "3805," CC, *09*		900
11153	Stourbridge Lion Steam Locomotive, *09–10*		430

Exc Mint

11154	PRR CC2s 0-8-8-0 Mallet Locomotive "8183," CC, *09–10*	2000____
11155	ATSF 2-10-10-2 Mallet Locomotive "3000," CC, *09–10*	2500____
11156	C&O 4-6-0 Ten-Wheeler Locomotive, CC, *10*	740____
11157	WM Shay Locomotive "6," CC, *10*	800____
11162	Lone Ranger Add-on 3-pack, *10*	165____
11164	Dewitt Clinton Passenger Set, *10*	630____
11165	Dewitt Clinton Add-on Coach, *10*	70____
11166	CSX Merger Freight 2-pack #1, *10–11*	130____
11167	CSX Merger Freight 2-pack #2, *10–11*	105____
11168	CSX Merger Freight 2-pack #3, *10–11*	130____
11169	Strasburg Freight Add-on 2-pack, *10*	100____
11170	Three Rivers Fast Freight Set, *10–12*	400____
11172	Santa Fe 4-4-2 Steam Freight Set, *13*	200____
11173	Texan Freight Add-on 2-pack, *10–11*	130____
11174	Maple Leaf Freight Add-on 2-pack, *10–11*	110____
11175	Operation Eagle Justice Add-on 2-pack, *10–11*	125____
11180	Motor City Express Diesel Freight Train Set, CC, *12–13*	1150____
11181	CN GP9 Diesel Piggyback Train Set, CC, *12*	850____
11182	Dixie Special FT Diesel Freight Set, *11*	700____
11183	Lincoln Funeral Train, *13*	1140____
11194	Texas Special Diesel Passenger Set, CC, *13–14*	1110____
11195	PRR Diesel Passenger Set, CC, *13–14*	1110____
11199	UP NW2 Diesel Switcher Work Train Set, CC, *12*	600____
11200	UP LionMaster Challenger Locomotive "3985," CC, *10*	900____
11201	WM LionMaster Challenger Locomotive "1204," CC, *10*	900____
11202	CP 4-6-0 Ten-Wheeler Locomotive "914," CC, *10*	740____
11203	Pere Marquette Berkshire Locomotive "1225," CC, *09*	980____
11204	Pere Marquette Tender, RailSounds, *09*	440____
11207	PRR LionMaster T1 Duplex Locomotive "5511," CC, *10*	800____
11208	UP LionMaster Big Boy Locomotive "4011," CC, *10*	900____
11209	Vision NYC Hudson Locomotive "5344," CC, *10*	1600____
11210	UP Challenger Locomotive "3967," CC, *10*	1825____
11211	UP 4-6-6-4 Challenger Locomotive "3976," CC, *10*	1825____
11212	NKP Berkshire Locomotive "765," CC, *10*	1400____
11215	LV 4-6-0 Camelback Locomotive "1598," CC, *10*	550____
11216	Jersey Central 4-6-0 Camelback Locomotive, CC, *10*	550____
11217	PRR 4-6-0 Camelback Locomotive "822," CC, *10*	550____
11218	Vision NYC Hudson Locomotive "5331," CC, *10*	1600____
11219	Clinchfield Challenger Locomotive "672," CC, *10*	1825____
11220	UP Challenger Locomotive "3989," CC, *10*	1825____
11221	UP Challenger Locomotive "3983," CC, *10*	1825____
11224	PRR Atlantic Locomotive "460," CC, *10–11*	700____
11225	B&O Atlantic Locomotive "1440," CC	700____
11226	UP Water Tender, black, CC, *11*	300____

		Exc	Mint
___11227	UP Water Tender, gray, CC, *11*		300
___11228	Clinchfield Water Tender, CC, *11*		300
___11229	MILW 4-8-4 Northern Locomotive "261," CC, *11*		995
___11230	MILW 4-8-4 Northern Locomotive "267," CC, *11*		995
___11232	Reading Atlantic Locomotive "351," CC, *11*		700
11233	Pennsylvania Power & Light 2-Truck Shay Locomotive, CC, *11*		900
11234	Pennsylvania Power & Light 2-Truck Shay Locomotive, *11*		750
11235	West Side Lumber 2-Truck Shay Steam Locomotive, CC, *11*		900
11236	West Side Lumber 2-Truck Shay Steam Locomotive, *11*		750
___11237	Sugar Pine Lumber Shay Locomotive "4," CC, *11*		900
___11238	Sugar Pine Lumber Shay Locomotive "5," *11*		750
11239	Merrill & Ring Lumber 2-Truck Shay Steam Locomotive, CC, *11*		900
11240	Merrill & Ring Lumber 2-Truck Shay Steam Locomotive, *11*		750
11247	Erie USRA 0-8-0 Steam Switcher "121," CC, *11–12*		700
___11248	Erie USRA 0-8-0 Steam Switcher "127," *11–12*		550
11249	L&N USRA 0-8-0 Steam Switcher "2119," CC, *11–12*		700
___11250	L&N USRA 0-8-0 Steam Switcher "2121," *11–12*		550
11251	Pere Marquette USRA 0-8-0 Steam Switcher "1300," CC, *11–12*		700
11252	Pere Marquette USRA 0-8-0 Steam Switcher "1307," *11–12*		550
___11253	NH 0-8-0 Steam Switcher "3603," CC, *11–13*		700
___11254	NH 0-8-0 Steam Switcher "3606," *11–13*		550
11255	C&O 2-8-2 Mikado Steam Locomotive "1062," CC, *12*		900
11256	NH 2-8-2 Mikado Steam Locomotive "3021," CC, *12*		900
11257	PRR 2-8-2 Mikado Steam Locomotive "8631," CC, *12*		900
11258	Southern 2-8-2 Mikado Steam Locomotive "4501," CC, *12*		900
11259	UP 2-8-2 Mikado Steam Locomotive "2840," CC, *12*		900
11260	Rio Grande 2-8-2 Mikado Steam Locomotive "1207," CC, *12*		900
11261	DM&I 2-8-2 Mikado Steam Locomotive "1305," CC, *12*		900
11262	Erie 2-8-2 Mikado Steam Locomotive "3007," CC, *12*		900
11264	PRR K4 4-6-2 Pacific Steam Locomotive "1361," CC, *11*		900
11265	PRR K4 4-6-2 Pacific Steam Locomotive "1330," CC, *11*		900
11266	PRR K4 4-6-2 Pacific Steam Locomotive "1361," *11*		750
11268	Strasburg 2-6-0 Mogul Steam Locomotive "89," *11*		550
___11269	RI 2-6-0 Mogul Steam Locomotive "750," *11–13*		550

Exc Mint

		Exc	Mint
11270	GN 2-6-0 Mogul Steam Locomotive "453," *11*	550	____
11271	C&O 2-6-0 Mogul Steam Locomotive "49," *11–12*	550	____
11272	ATSF 2-6-0 Mogul Steam Locomotive "573," *11*	550	____
11273	Central Pacific 2-6-0 Mogul Steam Locomotive "1470," *11–13*	550	____
11274	MKT USRA 0-8-0 Steam Switcher "46," CC, *11–12*	700	____
11275	MKT 0-8-0 Steam Switcher "51," CC, *11*	550	____
11276	Lionelville & Western 0-8-0 Steam Switcher "1," CC, *11–13*	700	____
11277	Lionelville & Western 0-8-0 Steam Switcher "2," *11–13*	550	____
11278	WP 2-8-2 Mikado Steam Locomotive "322," CC, *11*	900	____
11279	WP 2-8-2 Mikado Steam Locomotive "327," *11*	750	____
11280	B&O 2-8-2 Mikado Steam Locomotive "4507," CC, *11*	900	____
11281	B&O 2-8-2 Mikado Steam Locomotive "451," *11*	750	____
11282	GN 2-8-2 Mikado Steam Locomotive "3125," CC, *11*	900	____
11284	MP 2-8-2 Mikado Steam Locomotive "1310," CC, *11*	900	____
11286	RI 2-8-2 Mikado Steam Locomotive "2302," CC, *11*	900	____
11287	RI 2-8-2 Mikado Steam Locomotive "2305," *11*	750	____
11288	T&P 2-8-2 Mikado Steam Locomotive "552," CC, *11*	900	____
11289	T&P 2-8-2 Mikado Steam Locomotive "557," *11*	750	____
11290	Bethlehem Steel 2-6-0 Mogul Steam Locomotive "28," *11*	550	____
11291	Weyerhaeuser 2-6-0 Mogul Locomotive "288," *11–13*	550	____
11295	Elk River Lumber 2-Truck Shay Locomotive "1," CC, *11*	900	____
11296	Elk River Lumber 2-Truck Shay Locomotive "2," *11*	750	____
11297	P. Bunyan Lumber 2-Truck Shay Locomotive "18," CC, *11*	900	____
11298	P. Bunyan Lumber 2-Truck Shay Locomotive "23," *11*	750	____
11299	C&O 2-6-6-2 Mallet Steam Locomotive "875," CC, *12*	1300	____
11300	PRR 2-10-4 Texas Steam Locomotive "6479," CC, *11*	1300	____
11301	PRR 2-10-4 Texas Steam Locomotive "6498," CC, *11*	1300	____
11303	C&O 2-10-4 Texas Steam Locomotive "3011," CC, *11*	1300	____
11304	C&O 2-10-4 Texas Steam Locomotive "3025," CC, *11*	1300	____
11306	NKP 2-10-4 Texas Steam Locomotive "801," CC, *11*	1300	____
11308	Erie 2-10-4 Texas Steam Locomotive "3405," CC, *11*	1300	____
11310	Pere Marquette 2-10-4 Texas Locomotive "1241," CC, *11*	1300	____

Exc Mint

		Exc	Mint
11312	MILW S3 4-8-4 Northern Steam Locomotive "265," CC, _11_		995
11315	Pennsylvania-Reading Seashore Atlantic Locomotive, _11_		550
11316	PRR 4-4-2 Atlantic Steam Locomotive "272," _11_		550
11317	Southern 4-4-2 Atlantic Steam Locomotive "1910," _11_		550
11318	CN 4-4-2 Atlantic Steam Locomotive "1630," _11_		550
11319	PRR K4 4-6-2 Pacific Locomotive "5409," _13_		900
11320	PRR K4 4-6-2 Pacific Locomotive, "5436," _13_		750
11321	C&O 2-6-6-2 Mallet Steam Locomotive "1525," CC, _12_		1300
11322	NKP 2-6-6-2 Mallet Steam Locomotive "943," CC, _12_		1300
11323	W&LE 2-6-6-2 Mallet Steam Locomotive "8002," CC, _12_		1300
11327	PRR Prewar K4 4-6-2 Pacific Locomotive "3667," CC, _11_		900
11328	PRR Prewar K4 4-6-2 Pacific Locomotive "3672," CC, _11_		900
11329	PRR Prewar K4 4-6-2 Pacific Locomotive "3678," _11_		750
11330	Polar K4 4-6-2 Pacific Locomotive, CC, _11–14_		900
11331	Polar K4 4-6-2 Pacific Locomotive, _11_		750
11332	ATSF 4-8-4 Northern Steam Locomotive "3751," CC, _12_		1300
11333	ATSF 4-8-4 Northern Steam Locomotive "3759," CC, _12_		1300
11334	Southern Crescent Limited 4-6-2 Pacific Locomotive, CC, _12_		1100
11335	Blue Comet 4-6-2 Pacific Steam Locomotive "832," CC, _12_		1100
11337	B&O 2-8-8-4 Steam Locomotive "7621," CC, _12_		1300
11338	Alton Limited 4-6-2 Pacific Steam Locomotive "657," CC, _12_		1100
11339	N&W 2-6-6-2 Mallet Steam Locomotive "1409," CC, _12_		1300
11340	B&O 2-8-8-4 Steam Locomotive "659," CC, _12_		1300
11341	Pilot 4-12-2 Locomotive, CC, _13_		1300
11342	UP 4-12-2 Steam Locomotive "9004," CC, _12–13_		1300
11343	UP 4-12-2 Steam Locomotive, black, "9000," CC, _12–13_		1300
11344	UP 4-12-2 Steam Locomotive, greyhound, "9000," CC, _12_		1300
11363	Cass Scenic RR 2-Truck Shay Steam Locomotive "3," CC, _12_		900
11364	Meadow River 2-Truck Shay Steam Locomotive "1," CC, _12–13_		900
11365	Weyerhaeuser 2-Truck Shay Steam Locomotive "3," CC, _12–13_		900
11366	Pickering Lumber 2-Truck Shay Locomotive "3," CC, _12–13_		900
11367	CP 2-Truck Shay Steam Locomotive "111," CC, _12–13_		900
11368	WM 2-Truck Shay Steam Locomotive "2," CC, _12_		900

		Exc	Mint
11369	Bethlehem Steel 2-Truck Shay Steam Locomotive "5," CC, *12–13*	900	___
11374	DM&I 2-8-8-4 Steam Locomotive "223," CC, *12*	1300	___
11375	WP 2-8-8-4 Steam Locomotive "258," CC, *12*	1300	___
11376	NP 2-8-8-4 Steam Locomotive "5000," CC, *12*	1300	___
11377	GN 2-8-8-4 Steam Locomotive "2060," CC, *12*	1300	___
11379	PRR 0-4-0 Shifter Steam Locomotive "112," *12*	450	___
11380	PRR 0-4-0 Shifter Steam Locomotive "94," *12*	450	___
11381	North Pole Central 0-4-0 Switcher (std O), *12*	450	___
11382	Transylvania 0-4-0 Shifter Steam Locomotive "13," *12*	450	___
11383	Bethlehem Steel 0-4-0 Shifter Steam Locomotive "134," *12*	450	___
11384	ATSF 0-4-0 Shifter Steam Locomotive "2301," *13*	450	___
11385	UP 0-4-0 Shifter Steam Locomotive "206," *13*	450	___
11386	B&M 2-8-4 Berkshire Steam Locomotive "4018," CC, *12–13*	1250	___
11387	ATSF 2-8-4 Berkshire Steam Locomotive "4199," CC, *12–13*	1250	___
11388	SP 2-8-4 Berkshire Steam Locomotive "3505," CC, *12–13*	1250	___
11389	B&A 2-8-4 Berkshire Steam Locomotive "1404," CC, *12–13*	1250	___
11390	Lima Demonstrator 2-8-4 Berkshire Locomotive "1," CC, *12–13*	1250	___
11391	IC 2-8-4 Berkshire Steam Locomotive "7020," CC, *12–13*	1250	___
11392	Michigan Central 2-8-4 Berkshire Locomotive "1420," CC, *12–13*	1250	___
11399	UP H7 Class 2-8-8-2 Steam Locomotive "3595," CC, *13–14*	1350	___
11400	C&O H7 Class 2-8-8-2 Steam Locomotive "1578," CC, *13–14*	1350	___
11401	Pilot H7 Class 2-8-8-2 Locomotive, CC, *14–15*	1350	___
11402	Virginian USRA Y3 2-8-8-2 Locomotive, CC, *13–14*	1350	___
11403	Pilot USRA 2-8-8-2 Locomotive, CC, *13–15*	1350	___
11404	ATSF USRA Y3 2-8-8-2 Locomotive, CC, *13–14*	1350	___
11405	N&W USRA Y3 2-8-8-2 Locomotive, CC, *13–14*	1350	___
11410	Pilot 4-8-2 Mohawk Locomotive, CC, *13–15*	1300	___
11411	NYC 4-8-2 Mohawk Locomotive "2854," CC, *12–13*	1300	___
11412	NYC 4-8-2 Mohawk Locomotive "2867," CC, *12–13*	1300	___
11413	Pilot 4-8-4 J-Class Locomotive, CC, *13–15*	1300	___
11414	N&W 4-8-4 Steam Locomotive "612," CC, *12–13*	1300	___
11415	Pilot S2 6-8-6 Turbine Locomotive, CC, *14–15*	1300	___
11416	PRR S2 6-8-6 Steam Turbine Locomotive "6200," CC, *12–14*	1300	___
11417	PRR S2 6-8-6 Steam Turbine Locomotive "6200," CC, *12–13*	1300	___
11418	Pilot GS-6 Locomotive, CC, *13–14*	1300	___
11419	SP 4-8-4 GS-2 Locomotive, black, CC, *12–13*	1300	___
11420	SP 4-8-4 GS-2 Locomotive, Daylight, CC, *12*	1300	___
11421	SP 4-8-4 GS-6 Locomotive, black, CC, *12*	1300	___

			Exc	Mint
____	11422	WP 4-8-4 GS-64 Locomotive "482," CC, 12		1300
____	11423	CNJ Blue Comet Locomotive "833," CC, 12–13		1100
____	11425	Alaska 0-4-0 Locomotive, RailSounds, 12–13		1100
____	11426	Rio Grande 0-4-0 Locomotive, RailSounds, 12–13		450
____	11427	SP 0-4-0 Locomotive "14," RailSounds, 12–13		450
____	11428	MILW 0-4-0 Locomotive, RailSounds, 12–13		450
____	11429	Southern 0-4-0 Locomotive, RailSounds, 12–13		450
____	11430	GN 0-4-0 Locomotive "1066," RailSounds, 12–13		450
____	11431	N&W 4-8-4 Locomotive "611," CC, 12		1300
____	11432	LL S2 6-8-6 Steam Turbine Locomotive, CC, 13–14		1300
____	11433	PRR S2 6-8-6 Steam Turbine Locomotive CC, 13–14		1300
____	11434	UP Big Boy Locomotive "4006," CC, 14		2700
____	11435	UP Big Boy Locomotive "4018," CC, 14		2700
____	11436	UP Big Boy Locomotive "4005," CC, 14		2700
____	11437	UP Big Boy Locomotive "4014," CC, 14		2700
____	11438	UP Big Boy Locomotive "4017," CC, 14		2700
____	11446	UP USRA Y3 2-8-8-2 Locomotive "3671," CC, 13–14		1350
____	11447	PRR USRA Y3 2-8-8-2 Locomotive "376," CC, 13–14		1350
____	11448	UP Big Boy Locomotive "4012," CC, 14		2700
____	11449	UP Big Boy Locomotive "4004," CC, 14		2700
____	11450	Polar Express Berkshire Scale Locomotive, gold, CC, 14		1500
____	11451	Polar Express Berkshire Scale Locomotive, black, CC, 14		1500
____	11452	C&O 2-8-4 Berkshire Locomotive "2687," CC, 14		1500
____	11453	Erie 2-8-4 Berkshire Locomotive "3321," CC, 14		1500
____	11454	NKP 2-8-4 Berkshire Locomotive "765," CC, 14		1500
____	11455	Pere Marquette 2-8-4 Berkshire Locomotive "1225," CC, 14		1500
____	11456	Pere Marquette 2-8-4 Berkshire Locomotive "1227," CC, 14		1500
____	11462	SP AC-12 Cab-Forward Locomotive "4291," CC, 14		1700
____	11463	SP AC-12 Cab-Forward Locomotive "4286," CC, 14		1700
____	11464	SP AC-12 Cab-Forward Locomotive "4294," CC, 14		1700
____	11465	SP AC-12 Cab-Forward Locomotive "4275," CC, 14		1700
____	11469	Pilot AC-12 Cab-Forward Locomotive, CC, 14–15		1700
____	11528	Frosty the Snowman Figure Pack, 14, 16		30
____	11650	Alderney Dairy General American Milk Car 2-pack (std O), 07		130
____	11651	Freeport General American Milk Car 2-pack (std O), 07		130
____	11652	BNSF Mechanical Reefer 2-pack (std O), 07–09		140
____	11653	SPFE Mechanical Reefer 2-pack (std O), 07		140
____	11654	UPFE Mechanical Reefer 2-pack (std O), 07		140
____	11655	GN WFE Mechanical Reefer 2-pack (std O), 07		140
____	11657	PFE Wood-sided Reefer 3-pack (std O), 06		190
____	11658	John Bull Add-on Coach, 08		80

		Exc	Mint	
11700	Conrail Limited Set, *87*	320	370	___
11701	Rail Blazer Set, *87–88*		60	___
11702	Black Diamond Set, *87*	195	265	___
11703	Iron Horse Freight Set, *88–91*	100	105	___
11704	Southern Freight Runner Set (SSS), *87*	210	285	___
11705	Chessie System Unit Train, *88*	360	450	___
11706	Dry Gulch Line Set (SSS), *88*	190	260	___
11707	Silver Spike Set, *88–89*	175	245	___
11708	Midnight Shift Set, *88 u, 89*	60	75	___
11710	CP Rail Freight Set, *89*	375	447	___
11711	Santa Fe F3 Diesel ABA Set, *91*	480	590	___
11712	Great Lakes Express Set (SSS), *90*	260	280	___
11713	Santa Fe Dash 8-40B Set, *90*	395	480	___
11714	Badlands Express Set, *90–91*	49	60	___
11715	Lionel 90th Anniversary Set, *90*	339	361	___
11716	Lionelville Circus Special Set, *90–91*	155	190	___
11717	CSX Freight Set, *90*	230	240	___
11718	Norfolk Southern Dash 8-40C Unit Train, *92*	445	481	___
11719	Coastal Freight Set (SSS), *91*	165	215	___
11720	Santa Fe Special Set, *91*	49	60	___
11721	Mickey's World Tour Train Set, *91, 92 u*	118	158	___
11722	Girls Train Set, *91*	547	817	___
11723	Amtrak Maintenance Train, *91, 92 u*	210	245	___
11724	GN F3 Diesel ABA Set, *92*	730	840	___
11726	Erie-Lackawanna Freight Set, *91 u*	225	275	___
11727	Coastal Limited Set, *92*	90	110	___
11728	High Plains Runner Set, *92*	120	130	___
11733	Feather River Set (SSS), *92*	285	330	___
11734	Erie Alco Diesel ABA Set (FF 7), *93*	250	305	___
11735	NYC Flyer Freight Set "1735WS," *93–99*	125	160	___
11736	Union Pacific Express Set, *93–95*	110	130	___
11738	Soo Line Set (SSS), *93*	250	280	___
11739	Super Chief Set, *93–94*	135	155	___
11740	Conrail Consolidated Set, *93*	200	240	___
11741	Northwest Express Set, *93*	130	155	___
11742	Coastal Limited Set, *93 u*	90	115	___
11743	Chesapeake & Ohio Freight Set, *94*	240	280	___
11744	NYC Passenger/Freight Set (SSS), *94*	295	335	___
11745	U.S. Navy Set, *94–95*	253	295	___
11746	Seaboard Freight Set, *94, 95 u*	90	115	___
11747	Lionel Lines Steam Set, *95*	310	340	___
11748	Amtrak Alco Diesel Passenger Set, *95–96*	130	185	___
11749	Western Maryland Set (SSS), *95*	275	300	___
11750	McDonald's Nickel Plate Special Set, *87 u*	143	153	___
11751	Sears PRR Passenger Set, *87 u*	120	155	___
11752	JCPenney Timber Master Set, *87 u*	75	115	___
11753	Kay Bee Toys Rail Blazer Set, *87 u*	80	100	___
11754	Key America Set, *87 u*	150	165	___
11755	Timber Master Set, *87 u*	150	165	___
11756	Hawthorne Freight Flyer Set, *87–88 u*	65	85	___
11757	Chrysler Mopar Express Set, *88 u*	318	366	___
11758	Desert King Set (SSS), *89*	195	250	___

		Exc	Mint
____11759	JCPenney Silver Spike Set, *88 u*	175	250
____11761	JCPenney Iron Horse Freight Set, *88 u*	120	125
____11762	True Value Cannonball Express Set, *89 u*	95	145
____11763	United Model Freight Hauler Set, *88 u*	135	145
____11764	Sears Iron Horse Freight Set, *88 u*	155	190
____11765	Spiegel Silver Spike Set, *88 u*	175	250
____11767	Shoprite Freight Flyer Set, *88 u*	80	125
____11769	JCPenney Midnight Shift Set, *89 u*	100	175
____11770	Sears Circus Set, *89 u*	185	220
____11771	K-Mart Microracers Set, *89 u*	80	110
____11772	Macy's Freight Flyer Set, *89 u*	170	220
____11773	Sears NYC Passenger Set, *89 u*	175	200
____11774	Ace Hardware Cannonball Express Set, *89 u*	145	175
____11775	Anheuser-Busch Set, *89–92 u*	247	343
____11776	Pace Iron Horse Freight Set, *89 u*	115	135
____11777	Sears Lionelville Circus Set, *90 u*	175	190
____11778	Sears Badlands Express Set, *90 u*	49	60
____11779	Sears CSX Freight Set, *90 u*	190	230
____11780	Sears NP Passenger Set, *90 u*	155	190
____11781	True Value Cannonball Express Set, *90 u*	75	115
____11783	Toys "R" Us Heavy Iron Set, *90–91 u*	135	160
____11784	Pace Iron Horse Freight Set, *90 u*	115	135
____11785	Costco Union Pacific Express Set, *90 u*	200	230
____11789	Sears Illinois Central Passenger Set, *91 u*	170	200
____11793	Santa Fe Set, *91 u*	49	60
____11794	Mickey's World Tour Set, *91 u*	80	100
____11796	Union Pacific Express Set, *91 u*	150	160
____11797	Sears Coastal Limited Set, *92 u*	80	100
11800	Toys "R" Us Heavy Iron Thunder Limited Set, *92–93 u*	235	295
____11803	Nickel Plate Special Set, *92 u*	135	145
____11804	K-Mart Coastal Limited Set, *92 u*	80	100
____11809	Village Trolley Set, *95–97*	55	85
____11810	Budweiser Modern Era Set, *93–94 u*	206	215
____11811	United Auto Workers Set, *93 u*	189	447
____11812	Coastal Limited Special Set, *93 u*	95	115
____11813	Crayola Activity Train Set, *94 u, 95*	112	128
____11814	Ford Limited Edition Set, *94 u*	212	257
____11818	Chrysler Mopar Set, *94 u*	227	264
____11819	Georgia Power Set, *95 u*	517	542
____11820	Red Wing Shoes NYC Flyer Set, *95 u*	258	313
____11821	Sears Zenith Set, *95 u*		775
____11822	Chevrolet Set, *96 u*	277	322
____11825	Bloomingdale's Set, *96 u*		318
____11826	Sears Freight Set, *95–96 u*		762
____11827	Zenith Employees Set, *96 u*		800
____11828	NJ Transit Passenger Set, *96 u*		180
____11833	NJ Transit GP38 Diesel Passenger Set, *97*	275	300
____11837	Union Pacific GP9 Diesel Set, *97*		520
____11838	ATSF Warhorse Hudson Freight Set, *97*		810
____11839	SP&S 4-6-2 Steam Freight Set, *97*		280
____11841	Bloomingdale's Set, *97 u*		297

		Exc	Mint
11843	Boston & Maine GP9 Diesel ABA Set, *98*		510____
11844	Union Pacific Die-cast Ore Cars 4-pack, *98*		225____
11846	Kal Kan Pet Care Train Set, *97 u*		796____
11849	Lionel Centennial Series Reefer 4-pack, *98*		115____
11850	Rice A Roni Trolley Set, *02 u*		265____
11851	PFE Reefer 6-pack (std O), *02*	225	255____
11852	Clinchfield PS-2 2-bay Hopper, *04*		70____
11853	B&M PS-2 2-bay Hopper 2-pack, *05*		128____
11854	N&W PS-2 Covered Hopper 2-pack, *04*		70____
11855	GN Offset Hopper with coal, 2-pack, *05*		120____
11856	Green Bay & Western Offset Hopper 2-pack, *05*		120____
11857	Baltimore & Ohio Offset Hopper 2-pack, *05*		120____
11858	PRR PS-4 Flatcar with trailers, 2-pack (std O), *05*		160____
11859	GN PS-4 Flatcar with trailers (std O), *05*		160____
11860	SP PS-4 Flatcar with trailers (std O), *05*		160____
11861	C&O PS-4 Flatcar with trailers (std O), *05*		160____
11863	Southern Pacific GP9 Diesel "2383," *98*		225____
11864	New York Central GP9 Diesel "2383," *98*		275____
11865	Alaska GP7 Diesel "1802," *98–99*		90____
11866	Govt. of Canada Cylindrical Hopper 2-pack (std O), *05*		120____
11867	CN Cylindrical Hopper 2-pack (std O), *05*		120____
11868	BN Husky Stack Car 2-pack (std O), *05*		160____
11869	SP Husky Stack Car 2-pack (std O), *05*		160____
11870	CSX Husky Stack Car 2-pack (std O), *05*		220____
11871	TTX Trailer Train Stack Car 2-pack (std O), *05*		160____
11872	PFE Orange Steel-sided Reefer 3-pack (std O), *05*		130____
11873	C&O Offset Hopper 3-pack (std O), *05*		130____
11874	PFE Orange Steel-sided Reefer 3-pack (std O), *05*		130____
11875	NP Steel-sided Reefer 3-pack (std O), *05*		130____
11876	PFE Silver Steel-sided Reefer 3-pack (std O), *05*		130____
11877	C&NW Steel-sided Reefer 3-pack (std O), *05*		130____
11878	Santa Fe PS-2 2-bay Covered Hopper 3-pack (std O), *06*		125____
11879	MKT PS-2 2-bay Covered Hopper 3-pack (std O), *06*		125____
11880	Boraxo PS-2 2-bay Covered Hopper 3-pack (std O), *06*		125____
11881	PRR PS-2 2-bay Covered Hopper 3-pack (std O), *06*		125____
11882	RI Offset Hopper with gravel, 3-pack (std O), *06*		125____
11883	CNJ Offset Hopper 3-pack (std O), *06*		145____
11884	Maine Central Offset Hopper 3-pack (std O), *06*		145____
11891	Pennsylvania 3-bay Hopper 3-pack (std O), *06*		155____
11892	Conrail ACF 3-bay Hopper 3-pack (std O), *06*		155____
11893	N&W 3-bay Hopper 3-pack (std O), *06*		155____
11894	UP 3-bay Hopper 3-pack (std O), *06*		155____
11895	GN Steel-sided Reefer 3-pack (std O), *06*		145____
11896	Santa Fe Steel-sided Reefer 3-pack (std O), *06*		145____
11897	Pepper Packing Steel-sided Reefer 3-pack (std O), *06*		145____
11900	SF Steam Freight Set, *96–01*		130____
11903	ACL F3 Diesel ABA Set, *96*		716____

		Exc	Mint
____11905	U.S. Coast Guard Set, *96*	160	180
____11906	Factory Selection Special Set, *95 u*		85
____11909	N&W J 4-8-4 Warhorse Set, *96*	560	720
____11910	Lionel Lines Set (027), *96*	140	160
____11912	"57" Switcher Service Exclusive, *96*		310
____11913	SP GP9 Diesel Freight Set, *97*		440
____11914	NYC GP9 Diesel Freight Set, *97*		370
11918	Conrail SD20 Service Exclusive "X1144" (SSS), *97*		255
____11919	Docksider Set, *97*		70
____11920	Port of Lionel City Dive Team Set, *97*		185
____11921	Lionel Lines Freight Set, *97*		130
____11929	ATSF Warbonnet Passenger Set, *97–99*		132
____11930	ATSF Warbonnet Passenger Car 2-pack, *97–99*		80
____11931	Chessie Flyer Freight Set "1931S," *97–99*		165
____11933	Dodge Motorsports Freight Set, *96 u*		290
____11934	Virginian Electric Locomotive Freight Set, *97–99*		260
____11935	NYC Flyer Freight Set, *97*		155
____11936	Little League Baseball Steam Set, *97*	225	291
____11939	SP&S 4-6-2 Steam Freight Set, *97*		220
____11940	Southern Pacific SD40 Warhorse Coal Set, *98*		600
____11944	Lionel Lines 4-4-2 Steam Freight Set, *98*		175
____11956	UP GP9 Diesel Set, *97*	325	375
____11957	Mobil Oil Steam Special Set, *97*		408
____11971	D&H 4-4-2 Steam Freight Set, *98*	125	155
____11972	Alaska GP7 Diesel Set, *98–99*	180	215
____11974	Station Accessory Set, *98*		22
____11975	Freight Accessory Pack, *98*		23
____11977	NP Freight Cars 4-pack, *98*		170
____11979	N&W 4-4-2 Steam Freight Set, *98*		75
____11981	1998 Holiday Trolley Set, *98*		75
____11982	New Jersey Transit Ore Car Set, *98*		250
____11983	Farmrail Agricultural Set, *99*		455
____11984	Corvette GP7 Diesel Set, *99*		451
11988	NYC Firecar "18444" and Instruction Car "19853," *99*		210
____12000	NY Yankees Berkshire Passenger Set, *13*		380
____12004	Philadelphia Phillies Berkshire Passenger Set, *13*		380
____12008	Boston Red Sox Berkshire Passenger Set, *13*		380
____12012	Chicago Cubs Berkshire Passenger Set, *13*		380
____12013	NY Mets and Yankees Subway Series Set, *13*		400
____12014	10" Straight Track (FasTrack), *03–16*		5
____12015	O36 Curved Track (FasTrack), *03–16*		4
____12016	10" Terminal Track (FasTrack), *03–14, 16*		6
____12017	O36 Manual Switch, left hand (FasTrack), *03–16*		50
____12018	O36 Manual Switch, right hand (FasTrack), *03–16*		50
____12019	90-degree Crossover (FasTrack), *03–16*		26
____12020	5" Uncoupling Track (FasTrack), *03–16*		42
____12022	O36 Half Curved Track (FasTrack), *03–14, 16*		5
____12023	O36 Quarter Curved Track (FasTrack), *03–14, 16*		5
____12024	5" Straight Track (FasTrack), *03–16*		5
____12025	4" Straight Track (FasTrack), *03–14, 16*		5
____12026	1" Straight Track (FasTrack), *03–14, 16*		5

Exc Mint

		Exc	Mint
12027	10" Insulated Track (FasTrack), *03–14, 16*		5____
12028	Inner Passing Loop Track Pack (FasTrack), *03–16*		115____
12029	Accessory Activator Pack (FasTrack), *03–16*		21____
12030	Figure 8 Track Pack (FasTrack), *03–16*		75____
12031	Outer Passing Loop Track Pack (FasTrack), *03–16*		145____
12032	10" Straight Track 4-pack (FasTrack), *03–16*		22____
12033	O36 Curved Track, card of 4 (FasTrack), *03–16*		22____
12035	FasTrack Lighted Bumper 2-pack, *05–16*		33____
12036	Grade Crossing (FasTrack), *05–16*		14____
12037	Graduated Trestle Set (FasTrack), *05–16*		85____
12038	Elevated Trestle Set (FasTrack), *05–16*		45____
12039	Railer (FasTrack), *04–16*		9____
12040	O Gauge Transition Piece (FasTrack), *04–14, 16*		9____
12041	O72 Curved Track (FasTrack), *04–14, 16*		7____
12042	30" Straight Track (FasTrack), *04–14, 16*		15____
12043	O48 Curved Track (FasTrack), *04–14, 16*		5____
12044	Siding Track Add-on Track Pack (FasTrack), *04–16*		120____
12045	O36 Remote Switch, left hand (FasTrack), *04–16*		95____
12046	O36 Remote Switch, right hand (FasTrack), *04–16*		95____
12047	O72 Wye Remote Switch (FasTrack), *04–14*		97____
12048	O72 Remote Switch, left hand (FasTrack), *04–14*		104____
12049	O72 Remote Switch, right hand (FasTrack), *04–14*		104____
12050	22 1/2-degree Crossover (FasTrack), *04–14, 16*		46____
12051	45-degree Crossover (FasTrack), *04–14, 16*		24____
12052	Grade Crossing with flashers (FasTrack), *05–16*		100____
12053	Accessory Power Wire (FasTrack), *04–16*		6____
12054	Operating Track with half straight (FasTrack), *05–16*		45____
12055	O72 Half Curved Track (FasTrack), *04–14, 16*		6____
12056	O60 Curved Track (FasTrack), *05–14, 16*		7____
12057	O60 Remote Switch, left hand, *05–14*		104____
12058	O60 Remote Switch, right hand (FasTrack), *05–14*		104____
12059	Earthen Bumper (FasTrack), *04–16*		9____
12060	Block Section (FasTrack), *05–14, 16*		9____
12061	O84 Curved Track (FasTrack), *05–14, 16*		7____
12062	Grade Crossing with gates and flashers (FasTrack), *06–14*		160____
12065	O48 Remote Switch, left hand (FasTrack), *07–14*		104____
12066	O48 Remote Switch, right hand (FasTrack), *07–14*		104____
12073	1⅜" Track Section (FasTrack), *07–14, 16*		5____
12074	1⅜" Track Section, no roadbed (FasTrack), *07–14, 16*		5____
12080	42" Path Remote Switch, right hand, *07–12*		80____
12081	42" Path Remote Switch, left hand, *07–12*		80____
12700	Erie Magnetic Gantry Crane, *87*	125	150____
12701	Operating Fueling Station, *87*	60	74____
12702	Control Tower, *87*	60	75____
12703	Icing Station, *88–89*	60	65____
12704	Dwarf Signal, *88–93*	9	11____

Exc Mint

		Exc	Mint
____12705	Lumber Shed Kit, *88–99*		9
____12706	Barrel Loader Building Kit, *87–99*		10
____12707	Billboards, set of 3, *87–99*		5
____12708	Street Lamps, set of 3, *88–93*	6	9
____12709	Banjo Signal, *87–91, 95–00*		29
____12710	Engine House Kit, *87–91*	21	25
____12711	Water Tower Kit, *87–99*		13
____12712	Automatic Ore Loader, *87–88*	17	21
____12713	Automatic Gateman, *87–88, 94–00*	30	40
____12714	Crossing Gate, *87–91, 93–16*		50
____12715	Illuminated Bumpers, set of 2, *87–15*		13
____12716	Searchlight Tower, *87–89, 91–92*	15	22
____12717	Nonilluminated Bumpers, set of 3, *87–16*		7
____12718	Barrel Shed Kit, *87–99*		10
____12719	Animated Refreshment Stand, *88–89*	65	70
____12720	Rotary Beacon, *88–89*	40	45
____12721	Illuminated Extension Bridge, rock piers, *89*	26	38
____12722	Roadside Diner, smoke, *88–89*	27	38
____12723	Microwave Tower, *88–91, 94–95*	14	19
____12724	Double Signal Bridge, *88–90*	39	50
____12725	Lionel Tractor and Trailer, *88–89*	10	18
____12726	Grain Elevator Kit, *88–91, 94–99*		36
____12727	Operating Semaphore, *89–99*		26
____12728	Illuminated Freight Station, *89*	29	38
____12729	Mail Pickup Set, *88–91, 95*	12	16
____12730	Girder Bridge, *88–03, 08–16*		21
____12731	Station Platform, *88–00*		8
____12732	Coal Bag, *88–16*		7
____12733	Watchman Shanty Kit, *88–99*		5
____12734	Passenger/Freight Station, *89–99*		18
____12735	Diesel Horn Shed, *88–91*	19	24
____12736	Coaling Station Kit, *88–91*	21	31
____12737	Whistling Freight Shed, *88–99*		28
____12739	Lionel Gas Company Tractor and Tanker, *89*	20	25
12740 ____	Genuine Wood Logs, set of 3, *88–92, 94–95, 97–99*		5
____12741	Union Pacific Intermodal Crane, *89*	165	185
____12742	Gooseneck Lamps, set of 2, *89–00*		21
____12743	Track Clips, dozen (O), *89–16*		12
____12744	Rock Piers, set of 2, *89–92, 94–05, 08, 11–15*		15
____12745	Barrel Pack, set of 6, *89–16*		8
____12746	Operating/Uncoupling Track (O27), *89–16*		10
____12748	Illuminated Passenger Platform, *89–99*		18
____12749	Rotary Radar Antenna, *89–92, 95*	28	38
____12750	Crane Kit, *89–91*	8	10
____12751	Shovel Kit, *89–91*	8	10
____12752	History of Lionel Trains Video, *89–92, 94*	19	21
____12753	Ore Load, set of 2, *89–91, 95*	1	2
____12754	Graduated Trestle Set, 22 pieces, *89–15*		27
____12755	Elevated Trestle Set, 10 pieces, *89–15*		27
____12756	The Making of the Scale Hudson Video, *91–94*	20	22
____12759	Floodlight Tower, *90–00*		25

		Exc	Mint
12760	Automatic Highway Flasher, *90–91*	23	27____
12761	Animated Billboard, *90–91, 93, 95*	12	23____
12763	Single Signal Bridge, *90–91, 93*	31	35____
12767	Steam Clean and Wheel Grind Shop, *92–93, 95*	240	290____
12768	Burning Switch Tower, *90, 93*	85	90____
12770	Arch-Under Bridge, *90–03, 08–16*		30____
12771	Mom's Roadside Diner, smoke, *90–91*	34	50____
12772	Truss Bridge, flasher and piers, *90–16*		70____
12773	Freight Platform Kit, *90–98*		32____
12774	Lumber Loader Kit, *90–99*		19____
12777	Chevron Tractor and Tanker, *90–91*	9	15____
12778	Conrail Tractor and Trailer, *90*	9	16____
12779	Lionelville Grain Company Tractor and Trailer, *90*	11	19____
12780	RS-1 50-watt Transformer, *90–93*	95	130____
12781	N&W Intermodal Crane, *90–91*	145	160____
12782	Lift Bridge, *91–92*	428	518____
12783	Monon Tractor and Trailer, *91*	11	19____
12784	Intermodal Containers, set of 3, *91*	12	17____
12785	Lionel Gravel Company Tractor and Trailer, *91*	9	15____
12786	Lionel Steel Company Tractor and Trailer, *91*	10	16____
12791	Animated Passenger Station, *91*	45	60____
12794	Lionel Tractor, *91*	7	13____
12795	Cable Reels, pair, *91–98*	3	5____
12798	Forklift Loader Station, *92–95*	33	44____
12800	Scale Hudson Replacement Pilot Truck, *91 u*	13	17____
12802	Chat & Chew Roadside Diner, smoke and lights, *92–95*	41	50____
12804	Highway Lights, set of 4, *92–99, 02–04, 13–16*	9	27____
12805	Intermodal Containers, set of 3, *92*	10	14____
12806	Lionel Lumber Company Tractor and Trailer, *92*	10	15____
12807	Little Caesars Tractor and Trailer, *92*	9	14____
12808	Mobil Tractor and Tanker, *92*	8	13____
12809	Animated Billboard, *92–93*	12	22____
12810	American Flyer Tractor and Trailer, *94*	12	18____
12811	Alka Seltzer Tractor and Trailer, *92*	11	19____
12812	Illuminated Freight Station, *93–00*		27____
12818	Animated Freight Station, *92, 94–95*	50	60____
12819	Inland Steel Tractor and Trailer, *92*	9	16____
12821	Lionel Catalog Video, *92*	13	17____
12826	Intermodal Containers, set of 3, *93*	10	16____
12831	Rotary Beacon, *93–95*	22	32____
12832	Block Target Signal, *93–98*		25____
12833	RoadRailer Tractor and Trailer, *93*	9	15____
12834	Pennsylvania Magnetic Gantry Crane, *93*	130	170____
12835	Operating Fueling Station, *93*	55	60____
12836	Santa Fe Quantum Tractor and Trailer, *93*	8	14____
12837	Humble Oil Tractor and Tanker, *93*	9	16____
12838	Crate Load, set of 2, *93–97*		3____
12839	Grade Crossings, set of 2, *93–16*		7____
12840	Insulated Straight Track (O), *93–16*		8____
12841	Insulated Straight Track (O27), *93–16*		5____
12842	Dunkin' Donuts Tractor and Trailer, *92 u*	13	25____

		Exc	Mint
____12843	Die-cast Sprung Trucks, pair, *93–99*		10
____12844	Coil Covers, pair (O), *93–98*		3
____12847	Animated Ice Depot, *94–99*		65
____12848	Lionel Oil Company Derrick, *94*	55	75
____12849	Lionel Controller with wall pack, *94, 95 u*		NRS
____12852	Die-cast Intermodal Trailer Frame, *94–01*		6
____12853	Coil Covers, pair (std O), *94–98*		7
____12854	U.S. Navy Tractor and Tanker, *94–95*		33
____12855	Intermodal Containers, set of 3, *94–95*	9	13
____12860	Lionel Visitor's Center Tractor and Trailer, *94 u*	10	14
____12861	Lionel Leasing Company Tractor, *94*	8	13
____12862	Oil Drum Loader, *94–95*	75	85
____12864	Little Caesars Tractor and Trailer, *94*	8	14
____12865	Wisk Tractor and Trailer, *94*	12	55
____12866	TMCC 135-watt PowerHouse Power Supply, *94 u, 95–03*		46
12867	TMCC 135 PowerMaster Power Distribution Center, *94 u, 95–04*		49
____12868	TMCC CAB-1 Remote Controller, *94 u, 95–09*		115
____12869	Marathon Oil Tractor and Tanker, *94*	15	22
____12873	Operating Sawmill, *95–97*		70
____12874	Classic Street Lamps, set of 3, *94–00*		13
____12877	Operating Fueling Station, *95*	75	85
____12878	Control Tower, *95*	49	60
____12881	Chrysler Mopar Tractor and Trailer, *94 u*	41	52
____12882	Lighted Billboard, *95*	9	14
____12883	Dwarf Signal, *95–16*		27
____12884	Truck Loading Dock Kit, *95–98*		16
____12885	40-watt Control System, *94 u, 95–05*		35
____12886	Floodlight Tower, *95–98*		31
____12888	Railroad Crossing Flasher, *95–16*		56
____12889	Operating Windmill, *95–98*		34
____12890	Big Red Control Button, *94 u, 95–00*		43
____12891	Lionel Refrigerator Lines Tractor and Trailer, *95*	12	16
____12892	Automatic Flagman, *92–98*		25
12893	TMCC PowerMaster Power Adapter Cable, *94 u, 95–13, 16*		20
____12894	Signal Bridge, *95–01*		22
____12895	Double-track Signal Bridge, *95–00*		44
____12896	Tunnel Portals, pair, *95–16*		20
____12897	Engine House Kit, *96–98*		29
____12898	Flagpole, *95–97*		9
____12899	Searchlight Tower, *95–98*	10	25
____12900	Crane Kit, *95–98*		8
____12901	Shovel Kit, *95–98*		7
____12902	Marathon Oil Derrick, *94 u, 95*	103	156
____12903	Diesel Horn Shed, *95–98*		29
____12904	Coaling Station Kit, *95–98*		19
____12905	Factory Kit, *95–98*		20
____12906	Maintenance Shed Kit, *95–98*		20
____12907	Intermodal Containers, set of 3, *95*	9	14
____12911	TMCC Command Base, *95–09*		80
____12912	Oil Pumping Station, *95–98*	38	65

Exc Mint

		Exc	Mint
12914	SC-1 Switch and Accessory Controller, *95–98*		35____
12915	Log Loader, *96*		115____
12916	Water Tower, *96–97*		56____
12917	Animated Switch Tower, *96–98*		29____
12922	NYC Operating Gantry Crane, coil covers, *96*	75	90____
12923	Red Wing Shoes Tractor and Trailer, *95 u*	34	38____
12925	42" Diameter Curved Track Section (O), *96–16*		4____
12926	Globe Street Lamps, set of 3, *96–03, 08–09, 16*		25____
12927	Yard Light, set of 3, *96–16*		27____
12929	Rail-truck Loading Dock, *96*		44____
12930	Lionelville Oil Company Derrick, *95 u, 96*	55	75____
12931	Electrical Substation, *96*		22____
12932	Laimbeer Packaging Tractor and Trailer Set, *96*		14____
12933	GM Parts Tractor and Trailer, *95*		NRS____
12935	Zenith Tractor and Trailer, *96*		24____
12936	SP Intermodal Crane, *97*		195____
12937	NS Intermodal Crane, *97*		200____
12938	PowerStation Controller and PowerHouse 135-watt Power Supply, *97–00*		150____
12943	Illuminated Station Platform, *97–00*		24____
12944	Sunoco Oil Derrick, *97*		85____
12945	Sunoco Pumping Oil Station, *97*		80____
12948	Bascule Bridge, *97*		315____
12949	Billboards, set of 3, *97–00*		7____
12951	Airplane Hangar Kit, *97–98*		29____
12952	Big L Diner Kit, *97*		24____
12953	Linex Gas Tall Oil Tank, *97*		9____
12954	Linex Gas Wide Oil Tank, *97*		10____
12955	Road Runner and Wile E. Coyote Ambush Shack, *97*		93____
12958	Industrial Water Tower, *97–98*		50____
12960	Rotary Radar Antenna, *97*		26____
12961	Newsstand with diesel horn, *97*		30____
12962	LL Passenger Service Train Whistle, *97–99*		30____
12964	Donald Duck Radar Antenna, *97*		64____
12965	Goofy Rotary Beacon, *97*		52____
12966	Rotary Aircraft Beacon, *97–00*		35____
12968	Girder Bridge Building Kit, *97*		22____
12969	TMCC Command Set, *97–09*		148____
12974	Blinking Light Billboard, *97–00*		15____
12975	Steiner Victorian Building Kit, *97–98*		33____
12976	Dobson Victorian Building Kit, *97–98*		24____
12977	Kindler Victorian Building Kit, *97–98*		35____
12982	Culvert Loader, conventional, *98–00*		190____
12983	Culvert Unloader, conventional, *99*		185____
12987	Intermodal Containers, set of 3, *98*		15____
12989	Lionel Tractor and Trailer, *98*		16____
12991	Linex Gas Tractor-Tanker, *98*		16____
14000	Operating Forklift Platform, *00*		160____
14001	Operating Belt Lumber Loader, *00*		95____
14002	ZW Amp/Volt Meter, *00–04*		80____
14003	80-watt Transformer/Controller, *00–03*		70____
14004	Operating Coal Loader, *00*		135____

			Exc	Mint
____	**14005**	Operating Coal Ramp, *00*		130
	14018	ElectroCoupler Kit for Command Upgradeable		
____		GP9s, *00*		20
____	**14062**	31" Path Remote Switch, left hand, *01–14*		55
____	**14063**	31" Path Remote Switch, right hand, *01–14*		75
____	**14065**	Nuclear Reactor, *00*		233
____	**14071**	Yard Light, *00–16*		35
____	**14072**	Haunted House, *01*		181
____	**14073**	History of Lionel, The First 90 Years Video, *00*		15
____	**14075**	A Century of Lionel, 1900-1969 Video, *00*		15
____	**14076**	A Century of Lionel, 1970-2000 Video, *00*		15
____	**14077**	ZW Amp/Volt Meter, *00–03*		70
____	**14078**	Die-cast Sprung Trucks, *00–05, 07–16*		24
____	**14079**	Operating North Pole Pylon, *01*		70
____	**14080**	Hobo Hotel, *01*	30	65
____	**14081**	Shell Oil Derrick, *01*		100
____	**14082**	Pedestrian Walkover, speed sensor, *01–03*		50
____	**14083**	Pedestrian Walkover, *01–03, 08, 12–16*		55
____	**14084**	Lionel Heliport, *01*		85
____	**14085**	Newsstand, *01*		75
____	**14086**	Water Tower, *00*		105
____	**14087**	Lighthouse, *01*		95
____	**14090**	Banjo Signal, *01–16*		60
____	**14091**	Automatic Gateman, *01–03, 07–09*		38
____	**14092**	Floodlight Tower, *01–05, 08–16*		48
____	**14093**	Single Signal Bridge, *01–04, 08*		22
____	**14094**	Double Signal Bridge, *01–04, 08*		30
____	**14095**	Illuminated Station Platform, *01–04*		20
____	**14096**	Station Platform, *01–04*		10
____	**14097**	Rotary Aircraft Beacon, *01–04, 07–10*		40
____	**14098**	Auto Crossing Gate, *01–16*		100
____	**14099**	Block Target Signal, *01–04, 07–08*		22
____	**14100**	Blinking Light Billboard, *01–03*		23
____	**14101**	Red Baron Pylon, *01*		85
____	**14102**	Rocket Launcher, *01*		250
____	**14104**	Burning Switch Tower, *00*		70
____	**14105**	Aquarium, *01*		175
____	**14106**	Operating Freight Station, *00*		70
____	**14107**	Coaling Station, *01–03*		95
____	**14109**	Carousel, *01*		230
____	**14110**	Operating Ferris Wheel, *01–02, 04*		170
____	**14111**	1531R Controller, *00–16*		46
____	**14112**	Lighted Lockon, *01–10, 13–16*		6
____	**14113**	Engine Transfer Table, *01*		210
____	**14114**	Engine Transfer Table Extension, *01*		75
____	**14116**	PRR Die-cast Girder Bridge, *01*		20
____	**14117**	NYC Die-cast Girder Bridge, *01*		20
____	**14119**	Gooseneck Lamps, set of 2, *01–04, 07*		22
____	**14121**	Classic Billboards, set of 3, *01–03*		10
____	**14124**	ZW Controller with 2 transformers, *01*		300
____	**14125**	Christmas Tree with 400E Train, *00*		65
____	**14126**	Exploding Ammo Dump		55

		Exc	Mint
14133	Madison Hobby Shop, *01*	290	___
14134	Triple Action Magnetic Crane, *01*	230	___
14135	NS Black Die-cast Girder Bridge, *02*	15	___
14137	Die-cast Girder Bridge, *01–07*	25	___
14138	Snap-On Tool Animated Billboard, *01 u*	NRS	___
14142	Industrial Smokestack, *02–04*	50	___
14143	Industrial Tank, *02–04*	40	___
14145	Operating Lumberjacks, *02–03*	65	___
14147	Die-cast Old Style Clock Tower, *02–04, 08–16*	47	___
14148	Operating Billboard Signmen, *02–03*	60	___
14149	Scale-sized Banjo Signal, *02–05*	40	___
14151	Mainline Dwarf Signal, *02–08*	43	___
14152	Passenger Station, *02–04*	37	___
14153	Lion Oil Derrick, *02–03*	50	___
14154	Water Tower, *01–02*	65	___
14155	Floodlight Tower, *02–03*	55	___
14156	Lion Oil Diesel Fueling Station, *02–03*	70	___
14157	Coal Loader, *01–03*	120	___
14158	Icing Station, *01–02*	75	___
14159	Animated Billboard, *02–04*	20	___
14160	Frank's Hotdog Stand, *03–04*	55	___
14161	Smoking Hobo Shack, *02*	60	___
14162	Missile Launching Platform, *02–03*	48	___
14163	Industrial Power Station, *02–03*	550	___
14164	Lionelville Bandstand, *02*	140	___
14166	Train Orders Building, *04–05*	49	___
14167	Operating Lift Bridge, *02*	380	___
14168	Operating Harry's Barber Shop, *02–04*	100	___
14170	Amusement Park Swing Ride, *03–04*	150	___
14171	Pirate Ship Ride, *02–04*	130	___
14172	NYC Railroad Tugboat, *02*	180	___
14173	Drawbridge, *02–04*	70	___
14175	Santa Fe Die-cast Girder Bridge, *01–03*	17	___
14176	Norfolk Southern Die-cast Girder Bridge, *02–03*	18	___
14178	TMCC Direct Lockon, *02–03*	25	___
14179	TMCC Track Power Controller, *02–13*	230	___
14180	B&O Railroad Tugboat, *02–03*	155	___
14181	TMCC Action Recorder Controller, *02–13*	115	___
14182	TMCC Accessory Switch Controller, *02–13*	115	___
14183	TMCC Accessory Motor Controller, *02–13*	115	___
14184	TMCC Block Power Controller, *02–12*	90	___
14185	TMCC Operating Track Controller, *02–13*	100	___
14186	TMCC Accessory Voltage Controller, *02–13*	160	___
14187	TMCC How-to Video, *02–04*	11	___
14189	TMCC Track Power Controller, *02–13*	175	___
14190	The Lionel Train Book, *04–14*	30	___
14191	TMCC Command Base Cable, 6 feet, *02–13*	14	___
14192	TMCC 3-wire Command Base Cable, *02–13*	15	___
14193	TMCC Controller to Controller Cable, 1 foot, *02–13*	6	___
14194	TMCC TPC Cable Set, *02–13*	16	___
14195	TMCC Command Base Cable, 20 feet, *02–07*	12	___

		Exc	Mint
14196	TMCC Controller to Controller Cable, 6 feet, *02–13*		9
14197	TMCC Controller to Controller Cable, 20 feet, *02–07*		9
14198	CW-80 80-watt Transformer, *03–16*	65	150
14199	Playground Swings, *03–04, 08–09*		50
14201	Burning Switch Tower, *05*		70
14202	Water Tower, *05*		140
14203	Amusement Park Swing Ride, *06–07*		230
14209	U.S. Steel Gantry Crane, *05*		180
14210	Pony Ride, *06–07*		70
14211	Road Crew, *07–08*		90
14214	Lionelville Mini Golf, *06*		80
14215	Tug-of-War, *06–08*		60
14217	Helicopter Pylon, *06–09*		140
14218	Downtown People Pack, *06–16*		27
14219	Ice Rink, *06–08*		80
14220	Lionelville Water Tower, *06–08*		21
14221	Witches Cauldron, *06–08*		70
14222	Die-cast Girder Bridge, *06–09*		30
14225	Sunoco Industrial Tank, *06–09*		70
14227	Yard Tower, *06–08*		45
14229	Crossing Shanty, *06–09*		20
14230	Milk Bottle Toss Midway Game, *06*		20
14231	Cotton Candy Midway Booth, *06*		20
14236	Operating Freight Station, *06–07*		105
14237	Rocket Launcher, *06–07*		320
14240	Ice Block Pack, *06–16*		6
14241	Work Crew People Pack, *06–16*		27
14242	Hard Rock Cafe, *06*		50
14243	U.S. Army Water Tower, *06–08*		95
14244	Ammo Loader, *06–07*		105
14251	Die-cast Sprung Trucks, rotating bearing caps, *07–16*		25
14255	Sand Tower, *06–16*		35
14257	Passenger Station, *06–13*		60
14258	North Pole Passenger Station, *06–10*		53
14259	Christmas People Pack, *06–12*		23
14260	Christmas Tractor and Trailer, *06–08*		25
14261	Christmas Tree Lot, *06*		70
14262	Elevated Tank, *07*		70
14265	Sawmill with sound, *08*		130
14267	Sir Topham Hatt Gateman, *07–12*		80
14273	Polar Express Add-on Figures, *06–07, 12–14, 16*		30
14289	Operating Santa Gateman, *08*		80
14290	UPS Store, *06*		30
14291	Operating Milk Loading Depot, K-Line, *08*		100
14294	993 Legacy Expansion Set, *07–16*		290
14295	990 Legacy Command Set, *07–16*		400
14297	Halloween Witch Pylon, *07–08*		140
14500	KCS F3 Diesel AA Set, Railsounds, CC, *01*	380	660
14512	F3 Diesel ABA Demonstrator "291," CC, *01*	360	425
14517	Santa Fe F3 Diesel B Unit "2343C," powered, *01*		280

Exc Mint

		Exc	Mint
14518	CP F3 Diesel B Unit "2373C," RailSounds, CC, *01*		345____
14520	Texas Special F3 Diesel B Unit, RailSounds, *01*		360____
14521	Rock Island E6 Diesel AA Set, *01*		530____
14524	Atlantic Coast Line E6 Diesel AA Set, *01*		630____
14536	Santa Fe F3 Diesel AA Set, RailSounds, CC, *03–04*		800____
14539	Santa Fe F3 Diesel B Unit, *03*		300____
14540	D&RGW F3 Diesel B Unit, RailSounds, CC, *01*		315____
14541	C&O F3 Diesel B Unit, RailSounds, CC, *01*		300____
14542	KCS F3 Diesel B Unit "2388C," RailSounds, CC, *01*		375____
14543	SP F3 Diesel B Unit, RailSounds, CC, *01*		282____
14544	Southern E6 AA Diesel Set, CC, *02*		560____
14547	Burlington E5 AA Diesel Set, CC, *02*		570____
14552	NYC F3 Diesel AA Set, RailSounds, CC, *03–04*		740____
14555	NYC F3 Diesel B Unit, *03*		200____
14557	WP F3 Diesel B Unit, nonpowered, *03–04*		190____
14558	B&O F3 Diesel B Unit, nonpowered, *03–04*		155____
14559	D&RGW F3 Diesel AA Set, *01*		620____
14560	NP F3 Diesel A Unit "2390B," freight, *02*		175____
14561	NP F3 Diesel A Unit "2390B," passenger, *02*		190____
14562	Milwaukee Road F3 Diesel A Unit "75C," *02*		190____
14563	Erie-Lackawanna F3 Diesel A Unit "7094," *02*		175____
14564	CP F3 Diesel B Unit "237C," CC, *02*		350____
14565	B&O F3 Diesel AA Set, *03–04*		650____
14568	WP F3 Diesel AA Set, *03–04*		780____
14571	Santa Fe PA Diesel AA Set, CC, *03*		660____
14574	D&H PA Diesel AA Set, CC, *03*		580____
14584	Wabash F3 Diesel A Unit, nonpowered, *03*		180____
14586	D&H PB Unit, *03*		125____
14587	Santa Fe PB Unit, *03*		125____
14588	Santa Fe F3 Diesel ABA Set, CC, *04–05*		980____
14592	PRR F3 Diesel ABA Set, CC, *04–05*		750____
14596	NH Alco PA Diesel AA Set, *04–05*		700____
14599	NH Alco PB Diesel B Unit "0767-B," *04–05*		150____
15000	D&RGW Waffle-sided Boxcar, *95*	12	18____
15001	Seaboard Waffle-sided Boxcar, *95*	14	19____
15002	Chesapeake & Ohio Waffle-sided Boxcar, *96*	16	20____
15003	Green Bay & Western Waffle-sided Boxcar, *96*	16	20____
15004	Bloomingdale's Boxcar, *97 u*		40____
15005	"I Love NY" Boxcar, *97 u*		65____
15008	CP Rail Boxcar		30____
15013	L&N Waffle-sided Boxcar "102402," *00*		29____
15014	Seaboard Waffle-sided Boxcar "125925," *00*		25____
15015	C&NW Waffle-sided Boxcar "161013," *03*		18____
15016	IC Waffle-sided Boxcar "12981," *04*		20____
15017	CSX Waffle-sided Boxcar, *05*		27____
15018	D&H Waffle-sided Boxcar "24052," *06*		30____
15020	NH Waffle-sided Boxcar, *07*		30____
15021	MKT Waffle-sided Boxcar, *08*		35____
15024	UP Waffle Boxcar "960860," *09–11*		40____
15028	Southern Waffle-sided Boxcar "539889," *10*		40____
15029	Western & Atlantic Wood-sided Reefer, *10*		53____

Exc Mint

			Exc	Mint
____	15033	MTK Stock Car, *10*		65
____	15038	CSX Hi-Cube Boxcar, *11–12*		40
____	15039	NS Waffle-sided Boxcar, *11–12*		40
____	15041	BNSF Hi-Cube Boxcar, *10*		50
____	15042	CSX Waffle-sided Boxcar, *11*		40
____	15051	Lionel Lines Boxcar, *11–12*		40
____	15052	Amtrak Hi-Cube Boxcar, *11–12*		40
____	15053	REA Waffle-sided Boxcar, *11–12*		40
____	15054	C&NW Wood-sided Reefer, *11–12*		40
____	15060	K-Line Boxcar, *06*		40
____	15063	U.S.A.F. Minuteman Boxcar, *11*		55
____	15069	Coke Wood-sided Reefer #1, *09–16*		65
____	15071	Coca-Cola Christmas Boxcar, *12*		70
____	15072	Halloween Boxcar, *09–11*		55
____	15074	Mr. Goodbar Wood-sided Reefer, *09-11*		55
	15075	Boy Scouts of America Eagle Scout Boxcar, *11–14*		60
____	15077	ATSF Stock Car, *11*		55
____	15078	Pabst Wood-sided Reefeer, *11*		58
____	15079	Schlitz Wood-sided Reefer, *11*		55
____	15080	C&O 40' Boxcar, *11*		55
____	15083	CP Rail Waffle-sided Boxcar, *13*		43
____	15084	GN Hi-Cube Boxcar, *13–14*		43
____	15086	Alaska Wood-Sided Reefer, *12*		40
	15091	Angela Trotta Thomas "High Hopes" Hi-Cube Boxcar, *12*		55
____	15094	Sleepy Hollow Halloween Reefer, *14–15*		60
____	15095	1953 Lionel Catalog Art Reefer, *13*		55
____	15096	Hershey's Kisses Christmas Boxcar, *12*		65
____	15097	Peanuts Christmas Boxcar, *12–13*		70
____	15098	Lone Ranger Boxcar, *12–14*		60
____	15100	Amtrak Passenger Coach, *95–97*		35
____	15101	Reading Baggage Car (027), *96*		34
____	15102	Reading Combination Car (027), *96*		23
____	15103	Reading Passenger Coach (027), *96*		23
____	15104	Reading Vista Dome Car (027), *96*		26
____	15105	Reading Full Vista Dome Car (027), *96*		26
____	15106	Reading Observation Car (027), *96*		23
____	15107	Amtrak Vista Dome Car, *96*		38
____	15108	Northern Pacific Vista Dome Car, *96*		34
____	15109	ATSF Combine Car "2407," *97*		35
____	15110	ATSF Vista Dome Car 2404," *97*		35
____	15111	ATSF Observation Car "2406," *97*		35
____	15112	ATSF Albuquerque Coach "2405," *97*		34
____	15113	ATSF Culebra Vista Dome Car "2404," *97*		34
____	15114	NJ Transit Coach "5610," *96 u*		45
____	15115	NJ Transit Coach "5611," *96 u*		45
____	15116	NJ Transit Coach "5612," *96 u*		45
____	15117	Annie Passenger Coach, *97*		26
____	15118	Clarabel Passenger Coach, *97*		26
____	15122	NJ Transit Passenger Coach "5613," *97 u*		45
____	15123	NJ Transit Passenger Coach "5614," *97 u*		45
____	15124	NJ Transit Passenger Coach "5615," *97 u*		45

		Exc	Mint
15125	Amtrak Observation Car, *97 u*		50____
15126	Stars & Stripes Abraham Lincoln General Coach, *99*		60____
15127	Stars & Stripes Ulysses S. Grant General Coach, *99*		60____
15128	Pride of Richmond Robert E. Lee General Coach, *99*		60____
15129	Pride of Richmond Jefferson Davis General Coach, *99*		60____
15136	Custom Series Short Observation Car, blue, *99*		40____
15137	Custom Series Short Observation Car, red, *99*		34____
15138	Pratt's Hollow Baggage Car, *98*		100____
15139	Pratt's Hollow Vista Dome Car, *98*		100____
15140	Pratt's Hollow Coach, *98*		100____
15141	Pratt's Hollow Observation, *98*		100____
15142	U.S. Army Baby Heavyweight Coach, *00*		50____
15143	U.S. Army Baby Heavyweight Coach, *00*		50____
15153	Pullman Baby Madison Set 4-pack, *01*		190____
15163	T&P Baby Heavyweight Coach, *01*		30____
15166	Union Pacific Whistling Baggage Car, *04*		41____
15169	C&O Streamliner Car 4-pack, *03*		140____
15170	L&N Streamliner Car 4-pack, *03*		140____
15180	NYC Streamliner Car 4-pack, *04*		340____
15185	UP Streamliner Car 4-pack, *04*		340____
15300	NYC Superliner Aluminum Passenger Car 4-pack, *02*		360____
15301	NYC Manhattan Superliner Passenger Coach, *02*		90____
15302	NYC Queens Superliner Passenger Coach, *02*		90____
15304	NYC Staten Island Superliner Passenger Coach, *02*		90____
15305	NYC Brooklyn Superliner Passenger Coach, *02*		90____
15311	CB&Q California Zephyr Aluminum Passenger Car 4-pack, *03*		350____
15312	Santa Fe Super Chief Aluminum Passenger Car 4-pack, *03*		275____
15313	D&H Aluminum Passenger Car 4-pack, *03*		415____
15314	Amtrak Superliner 2-pack, *03*		220____
15315	Santa Fe Superliner 2-pack, *03*		200____
15316	NYC Superliner 2-pack, *03*		195____
15317	Southern Aluminum Passenger Car 4-pack, *03*		350____
15318	Lionel Lines Aluminum Passenger Car 2-pack, *03*		125____
15319	Santa Fe Superliner Aluminum Passenger Car 2-pack, *03*		145____
15326	NYC 20th Century Limited Aluminum Passenger Car 6-pack, *02*		485____
15333	N&W Powhatan Arrow Aluminum Passenger Car 6-pack, *02*		435____
15340	PRR South Wind Aluminum Passenger Car 6-pack, *02*		435____
15379	Lionel Lines Silver Valley Aluminum Combination Car, *03*		100____
15380	Lionel Lines Silver Spoon Aluminum Diner, *03*		100____
15381	Santa Fe Aluminum Baggage Car "2571," *03*		100____
15382	Santa Fe Regal Dome Aluminum Vista Dome Car, *03*		100____

		Exc	Mint
____15383	NYC 20th Century Limited Diner, StationSounds, *03*		195
____15384	N&W Powhatan Arrow Diner, StationSounds, *03*		190
15385	Pennsylvania South Wind Diner, StationSounds, *03*		190
____15394	Amtrak Streamliner Car 4-pack, *03–04*		450
____15395	Alaska Streamliner Car 4-pack, *03–04*		355
____15396	Amtrak Superliner Diner, StationSounds, *03*		220
____15397	Santa Fe Superliner Diner, StationSounds, *03*		200
____15398	NYC Superliner Diner, StationSounds, *03*		200
15405	50th Anniversary Hillside Heavyweight Diner, StationSounds, *02*		195
15406	Blue Comet Giacobini Heavyweight Diner, StationSounds, *02*		300
____15504	Alton Limited Diner, StationSounds, *03*		230
15507	Phantom III Passenger Car 4-pack (15508 Baggage, 15509 Vista Dome, 15510 Coach, 15511 Observation), *02*		245
____15512	Phantom II Passenger Car 4-pack, *02*		250
15517	Southern Crescent Limited Heavyweight Passenger Car 2-pack, *03–04*		205
15520	Southern Crescent Limited Heavyweight Diner, StationSounds, *03–04*		220
15521	NYC 20th Century Limited Heavyweight Passenger Car 4-pack, *04*		345
15526	Santa Fe Chief Heavyweight Passenger Car 4-pack, *04*		370
15538	NYC 20th Century Limited Heavyweight Passenger Car 2-pack, *04*		200
15541	NYC 20th Century Limited Heavyweight Diner, StationSounds, *04*		200
15542	Santa Fe Chief Heavyweight Passenger Car 2-pack, *04*		195
15545	Santa Fe Chief Heavyweight Diner, StationSounds, *04*		200
____15546	Napa Valley Wine Train Heavyweight 2-pack, *05*		250
____15549	Napa Valley Wine Train Diner, StationSounds, *05*		280
____15554	Pennsylvania Heavyweight Car 3-pack (std O), *05*		375
15558	Pennsylvania Heavyweight Add-on Coach (std O), *05*		140
15559	PRR Reading Seashore Heavyweight Car 3-pack (std O), *05*		370
15563	PRR Reading Seashore Heavyweight Add-on Coach, *05*		130
____15564	LIRR Heavyweight Car 3-pack (std O), *05*		370
____15568	LIRR Heavyweight Add-on Coach (std O), *05*		130
____15570	LIRR Heavyweight Car 3-pack (std O), *06*		230
____15574	LIRR Heavyweight Car Add-on (std O), *06*		140
15575	C&O Heavyweight Diner, StationSounds (std O), *06–07*		295
15576	C&O Heavyweight Passenger Car 2-pack (std O), *06–07*		265
____15577	NYC Heavyweight 3-pack (std O), *05–06*		370
____15581	NYC Heavyweight Add-on Coach (std O), *05–06*		130
____15584	Amtrak Acela Passenger Car 3-pack (std O), *06*		580
____15588	Southern Heavyweight Passenger Car 4-pack, *06*		495

Exc Mint

		Exc	Mint
15593	Southern Heavyweight Passenger Car 2-pack, *06*		265____
15596	Southern Heavyweight Diner, StationSounds, *06*		295____
15597	C&O Heavyweight Passenger Car 4-pack (std O), *06–07*		495____
15906	RailSounds Trigger Button, *90–95*		12____
16000	PRR Vista Dome Car (027), *87–88*	37	55____
16001	PRR Passenger Coach (027), *87–88*	33	41____
16002	PRR Passenger Coach (027), *87–88*	24	29____
16003	PRR Observation Car (027), *87–88*	24	29____
16009	PRR Combination Car (027), *88*	36	38____
16010	Virginia & Truckee Passenger Coach (SSS), *88*	36	47____
16011	Virginia & Truckee Passenger Coach (SSS), *88*	36	47____
16012	Virginia & Truckee Baggage Car (SSS), *88*	36	47____
16013	Amtrak Combination Car (027), *88–89*	21	34____
16014	Amtrak Vista Dome Car (027), *88–89*	21	34____
16015	Amtrak Observation Car (027), *88–89*	21	34____
16016	NYC Baggage Car (027), *89*	36	55____
16017	NYC Combination Car (027), *89*	21	29____
16018	NYC Passenger Coach (027), *89*	21	29____
16019	NYC Vista Dome Car (027), *89*	21	29____
16020	NYC Passenger Coach (027), *89*	23	33____
16021	NYC Observation Car (027), *89*	20	28____
16022	Pennsylvania Baggage Car (027), *89*	27	38____
16023	Amtrak Passenger Coach (027), *89*	21	30____
16024	Northern Pacific Diner (027), *92*	39	44____
16027	LL Combination Car (027, SSS), *90*	39	48____
16028	LL Passenger Coach (SSS, 027), *90*	35	42____
16029	LL Passenger Coach (SSS, 027), *90*	35	42____
16030	LL Observation Car (SSS, 027), *90*	35	42____
16031	Pennsylvania Diner (027), *90*	35	39____
16033	Amtrak Baggage Car (027), *90*	28	38____
16034	NP Baggage Car (027), *90–91*	30	45____
16035	NP Combination Car (027), *90–91*	18	26____
16036	NP Passenger Coach (027), *90–91*	21	30____
16037	NP Vista Dome Car (027), *90–91*	18	26____
16038	NP Passenger Coach (027), *90–91*	17	25____
16039	NP Observation Car (027), *90–91*	21	30____
16040	Southern Pacific Baggage Car, *90–91*	22	30____
16041	NYC Diner (027), *91*	37	47____
16042	Illinois Central Baggage Car (027), *91*	24	34____
16043	Illinois Central Combination Car (027), *91*	22	30____
16044	Illinois Central Passenger Coach (027), *91*	24	34____
16045	Illinois Central Vista Dome Car (027), *91*	22	30____
16046	Illinois Central Passenger Coach (027), *91*	24	34____
16047	Illinois Central Observation Car (027), *91*	24	34____
16048	Amtrak Diner (027), *91–92*	33	40____
16049	Illinois Central Diner (027), *92*	27	38____
16050	C&NW Baggage Car "6620," *93*	44	55____
16051	C&NW Combination Car "6630," *93*	40	50____
16052	C&NW Passenger Coach "6616," *93*	34	42____
16053	C&NW Passenger Coach "6602," *93*	37	46____
16054	C&NW Observation Car "6603," *93*	38	47____

		Exc	Mint
___**16055**	Santa Fe Passenger Coach (027), *93–94*	29	38
___**16056**	Santa Fe Vista Dome Car (027), *93–94*	25	32
___**16057**	Santa Fe Passenger Coach (027), *93–94*	30	40
___**16058**	Santa Fe Combination Car (027), *93–94*	27	35
___**16059**	Santa Fe Vista Dome Car (027), *93–94*	26	34
___**16060**	Santa Fe Observation Car (027), *93–94*	25	31
___**16061**	N&W Baggage Car "6061," *94*	60	85
___**16062**	N&W Combination Car "6062," *94*	38	50
___**16063**	N&W Passenger Coach "6063," *94*	43	55
___**16064**	N&W Passenger Coach "6064," *94*	43	55
___**16065**	N&W Observation Car "6065," *94*	36	48
___**16066**	NYC Combination Car "6066" (SSS), *94*	55	70
___**16067**	NYC Passenger Coach "6067" (SSS), *94*	38	47
___**16068**	UP Baggage Car "6068" (027), *94*	50	65
___**16069**	UP Combination Car "6069" (027), *94*	36	43
___**16070**	UP Passenger Coach "6070" (027), *94*	36	43
___**16071**	UP Diner "6071" (027), *94*	36	46
___**16072**	UP Vista Dome Car "6072" (027), *94*	36	43
___**16073**	UP Passenger Coach "6073" (027), *94*	36	42
___**16074**	UP Observation Car "6074" (027), *94*	36	43
___**16075**	Missouri Pacific Baggage Car "6620," *95*	44	55
___**16076**	Missouri Pacific Combination Car "6630," *95*	34	41
___**16077**	Missouri Pacific Passenger Coach "6616," *95*	34	41
___**16078**	Missouri Pacific Passenger Coach "7805," *95*	34	39
___**16079**	Missouri Pacific Observation Car "6609," *95*	34	41
___**16080**	New Haven Baggage Car "6080" (027), *95*	35	44
___**16081**	New Haven Combination Car "6081" (027), *95*	28	37
___**16082**	New Haven Passenger Coach "6082" (027), *95*	28	37
___**16083**	New Haven Vista Dome Car "6083" (027), *95*	30	39
___**16084**	New Haven Full Vista Dome Car "6084" (027), *95*	33	39
___**16086**	New Haven Observation Car "6086" (027), *95*	31	40
___**16087**	NYC Baggage Car "6087" (SSS), *95*	48	65
___**16088**	NYC Passenger Coach "6088" (SSS), *95*	36	43
___**16089**	NYC Diner "6089" (SSS), *95*	36	43
___**16090**	NYC Observation Car "6090" (SSS), *95*	38	46
___**16091**	NYC Passenger Cars, set of 4 (SSS), *95*	140	165
___**16092**	Santa Fe Full Vista Dome Car (027), *95*	30	38
___**16093**	Illinois Central Full Vista Dome Car (027), *95*	29	38
___**16094**	Pennsylvania Full Vista Dome Car (027), *95*	30	39
___**16095**	Amtrak Combination Car (027), *95*	19	23
___**16096**	Amtrak Vista Dome Car (027), *95*	19	23
___**16097**	Amtrak Observation Car (027), *95*	19	23
___**16098**	Amtrak Passenger Coach, *95–97*	20	33
___**16099**	Amtrak Vista Dome Car, *95–97*	20	33
___**16102**	Southern 3-D Tank Car (SSS), *87*	23	30
___**16103**	Lehigh Valley 2-D Tank Car (027), *88*	19	25
___**16104**	Santa Fe 2-D Tank Car (027), *89*	19	23
___**16105**	D&RGW 3-D Tank Car (SSS), *89*	48	65
___**16106**	Mopar Express 3-D Tank Car, *88 u*	100	151
___**16107**	Sunoco 2-D Tank Car (027), *90*	16	20
16108 ___	Racing Fuel 1-D Tank Car "6108" (027), *89 u, 92 u*	9	13

		Exc	Mint
16109	B&O 1-D Tank Car (SSS), *91*	29	34____
16110	Circus Animals Operating Stock Car "1989" (027), *89 u*	24	34____
16111	Alaska 1-D Tank Car (027), *90–91*	22	27____
16112	Dow Chemical 3-D Tank Car, *90*	20	26____
16113	Diamond Shamrock 2-D Tank Car (027), *91*	20	25____
16114	Hooker Chemicals 1-D Tank Car (027), *91*	13	17____
16115	MKT 3-D Tank Car, *92*	13	16____
16116	U.S. Army 1-D Tank Car, *91 u*	36	42____
16119	MKT 2-D Tank Car (027), *92, 93 u*	14	19____
16121	C&NW Stock Car (SSS), *92*	33	43____
16123	Union Pacific 3-D Tank Car, *93–95*	16	22____
16124	Penn Salt 3-D Tank Car, *93*	21	26____
16125	Virginian Stock Car, *93*	19	24____
16126	Jefferson Lake 3-D Tank Car, *93*	22	26____
16127	Mobil 1-D Tank Car, *93*	28	33____
16128	Alaska 1-D Tank Car, *94*	24	29____
16129	Alaska 1-D Tank Car (027), *93 u, 94*	21	28____
16130	SP Stock Car (027), *93 u, 94*	10	13____
16131	T&P Reefer, *94*	19	24____
16132	Deep Rock 3-D Tank Car, *94*	25	30____
16133	Santa Fe Reefer, *94*	22	28____
16134	Reading Reefer, *94*	17	21____
16135	C&O Stock Car, *94*	23	27____
16136	B&O 1-D Tank Car, *94*	28	32____
16137	Ford 1-D Tank Car "12," *94 u*	34	39____
16138	Goodyear 1-D Tank Car, *95*	28	34____
16140	Domino Sugar 1-D Tank Car, *95*	24	29____
16141	Erie Stock Car, *95*	22	30____
16142	Santa Fe 1-D Tank Car, *95*	26	30____
16143	Reading Reefer, *95*	18	23____
16144	San Angelo 3-D Tank Car, *95*	22	25____
16146	Dairy Despatch Reefer, *95*	15	20____
16147	Clearly Canadian 1-D Tank Car (027), *94 u*	25	40____
16149	Zep Chemical 1-D Tank Car (027), *95 u*	60	75____
16150	Sunoco 1-D Tank Car "6315," *97*	35	38____
16152	Sunoco 3-D Tank Car "6415," *97*		26____
16153	AEC Reactor Fluid 1-D Tank Car "6515-1," *97*		88____
16154	AEC Reactor Fluid 1-D Tank Car "6515-2," *97*		99____
16155	AEC Reactor Fluid 1-D Tank Car "6515-3," *97*		100____
16157	Gatorade Little League Baseball 1-D Tank Car "6315," *97 u*		55____
16160	AEC Tank Car "6515" with reactor fluid, *98*		77____
16162	Hooker 1-D Tank Car "6315-1," *97*		50____
16163	Hooker 1-D Tank Car "6315-2," *97*		50____
16164	Hooker 1-D Tank Car "6315-3," *97*		50____
16165	Mobilfuel 3-D Tank Car "6415," *97 u*		50____
16171	Alaska 1-D Tank Car "6171," *98–99*		33____
16173	Harold the Helicopter Flatcar, *98*	45	60____
16175	NJ Transit Port Morris Ore Car "9125," *98*		45____
16176	NJ Transit Raritan Yard Ore Car "9126," *98 u*		45____
16177	NJ Transit Gladstone Yard Ore Car "9127," *98 u*		45____
16178	NJ Transit Bay Head Yard Ore Car "9128," *98 u*		45____

		Exc	Mint
____16179	NJ Transit Dover Yard Ore Car "9129," *98 u*		45
____16180	Tabasco 1-D Tank Car, *98*	63	77
____16181	Biohazard Tank Car with Lights, *98*		80
____16182	Gatorade 1-D Tank Car "6315," *98 u*		64
____16187	Linex 3-D Tank Car "6425," *99*		30
____16188	Kodak 1-D Tank Car "6515," *99*	74	91
____16199	UP 1-D Tank Car "6035," *99–00*		25
____16200	Rock Island Boxcar (027), *87–88*	7	10
____16201	Wabash Boxcar (027), *88–91*	7	10
____16203	Key America Boxcar (027), *87 u*	45	65
____16204	Hawthorne Boxcar (027), *87 u*	50	85
____16205	Mopar Express Boxcar "1987" (027), *87–88 u*	50	60
____16206	D&RGW Boxcar (SSS), *89*	37	42
____16207	True Value Boxcar (027), *88 u*	32	47
____16208	PRR Auto Carrier, 3-tier, *89*	24	37
____16209	Disney Magic Boxcar (027), *88 u*	90	110
____16211	Hawthorne Boxcar (027), *88 u*	45	65
____16213	Shoprite Boxcar (027), *88 u*	55	80
____16214	D&RGW Auto Carrier, *90*	24	32
____16215	Conrail Auto Carrier, *90*	27	38
____16217	Burlington Northern Auto Carrier, *92*	24	36
____16219	True Value Boxcar (027), *89 u*	55	75
____16220	Ace Hardware Boxcar (027), *89 u*	55	80
____16221	Macy's Boxcar (027), *89 u*	55	80
____16222	Great Northern Boxcar (027), *90–91*	8	15
____16223	Budweiser Reefer, *89–92 u*	60	82
____16224	True Value "Lawn Chief" Boxcar (027), *90 u*	45	60
____16225	Budweiser Vat Car, *90–91 u*	123	161
____16226	Union Pacific Boxcar "6226" (027), *90–91 u*	15	19
____16227	Santa Fe Boxcar (027), *91*	13	17
____16228	Union Pacific Auto Carrier, *92*	26	33
____16229	Erie-Lackawanna Auto Carrier, *91 u*	45	55
____16232	Chessie System Boxcar, *92, 93 u, 94, 95 u*	25	30
____16233	MKT DD Boxcar, *92*	20	29
____16234	ACY Boxcar (SSS), *92*	34	41
____16235	Railway Express Agency Reefer, *92*	19	23
____16236	NYC Pacemaker Boxcar, *92 u*	18	24
____16237	Railway Express Agency Boxcar, *92 u*	21	23
____16238	NYNH&H Boxcar, *93–95*		3
____16239	Union Pacific Boxcar, *93–95*	15	20
____16241	Toys "R" Us Boxcar, *92–93 u*	35	45
____16242	Grand Trunk Western Auto Carrier, *93*	35	40
____16243	Conrail Boxcar, *93*	26	34
____16244	Duluth, South Shore & Atlantic Boxcar, *93*	20	24
____16245	Contadina Boxcar, *93*	16	20
____16247	ACL Boxcar, *94*	15	19
____16248	Budweiser Boxcar, *93–94 u*	44	60
____16249	United Auto Workers Boxcar, *93 u*		55
____16250	Santa Fe Boxcar (027), *93 u, 94*	8	10
____16251	Columbus & Greenville Boxcar, *94*	8	15
____16252	U.S. Navy Boxcar "6106888," *94–95*		30
____16253	Santa Fe Auto Carrier, *94*	32	38

		Exc	Mint
16255	Wabash DD Boxcar, *95*	20	26
16256	Ford DD Boxcar, *94 u*	30	34
16257	Crayola Boxcar, *94 u, 95*	17	23
16258	Lehigh Valley Boxcar, *95*	17	22
16259	Chrysler Mopar Boxcar, *97 u*	33	43
16260	Chrysler Mopar Auto Carrier, *96 u*	54	64
16261	Union Pacific DD Boxcar, *95*	26	29
16263	ATSF Boxcar, *96–99*		25
16264	Red Wing Shoes Boxcar, *95*	24	28
16265	Georgia Power "Atlanta '96" Boxcar, *95 u*	192	232
16266	Crayola Boxcar, *95*	17	23
16267	Sears Zenith Boxcar, *95–96 u*		55
16268	GM/AC Delco Boxcar, *95 u*		51
16269	Lionel Lines Boxcar, *96*		10
16272	Christmas Boxcar, *97*		36
16273	Lionel Employee Christmas Boxcar, *97*		55
16274	Marvin the Martian Boxcar, *97*		50
16279	Dodge Motorsports Boxcar, *96 u*	137	178
16284	Galveston Wharves Boxcar, *98*		28
16285	Savannah State Docks Boxcar, *98*		26
16291	Christmas Boxcar, *98*		34
16292	Lionel Employee Christmas Boxcar, *98*	309	369
16293	JCPenney Boxcar, *97*		100
16294	Pedigree Boxcar, *97*	140	160
16295	Kal Kan Boxcar, *97*	143	163
16296	Whiskas Boxcar, *97*	132	155
16297	Sheba Boxcar, *97*	130	154
16298	Mobil Boxcar, *97*		50
16300	Rock Island Flatcar with fences (027), *87–88*	8	10
16301	Lionel Barrel Ramp Car, *87*	14	19
16303	PRR Flatcar with trailers, *87*	26	33
16304	RI Gondola with cable reels (027), *87–88*	5	9
16305	Lehigh Valley Ore Car, *87*	80	130
16306	Santa Fe Barrel Ramp Car, *88*	12	16
16307	NKP Flatcar with trailers, *88*	30	40
16308	Burlington Northern Flatcar with trailer, *88–89*	20	25
16309	Wabash Gondola with canisters, *88–91*	9	13
16310	Mopar Express Gondola with canisters, *87–88 u*	35	39
16311	Mopar Express Flatcar with trailers, *87–88 u*	116	160
16313	PRR Gondola with cable reels (027), *88 u, 89*	5	10
16314	Wabash Flatcar with trailers, *89*	26	30
16315	PRR Flatcar with fences (027), *88 u, 89*	7	9
16317	PRR Barrel Ramp Car, *89*	18	22
16318	LL Depressed Center Flatcar with cable reels, *89*	22	26
16320	Great Northern Barrel Ramp Car, *90*	13	19
16321/22	Sealand TTUX Flatcar Set with trailers, *90*	65	73
16323	Lionel Lines Flatcar with trailers, *90*	21	25
16324	PRR Depressed Center Flatcar with cable reels, *90*	16	20
16325	Microracers Exhibition Ramp Car, *89 u*	21	28
16326	Santa Fe Depressed Center Flatcar with cable reels, *91*	16	21

		Exc	Mint
16327	"The Big Top" Circus Gondola with canisters, *89 u*	19	24
___16328	NKP Gondola with cable reels, *90–91*	17	23
___16329	SP Flatcar with horses (O27), *90–91*	19	24
___16330	MKT Flatcar with trailers, *91*	25	30
___16332	LL Depressed Center Flatcar with transformer, *91*	28	33
___16333	Frisco Bulkhead Flatcar with lumber, *91*	17	22
16334	C&NW Flatcar Set ("16337, 16338") with trailers, *91*	55	60
___16335	NYC Pacemaker Flatcar with trailer (SSS), *91*	46	65
___16336	UP Gondola "6336" with canisters, *90–91 u*	17	21
16339	Mickey's World Tour Gondola with canisters (O27), *91, 92 u*	17	21
16341	NYC Depressed Center Flatcar with transformer, *92*	29	32
___16342	CSX Gondola with coil covers, *92*	18	23
___16343	Burlington Gondola with coil covers, *92*	20	23
___16345/46	SP TTUX Flatcar Set with trailers, *92*	55	65
16347	Ontario Northland Bulkhead Flatcar with pulp load, *92*	22	26
___16348	Erie Liquefied Petroleum Car, *92*	23	25
___16349	Allis Chalmers Condenser Car, *92*	28	35
___16350	CP Rail Bulkhead Flatcar with lumber, *91 u*	20	29
___16351	Flatcar with U.S. Navy submarine, *92*	27	33
___16352	U.S. Military Flatcar with cruise missile, *92*	33	43
___16353	B&M Gondola with coil covers, *91 u*	33	39
___16355	Burlington Gondola, *92, 93 u, 94–95*	11	17
16356	MKT Depressed Center Flatcar with cable reels, *92*	17	21
___16357	L&N Flatcar with trailer, *92*	24	31
___16358	L&N Gondola with coil covers, *92*	17	21
___16359	Pacific Coast Gondola with coil covers (SSS), *92*	33	38
16360	N&W Maxi-Stack Flatcar Set ("16361, 16362") with containers, *93*	44	55
16363	Southern TTUX Flatcar Set ("16364, 16365") with trailers, *93*	38	49
___16367	Clinchfield Gondola with coil covers, *93*	18	21
___16368	MKT Liquid Oxygen Car, *93*	21	22
___16369	Amtrak Flatcar with wheel load, *92 u*	19	28
___16370	Amtrak Flatcar with rail load, *92 u*	19	28
___16371	BN I-Beam Flatcar with load, *92 u*	24	29
___16372	Southern I-Beam Flatcar with load, *92 u*	24	34
___16373	Erie-Lackawanna Flatcar with stakes, *93*	19	23
___16374	D&RGW Flatcar with trailer, *93*	25	28
___16375	NYC Bulkhead Flatcar, *93–95*	21	25
___16376	UP Flatcar with trailer, *93–95*	31	37
___16378	Toys "R" Us Flatcar with trailer, *92–93 u*	60	95
___16379	NP Bulkhead Flatcar with pulp load, *93*	16	23
___16380	UP I-Beam Flatcar with load, *93*	20	26
___16381	CSX I-Beam Flatcar with load, *93*	20	25
___16382	Kansas City Southern Bulkhead Flatcar, *93*	14	18
___16383	Conrail Flatcar with trailer, *93*	50	58
___16384	Soo Line Gondola with cable reels, *93*	14	19
___16385	Soo Line Ore Car, *93*	65	75

		Exc	Mint	
16386	SP Flatcar with lumber, *94*	15	19	___
16387	KCS Gondola with coil covers, *94*	13	16	___
16388	LV Gondola with canisters, *94*	16	20	___
16389	PRR Flatcar with wheel load, *94*	27	32	___
16390	Flatcar with water tank, *94*	24	27	___
16391	Lionel Lines Gondola, *93 u*		15	___
16392	Wabash Gondola with canisters (O27), *93 u, 94*	7	9	___
16393	Wisconsin Central Bulkhead Flatcar, *94*	13	19	___
16394	Vermont Central Bulkhead Flatcar, *94*	20	30	___
16395	CP Flatcar with rail load, *94*	18	23	___
16396	Alaska Bulkhead Flatcar, *94*	17	22	___
16397	Milwaukee Road I-Beam Flatcar with load, *94*	30	34	___
16398	C&O Flatcar with trailer, *94*	80	85	___
16399	Western Pacific I-Beam Flatcar with load, *94*	31	35	___
16400	PRR Hopper (O27), *88 u, 89*	15	18	___
16402	Southern Quad Hopper with coal (SSS), *87*	30	42	___
16406	CSX Quad Hopper with coal, *90*	29	34	___
16407	B&M Covered Quad Hopper (SSS), *91*	28	37	___
16408	UP Hopper "6408" (O27), *90–91 u*	17	21	___
16410	MKT Hopper (O27), *92, 93 u*	19	24	___
16411	L&N Quad Hopper with coal, *92*	28	32	___
16412	C&NW Covered Quad Hopper, *94*	16	21	___
16413	Clinchfield Quad Hopper with coal, *94*	16	22	___
16414	CCC&StL Hopper (O27), *94*	18	25	___
16416	D&RGW Covered Quad Hopper, *95*	16	20	___
16417	Wabash Quad Hopper with coal, *95*	19	21	___
16418	C&NW Hopper with coal (O27), *95*	15	21	___
16419	Tennessee Central Hopper, *96*		17	___
16420	WM Quad Hopper with coal (SSS), *95*	30	34	___
16421	WM Quad Hopper with coal (SSS), *95*	30	33	___
16422	WM Quad Hopper with coal (SSS), *95*		33	___
16423	WM Quad Hopper with coal (SSS), *95*		30	___
16424	WM Covered Quad Hopper (SSS), *95*	34	39	___
16425	WM Covered Quad Hopper (SSS), *95*	25	29	___
16426	WM Covered Quad Hopper (SSS), *95*	24	27	___
16427	WM Covered Quad Hopper (SSS), *95*	27	30	___
16429	WM Quad Hopper with coal, set of 2		70	___
16430	Georgia Power Quad Hopper "82947" with coal, *95 u*		109	___
16431	Lionel Corporation 2-bay Hopper "6456-1," *96*		30	___
16432	Lionel Corporation 2-bay Hopper "6456-2," *96*		64	___
16433	Lionel Corporation 2-bay Hopper "6456-3," *96*		18	___
16434	LV 2-bay Hopper "6456," "TLDX," *97*		25	___
16435	Virginian 2-bay Hopper "6456-1," *97*		30	___
16436	N&W 2-bay Hopper "6456-2," *97*		33	___
16437	C&O 2-bay Hopper "6456-3," *97*		33	___
16438	Frisco 4-bay Covered Hopper "87538," *98*		34	___
16439	Southern 4-bay Covered Hopper "77836," *98*		34	___
16440	Alaska 2-bay Hopper "7100," *98–99*		35	___
16441	New York Central 4-bay Hopper, *99*		26	___
16442	Bethlehem Gondola "6462" (SSS), *99*		40	___
16443	GN 2-bay Hopper "172364," *99–00*		20	___

		Exc	Mint
____**16444**	CNJ 2-bay Hopper "643," *00*		20
____**16445**	Frisco 2-bay Hopper "93108," *00*		20
____**16446**	Burlington 2-bay Hopper, *00*		20
____**16447**	PRR Tuscan 2-bay Hopper, *00 u*		30
____**16448**	PRR Gray 2-bay Hopper, *00 u*		30
____**16449**	PRR Black 2-bay Hopper, *00 u*		30
____**16450**	PRR Green 2-bay Hopper, *00 u*		30
____**16451**	Lionel Mines 2-bay Hopper, *00 u*		50
____**16453**	SP 2-bay Hopper "460604," *01*		15
____**16454**	Bethlehem Steel Hopper "41025," *01*		37
____**16455**	Pioneer Seed 2-bay Hopper, *00 u*		50
____**16456**	B&O 2-bay Hopper, *01*		20
____**16459**	LV 2-bay Hopper "51102," *01*		23
____**16460**	Reading 2-bay Hopper "79636," *02*		25
____**16463**	Rio Grande Icebreaker Tunnel Car "18936," *02*		32
____**16464**	NYC Icebreaker Tunnel Car "X3200," *02*		32
____**16465**	WP 2-bay Hopper "100340," *03*		19
____**16466**	Pennsylvania Icebreaker Tunnel Car, *03*		33
____**16467**	"Naughty and Nice" Hopper 2-pack, *02*		60
____**16469**	B&O Hopper "435351," *02*		22
____**16470**	"Naughty and Nice" Ore Car 2-pack, *03*		43
____**16473**	Rock Island Ore Car "99122," *03*		18
____**16474**	Alaska Ore Car "16474," *04*		21
____**16475**	Santa Fe Hopper "16475," *04*		18
____**16480**	Lionelville Snow Transport Quad Hopper, *04*		45
____**16482**	Norfolk Southern Hopper, traditional, *05*		27
____**16487**	Alaska 2-bay Hopper, *05*		35
____**16489**	BNSF Ore Car, traditional, *05*		15
____**16490**	Sodor Mining Hopper, *05, 13*		35
____**16491**	CNJ Hopper "60714," *06*		30
____**16492**	C&NW Ore Car "114023," *06*		30
____**16493**	Christmas Ice Breaker Car, *06*		55
____**16500**	Rock Island Bobber Caboose, *87–88*	9	13
____**16501**	Lehigh Valley SP-type Caboose, *87*	19	24
____**16503**	NYC Transfer Caboose, *87*	16	22
____**16504**	Southern N5c Caboose (SSS), *87*	17	30
____**16505**	Wabash SP-type Caboose, *88–91*	10	15
____**16506**	Santa Fe Bay Window Caboose, *88*	18	28
____**16507**	Mopar Express SP-type Caboose, *87–88 u*	42	54
____**16508**	Lionel Lines SP-type Caboose "6508," *89 u*	13	17
____**16509**	D&RGW SP-type Caboose (SSS), *89*	19	24
____**16510**	New Haven Bay Window Caboose, *89*	25	30
____**16511**	PRR Bobber Caboose, *88 u, 89*	9	13
____**16513**	Union Pacific SP-type Caboose, *89*	14	21
____**16515**	Lionel Lines SP-type Caboose, RailScope, *89*	20	23
____**16516**	Lehigh Valley SP-type Caboose, *90*	15	26
____**16517**	Atlantic Coast Line Bay Window Caboose, *90*	22	26
____**16518**	Chessie System Bay Window Caboose, *90*	41	50
____**16519**	Rock Island Transfer Caboose, *90*	13	17
16520 ____	"Welcome to the Show" Circus SP-type Caboose, *89 u*	13	21
____**16521**	PRR SP-type Caboose, *90–91*	8	11

		Exc	Mint
16522	"Chills & Thrills" Circus N5c Caboose, *90–91*	10	15___
16523	Alaska SP-type Caboose, *91*	24	31___
16524	Anheuser-Busch SP-type Caboose, *89–92 u*	32	42___
16525	D&H Bay Window Caboose (SSS), *91*	30	39___
16526	Kansas City Southern SP-type Caboose, *91*	17	21___
16528	UP SP-type Caboose "6528," *90–91 u*	17	21___
16529	Santa Fe SP-type Caboose "16829," *91*	9	13___
16530	Mickey's World Tour SP-type Caboose "16830," *91, 92 u*	13	17___
16531	Texas & Pacific SP-type Caboose, *92*	18	23___
16533	C&NW Bay Window Caboose, *92*	29	40___
16534	Delaware & Hudson SP-type Caboose, *92*	14	19___
16535	Erie-Lackawanna Bay Window Caboose, *91 u*	42	50___
16536	Chessie System SP-type Caboose, *92, 93 u, 94, 95 u*		23___
16537	MKT SP-type Caboose, *92, 93 u*	17	21___
16538	L&N Bay Window Caboose "1041," *92 u*	29	33___
16539	WP Steelside Caboose "539," smoke, SSS (std O), *92*	50	55___
16541	Montana Rail Link Extended Vision Caboose "10131" with smoke, *93*	55	65___
16543	NYC SP-type Caboose, *93–95*		20___
16544	Union Pacific SP-type Caboose, *93–95*	22	26___
16546	Clinchfield SP-type Caboose, *93*	22	26___
16547	"Happy Holidays" SP-type Caboose, *93–95*	46	55___
16548	Conrail SP-type Caboose, *93*	15	20___
16549	Soo Line Work Caboose, *93*	18	26___
16550	U.S. Navy Searchlight Caboose, *94–95*	17	21___
16551	Budweiser SP-type Caboose, *93–94 u*	27	31___
16552	Frisco Searchlight Caboose, *94*	23	26___
16553	United Auto Workers SP-type Caboose, *93 u*		40___
16554	GT Extended Vision Caboose "79052," smoke, *94*	40	47___
16555	C&O SP-type Caboose, *94*	22	26___
16557	Ford SP-type Caboose, *94 u*	19	24___
16558	Crayola SP-type Caboose, *94 u, 95*	17	21___
16559	Seaboard Center Cupola Caboose "5658," *95*	23	24___
16560	Chrysler Mopar Caboose, *94 u*	24	26___
16561	UP Center Cupola Caboose "25766," *95*	27	31___
16562	Reading Center Cupola Caboose, *95*	25	29___
16563	Lionel Lines SP-type Caboose, *95*	22	26___
16564	Western Maryland Center Cupola Caboose (SSS), *95*	30	34___
16565	Milwaukee Road Bay Window Caboose, *95*	50	60___
16566	U.S. Army SP-type Caboose "907," *95*		28___
16568	ATSF SP-type Caboose, *96–99*		23___
16571	Georgia Power SP-type Caboose "52789," *95 u*		68___
16575	Sears Zenith SP-type Caboose, *95*		38___
16577	U.S. Coast Guard Work Caboose, *96*		26___
16578	Lionel Lines SP-type Caboose, *95 u*		20___
16579	GM/AC Delco, SP-type Caboose, *95*		35___
16580	SP-type Caboose, *96–99*		11___
16581	UP Illuminated Caboose, *96*		30___
16586	SP Illuminated Caboose "6357," *97*		42___

		Exc	Mint
____16590	Dodge Motorsports SP-type Caboose "6950," *96*		54
16591	Little League Baseball SP-type Caboose "6397," *97*		40
____16593	Lionel Belt Line Caboose "6257," *98*		32
____16594	Caboose "6357," *98*		29
____16600	Illinois Central Coal Dump Car, *88*	14	23
____16601	Canadian National Searchlight Car, *88*	19	24
____16602	Erie-Lackawanna Coal Dump Car, *87*	16	26
____16603	Detroit Zoo Giraffe Car (027), *87*	40	49
____16604	NYC Log Dump Car, *87*	15	27
____16605	Bronx Zoo Giraffe Car (027), *88*	39	44
____16606	Southern Searchlight Car, *87*	13	21
____16607	Southern Coal Dump Car "16707" (SSS), *87*	18	26
____16608	Lehigh Valley Searchlight Car, *87*	22	30
____16609	Lehigh Valley Derrick Car, *87*	22	30
____16610	Track Maintenance Car, *87–88*	15	25
____16611	Santa Fe Log Dump Car, *88*	15	23
____16612	Soo Line Log Dump Car, *89*	14	24
____16613	MKT Coal Dump Car, *89*	17	26
____16614	Reading Cop and Hobo Car (027), *89*	24	25
____16615	Lionel Lines Extension Searchlight Car, *89*	20	28
____16616	D&RGW Searchlight Car (SSS), *89*	22	30
____16617	C&NW Boxcar with ETD, *89*	23	34
____16618	Santa Fe Track Maintenance Car, *89*	11	19
____16619	Wabash Coal Dump Car, *90*	14	25
____16620	C&O Track Maintenance Car, *90–91*	16	19
____16621	Alaska Log Dump Car, *90*	24	31
____16622	CSX Boxcar with ETD, *90–91*	20	28
____16623	MKT DD Boxcar with ETD, *91*	16	23
____16624	NH Cop and Hobo Car (027), *90–91*	23	31
____16625	NYC Extension Searchlight Car, *90*	22	30
____16626	CSX Searchlight Car, *90*	18	26
____16627	CSX Log Dump Car, *90*	19	23
____16628	Cop and Hobo Circus Gondola, *90–91*	36	43
____16629	Operating Circus Elephant Car (027), *90–91*	38	50
____16630	SP Operating Cowboy Car (027), *90–91*	22	26
____16631	RI Boxcar, steam RailSounds, *90*	110	130
____16632	BN Boxcar, diesel RailSounds, *90*	90	100
____16634	WM Coal Dump Car, *90*	26	32
____16636	D&RGW Log Dump Car, *91*	19	25
____16637	WP Extension Searchlight Car, *91*	27	30
____16638	Operating Circus Animal Car (027), *91*	50	55
____16639	B&O Boxcar, steam RailSounds, *91*	100	120
____16640	Rutland Boxcar, diesel RailSounds, *91*	100	120
____16641	Toys "R" Us Giraffe Car (027), *90–91 u*	45	65
____16642	Mickey's World Tour Goofy Car (027), *91, 92 u*	33	41
____16644	Amtrak Crane Car, *91, 92 u*	36	42
____16645	Amtrak Searchlight Caboose, *91*	27	30
16649	Railway Express Agency Boxcar, steam RailSounds, *92*	110	140
____16650	NYC Pacemaker Boxcar, diesel RailSounds, *92*	100	135
____16651	Operating Circus Clown Car (027), *92*	24	30
____16652	Radar Car, *92*	25	29

		Exc	Mint
16653	Western Pacific Crane Car (SSS), *92*	44	60___
16655	Steam Tender "1993," RailSounds, *93*	115	140___
16656	Burlington Log Dump Car, *92 u*	18	25___
16657	Lehigh Valley Coal Dump Car, *92 u*	22	29___
16658	Erie-Lackawanna Crane Car, *93*	47	65___
16659	Union Pacific Searchlight Car, *93–95*	15	18___
16660	Fire Car with ladders, *93–94*	28	33___
16661	Flatcar with boat, *93*	20	22___
16662	Bugs Bunny and Yosemite Sam Outlaw Car (027), *93–94*	28	30___
16663	Missouri Pacific Searchlight Car, *93*	16	19___
16664	L&N Coal Dump Car, *93*	22	25___
16665	Maine Central Log Dump Car, *93*	23	27___
16666	Toxic Waste Car, *93–94*	25	32___
16667	Conrail Searchlight Car, *93*	27	30___
16668	Ontario Northland Log Dump Car, *93*	20	24___
16669	Soo Line Searchlight Car, *93*	17	21___
16670	TV Car, *93–94*	12	22___
16673	Lionel Lines Tender, whistle, *94–97*	33	42___
16674	Pinkerton Animated Gondola, *94*	28	32___
16675	Great Northern Log Dump Car, *94*	21	25___
16676	Burlington Coal Dump Car, *94*	23	28___
16677	NATO Flatcar with Royal Navy submarine, *94*	34	44___
16678	Rock Island Searchlight Car, *94*	12	23___
16679	U.S. Mail Operating Boxcar, *94*	45	50___
16680	Cherry Picker Car, *94*	25	28___
16681	Aquarium Car, *95*	35	44___
16682	Lionelville Farms Operating Stock Car (027), *94*	23	27___
16683	Los Angeles Zoo Elephant Car (027), *94*	22	26___
16684	U.S. Navy Crane Car, *94–95*	35	40___
16685	Erie Extension Searchlight Car, *95*	30	34___
16686	Mickey Mouse Animated Boxcar, *95*	28	35___
16687	U.S. Mail Operating Boxcar, *94*	29	37___
16688	Fire Car with ladders, *94*	35	43___
16689	Toxic Waste Car, *94*	29	32___
16690	Bugs Bunny and Yosemite Sam Outlaw Car (027), *94*	30	34___
16701	Southern Tool Car (SSS), *87*	43	55___
16702	Amtrak Bunk Car, *91, 92 u*	25	27___
16703	NYC Tool Car, *92*	24	31___
16704	TV Car, *94*	27	29___
16705	Chesapeake & Ohio Cop and Hobo Car, *95*	28	34___
16706	Animal Transport Service Giraffe Car, *95*	27	30___
16708	C&NW Track Maintenance Car, *95*	24	31___
16709	New York Central Derrick Car, *95*	22	28___
16710	U.S. Army Operating Missile Car, *95*	40	42___
16711	Pennsylvania Searchlight Car, *95*	27	31___
16712	Pinkerton Animated Gondola, *95*	34	39___
16715	ATSF Log Dump Car, *96–99*		24___
16717	Jersey Central Crane Car, *96*		41___
16718	USMC Missile Launching Flatcar, *96*	26	31___
16719	Exploding Boxcar, *96*		38___
16720	Lionel Lines Searchlight Car "3650," *96–97*		50___

		Exc	Mint
___ 16724	Mickey and Friends Submarine Car, 96		39
___ 16725	Rhino Transport Car, 97		31
___ 16726	U.S. Army Fire Ladder Car, 96		43
___ 16734	U.S. Coast Guard Searchlight Car, 96		30
___ 16735	U.S. Coast Guard Flatcar with radar, 96	28	35
___ 16736	U.S. Coast Guard Derrick Car, 96		34
16737	Road Runner and Wile E. Coyote Gondola "3444," 96		60
___ 16738	Pepe LePew Boxcar "3370," 96		40
___ 16739	Foghorn Leghorn Poultry Car "6434," 96		44
___ 16740	Lionel Corporation Mail Car "3428," 96		37
___ 16741	Union Pacific Illuminated Bunk Car, 97		25
___ 16742	Trout Ranch Aquarium Car "3435," 96		32
___ 16744	Port of Lionel City Searchlight Car, 97		30
___ 16745	Port of Lionel City Flatcar with radar, 97		30
___ 16746	Port of Lionel City Derrick Car, 97		30
___ 16747	Breyer Animated Horse Car "6473," 97		34
___ 16748	U.S. Forest Service Log-Dump Car "3361," 97		30
___ 16749	Midget Mines Ore-Dump Car "3479," 97		36
___ 16750	Lionel City Aquarium Car "3436," 97		32
___ 16751	AIREX Sports Channel TV Car "3545," 97		25
16752	Marvin the Martian Missile Launching Flatcar "6655," 97	127	135
___ 16754	Porky Pig and Instant Martians Flatcar "6805," 97	128	177
___ 16755	Daffy Duck Animated Balloon Car "3470," 97	129	165
___ 16760	Pluto and Cats Animated Gondola "3444," 97		55
___ 16765	Bureau of Land Management Log Car "3351," 98		30
___ 16766	Bureau of Land Management Ore Car "3479," 98		31
___ 16767	New York Central Ice Docks Ice Car "6352," 98		47
___ 16776	Holiday Boxcar, RailSounds, 98		68
___ 16777	Animated Cola Car and Platform, 98		100
___ 16782	Bethlehem Ore Dump Car "3479," 99		95
___ 16783	Westside Lumber Log Dump Car "3351," 99		32
___ 16784	Pratt's Hollow Seed Dump Car "3479," 99		36
___ 16785	"Happy Holidays" Music Reefer "5700," 99		100
___ 16789	Easter Operating Boxcar, 99		39
___ 16790	UP Stock Car "3356," Crowsounds, 99		90
___ 16791	New York City Lights Boxcar, 99		44
___ 16792	Constellation Boxcar "9600," 99		37
___ 16793	Animated Glow-in-the-Dark Alien Boxcar, 99		44
___ 16794	Wicked Witch Halloween Boxcar, 99		46
___ 16795	Elf Chasing Rudolph Gondola "6462," 99		55
___ 16796	Snowman Loading Ice Car "6352," 99		55
___ 16805	Budweiser Malt Nutrine Reefer "3285," 91–92 u	76	102
___ 16806	Toys "R" Us Boxcar, 92 u	21	26
___ 16807	H.J. Heinz Reefer "301," 93	23	27
___ 16808	Toys "R" Us Boxcar, 93 u	28	30
___ 16817	Ambassador 1-D Tank Car, 00 u		168
___ 16818	Engineer Award Tank Car, 00 u		706
___ 16819	JLC Award Tank Car, 00 u		756
___ 16820	Ambassador Boxcar, 00 u	309	505
___ 16822	CSX Water Tower, 08		23

		Exc	Mint
16824	O36 Command Control Switch, left hand (FasTrack), *09–14*		110____
16825	O36 Command Control Switch, right hand (FasTrack), *09–14*		110____
16826	O72 Command Control Switch, left hand (FasTrack), *09–14*		120____
16827	O72 Command Control Switch, right hand (FasTrack), *09–14*		120____
16828	O60 Command Control Switch, left hand (FasTrack), *09–14*		120____
16829	O60 Command Control Switch, right hand (FasTrack), *09–14*		120____
16830	O48 Command Control Switch, left hand (FasTrack), *09–14*		120____
16831	O48 Command Control Switch, right hand (FasTrack), *09–14*		120____
16832	O72 Command Control Wye Switch (FasTrack), *09–14*		115____
16834	O48 Half-Curved Track (FasTrack), *09–14, 16*		5____
16835	O48 Quarter-Curved Track (FasTrack), *09–14, 16*		5____
16836	Christmas Girder Bridge, *09*		21____
16837	Christmas Operating Billboard, *09*		45____
16841	Halloween Gateman, *09*		80____
16842	Big Moe Crane, *10*		70____
16843	City and Western Diorama, *10–11*		15____
16845	Bookstore, *09–10*		60____
16846	Burning Hobo Depot, *09*		90____
16847	Legacy Hotel, *10–11*		70____
16848	Creature Comforts Pet Store, sound, *09–10*		80____
16849	Rotary Dumper with coal conveyor, CC, *10*		600____
16850	Operating Wind Turbine, 3-pack, *09–11*		225____
16851	Sunoco Cylindrical Oil Tank, gray, *10–11*		100____
16852	Sunoco Cylindrical Oil Tank, yellow, *10–11*		90____
16853	Polar Express Diorama, *09–11, 13*		18____
16854	MTA LIRR Blinking Billboard, *09*		30____
16855	MTA LIRR Illuminated Station Platform, *09*		37____
16856	MTA LIRR Passenger Station, *09*		60____
16857	Thomas & Friends Diorama, *10–16*		18____
16859	Grand Central Terminal, *09*		1500____
16861	50,000-gallon Water Tank, *09–11*		150____
16863	Santa's Christmas Wish Station, *09–11*		125____
16868	Straight O Gauge Tunnel, *09–16*		55____
16871	Winter Wonderland Diorama, *09–11*		15____
16872	Illuminated Christmas Station Platform, *09*		35____
16873	Bathtub Gondola Coal Load 3-pack, *10–16*		20____
16874	Coaling Station, *10–11*		80____
16880	Freight Platform, *10–12*		30____
16881	Barrel Shed, *10–11*		30____
16882	12" Covered Bridge, *10–16*		60____
16883	Neil's Guitar Shop, *10–11*		60____
16889	Coal Tipple Pack, *11–16*		15____
16891	Tank Car Accident, *10–11*		130____
16896	Flagpole with lights, *10–16*		28____
16897	75th Anniversary Gateman, *10*		75____

		Exc	Mint
____16903	CP Bulkhead Flatcar with pulp load (SSS), *94*	22	25
____16904	NYC Pacemaker Flatcar Set with trailers, *94*	55	60
____16907	Flatcar with farm tractors, *94*	27	33
16908	U.S. Navy Flatcar "04039" with submarine, *94–95*	39	46
16909	U.S. Navy Gondola "16556" with canisters, *94–95*	16	22
____16910	Missouri Pacific Flatcar with trailer, *94*	22	27
____16911	B&M Flatcar with trailer, *94*	28	34
____16912	CN Maxi-Stack Flatcar Set with containers, *94*	70	75
____16915	Lionel Lines Gondola (027), *93–94 u*	7	10
____16916	Ford Flatcar with trailer, *94 u*	38	45
____16917	Crayola Gondola with crayons, *94 u, 95*	8	9
____16919	Chrysler Mopar Gondola with coil covers, *94–96*	33	36
____16922	Chesapeake & Ohio Flatcar with trailer, *95*	25	31
____16923	Intermodal Service Flatcar with wheel chocks, *95*	15	22
____16924	Lionel Corporation Flatcar "6424" with trailer, *96*		24
____16925	New York Central Flatcar with trailer, *95*	65	85
____16926	Frisco Flatcar with trailers, *95*	24	31
____16927	New York Central Flatcar with gondola, *95*	17	22
____16928	Soo Line Flatcar with dump bin (027), *95*	12	15
____16929	BC Rail Gondola with cable reels, *95*	21	25
____16930	Santa Fe Flatcar with wheel load, *95*	20	25
____16932	Erie Flatcar with rail load, *95*	17	22
____16933	Lionel Lines Flatcar with autos, *95*	23	25
____16934	Pennsylvania Flatcar with Ertl road grader, *95*	28	39
16935	UP Depressed Center Flatcar with Ertl bulldozer, *95*	22	35
16936	Sealand Maxi-Stack Flatcar Set with containers, *95*	70	85
____16939	U.S. Navy Flatcar "04040" with boat, *95*	25	30
____16940	ATSF Flatcar with trailer, *96–99*		40
____16941	ATSF Flatcar with autos, *96–99*		25
____16943	Jersey Central Gondola, *96*		18
16944	Georgia Power Depressed Center Flatcar "31438" with transformer, *95 u*		50
16945	Georgia Power Depressed Center Flatcar "31950" with cable reels, *95 u*		53
____16946	C&O F9 Well Car "3840," *96*		31
____16951	Southern I-Beam Flatcar "9823" with load, *97*		25
____16952	U.S. Navy Flatcar with Ertl helicopter, *96*		25
____16953	NYC Flatcar with Red Wing Shoes trailer, *95 u*	39	45
____16954	NYC Flatcar "6424" with Ertl scraper, *96*		30
____16955	ATSF Flatcar with Ertl Challenger, *96*		30
____16956	Zenith Flatcar with trailer, *95 u*		134
16957	Depressed Center Flatcar "6461" with Ertl Case tractor, *96*		29
____16958	Flatcar with Ertl New Holland loader, *96*		26
____16960	U.S. Coast Guard Flatcar with boat, *96*		40
____16961	GM/AC Delco Flatcar with trailer, *95*		73
____16963	Lionel Corporation Flatcar "6411," *96–97*		34
____16964	Lionel Corporation Gondola "6462," *97*		22
____16965	Scout Flatcar "6424" with stakes, *96–97*		20

Exc Mint

		Exc	Mint
16967	Depressed Center Flatcar "6461" with transformer, *96*		21___
16968	Depressed Center Flatcar "6461" with Ertl Helicopter, *96*		35___
16969	Flatcar "6411" with Beechcraft Bonanza, *96*		33___
16970	LA County Flatcar "6424" with motorized powerboat, *96*		20___
16971	Port of Lionel City Flatcar with boat, *97*		35___
16972	P&LE Gondola "6462," *97*		22___
16975	Well Car Doublestack Set, *97*		75___
16978	MILW Flatcar "6424" with P&H shovel, *97*		43___
16980	Speedy Gonzales Missile Flatcar "6823," *97*		43___
16982	BC Rail Bulkhead Flatcar "9823" with lumber, *97*		28___
16983	PRR F9 Well Car "6983" with cable reels, *97*		39___
16986	Sears Zenith Bulkhead Flatcar, *96 u*		45___
16987	Musco Lighting Bulkhead Flatcar, *97 u*		35___
16997	Lionel Lines Recovery Crane Car, *99*		50___
17002	Conrail 2-bay ACF Hopper (std O), *87*	42	47___
17003	Du Pont 2-bay ACF Hopper (std O), *90*	39	45___
17004	MKT 2-bay ACF Hopper (std O), *91*	23	27___
17005	Cargill 2-bay ACF Hopper (std O), *92*	29	37___
17006	Soo Line 2-bay ACF Hopper (std O, SSS), *93*	31	36___
17007	GN 2-bay ACF Hopper "173872" (std O), *94*	26	31___
17008	D&RGW 2-bay ACF Hopper "10009" (std O), *95*		31___
17009	New York Central 2-bay ACF Hopper, *96*		35___
17010	Govt. of Canada ACF 2-bay Covered Hopper "7000," *98*		32___
17011	NP ACF 2-bay Covered Hopper "75052," *98*		44___
17012	Govt. of Canada ACF 2-bay Covered Hopper "7001," *98*		30___
17013	NYC Graffiti 2-bay Covered Hopper "7000," *99*		55___
17014	Graffiti 2-bay Covered Hopper "7000" (std O), *99*		45___
17015	Corning 2-bay Hopper "90409" (std O), *01*		40___
17016	C&NW 2-bay Hopper "96644" (std O), *01*		46___
17017	Chessie System 2-bay Hopper "605527" (std O), *02*		32___
17018	Nickel Plate Road Offset Hopper "33074," *02*		43___
17019	Santa Fe Offset Hopper "78299," *02*		43___
17020	Frisco Offset Hopper "92092," *02*		43___
17021	NYC Offset Hopper "867999," *02*		43___
17022	Burlington 2-bay ACF Hopper "183925" (std O), *03*		30___
17023	BNSF 2-bay Hopper "409038" (std O), *04*		30___
17024	Reading Offset Hopper "81089" (std O), *03–04*		43___
17025	C&O Offset Hopper "300027" (std O), *03–04*		43___
17026	D&H Offset Hopper "7215" (std O), *03–04*		41___
17027	IC Offset Hopper "92142" (std O), *03–04*		49___
17028	GE PS-2 2-bay Covered Hopper "326" (std O), *03–04*		35___
17029	CNJ PS-2 2-bay Covered Hopper "803" (std O), *03–04*		35___
17030	MILW PS-2 2-bay Covered Hopper "99708" (std O), *03–04*		35___

		Exc	Mint
17031	SP PS-2 2-bay Covered Hopper "401306" (std O), 03–04		38
17038	Clinchfield PS-2 Covered Hopper, 05		70
17039	Boston & Maine PS-2 2-bay Covered Hopper, 05		55
17040	Norfolk & Western PS-2 2-bay Covered Hopper, 05		55
17041	Great Northern Offset Hopper, 05		60
17042	Green Bay & Western Offset Hopper, 05		60
17043	Baltimore & Ohio Offset Hopper, 05		60
17063	Santa Fe PS-2 2-bay Covered Hopper "82297" (std O), 06		55
17064	MKT PS-2 2-bay Covered Hopper "1311" (std O), 06		55
17065	Boraxo PS-2 2-bay Covered Hopper "31062" (std O), 06		55
17066	PRR PS-2 2-bay Covered Hopper "256177" (std O), 06		55
17067	Rock Island Offset Hopper "89500" with gravel (std O), 06		65
17068	CNJ Offset Hopper "61261" (std O), 06		65
17069	Maine Central Offset Hopper "3785" (std O), 06		65
17070	P&LE Offset Hopper "4990" (std O), 06		65
17083	C&O Offset Hopper "47386" (std O), 05		40
17100	Chessie System 3-bay ACF Hopper	49	85
17101	Chessie System 3-bay ACF Hopper (std O), 88	37	45
17102	Chessie System 3-bay ACF Hopper (std O), 88	35	41
17103	Chessie System 3-bay ACF Hopper (std O), 88	31	34
17104	Chessie System 3-bay ACF Hopper (std O), 88	38	46
17105	Chessie System 3-bay ACF Hopper (std O), 88	39	46
17107	Sinclair 3-bay ACF Hopper (std O), 89	40	48
17108	Santa Fe 3-bay ACF Hopper (std O), 90	42	48
17109	N&W 3-bay ACF Hopper (std O), 91	24	31
17110	UP Hopper with coal (std O), 91	24	30
17111	Reading Hopper with coal (std O), 91	23	28
17112	Erie-Lack. 3-bay ACF Hopper (std O), 92	24	34
17113	LV Hopper with coal (std O), 92–93	25	32
17114	Peabody Hopper with coal (std O), 92–93	26	30
17118	Archer Daniels Midland 3-bay ACF Hopper "60029" (std O), 93	28	35
17120	CSX Hopper "295110" with coal (std O), 94	28	30
17121	ICG Hopper "72867" with coal (std O), 94	26	33
17122	RI 3-bay ACF Hopper "800200" (std O), 94	32	39
17123	Cargill Covered Grain Hopper "844304" (std O), 95	25	34
17124	Archer Daniels Midland 3-bay ACF Hopper "50224" (std O), 95	24	30
17127	Delaware & Hudson 3-bay Hopper, 96		34
17128	Chesapeake & Ohio 3-bay Hopper, 96		30
17129	WM 3-bay Hopper "9300" with coal (std O), 97		34
17132	PRR 3-bay ACF Hopper "260815," 98		40
17133	BNSF ACF 3-bay Covered Hopper "403698," 98		38
17134	BNSF 3-bay Covered Hopper "403698" (std O), 01		38
17135	BNSF ACF 3-bay Covered Hopper with ETD, 98		39

Exc Mint

		Exc	Mint
17137	Cargill 3-bay Covered Hopper "1219" (std O), *99*	45	
17138	Farmers Elevator 3-bay Covered Hopper (std O), *99*	45	
17139	"Grain Train" 3-bay Hopper "BLMR 1025," *99–00*	39	
17140	Virginian 3-bay Hopper 6-pack, "5260-5265," *99*	230	
17147	C&O 3-bay Hopper 6-pack, "156330-156335," *99*	230	
17154	Alberta Cylindrical Hopper "628373" (std O), *01*	40	
17155	Shell Cylindrical Hopper "3527" (std O), *01*	40	
17156	ACF Pressureaide 3-bay Hopper "59267" (std O), *01*	27	
17157	Wonder Bread "56670" 3-bay Hopper (std O), *01*	40	
17158	Conrail Coal Hopper "487739" (std O), *01*	42	
17159	N&W Coal Hopper "1776" (std O), *01*	45	
17163	C&O 3-bay Hopper (std O), *01*	30	
17170	General Mills 3-bay Covered Hopper (std O), *00 u*	60	
17171	Lionel Lion Cylindrical Hopper (std O), *01*	45	
17172	CP Rail Cylindrical Hopper "385206" (std O), *02*	37	
17173	Govt. of Canada Cylindrical Hopper "111031" (std O), *02*	33	
17174	GN 3-bay Hopper "171250" (std O), *02*	29	
17175	IC PS-2CD 4427 Covered Hopper "57031" (std O), *02*	40	
17176	Cargill PS-2CD 4427 Covered Hopper "2514" (std O), *02*	46	
17177	PS-2CD 4427 Covered Hopper "2500" (std O), *02*	40	
17178	Santa Fe PS-2CD 4427 Covered Hopper "304774" (std O), *02*	40	
17179	Indianapolis Power & Light Coal Hopper "10074" (std O), *02*	40	
17180	Rock Island Coal Hopper "700665" (std O), *02*	40	
17181	NYC 4-bay ACF Centerflow Hopper "892138" (std O), *03*	45	
17182	Sigco Hybrids 4-bay ACF Centerflow Hopper "1100" (std O), *03*	46	
17183	C&O Hopper "156341" (std O), *01*	30	
17184	Virginian Hopper "5271" (std O), *01*	30	
17185	LLCX Bathtub Gondola "877900" (std O), *01*	36	
17186	Cannonaide 4-bay ACF Centerflow Hopper "96169" (std O), *03*	40	
17187	Rio Grande 4-bay ACF Centerflow Hopper "15521" (std O), *03*	40	
17188	Govt. of Canada 3-bay Cylindrical Hopper (std O), *03*	48	
17189	Saskatchewan Grain 3-bay Cylindrical Hopper (std O), *03*	48	
17190	Soo/CP 3-bay ACF Hopper "119303" (std O), *03*	37	
17191	BN PS-2CD 4427 Hopper "450669" (std O), *03–04*	45	
17192	Lehigh Valley PS-2CD 4427 Hopper "51118" (std O), *03–04*	40	
17193	Chessie System/WM PS-2CD 4427 Hopper "4673" (std O), *03–04*	30	
17194	MKT PS-2CD 4427 Hopper "1122" (std O), *03–04*	40	
17195	L&N 3-bay Hopper "240850" (std O), *04*	40	

		Exc	Mint
___17196	Firestone 4-bay Hopper "53240" (std O), *04*		40
17197	Diamond Chemicals 4-bay Hopper "53286" (std O), *04*		40
___17198	Hercules 4-bay Hopper "50503" (std O), *04*		40
___17199	Conrail 4-bay Hopper "888367" (std O), *04*		46
___17200	Canadian Pacific Boxcar (std O), *89*	26	32
___17201	Conrail Boxcar (std O), *87*	33	38
___17202	Santa Fe Boxcar (std O), diesel RailSounds, *90*	80	85
___17203	Cotton Belt DD Boxcar (std O), *91*	33	38
___17204	Missouri Pacific DD Boxcar (std O), *91*	27	30
___17207	C&IM DD Boxcar (std O), *92*	36	42
___17208	Union Pacific DD Boxcar (std O), *92*	35	40
___17209	B&O DD Boxcar "296000" (std O), *93*	37	43
17210	Chicago & Illinois Midland Boxcar "16021" (std O), *92 u*	30	39
17211	Chicago & Illinois Midland Boxcar "16022" (std O), *92 u*	30	39
17212	Chicago & Illinois Midland Boxcar "16023" (std O), *92 u*	24	31
___17213	Susquehanna Boxcar "501" (std O), *93*	28	31
___17214	Railbox Boxcar (std O), diesel RailSounds, *93*	75	85
___17216	PRR DD Boxcar "60155" (std O), *94*	34	38
17217	New Haven State of Maine Boxcar "45003" (std O), *95*	28	35
___17218	BAR State of Maine Boxcar "2184" (std O), *95*	23	36
___17219	Tazmanian Devil 40th Birthday Boxcar (std O), *95*	40	50
___17220	Pennsylvania Boxcar (std O), *96*		23
___17221	NYC Boxcar (std O), *96*		34
___17222	Western Pacific Boxcar (std O), *96*	28	34
___17223	Milwaukee Road DD Boxcar (std O), *96*		34
___17224	Central of Georgia Boxcar "9464-197" (std O), *97*	15	29
___17225	Penn Central Boxcar "9464-297" (std O), *97*	13	26
___17226	Milwaukee Road Boxcar "9464-397" (std O), *97*		23
___17227	UP DD Boxcar "9200" (std O), *97*		35
17231	Wisconsin Central DD Boxcar "9200" with auto frames, *98*		40
___17232	SP/UP Merger DD Boxcar "9200," *98*		33
___17233	Western Pacific Boxcar "9464-198," *98*		27
___17234	Port Huron & Detroit Boxcar "9464-298," *98*		33
___17235	Boston & Maine Boxcar "9464-398," *98*		41
___17239	ATSF "Texas Chief" Boxcar "9464-1," *97*		50
___17240	ATSF "Super Chief" Boxcar "9464-2," *97*		50
___17241	ATSF" El Capitan" Boxcar "9464-3," *97*		50
___17242	ATSF "Grand Canyon" Boxcar "9464-4," *97*		60
___17243	NP Boxcar "8722," *98*		48
___17244	Santa Fe "Chief" Boxcar, *98*		37
___17245	C&O Boxcar with Chessie kitten, *98*		44
___17246	NYC Pacemaker Rolling Stock 4-pack, *98*		200
___17247	NYC 9464 Boxcar "174940," *98*		135
___17248	NYC 9464 Boxcar "174945," *98*		115
___17249	NYC 9464 Boxcar "174949," *98*		60
___17250	UP Boxcar "507406" (std O), *99*		45
___17251	BNSF Boxcar "103277," *99*		41

Exc Mint

		Exc	Mint
17252	NS Boxcar "564824" (std O), *99*		41___
17253	CSX Boxcar "141756" (std O), *99*		35___
17254	UP Boxcar "551967" (std O), *99*		42___
17255	Chevy DD Boxcar "9200" (std O), *99*		38___
17257	Atlantic Coast Line Boxcar "28809" (std O), *99*		36___
17258	D&H 9464 Boxcar "29055" std O, *99*		41___
17259	MKT 9464 Boxcar "1422" (std O), *99*		34___
17260	CP Rail 9464 Boxcar "286138" (std O), silver, *00*		45___
17261	CP Rail 9464 Boxcar "85154," green, *00*		44___
17262	CP Rail 9464 Boxcar "56776," red (std O), *00*		48___
17263	NYC Boxcar "45725" (std O), *00*		46___
17264	C&O Boxcar "6054" (std O), *00*		44___
17265	U.S. Army Boxcar (std O), *00*		35___
17266	Monon Boxcar "911" (std O), *00*		45___
17268	C&O 9464 Boxcar "12700" (std O), *01*		44___
17269	Western Maryland 9464 Boxcar "29140" (std O), *01*		44___
17270	B&O Time-Saver 9464 Boxcar "467439" (std O), *01*		42___
17271	"The Rock" Boxcar "300324" (std O), *01*		37___
17272	Railbox Boxcar "15150" (std O), *01*		27___
17273	DT&I DD Boxcar "26852" (std O), *01*		44___
17274	Soo Line DD Boxcar "177587" (std O), *01*		42___
17275	NYC PS-1 Boxcar "175008" (std O), *02*		43___
17276	Cotton Belt PS-1 Boxcar "75000" (std O), *02*		44___
17277	Rio Grande PS-1 Boxcar "69676" (std O), *02*		40___
17278	WP PS-1 Boxcar "1953" (std O), *02*		44___
17279	Ontario Northland Boxcar "7428" (std O), *02*		40___
17280	Santa Fe Boxcar "600194" with auto frames (std O), *02*		45___
17281	PRR DD Boxcar "83158" (std O), *04*		42___
17282	UP DD Boxcar "160300" (std O), *04*		42___
17283	GM&O DD Boxcar "9077" (std O), *04*		41___
17284	Erie DD Boxcar "66000" (std O), *04*		41___
17285	CSX Big Blue Boxcar "151296" (std O), *03*		36___
17287	BAR Boxcar "5976" (std O), *03*		35___
17288	NYC PS-1 Boxcar "175012" (std O), *03–04*		38___
17289	GN PS-1 Boxcar "18485" (std O), *03*		40___
17290	Seaboard PS-1 Boxcar "24452" (std O), *03–04*		42___
17291	RI PS-1 Boxcar "21110" (std O), *03–04*		42___
17292	B&M PS-1 Boxcar "76182" (std O), *04*		34___
17293	IC PS-1 Boxcar "400666" (std O), *04*		40___
17294	TP&W PS-1 Boxcar "5036" (std O), *04*		36___
17295	Santa Fe PS-1 Boxcar "276749" (std O), *04*		40___
17297	UP PS-1 Boxcar, *03*		100___
17300	Canadian Pacific Reefer (std O), *89*	28	33___
17301	Conrail Reefer (std O), *87*	35	42___
17302	Santa Fe Reefer with ETD (std O), *90*	35	41___
17303	C&O Reefer "7890" (std O), *93*	23	30___
17304	Wabash Reefer "26269" (std O), *94*	29	37___
17305	Pacific Fruit Express Reefer "459400" (std O), *94*	27	40___
17306	Pacific Fruit Express Reefer "459401" (std O), *94*	19	27___
17307	Tropicana Reefer "300" (std O), *95*	44	65___

		Exc	Mint
____**17308**	Tropicana Reefer "301" (std O), *95*	22	35
____**17309**	Tropicana Reefer "302" (std O), *95*	21	29
____**17310**	Tropicana Reefer "303" (std O), *95*	20	27
____**17311**	REA Reefer (std O), *96*	28	30
____**17314**	PFE Reefer "9800-198," *98*		42
____**17315**	PFE Reefer "9800-298," *98*		39
____**17316**	NP Reefer "98583," *98*		50
____**17317**	PRR Reefer FGE "91904," *98*		36
____**17318**	UP Reefer "170650" (std O), *99*		47
____**17319**	PFE Reefer 6-pack (std O), *01*		300
17331	Hood's General American Milk Car "802" (std O), ____ *02*		100
17332	Pfaudler General American Milk Car "501" (std O), *02* ____		70
17334	REA General American Milk Car "1741" (std O), ____ *02*		100
17335	New Haven General American Milk Car "102" (std O), *02* ____		75
____**17336**	PFE Steel-sided Reefer "17760" (std O), *03*		45
____**17337**	CN Steel-sided Reefer "209712" (std O), *03*		38
17338	Merchants Dispatch Transit Steel-sided Reefer "12322" (std O), *03* ____		39
____**17339**	Burlington Steel-sided Reefer "74825" (std O), *03*		45
17340	White Bros. General American Milk Car "891" (std O), *03* ____		44
17341	Dairymen's League General American Milk Car "779" (std O), *03* ____		43
____**17342**	Miller Beer Steel-sided Reefer (std O), *03 u*		58
____**17343**	Miller Beer Steel-sided Reefer (std O), *03 u*		64
17349	NYC General American Milk Car "6581" (std O), *03 u* ____		42
17350	Hood's General American Milk Car "503" (std O), *03 u* ____		45
____**17351**	Santa Fe Steel-sided Reefer "3526" (std O), *04*		43
____**17352**	PFE Steel-sided Reefer "20043" (std O), *04*		41
17353	Needham Packing Steel-sided Reefer "60507" (std O), *04* ____		44
____**17354**	Swift Steel-sided Reefer "15392" (std O), *04*		42
____**17355**	Hood's Steel-sided Reefer "550" (std O), *04*		40
____**17356**	Nestle Nesquik Steel-sided Reefer (std O), *04*		44
____**17357**	Borden's Steel-sided Reefer "522" (std O), *04*		47
____**17358**	Fairfield Farms Steel-sided Reefer (std O), *04*		44
17360	Hood's General American Milk Car "810" (std O), *03* ____		46
17361	Hood's General American Milk Car "811" (std O), *03* ____		43
17362	Pfaudler General American Milk Car "502" (std O), *03* ____		47
17363	Pfaudler General American Milk Car "503" (std O), *03* ____		40
17364	REA General American Milk Car "1742" (std O), *03* ____		38
17365	REA General American Milk Car "1743" (std O), *03* ____		44
____**17366**	NH General American Milk Car "103" (std O), *03*		43

		Exc	Mint
17367	NH General American Milk Car "104" (std O), *03*		47____
17368	White Brothers General American Milk Car "892" (std O), *03*		43____
17369	White Brothers General American Milk Car "893" (std O), *03*		47____
17370	Dairymen's League General American Milk Car "780" (std O), *03*		47____
17371	Dairymen's League Milk Car "781" (std O), *03*		47____
17372	NYC General American Milk Car "6582" (std O), *03*		47____
17373	NYC General American Milk Car "6583" (std O), *03*		40____
17374	Hood's General American Milk Car "504" (std O), *03*		43____
17375	Hood's General American Milk Car "505" (std O), *03*		47____
17377	Railway Express Operating Milk Car "302" (std O), *05*		172____
17378	Supplee General American Milk Car (std O), *05*		63____
17379	NP Steel-sided Reefer "91353" (std O), *05*		60____
17380	PFE Silver Steel-sided Reefer "45698" (std O), *05*		60____
17381	North Western Steel-sided Reefer "751" (std O), *05*		40____
17397	PFE Steel-sided Reefer "47767" (std O), *05*		45____
17398	A&P General American Milk Car "737" (std O), *06*		65____
17399	Bowman Dairy General American Milk Car "117" (std O), *06*		65____
17400	CP Rail Gondola with coal (std O), *89*	30	34____
17401	Conrail Gondola with coal (std O), *87*	24	26____
17402	Santa Fe Gondola with coal (std O), *90*	19	25____
17403	Chessie System Gondola "371629" with coil covers (std O), *93*	18	25____
17404	ICG Gondola "245998" with coil covers (std O), *93*	26	32____
17405	Reading Gondola "24876" with coil covers (std O), *94*	27	31____
17406	PRR Gondola "385405" with coil covers (std O), *95*	37	42____
17407	NKP Gondola with scrap load, *96*		24____
17408	Cotton Belt Gondola "9820" with scrap load (std O), *97*		32____
17410	UP Gondola "903004" with scrap load (std O), *99*		30____
17412	Gondola, blue, online store, *98*		20____
17413	Service Center Gondola with parts load (SSS), *00*		24____
17414	Nickel Plate PS-5 Gondola "44801" (std O), *01–02*		40____
17415	Frisco PS-5 Gondola "61878" (std O), *01–02*		35____
17416	D&H Gondola "14011" with scrap load (std O), *01*		33____
17417	BN Rotary Bathtub Gondola 3-pack, *01*		140____
17421	CSX Rotary Bathtub Gondola 3-pack, *01*		135____
17425	Western Maryland PS-5 Gondola "354903" (std O), *01–02*		36____
17426	Maine Central PS-5 Gondola "1116" (std O), *01–02*		40____
17427	CSX Rotary Bathtub Gondola Add-on Unit (std O), *02*		47____

		Exc	Mint
17428	BN Rotary Bathtub Gondola Add-on Unit (std O), 02		42
17429	Conrail Rotary Bathtub Gondola 3-pack (std O), 02–03		115
17433	BNSF Rotary Bathtub Gondola 3-pack (std O), 02–03		145
17439	UP PS-5 Gondola "229606" (std O), 03		35
17440	Algoma Central PS-5 Gondola "801" (std O), 03		32
17441	Conrail Rotary Bathtub Gondola "507673" (std O), 03		39
17442	BNSF Rotary Bathtub Gondola "668330" (std O), 03		46
17443	NS Rotary Bathtub Gondola 3-pack (std O), 03		90
17447	UP Rotary Bathtub Gondola 3-pack (std O), 03		100
17457	GN PS-5 Gondola "72839" (std O), 03		35
17458	Reading PS-5 Gondola "33267" (std O), 03		35
17459	CP Rail PS-5 Gondola "338966" (std O), 04		35
17460	NYC PS-5 Gondola "749592" (std O), 04		40
17461	Pennsylvania PS-5 Gondola "374256" (std O), 04		36
17462	Santa Fe PS-5 Gondola "167340" (std O), 04		35
17463	NS Bathtub Gondola "10303" (std O), 04		40
17464	UP Bathtub Gondola "28100" (std O), 04		35
17465	CP Rail Bathtub Gondola 3-pack (std O), 04		105
17470	CP Rail Bathtub Gondola, 05		50
17471	Burlington PS-5 Gondola with covers (std O), 05		44
17472	New Haven PS-5 Gondola with covers (std O), 05		53
17473	NYC PS-5 Gondola "502351" (std O), 06–07		65
17474	D&H PS-5 Gondola "13816" (std O), 06–07		65
17475	Koppers PS-5 Gondola "213" (std O), 06–07		65
17477	L&N PS-5 Gondola "170012" (std O), 06–07		46
17478	N&W PS-5 Gondola "275005" with containers (std O), 08		70
17479	LV PS-5 Gondola "33455" with containers (std O), 08		70
17480	RI PS-5 Gondola with coke containers (std O), 08–09		70
17488	UP Bathtub Gondola 3-pack (std O), 09		190
17500	CP Flatcar with logs (std O), 89	17	29
17501	Conrail Flatcar with stakes (std O), 87	37	45
17502	Santa Fe Flatcar with trailer (std O), 90	70	75
17503	NS Flatcar with trailer (std O), 92	55	65
17504	NS Flatcar with trailer (std O), 92	55	65
17505	NS Flatcar with trailer (std O), 92	50	55
17506	NS Flatcar with trailer (std O), 92	46	55
17507	NS Flatcar with trailer (std O), 92	50	55
17510	NP Flatcar "61200" with logs (std O), 94	31	36
17511	WM Flatcar with logs, set of 3 (std O), 95		145
17512	WM Flatcar with logs (std O), 95	35	41
17513	WM Flatcar with logs (std O), 95	43	50
17514	WM Flatcar with logs (std O), 95	39	45
17515	Norfolk Southern Flatcar with tractors (std O), 95	24	42
17516	T&P Flatcar "9823" with 2 Beechcraft Bonanzas (std O), 97		50

Exc Mint

		Exc	Mint
17517	WP Flatcar "9823" with Ertl Caterpillar frontloader (std O), *97*		39___
17518	PRR Flatcar "9823" with 2 Corgi Mack trucks (std O), *97*	29	50___
17522	Flatcar with Plymouth Prowler, *98*		41___
17527	Flatcar with 2 Dodge Vipers, *98*		38___
17529	ATSF Flatcar "90010" with Ford milk truck, *99*		55___
17533	MTTX Ford Flatcar with auto frames, *99*		38___
17534	Diamond T Flatcar with Mack trucks "9823," *99*		55___
17536	Route 66 Flatcar "9823-3" with 2 luxury coupes, *99*		37___
17537	Route 66 Flatcar "9823-4" with 2 touring coupes, *99*		32___
17538	NYC Flatcar with Ford tow truck, *99*		43___
17539	Flatcar "9823" with 2 Corvettes (std O), *99*		70___
17540	Flatcar "9823" with 2 Corvettes (std O), *99*		70___
17546	LL Recovery Flatcar "6424" with rail load, *99*		50___
17547	Lionel Lines Recovery Flatcar "6429" with machinery, *99*		50___
17548	Route 66 Flatcar "9823-6" with 2 luxury coupes, *99*		42___
17549	Route 66 Flatcar "9823-5" with station wagon and trailer, *99*		42___
17550	BN Center Beam Flatcar "6216" with lumber (std O), *99*		39___
17551	NYC Flatcar with NYC pickups "499," *99*		49___
17553	Trailer Train Flatcar "98102" with combine (std O), *99*		125___
17554	GN Flatcar "61042" with logs, *00*		32___
17555	Ford Mustang Flatcar with 2 cars (std O), *01*		NRS___
17556	Ford Mustang Flatcar with 2 cars (std O), *01*		NRS___
17557	Route 66 Flatcar "9823-7" with black sedans, *99–00*		39___
17558	Route 66 Flatcar "9823-8" with brown sedans, *99*		39___
17559	Route 66 Flatcar "9823-9" with 2 wagons (std O), *01*		40___
17560	Route 66 Flatcar "9823-10" with 2 sedans (std O), *01*		40___
17563	Santa Fe Flatcar "90011" with pickup trucks (std O), *01*		49___
17564	West Side Lumber Shay Log Car 3-pack #2 (std O), *01*		95___
17568	PRR Flatcar "470333" with pickup trucks (std O), *02*		50___
17571	UP Flatcar "909231" with pickup trucks (std O), *03*		50___
17572	Pioneer Seed Flatcar with pedal cars, *02 u*		190___
17573	WM PS-4 Flatcar "2631" (std O), *03*		35___
17574	Santa Fe PS-4 Flatcar "90081" (std O), *03*		35___
17575	NYC PS-4 Flatcar "506098" (std O), *03*		40___
17576	Ontario Northland PS-4 Flatcar "2020" (std O), *03*		35___
17577	B&O PS-4 Flatcar "8651" (std O), *04*		35___
17578	B&M PS-4 Flatcar "34007" (std O), *04*		35___
17579	Milwaukee Road PS-4 Flatcar "64073" (std O), *04*		35___

		Exc	Mint
____17580	UP PS-4 Flatcar "54603" (std O), *04*		35
17581	GN Flatcar "X4168" with pickup trucks (std O), *04*		42
17582	PRR PS-4 Flatcar "469617" with trailers (std O), *05*		110
____17583	GN PS-4 Flatcar with trailers, *05*		80
____17584	SP PS-4 Flatcar with trailers, *05*		80
17585	C&O PS-4 Flatcar "81000" with trailers (std O), *05*		80
____17586	BN Husky Stack Car "63322" (std O), *05*		80
____17587	SP Husky Stack Car "513915" (std O), *05*		80
____17588	CSX Husky Stack Car "620350" (std O), *05*		80
17589	TTX Trailer Train Husky Stack Car "456249" (std O), *05*		65
____17600	NYC Wood-sided Caboose (std O), *87 u*	35	45
____17601	Southern Wood-sided Caboose (std O), *88*	35	44
____17602	Conrail Wood-sided Caboose (std O), *87*	65	75
____17603	RI Wood-sided Caboose (std O), *88*	19	34
____17604	Lackawanna Wood-sided Caboose (std O), *88*	42	53
____17605	Reading Wood-sided Caboose (std O), *89*	34	37
____17606	NYC Steel-sided Caboose, smoke (std O), *90*	49	65
____17607	Reading Steel-sided Caboose, smoke (std O), *90*	55	65
____17608	C&O Steel-sided Caboose, smoke (std O), *91*	46	55
____17610	Wabash Steel-sided Caboose, smoke (std O), *91*	39	55
____17611	NYC Wood-sided Caboose "6003" (std O), *90 u*	40	55
____17612	NKP Steel-sided Caboose, smoke (FF 6), *92*	60	65
17613	Southern Steel-sided Caboose "7613," smoke (std O), *92*	60	65
____17615	NP Wood-sided Caboose, smoke (std O), *92*	65	70
____17617	D&RGW Steel-sided Caboose (std O), *95*	50	55
____17618	Frisco Wood-sided Caboose (std O), *95*	65	75
____17620	NP Wood-sided Caboose "1746," *98*		70
____17623	Farmrail Extended Vision Caboose, *99*		74
____17624	Conrail Extended Vision Caboose "6900," *99*		43
17625	Burlington Northern Steel-sided Caboose "7606," *99*		65
17626	Service Center Extended Vision Caboose (SSS), *00*		29
____17627	C&O Extended Vision Caboose, *01*		65
____17628	BNSF Extended Vision Caboose, *01*		65
____17629	Santa Fe Extended Vision Caboose, *01*		80
____17630	UP Extended Vision Caboose, *01*		85
____17631	Virginian Bay Window Caboose, *01*		85
____17632	CSX Bay Window Caboose, *01*		75
____17633	NYC Bay Window Caboose, *01*		90
____17634	Delaware & Hudson Bay Window Caboose, *01*		75
____17635	100th Anniversary Die-cast Gold Caboose, *00*		345
____17636	NYC Die-cast Caboose "18096," *00–01*		100
____17637	NYC "Quicker via Peoria" Die-cast Caboose, *00*		135
____17638	RI Extended Vision Caboose "17011" (std O), *02*		55
17639	Chessie Extended Vision Caboose "3322" (std O), *02*		55
17640	CP Extended Vision Caboose "434604" (std O), *02*		57

Exc Mint

17641	Soo Line Extended Vision Caboose "2" (std O), *02*	55	
17642	Conrail Bay Window Caboose "21023" (std O), *02*	65	
17643	NKP Bay Window Caboose "480" (std O), *02*	60	
17644	Erie Bay Window Caboose "C307," (std O), *02*	55	
17645	N&W Bay Window Caboose "C-6," (std O), *02*	55	
17646	UP Bay Window Caboose "24555," (std O), *02*	65	
17647	B&O Caboose "C-2820" (std O), *03–04*	65	
17648	Chessie System Caboose "C-2800" (std O), *03–04*	75	
17649	Lionel Lines Caboose "7649" (std O), *03–04*	65	
17650	Rio Grande Extended Vision Caboose "01500" (std O), *03*	65	
17651	BN Extended Vision Caboose "10531" (std O), *03–05*	80	
17652	NYC Bay Window Caboose "20200" (std O), *03*	75	
17653	SP Bay Window Caboose "1337" (std O), *03*	65	
17654	Alaska Extended Vision Caboose "989" (std O), *03*	75	
17655	WP Bay Window Caboose "448" (std O), *03–04*	75	
17657	Norman Rockwell Holiday Caboose, *03*	30	
17658	Burlington Extended Vision Caboose "13611" (std O), *04*	70	
17659	CN Extended Vision Caboose "79646" (std O), *04*	70	
17660	Seaboard Extended Vision Caboose "5700" (std O), *04*	65	
17661	C&NW Bay Window Caboose "10871" (std O), *04*	65	
17662	PC Bay Window Caboose "21001" (std O), *04*	65	
17663	Southern Bay Window Caboose "X546" (std O), *04*	65	
17664	B&O Caboose "C-2824" (std O), *03–04*	65	
17665	Chessie System Caboose "C-2802" (std O), *03–04*	75	
17669	NYC Bay Window Caboose, smoke, *05*	85	
17670	CP Rail Bay Window Caboose, smoke, *05*	85	
17671	BN Extended Vision Caboose, *05*	85	
17672	GN Extended Vision Caboose "X-106" (std O), *05*	85	
17673	Santa Fe Extended Vision Caboose, *05*	85	
17674	Reading Extended Vision Caboose "94119" (std O), *05*	75	
17675	Rio Grande Extended Vision Caboose "01507" (std O), *06*	90	
17676	NYC Bay Window Caboose "20300," *07*	60	
17677	Erie-Lack. Bay Window Caboose "C359" (std O), *06*	90	
17678	B&O I-12 Caboose "C2421" (std O), *06*	90	
17679	Long Island Bay Window Caboose "C-62" (std O), *06*	90	
17682	Reading Northeastern Caboose "92841" (std O), *06–07*	85	
17683	Chessie System Northeastern Caboose "1893" (std O), *07*	85	
17684	Conrail Northeastern Caboose "18873" (std O), *07*	85	
17685	Jersey Central Northeastern Caboose "91533" (std O), *07*	85	

		Exc	Mint
___17690	UP CA-4 Caboose "3826" (std O), *06*		90
___17691	UP CA-4 Caboose "25103" (std O), *06*		90
___17692	LL CA-4 B22 Caboose "7629" (std O), *06*		90
17693	Chessie Extended Vision Caboose "3285" (std O), *06*		90
17694	NS Extended Vision Caboose "555582" (std O), *06*		90
___17695	Alaska I-12 Caboose "1001" (std O), *06*		90
___17696	CP Bay Window Caboose "437266" (std O), *06*		90
___17697	CN Extended Vision Caboose "78128" (std O), *06*		90
___17699	UP Ca-4 Caboose "25193" (std O), *07*		90
___17700	UP ACF 40-ton Stock Car "47456" (std O), *01–02*		85
17701	Rio Grande ACF 40-ton Stock Car "39269" (std O), *01–02*		60
17702	CP ACF 40-ton Stock Car "277083" (std O), *01–02*		75
17703	NYC ACF 40-ton Stock Car "23334" (std O), *01–02*		85
___17704	B&O ACF 40-ton Stock Car "110234" (std O), *02*		40
___17705	CB&Q ACF 40-ton Stock Car "52886" (std O), *02*		40
___17707	PRR ARF 40-ton Stock Car "128994" (std O), *03*		35
17708	CP Rail ACF 40-ton Stock Car "277313" (std O), *03*		38
___17709	UP Stock Car "48154" (std O), *04*		45
___17710	Great Northern Stock Car "56385" (std O), *04*		40
___17711	C&O ACF 40-ton Stock Car "95237" (std O), *06*		60
___17712	N&W ACF 40-ton Stock Car "33000" (std O), *06*		60
___17713	MKT ACF 40-ton Stock Car "47150" (std O), *06*		60
___17714	CN 40-ton Stock Car "172755" (std O), *06*		60
___17715	MP 40-ton Stock Car "52428" (std O), *06*		60
___17716	CGW 40-ton Stock Car "838," *08*		60
___17717	UP 40-ton Stock Car "48217," *08*		60
___17718	NS Heritage 3-bay Hopper 2-pack (std O), *12*		160
___17719	C&BQ ACF Stock Car "52925" (std O), *09*		70
___17720	UP ACF Stock Car (std O), *10*		70
___17721	Postwar Scale Stock Car 2-pack, *10–11*		140
17724	CN Scale Steel-sided Reefer "210552," (std O), *11*		80
___17725	NP Scale Steel-sided Reefer "98528," (std O), *11*		80
___17726	IC Scale Steel-sided Reefer "16644," (std O), *11*		80
17727	Mopac/Wabash Scale Steel-sided Reefer "30790," (std O), *11*		80
___17729	C&O Scale PS-1 Boxcar "2992" (std O), *12*		70
17730	Seaboard Scale Round-roof Boxcar "19293" (std O), *11*		70
___17731	Pere Marquette Scale Boxcar "81805" (std O), *12*		70
___17732	L&N Scale PS-1 Boxcar "4798" (std O), *12*		70
17733	PRR Scale Round-roof Boxcar "78948" (std O), *11*		70
17734	PRR Scale Round-roof Boxcar "76644" (std O), *11*		70
___17735	PRR Round-roof DD Boxcar "77851" (std O), *12*		70
___17736	PRR Round-roof DD Boxcar "60156" (std O), *12*		70

		Exc	Mint
17737	N&W Scale Round-roof Boxcar "46494" (std O), *11*		70____
17738	NP Round-roof DD Boxcar "39300" (std O), *12*		70____
17739	DT&I Round-roof DD Boxcar "12250" (std O), *12*		70____
17740	Alaska Scale Round-roof Boxcar "27781" (std O), *11*		70____
17741	Santa Fe Scale Slogan Reefer 5-car Set (std O), *12*		320____
17747	Santa Fe Scale Boxcar "39009" (std O), *12*		70____
17748	Grave's Mortuary Supply Scale PS-1 Boxcar (std O), *12-13*		70____
17749	Erie Scale PS-1 Boxcar "90300" (std O), *12*		70____
17750	NYC Round-roof DD Boxcar "77147" (std O), *12*		70____
17751	NKP Scale PS-1 Boxcar "6605" (std O), *12*		70____
17752	Polar Round-roof Boxcar "1202" (std O), *12–13, 16*		70____
17753	LV Scale PS-1 Boxcar "65124" (std O), *12*		70____
17754	EL DD Boxcar "65000" (std O), *12*		75____
17755	D&H DD Boxcar "25025" (std O), *12*		75____
17756	CP Rail DD Boxcar "42630" (std O), *12*		75____
17757	Milwaukee Road DD Boxcar "13441" (std O), *12*		75____
17758	ATSF Map and Slogan Reefer 3-pack, *12*		190____
17762	BN 57' Mechanical Reefer "9618" (std O), *12*		85____
17763	NYC 57' Mechanical Reefer "6762" (std O), *12*		85____
17764	ATSF 57' Mechanical Reefer "56244" (std O), *12*		85____
17765	Virginian Round-roof DD Boxcar "3131" (std O), *13–14*		80____
17766	NH Round-roof Boxcar "39303" (std O), *13*		70____
17767	SP Round-roof DD Boxcar "166052" (std O), *13–14*		80____
17768	Grave's Mortuary Supply Round-roof Boxcar (std O), *13*		70____
17769	D&RGW PS-1 Boxcar "60046" (std O), *13*		70____
17770	MILW PS-1 Boxcar "8777" (std O), *13*		70____
17771	CNJ PS-1 Boxcar "23522" (std O), *13–14*		80____
17772	Central of Georgia PS-1 Boxcar (std O), *13*		70____
17773	D&M Round-roof Boxcar "3148" (std O), *13–14*		80____
17774	D&M PS-1 Boxcar "2833" (std O), *13*		70____
17775	NS Heritage 3-bay Hopper 3-pack (std O), *13–15*		240____
17779	NS Heritage 3-bay Hopper 3-pack (std O), *13–15*		240____
17783	NS Heritage 3-bay Hopper 3-pack (std O), *13–15*		240____
17787	NS Heritage 3-bay Hopper 3-pack (std O), *13*		240____
17791	NS Heritage 3-bay Hopper 3-pack (std O), *13*		240____
17795	NS Heritage 3-bay Hopper 3-pack (std O), *13*		240____
17800	Ontario Northland Ore Car "6126," *00*		30____
17801	CN Ore Car "345165," *00*		37____
17802	CP Ore Car "377249," *00*		28____
17803	DMIR Ore Car "51456," *00*		30____
17804	UP Ore Car "8023," *01*		29____
17805	CP Rail Ore Car "377238," *01*		29____
17806	UP Ore Car "27250," *03*		30____
17807	BN Ore Car "95887," *02*		28____
17900	Santa Fe Unibody Tank Car (std O), *90*	37	46____
17901	Chevron Unibody Tank Car (std O), *90*	26	32____

		Exc	Mint
____17902	NJ Zinc Unibody Tank Car (std 0), *91*	26	34
____17903	Conoco Unibody Tank Car (std 0), *91*	24	29
____17904	Texaco Unibody Tank Car (std 0), *92*	34	43
____17905	Archer Daniels Midland Unibody Tank Car (std 0), *92*	24	33
____17906	SCM Unibody Tank Car "78286" (std 0), *93*	47	55
____17908	Marathon Oil Unibody Tank Car (std 0), *95*	51	56
____17909	Hooker Chemicals Unibody Tank Car (std 0), *96*		55
____17910	Sunoco Unibody Tank Car "7900," *97*		37
____17913	J.M. Huber Tank Car, *98*		29
____17914	Englehard Tank Car, *98*		36
____17915	Gulf Unibody Tank Car "8438," *00*		43
____17916	Burlington Unibody Tank Car "130000," *00*	24	38
____17918	Southern Unibody Tank Car, *01*		32
____17919	Koppers Unibody Tank Car, *01*		39
17924	Safety Kleen Unibody Tank Car "77603" (std 0), *02*		40
17925	Beefmaster Unibody Tank Car "120021" (std 0), *02*		38
____17926	Cargill Unibody 1-D Tank Car "5836" (std 0), *03*		40
17927	Union Starch Unibody 1-D Tank Car "59137" (std 0), *03*		35
____17928	Merck 1-D Tank Car "25421" (std 0), *03*		35
17929	Wyandotte Chemicals 1-D Tank Car "1325" (std 0), *03*		34
____17930	CSX Unibody Tank Car "993369" (std 0), *04*		35
____17931	UP Unibody Tank Car "6" (std 0), *04*		35
17932	CIBRO TankTrain Intermediate Car "26263" (std 0), *04*		35
17933	GATX TankTrain Intermediate Car 3-pack (std 0), *04*		100
____17946	Candy Cane Unibody Tank Car, *04*		60
17948	Philadelphia Quartz 1-D Tank Car "806" (std 0), *06*		55
____17949	Skelly Oil 1-D Tank Car "2293" (std 0), *06*		55
____17950	ADM Unibody Tank Car "19020" (std 0), *06*		60
____17951	Cerestar Unibody Tank Car "190177" (std 0), *06*		60
____17959	Dow 1-D Tank Car "310101" (std 0), *07*		55
____17960	Amaizo 1-D Tank Car "15440" (std 0), *07*		55
____17962	Domino Sugar 1-D Tank Car "3008" (std 0), *07*		60
____17966	Procor 1-D Tank Car "82607" (std 0), *07*		60
____17972	Union Starch 1-D Tank Car "724" (std 0), *08*		60
____17973	UP 1-D Tank Car "907838" (std 0), *08*		60
17975	Cargill Foods Unibody Tank Car 3-pack (std 0), *08–09*		195
____17976	Huber Unibody Tank Car 3-pack (std 0), *08–09*		195
____17983	GATX TankTrain Intermediate Car 3-pack, *08*		195
____18000	PRR 0-6-0 Locomotive "8977," *89, 91*	258	405
____18001	Rock Island 4-8-4 Locomotive "5100," *87*	305	315
____18002	NYC 4-6-4 Locomotive "785," *87 u*	510	576
____18003	DL&W 4-8-4 Locomotive "1501," *88*	235	294
____18004	Reading 4-6-2 Locomotive "8004," *89*	185	205
____18005	NYC 4-6-4 Locomotive "5340," display case, *90*	705	799
____18006	Reading 4-8-4 Locomotive "2100," *89 u*	490	528

Exc Mint

		Exc	Mint	
18007	Southern Pacific 4-8-4 Locomotive "4410," *91*	374	392	___
18008	Disneyland 35th Anniversary 4-4-0 Locomotive, display case, *90*	252	300	___
18009	NYC 4-8-2 Locomotive "3000," *90 u, 91*	370	561	___
18010	PRR 6-8-6 Steam Turbine Locomotive "6200," *91–92*	900	1041	___
18011	Chessie System 4-8-4 Locomotive "2101," *91*	440	536	___
18012	NYC 4-6-4 Locomotive "5340," *90*	710	900	___
18013	Disneyland 35th Anniversary 4-4-0 Locomotive, *90*	243	278	___
18014	Lionel Lines 2-6-4 Locomotive "8014," *91*	145	190	___
18016	Northern Pacific 4-8-4 Locomotive "2626," *92*	385	440	___
18018	Southern 2-8-2 Locomotive "4501," *92*	640	650	___
18022	Pere Marquette 2-8-4 Locomotive "1201," *93*	550	650	___
18023	Western Maryland Shay Locomotive "6," *92*	1050	1350	___
18024	Sears T&P 4-8-2 Locomotive "907," display case, *92 u*	750	790	___
18025	T&P 4-8-2 Locomotive "907," *92 u*		640	___
18026	NYC 4-6-4 Dreyfuss Hudson Locomotive, 2-rail, *92 u*		2350	___
18027	NYC 4-6-4 Dreyfuss Hudson Locomotive, 3-rail, *93 u*		1450	___
18028	Smithsonian PRR 4-6-2 Locomotive "3768," 2-rail, *93 u*		2150	___
18029	NYC 4-6-4 Dreyfuss Hudson Locomotive, 3-rail, *93 u*	1900	2150	___
18030	Frisco 2-8-2 Locomotive "4100," *93 u*	530	625	___
18031	2-10-0 Bundesbahn BR-50 Locomotive, 2-rail, *93 u*		NRS	___
18034	Santa Fe 2-8-2 Locomotive "3158," *94*	540	620	___
18035	2-10-0 Reichsbahn BR-50 Locomotive, 2-rail, *93 u*		NRS	___
18036	2-10-0 French BR-50 Locomotive, 2-rail, *93 u*		NRS	___
18040	N&W 4-8-4 Locomotive "612," *95*	640	710	___
18042	Boston & Albany 4-6-4 Locomotive "618," *95*		250	___
18043	Chesapeake & Ohio 4-6-4 Locomotive "490," *95*	680	750	___
18044	Southern 4-6-2 Locomotive "1390," *96*		255	___
18045	Commodore Vanderbilt Locomotive "777," *96*		678	___
18046	Wabash 4-6-4 Locomotive "700," *96*	190	375	___
18049	N&W Warhorse 4-8-4 Locomotive "600," *96*		490	___
18050	JCPenney 4-6-2 Locomotive "2055," *96*	235	245	___
18052	Pennsylvania Torpedo Locomotive "238E," *97*		455	___
18054	NYC 0-4-0 Switcher "1665," black, *97*		145	___
18056	NYC J1-e Hudson Locomotive "763E," Vanderbilt tender, *97*		603	___
18062	ATSF 4-6-4 Hudson Locomotive "3447," *97*		680	___
18063	NYC 4-6-4 Commodore Vanderbilt Locomotive, *99*		952	___
18064	NYC 4-8-2 Mohawk L-3A Locomotive "3005," tender, *98*	275	450	___
18067	NYC Weathered Commodore Vanderbilt Scale Hudson Locomotive, *97*		840	___
18071	SP Daylight Locomotive "4449," *98*		680	___
18072	Lionel Lines Torpedo Locomotive, tender, *98*		360	___
18079	NYC 2-8-2 Mikado Locomotive "1967," *99*		710	___

		Exc	Mint
____**18080**	D&RGW 2-8-2 Mikado Locomotive "1210," *99*		720
____**18082**	NYC 4-6-4 Hudson Locomotive "5404," *99*		230
____**18083**	C&O 4-6-4 Hudson Locomotive "305," *99*		205
____**18084**	Santa Fe 4-6-4 Hudson Locomotive "305," *99*		225
____**18085**	NH 4-6-2 Pacific Locomotive "1334," *99*		275
____**18086**	NYC 4-6-2 Pacific Locomotive "4929," *99*		235
____**18087**	Santa Fe 4-6-2 Pacific Locomotive "3448," *99*		265
____**18088**	SP 4-6-2 Pacific Locomotive "1407," *99*		350
____**18089**	CNJ 4-6-0 Camelback Locomotive "771," *99*		405
____**18091**	PRR 4-6-0 Camelback Locomotive "821," *99*		405
____**18092**	SP 4-6-0 Camelback Locomotive "2283," *99*		395
____**18093**	C&NW 4-6-0 Camelback Locomotive "3006," *99*		285
____**18094**	B&O 4-4-2 E6 Atlantic Locomotive, CC, *99–00*		345
____**18095**	PRR 4-4-2 E6 Atlantic Locomotive, CC, *99–00*	275	455
____**18096**	ATSF 4-4-2 E6 Atlantic Locomotive, CC, *99–00*		370
____**18097**	CNJ 4-6-0 Camelback Locomotive "770," *99*		330
____**18098**	PRR 4-6-0 Camelback Locomotive "820," *99*		355
____**18099**	SP 4-6-0 Camelback Locomotive "2282," *99*		360
____**18100**	Santa Fe F3 Diesel A Unit "8100" (see 11711)		NRS
____**18101**	Santa Fe F3 Diesel B Unit "8101" (see 11711)		NRS
18102	Santa Fe F3 Diesel A Unit "8102," dummy (see 11711)		
____	11711)		NRS
____**18103**	Santa Fe F3 Diesel B Unit "8103," dummy, *91 u*	180	190
____**18104**	GN F3 Diesel A Unit "366A," dummy (see 11724)		500
____**18105**	GN F3 Diesel B Unit "370B," dummy (see 11724)		NRS
____**18106**	GN F3 Diesel A Unit "351C," dummy (see 11724)		NRS
____**18107**	D&RGW Alco PA1 Diesel ABA Set, *92*	640	740
____**18108**	Great Northern F3 Diesel B Unit "371B," *93*	85	105
____**18109**	Erie Alco Diesel A Unit "725A" (see 11734)		NRS
____**18110**	Erie Alco Diesel B Unit "725B" (see 11734)		160
18111	Erie Alco Diesel A Unit "736A," dummy (see		
____	11734)		NRS
____**18115**	Santa Fe F3 Diesel B Unit, *93*	90	115
____**18116**	Erie-Lackawanna Alco PA1 Diesel AA Set, *93*	450	490
____**18117/18**	Santa Fe F3 Diesel AA Set "200," *93*	330	410
____**18119/20**	UP Alco Diesel AA Set, *94*	200	235
____**18121**	Santa Fe F3 Diesel B Unit "200A," *94*	75	95
____**18122**	Santa Fe F3 Diesel B Unit "200B," *95*	140	150
____**18123**	ACL F3 Diesel A Unit "342" (see 11903)		NRS
____**18124**	ACL F3 Diesel B Unit "342B" (see 11903)		NRS
____**18125**	ACL F3 Diesel A Unit "343," dummy (see 11903)		NRS
____**18128**	Santa Fe F3 Diesel A Unit "2343," *96*		435
____**18129**	Santa Fe F3 Diesel B Unit "2343C," *96*		245
____**18130**	Santa Fe F3 Diesel AB Set, *96*		580
____**18131**	NP F3 Diesel AB Set, "2390A, 2390C," *97*	295	360
____**18132**	NP F3 Diesel A Unit, powered		300
____**18133**	NP F3 Diesel B Unit, dummy		150
____**18134**	Santa Fe F3 Diesel A Unit "2343," dummy, *97*		195
____**18136**	Santa Fe F3 Diesel B Unit "2343C,," *97*	135	240
____**18138**	Milwaukee Road F3 Diesel A Unit "75A," *98*		400
____**18139**	Milwaukee Road F3 Diesel B Unit "2378B," *98*		250
____**18140**	Milwaukee Road F3 Diesel AB Set, *98*	390	600
____**18145**	NP F3 Diesel A Unit "2390A," *97*	300	360

		Exc	Mint
18146	NP F3 Diesel B Unit "2390C," *97*		170____
18147	NP F3 Diesel AB Set, *97*	450	580____
18149	UP Veranda Gas Turbine Locomotive "61," *98*	860	900____
18154	Deluxe Santa Fe FT Diesel AA Set, *98–00*		375____
18155	Deluxe Santa Fe FT Diesel A Unit, powered (see 18154)		NRS____
18156	Deluxe Santa Fe FT Diesel A Unit, dummy (see 18154)		NRS____
18157	Santa Fe FT Diesel AA Set, *98–00*		240____
18158	Santa Fe FT Diesel A Unit, powered (see 18157)		NRS____
18159	Santa Fe FT Diesel A Unit, dummy (see 18157)		NRS____
18160	NYC Deluxe FT Diesel AA Set, "1602, 1603," *98–00*		500____
18163	NYC FT Diesel AA Set, "1600, 2400," *98–00*		300____
18166	B&O FT Diesel AA Set, CC, *99–00*		340____
18169	B&O FT Diesel AA Set, traditional, *99–00*		240____
18189	Army of Potomac Operating Stock Car, *99*		45____
18190	McNeil's Rangers Operating Stock Car "2," *99*		45____
18191	WP F3 Diesel AA Set, *98*	153	570____
18192	WP F3 Diesel A Unit, powered, *98*		485____
18193	WP F3 Diesel A Unit, dummy, *98*		495____
18197	WP F3 Diesel B Unit "2355C," *99*	88	255____
18198	WP F3 Diesel B Unit "2345C" CC, *99*		360____
18200	Conrail SD40 Diesel "8200," *87*	180	200____
18201	Chessie System SD40 Diesel "8201," *88*	245	340____
18202	Erie-Lack. SD40 Diesel Unit "8459," dummy, *89 u*	90	140____
18203	CP Rail SD40 Diesel "8203," *89*	195	250____
18204	Chessie SD40 Diesel Unit "8204," dummy, *90 u*	135	190____
18205	Union Pacific Dash 8-40C Diesel "9100," *89*	275	335____
18206	Santa Fe Dash 8-40B Diesel "8206," *90*	195	235____
18207	Norfolk Southern Dash 8-40C Diesel "8689," *92*	230	270____
18208	BN SD40 Diesel Dummy Unit "8586," *91 u*	115	165____
18209	CP Rail SD40 Diesel Dummy Unit "8209," *92 u*	135	165____
18210	Illinois Central SD40 "6006," *93*	220	250____
18211	Susquehanna Dash 8-40B Diesel "4002," *93*	145	165____
18212	Santa Fe Dash 8-40B Diesel Dummy Unit "8212," *93*	155	180____
18213	Norfolk Southern Dash 8-40C Diesel "8688," *94*	225	240____
18214	CSX Dash 8-40C Diesel "7500," *94*	235	255____
18215	CSX Dash 8-40C Diesel "7643," *94*	240	260____
18216	Conrail SD-60M Diesel "5500," *94*	355	380____
18217	Illinois Central SD40 Diesel "6007," *94*	170	175____
18218	Susquehanna Dash 8-40B Diesel "4004," *94*	205	225____
18219	C&NW Dash 8-40C Diesel "8501," *95*	325	330____
18220	C&NW Dash 8-40C Diesel "8502," *95*	215	315____
18221	D&RGW SD50 Diesel "5512," *95*	455	520____
18222	D&RGW SD50 Diesel "5517," *95*	280	325____
18223	Milwaukee Road SD40 Diesel "154," *95*	375	380____
18224	Milwaukee Road SD40 Diesel "155," *95*	240	265____
18226	GE Dash 9 Diesel, *97*		295____
18228	SP Dash 9 Diesel "8228," gray with red nose, *97*		340____
18229	SP SD40 Diesel "7333," *98*	300	425____
18231	BNSF Dash 9 Diesel "739," *98*		435____

___18232	Soo Line SD60 Diesel "5500," *97*		350
___18233	BNSF Dash 9 Diesel "745," *98*		330
___18234	BNSF Dash 9 Diesel "740," CC, *98–99*		405
___18235	BNSF Dash 9 Diesel 2-pack, "739, 740," *98*		710
___18238	Conrail SD70 Diesel "4145," *99–00*		300
___18240	Conrail Dash 8-40B Diesel "5065" CC, *98*		260
___18241	BN SD70 Diesel "9413," *99–00*		345
___18245	PRR Alco PA1 Diesel AA Set, *99*		495
___18248	PRR Alco PB-1 Diesel "5750B," *99*		215
___18249	Erie Alco PB-1 Diesel "850B," *00*		250
___18250	BNSF SD70 Diesel "9870," *99–00*		365
___18251	CSX SD60 Diesel "8701," *99–00*		300
___18252	Amtrak Dash 9 Diesel, CC, *99*		285
___18253	BNSF Dash 9 Diesel, CC, *99*		305
___18254	ATSF Dash 9 Diesel, CC, *99*		340
___18255	NS Dash 9 Diesel, CC, *99*		315
___18256	Amtrak Dash 9 Diesel, traditional, *99*		200
___18257	BNSF Dash 9 Diesel, traditional, *99*		190
___18258	ATSF Dash 9 Diesel, traditional, *99*		205
___18259	NS Dash 9 Diesel, traditional, *99*		215
___18260	Conrail SD70 Diesel "4144," *99–00*		280
___18261	BN SD60 Diesel "9412," *99–00*		255
___18262	BNSF SD70 Diesel "9869," *99–00*		250
___18263	CSX SD60 Diesel "8700," *99–00*		255
___18264	Southern Pacific SD70M Diesel "8238," *99–00*		245
___18265	Southern Pacific SD70M Diesel "9803," *99–00*		340
___18266	Norfolk Southern SD60 Diesel "6552," CC, *01–02*		400
___18268	Lionel Centennial SD90MAC Diesel, CC, *00*		415
___18269	UP SD90MAC Diesel "8006," CC, *00*		405
___18271	CP SD90MAC Diesel "9129," CC, *00*		440
___18273	UP SD40 Diesel "8071," *99–00*		330
___18274	Burlington U30C Diesel "891," CC, *01*		370
___18276	Seaboard U30C Diesel "7274," CC, *01*		325
___18278	UP U30C Diesel "2938," CC, *01*		330
___18280	Maersk SD70 Diesel, CC, *00*		345
___18281	BNSF Dash 9-44CW Diesel "788," CC, *00*		340
___18282	BNSF Dash 9-44CW Diesel "789," traditional, *00*		225
___18283	CSX Dash 9-44CW Diesel "9019," CC, *00*		340
___18284	CSX Dash 9-44CW Diesel "9020," traditional, *00*		300
___18285	UP Dash 9-44C Diesel "9659," CC, *01*		325
___18286	UP Dash 9-44CW Diesel "9717," CC, *01*		355
___18287	CN Dash 9-44C Diesel "2529," CC, *01*		460
___18288	Odyssey System SD70 Diesel, CC, *00 u*		400
___18290	Amtrak Dash 8-32BWH Diesel "509," CC, *01*		325
___18291	BNSF Dash 8-32BWH Diesel "580," CC, *02*		340
___18292	Chessie GE U30C Diesel "3312," CC, *02*		340
___18293	Santa Fe U30C Diesel, CC, *03*		395
___18294	Alaska SD70MAC Diesel "4005," CC, *01–02*		435
___18295	Conrail SD80MAC Diesel "7200," CC, *02–03*		365
___18296	CSX SD80MAC Diesel "801," CC, *02–03*		405
___18297	NYC SD80MAC Diesel "9914," CC, *02–03*		405

Exc Mint

No.	Description	Exc	Mint
18298	UP "Desert Victory" SD40-2 Diesel "3593," CC, *02–03*		380___
18299	CP Rail SD40-2 Diesel "5420," CC, *02–03*		375___
18300	PRR GG1 Electric Locomotive "8300," *87*	285	335___
18301	Southern FM Train Master Diesel "8301," *88*	150	204___
18302	GN EP-5 Electric Locomotive "8302" (FF 3), *88*	190	250___
18303	Amtrak GG1 Electric Locomotive "8303," *89*	275	338___
18304	Lackawanna MU Commuter Car Set, *91*	380	435___
18305	Lackawanna MU Commuter Car Dummy Set, *92*	230	255___
18306	PRR MU Commuter Car Set, *92*	260	330___
18307	PRR FM Train Master Diesel "8699," *94*	170	202___
18308	PRR GG1 Electric Locomotive "4866," *92*	193	278___
18309	Reading FM Train Master Diesel "863," *93*	173	212___
18310	PRR MU Commuter Car Dummy Set, *93*	265	345___
18311	Disney EP-5 Electric Locomotive "8311," *94*	296	397___
18313	Pennsylvania GG1 Electric Locomotive "4907," *96*	75	297___
18314	PRR GG1 Electric Locomotive "2332," 5 gold stripes, *97*	300	507___
18315	Virginian E33 Electric Locomotive "2329," *97*		240 ___
18319	New Haven EP-5 Electric Locomotive, *99*	200	365___
18321	CNJ Train Master Diesel "2341," *99*		405___
18322	Lackawanna Train Master Diesel "2321," *99*		465___
18326	PRR Congressional GG1 Electric Locomotive, *00*		600___
18327	Virginian FM Train Master Diesel "2331," *99–00*		410___
18328	NH MU Commuter Car Set, CC, *00*		385___
18331	Reading MU Commuter Car Set, CC, *00*		460___
18334	NH MU Commuter Car Dummy Set, CC, *01*		180___
18337	Reading MU Commuter Car Dummy Set, CC, *01*		200___
18343	PRR GG1 Electric Locomotive "2332," CC, *01*		610___
18344	LIRR MU Commuter Car Set, powered, CC, *01*		470___
18347	IC MU Commuter Car Set, powered, CC, *01*		470___
18351	NYC S1 Electric Locomotive, *03*		400___
18352	JCPenney SP MU Commuter Car, display case, *02*		140___
18353	Pennsylvania E33 Electric Locomotive "4403," CC, *02*		280___
18354	PRR GG1 Electric Locomotive "4918," tuscan, CC, *04*		790___
18355	PRR GG1 Electric Locomotive "4876," green, CC, *04*		900___
18356	Penn Central GG1 Electric Locomotive "4901," CC, *04*		1050___
18364	PRR BB1 Electric Locomotive "3900," CC, *05–07*		530___
18367	LIRR BB3 Electric Locomotive "328 A," CC, *05*		530___
18371	PRR GG1 Electric Locomotive "4912," tuscan, 5 stripes, CC, *05–07*		780___
18372	PRR GG1 Electric Locomotive "4925," green, 1 stripe, CC, *05–07*		780___
18373	NYC S2 Electric Locomotive "125," CC, *05–07*		410___
18374	PRR GG1 Electric Locomotive "4866," silver, CC, *06–08*		900___
18375	Lackawanna FM Train Master Diesel "850," CC, *06*		400___
18376	Lackawanna FM Train Master Diesel "851," nonpowered (std O), *06*		130___

			Exc	Mint
____	18378	New York City R27 Subway Car 2-pack, *07*		360
____	18384	MILW EP-2 Electric Locomotive, CC, *07–08*		950
____	18385	NYC H-16-44 Diesel "7001," *07–09*		202
____	18386	NYC H-16-44 Diesel "7002," nonpowered (std O), *07–09*		123
____	18389	MILW EP-2 Electric Locomotive "E-1," CC, *07–08*		950
____	18399	NH EF-4 Rectifier Locomotive "306," CC, *09*		360
____	18400	Santa Fe Vulcan Rotary Snowplow "8400," *87*	135	170
____	18401	Workmen Handcar, *87–88*	30	37
____	18402	Lionel Lines Burro Crane, *88*	65	80
____	18403	Santa Claus Handcar, *88*	26	29
____	18404	San Francisco Trolley "8404," *88*	55	85
____	18405	Santa Fe Burro Crane, *89*	70	83
____	18406	Track Maintenance Car, *89, 91*	34	49
____	18407	Snoopy and Woodstock Handcar, *90–91*	89	103
____	18408	Santa Claus Handcar, *89*	26	35
____	18410	PRR Burro Crane, *90*	100	115
____	18411	Canadian Pacific Fire Car, *90*	70	98
____	18413	Charlie Brown and Lucy Handcar, *91*	40	68
____	18416	Bugs Bunny and Daffy Duck Handcar, *92–93*	117	165
____	18417	Section Gang Car, *93*	65	80
____	18419	Lionelville Electric Trolley "8419," *94*	75	90
____	18421	Sylvester and Tweety Handcar, *94*	44	50
____	18422	Santa and Snowman Handcar, *94*	32	37
____	18423	On-track Step Van, *95*	23	28
____	18424	On-track Pickup Truck, *95*	20	25
____	18425	Goofy and Pluto Handcar, *95*	36	50
____	18426	Santa and Snowman Handcar, *95*	25	30
____	18427	Tie-Jector Car "55," *97*		60
____	18429	Workmen Handcar, *96*	28	34
____	18430	Crew Car, *96*		28
____	18431	Trolley Car, *96–97*		46
____	18433	Mickey and Minnie Handcar, *96–97*	43	82
____	18434	Porky and Petunia Handcar, *96*		35
____	18436	Dodge Ram Track Inspection Vehicle, *97*		39
____	18438	PRR High-rail Inspection Vehicle, *98*		50
____	18439	Union Pacific High-rail Inspection Vehicle, *98*		42
____	18440	NJ Transit High-rail Inspection Vehicle, *98*		50
____	18444	Lionelville Fire Car (SSS), *98*		150
____	18445	NYC Fire Car, *98*		90
____	18446	Postwar "58" GN Rotary Snowplow, *99*		181
____	18447	Executive Inspection Vehicle, *99*		125
____	18452	Boston Trolley "3321," *99–00*		65
____	18454	Executive Inspection Vehicle, blue, *00*		105
____	18455	NYC Tie-Jector Car "X-2," *00–01*		74
____	18456	Postwar "59" Minuteman Motorized Unit, *01–02*		290
____	18457	Postwar "65" Handcar, *00–01*		45
____	18458	Postwar "53" D&RGW Snowplow, *00*		160
____	18459	Christmas Handcar, *01*		35
____	18461	Track Cleaning Car, *02–03*		90
____	18463	Hot Rod Inspection Vehicle, *01–02*		100
____	18464	Postwar "54" Track Ballast Tamper, *02–03*		170

		Exc	Mint
18465	Postwar "50" Gang Car, *03*		78____
18466	UP Rotary Snow Plow, *01–02*		150____
18467	Train Robbery Handcar, *02*		45____
18468	CN Railroad Speeder, *03–04*		49____
18469	Chessie System Railroad Speeder, *03–04*		49____
18470	Postwar "52" Fire Car, *02*		105____
18471	UP GP20 Diesel "1977," *03*		105____
18473	Lehigh Valley GP38 Diesel "310," *03*		160____
18474	Postwar "41" U.S. Army Switcher, *03–04*		145____
18475	Toy Story Handcar, *03*		55____
18476	Mickey and Minnie Mouse Handcar, *03–04*		55____
18480	Hobo Motorized Handcar, *03–04*		35____
18481	Christmas Yuletide Trolley, *03*		50____
18482	New Haven Rail Bonder "16," *04*		35____
18483	C&O Ballast Tamper "48," *04*		55____
18484	NS Dodge Inspection Vehicle, *04–05*		55____
18485	NYC Gang Car, *04–05*		100____
18486	Donald and Daisy Duck Handcar, *04–05*		63____
18487	Postwar "56" M&StL Mine Transport Car, *04–05*		230____
18489	Great Northern Rail Bonder "HR-73," *04*		35____
18490	UP Ballast Tamper, *04–05*		150____
18491	MOW Ballast Tamper "325," *04*		44____
18492	MOW Rail Bonder "58," *04*		35____
18493	Santa's Speeder, *05*		60____
18497	N&W Speeder "541005," traditional, *05*		65____
18498	New York Central Rotary Snowplow, *05*		210____
18500	Milwaukee Road GP9 Diesel "8500" (FF 2), *87*	175	230____
18501	WM NW2 Switcher "8501" (FF 4), *89*	185	215____
18502	LL 90th Anniversary GP9 Diesel "1900," *90*	148	173____
18503	Southern Pacific NW2 Switcher "8503," *90*	250	280____
18504	Frisco GP7 Diesel "504" (FF 5), *91*	155	240____
18505	NKP GP7 Diesel Set "400, 401" (FF 6)	295	365____
18506	CN Budd RDC Set, "D202, D203"	210	261____
18507	CN Budd RDC Baggage Car "D202," powered, *92*	50	75____
18508	CN Budd RDC Passenger Dummy Unit "D203," *92*	125	150____
18510	CN Budd RDC Passenger Dummy Unit "D200"	50	75____
18511	CN Budd RDC Passenger Dummy Unit "D250"	50	75____
18512	CN Budd RDC Dummy Set, "D200, D250," *93*	125	195____
18513	NYC GP7 Diesel "7420," *94*	90	125____
18514	Missouri Pacific GP7 Diesel "4124," *95*	245	310____
18515	Lionel Steel Vulcan Diesel "57" (SSS), *96*		190____
18516	Phantom III Locomotive, CC, *02*		345____
18550	JCPenney MILW GP9 Diesel "8500," display case, *87 u*	180	245____
18551	JCPenney Susquehanna RS3 Diesel "8809," display case, *89 u*	180	195____
18552	JCPenney DM&IR SD18 Diesel "8813," display case, *90 u*	170	195____
18553	Sears UP GP9 Diesel "150," display case, *91 u*	100	150____
18554	JCPenney GM&O RS3 "721," display case, *92–93 u*	160	180____
18555	Sears C&IM SD9 Diesel "52," *92 u*	165	190____

Exc Mint

		Exc	Mint
18556	Sears Chicago & Illinois Midland Freight Car Set, *92 u*	110	120
18557	Chessie System 4-8-4 Locomotive "2101," display case, export, *92 u*		NRS
18558	JCPenney MKT GP9 Diesel "91," display case, *94 u*	160	180
18562	SP GP9 Diesel "2380," *96*		195
18563	NYC GP9 Diesel "2380," *96*		230
18564	CP GP9 Diesel "2380," *97*		265
18565	Milwaukee Road GP9 Diesel "2338," *97*		220
18566	CR SD20 Diesel "8495" (SSS), *97*		150
18567	PRR GP9 Diesel "2028," *97*		225
18569	CB&Q GP9 Diesel "2380," *98*		190
18573	Santa Fe GP9 Diesel "2380," *98*		155
18574	Milwaukee Road GP20 Diesel "975," *98*		250
18575	Custom Series I GP9 Diesel "2398," *98*		350
18576	SP GP9 Diesel B Unit "2385," nonpowered, *98*		135
18577	NYC GP9 Diesel B Unit "2385," nonpowered, *98*		145
18579	MILW GP9 Diesel "2384," nonpowered, *99*		135
18580	Pennsylvania GP9 Diesel B Unit "2027," *98*		165
18582	Seaboard NW2 Switcher, *98*	250	455
18583	AEC Switcher "57," *98*		217
18585	Centennial SD40 Diesel, *99*		447
18587	NKP Alco C420 Switcher "577," CC, *99–01*	215	255
18588	D&H Alco C420 Switcher "412," CC, *99–01*	250	275
18589	LV Alco C420 Switcher "409," CC, *99–01*	255	300
18590	NKP Alco C420 Switcher "578," traditional, *99–01*		170
18591	D&H Alco C420 Switcher "411," traditional, *99–01*		215
18592	LV Alco C420 Switcher "410," traditional, *99–01*		175
18596	D&H Alco RS-11 Switcher "5001," CC, *99–01*		370
18598	NYC Alco RS-11 Switcher "8010," CC, *99–01*		380
18599	C&O GP38 Diesel "3855," *99–00*		145
18600	ACL 4-4-2 Locomotive "8600," *87 u*	65	75
18601	Great Northern 4-4-2 Locomotive "8601," *88*	80	95
18602	PRR 4-4-2 Locomotive "8602," *87*	75	85
18604	Wabash 4-4-2 Locomotive "8604," *88–91*	65	75
18605	Mopar Express 4-4-2 Locomotive "1987," *87–88 u*	75	120
18606	NYC 2-6-4 Locomotive "8606," *89*	170	190
18607	Union Pacific 2-6-4 Locomotive "8607," *89*	130	155
18608	D&RGW 2-6-4 Locomotive "8608" (SSS), *89*	90	105
18609	Northern Pacific 2-6-4 Locomotive "8609," *90*	170	195
18610	Rock Island 0-4-0 Locomotive "8610," *90*	105	115
18611	Lionel Lines 2-6-4 Locomotive (SSS), *90*	125	140
18612	C&NW 4-4-2 Locomotive "8612," *89*	75	100
18613	NYC 4-4-2 Locomotive "8613," *89 u*	75	95
18614	Circus Train 4-4-2 Locomotive "1989," *89 u*	95	125
18615	GTW 4-4-2 Locomotive "8615," *90*	70	85
18616	Northern Pacific 4-4-2 Locomotive "8616," *90 u*	85	110
18617	Adolphus III 4-4-2 Locomotive, *89–92 u*	100	125
18620	Illinois Central 2-6-2 Locomotive "8620," *91*	165	190

		Exc	Mint	
18622	Union Pacific 4-4-2 Locomotive "8622," *90–91 u*	65	80	___
18623	Texas & Pacific 4-4-2 Locomotive "8623," *92*	80	110	___
18625	Illinois Central 4-4-2 Locomotive "8625," *91 u*	70	95	___
18626	Delaware & Hudson 2-6-2 Locomotive "8626," *92*	105	115	___
18627	C&O 4-4-2 Locomotive "8627" or "8633," *92, 93 u, 94, 95 u*	75	95	___
18628	MKT 4-4-2 Locomotive "8628," *92, 93 u*	70	85	___
18630	C&NW 4-6-2 Locomotive "2903," *93*	325	370	___
18632	C&O Columbia 4-4-2 Locomotive "8632," *97–99*	75	95	___
18632	NYC 4-4-2 Locomotive "8632," *93–95*	75	95	___
18633	C&O 4-4-2 Locomotive "8633," *94–95*	65	85	___
18633	UP 4-4-2 Locomotive "8633," *93–95*	65	85	___
18635	Santa Fe 2-6-4 Locomotive "8625," *93*	135	155	___
18636	B&O 4-6-2 Locomotive "5300," *94*	295	315	___
18637	United Auto Workers 4-4-2 Locomotive "8633," *93 u*		90	___
18638	Norfolk & Western 2-6-4 Locomotive "638," *94*	170	220	___
18639	Reading 4-6-2 Locomotive "639," *95*	145	170	___
18640	Union Pacific 4-6-2 Locomotive "8640," *95*	110	130	___
18641	Ford 4-4-2 Locomotive "8641," *94 u*	65	85	___
18642	Lionel Lines 4-6-2 Locomotive, *95*	110	130	___
18644	ATSF 4-4-2 Columbia Locomotive "8644," *96–99*	75	90	___
18648	Sears Zenith 4-4-2 Locomotive "8632," *96 u*		132	___
18649	Chevrolet 4-4-2 Locomotive "USA-1," *96 u*		112	___
18650	LL 4-4-2 Columbia Locomotive "X-1110," *96–99*	95	120	___
18653	B&A 4-6-2 Pacific Locomotive "2044," *97*		140	___
18654	SP 4-6-2 Pacific Locomotive "2044," *97*		140	___
18656	Bloomingdale's 4-4-2 Columbia Locomotive "8632," *96*		108	___
18657	Sears Zenith 4-4-2 Columbia Locomotive "8632," *96*		115	___
18658	LL Little League 4-4-2 Columbia Locomotive "X-1110," *97*		90	___
18660	CN 4-6-2 Locomotive "2044," tender, *98*		175	___
18661	N&W 4-6-2 Locomotive "2044," tender, *98*		160	___
18662	Pennsylvania 0-4-0 Switcher, *98*	165	230	___
18666	SP&S 4-6-2 Pacific Locomotive "2044," *97*		200	___
18668	Bloomingdale's 4-4-2 Columbia Locomotive "8632," *97*		130	___
18669	JCPenney IC 4-6-2 Pacific Locomotive "2099," *98*		205	___
18670	D&H Columbia 4-4-2 Locomotive "1400," *98*		80	___
18671	N&W Columbia 4-4-2 Locomotive "1201," *98*		70	___
18678	Quaker Oats Columbia 4-4-2 Locomotive "8632," *98*		162	___
18679	JCPenney T&P 4-6-2 Locomotive "2000," traditional, *99, 00 u*		250	___
18681	PRR 4-4-2 Locomotive "460," *99*		75	___
18682	Santa Fe 4-4-2 Columbia Locomotive "524," traditional, *00–01*		70	___
18696	ACL 4-6-4 Locomotive "1800," *01*		120	___
18697	Santa Fe 4-6-4 Locomotive "3465," *01*		100	___
18699	Alaska 4-4-2 Locomotive "64," *01*		105	___

		Exc	Mint
____18700	Rock Island 0-4-0T Locomotive "8700," *87–88*	36	43
____18702	V&TRR 4-4-0 Locomotive "8702" (SSS), *88*	160	195
____18704	Lionel Lines 2-4-0 Locomotive, *89 u*	36	43
____18705	Neptune 0-4-0T Locomotive "8705," *90–91*	35	42
____18706	Santa Fe 2-4-0 Locomotive "8706," *91*	36	43
18707	Mickey's World Tour 2-4-0 Locomotive "8707," *91, 92 u*	58	68
18709	Lionel Employee Learning Center 0-4-0T Locomotive, *92 u*		140
____18710	SP 2-4-0 Locomotive "2000," *93*	30	38
____18711	Southern 2-4-0 Locomotive "2000," *93*	30	38
____18712	Jersey Central 2-4-0 Locomotive "2000," *93*	30	38
18713	Chessie System 2-4-0 Locomotive "1993," *94–95*	30	38
____18716	Lionelville Circus 4-4-0 Locomotive, *90–91*	90	110
____18718	LL 0-4-0 Dockside Switcher "8200," *97–98*		40
____18719	Thomas the Tank Engine "1," *97*		158
____18720	Union 4-4-0 General Locomotive "1865," *99*		175
18721	Confederate 4-4-0 General Locomotive "1861," *99*		175
____18722	Percy the Tank Engine "6," *99*		170
____18723	Union Pacific 4-4-0 General Locomotive, *05*		100
18730	Transylvania RR 4-4-0 Locomotive "13," traditional, *05*		105
____18732	North Pole Central 4-4-0 Locomotive "25," *06*		110
____18733	Percy the Tank Engine "6," *05–12*		120
____18734	James the Tank Engine "5," *06–12*		120
____18741	Thomas the Tank Engine, *08–13*		120
____18745	Hallow's Eve 4-6-0 Steam Locomotive, *11–12*		190
____18753	Route of the Reindeer RS3 Diesel, *11*		190
18754	Polar Express 2-8-4 Berkshire Steam Locomotive, *11, 13*		300
18755	C&O Berkshire Steam Locomotive "2751," with TrainSounds, *11*		290
____18771	Percy, remote system, *13–16*		140
____18774	James, remote system, *13–16*		140
____18775	Diesel, remote system, *13–16*		140
____18799	Bethlehem Steel Switcher "44," *99*		100
____18800	Lehigh Valley GP9 Diesel "8800," *87*	80	95
____18801	Santa Fe U36B Diesel "8801," *87*	100	120
____18802	Southern GP9 Diesel "8802" (SSS), *87*	100	115
____18803	Santa Fe RS3 Diesel "8803," *88*	90	105
____18804	Soo Line RS3 Diesel "8804," *88*	95	115
____18805	Union Pacific RS3 Diesel "8805," *89*	100	125
____18806	New Haven SD18 Diesel "8806," *89*	100	115
____18807	Lehigh Valley RS3 Diesel "8807," *90*	90	120
____18808	ACL SD18 Diesel "8808," *90*	85	105
____18809	Susquehanna RS3 Diesel "8809," *89 u*		130
____18810	CSX SD18 Diesel "8810," *90*	95	130
____18811	Alaska SD9 Diesel "8811," *91*	95	135
____18812	Kansas City Southern GP38 Diesel "4000," *91*	120	140
____18813	DM&IR SD18 Diesel "8813," *90 u*	90	145
____18814	D&H RS3 Diesel "8814" (SSS), *91*	90	120
____18815	Amtrak RS3 Diesel "1815," *91, 92 u*	100	130

		Exc	Mint
18816	C&NW GP38-2 Diesel "4600," *92*	105	130___
18817	UP GP9 Diesel "150" (see 18553), *91 u*		135___
18819	L&N GP38-2 Diesel "4136," *92*	115	145___
18820	WP GP9 Diesel "8820" (SSS), *92*	120	140___
18821	Clinchfield GP38-2 Diesel "6005," *93*	125	150___
18822	Gulf, Mobile & Ohio RS3 Diesel "721," *92–93 u*		NRS___
18823	Chicago & Illinois Midland SD9 Diesel "52," *92 u*		235___
18824	Montana Rail Link SD9 Diesel "600," *93*	185	230___
18825	Soo Line GP38-2 Diesel "4000" (SSS), *93*	120	145___
18826	Conrail GP7 Diesel "5808," *93*	100	120___
18827	"Happy Holidays" RS3 Diesel "8827," *93*	165	220___
18830	Budweiser GP9 Diesel "1947," *93–94 u*	118	158___
18831	SP GP20 Diesel "4060," *94*	105	120___
18832	PRR RSD-4 Diesel "8446," *95*	110	135___
18833	Milwaukee Road RS3 Diesel "2487," *94*	100	110___
18834	C&O SD28 Diesel "8834," *94*	110	140___
18835	NYC RS3 Diesel "8223" (SSS), *94*	135	195___
18836	CN (Grand Trunk) GP38-2 Diesel "5800," *94*	135	160___
18837	"Happy Holidays" RS3 Diesel "8837," *94–95*	150	190___
18838	Seaboard RSC-3 Diesel "1538," *95*	110	140___
18840	U.S. Army GP7 Diesel "1821," *95*	85	124___
18841	Western Maryland GP20 Diesel "27" (SSS), *95*	120	150___
18842	JCPenney B&LE SD38 Diesel "868," *95 u*		265___
18843	Great Northern RS3 Diesel "197," *96*		145___
18845	D&RGW RS3 Diesel "5204," *97*		100___
18846	Lionel Centennial Series GP9 Diesel, *98*		415___
18847	Santa Fe H-12-44 Switcher "602," *99*		385___
18848	PRR H-12-44 Switcher "9087," *99*		420___
18853	JCPenney Santa Fe GP9 Diesel "2370," *97 u*		150___
18854	UP GP9 Diesel Dummy Set, "2380, 2387," *97*		450___
18856	NJ Transit GP38-2 Diesel "4303," *99*		315___
18857	Union Pacific GP9 Diesel "2397," *97*		240___
18858	Lionel Centennial GP20 Diesel, *98*		450___
18859	Phantom II, *99*		360___
18860	Pratt's Hollow Collection I: Phantom, *98*		400___
18864	Southern Pacific GP9 Diesel B Unit, *98*		140___
18865	New York Central GP9 Diesel B Unit, *98*		170___
18866	Milwaukee Road GP7 Diesel "2383," *98*		205___
18868	NJ Transit GP38-2 Diesel "4300," *98 u*		140___
18870	Pennsylvania GP9 Diesel "2029," *98*		180___
18872	Wabash GP7 Diesel Set, "453, 454, 455," *99*		560___
18876	C&NW H-12-44 Switcher "1053," *99*	125	363___
18877	Union Pacific GP9 Diesel "2399," nonpowered, *99*		175___
18878	Alaska GP7 Diesel "1803," *99*		115___
18879	B&O GP9 Diesel "5616," *99*		260___
18881	Custom GP9 Diesel "5616," *99*		350___
18892	Burlington GP9 Diesel "2328," *99*		205___
18897	Christmas GP7 Diesel "1999," *99*		200___
18900	PRR Switcher "8900," *88 u, 89*	26	34___
18901/02	PRR Alco Diesel AA Set, *88*	110	130___
18903/04	Amtrak Alco Diesel AA Set, *88–89*	90	130___
18903	Amtrak "Mopar Express," *99*		500___

			Exc	Mint
____	18905	PRR 44-ton Switcher "9312," *92*	80	116
____	18906	Erie-Lackawanna RS3 Diesel "8906," *91 u*	70	90
____	18907	Rock Island 44-ton Switcher "371," *93*	95	110
____	18908/09	NYC Alco Diesel AA Set, *93*	105	115
____	18910	CSX Switcher "8910," *93*	40	46
____	18911	UP Switcher "8911," *93*	33	37
____	18912	Amtrak Switcher "8912," *93*	37	43
____	18913	Santa Fe Alco Diesel A Unit "8913," *93–94*	55	65
____	18915	WM Alco Diesel A Unit "8915," *93*	65	80
____	18916	WM Alco Diesel A Unit "8916," dummy, *93*	38	42
____	18917	Soo Line NW2 Switcher, *93*	65	75
____	18918	B&M NW2 Switcher "8918," *93*	75	90
	18919	Santa Fe Alco Diesel A Unit "8919," dummy, *93–94*	36	55
____	18920	Frisco NW2 Switcher "254," *94*	70	75
____	18921	C&NW NW2 Switcher "1017," *94*	60	80
____	18922	New Haven Alco Diesel A Unit "8922," *94*	75	105
	18923	New Haven Alco Diesel A Unit "8923," dummy, *94*	50	55
____	18924	IC Switcher "8924," *94–95*	37	44
____	18925	D&RGW Switcher "8925," *94–95*	32	37
____	18926	Reading Switcher "8926," *94–95*	31	39
____	18927	U.S. Navy NW2 Switcher "65-00637," *94–95*	65	85
____	18928	C&NW NW2 Switcher Calf Unit, *95*	50	55
____	18929	B&M NW2 Switcher Calf Unit, *95*	44	49
____	18930	Crayola Switcher, *94 u, 95*	27	30
____	18931	Chrysler Mopar NW2 Switcher "1818," *94 u*	76	88
____	18932	Jersey Central NW2 Switcher "8932," *96*		65
	18933	Jersey Central NW2 Switcher Calf Unit "8933," *96*		55
____	18934/35	Reading Alco Diesel AA Set, *95*	75	95
____	18936	Amtrak Alco Diesel A Unit "8936," *95*		65
____	18937	Amtrak FA2 Alco Diesel, nonpowered, *95–97*		50
____	18938	U.S. Navy NW2 Switcher Calf Unit, *95*	55	65
____	18939	Union Pacific NW2 Switcher Set, *96*		145
____	18943	Georgia Power NW2 Switcher "1960," *95 u*		170
____	18946	U.S. Coast Guard NW2 Switcher "8946," *96*		80
____	18947	Port of Lionel City Alco FA2 Diesel "2030," *97*		70
____	18948	Port of Lionel City Alco FB2 Diesel "2030B," *97*		45
____	18952	ATSF Alco PA1 Diesel "2000," *97*		345
____	18953	NYC Alco PA1 Diesel "2000," *97*		260
____	18954	ATSF Alco FA2 Diesel "212," powered, *97–99*		80
____	18955	NJ Transit NW2 Switcher "500," *96 u*		110
____	18956	Dodge Motorsports NW2 Switcher "8956," *96 u*		168
____	18959	New York Central NW2 Switcher "622," *97*		475
____	18961	Erie Alco PA1 Diesel "850," *98*		315
____	18965	Santa Fe Alco PB1 Diesel, *98*		255
____	18966	New York Central Alco BP1 Diesel "2008," *98*		250
____	18971	Alco Diesel A Unit, nonpowered, *98*		60
____	18973	RI Alco FA2 Diesel "2031," powered, *98–99*		NRS
____	18974	RI Alco FA2 Diesel Dummy Unit, *98–99*		NRS
____	18975	Southern 44-ton Switcher "1955," *99*		190
____	18978	C&O NW2 Switcher "624," *99–00*		410

		Exc	Mint
18981	Pennsylvania Railroad Speeder "16," *04*		45___
18982	Santa Fe Railroad Speeder "122," *04–05*		65___
18988	MP15 Diesel, K-Line, *06*		140___
18989	Bethlehem Steel Plymouth Switcher, traditional, K-Line, *06*		100___
18992	SP S2 Diesel Switcher "1440," CC, *08*		410___
18993	C&NW S2 Diesel Switcher "1031," CC, *08*		410___
18994	Lionel Lines FA Diesel, traditional, *08–09*		90___
19000	Blue Comet Diner, *87 u*	60	75___
19001	Southern Diner, *87 u*	55	65___
19002	Pennsylvania Diner, *88 u*	29	41___
19003	Milwaukee Road Diner, *88 u*	29	44___
19010	B&O Diner, *89 u*	36	55___
19011	Lionel Lines Baggage Car, *93*	268	398___
19015	Lionel Lines Passenger Coach, *91*	125	180___
19016	Lionel Lines Passenger Coach, *91*	100	135___
19017	Lionel Lines Passenger Coach, *91*	85	110___
19018	Lionel Lines Observation Car, *91*	95	120___
19019	SP Baggage Car "9019," *93*	120	153___
19023	SP Passenger Coach "9023," *92*	125	160___
19024	SP Passenger Coach "9024," *92*	85	100___
19025	SP Passenger Coach "9025," *92*	100	115___
19026	SP Observation Car "9026," *92*	85	100___
19038	Adolphus Busch Observation Car, *92–93 u*		85___
19039	Pere Marquette Baggage Car, *93*		75___
19040	Pere Marquette Passenger Coach "1115," *93*		75___
19041	Pere Marquette Passenger Coach "1116," *93*		75___
19042	Pere Marquette Observation Car "36," *93*		75___
19047	Baltimore & Ohio Combination Car "9047," *96*		55___
19048	Baltimore & Ohio Passenger Coach "9048," *96*		50___
19049	Baltimore & Ohio Diner "9049," *96*		42___
19050	Baltimore & Ohio Observation Car "9050," *96*		42___
19056	NYC Heavyweight Baggage Car, *96*		105___
19057	NYC Willow Run Heavyweight Coach, *96*		95___
19058	NYC Willow Trail Heavyweight Coach, *96*		90___
19059	NYC Seneca Valley Heavyweight Observation Car, *96*		100___
19060	Pullman Heavyweight Set, *96*		473___
19061	Wabash Passenger Set, *97*		235___
19062	Wabash City of Columbia Coach "2361," *97*		90___
19063	Wabash City of Danville Coach "2362," *97*		75___
19064	Wabash REA Baggage Car "2360," *97*		47___
19065	Wabash Windy City Observation Car "2363," *97*		90___
19066	Commodore Vanderbilt Pullman Heavyweight 2-pack, *97*		190___
19067	Commodore Vanderbilt Willow River Pullman "2543," *97*		115___
19068	Commodore Vanderbilt Willow Valley Pullman "2544," *97*		100___
19069	Pullman Baby Madison Set "9500-02," *97*		155___
19070	Baby Madison Combination Car "9501," *97*		40___
19071	Laurel Gap Baby Madison Coach "9500," *97*		34___
19072	Laurel Summit Baby Madison Coach "9500," *97*		40___

		Exc	Mint
___19073	Catskill Valley Baby Madison Observation Car "9502," *97*		34
___19074	Legends of Lionel Madison Set, *97*		385
___19075	Mazzone Lionel Legends Coach "2621," *97*		105
___19076	Caruso Lionel Legends Coach "2624," *97*		90
___19077	Raphael Lionel Legends Coach "2652," *97*		90
___19078	Cowen Lionel Legends Observation Car "2600," *97*		95
___19079	NYC Heavyweight Passenger Car Set, *97*		275
___19080	NYC Heavyweight REA Baggage Car "2564," *97*		100
___19081	NYC Park Place Heavyweight Coach "2565," *97*		100
___19082	NYC Star Beam Heavyweight Coach "2566," *97*		100
___19083	NYC Hudson Valley Heavyweight Observation Car "2567," *97*		100
___19087	C&O Heavyweight Passenger Car 4-pack, "2571-74," *97*		290
___19088	C&O Heavyweight Baggage Car "2571," *97*		100
___19089	C&O Heavyweight Sleeper Car "2572," *97*		100
___19090	C&O Heavyweight Diner "2573," *97*		110
___19091	C&O Heavyweight Observation Car "2574," *97*		100
___19093	Commodore Vanderbilt Heavyweight Sleeper Car 2-pack, *98*		170
___19094	Commodore Vanderbilt Niagara Falls Sleeper, *98*		75
___19095	Commodore Vanderbilt Highland Falls Sleeper, *98*		75
___19096	Legends of Lionel Madison Car 2-pack, *98*		130
___19097	Bonnano Lionel Legends Coach "2653," *98*		80
___19098	Pagano Lionel Legends Coach "2654," *98*		105
___19099	PRR Liberty Gap Baggage Car "2623," *99*		80
___19100	Amtrak Baggage Car "9100," *89*	125	165
___19101	Amtrak Combination Car "9101," *89*	75	85
___19102	Amtrak Passenger Coach "9102," *89*	75	85
___19103	Amtrak Vista Dome Car "9103," *89*	70	90
___19104	Amtrak Diner "9104," *89*	65	80
___19105	Amtrak Full Vista Dome Car "9105," *89 u*	70	80
___19106	Amtrak Observation Car "9106," *89*	75	90
___19107	SP Full Vista Dome Car, *90 u*	70	88
___19108	N&W Full Vista Dome Car "576," *91 u*	75	85
___19109	Santa Fe Baggage Car "3400," *91*	225	300
___19110	Santa Fe Combination Car "3500," *91*	80	110
___19111	Santa Fe Diner "601," *91*	100	135
___19112	Santa Fe Passenger Coach, *91*	125	175
___19113	Santa Fe Vista Dome Car, *91*	100	135
___19116	Great Northern Baggage Car "1200," *92*	135	165
___19117	Great Northern Combination Car "1240," *92*	65	80
___19118	Great Northern Passenger Coach "1212," *92*	75	95
___19119	Great Northern Vista Dome Car "1322," *92*	75	95
___19120	Great Northern Observation Car "1192," *92*	75	95
___19121	Union Pacific Vista Dome Car "9121," *92 u*	90	100
___19122	D&RGW California Zephyr Baggage Car, *93*	170	210
___19123	D&RGW California Zephyr Silver Bronco Vista Dome Car, *93*	95	115
___19124	D&RGW California Zephyr Silver Colt Vista Dome Car, *93*	95	115

Exc Mint

		Exc	Mint
19125	D&RGW California Zephyr Silver Mustang Vista Dome Car, *93*	100	125____
19126	D&RGW California Zephyr Silver Pony Vista Dome Car, *93*	95	115____
19127	D&RGW California Zephyr Vista Dome Car, *93*	85	100____
19128	Santa Fe Full Vista Dome Car "507," *92 u*	175	185____
19129	IC Full Vista Dome Car "9129," *93*	75	85____
19130	Lackawanna Passenger Cars, set of 4, *94*	280	350____
19131	Lackawanna Baggage Car "2000" (see 19130)		150____
19132	Lackawanna Diner "469" (see 19130)		100____
19133	Lackawanna Passenger Coach "260" (see 19130)		100____
19134	Lackawanna Observation Car "789" (see 19130)		85____
19135	Lackawanna Combination Car "425," *94*	85	100____
19136	Lackawanna Passenger Coach "211," *94*	65	75____
19137	New York Central Roomette Car, *95*	90	105____
19138	Santa Fe Roomette Car, *95*	75	95____
19139	N&W Baggage Car "577," *95*	150	200____
19140	N&W Combination Car "494," *95*	60	80____
19141	N&W Diner "495," *95*	105	135____
19142	N&W Passenger Coach "538," *95*	75	95____
19143	N&W Passenger Coach "537," *95*	75	95____
19144	N&W Observation Car "582," *95*	80	95____
19145	C&O Combination Car "1403," *96*		65____
19146	C&O Passenger Coach "1623," *96*		60____
19147	C&O Passenger Coach "1803," *96*		55____
19148	C&O Chessie Club Coach "1903," *96*		55____
19149	C&O Coach/Diner "1950," *96*		50____
19150	C&O Observation Car "2504," *96*		55____
19151	Norfolk & Western Duplex Roomette car, *96*		108____
19152	Union Pacific Duplex Roomette Car, *96*		75____
19153	C&O Passenger Cars, set of 4, *96*		340____
19154	Atlantic Coast Line Passenger Car Set, *96*		340____
19155	ACL Combination Car "101," *96*		90____
19156	ACL Talladega Diner, *96*		90____
19157	ACL Moultrie Coach, *96*		95____
19158	ACL Observation Car "256," *96*		90____
19159	N&W Passenger Cars, set of 4, *95 u*	300	385____
19160	LL REA Baggage Car, *96*		90____
19161	LL Silver Mesa Coach, *96*		80____
19162	LL Silver Sky Vista Dome Car, *96*		75____
19163	LL Silver Rail Observation Car, *96*		75____
19164	Chesapeake & Ohio Passenger Cars, *96*		160____
19165	ATSF Super Chief Set, *96*		305____
19166	NP Vista Dome Car Set, *97*		305____
19167	NP Pullman Coach "2571," *97*		105____
19168	NP Pullman Coach "2571," *97*		105____
19169	NP Pullman Coach "2570," *97*		95____
19170	NP Pullman Coach "2571," *97*		100____
19171	NYC Streamliner Car 4-pack, *97*		285____
19172	NYC Aluminum Passenger/Baggage Car "2570," *97*		95____
19173	NYC Manhattan Island Aluminum Passenger Diner, *97*		100____

		Exc	Mint
19174	NYC Queensboro Bridge Aluminum Passenger Coach, *97*		100
19175	NYC Windgate Brook Aluminum Observation Car, *97*		90
19176	ATSF Indian Arrow Diner "2572," *97*		90
19177	ATSF Grass Valley Coach "2573," *97*		90
19178	ATSF Citrus Valley Coach "2574," *97*		90
19179	ATSF Vista Heights Coach "2575," *97*		90
19180	ATSF Surfliner Passenger Car 4-pack, *97*		250
19181	GN Empire Builder Prairie View Full Vista Dome Car, *98*		75
19182	GN Empire Builder River View Full Vista Dome Car, *98*		75
19183	GN Empire Builder Vista Dome Car 2-pack, *98*		125
19184	Milwaukee Road Passenger Car 4-pack, *99*		390
19185	MILW Red River Valley Aluminum Passenger Coach "194," *99*		125
19186	MILW Aluminum Coach/Diner "170," *99*		110
19187	MILW Cedar Rapids Aluminum Observation Car "186," *99*		120
19188	MILW Aluminum REA Passenger/Baggage Car "1336," *99*		95
19194	KCS Aluminum Passenger Car 4-pack, *00*		380
19200	Tidewater Southern Boxcar, *87*	14	21
19201	Lancaster & Chester Boxcar, *87*	23	37
19202	PRR Boxcar, *87*	22	30
19203	D&TS Boxcar, *87*	11	18
19204	Milwaukee Road Boxcar (FF 2), *87*	29	41
19205	Great Northern DD Boxcar (FF 3), *88*	20	24
19206	Seaboard System Boxcar, *88*	18	23
19207	CP Rail DD Boxcar, *88*	17	22
19208	Southern DD Boxcar, *88*	11	13
19209	Florida East Coast Boxcar, *88*	15	19
19210	Soo Line Boxcar, *89*	19	23
19211	Vermont Railway Boxcar, *89*	18	21
19212	PRR Boxcar, *89*	21	25
19213	SP&S DD Boxcar, *89*	16	19
19214	Western Maryland Boxcar (FF 4), *89*	23	27
19215	Union Pacific DD Boxcar, *90*	17	21
19216	Santa Fe Boxcar, *90*	17	22
19217	Burlington Boxcar, *90*	16	21
19218	New Haven Boxcar, *90*	16	20
19219	Lionel Lines 1900-1906 Boxcar, diesel RailSounds, *90*	120	145
19220	Lionel Lines 1926-1934 Boxcar, *90*	27	30
19221	Lionel Lines 1935-1937 Boxcar, *90*	27	30
19222	Lionel Lines 1948-1950 Boxcar, *90*	27	30
19223	Lionel Lines 1979-1989 Boxcar, *90*	18	25
19228	Cotton Belt Boxcar, *91*	16	22
19229	Frisco Boxcar, diesel RailSounds (FF 5), *91*	75	90
19230	Frisco DD Boxcar (FF 5), *91*	21	26
19231	TA&G DD Boxcar, *91*	13	16
19232	Rock Island DD Boxcar, *91*	17	20
19233	Southern Pacific Boxcar, *91*	15	19

		Exc	Mint
19234	NYC Boxcar, *91*	60	65____
19235	MKT Boxcar, *91*	55	65____
19236	NKP DD Boxcar (FF 6), *92*	22	30____
19237	C&IM Boxcar, *92*	17	24____
19238	Kansas City Southern Boxcar, *92*	18	23____
19239	Toronto, Hamilton & Buffalo DD Boxcar, *92*	15	20____
19240	Great Northern DD Boxcar, *92*	15	20____
19241	Mickey Mouse 60th Anniversary Hi-Cube Boxcar, *91 u*	130	175____
19242	Donald Duck 50th Anniversary Hi-Cube Boxcar, *91 u*	130	140____
19243	Clinchfield Boxcar "9790," *91 u*	35	41____
19244	L&N Boxcar "9791," *92*	35	38____
19245	Mickey's World Tour Hi-Cube Boxcar, *92 u*	35	40____
19246	Disney World 20th Anniversary Hi-Cube Boxcar, *92 u*	33	40____
19247	Postwar "6464" Series Boxcar Set I, 3 cars, *93*	445	610____
19248	Western Pacific Boxcar "6464," *93*	75	95____
19249	Great Northern Boxcar "6464," *93*	75	95____
19250	M&StL Boxcar "6464," *93*	80	105____
19251	Montana Rail Link DD Boxcar "10001," *93*	21	27____
19254	Erie Boxcar (FF 7), *93*	21	25____
19255	Erie DD Boxcar (FF 7), *93*	22	26____
19256	Goofy Hi-Cube Boxcar, *93*	23	26____
19257	Postwar "6464" Series Boxcar Set II, 3 cars, *94*	80	97____
19258	Rock Island Boxcar "6464," *94*	25	34____
19259	Western Pacific Boxcar "6464100," *94*	33	46____
19260	Western Pacific Boxcar "6464100," *94*	35	49____
19261	Perils of Mickey Hi-Cube Boxcar #1, *93*	20	30____
19262	Perils of Mickey Hi-Cube Boxcar #2, *93*	20	28____
19263	NYC DD Boxcar (SSS), *94*	36	42____
19264	Perils of Mickey Hi-Cube Boxcar #3, *94*	28	31____
19265	Mickey Mouse 65th Anniversary Hi-Cube Boxcar, *94*	22	44____
19266	Postwar "6464" Series Boxcar Set III, 3 cars, *95*	75	90____
19267	NYC Pacemaker Boxcar "6464125," *95*	37	42____
19268	Missouri Pacific Boxcar "6464150," *95*	25	29____
19269	Rock Island Boxcar "6464," *95*	25	26____
19270	Donald Duck 60th Anniversary Hi-Cube Boxcar, *95*	30	34____
19271	Minnie Mouse Hi-Cube Boxcar, *95*	21	43____
19272	Postwar "6464" Series Boxcar Set IV, 3 cars, *96*	70	85____
19273	BAR State of Maine Boxcar "6464275," *96*		35____
19274	SP Overnight Boxcar "6464225," *96*		28____
19275	Pennsylvania Boxcar "6464," *96*		44____
19276	Postwar "6464" Series Boxcar Set V, 3 cars, *96*	65	85____
19277	Rutland Boxcar "6464-300," *96*		26____
19278	B&O Boxcar "6464-325," *96*		30____
19279	Central of Georgia Boxcar "6464-375," *96*		29____
19280	Mickey's Wheat Hi-Cube Boxcar, *96*		32____
19281	Mickey's Carrots Hi-Cube Boxcar, *96*		40____
19282	Santa Fe "Super Chief" Boxcar "6464-196," *96*		24____
19283	Erie Boxcar "6464-296," *96*		22____

		Exc	Mint
____19284	Northern Pacific Boxcar "6464-396," *96*		29
____19285	B&A State of Maine Boxcar "6464-275," *96*		27
____19286	Tweety and Sylvester Boxcar, *96*		46
____19287	NYC/PC Merger Boxcar "6464-125X" (SSS), *97*	50	75
____19288	PRR/CR Merger Boxcar "6464-200X" (SSS), *97*	43	56
____19289	Monon "Hoosier Line" Boxcar "6464," *97*		27
____19290	Seaboard "Silver Meteor" Boxcar "6464," *97*		24
____19291	GN Boxcar "6464-397," *97*		26
____19292	Postwar "6464" Series Boxcar Set VI, 3 cars, *97*		90
____19293	MKT Boxcar "6464-350," *97*	28	32
____19294	B&O Boxcar "6464-400," *97*	27	34
____19295	NH Boxcar "6464-425," *97*	25	34
____19300	PRR Ore Car, *87*	15	23
____19301	Milwaukee Road Ore Car, *87*	20	25
19302 ____	Milwaukee Road Quad Hopper with coal (FF 2), *87*	24	35
____19303	Lionel Lines Quad Hopper with coal, *87 u*	20	31
____19304	GN Covered Quad Hopper (FF 3), *88*	18	25
____19305	Chessie System Ore Car, *88*	18	23
____19307	B&LE Ore Car with load, *89*	19	25
____19308	GN Ore Car with load, *89*	18	23
____19309	Seaboard Covered Quad Hopper, *89*	16	19
____19310	L&C Quad Hopper with coal, *89*	16	30
____19311	SP Covered Quad Hopper, *90*	14	19
____19312	Reading Quad Hopper with coal, *90*	21	36
____19313	B&O Ore Car with load, *90–91*	20	25
____19315	Amtrak Ore Car with load, *91*	22	30
____19316	Wabash Covered Quad Hopper, *91*	18	23
____19317	Lehigh Valley Quad Hopper with coal, *91*	47	55
____19318	NKP Quad Hopper with coal (FF 6), *92*	30	34
____19319	Union Pacific Covered Quad Hopper, *92*	19	23
____19320	PRR Ore Car with load, *92*	21	30
____19321	B&LE Ore Car with load, *92*	21	30
____19322	C&NW Ore Car with load, *93*	27	34
____19323	Detroit & Mackinac Ore Car with load, *93*	20	29
____19324	Erie Quad Hopper with coal (FF 7), *93*	25	33
____19325	N&W 4-bay Hopper "6446-1" with coal, *97*		65
____19326	N&W 4-bay Hopper "6446-2" with coal, *96*		60
____19327	N&W 4-bay Hopper "6446-3" with coal, *96*		60
____19328	N&W 4-bay Hopper "6446-4" with coal, *96*		60
____19329	N&W 4-bay Hopper "6436" with coal, *97*		55
____19330	Cotton Belt 4-bay Hopper "64661" with coal, *98*		45
____19331	Cotton Belt 4-bay Hopper "64662" with coal, *98*		45
____19332	Cotton Belt 4-bay Hopper "64663" with coal, *98*		45
____19333	Cotton Belt 4-bay Hopper "64664" with coal, *98*		45
____19338	Cotton Belt 4-bay Hopper 2-pack, *99*		120
____19339	Cotton Belt 4-bay Hopper "64469," *99*		NRS
____19340	Cotton Belt 4-bay Hopper "64470," *99*		NRS
____19341	LV 2-bay Hopper "6456," *99*		30
19344 ____	D&RGW 3-bay Cylindrical Hopper "15990," *99–00*		42
____19345	CN 3-bay Cylindrical Hopper "370708," *99–00*		95
____19346	PRR 4-bay Hopper with coal "744433," *01*		40

Exc Mint

		Exc	Mint
19347	LV 2-bay Hopper "643657," *01*		40____
19348	Duluth, Missabe & Iron Range Ore Car "28000," *03*		25____
19349	U.S. Steel Ore Car "19349," *03*		29____
19350	Postwar "6636" Alaska Quad Hopper, *03*		34____
19357	N&W Hopper "6446-25," Archive Collection, *07*		50____
19361	Twizzlers Quad Hopper, *10*		55____
19362	Coursers Christmas Hopper with gifts, *10*		60____
19364	Milk Duds Covered Hopper, *11*		55____
19365	Coca-Cola Quad Hopper, *10*		60____
19366	Santa's Little Hopper, *10–11*		55____
19367	ATSF Quad Hopper, *11*		60____
19368	Southern Offset Hopper "106723," (std O), *11*		70____
19369	Alaska Quad Hopper "20756," *12*		60____
19371	Burlington Northern I-Beam Car, *04*		60____
19374	NS Bathtub Gondola 2-pack (std O), *15*		140____
19377	DETX Bathtub Gondola 2-pack (std O), *15*		140____
19380	CSX Bathtub Gondola 2-pack (std O), *15*		140____
19383	UP PS-4 Flatcar "57125" (std O), *13*		70____
19384	ATSF PS-4 Flatcar "90088" (std O), *13*		70____
19385	CNJ PS-4 Flatcar "339" (std O), *13*		70____
19386	BN PS-4 Flatcar "613200" (std O), *13*		70____
19388	BN 89' Auto Carrier (std O), *13–14*		110____
19389	SP 89' Auto Carrier (std O), *13–14*		110____
19390	CP 89' Auto Carrier (std O), *13–14, 16*		110____
19391	Soo Line 89' Auto Carrier (std O), *13–14, 16*		110____
19393	BNSF Auto Carrier 2-pack (std O), *12*		220____
19394	UP Auto Carrier 2-pack (std O), *12*		220____
19395	Grand Trunk Auto Carrier 2-pack (std O), *12*		220____
19396	CSX Auto Carrier 2-pack (std O), *12*		220____
19397	CN Auto Carrier 2-pack (std O), *12*		220____
19398	Conrail Auto Carrier 2-pack (std O), *12*		220____
19400	Milwaukee Road Gondola with cable reels (FF 2), *87*	23	31____
19401	GN Gondola with coal (FF 3), *88*	14	16____
19402	GN Crane Car (FF 3), *88*	47	65____
19403	WM Gondola with coal (FF 4), *89*	20	25____
19404	Trailer Train Flatcar with WM trailers (FF 4), *89*	29	33____
19405	Southern Crane Car, *91*	42	65____
19406	West Point Mint Car, *91 u*	38	50____
19408	Frisco Gondola with coil covers (FF 5), *91*	26	31____
19409	Southern Flatcar with stakes, *91*	18	22____
19410	NYC Gondola with canisters, *91*	47	55____
19411	NKP Flatcar with Sears trailer (FF 6), *92*	50	59____
19412	Frisco Crane Car, *92*	49	65____
19413	Frisco Flatcar with stakes, *92*	16	21____
19414	Union Pacific Flatcar with stakes (SSS), *92*	19	26____
19415	Erie Flatcar with trailer "7200" (FF 7), *93*	28	39____
19416	ICG TTUX Flatcar Set with trailers (SSS), *93*	70	75____
19419	Charlotte Mint Car, *93*	25	32____
19420	Lionel Lines Vat Car, *94*	18	22____
19421	Hirsch Brothers Vat Car, *95*	16	21____

		Exc	Mint
19423	Circle L Racing Flatcar "6424" with stock cars, *96*		27
19424	Edison Electric Depressed Center Flatcar "6461" with transformer, *97*		31
19427	Evans Auto Loader "6414," *99*		55
19428	Evans Boat Loader "6414," *99*		70
19429	Culvert Gondola "6342," *98–99*		48
19430	ATSF Flatcar "6411" with Beechcraft Bonanza, *98*		47
19438	Christmas Gondola (std O), *98*		42
19439	Flatcar with safes, *98*		35
19440	Flatcar with FedEx trailer, *98*		34
19441	Lobster Vat Car, *98*		35
19442	Water Supply Flatcar with tank (SSS), *98*		31
19444	Flatcar with VW Bug, *98*		38
19445	Borden Milk Tank Car "520," *99*		38
19446	Pittsburgh Paint Vat Car, *99*		43
19447	Mama's Baked Beans Vat Car, *99*		35
19448	Easter Gondola "6462" with candy, *99*		27
19449	Liquified Gas Tank Car "6469," *99*		31
19450	Barrel Ramp Car "6343," *99*		31
19451	Wheel Car "6262," *99*		32
19454	PRR Flatcar "6424" with gondola, *99*		25
19455	Lionel Lines Flatcar "6430" with Cooper-Jarrett trailers, *99*		60
19457	Lionel Lines Extension Searchlight Car, *99*		40
19459	Valentine Gondola "6462" with candy, *99*		50
19471	Mobil Flatcar with 2 trailers, *00 u*		96
19472	Mobil Bulkhead Flatcar with tank, *00 u*		68
19474	L&N Flatcar "6424" with trailer frames, *99*		26
19476	Zoo Gondola "6462" with animals, *99–00*		43
19477	Monday Night Football Flatcar with trailer, *01*		30
19478	Culvert Gondola "6342," *99*		45
19479	Borden Milk Car "521," *00*		38
19480	Valentine's Vat Car "6475," *99–00*		30
19481	Easter Vat Car, *99–00*		38
19482	NYC Flat with trailer "6424," *00*		50
19483	VW Beetle Flatcar, *00*		48
19484	Flatcar "6264" with timber, *00*		34
19485	PRR Culvert Gondola "347004," *01*		41
19486	NYC Lumber Flatcar, *01*		34
19487	Flatcar "6800" with airplane, *00*		41
19489	Evans Auto Loader "500085," *00*		50
19490	Postwar "6475" Libby's Vat Car, *01–02*		36
19491	Christmas Vat Car, *01*		30
19492	WM Skeleton Log Car 3-pack, *01*		95
19496	Westside Lumber Skeleton Log Car 3-pack, *01*		112
19500	Milwaukee Road Reefer (FF 2), *87*	30	39
19502	C&NW Reefer, *87*	30	33
19503	Bangor & Aroostook Reefer, *87*	22	25
19504	Northern Pacific Reefer, *87*	16	22
19505	Great Northern Reefer (FF 3), *88*	29	35
19506	Thomas Newcomen Reefer, *88*	18	23

		Exc	Mint
19507	Thomas Edison Reefer, *88*	21	27____
19508	Leonardo da Vinci Reefer, *89*	19	27____
19509	Alexander Graham Bell Reefer, *89*	17	20____
19510	PRR Stock Car (FARR 5), *89 u*	18	26____
19511	WM Reefer (FF 4), *89*	22	28____
19512	Wright Brothers Reefer, *90*	17	21____
19513	Ben Franklin Reefer, *90*	17	20____
19515	Milwaukee Road Stock Car (FF 2), *90 u*	33	41____
19516	George Washington Reefer, *89 u, 91*	14	19____
19517	Civil War Reefer, *89 u, 91*	14	19____
19518	Man on the Moon Reefer, *89 u, 91*	13	17____
19519	Frisco Stock Car (FF 5), *91*	26	31____
19520	CSX Reefer, *91*	18	23____
19522	Guglielmo Marconi Reefer, *91*	19	23____
19523	Dr. Robert Goddard Reefer, *91*	19	23____
19524	Delaware & Hudson Reefer (SSS), *91*	29	32____
19525	Speedy Alka Seltzer Reefer, *91 u*	31	32____
19526	Jolly Green Giant Reefer, *91 u*	21	33____
19527	Nickel Plate Road Reefer (FF 6), *92*	20	29____
19528	Joshua L. Cowen Reefer, *92*	23	28____
19529	A.C. Gilbert Reefer, *92*	18	23____
19530	Rock Island Stock Car, *92 u*	34	38____
19531	Rice Krispies Reefer, *92 u*	23	33____
19532	Hormel Reefer "901," *92 u*	18	24____
19535	Erie Reefer (FF 7), *93*	23	26____
19536	Soo Line REA Reefer (SSS), *93*	25	30____
19538	Hormel Reefer "102," *94*	22	25____
19539	Heinz Reefer, *94*	38	47____
19540	Broken Arrow Ranch Stock Car "3356," *97*		28____
19552	Rutland Reefer "395" (std O), *00*		32____
19553	ATSF Stock Car "23003," *00*		37____
19554	Postwar Celebration Milk Car "36621," *00*		125____
19555	Swift Reefer "5839," red, *01*		33____
19556	Swift Reefer "1020," silver, *01*		31____
19557	Circus Stock Car "6376," *00*		32____
19558	Postwar "6556" MKT Stock Car, *02*		27____
19559	MKT Stock Car, girls set add-on, *02*		95____
19560	NP 2-door Stock Car "6356," Archive Collection, *02*		33____
19561	Norman Rockwell Holiday Reefer, *03*		25____
19562	Norman Rockwell Holiday Reefer, *03*		25____
19563	Norman Rockwell Holiday Reefer, *03*		25____
19564	Postwar "6672" Santa Fe Reefer, *03*		35____
19565	Burlington Reefer "6672," Archive Collection, *03*		35____
19567	Postwar "6572" Railway Express Agency Reefer, *05*		45____
19568	GN Reefer, Archive Collection, *05*		45____
19569	Pillsbury Reefer, traditional, *05*		53____
19570	Nestle Nesquik Reefer, traditional, *05*		53____
19572	NYC Reefer "6672," Archive Collection, *06*		45____
19573	Postwar "6356" NYC Stock Car, *06–07*		50____
19574	GN Stock Car, *08*		50____
19575	REA Reefer "6721," *08–09*		50____

			Exc	Mint
____	19576	Alaska Reefer, *08*		50
____	19577	Krey's Reefer, *10–11*		60
____	19578	Granny Smith Apples Wood-sided Reefer, *10–11*		53
____	19585	NS Transparent Instruction Car, *10–11*		75
____	19586	Alaska Husky Transport Car, *10–11*		75
____	19587	Hershey's Chocolate Wood-sided Reefer, *10*		75
____	19588	Santa's Wish Transparent Gift Car, *10*		75
____	19589	Blood Transfusion Bunk Car, *10–11*		60
____	19590	Wood-sided Reefer 2-pack, *10*		110
____	19593	Hershey's Kisses Wood-sided Reefer, *11–15*		60
____	19594	York Peppermint Patty Wood-sided Reefer, *10–11*		55
____	19599	Old Glory Reefers, set of 3, *89 u, 91*	37	43
____	19600	Milwaukee Road 1-D Tank Car (FF 2), *87*	33	40
____	19601	North American 1-D Tank Car (FF 4), *89*	17	29
____	19602	Johnson 1-D Tank Car (FF 5), *91*	24	30
____	19603	GATX 1-D Tank Car (FF 6), *92*	32	41
____	19604	Goodyear 1-D Tank Car (SSS), *93*	33	36
____	19605	Hudson's Bay 1-D Tank Car (SSS), *94*	25	29
____	19607	Sunoco 1-D Tank Car "6315," *96*		23
	19608	Sunoco Aviation Services 1-D Tank Car "6315" (SSS), *97*		38
____	19611	Gulf Oil 1-D Tank Car "6315," *98*		33
____	19612	Gulf Oil 3-D Tank Car "6425," *98*		30
____	19614	BASF 1-D Tank Car "UTLX 78252," *99–00*		25
____	19615	Vulcan Chemicals 1-D Tank Car, *99–00*		25
____	19621	Centennial 1-D Tank Car "6015-1," *99*		53
____	19622	Centennial 1-D Tank Car "6015-2," *99*		59
____	19623	Centennial 1-D Tank Car "6015-3," *99*		58
____	19624	Centennial 1-D Tank Car "6015-4," *99*		55
____	19625	Ethyl Tank Car " 6236," *01*		31
____	19626	Diamond Chemical Tank Car "19419," *01*		29
____	19627	Shell 1-D Tank Car "1227," *01*		37
____	19628	Lion Oil 1-D Tank Car "2256," *01*		35
____	19634	General American 1-D Tank Car, *01*		30
____	19635	U.S. Army 1-D Tank Car "10936," *01*		31
____	19636	Hooker Chemicals 1-D Tank Car "6180," *01*		36
	19637	GATX TankTrain Intermediate Car "44589" (std O), *02*		5!
	19638	CN TankTrain Intermediate Car "75571" (std O), *02*		65
	19639	GATX TankTrain Intermediate Car 3-pack (std O), *02*		14(
____	19644	Union Texas 1-D Tank Car "9922," *02*		3?
____	19645	Penn Salt 1-D Tank Car "4730," *02*		3
	19646	CN TankTrain Intermediate Car "75571" (std O), *03*		4
	19647	GATX TankTrain Intermediate Car "44589" (std O), *03*		4!
____	19649	Scrooge McDuck Mint Car, *05*		19?
____	19651	Santa Fe Tool Car, *87*	30	35
____	19652	Jersey Central Bunk Car, *88*	25	3?
____	19653	Jersey Central Tool Car, *88*	26	28
____	19654	Amtrak Bunk Car, *89*	22	25

		Exc	Mint	
19655	Amtrak Tool Car, *90–91*	23	30	___
19656	Milwaukee Road Bunk Car, smoke, *90*	40	50	___
19657	Wabash Bunk Car, smoke, *91–92*	36	42	___
19658	Norfolk & Western Tool Car, *91*	24	29	___
19660	Mint Car, *98*		40	___
19663	Pratt's Hollow Bunk Car "5717," *99*		40	___
19664	Ambassador Award Bunk Car, bronze, *99 u*		400	___
19665	Ambassador Engineer Bunk Car, silver, *99 u*		585	___
19666	Ambassador Cowen Bunk Car, gold, *99 u*		425	___
19667	Wellspring Gold Bullion Car, *99*		56	___
19669	King Tut Museum Car "9660," *99*		70	___
19670	NY Federal Reserve Bullion Car "6445," *00*		44	___
19671	Lionel Model Shop Display Car "6445-01," *99–00*		50	___
19672	Lionel Mines Mint Car, *00 u*		250	___
19673	Wellspring Capital Management Mint Car, *99 u*		215	___
19674	Lionel Lines Platinum Car, *00*		43	___
19675	Lionel Model Shop Display "6445-2," *01*		42	___
19676	Philadelphia Mint Car, *01*		40	___
19677	Fort Knox Mint Car "6445," *00*		50	___
19678	U.S. Army Bunk Car, *02*		45	___
19679	St. Louis Federal Reserve Mint Car, *02*		38	___
19681	Area 51 Alien Suspension Car, *02*		47	___
19682	Alaska Klondike Mining Mint Car, *02*		40	___
19683	Pony Express Mint Car, *02*		50	___
19686	Chicago Federal Reserve Mint Car "6445," *03–04*		45	___
19687	UP Bunk Car "3887," smoke, *03*		40	___
19688	Postwar "6445" Fort Knox Mint Car, *02–03*		39	___
19689	CIBRO TankTrain Intermediate Car 3-pack (std O), *03*		100	___
19694	Pony Express Mint Car, *03*		50	___
19696	U.S. Savings Bond Mint Car, *00*		150	___
19697	U.S. Bureau of Engraving and Printing Mint Car "19697," *04*		40	___
19698	San Francisco Federal Reserve Mint Car, *04*		40	___
19700	Chessie System Extended Vision Caboose, *88*	43	50	___
19701	Milwaukee Road N5c Caboose (FF 2), *88*	50	65	___
19702	PRR N5c Caboose, *87*	44	55	___
19703	GN Extended Vision Caboose (FF 3), *88*	42	49	___
19704	WM Extended Vision Caboose, smoke (FF 4), *89*	42	49	___
19705	CP Rail Extended Vision Caboose, smoke, *89*	43	47	___
19706	UP Extended Vision Caboose "9706," smoke, *89*	40	56	___
19707	SP Work Caboose with searchlight, smoke, *90*	55	60	___
19708	Lionel Lines Bay Window Caboose, *90*	43	46	___
19709	PRR Work Caboose, smoke, *89, 91*	49	70	___
19710	Frisco Extended Vision Caboose, smoke (FF 5), *91*	43	47	___
19711	NS Extended Vision Caboose, smoke, *92*	47	65	___
19712	PRR N5c Caboose, *91*	44	47	___
19714	NYC Work Caboose with searchlight, smoke, *92*	100	130	___
19715	DM&IR Extended Vision Caboose "C-217," *92 u*	50	60	___
19716	IC Extended Vision Caboose "9405," smoke, *93*	105	135	___
19717	Susquehanna Bay Window Caboose "0121," *93*	44	55	___
19718	C&IM Extended Vision Caboose "74," *92 u*	38	45	___
19719	Erie Bay Window Caboose "C-300" (FF 7), *93*	47	55	___

			Exc	Mint
____	**19720**	Soo Line Extended Vision Caboose (SSS), *93*	32	41
____	**19721**	GM&O Extended Vision Caboose "2956," *93 u*	47	50
____	**19723**	Disney Extended Vision Caboose, *94*	36	45
____	**19724**	JCPenney MKT Extended Vision Caboose "125," *94 u*	38	43
____	**19726**	NYC Bay Window Caboose (SSS), *95*	50	60
____	**19727**	Pennsylvania N5c Caboose "477938," *96*		30
____	**19728**	N&W Bay Window Caboose, *96*		70
____	**19732**	ATSF Bay Window Caboose "6517," *96*		43
____	**19733**	New York Central Caboose "6357," *96*		30
____	**19734**	Southern Pacific Caboose "6357," *96*		26
____	**19736**	PRR N5c Caboose "6417," *97*		27
____	**19737**	Lackawanna Searchlight Caboose "2420," *97*		75
____	**19738**	Conrail N5c Caboose "6417" (SSS), *97*		55
____	**19739**	NYC Wood-sided Caboose "6907," *97*		60
____	**19740**	Virginian N5c Caboose "6427," *97 u*		65
____	**19741**	Pennsylvania N5c Caboose "6417," *98*		50
	19742	Erie Bay Window Caboose "C301," Caboose Talk, *98*		95
____	**19748**	SP&S Bay Window Caboose "6517," *97 u*		50
____	**19749**	SP Bay Window Caboose "6517," *98*		100
____	**19750**	Holiday Music Bay Window Caboose, *98*		160
____	**19751**	PRR N5c Caboose "492418," *98*		30
____	**19752**	NP Bay Window Caboose "407," *98*		50
____	**19753**	UP Extended Vision Caboose "25641," *98*		55
____	**19754**	NYC Caboose "20112," *98*		55
____	**19755**	Centennial Porthole Caboose, *99*		68
____	**19756**	Lionel Lines Bay Window Caboose, *99*		50
____	**19758**	DL&W Work Caboose "6419," *99*		55
____	**19759**	Corvette N5c Caboose, *99*		60
____	**19772**	Lionel Visitor's Center Vat Car, *99 u*		40
____	**19773**	Lionel Kids Club Barrel Ramp Car "6343," *96 u*		48
	19778	Case Cutlery Wood-sided Caboose "1889" (std O), *99 u*		NRS
____	**19779**	SP Bay Window Caboose "1908," *99*		65
____	**19780**	LV Porthole Caboose "641751," *99–00*		43
	19781	Vapor Records Holiday Porthole Caboose "6417," *99–00*		58
____	**19782**	NYC Bay Window Caboose "21719," *00*		65
____	**19783**	Ford Mustang Extended Vision Caboose, *01*		50
____	**19785**	SP Bay Window Caboose "6517," *00*		55
____	**19786**	PRR Extended Vision Caboose, *00 u*		40
____	**19787**	PRR Extended Vision Caboose "477927," *01*		40
____	**19790**	Postwar "6417" Lehigh Valley Caboose, *02*		41
____	**19792**	Postwar "C301" Erie Bay Window Caboose, *03*		45
____	**19796**	C&O Bay Window Caboose, *03*		50
____	**19800**	Circle L Ranch Operating Cattle Car, *88*	75	95
____	**19801**	Poultry Dispatch Chicken Car, *87*	20	27
____	**19802**	Carnation Milk Car, *87*	87	102
____	**19803**	Reading Ice Car, *87*	38	44
____	**19804**	Wabash Operating Hopper, *87*	25	34
____	**19805**	Santa Fe Operating Boxcar, *87*	28	36
____	**19806**	PRR Operating Hopper, *88*	28	32

		Exc	Mint
19807	PRR Extended Vision Caboose, smoke, *88*	39	47___
19808	NYC Ice Car, *88*	38	49___
19809	Erie-Lackawanna Operating Boxcar, *88*	27	35___
19810	Bosco Milk Car, *88*	80	89___
19811	Monon Brakeman Car, *90*	50	55___
19813	Northern Pacific Ice Car, *89 u*	41	46___
19815	Delaware & Hudson Brakeman Car, *92*	49	60___
19816	Madison Hardware Operating Boxcar "190991," *91 u*	80	102___
19817	Virginian Ice Car, *94*	31	35___
19818	Dairymen's League Milk Car "788," *94*	65	80___
19819	Poultry Dispatch Car (SSS), *94*	36	43___
19820	Die-cast Tender, RailSounds II, *95–96*		175___
19821	UP Operating Boxcar, *95*	31	36___
19822	Pork Dispatch Car, *95*	29	39___
19823	Burlington Ice Car, *94 u, 95*	39	49___
19824	U.S. Army Target Launcher, *96*		30___
19825	Generator Car, *96*		48___
19827	NYC Operating Boxcar, *97*		37___
19828	C&NW Animated Stock Car "3356" and Stockyard, *96–97*		100___
19830	U.S. Mail Operating Boxcar "3428," *97*		39___
19831	GM Generator Car "3530," power pole and wire, *97*		46___
19832	Cola Ice Car "6352," *97*		47___
19833	Tender "2426RS," RailSounds II, *97*		240___
19834	LL 6-wheel Crane Car "2460," *97*		60___
19835	FedEx Animated Boxcar "3464X," *97*		38___
19837	Bucyrus 6-wheel Crane Car "2460," *99*		49___
19845	Aquarium Car "3435," CC, *98*		151___
19846	Animated Giraffe Car "3376C," *98*		105___
19850	Stock Car "33760," RailSounds, *00*		130___
19853	Firefighting Instruction Generator Car (SSS), *98*		60___
19854	Lionelville Fire Car (SSS), *98*		55___
19855	Christmas Aquarium Car, *98*		60___
19856	Mermaid Transport, *98*		65___
19857	NYC Firefighting Instruction Car "19853," *98–99*		175___
19858	Lionelville Operating Searchlight Car "19854," *99*		65___
19859	REA Boxcar "6267," steam RailSounds, *99*		170___
19860	Conrail Boxcar "169671," diesel RailSounds, *99*		140___
19864	Animated Ostrich Boxcar, *99*		37___
19867	Operating Poultry Dispatch Car "3434," *99*		48___
19868	Shark Aquarium Car "3435," *99*		190___
19869	Alien Aquarium Car "3435," *99*		49___
19877	ATSF Operating Barrel Car, *99*		55___
19878	Operating Helium Tank Flatcar "3362," *99*		40___
19880	Lionel Lines Extension Searchlight Car, *00*		50___
19882	Sanderson Farms Poultry Car "3434," *99*		41___
19883	LL Bucyrus Erie Crane Car "64608," *99*		45___
19884	Atlantis Travel Aquarium Car, *00 u*		95___
19885	N&W Operating Hopper Car, *00*		31___
19886	Seaboard Boxcar "16126," steam RailSounds, *00*		140___
19887	SP Boxcar "651663," diesel RailSounds, *00*		140___

		Exc	Mint
___19888	Christmas Music Boxcar, *01*		65
19889	PRR Bay Window Caboose "477719," Crewtalk, *00*		140
19890	Santa Fe Bay Window Caboose "999211," Crewtalk, *00*		100
___19894	Hood's Operating Milk Car with platform, *03–04*		95
___19894	Pony Express Mint Car, *03*		50
___19895	3356 Santa Fe Horse Car with corral, *04*		120
___19896	USMC Missile Launch Sound Car "45," *03–04*		165
___19897	NYC Crane Car, TMCC, *04*		255
19898	Nestle Nesquik Operating Milk Car with platform, *04*		95
___19899	Pennsylvania Crane Car "19899" CC, *03–05*		260
___19900	Toy Fair Boxcar, *87 u*	65	80
___19901	"I Love Virginia" Boxcar, *87*	25	35
___19902	Toy Fair Boxcar, *88 u*	55	80
___19903	Christmas Boxcar, *87 u*	22	34
___19904	Christmas Boxcar, *88 u*	32	43
___19905	"I Love California" Boxcar, *88*	20	24
___19906	"I Love Pennsylvania" Boxcar, *89*	26	32
___19907	Toy Fair Boxcar, *89 u*	38	55
___19908	Christmas Boxcar, *89 u*	30	39
___19909	"I Love New Jersey" Boxcar, *90*	19	25
___19910	Christmas Boxcar, *90 u*	35	38
___19911	Toy Fair Boxcar, *90 u*	75	95
___19912	"I Love Ohio" Boxcar, *91*	21	28
___19913	Christmas Boxcar, *91*	34	52
___19913	Lionel Employee Christmas Boxcar, *91 u*	150	200
___19914	Toy Fair Boxcar, *91 u*	38	50
___19915	"I Love Texas" Boxcar, *92*	35	60
___19916	Lionel Employee Christmas Boxcar, *92 u*	190	220
___19917	Toy Fair Boxcar, *92 u*	45	53
___19918	Christmas Boxcar, *92 u*	49	70
___19919	"I Love Minnesota" Boxcar, *93*	40	60
___19920	Lionel Visitor's Center Boxcar, *92 u*	16	28
___19921	Lionel Employee Christmas Boxcar, *93 u*	140	185
___19922	Christmas Boxcar, *93*	33	41
___19923	Toy Fair Boxcar, *93 u*	65	95
___19925	Lionel Employee Learning Center Boxcar, *93 u*	55	63
___19926	"I Love Nevada" Boxcar, *94*	21	26
___19927	Lionel Visitor's Center Boxcar, *93 u*	26	33
___19928	Lionel Employee Christmas Boxcar, *94 u*	205	230
___19929	Christmas Boxcar, *94*	30	40
___19931	Toy Fair Boxcar, *94 u*	49	65
___19932	Lionel Visitor's Center Boxcar, *94 u*	26	33
___19933	"I Love Illinois" Boxcar, *95*	21	27
___19934	Lionel Visitor's Center Boxcar, *95 u*	18	22
___19937	Toy Fair Boxcar, *95 u*	55	75
___19938	Christmas Boxcar, *95*	26	34
___19939	Lionel Employee Christmas Boxcar, *95 u*	100	128
___19941	"I Love Colorado" Boxcar, *95*	23	30
___19942	"I Love Florida" Boxcar, *96*	19	27
___19943	"I Love Arizona" Boxcar, *96*	20	25

Exc Mint

		Exc	Mint
19944	Lionel Visitor's Center Tank Car, *96 u*		35____
19945	Holiday Boxcar, *96*		29____
19946	Lionel Employee Christmas Boxcar, *96 u*		195____
19947	Lionel Toy Fair Boxcar, *96 u*		200____
19948	Visitor's Center Flatcar with trailer, *96 u*		34____
19949	"I Love NY" Boxcar, *97*		50____
19950	"I Love Montana" Boxcar, *97*		30____
19951	"I Love Massachusetts" Boxcar, *98*		26____
19952	"I Love Indiana" Boxcar, *98*		31____
19955	Lionel Visitor's Center Gondola with coil covers, *98 u*		20____
19956	Toy Fair Boxcar "777," *98 u*		65____
19957	Ambassador Caboose, *97 u*		484____
19958	Ambassador Caboose, silver (std O), *98 u*		553____
19959	Ambassador Caboose, gold (std O), *98 u*		744____
19964	U.S. JCI Senate Boxcar, *92 u*	55	63____
19968	"I Love Maine" Boxcar, *99*		40____
19969	"I Love Vermont" Boxcar, *99*		40____
19970	"I Love New Hampshire" Boxcar, *99*		34____
19971	"I Love Rhode Island" Boxcar, *99*		34____
19976	Lionel Employee Holiday Boxcar, *99 u*		150____
19977	Toy Fair Boxcar, *99 u*		50____
19981	Lionel Centennial Boxcar, *99*		36____
19982	Lionel Centennial Boxcar, *99*		36____
19983	Lionel Centennial Boxcar, *99*		36____
19984	Lionel Centennial Boxcar, *99*		36____
19985	"I Love Georgia" Boxcar, *99–00*		45____
19986	"I Love North Carolina" Boxcar, *99–00*		40____
19987	"I Love South Carolina" Boxcar, *99–00*		40____
19988	"I Love Tennessee" Boxcar, *99–00*		55____
19989	Toy Fair Boxcar, *00 u*		55____
19996	Toy Fair Boxcar, *01 u*		50____
19997	Lionel Employee Boxcar, *01 u*		125____
19998	Christmas Boxcar, *01*		33____
19999	Lionel Visitor's Center 4-bay Hopper, *02 u*		153____
20000	PRR Senator Coach 4-pack (std O), *13, 15*		640____
20005	SP Sunset Limited Coach 4-pack (std O), *13, 15*		640____
20010	UP City of Los Angeles Coach 4-pack (std O), *13, 15*		640____
20015	B&O Capitol Limited Coach 4-pack (std O), *13*		640____
20020	FEC City of Miami Coach 4-pack (std O), *13*		640____
20025	KCS Southern Belle Coach 4-pack (std O), *13*		640____
20030	MILW Olympian Coach 4-pack (std O), *13, 15*		640____
21029	World of Little Choo Choo Set, *94u, 95*	36	43____
21141	North Dakota State Quarter Gondola Bank, *07*		60____
21142	South Dakota State Quarter Hopper Bank, *07*		60____
21163	SuperStreets FasTrack Grade Crossing, *08–10*		20____
21164	SuperStreets 10" Transition to FasTrack, *08–10*		9____
21165	SuperStreets Transition to FasTrack, 2 pieces, *08–10*		17____
21168	City Traction Trolley Add-on, *08*		75____
21169	City Traction Speeder Add-on, *08*		75____
21170	NYC 15" Heavyweight Passenger Car 4-pack, *07*		250____

			Exc	Mint
____	**21175**	NYC 15" Heavyweight Passenger Car 2-pack, *07*		125
____	**21198**	ATSF Alco Diesel AA Set, horn, *08*		200
____	**21199**	ATSF Midnight Chief Streamliner Car 4-pack, *08*		200
____	**21204**	ATSF Midnight Chief Streamliner Car 2-pack, *08*		100
____	**21207**	SP Diesel Work Train, *07*		175
____	**21212**	NH Diesel Freight Set, *07*		250
____	**21217**	Southern Diesel Executive Inspection Train, *07*		175
____	**21229**	Ringling Bros. S2 Diesel Switcher, horn, *07*		80
____	**21230**	Ringling Bros. Porter Locomotive, *07*		105
____	**21231**	Ringling Bros. Streamliner Car 4-pack, *07*		210
____	**21234**	Ringling Bros. Streamliner Car 2-pack, *07*		105
____	**21237**	Ringling Bros. Flatcar with 3 wagons, *07*		50
____	**21238**	Ringling Bros. Flatcar with 3 wagons, *07*		50
____	**21239**	Ringling Bros. Flatcar with crates, *07*		45
____	**21240**	Ringling Bros. Flatcar with front end loader and poles, *07*		45
____	**21252**	Boy Flying Kite, *08*		60
____	**21253**	Operating Bunk Car Yard Office, *07*		80
____	**21261**	SuperStreets 2.5" Straight-to-Curve Connector, 4 pieces, *08–10*		9
____	**21265**	Operating Voltmeter Car, *07*		75
____	**21266**	SuperStreets Intersection, 4 pieces, *08–10*		40
____	**21267**	PRR Boxcab Electric Locomotive, horn, *07*		77
____	**21271**	WP Operating Coal Dump Car with vehicle, *07*		33
____	**21276**	Congressional Diner, smoke, *07*		110
____	**21277**	Operating Flagman's Shanty, *08*		70
____	**21279**	Roach Wranglers Pest Control Van, *08*		30
____	**21281**	SuperStreets D21 Curve, *08–10*		3
____	**21282**	SuperStreets 2.5" Curve-to-Curve Connector, 4 pieces, *08–10*		9
____	**21283**	SuperStreets Tubular Track Grade Crossing, *08–10*		18
____	**21284**	SuperStreets 10" Tubular Transition, *08–10*		8
____	**21285**	SuperStreets 10" Tubular Transition, 2 pieces, *08–10*		14
____	**21286**	SuperStreets Intersection, *08–10*		10
____	**21287**	SuperStreets Y Roadway, *08–10*		12
____	**21288**	SuperStreets O Gauge Conversion Pins, *08–10*		2
____	**21289**	SuperStreets Connector Pins, *08–10*		2
____	**21290**	SuperStreets Hookup Wires, 2 pieces, *08–10*		3
____	**21291**	Dogbone Expander pack, *08–10*		25
____	**21296**	City Traction Classic Truck, *07*		30
____	**21298**	NYC 4-6-4 Hudson Locomotive "5279," CC, *07*		500
____	**21316**	PE RS3 Diesel "2815," CC, *07*		350
____	**21324**	Acrobats and Clowns Figures, 10 pieces, *08–10*		12
____	**21325**	Ringmaster Circus Figures, 5, with accessories, *08–10*		12
____	**21326**	PRR 15" Interurban Car 2-pack, *07*		200
____	**21354**	Fresh Never Frozen Fish Transport Car, *07*		80
____	**21355**	Dump Bin, *08–10*		20
____	**21358**	Special Addition Boxcar, Girl, *08–10*		25
____	**21359**	Special Addition Boxcar, Boy, *08–10*		25
____	**21368**	Passenger Coach Figures, 9 pieces, *08–10*		11

Exc Mint

		Exc	Mint
21369	Walking Figures, 8 pieces, *08–10*	11	___
21370	Sitting Figures, 6, with benches, *08–10*	11	___
21371	Standing Figures, 8 pieces, *08–10*	11	___
21372	Railroad Station Figures, 6, with accessories, *08–10*	11	___
21373	School Figures, 7, with accessories, *08–10*	11	___
21374	Service Station Figures, 5, with accessories, *08–10*	11	___
21375	Police Figures, 10, with dog, *08*	20	___
21376	Seated Passenger Figures, 40 pieces, *08*	27	___
21377	Mounted Police, 3, with horses, *08–10*	11	___
21378	Factory, *08–10*	18	___
21379	Police Station, *08–10*	16	___
21380	Colonial House, *08–10*	16	___
21381	Suburban Station, *08–10*	16	___
21382	School, *08–10*	17	___
21383	Suburban Ranch House, *08–10*	15	___
21384	Service Station with gas pumps, *08–10*	17	___
21385	Barn and Chicken Coop, *08–10*	20	___
21386	Firehouse, *08–10*	17	___
21387	Church, *08–10*	15	___
21388	Country L-shaped Ranch House, *08–10*	16	___
21389	Supermarket, *08–10*	12	___
21390	Diner, *08–10*	15	___
21394	Rotating Beacon, *08–09*	31	___
21396	Single Tunnel Portals, pair, *08–10*	15	___
21397	SuperSnap 31" Remote Switch, left hand, *08–09*	55	___
21398	SuperSnap 31" Remote Switch, right hand, *08–09*	55	___
21399	SuperSnap 72" Remote Switch, left hand, *08–09*	70	___
21400	SuperSnap 72" Remote Switch, right hand, *08–09*	70	___
21412	NYC Plymouth Switcher Freight Set, *07*	155	___
21430	SuperStreets D16 Curve, *08–10*	2	___
21431	SuperStreets 10" Straight Track, *08–10*	2	___
21432	SuperStreets D16 Curved Track, 8 pieces, *08–10*	18	___
21433	SuperStreets 5" Straight Track, 4 pieces, *08–10*	14	___
21434	SuperStreets 10" Straight Track, 8 pieces, *08–10*	19	___
21435	World War II Seated Soldiers, 9, with benches, *08–09*	20	___
21436	Rings and Things Circus Accessories, *08–09*	10	___
21438	Remote Controller, *07–10*	35	___
21442	City Figures, 7, with scooter, *08–10*	11	___
21443	Factory Figures, 6, with accessories, *08–10*	11	___
21444	Church Figures, 5, with accessories, *08–10*	11	___
21445	Firefighting Figures, 11, with accessories, *08–10*	20	___
21449	Operating Loading Platform with flatcar, *07–08*	80	___
21450	Unloading Station with dump bins, *07*	100	___
21451	Girder Bridge with stone piers, *07*	40	___
21452	Graduated Trestle Set, 26 pieces, *07*	50	___
21453	Elevated Trestle Set, 10 pieces, *07*	40	___
21454	Double Tunnel Portals, 2 pieces, *08–10*	20	___
21456	UPS Step Van, *07*	30	___

			Exc	Mint
____	21466	Ringling Bros. 15" Aluminum Advertising Car, *07*		110
____	21469	Ringling Bros. Flatcar, white, with container, *07*		45
____	21470	Ringling Bros. Flatcar, blue, with container, *07*		45
____	21471	Ringling Bros. Flatcar with 2 trailers, *08–10*		60
____	21472	Ringling Bros. Flatcar with 2 trailers, *08–10*		60
____	21476	Strasburg Plymouth Diesel Switcher, *07*		100
____	21494	WM RS3 Diesel "189," CC, *07*		350
____	21529	Montana State Quarter Boxcar Bank, *08*		45
____	21542	Washington State Quarter Tank Car Bank, *08*		45
____	21543	Boyd Bros. Ford Classic Truck, *08*		33
____	21549	Ringling Bros. Crew Bus, *08*		33
____	21552	S.W.A.T. Team Step Van, *08*		30
____	21560	Reading Flatcar with rail load, *07*		25
____	21567	School Bus SuperStreets Set, *08*		110
____	21568	Dirty Dogz Van SuperStreets Set, *08*		100
____	21569	Angelo's Pizza Delivery Van, *08*		30
____	21570	Flying Colors Painting Van, *08*		30
____	21571	SuperStreets 10" Insulated Roadway, 2 pieces, *08–10*		8
____	21572	SuperStreets 5" Straight School, 2 pieces, *08–10*		8
____	21573	SuperStreets 5" Straight Stop Ahead, 2 pieces, *08–10*		8
____	21574	SuperStreets 5" Straight Crosswalk, 2 pieces, *08–10*		8
____	21575	SuperStreets 10" Crossing, 2 pieces, *08–10*		10
____	21576	SuperStreets Skid Mark Roadway Pack, *08–10*		13
____	21577	Snack-On Step Van, *08*		30
____	21582	Keystone Coal Porter Locomotive, *08*		100
____	21583	Keystone Coal Freight Car 4-pack, *08*		100
____	21590	ATSF "Midnight Chief" 2-bay Hopper "162277," *08*		25
____	21591	ATSF "Midnight Chief" Flatcar "94468" with trailer, *08*		43
____	21592	ATSF "Midnight Chief" Caboose, *08*		25
____	21593	ATSF "Midnight Chief" Boxcar "621593," *08*		35
____	21594	NYC Empire State Express 15" Aluminum Car 4-pack, *08–09*		420
____	21599	SP flatcar with wheel load, *07*		35
____	21600	B&M RS3 Diesel "1538," CC, *08–09*		350
____	21607	Jack Frost Hopper "327" with sugar load, *08*		25
____	21609	Elephants and Giraffes, 2 pair, *08–10*		13
____	21610	Lions and Tigers, 2 pair, *08–10*		13
____	21611	Horses, 4 pieces, *08*		13
____	21621	ATSF Operating Boxcar "22658," *08–09*		90
____	21623	Rutland Operating Milk Car with platform, *08–10*		150
____	21626	Rath Wood-sided Reefer "622," *09*		45
____	21627	Greenlee Packing Wood-sided Reefer "3862," *10*		45
____	21628	CNJ Reefer "1438," *08–09*		35
____	21629	C&O Reefer "7783," *08–09*		35
____	21630	UP Stock Car "42005," *09*		45
____	21631	Reading Boxcar "107984," *08–09*		35
____	21632	GN Boxcar "34285," *08–09*		35
____	21633	RI "Route of the Rockets" Boxcar "21110," *09–10*		40

		Exc	Mint
21634	Tidewater Flying A 1-D Tank Car "1367," *09*		40____
21635	Southern Depressed Center Flatcar, 2 transformers, *09*		43____
21636	NS Flatcar with bulkheads and stakes, *08–09*		35____
21637	Ontario Northland Ribbed Hopper with coal, *09*		40____
21639	Pan Am Boxcar "32126," *08–09*		55____
21640	UP Modern Steel-sided Reefer "499030," *08–09*		55____
21641	Ringling Bros. Merchandise Flatcar, *08*		50____
21643	PRR Die-cast Gondola with covers, *09*		73____
21644	PRR 16-wheel Flatcar with transformer, *08–09*		80____
21646	DT&I Work Crane and Boom Car, *09*		85____
21649	City Traction Trolley with Ringling Bros. banner, *08–09*		80____
21651	Moo-Town Creamery Step Van, *08–09*		38____
21656	Quikrete Step Van, *08–09*		42____
21658	Ringling Bros. Vintage Truck, *08–09*		42____
21659	DT&I Flatcar "90059" with Ford trailer, *08–09*		60____
21662	Moo-Town Creamery Vending Machine, *08–09*		13____
21663	Moo-Town Creamery Bunk Car Ice Cream Shop, *08–09*		115____
21664	RI Operating Coal Dump Car with vehicle, *08–09*		40____
21665	Alaska Operating Log Dump Car with vehicle, *09*		40____
21667	Red River Lumber Boxcab Diesel with horn, *08–09*		100____
21668	CP Operating Hopper "9628," *08–09*		45____
21675	Mountain View Creamery Loading Depot, *08–10*		130____
21676	Beaver Creek Logging Die-cast Porter Locomotive, *08–09*		120____
21677	Ford Factory, *09*		22____
21679	Assured Comfort HVAC Van, *08–09*		38____
21680	Division of Prisons Bus SuperStreets Set, *08–09*		150____
21688	Ringling Bros. Heavyweight Coach 2-pack, *08–11*		240____
21691	Ringling Bros. Flatcar with 2 trailers, *08–10*		60____
21692	C&NW MP15 Diesel with Ringling Bros. banner, *08–09*		140____
21693	Southern MP15 Diesel Pair, powered and dummy, *10*		200____
21696	Ford Flatcar with 2 trucks, *08–09*		53____
21698	Lionel Van SuperStreets Set, *08–10*		130____
21701	Star Spangled GG1 Electric Locomotive "4837," *08–10*		260____
21702	Milwaukee Road Girder Bridge, *08–09*		15____
21703	ATSF Black Mesa Aluminum Business Car, *09–10*		160____
21704	C&O Double Searchlight Car with vehicle, *08–09*		50____
21706	Chatham Police Van, *08–09*		38____
21707	NYC Aluminum Business Car, *09*		160____
21708	CN Operating Log Dump Car, *10*		120____
21709	PRR Girder Bridge, *08–09*		15____
21715	Ringling Bros. Stock Car, *08–09*		60____
21717	Pullman-Standard 1-D Tank Car, *08–09*		35____
21719	NYC Bay Window Caboose, *99*		70____
21720	Ringling Bros. Billboard Set #2, *08–09*		10____
21721	Warning Sign Pack, 12 pieces, *08–10*		25____
21730	Regulatory Sign Pack, 12 pieces, *08–10*		25____

		Exc	Mint
___21738	Railroad Crossing Sign Pack, 6 pieces, *08–10*		21
___21750	NKP Rolling Stock 4-pack, *98*		160
___21751	PRR Rolling Stock 4-pack, *98*		145
___21752	Conrail Unit Trailer Train, *98*		285
___21753	Service Station Fire Rescue Train, *98*	500	585
___21754	BNSF 3-bay Covered Hopper 2-pack (std O), *98*		65
___21755	4-bay Covered Hoppers 2-pack, *98*		65
___21756	6464-style Overstamped Boxcars 2-pack, *98*		65
___21757	UP Freight Car Set, *98*		188
___21758	Bethlehem Steel "44" (SSS), *99*		375
___21759	Canadian Pacific F3 Diesel Passenger Set, *99*		930
___21761	B&M Boxcar Set, 4-pack, *99*		180
___21763	New Haven Freight Set, *99*		265
___21766	ACL Passenger Car 2-pack, *99*		385
___21769	Centennial 1-D Tank Car Set, 4-pack, *99*		225
___21770	NYC Reefer Set, 4-pack, *99*		225
___21771	D&RGW Stock Car Set, 4-pack, *99*		230
___21774	Custom Series Consist I, 3-pack, *99*		150
___21775	Train Wreck Recovery Set, *99*		190
___21778	ATSF Train Master Diesel Freight Set, *99*		NRS
___21779	Seaboard Freight Car Set, *99*		280
___21780	NYC Aluminum Passenger Car 2-pack, *99*		160
___21781	Case Cutlery Freight Set, *99 u*		985
___21782	PRR Congressional Set, *00*		930
___21783	Monday Night Football 2-pack, *01–02*		50
___21784	QVC PRR Coal Freight Steam Set, *00 u*		356
___21785	QVC Gold Mine Freight Steam Set, *00 u*		386
___21786	Santa Fe F3 Diesel ABBA Passenger Set, *00*		1500
___21787	Blue Comet Steam Passenger Set, *01–02*		1050
___21788	Postwar Missile Launch Freight Set, *02–03*		350
___21789	Norfolk Southern Piggyback Set, CC (SSS), *01*		370
___21790	CN TankTrain Dash 9 Diesel Freight Set, *02*		630
21791	Freedom Train Diesel Passenger Set, RailSounds, *03*		540
___21792	C&O Coal Hopper 6-pack #2 (std O), *01*		145
___21793	Virginian Coal Hopper 6-pack #2 (std O), *01*		160
___21794	Pioneer Seed GP7 Diesel Freight Set, *01 u*		885
___21795	Case Farmall Freight Set, *01 u*		965
___21796	NJ Medical Steam Freight Set, *01 u*		483
___21797	SP Daylight Passenger Set, *01*		670
___21852	MILW PS-2CD Hopper 3-pack (std O), *06*		155
___21853	BNSF PS-2CD Hopper 3-pack (std O), *06*		155
___21854	N&W PS-2CD Hopper 3-pack (std O), *06*		155
___21855	A&P Milk Car 3-pack, *06*		150
___21856	Bowman Dairy Milk Car 3-pack (std O), *06*		150
___21857	Western Dairy Milk Car 3-pack (std O), *06*		150
___21858	NP PS-4 Flatcar with trailers, 2-pack (std O), *06*		170
21859	C&NW PS-4 Flatcar with trailers, 2-pack (std O), *06*		170
___21860	UP PS-4 Flatcar with trailers, 2-pack (std O), *06*		170
___21861	PRR PS-4 Flatcar with trailers (std O), *06*		170
___21863	ADM Unibody Tank Car 3-pack (std O), *06*		135
___21864	Cerestar Unibody Tank Car 3-pack (std O), *06*		135

Exc Mint

		Exc	Mint
21865	Coe Rail Husky Stack Car 2-pack (std O), *06*		170____
21866	Santa Fe Husky Stack Car 2-pack (std O), *06*		170____
21872	C&O Offset Hopper 3-pack (std O), *05*		130____
21873	P&LE Offset Hopper 3-pack (std O), *06*		145____
21874	TTX Trailer Train 2-pack (std O), *06*		170____
21875	CSX Husky Stack Car 2-pack (std O), *06*		170____
21876	Disney Villain Hi-Cube Boxcar 3-pack, *05–06*		135____
21877	Domino Sugar 1-D Tank Car 3-pack (std O), *07*		135____
21878	Procor 1-D Tank Car 3-pack (std O), *07*		135____
21879	C&EI Offset Hopper 3-pack (std O), *07*		145____
21880	Erie Offset Hopper 3-pack (std O), *07*		145____
21881	Frisco Offset Hopper 3-pack (std O), *07–08*		200____
21882	Chessie System Offset Hopper 3-pack (std O), *07*		145____
21883	C&O 3-bay Hopper 2-pack (std O), *07–08*		140____
21884	Pennsylvania Power & Light 3-bay Hopper 2-pack (std O), *07*		140____
21885	Santa Fe 3-bay Hopper 2-pack (std O), *07*		140____
21886	C&NW 3-bay Hopper 2-pack (std O), *07–08*		140____
21888	IMC Canada Cylindrical Hopper 2-pack, *06*		130____
21893	Greenbrier Husky Stack Car 2-pack (std O), *07*		170____
21894	CSX Husky Stack Car 2-pack (std O), *07*		170____
21895	BN Husky Stack Car 2-pack (std O), *07*		170____
21896	Arizona & California Husky Stack Car 2-pack (std O), *07*		170____
21897	REA PS-4 Flatcar with trailers, 2-pack (std O), *07–08*		170____
21898	NYC PS-4 Flatcar with trailers, 2-pack (std O), *07–08*		170____
21899	Lackawanna PS-4 Flatcar with trailers, 2-pack (std O), *07*		170____
21900	Civil War Union Train Set, *99*		375____
21901	Civil War Confederate Train Set, *99*		375____
21902	Construction Zone Set, *99 u*		87____
21902	MILW PS-4 Flatcar with trailers, 2-pack (std O), *07–08*		170____
21904	Safari Adventure Set, *99 u*		90____
21904	UP PS-2 Covered Hopper 2-pack (std O), *07*		120____
21905	NYC Flyer Set, *99 u*		100____
21909	AGFA Film Steam Freight Set, *98 u*		1400____
21914	Lionel Lines Freight Set, *99*		120____
21916	Lionel Village Trolley, *99*		75____
21917	N&W Freight Set, *99*		70____
21918	Thomas Circus Play Set, *00*		100____
21918	PC PS-2 Covered Hopper 2-pack (std O), *07*		120____
21921	Imco PS-2 Covered Hopper 2-pack (std O), *07–08*		120____
21924	Holiday Trolley Set, *99*		65____
21925	Thomas the Tank Engine Island of Sodor Train Set, *99–00*		150____
21930	NYC PS-2 Covered Hopper 2-pack (std O), *07*		120____
21932	JCPenney NYC Freight Flyer Steam Set, *00 u*		170____
21934	Custom Series Consist II, 3-pack, *99*		140____
21936	Looney Tunes Train Set, *00 u*		380____
21937	NYC Steel-sided Reefer 2-pack (std O), *07*		130____

		Exc	Mint
___21939	Dubuque Steel-sided Reefer 2-pack (std O), 07–08		130
___21940	ADM Steel-sided Reefer 2-pack (std O), 07		130
21941	National Car Steel-sided Reefer 2-pack (std O), 07		130
___21944	"Celebrate a Lionel Christmas" Steam Set, 00–01		165
___21945	Christmas Trolley Set, 00		100
___21948	NYC Freight Flyer Set, air whistle, 00		240
___21950	Maersk SD70 Diesel Maxi-Stack Set, 00	560	700
___21951	World War II Troop Train, 00		410
___21952	Lionel Lines Service Station Special Set, 00		294
___21953	Ford Mustang GP7 Diesel Set, CC, 01		345
___21955	D&RGW F3 Diesel AA Passenger Set, CC, 01		740
___21956	New York Central Freight Set, 99–00		355
___21969	Lionel Village Trolley Set, 00		85
___21970	SP RS3 Diesel Freight Set, horn, 00–01		110
___21971	Pennsylvania Flyer Steam Set, 00		150
___21972	Frisco GP7 Diesel Freight Set, horn, 00		150
___21973	ATSF Passenger Set, RailSounds, 00–01		375
___21974	ATSF Passenger Set, SignalSounds, 00–01		240
___21975	Burlington Steam Freight Set, SignalSounds, 00		275
___21976	Centennial Steam Freight Starter Set, 00		600
___21977	NYC Train Master Steam Freight Set, 99–00		620
___21978	ATSF Train Master Diesel Freight Set, 99–00		500
___21981	JCPenney NYC Flyer Set, 00 u		150
___21988	NYC Freight Set, RailSounds, 00		325
___21989	Burlington Steam Freight Set, RailSounds, 00		300
___21990	NYC Flyer Freight Set, RailSounds, 00		175
___21999	Whirlpool Steam Freight Set, 00 u		710
___22103	PRR A5 Scale Switcher "411," CC, 08–09		330
___22104	PRR Freight Car 3-pack, 08		135
22105	NYC Empire State Express 4-6-4 Hudson Locomotive "5429," CC, 08–09		420
22113	NYC Empire State Express 15" Aluminum Car 2-pack, 08–10		210
___22116	Ringling Bros. Diesel Freight Set, 08–10		245
___22121	Ringling Bros. Freight Set, 08–10		390
___22126	Ringling Bros. Expansion Pack, 08–10		135
___22131	NH Streamliner Car 3-pack, 07		150
___22135	CB&Q S2 Diesel Switcher "9305," horn, 07		80
___22136	Erie S2 Diesel Switcher "522," horn, 07		80
___22137	Alaska MP15 Diesel "1552," horn, 07		100
___22138	Astoria Heat & Power Porter Locomotive "4," 07		100
___22139	LIRR Speeder, 08		50
___22140	CNJ Boxcab Diesel "1000," horn, 08		90
___22141	Lackawanna 15" Interurban Car 2-pack, 07		200
___22142	FEC Operating Dump Car, 07		70
___22143	B&A Operating Log Dump Car, 08–09		70
___22144	Alaska Operating Coal Dump Car with vehicle, 08		33
___22145	WM Operating Log Dump Car with vehicle, 08		33
___22146	PFE Operating Boxcar, 08		80
___22147	B&O Operating Hopper with coal, 08		35
___22148	GN Operating Hopper with coal, 08		35

			Exc	Mint
22149	Dairymen's League Operating Milk Car, green, with platform, *08*			140____
22150	D&RGW Bunk Car, smoke, *08*			65____
22151	Alaska Searchlight Car with vehicle, *08*			45____
22152	NKP 2-bay Outside-braced Hopper "31299," *08*			50____
22153	L&N 2-bay Offset Hopper "78660," *08*			50____
22154	D&H 2-bay Rib Side Hopper "5737," *07*			50____
22155	Erie-Lack. 2-bay Aluminum Hopper "21353," *08*			60____
22156	ACF Demonstrator 2-bay Aluminum Hopper "44586," *07*			60____
22157	GN Aluminum Tank Car "74787," *08*			60____
22158	MILW Bulkhead Flatcar "967116" with wood, *08–09*			43____
22159	BNSF Flatcar "585011" with trailer, *08*			43____
22160	UP Flatcar "58059" with container, *08*			43____
22161	Conrail Flatcar "705910" with NS container, *08*			43____
22162	Foppiano Wine 3-D Tank Car "1112," *08*			45____
22163	PRR Weed Control Car "6321226," *07*			45____
22166	PRR Reefer "19492," *08*			25____
22167	Seaboard Reefer "16622," *08*			25____
22168	N&W Boxcar "645772," *08*			25____
22169	ATSF Reefer "11744," *07*			25____
22170	P&LE Reefer "22300," *07*			25____
22171	B&O DD Boxcar "495289," *08*			25____
22172	CB&Q Stock Car "52731," *08*			25____
22174	Erie-Lack. Transfer Caboose, *07*			25____
22176	PRR Caboose "478884," *07*			25____
22177	L&N Caboose "100," *07*			25____
22179	NYC Depressed Center Flatcar "66256" with 2 girders, *08*			25____
22180	IC Depressed Center Flatcar with 2 transformers, *07*			25____
22182	RI Gondola "180043" with coils, *08*			25____
22184	B&O Covered Hopper "604321," *08*			25____
22185	UP Covered Hopper "53186," *08*			25____
22186	P&LE (NYC) Gondola "17243," *08–09*			35____
22187	PRR 2-D Tank Car "6351815," *07*			25____
22188	Deep Rock 3-D Tank Car "2152," *08*			25____
22189	NP Java Diner, smoke, *08*			110____
22190	C&O Operating Billboard, *08*			65____
22191	Operating Passenger Station, *08–09*			105____
22192	Hot Box Operating BBQ Shack, *07*			80____
22193	Cold Drinks Vending Machine, *08*			12____
22194	Water Tower with light, *08–09*			20____
22199	City Traction Trolley Barn, *08–09*			65____
22202	Loading Ramp, *08–10*			20____
22203	Dairymen's League Operating Milk Car, white, with platform, *07*			140____
22204	Snacks Vending Machine, *08*			12____
22205	Soup and Sandwich Vending Machine, *08*			12____
22206	PRR Crew Bus, *08*			30____
22222	Ringling Bros. Speeder Chase Set, *08–10*			92____
22225	Ringling Bros. Jomar Heavyweight Private Car, *08–11*			120____

		Exc	Mint
22226	Ringling Bros. 18" Caledonia Heavyweight Private Car, *08*		100
22227	Ringling Bros. 18" Advertising Car, *08*		100
22228	Ringling Bros. Flatcar with 3 wagons, *08*		50
22231	Ringling Bros. Flatcar with 3 wagons, *08*		50
22235	Ringling Bros. Flatcar with pole wagon and truck, *08*		75
22238	Ringling Bros. Work Caboose with calliope wagon, *08*		40
22240	Ringling Bros. Flatcar/Stock Car with wagon, *08*		50
22243	Ringling Bros. Human Cannonball Car, *08*		45
22244	Ringling Bros. Operating Searchlight Car with 3 spotlights, *08*		60
22247	Ringling Bros. Stock Car "54," *08*		50
22248	Ringling Bros. Stock Car "47," *08*		50
22249	Ringling Bros. Dining Dept. Billboard Reefer, *08*		80
22250	Ringling Bros. Dining Dept. Wood-sided Reefer, *08–09*		90
22251	Ringling Bros. Dormitory Bunk Car "22," *08*		75
22252	Ringling Bros. Operating Billboard, *08–09*		75
22253	Ringling Bros. Vintage Billboard Set #1, *08*		9
22255	Ringling Bros. Aluminum Coach "40010," *08–10*		165
22257	Ringling Bros. Aluminum Shop Car "63002," *08–10*		165
22258	Ringling Bros. 18" Aluminum Large Animal Car, *08–10*		165
22259	Ringling Bros. Flatcar with trailer, *08*		53
22260	Ringling Bros. Tractor Trailer, *08*		30
22261	Idaho State Quarter Hopper Bank, *08*		65
22262	Wyoming State Quarter Tank Car Bank, *08*		50
22263	Utah State Quarter Boxcar Bank, *08*		45
22264	SuperStreets Figure-8 Expander Pack, *08–10*		35
22267	Mulligan Spring Water Step Van, *08*		30
22270	Quikrete Classic Truck with 2 pallets, *08*		33
22271	MILW EP-5 Electric Locomotive "E20," CC, *08–09*		460
22272	MILW Olympian Hiawatha 18" Aluminum Car 4-pack, *08*		480
22277	MILW Olympian Hiawatha 18" Aluminum Car 2-pack, *08*		250
22280	Erie-Lack. RS3 Diesel "933," CC, *08–09*		350
22281	Southern Train Master Diesel "6300," CC, *08–09*		420
22282	Southern Bay Window Caboose "X270," *08–09*		70
22283	UP S2 Diesel Switcher "1103" and Caboose "25384," *08*		130
22286	GN Boxcab Electric Locomotive "5008-A," horn, *08*		90
22287	North Shore Line 15" Interurban Car 2-pack, *08*		230
22288	Commuter Train Station, 6 road name stickers, *09*		25
22289	Ringling Bros. 18" Aluminum Passenger Car 2-pack, *08*		270
22290	Erie Boxcar "86448" with graffiti, *08*		46
22291	C&NW Stock Car "14303," *08*		46
22292	Land o' Lakes Butter Billboard Reefer, *08*		75
22293	PRR 4-bay Hopper "253776," *08*		65

No.	Description	Exc	Mint
22294	Montana Rail Link 3-bay Aluminum Hopper "50049," *08*		70___
22295	Canada Wheat 4-bay Aluminum Hopper "606418," *08*		73___
22296	Eaglebrook Aluminum Tank Car "19039," *08*		70___
22297	Petri Wine 3-D Tank Car "904," *08–09*		45___
22298	Cotton Belt Offset Cupola Wood-sided Caboose "2230," *08*		80___
22299	MILW Bay Window Caboose "980502," *08–09*		70___
22300	Detroit, Toledo & Ironton Coil Car "1352," *08*		60___
22301	NYC Flatcar "506090" with freight kit, *08*		35___
22302	C&O Flatcar "80951" with freight kit, *08*		35___
22303	Extruded Aluminum I-Beam, 3 pieces, *08–09*		6___
22304	Rails, 12 pieces, *08–09*		6___
22305	Small Transformer Load, pair, *08–09*		15___
22306	Large Transformer Load, *08*		19___
22307	Forklifts, 3, with pallets, *08–09*		27___
22308	Loaders with crates, pair, *08–09*		13___
22309	Loaders with logs, pair, *08–09*		13___
22310	KBL Logistics Container 2-pack, *08*		40___
22312	Commemorative Quarter Extended Vision Caboose, *09*		80___
22313	ATSF Boxcar "137460," *08*		25___
22314	Coastal King Seafood Wood-sided Reefer, *08*		25___
22315	Wisconsin & Southern "God Bless America" Boxcar, *09*		43___
22316	NP Depressed Center Flatcar "66130" with water tank, *08*		25___
22317	U.S. Air Force Hopper "55175" with ballast load, *08*		25___
22318	DM&IR Ore Car "29991," *08*		25___
22319	Celanese Chemicals 1-D Tank Car "12730," *08*		25___
22320	Baldwin Locomotives Works 1-D Tank Car "6809," *08*		25___
22321	B&O Operating Boxcar, *08*		45___
22322	PRR Operating Ballast Dump Car, *08*		75___
22323	FEMA Voltmeter Car, *08*		75___
22324	C&NW Cop and Robber Chase Gondola, *08–09*		55___
22325	White Milk Cans, 10 pieces, *08–10*		8___
22326	Twin Searchlight Tower, *08–10*		33___
22327	Tommy's Bunk Car Grill, *08–09*		100___
22328	Santa Fe Operating Freight Transfer Platform, *08–09*		130___
22329	Dual Track Signal Bridge, *08–10*		45___
22330	Stella's Heavyweight Diner, smoke, *08–09*		140___
22331	Coffee Vending Machine, *08*		12___
22332	Spring Water Vending Machine, *08*		12___
22333	Candy Vending Machine, *08*		12___
22334	Ford Plymouth Diesel Switcher and Ore Car 6-pack, *08*		200___
22335	NS Operating Paint Shop with boxcar, *08–09*		140___
22344	KBL Logistics ISO Tank, *08*		19___
22346	Tableau Circus Wagons, *08*		13___
22349	Forklift with 6 pallets, *08–09*		23___

			Exc	Mint
___	22350	Twin Lamp Posts, 3 pieces, *08–09*		22
___	22352	Lamp Posts, 4 pieces, *08–09*		20
___	22354	Portable Spotlights, 3 pieces, *08–09*		15
___	22356	High Tension Poles, 4 pieces, *08–09*		8
___	22358	Rail Yard Signs, 12 pieces, *08–09*		10
___	22360	Telephone Poles, 6 pieces, *08–09*		7
___	22362	Girder Bridge, *08–09*		8
___	22363	Stone Bridge Piers, pair, *08–10*		27
___	22365	Heavyweight Passenger Coach 6-wheel Scale Trucks, pair, *08–09*		25
	22366	Aluminum Passenger Coach 4-wheel Scale Trucks, pair, *08–09*		25
___	22367	Timkin Scale Sprung Trucks, pair, *08–09*		19
___	22368	Bettendorf Scale Sprung Trucks, pair, *08–09*		19
___	22369	Scale Couplers, pair, *08–09*		6
___	22379	SuperStreets Barricade, 2 pieces, *08–10*		11
___	22387	Kiosk with 3 vending machines, *08–09*		40
___	22391	Ford MP15 Diesel "10021," horn, *08*		115
___	22392	Ford Farming Boxcar "1681," *08*		30
___	22393	Ford Stampings DD Boxcar "101," *08*		35
___	22394	Ford 2-bay Covered Hopper "1667," *08*		30
___	22395	Ford Speeder "14," *08*		65
___	22396	Ford Water Tower, *08*		25
___	22397	Ford Rotating Sign Tower, *08*		55
___	22398	Boyd Bros. and Ford Barn and Chicken Coop, *08*		25
___	22399	Ford ISO Tank, *08–09*		21
___	22402	PRR Streamlined K4 4-6-2 Pacific Locomotive, tender, *09–10*		500
___	22408	Ringling Bros. Tractor Trailer #1, *08–09*		35
___	22411	Tableau Wagon Set #2, *08–10*		18
___	22412	PRR Operating Flagman's Shanty, *08–09*		90
___	22414	Linde Union Carbide Boxcar with aluminum tank, *08–09*		70
___	22415	Ringling Bros. Flatcar with circus wagon, *08*		50
___	22417	Ringling Bros. Flatcar with container, *09*		55
___	22420	PRR Broadway Limited Aluminum Passenger Car 2-pack, *09–10*		300
___	22423	GN Aluminum Passenger Car 2-pack, *09–10*		360
___	22426	Ford Gondola "13447" with coils, *08–09*		43
___	22427	Ford Operating Billboard, *08–09*		75
___	22428	Ford Tin Sign Replica 4-pack, *08–09*		17
___	22433	PRR Broadway Limited Aluminum Passenger Car 4-pack, *09–10*		600
___	22438	Mail Crane, *08–10*		30
___	22439	Milwaukee Road Aluminum Passenger Car 2-pack, *09–11*		360
___	22447	Wabash Die-cast 2-bay Ribbed Hopper "37751," *08–09*		60
___	22449	UP Crew Bus, *08–09*		38
___	22450	Seaboard Die-cast Hopper with gravel, *10*		80
___	22454	Oklahoma State Quarter Die-cast Hopper Bank, *08–09*		75
___	22455	New Mexico State Quarter Die-cast Gondola Bank, *08–09*		74

		Exc	Mint
22456	Arizona State Quarter Tank Car Bank, *08–09*	55	____
22457	Alaska State Quarter Boxcar Bank, *09*	55	____
22458	Hawaii State Quarter Die-cast Hopper Bank, *09*	75	____
22459	Southern Aluminum Passenger Car 2-pack #1, *09*	300	____
22460	Southern Aluminum Passenger Car 2-pack #2, *09*	300	____
22461	Scale Skeleton Log Car 4-pack, *08–09*	160	____
22467	Railroad Water Tower, *08–09*	23	____
22468	Fast Eddie's Used Car Lot with 2 die-cast vehicles, *08–09*	50	____
22469	Cola Illuminated Vending Machine, *08–09*	13	____
22470	SuperStreets Guard Rails, *08–10*	20	____
22472	Ringling Bros. Tin Sign Replica 4-pack, *08–09*	17	____
22477	Lionel Tin Sign Replica 4-pack, *08–09*	15	____
22482	Vintage Tin Sign Replica 4-pack, *08–09*	15	____
22487	Scooter Gang with scooters, *09–10*	13	____
22492	Airport Revolving Searchlight, *10*	40	____
22493	Ringling Bros. Lighted Clown Wood-sided Reefer, *09*	75	____
22494	Ford Flatcar with 2 Thunderbird convertibles, *09*	53	____
22496	Vita O Flavored Water Vending Machine, *09*	13	____
22497	Top Pop Soda Illuminated Vending Machine, *09*	13	____
22498	Ringling Bros. Flatcar with 3 circus wagons, *09–10*	55	____
22500	Defense Dept. Flatcar with 2 jeeps and soldier, *09*	50	____
22501	C&NW Railroad Van, CC, *09–10*	100	____
22502	Ringling Bros. Flatcar with 3 circus wagons, *09–10*	55	____
22504	Ford Water Tower with vintage Ford logo, *09–10*	25	____
22505	Sparkling Springs Beverage Truck, *09*	45	____
22506	SuperStreets Fishtail Roadway, *09*	25	____
22507	Ringling Bros. Flatcar with boxcar and ticket wagon, *09*	60	____
22509	Pallet Pack with banded loads, *09*	20	____
22510	Lionel Step Van, CC, *09–10*	100	____
22511	BNSF Flatcar with helicopter, *09*	50	____
22513	Ringling Bros. Heavyweight Advertising Car, *09*	120	____
22514	NYC Girder Bridge, *09–10*	15	____
22515	Milwaukee Road/REA Scale Boxcar "6436," *09*	55	____
22516	BNSF MP15 Diesel "3704" with horn, *09*	120	____
22517	Quick Lane Ford Motorcraft Auto Parts Van, *09–10*	42	____
22518	Lionel Tank Container Leasing ISO Tank, *09–10*	23	____
22519	Roma Wine Wood-sided Billboard Reefer, *09–10*	70	____
22520	WWII Soldiers in Action, 10 pieces, *09–10*	20	____
22521	1959 Ford Billboard Set, *09*	10	____
22523	American Flyer Vintage Truck, *09*	38	____
22524	Ford Coil Car "749772," *09*	73	____
22525	Vermont Railway Operating Boxcar "177," *09*	50	____
22526	Crabby Matt's Smoking Heavyweight Diner, *09*	150	____
22527	Toledo, Peoria & Western Boxcar "5067," *09–10*	55	____
22528	GN Stock Car "55973," *09–10*	55	____
22529	U.S. Army 1-D Tank Car "11278," *09*	35	____
22530	Milwaukee Road Aluminum Coach "627," *09–11*	180	____

			Exc	Mint
____	22531	Southern Girder Bridge, *09*		15
____	22532	Montana Rail Link 1-D Tank Car "100017," *09*		35
____	22533	GN Aluminum Coach "1377," *09–10*		180
____	22534	SuperStreets D16 Curve Guard Rails, *09–10*		20
____	22536	SuperStreets D21 Curve Guard Rails, *09–10*		22
____	22538	Ford Modern Aluminum Tank Car "30166," *09*		90
____	22539	BNSF Flatcar "922267" with Ford trailer, *09–10*		60
____	22542	PRR Flatcar "480227" with freight kit, *09*		40
____	22543	Biodiesel 2-D Tank Car "1544," *09*		40
____	22544	Ringling Bros. Wood-sided Gondola with equipment, *09*		63
____	22548	Kiosk #2 with 3 illuminated vending machines, *09*		40
____	22553	Convenience Mart, *09–10*		25
____	22554	Auto Parts Store, *09–10*		20
____	22555	Ringling Bros. Tractor with Gold Tour container, *09–10*		55
____	22558	PRR Flatcar "469301" with milk containers, *09*		50
____	22559	UP Gondola "229794" with freight kit, *09–10*		80
____	22560	CB&Q Wood-sided Gondola "85150" with spools, *09–10*		60
____	22561	Gondola Scrap Load, *09*		9
____	22562	Operation Lifesaver Boxcar with flashing LEDs, *09*		65
____	22563	Ringling Bros. Handcar and Trailer Set, *10–11*		70
____	22566	SuperStreets 2.5" Straight Roadway, 4 pieces, *10*		12
____	22568	Generators, 2 pieces, *09*		9
____	22570	Large transformer, *09*		22
____	22571	Cage Wagon Set, *09–10*		18
____	22573	Display Base, *09*		20
____	22574	Ringling Bros. Flatcar "39" with trailer, *09*		60
____	22577	Biodiesel Storage Tank with 2 figures, *09–10*		40
____	22578	Ringling Bros. Heavyweight Coach "70," *09*		120
____	22579	Circus Horses, 4 pieces, *09–10*		15
____	22580	Bollards and Chains, *09–10*		20
____	22582	Pipe Stack Load, *09*		30
____	22583	KBL Operating Wind Turbine, *09–10*		75
____	22584	KBL Die-cast 16-wheel Flatcar "34807," *09*		85
____	22587	Old Reading Flatcar Foot Bridge with stone piers, *09–10*		50
____	22590	Roadside Fender Bender, *09–10*		75
____	22592	SuperStreets D16 Turn Roadways, left and right, *10*		35
____	22595	SuperStreets D21 Turn Roadways, left and right, *10*		39
____	22598	SuperStreets Adjustable Straight Kit, *09–10*		20
____	22600	Wire Spool Load, 6 pieces, *09*		20
____	22610	Napa Valley Wine Train Alco FA Diesel AA Set, *10*		230
____	22613	Napa Valley Wine Train 15" Passenger Car 4-pack, *10*		450
____	22618	Signal Oil Co. 1-D Tank Car, *10*		40
____	22619	PRR Paoli MU Commuter Train 2-pack, *10*		290
____	22622	RR Paoli Motorized Combine, *10*		200
____	22623	PRR Commuter Train Station, *10*		35

No.	Description	Exc	Mint
22624	NH Die-cast Plymouth Switcher with snowplow, *10*		160___
22625	Ringling Bros. 18" Aluminum Generator Car, *10–11*		180___
22627	Ringling Bros. Lighted Clown Wood-sided Reefer, *10–11*		90___
22628	Ringling Bros. 18" Aluminum Advertising Car, *10–11*		180___
22629	Ringling Bros. Stock Car, *10–11*		60___
22630	Ringling Bros. Tractor and Trailer, *10–11*		35___
22633	Ringling Bros. 18" Aluminum Coach, *10–11*		180___
22634	Ringling Bros. 18" Heavyweight Advertising Car, *10–11*		146___
22635	Ringling Bros. Operating Dual Searchlight Car, *10–11*		60___
22637	Quikrete Step Van, *10*		48___
22638	PRR Crew Bus, *10*		45___
22639	B&O Boxcab Diesel "195," *10*		100___
22640	Central of Georgia Boxcar "5823," *10*		45___
22641	New Haven Boxcar "36438," *10*		45___
22642	Ringling Bros. Operating Large Animal Feed Car, *10–11*		150___
22643	Ford MP15 Diesel "10022," *10–11*		135___
22644	Ford Motorcraft 48' Aluminum Tank Car, *10–11*		95___
22645	Ringling Bros. Operating Tent Pole Dump Car, *10–11*		130___
22646	Ford Speeder, *10–11*		75___
22647	Rock Island Gondola "180044," *10*		35___
22648	PRR Gondola "353381," *10*		35___
22651	Central Vermont Operating Milk Car with platform, *10*		175___
22653	Starlite Diner with parking lot, *10*		200___
22654	Ringling Bros. Flatcar with 3 circus wagons, *10–11*		60___
22656	Ringling Bros. Flatcar with 3 circus wagons, *10–11*		60___
22658	Operating Flagman's Shanty, *10*		100___
22659	Union 76 1-D Tank Car "6322," *10*		40___
22660	Moose Pond Creamery Operating Loading Depot, *10*		140___
22661	WM 2-Bay Covered Hopper "5051," *10*		35___
22662	PRR Reefer "19494," *10*		45___
22663	New Haven Illuminated Caboose, *10*		40___
22667	Acme Scrap Platform Crane, *10*		60___
22670	ATSF Operating Boxcar, *10*		140___
22671	Smoking Southern Bay Window Caboose, *10*		90___
22672	Ringling Bros. 18" Sarasota Observation Car, *10–11*		146___
22673	Ford Water Tower with light, *10*		27___
22674	MILW 21" Aluminum Passenger Car 2-pack, *10–11*		400___
22679	Ringling Bros. Operating Billboard, *10–11*		100___
22902	Quonset Hut, *98–99*		22___
22907	Die-cast Girder Bridge, *98–01*		10___
22910	Gilbert Tractor Trailer, *98*		20___

		Exc	Mint
____22914	PowerHouse Lockon, *98–01*		24
____22915	Municipal Building, *98–99*		28
____22916	190-watt Power Accessory System, *98*		425
____22918	Locomotive Backshop, *98*	300	460
____22919	ElectroCouplers Kit for GP9 Diesel, *98–00*		20
____22922	Intermodal Crane, *98*		195
____22931	Die-cast Cantilever Signal Bridge, *98–06*		35
____22934	Walkout Cantilever Signal, *98–03*		42
____22936	Coaling Tower, 3 pieces, *98*		85
____22940	Mast Signal, *98–00*		37
____22942	Accessories Box, *98–01*		20
____22944	Automatic Operating Semaphore, *98–03, 08*		35
____22945	Block Target Signal, *98–00*		39
____22946	Automatic Crossing Gate and Signal, *98–99*		45
____22947	Auto Crossing Gate, *98–00*		36
____22948	Gooseneck Street Lamps, set of 2, *98–00*		30
____22949	Highway Lights, set of 4, *98–99*		20
____22950	Classic Street Lamps, set of 3, *98–02*		20
____22951	Dwarf Signal, *98–00*		24
____22952	Classic Billboards, set of 3, *98–00*		15
____22953	Linex Gasoline Tall Oil Tank, *98–99*		6
____22954	Linex Gasoline Wide Oil Tank, *98–99*		6
22955	ElectroCouplers Kit for J Class and B&A tenders, *98–00*		20
____22956	ElectroCouplers Kit for NW2 Switcher, *98*		20
____22957	ElectroCouplers Kit for F3 Diesel, *98–01*		20
____22958	ElectroCouplers Kit for Dash 9 Diesel, *98–01*		20
22959	ElectroCoupler Conversion Kit for Atlantic Locomotive, *98–01*		13
____22960	Trainmaster Command Basic Upgrade Kit, *98–01*		34
____22961	Standard GP9 Diesel B Unit Upgrade Kit, *98–01*		30
22962	Deluxe GP9 Diesel B Unit Upgrade Kit, black trucks, *98–01*		44
22963	RailSounds Upgrade Kit, steam RailSounds, *98–01*		55
22964	RailSounds Upgrade Kit, diesel RailSounds, *98–01*		55
____22965	Culvert Loader, CC, *98–01*		255
____22966	Figure-8 Add-on Track Pack (027), *98–16*		17
____22967	Double Loop Add-on Track Pack (027), *98–16*		62
____22968	Double Loop Track Pack (027), *98–03*		65
____22969	Deluxe Complete Track Pack (O), *98–16*		120
____22972	Bascule Bridge, *98–99*		337
____22973	Lionel Corporation Tractor and Trailer, *98*		15
____22975	Culvert Unloader, CC, *99–00*		225
22979	GP9 Diesel B-Unit Deluxe Upgrade Kit, silver trucks, *98–01*		34
____22980	TMCC SC-2 Switch Controller, *99–16*		130
____22982	Postwar ZW Controller and Transformer Set, *98*		265
____22983	180-watt PowerHouse Power Supply, *99–16*		100
____22990	Flatcar with Route 66 autos, 4-pack, *99*		37
____22991	Christmas Tree and Blue Comet Train, *99–00*		60
____22993	Route 66 Sinclair Dino Cafe, *99–00*		210

		Exc	Mint
22997	Oil Drum Loader, *99–00*		100____
22998	Triple Action Magnetic Crane, *99*		220____
22999	Sound Dispatching Station, *99–00*		90____
23000	NYC Dreyfuss Hudson Operating Base, 2-rail, *92 u*		190____
23001	NYC Dreyfuss Hudson Operating Base, 3-rail, *93 u*		190____
23002	NYC Hudson Operating Base, *92 u, 93–94*		190____
23003	PRR B-6 Switcher Operating Base, *92 u, 93–94*		190____
23004	NP 4-8-4 Operating Base, *92 u, 93–94*		190____
23005	Reading T-1 Operating Base, *92 u, 93–94*		190____
23006	Chessie System T-1 Operating Base, *92 u, 93–94*		190____
23007	SP Daylight Operating Base, *92 u, 93–94*		190____
23008	NYC L-3 Mohawk Operating Base, *92 u, 93–94*		190____
23009	PRR S2 Turbine Locomotive Operating Base, *92 u, 93–94*		190____
23010	31" Remote Switch, left hand (O), *95–99*	30	37____
23011	31" Remote Switch, right hand (O), *95–99*	20	30____
23012	F3 Diesel ABA Operating Base, *92 u, 93–94*		190____
24018	PRR Boxcar, *05*		25____
24101	Mainline Color Position Signal, *04–08*		25____
24102	Industrial Water Tower, *03*		55____
24103	Double Floodlight Tower, *03, 05–09*		42____
24104	Hobo Tower, *03–05*		70____
24105	Track Gang, *03–06*		70____
24106	Exploding Ammunition Dump, *02*		25____
24107	Missile Firing Range Set, *02*		60____
24108	World War II Pylon, *03*		80____
24109	Santa Fe Railroad Tugboat, *03*		125____
24110	Pennsylvania Railroad Tugboat, *03*		118____
24111	Swing Bridge, *03*		215____
24112	Oil Field with bubble tubes, *03*		44____
24113	Lionelville Ford Auto Dealership, *03*		225____
24114	AMC/ARC Gantry Crane, CC, *03*		195____
24115	AMC/ARC Log Loader, CC, *03, 06–07*		140____
24117	Covered Bridge, *02–16*		60____
24119	Big Bay Lighthouse, *04–05*		170____
24122	Lionelville People Pack, *03, 08–09, 15–16*		27____
24123	Passenger Station People Pack, *03, 08–09, 15–16*		27____
24124	Carnival People Pack, *03, 08–11, 13–16*	5	27____
24130	TMCC 135/180 PowerMaster, *04–12*		79____
24131	Dumbo Pylon, *03*		70____
24134	Bethlehem Steel Gantry Crane, *02*		200____
24135	Lionel Lighthouse, *02–03*		100____
24137	Mr. Spiff and Puddles, *03, 08*		34____
24138	Playtime Playground, *03, 08*		50____
24139	Duck Shooting Gallery, *03*		110____
24140	Charles Bowdish Homestead, *03*		60____
24147	Lionel Sawmill, *03*		90____
24148	Coal Tipple Coal Pack, *602, 08–10, 13–15*		15____
24149	NYC Hobo Hotel, *02*		42____
24151	Hobo Campfire, *03*		25____

		Exc	Mint
____**24152**	Conveyor Lumber Loader, *03*		65
____**24153**	Railroad Control Tower, *03, 08–10*		40
____**24154**	Maiden Rescue, *03*		35
____**24155**	Blinking Light Billboard, *04–10*		21
____**24156**	Lionelville Street Lamps, set of 4, *04–05, 07–16*		30
____**24159**	Illuminated Station Platform, *04–08*		32
____**24160**	Rub-a-Dub-Dub, *04*		42
____**24161**	Test O' Strength, *04–06*		70
____**24164**	Summer Vacation, *04–05*		80
____**24168**	Tire Swing, *04–05*		70
____**24170**	Rover's Revenge, *04–05*		70
____**24171**	Campbell's Soup Water Tower, *04*		45
____**24172**	Balancing Man, *04–05*		70
____**24173**	Derrick Platform, *03–05*		60
____**24174**	Icing Station, *04–06*		100
____**24176**	Irene's Diner, *06–07*		65
____**24177**	Hot Air Balloon Ride, *04, 06*		95
____**24179**	Scrambler Amusement Ride, *04–07*		165
____**24180**	Choo Choo Barn Lionelville Zoo, *04–05*		105
____**24182**	Lionelville Firehouse, *04*		100
____**24183**	Lionelville Gas Station, *04, 06–09*		115
____**24187**	Classic Billboard Set: 3 stands and 5 inserts, *04–08*		10
____**24190**	Station Platform, *05–09*		17
____**24191**	Park People Pack, *04–16*		27
____**24192**	Park Benches People Pack, *04–09*		23
____**24193**	Railroad Yard People Pack, *04–08, 14–16*		27
____**24194**	Civil Servants People Pack, *04–16*		27
____**24196**	Farm People Pack, *04–09*		23
____**24197**	City Accessory Pack, *04–16*		27
____**24200**	Lionel FasTrack Book, *07–10, 13–15*		35
____**24201**	UPS Centennial Operating Billboard Signmen, *07*		100
____**24203**	Polar Express Original Figures, 4 pieces, *08–14, 16*		30
____**24204**	Christmas Tractor Trailer with trees, *08*		25
____**24205**	Classic Billboard Set, *08–10*		20
____**24206**	MOW Gantry Crane, *08*		280
____**24212**	Lionel Art Blinking Billboard, *08–09*		23
____**24213**	Universal Lockon, *12–16*		4
____**24214**	Postwar "395" Floodlight Tower, *08*		75
____**24215**	MTA Metro-North Passenger Station, *07*		53
____**24218**	Sunoco Elevated Tank, *08–09*		75
____**24219**	PRR Plastic Girder Bridge, *08*		18
____**24220**	ATSF Girder Bridge, *08–09*		18
____**24221**	UP Die-cast Girder Bridge, *08*		30
____**24222**	UPS Die-cast Girder Bridge, *08*		30
____**24223**	Santa's Sleigh Pylon, *08*		150
____**24224**	Postwar "38" Water Tower, *08–09*		150
____**24226**	Christmas Toy Store, *08*		52
____**24227**	Halloween Animated Billboard, *08–09*		54
____**24228**	Christmas Operating Billboard, *08*		38
____**24229**	Pennsylvania Water Tower, *08–09*		23
____**24230**	Maiden Rescue, *08*		60

Exc Mint

		Exc	Mint
24232	Burning Switch Tower, 08	80	___
24233	Exploding Ammunition Dump, 08	36	___
24234	Missile Firing Range, 08	43	___
24235	UPS Water Tower, 08	80	___
24236	Wimpy's All-Star Burger Stand, 08	97	___
24238	Sunoco Oil Derrick, 08	90	___
24240	MTA Metro-North Blinking Billboard, 07	21	___
24242	Postwar "352" Icing Station, 08	100	___
24243	Rosie's Roadside Diner, 08	85	___
24244	Commuter People, 08, 13–16	27	___
24245	MTA Metro-North Illuminated Station Platform, 07	32	___
24248	Manual Crossing Gate, 08–16	20	___
24250	Mainline Gooseneck Lamps, pair, 08–09	32	___
24251	Polar Express Caribou, 08–14, 16	27	___
24252	Polar Express Wolves and Rabbits, 08–14, 16	27	___
24264	Halloween People, 08–12	23	___
24265	Trick or Treat People, 08–13	23	___
24270	Operating Forklift Platform, 08–09	280	___
24272	Train Orders Building, 08	80	___
24273	Christmas Water Tower, 08–10	23	___
24274	Christmas Girder Bridge, 08	18	___
24279	PowerMaster Bridge, 08–13	55	___
24283	NYC Girder Bridge, 09–10	21	___
24284	Halloween Girder Bridge, 09–11	21	___
24285	CP Rail Girder Bridge, 08–09	30	___
24286	Polar Express Girder Bridge, 09–14	21	___
24287	ATSF Blinking Light Water Tower, 09	30	___
24288	NYC Blinking Light Water Tower, 09	30	___
24293	Legacy Module Garage, 08–09	50	___
24294	AEC Nuclear Reactor, 09–10	328	___
24295	Cowen's Corner Hobby Shop, 09	420	___
24296	Engine House, 09–12, 14	70	___
24299	Main Street Ice Cream Parlor, 08	37	___
24500	D&RGW Alco PA Diesel AA Set, 04	530	___
24503	D&RGW Alco PB Diesel, 04	150	___
24504	Santa Fe E6 Diesel AA Set, CC, 03	530	___
24507	Milwaukee Road E6 Diesel AA Set, CC, 03	530	___
24511	Burlington FT Diesel AA Set, RailSounds, 03	225	___
24516	Santa Fe F3 Diesel B Unit, 03	235	___
24517	NYC F3 Diesel B Unit "2404," powered, CC, 03	250	___
24518	WP F3 Diesel B Unit, 03	275	___
24519	B&O F3 Diesel B Unit, 03	270	___
24520	Alaska F3 Diesel AA Set, 03	650	___
24521	Alaska F3 Diesel B Unit, nonpowered, 03	200	___
24522	Alaska F3 Diesel B Unit "1519," powered, CC, 03	300	___
24528	Postwar "2379T" Rio Grande F3 Diesel A Unit, nonpowered, 04	175	___
24529	Santa Fe F3 Diesel AA Set, CC, 04	690	___
24532	Santa Fe F3 Diesel B Unit "18A," nonpowered, 04	150	___
24533	Santa Fe F3 Diesel B Unit "18B," 04	200	___
24534	Erie-Lack. F3 Diesel ABA Set, CC, 05	900	___
24538	Erie-Lack. F3 Diesel B Unit "8042," powered, CC, 05	225	___

			Exc	Mint
____	24544	NYC FA2 Diesel AA Set, CC, *05*		600
____	24547	NYC FB2 Diesel B Unit "3330" (std 0), *05*		150
____	24548	CN FPA-4 Diesel AA Set, CC, *05*		600
____	24551	CN FPB-4 Diesel B Unit "6865" (std 0), *05*		150
____	24552	UP F3 Diesel ABA Set, CC, *05*		680
____	24556	UP F3 Diesel B Unit "900C," powered, CC, *05*		285
____	24562	Santa Fe F3 Diesel B Unit, powered, *04–05*		300
____	24563	PRR F3 Diesel B Unit, powered, *04–05*		195
____	24570	Santa Fe FT Diesel B Unit, nonpowered, *05*		85
____	24573	Postwar "2383C" Santa Fe F3 Diesel B Unit, nonpowered, *05*		180
____	24574	UP E7 Diesel AA Set, CC, *06*		700
____	24577	UP E7 Diesel B Unit "990," nonpowered (std 0), *06*		150
____	24578	UP E7 Diesel B Unit "988," powered, *06*		300
____	24579	NYC E7 Diesel AA Set, CC, *06*		700
____	24582	NYC E7 Diesel B Unit "4105," nonpowered (std 0), *06*		150
____	24583	NYC E7 Diesel B Unit "4104," powered, *06*		300
____	24584	Pennsylvania F7 Diesel ABA Set, CC, *06*		900
____	24588	Pennsylvania F7 Diesel B Unit "9643B," powered, *06–07*		300
____	24589	Santa Fe F7 Diesel ABA Set, CC, *06–07*		900
____	24593	Santa Fe F7 Diesel B Unit "332B," powered, *06–07*		300
____	24594	PRR F7 Diesel Breakdown B Unit, RailSounds, *06–07*		160
____	24595	Santa Fe F7 Diesel Breakdown B Unit, RailSounds, *06–07*		270
____	24596	UP E7 Diesel Breakdown B Unit, RailSounds, *06*		270
____	24597	NYC E7 Diesel Breakdown B Unit, RailSounds, *06*		270
____	24928	Franklin Mutual Bank, *08*		60
____	25003	WP Boxcar, orange with silver feather, *05*		30
____	25008	Holiday Boxcar, *06*		50
____	25009	Santa Fe Hi-Cube Boxcar "14064," *06*		30
____	25010	NP Boxcar "48189," *06*		30
____	25011	Angela Trotta Thomas "Santa's Break" Boxcar, *06*		50
____	25014	PRR Boxcar, silver, *10*		30
____	25016	ATSF Boxcar, *10*		35
____	25022	NYC Boxcar, *06*		35
____	25025	Reading Boxcar "106502," *07–08*		35
____	25026	RI Hi-Cube Boxcar, *07–08*		35
____	25030	Billboard Boxcar with catalog art, *06*		20
____	25033	Holiday Boxcar, *07*		50
____	25034	Angela Trotta Thomas "Santa's Workshop" Boxcar, *07*		50
____	25035	Disney Holiday Boxcar, *06*		50
____	25041	UPS Centennial Boxcar #1, *06*		55
____	25042	UPS Centennial Boxcar #2, *07*		55
____	25043	Macy's Parade Boxcar, *06*		40
____	25050	British Columbia Hi-Cube Boxcar "8008," *08*		35
____	25051	Seaboard Boxcar, *08*		35
____	25052	Disney Holiday Boxcar, *07*		70
____	25053	NYC DD Boxcar "75500," *08*		55

Exc Mint

25054	Angela Trotta Thomas "Christmas Memories" Boxcar, *08*	55	
25057	PRR Boxcar "19751," *08*	20	
25058	Santa Fe Boxcar, *10*	30	
25059	Democrat 2008 Election Boxcar, *08*	50	
25060	Republican 2008 Election Boxcar, *08*	50	
25061	Holiday Boxcar, *08*	55	
25063	Conrail Boxcar "25063," *09*	40	
25064	CP Rail Hi-Cube Boxcar, *09–10*	40	
25065	Disney Holiday Boxcar, *08*	40	
25066	Holiday Boxcar, *09*	65	
25067	Angela Trotta Thomas "General Delivery" Boxcar, *09*	65	
25068	D&H Boxcar, *08 u*	60	
25077	Milwaukee Road Boxcar "8484," *09–10*	40	
25087	Wabash Boxcar "6439," *10–11*	40	
25093	Seaboard Boxcar, *10*	30	
25095	Texas Special Boxcar, *10*	100	
25096	CN Boxcar, *10*	45	
25103	Chessie "Steam Special" Madison Car 2-pack, *05*	100	
25106	Pennsylvania Madison Car 4-pack, *05*	210	
25111	Pennsylvania Madison Car 2-pack, *05*	120	
25114	Lionel Lines Passenger Car 3-pack, *05*	120	
25118	Lionel Lines Passenger Car 2-pack, *05*	80	
25121	Southern Streamliner Car 4-pack, *05*	210	
25126	Southern Streamliner Car 2-pack, *05–06*	120	
25134	Polar Express Add-on Diner, *05–14, 16*	70	
25135	Polar Express Add-on Baggage Car, *05–14,16*	70	
25148	B&O Madison Car 4-pack, *06–07*	220	
25153	B&O Madison Car 2-pack, *06–07*	125	
25156	California Zephyr Streamliner Car 4-pack (std O), *06–07*	220	
25161	California Zephyr Streamliner Car 2-pack, *06–07*	125	
25164	UP Madison Car 4-pack, *06–07*	220	
25169	UP Madison Car 2-pack, *06–07*	125	
25176	B&O Baggage Car, TrainSounds, *06–07*	160	
25177	UP Baggage Car, TrainSounds, *06–07*	160	
25178	California Zephyr Streamliner Baggage Car, TrainSounds, *06–07*	160	
25186	Polar Express Hot Chocolate Car Add-on, *06–14, 16*	70	
25187	GN Streamliner Car 4-pack, *07*	220	
25188	GN Streamliner Car 2-pack, *07*	125	
25189	GN Streamliner Baggage Car, TrainSounds, *07*	160	
25196	North Pole Central Vista Dome Car, *07–08*	45	
25197	North Pole Central Baggage Car, *07–10*	45	
25198	PRR Vista Dome Car "4058," *07–08*	45	
25199	PRR Baggage Car "9359," *07–09*	45	
25404	FEC Champion Aluminum Passenger Car 2-pack, *04–05*	290	
25407	FEC Champion Aluminum Diner, StationSounds, *04–05*	290	
25408	Santa Fe El Capitan Aluminum Passenger Car 2-pack, *05*	290	

			Exc	Mint
25411	Santa Fe El Capitan Aluminum Diner, StationSounds, *05*	____		290
25412	B&O Columbian Aluminum Passenger Car 2-pack, *05*	____		275
25415	B&O Columbian Aluminum Diner, StationSounds, *05*	____		290
25416	SP Daylight Aluminum Passenger Car 2-pack, *04–05*	____		290
25419	SP Daylight Aluminum Diner, StationSounds, *04–05*	____		290
25420	PRR Trail Blazer Aluminum Passenger Car 2-pack, *04–05*	____		290
25423	PRR Trail Blazer Aluminum Diner, StationSounds, *04–05*	____		290
25433	UP City of Denver Aluminum Passenger Car 4-pack (std O), *05*	____		1000
25438	Union Pacific Aluminum Passenger Car 2-pack, *05*	____		250
25441	UP City of Denver 18" Aluminum Diner, StationSounds, *05*	____		290
25446	Santa Fe Super Chief Streamliner Car 2-pack, *05*	____		150
25450	PRR Congressional Aluminum Passenger Car 4-pack (std O), *06–07*	____		580
25455	PRR Congressional Aluminum Passenger Car 2-pack (std O), *06–07*	____		300
25458	PRR Congressional Diner, StationSounds (std O), *06–07*	____		300
25473	NYC Commodore Vanderbilt Aluminum Passenger Car 2-pack (std O), *06*	____		300
25476	NYC Commodore Vanderbilt Diner, StationSounds (std O), *06*	____		300
25496	Texas Special 21" Streamliner Diner, StationSounds (std O), *07*	____		300
25503	Santa Fe Heavyweight Passenger Car 4-pack (std O), *07–09*	____		495
25504	Santa Fe Heavyweight Passenger Car 2-pack (std O), *07–09*	____		265
25505	Santa Fe Heavyweight Diner, StationSounds (std O), *07–09*	____		295
25506	SP Heavyweight Passenger Car 4-pack (std O), *07*	____		495
25507	SP Heavyweight Passenger Car 2-pack (std O), *07–08*	____		265
25508	SP Heavyweight Diner, StationSounds (std O), *07–08*	____		295
25512	Texas Special Streamliner Car 2-pack (std O), *07*	____		300
25514	Best Friend of Charleston Coach, *08*	____		125
25515	MILW Heavyweight Passenger Car 4-pack (std O), *07*	____		495
25516	MILW Heavyweight Passenger Car 2-pack (std O), *07*	____		265
25517	MILW Heavyweight Diner, StationSounds (std O), *07–08*	____		295
25518	PRR Heavyweight Passenger Car 4-pack (std O), *07*	____		495
25519	PRR Heavyweight Passenger Car 2-pack (std O), *07*	____		265

Exc Mint

		Exc Mint
25520	PRR Heavyweight Diner, StationSounds (std O), *07–08*	295____
25521	B&O Heavyweight Passenger Car 4-pack (std O), *07*	495____
25522	B&O Heavyweight Passenger Car 2-pack (std O), *07*	265____
25523	B&O Heavyweight Diner, StationSounds (std O), *07–08*	295____
25559	Phantom IV Passenger Car 4-pack, *08*	380____
25574	UP Streamlined Diner, StationSounds (std O), *08*	325____
25575	Polar Express Heavyweight Car 2-pack, *09*	400____
25576	Polar Express Scale Observation Car, *14, 16*	210____
25578	Polar Express Heavyweight Add-on Coach, *09*	200____
25582	New York City Transit R30 Subway 2-pack, *10*	400____
25586	Polar Express Heavyweight Baggage Car, *10, 12–14*	210____
25587	Polar Express Abandoned Toy Car, *10, 13*	200____
25595	New York City Transit R16 Subway 2-pack, *10*	400____
25598	Polar Express Heavyweight Combination Car, *12–14*	210____
25600	Postwar Scale CP 18" Aluminum Passenger Car 4-pack, *11*	640____
25605	Postwar Scale CP 18" Aluminum Passenger Car 2-pack, *11*	320____
25608	ATSF Super Chief 18" Aluminum Passenger Cars 4-pack, *11*	640____
25613	ATSF Super Chief 18" Aluminum Passenger Cars 2-pack, *11*	320____
25616	UP 18" Passenger Car 2-pack (std O), *11*	320____
25619	PRR "Lindbergh Special" Passenger Car 2-pack, *11*	280____
25622	Milwaukee Road 18" Passenger Car 4-pack, *11*	640____
25623	Milwaukee Road 18" Passenger Car 2-pack, *11*	320____
25630	Polar Express Scale Heavyweight Diner, *12–14, 16*	210____
25631	Lionel Funeral Set Add-on 2-pack (std O), *13*	300____
25635	PRR Red Arrow Heavyweight Coach 3-pack (std O), *13*	430____
25639	PRR Red Arrow Heavyweight Diner (std O), *13*	150____
25646	ATSF Scout Heavyweight Coach 4-pack (std O), *12–14*	550____
25651	ATSF Scout Heavyweight Coach 2-pack (std O), *12–14*	280____
25654	Southern Crescent Limited Heavyweight Passenger Car 2-pack, *12*	550____
25655	Blue Comet Heavyweight Passenger Car 2-pack, *12–13*	550____
25656	Alton Limited Heavyweight Passenger Car 2-pack, *12–14*	550____
25665	Amtrak Acela Passenger Car 2-pack, *12*	500____
25713	NYC 20th Century Limited Heavyweight Passenger Car 4-pack (std O), *12–14*	550____
25714	NYC 20th Century Limited Van Twiller Combo Car (std O), *12*	140____
25715	NYC 20th Century Limited Schuyler Mansion Sleeper Car (std O), *12*	140____

		Exc	Mint
25716	NYC 20th Century Limited Macomb House Sleeper Car (std O), *12*		140
25717	NYC 20th Century Limited Catskill Valley Observation Car (std O), *12*		140
25718	NYC 20th Century Limited Heavyweight Passenger Car 2-pack, *12–14*		280
25719	NYC 20th Century Limited Baggage Car "4857" (std O), *12*		140
25720	NYC 20th Century Limited Poplar Highlands Sleeper Car (std O), *12*		140
25721	NYC 20th Century Limited Heavyweight Diner "655" (std O), *12*		280
25722	D&RGW California Zephyr 18" Aluminum Passenger Car 4-pack, *12*		640
25727	WP California Zephyr 18" Aluminum Passenger Car 2-pack, *12*		320
25731	CB&Q California Zephyr 18" Aluminum Passenger Car 2-pack, *12*		320
25757	Texas Special Passenger Car 2-pack, *13–14*		400
25760	PRR Passenger Car 2-pack, *13–14*		400
25773	SAL Round-roof Boxcar "19297" (std O), *14*		80
25790	NYC 20th Century Limited Heavyweight Diner (std O), *12*		140
25795	Polar Express 10th Anniversary Scale Coach, *14*		215
25796	Polar Express 10th Anniversary Scale Observation Car, *14, 16*		215
25930	John Adams Boxcar, *13, 15–16*		70
25931	Andrew Johnson Boxcar, *13, 15–16*		70
25932	Calvin Coolidge Boxcar, *13, 15–16*		70
25933	Harry S. Truman Boxcar, *13, 15–16*		70
25934	Santa Fe Reefer 3-pack, *14–16*		145
25938	PRR Freight Expansion 3-pack, *13*		155
25942	Western Freight Expansion 3-pack, *13–16*		155
25946	SP Hi-Cube Boxcar "128132," *13, 15*		50
25947	North Pole Express Jack Frost Reefer, *13*		43
25958	Gingerbread Dough Vat Car, *13–14*		60
25959	Gingerbread 3-D Tank Car, *13*		55
25960	Christmas Tree Transparent Boxcar, *13–14*		75
25961	Thanksgiving on Parade Boxcar, *13*		60
25962	Thanksgiving Poultry Car, *13*		70
25963	A Christmas Story 30th Anniversary Boxcar, *13–14*		65
25964	Silver Bell Casting Co. Ore Car, *13*		55
25965	Polar Express 10th Anniversary Boxcar, *13*		65
25973	Seaboard Round-roof Boxcar "19297" (std O), *14*		80
25977	A Christmas Story Leg Lamp Mint Car, *13*		80
26000	C&O Flatcar with pipes, *01*		20
26001	BP Flatcar "6424" with trailers, *01 u*		150
26002	Monopoly Flatcar with airplane, *00 u*		NRS
26003	Lackawanna Flatcar with NH trailer, *01*		60
26004	Conrail Flatcar "71693" with trailer, *01*		50
26005	Nickel Plate Flatcar with trailer, *01*		55
26006	Southern Flatcar "50126" with trailer, *01*		50
26007	NW Flatcar "203029" with trailer, *01*		50

		Exc	Mint
26008	Farmall Flatcar, *01 u*		NRS____
26011	B&M Bulkhead Flatcar, *01 u*		NRS____
26013	CN Flatcar with Zamboni ice resurfacing machine, *01*		48____
26014	JCPenney Flatcar, *01 u*		145____
26016	Soo Line Flatcar with trucks, *01 u*		NRS____
26017	Soo Line Flatcar with trailer, *01 u*		NRS____
26018	Soo Line Flatcar with trailer, *01 u*		NRS____
26019	Alaska Gondola "13801," *02*		30____
26020	Postwar "3830" Flatcar with submarine, *02*		46____
26021	CN Flatcar with trailer, *02*		44____
26022	PFE Flatcar with trailer, *02*		32____
26023	Postwar "6816" Flatcar with bulldozer, *02*		65____
26024	Postwar "6817" Flatcar with scraper, *02*		65____
26025	Postwar "6407" Flatcar with rocket, *02*		42____
26026	Postwar "6413" Flatcar with Mercury capsules, *02*		95____
26027	Flatcar "6425" with U.S. Army boat, *02*		30____
26028	Conrail Well Car "768121," *02*		40____
26030	NYC Flatcar "601172" with stakes and bulkheads, *02*		22____
26033	NYC Gondola "6462," *01*		30____
26035	LL Flatcar with traffic helicopter, *01*		50____
26039	Lions Flatcar with 2 Zamboni ice resurfacing machines, *02*		39____
26042	B&O Gondola "601272" with canisters, *03*		19____
26043	Seaboard Flatcar "48109" with trailer, *03*		30____
26044	NYC Flatcar "506089" with trailers, *03*		35____
26045	Postwar "2411" Flatcar with pipes, *03*		40____
26046	Postwar "6561" Flatcar with cable reels, *03*		30____
26047	Postwar "2461" Flatcar with transformer, *03*		25____
26048	Postwar "6801" Flatcar with boat, *02*		29____
26049	Speedboat Willie Flatcar with boat, *03*		29____
26053	PRR Gondola with canisters, *04 05*		20____
26056	Southern Bulkhead Flatcar "50125," *02*		19____
26057	SP Flatcar "599365" with tractors, *02*		37____
26058	SP Flatcar "599366" with trailer frames, *02*		35____
26061	Lionelville Tree Transport Gondola, *03*		40____
26062	NYC Gondola "26062" with cable reels, *03*		19____
26063	Pennsylvania Bulkhead Flatcar "26063," *03*		19____
26064	Rock Island Flatcar "90088" with trailer, *04*		34____
26065	REA Flatcar with trailers "TLCX2," *04*		35____
26066	Great Northern Bulkhead Flatcar "26066," *04*		20____
26067	Southern Gondola "60141" with cable reels, *04*		20____
26070	Nestle Nesquik Flatcar "26070" with trailer, *03*		70____
26077	LL Flatcar "6424" with autos, girls set add-on, *03*		44____
26078	LL Flatcar "6801" with boat, boys set add-on, *03*		40____
26080	NJ Medical School Flatcar with handcar, *03*		80____
26082	Frisco Auto Carrier, 2-tier, *04*		20____
26085	New York Auto Carrier, 2-tier, *05*		27____
26086	Alaska Flatcar with bulkheads, *05*		25____
26087	Rock Island Gondola with canisters, traditional, *05*		27____

		Exc	Mint
____	26091	Elvis Flatcar with tractor and trailer, traditional, _05_	60
____	26099	PRR Auto Carrier "500423," 3-tier, _07_	30
____	26100	PRR 1-D Tank Car, _00_	27
____	26101	Lenoil 1-D Tank Car "6015," _00_	34
____	26102	AEC Glow-in-Dark 1-D Tank Car, _00_	50
____	26103	GATX Tank Train 1-D Tank Car "44588," _00_	34
____	26107	BP Petroleum 3-D Tank Car, _00 u_	99
____	26108	Lionel Visitor's Center Reefer "206482," _00 u_	38
____	26109	NYC (P&LE) 1-D Tank Car, _00_	42
____	26110	SP 3-D Tank Car "6415," _00–01_	15
____	26111	Frisco Tank Car, _00_	29
____	26112	Gulf Oil Tank Car, _00_	40
____	26113	U.S. Army 1-D Tank Car, _00_	35
____	26114	Service Station 1-D Tank Car (SSS), _00_	32
____	26115	Lionel Centennial Tank Car, _00 u_	86
____	26116	Pepe LePew 1-D Tank Car, _00 u_	85
____	26118	NYC Tank Car "101900," _01_	23
____	26119	Protex 3-D Tank Car "1054," _00_	29
____	26120	KCS Tank Car "1229," _00_	32
____	26122	Pioneer Seed Tank Car, _00 u_	NRS
____	26123	Santa Fe Stock Car "23002," _01_	35
____	26124	C&O 1-D Tank Car "X1019," _01_	30
____	26125	Winter Wonderland Clear Tank Car with confetti, _00_	50
____	26126	Cheerios Boxcar, _98_	60
____	26127	Wellspring Capital Management Tank Car with confetti, _00 u_	214
____	26131	Santa Fe 1-D Tank Car "335268," _02_	22
____	26132	UP 1-D Tank Car "69015, _02_	40
____	26133	Tootsie Roll 1-D Tank Car "26133," _02_	37
____	26135	Whirlpool Tank Car, _01_	NRS
____	26136	Southern 1-D Tank Car "8790011," _03_	20
____	26137	Jack Frost 1-D Tank Car "106," _03_	32
____	26138	Nestle Nesquik 1-D Tank Car "26138," _03_	40
____	26139	Lionel Lines Stock Car "26139" with horses, _03_	39
____	26141	Whirlpool 1-D Tank Car, _03 u_	94
____	26144	Chessie System 1-D Tank Car "2233," _02_	22
____	26145	Do It Best 1-D Tank Car, _03 u_	80
____	26146	Do It Best 1-D Tank Car, _03 u_	95
____	26147	Diamond Chemicals 1-D Tank Car "6315," Archive Collection, _02_	33
____	26149	Egg Nog 1-D Tank Car, _03_	43
____	26150	Alaska 3-D Tank Car "26150," _03_	23
____	26151	NP Wood-sided Reefer "26151," _03_	19
____	26152	Morton Salt 1-D Tank Car "26152," _04_	40
____	26153	Pillsbury 1-D Tank Car "26153," _04_	40
____	26154	NYC 3-D Tank Car "26154," _04_	25
____	26155	Pennsylvania 1-D Tank Car "26155," _04_	20
____	26156	North Western Wood-sided Reefer "15356," _04_	20
____	26157	Ballyhoo Brothers Circus Stock Car "26157," _04_	35
____	26158	Campbell's Soup 1-D Tank Car, _04_	35
____	26164	LL 1-D Tank Car "6315," girls set add-on, _03_	43

Exc Mint

26167	New Haven 1-D Tank Car, traditional, *05*	27____
26168	Conrail 3-D Tank Car, traditional, *05*	27____
26169	Santa Fe Wood-sided Reefer, traditional, *05*	27____
26171	Alaska 1-D Tank Car, *05*	30____
26176	Tidmouth Milk 1-D Tank Car, *05*	35____
26179	GN 3-D Tank Car, *06*	30____
26180	DM&IR 1-D Tank Car "S15," *06*	30____
26181	NYC Wood-sided Reefer, *06*	30____
26193	UP 1-D Tank Car, *07*	15____
26196	Candy Cane 1-D Tank Car, *06*	60____
26197	D&H 1-D Tank Car "55," *07–08*	35____
26198	D&RGW 3-D Tank Car, *07*	30____
26199	WP PFE Wood-sided Reefer "55327," *07*	30____
26200	NKP Boxcar "18211," *98*	35____
26201	Operation Lifesaver Boxcar, *98*	29____
26203	D&H Boxcar "1829," *98*	25____
26204	Alaska Boxcar "10806," *98–99*	35____
26205	Rocky & Bullwinkle Boxcar, *99*	36____
26206	Curious George Boxcar, *99*	40____
26208	Vapor Records Boxcar #2, *98*	55____
26214	Celebrate the Century Stamp Boxcar, *98 u*	97____
26215	AEC Glow-in-the-Dark Boxcar, *98*	93____
26216	Cheerios Boxcar, *98 u*	80____
26218	Quaker Oats Boxcar, *98 u*	430____
26219	Ace Hardware Boxcar, *98 u*	NRS____
26220	Smuckers Boxcar, *98 u*	84____
26222	Penn Central Boxcar "125962," *99*	31____
26223	FEC Boxcar "5027," *99*	31____
26224	D&H Boxcar, *99*	24____
26228	Vapor Records Holiday Boxcar, *99 u*	118____
26230	AEC Glow-in-the-Dark Boxcar #2, *99*	50____
26232	Martin Guitar Lumber Boxcar "9823," *99*	41____
26234	NYC Boxcar, *99*	29____
26235	Valentine Boxcar, *99*	40____
26236	Aircraft Boxcar, *99*	28____
26237	Boy Scout Boxcar, *99*	85____
26238	Detroit Historical Museum Boxcar, *99*	29____
26239	M.A.D.D. Boxcar, *99*	19____
26240	RailBox Boxcar, *99–00*	24____
26241	Norfolk & Western Boxcar, *99–00*	17____
26242	D.A.R.E. Boxcar, *99*	30____
26243	Christmas Boxcar, *99*	35____
26244	Woody Woodpecker Boxcar, *99*	43____
26247	Lionel Lines Boxcar, *99*	38____
26253	Acme Explosives Boxcar, *99 u*	NRS____
26254	Keebler Boxcar, *99 u*	NRS____
26255	NYC Boxcar "200495," *99 u*	30____
26256	Salvation Army Charity Boxcar, *99*	29____
26257	Wheaties Boxcar, *99*	74____
26264	Lionel Station Boxcar, *99*	44____
26265	NYC Pacemaker Boxcar, *00*	30____
26271	AEC Glow-in-the-Dark Boxcar, *99*	60____

		Exc	Mint
___ 26272	Christmas Boxcar, *00*		42
___ 26275	Boy Scout Boxcar, *00*		55
___ 26276	C&O Boxcar "23296," *99–00*		23
___ 26277	UP Boxcar "491050," *00*		20
___ 26278	Cap'n Crunch Christmas Boxcar, *99*		640
___ 26280	Tinsel Town Express Boxcar, music, *00*		50
___ 26284	Toy Fair Preview Boxcar, *99 u*		725
___ 26285	NYC Pacemaker Boxcar, *00*		40
___ 26288	AEC Glow-in-Dark Boxcar, *99*		44
___ 26290	SP Boxcar, *00*		20
___ 26291	Pennsylvania Boxcar "47158," *00*		20
___ 26292	Frisco Boxcar "22015," *00*		20
___ 26293	Burlington Boxcar, *00*		30
___ 26294	Centennial Express Boxcar, *00*		NRS
___ 26295	Trainmaster Boxcar, *99 u*		55
___ 26296	Service Station Boxcar Set (SSS), *00*		105
___ 26298	Taz Bobbing Boxcar, *00*		70
___ 26300	UPS Flatcar with trailers, *04*		50
___ 26301	UPS Flatcar with airplane, traditional, *05*		53
___ 26302	Troublesome Truck #1, *05*		35
___ 26303	Troublesome Truck #2, *05*		35
___ 26305	SP Auto Carrier, 2-tier, *06*		30
___ 26306	D&RGW Gondola "56135" with canisters, *06*		30
___ 26307	Chessie System Bulkhead Flatcar, *06*		30
___ 26308	Hard Rock Cafe Flatcar with billboards, *06*		55
26309	Alaska Depressed Center Flatcar with cable reels, *06*		50
___ 26310	CGW Flatcar "3707" with trailer, *06*		55
___ 26311	Santa Fe Flatcar with pickups, *06*		60
___ 26317	AEC Gondola with toxic waste containers		30
___ 26318	AEC Gondola with toxic waste containers		30
___ 26330	Gondola with trees and presents, *06*		60
___ 26331	Lionel Lines Bulkhead Flatcar, *07*		30
___ 26332	CP Rail Gondola "337061" with canisters, *07*		30
___ 26335	Domino Sugar Flatcar with trailer, *07–08*		60
___ 26357	CSX Flatcar "600514" with pipes, *07–08*		50
___ 26366	REA Flatcar with trailers, *07*		60
___ 26367	Santa's Egg Nog Flatcar with container, *07*		60
___ 26368	Gondola with trees and presents, *07*		60
___ 26378	Conrail Auto Carrier "786414," 2-tier, *08*		35
___ 26379	PRR Gondola with cable reels, *08–09*		35
___ 26380	NYC Bulkhead Flatcar, *08*		35
___ 26389	ATSF Flatcar "108477" with 2 pickups, *08*		60
___ 26390	ATSF Flatcar with bulkheads, *09–10*		40
___ 26391	NYC Gondola "263910" with containers, *09*		40
___ 26392	BNSF Auto Carrier, *09*		40
___ 26400	C&NW Hopper, *07–08*		35
___ 26401	NP Ore Car "78540," *08*		35
___ 26410	Chessie System Hopper "47806," *08*		35
___ 26411	Lionel Lines Ore Car "2026," *08–09*		35
___ 26412	Chessie System 4-bay Hopper "60573," *08*		35
___ 26418	B&M Hopper, *09*		40

Exc Mint

26421	PRR Ore Car, *11*	40___
26422	White Pass Ice Breaker Car, *09*	50___
26423	Soo Line Ore Car, *10*	40___
26424	LV Hopper, *11*	30___
26425	UP Hopper, *11*	40___
26429	PRR Hopper, *11*	40___
26435	B&M Ice Breaker Hopper, *11*	50___
26437	CSX Hopper, *11*	40___
26439	Central of Georgia Hopper, *11–12*	40___
26443	M&StL Ore Car "6700," *11*	40___
26445	Polar Hopper with presents, *11–14*	60___
26446	Thomas & Friends Troublesome Trucks Christmas 2-pack, *11–15*	70___
26448	U.S. Army Gondola with reels, *11*	40___
26449	CN Hi-Cube Boxcar "799346," *13*	55___
26451	DM&IR Ore Car "28003," *13*	43___
26452	PRR Hopper "153935," *13*	43___
26457	PRR Ore Car, *12*	40___
26473	Lackawanna NS Heritage 2-bay Hopper, *13*	55___
26474	NYC NS Heritage Quad Hopper, *13*	55___
26477	Monopoly Electric Company Hopper, *13*	65___
26481	Boy Scouts of America Christmas Gondola, *13*	65___
26488	Hershey's Ice Breakers Hopper, *13*	63___
26489	Hershey's Chistmas Bells Boxcar, *13*	65___
26491	Pennsylvania Power & Light Gondola with canisters, *13*	43___
26492	Area 51 3-D Tank Car, *13*	43___
26493	Monopoly Water Works 3-D Tank Car, *13*	65___
26494	PRR Truss Rod Gondola with vats, *13*	60___
26495	C&NW Poultry Car, *13*	60___
26496	Lionelville Aquarium Co. Fish Food Vat Car, *13–16*	65___
26497	Bethlehem Steel Depressed Flatcar with reels, *13*	43___
26499	CN Hi-Cube Boxcar "799346," *14*	55___
26502	UP Bay Window Caboose "6517," *97*	47___
26503	ATSF High-Cupola Caboose "7606R," *97*	85___
26504	Mobil Oil Square Window Caboose "6257," *97 u*	37___
26505	Rescue Unit Caboose, *98*	50___
26506	N&W Square Window Caboose "562748," *98*	15___
26507	D&H Square Window Caboose "35707," *98*	20___
26508	Alaska Square Window Caboose "1081," *98*	28___
26511	Quaker Oats Square Window Caboose, *98 u*	48___
26513	NYC Emergency Caboose "26505," *99*	47___
26515	Lionel Lines Bobber Caboose, *99*	10___
26516	Safari Bobber Caboose, *99 u*	10___
26519	Christmas Work Caboose "6496," *99*	41___
26520	Bethlehem Steel Work Caboose "6130" (SSS), *99*	55___
26523	Keebler Cheezit Square Window Caboose, *99 u*	NRS___
26524	NYC Square Window Caboose "295," *99 u*	20___
26526	Santa Fe Square Window Caboose "999471," *01*	30___
26527	Christmas Work Caboose with presents, *02*	27___
26528	PRR Square Window Caboose "6257," *99*	21___
26530	LL Square Window Caboose "6257," *99*	22___
26532	NYC Square Window Caboose "296," *00*	20___

Exc Mint

			Exc	Mint
____	26533	SP Square Window Caboose, *00*		20
____	26534	PRR Square Window Caboose "6257," *00*		20
____	26535	Frisco Square Window Caboose "1700," *00*		20
____	26536	Centennial Express Square Window Caboose, *00*		NRS
____	26537	Lionel Mines Square Window Caboose, *00 u*		45
____	26539	Whirlpool Square Window Caboose, *00 u*		NRS
____	26542	ACL Square Window Caboose "069," *01*		31
____	26543	GN Square Window Caboose "X66," *00–01*		28
____	26544	Alaska Square Window Caboose "1084," *01*		25
____	26545	Snap-On Square Window Caboose, *00 u*		NRS
____	26548	Pioneer Seed Square Window Caboose, *00 u*		NRS
____	26549	PRR Square Window Caboose "4977947," *01*		20
____	26550	NYC Square Window Caboose "19293," *01*		20
____	26551	Chessie System Center Cupola Caboose, *01*		25
____	26552	Santa Fe Square Window Caboose "999472," *01*		25
____	26553	C&O Center Cupola Caboose "A918," *01*		30
____	26554	Monopoly Short Line Square Window Caboose, *00 u*		NRS
____	26556	NH Center Cupola Caboose, *01*		35
____	26557	Farmall Square Window Caboose, *01 u*		NRS
____	26559	N&W Center Cupola Caboose "518408," *01*		20
____	26560	B&M Square Window Caboose, *01 u*		20
____	26564	Soo Line Center Cupola Caboose, *01 u*		20
____	26565	Lionel Employee Square Window Caboose, *01 u*		150
____	26566	WP Square Window Caboose "731," *02*		25
____	26568	NKP Square Window Caboose "1155," *02*		25
____	26569	Southern Square Window Caboose "252," *02*		25
____	26570	B&O Square Window Caboose "295," *02*		25
____	26572	Lionel 20th Century Square Window Caboose, *00 u*		25
____	26580	Wabash Square Window Caboose "2805," *03*		22
____	26581	C&O Square Window Caboose "C-1831," *03*		20
____	26582	L&N Square Window Caboose "318," *03*		20
____	26583	PRR Square Window Caboose "477814," *03*		25
____	26594	Ontario Northland Work Caboose "26594," *03*		25
____	26595	UP Caboose "26595," *03*		18
____	26596	NYC Caboose "17716," *04*		25
____	26597	Great Northern Caboose "X295," *04*		25
____	26598	UP Caboose "26598," *04*		25
____	26599	DM&IR Work Caboose "26599," *04*		25
____	26600	American Fire and Rescue Water Tank Car, *09–11*		55
____	26603	LV Depressed Flatcar with reels, *09*		40
____	26604	Halloween Spooky Grave Gondola, *09*		58
____	26609	NYC Gondola with Pacemaker canisters		40
____	26612	Christmas Gifts Gondola, *09*		60
____	26614	Tupelo Dairy Farms Milk Car, *10–11*		60
____	26616	UP Bulkhead Flatcar with pipes, *10*		40
____	26617	B&O Depressed Center Flatcar with generator, *10*		40
____	26629	PRR Flatcar with generators		35
____	26638	Pennsylvania Power & Light Flatcar with reels, *11*		40
____	26639	Cities Service 3-Tier Auto Carrier, *11–12*		40
____	26640	CN Maple Syrup Barrel Ramp Car, *11–12*		40
____	26641	Coca-Cola Flatcar with trailer, *11*		70

Exc Mint

26642	CN Jet Snowblower, *11–12*	65	___
26643	D&RGW Jet Snowblower, *11–13*	65	___
26644	BNSF Flatcar with generator, *11*	40	___
26645	BNSF Flatcar with trailer, *11*	40	___
26646	Pennsylvania Power & Light Flatcar with transformer, *11–12*	40	___
26647	IC Bulkhead Flatcar with pipes, *11*	40	___
26649	Erie-Lack. Gondola with canisters, *11*	40	___
26650	M&StL Flatcar with pipes, *11*	40	___
26651	ATSF Scout Heavyweight Passenger Car 2-pack (std O), *12*	280	___
26652	NYC Gondola with canisters, *11*	40	___
26653	PC Flatcar with generator, *11*	35	___
26654	Boy Scouts Flatcar with Pinewood Derby Kit, *11–13*	75	___
26660	Coca-Cola Vat Car, *11–16*	70	___
26661	Reindeer Feed Barrel Ramp Car, *09*	60	___
26665	Hershey's Special Dark Flatcar with trailer, *11*	60	___
26666	Boy Scouts Flatcar with trailer, *11*	70	___
26667	Flatcar with Santa's sleigh, *12*	70	___
26668	Strasburg Flatcar with wheels, *11*	55	___
26669	U.S. Navy Flatcar with Shark submarine, *12–13*	60	___
26673	B&M Flatcar with Milk Tank, *12*	60	___
26675	Monopoly Auto Loader, *12*	80	___
26676	Heinz Baked Beans Vat Car, *12*	60	___
26677	LIRR Gondola with canisters, *12*	40	___
26679	ATSF Gondola with reels, *12–13*	55	___
26683	Christmas Track Maintenance Car, *12–13*	67	___
26685	Flatcar with Santa's plane, *12*	55	___
26686	Hershey's Cocoa Vat Car, *12–13*	63	___
26687	Lone Ranger Gondola with gunpowder vats, *12–14*	65	___
26693	Hershey's Krackel Piggyback Flatcar with trailer, *12–13*	70	___
26694	Carnegie Science Center Flatcar with submarine, *13*	60	___
26696	NJ Transit Gondola with wood ties, *12*	75	___
26699	PRR Flatcar with wheel load," *12–14*	55	___
26706	Lighted Christmas Boxcar, *00*	47	___
26707	Lionel Steel Operating Welding Flatcar "1108," *00*	90	___
26709	Flatcar "6511" with psychedelic submarine, *99*	32	___
26710	Southern Stock Car, Carsounds, *99*	95	___
26712	Churchill Downs Horse Car "6473," *99–00*	38	___
26713	Shay Log Car 3-pack, *99*	105	___
26714	Westside Lumber Flatcar with logs (std O), *99*	45	___
26715	Westside Lumber Flatcar with logs (std O), *99*	45	___
26716	Westside Lumber Flatcar with logs (std O), *99*	45	___
26717	Orion Star Boxcar 9600, *00*	30	___
26718	Christmas Boxcar, RailSounds, *00*	160	___
26719	Bobbing Ghost Halloween Boxcar, *00*	46	___
26721	Lionel Lines Coal Dump Car "3379," *00*	31	___
26722	Lionel Lines Log Dump Car "3351," *00*	31	___
26723	Lion Chasing Trainer Gondola "3444," *00*	49	___

		Exc	Mint
____26724	Veterans Day Boxcar, *00*		70
____26725	NYC Jumping Hobo Boxcar "88160," *00*		38
____26726	T. Rex Bobbing Boxcar, *00*		41
____26727	San Francisco City Lights Boxcar, *00*		50
____26736	Lionel Birthday Boxcar, *02 u*		40
____26737	Operating Santa Gondola "6462," *00 u*		65
____26738	Lionel Mines Gondola, *00 u*		NRS
____26739	Santa and Snowman Boxcar, *00*		46
____26740	Reindeer Car, *00*		43
____26741	Operating Santa Boxcar, *00*		50
____26743	Christmas Reindeer Car, *01*		55
____26745	Traveling Aquarium Car "506," *01*		70
____26746	Bobbing Vampire Boxcar, *01*		46
____26747	Halloween Bats Aquarium Car, *01*		75
____26748	T&P Operating Hopper Car "9699," *01*		38
____26749	Alaska Log Dump Car, *01*		29
____26751	Chessie Coal Dump Car, *01*		27
____26752	Christmas Aquarium Car, *01*		55
____26753	Christmas Operating Dump Car, *01*		43
____26757	Operating Barrel Car "35621," *00*		55
____26758	AEC Nuclear Gondola "719766," *01*		90
____26759	Postwar "3459" Coal Dump Car, *02*		60
____26760	Postwar "3461" Log Dump Car, *02*		60
____26761	AEC Security Caboose 3535, *01*		63
____26762	Postwar "3665" Minuteman Car, *01*		55
____26763	Postwar "6448" Exploding Boxcar, *01*		40
____26764	Bethlehem Steel Operating Welding Car, *01*		75
____26765	Postwar "3370" Sheriff and Outlaw Car, *01–02*		49
____26766	Priority Mail Operating Boxcar, *01–02*		32
____26768	Postwar "6520" Searchlight Car, *02*		49
____26769	Santa Fe Crane Car "199793," CC, *03*		255
____26770	Wabash Brakeman Car "3424," *01*		70
____26773	Chessie Searchlight Car, *01*		20
____26774	Santa Fe Log Dump Car, *01*		25
____26775	U.S. Army Searchlight Car, *00*		50
____26776	U.S. Army Operating Boxcar "26413," *00*		55
____26777	U.S. Flag Boxcar, *01 u*		250
____26779	Burlington Operating Hopper "189312," *02*		40
____26780	Postwar "3376" Bronx Zoo Giraffe Car, *02*		36
____26781	Postwar "3540" Operating Radar Car, *02*		35
____26782	Lenny the Lion Bobbing Head Car, *02*		38
____26784	Stingray Express Aquarium Car, *02*		35
____26785	Flatcar with powerboat, *02*		31
____26786	Lionelville Operating Parade Car, *02*		40
____26787	Erie Jumping Hobo Boxcar, *01–02*		43
____26788	Christmas Music Boxcar, *02*		46
____26789	Kiss Kringle Chase Gondola, *02*		35
____26790	Lighted Christmas Boxcar, *02*		34
____26791	UP Animated Gondola, *02*		50
____26792	REA Operating Boxcar "6299," *03*		39
____26793	Alaska Extension Searchlight Car, *01*		44
____26794	Postwar "6352" PFE Ice Car, *01–02*		85

		Exc	Mint
26795	NYC Stock Car "3121," Cattle Sounds, 02	50	
26796	Lionel Farms Poultry Dispatch Car, 01	55	
26797	GN Log Dump Car "60011," 02	48	
26798	Bethlehem Steel Coal Dump Car "26798," 02	70	
26801	Jumping Bart Simpson Boxcar, 04	44	
26802	Simpsons Animated Gondola, 04	46	
26803	Santa Fe Derrick Car "26803," 04	25	
26804	NYC Coal Dump Car "26804," 04	22	
26805	Pennsylvania Log Dump Car "26805," 04	24	
26806	Pillsbury Operating Boxcar "3428," Archive Collection, 04	40	
26807	Blue Chip Line Motorized Animated Gondola, 04	40	
26808	Egg Nog Barrel Car, 04	55	
26809	Santa's Extension Searchlight Car, 04	42	
26810	NYC Operating Searchlight Car, 05	33	
26811	Pennsylvania Coal Dump Car, 05	33	
26812	Santa Fe Log Dump Car, 05	33	
26813	Lionel Lines Derrick Car, 05	33	
26814	NYC Walking Brakeman Car "174226," 05	40	
26815	PRR "Workin' on the Railroad" Boxcar "24255," 05	42	
26816	REA Boxcar, steam TrainSounds, 05	105	
26817	Alaska Boxcar, diesel TrainSounds, 05	145	
26818	Christmas Music Boxcar, 05	63	
26819	Holiday Animated Gondola, 05	55	
26820	Penguin Transport Aquarium Car, 05	60	
26821	NP Moe & Joe Lumber Flatcar, 05	75	
26826	Alaska Searchlight Car, 05	40	
26827	UPS Operating Boxcar "9237," Archive Collection, 05	63	
26828	Tornado Chaser Radar Tracking Car, 05	63	
26829	UPS Holiday Operating Boxcar, 05	59	
26832	Lionel Lines Tender, TrainSounds, 07–08	105	
26833	Wellspring Radar Car, 04	65	
26834	PFE Ice Car "20042" (std O), 05–06	63	
26835	MOW Track Cleaning Car, 05	140	
26836	Halloween Boxcar, SpookySounds, 05	105	
26841	PRR Log Dump Car, 05	27	
26842	NYC Coal Dump Car, 05	27	
26845	Southern Derrick Car, 06	35	
26846	GN Coal Dump Car, 06	38	
26847	C&O Coal Dump Car, 06–07	80	
26848	Lionel Lines Moe & Joe Flatcar, 06	80	
26849	SP Log Dump Car, 06–07	80	
26850	D&RGW Searchlight Car, 06	75	
26851	WM Log Dump Car, 06	35	
26852	Postwar "3562-25" Santa Fe Barrel Car, 06	75	
26853	SeaWorld Aquarium Car, 06	75	
26854	UP Walking Brakeman Car, 06–07	75	
26855	Halloween Animated Gondola, 06	65	
26856	Christmas Chase Gondola, 06	65	
26857	Alien Radar Tracking Car, 06	65	
26858	Christmas Music Boxcar, 06	65	

		Exc	Mint
26859	Christmas Parade Boxcar, *06*		75
26860	B&O Boxcar "466035," steam TrainSounds (std O), *06–07*		75
26861	Santa Fe Boxcar, diesel TrainSounds (std O), *06–07*		110
26862	Hard Rock Cafe Boxcar, *06*		35
26863	Railway Express Operating Milk Car with platform, *06*		140
26864	Domino Sugar Operating Boxcar, *06–07*		40
26865	CP Animated Caboose, *06–07*		80
26867	Boxcar, AlienSounds, *06–07*		110
26868	U.S. Steel Operating Welding Car, *06*		75
26869	REA Jumping Hobo Boxcar, *06–07*		70
26870	Christmas Dump Car with presents, *06*		80
26871	PRR Tender, steam TrainSounds (std O), *06*		105
26872	U.S. Army Security Car, *06*		75
26876	Missile Firing Trail Car, *06*		75
26877	U.S. Army Missile Launch Car, *06–07*		190
26888	Weyerhaeuser Timber Co. Log Car		40
26889	Weyerhaeuser Timber Co. Log Car		40
26891	PRR Coal Dump Car, *05*		30
26897	Great Western Flatcar with handcar, *07*		65
26898	NYC Log Dump Car, *05*		25
26905	Bethlehem Steel Gondola "6462" with canisters, *98*		29
26906	SP Flatcar "9823" with Corgi `57 Chevy, *98*		40
26908	TTUX Flatcar "6300" with Apple trailers, *98*		70
26913	East St. Louis Gondola "9820," *98*		29
26920	Union Pacific Die-cast Ore Car "64861," *97*		70
26921	Union Pacific Die-cast Ore Car "64862," *97*		55
26922	Union Pacific Die-cast Ore Car "64863," *97*		65
26923	Union Pacific Die-cast Ore Car "64864," *97*		55
26924	Union Pacific Die-cast Ore Car "64865," *97*		55
26925	Union Pacific Die-cast Ore Car "64866," *97*		60
26926	Union Pacific Die-cast Ore Car, *98*		55
26927	Union Pacific Die-cast Ore Car, *98*		55
26928	Union Pacific Die-cast Ore Car, *98*		55
26929	Union Pacific Die-cast Ore Car, *98*		40
26936	Die-cast Tank Car 4-pack, *98*		335
26937	Die-cast Hopper 4-pack, *98*		325
26938	NYC Reefer, *99*		80
26940	Rio Grande Stock Car "37710," *99*		80
26946	D&H Semi-Scale Hopper "9642"		85
26947	Gulf Die-cast Tank Car, *98*		120
26948	P&LE Die-cast Hopper, *98*		65
26949	NP Flatcar with trailer "6424-2017," *98*		47
26950	NP Flatcar with trailer "6424-2016," *98*		47
26951	TTX Flatcar "475185" with PRR trailer, *98*		55
26952	J.B. Hunt Flatcar with trailer, *98*		40
26953	J.B. Hunt Flatcar with trailer, *98*		40
26954	J.B. Hunt Flatcar with trailer, *98*		40
26955	J.B. Hunt Flatcar with trailer, *98*		40
26956	C&O Gondola (027), *98–99*		15

Exc Mint

26957	Delaware & Hudson Flatcar with stakes, *98*	20___
26971	Lionel Steel 16-wheel Depressed Center Flatcar, *98*	135___
26972	Pony Express Animated Gondola, *98*	36___
26973	Getty Die-cast Tank Car 3-pack, *98*	270___
26974	Getty Die-cast 1-D Tank Car "4003," *98*	80___
26975	Getty Die-cast 1-D Tank Car "4004," *98*	90___
26976	Getty Die-cast 1-D Tank Car "4005," *98*	80___
26977	Sinclair Die-cast Tank Car 3-pack, *98*	275___
26978	Sinclair Tank Car UTLX "64026," *98*	105___
26979	Sinclair Tank Car UTLX "64027," *98*	85___
26980	Sinclair Tank UTLX "64028," *98*	90___
26981	Gulf Die-cast Tank Car 2-pack, *99*	165___
26985	B&O Die-cast Hopper 2-pack, *99*	160___
26987	Chessie System (B&O) Die-cast 4-bay Hopper "235154," *99*	90___
26991	Lionelville Ladder Fire Car, *99*	47___
26992	NYC Reefer, *99*	75___
26993	NYC Reefer, *99*	85___
26994	NYC Reefer, *99*	135___
26995	Rio Grande Stock Car "37714," *99*	80___
26996	Rio Grande Stock Car "37715," *99*	80___
26997	Rio Grande Stock Car "37716," *99*	80___
27000	C&EI Offset Hopper "97393" (std O), *07*	65___
27001	Erie Offset Hopper "28001" (std O), *07*	65___
27002	Frisco Offset Hopper "92399" (std O), *07*	65___
27003	Chessie System Offset Hopper "234355" (std O), *07*	65___
27016	UP PS-2 Covered Hopper "1312" (std O), *07–08*	60___
27019	Imco PS-2 Covered Hopper "41001" (std O), *07–08*	60___
27022	PC PS-2 Covered Hopper "74217" (std O), *07*	60___
27025	NYC PS-2 Covered Hopper "883180" (std O), *07*	60___
27029	ATSF Offset Hopper 3-pack (std O), *08–09*	200___
27030	Monon Offset Hopper 3-pack (std O), *08–09*	200___
27031	MoPac Offset Hopper 3-pack (std O), *08–09*	200___
27032	NYC Offset Hopper 3-pack (std O), *08–09*	200___
27033	Chessie System PS-2 Hopper 3-pack (std O), *08–09*	180___
27034	Nickel Plate Road PS-2 Hopper 3-pack (std O), *08–09*	180___
27053	CB&Q ACF 2-bay Covered Hopper "183925" (std O), *08–09*	55___
27059	Bakelite Plastics PS-2 Hopper "61445" (std O), *10–11*	70___
27061	Clinchfield Freight Car 2-pack (std O), *10*	150___
27064	PRR Flatcar with PRR piggyback trailers (std O), *12*	98___
27065	SP Flatcar with SP piggyback trailers (std O), *12*	98___
27066	IC Flatcar with IC piggyback trailers (std O), *12*	98___
27067	C&O Flatcar with REA piggyback trailers (std O), *12*	98___
27068	ATSF Flatcar with Santa Fe piggyback trailers (std O), *12*	98___

		Exc	Mint
_____**27069**	Conrail PS-2 Hopper "878330" (std O), *12–13*		70
_____**27070**	N&W Scale Offset Hopper "279850" (std O), *12*		70
_____**27071**	CSX 4-Bay Covered Hopper "256300" (std O), *12*		90
_____**27072**	C&NW Scale PS-1 Boxcar "7" (std O), *12–13*		70
_____**27073**	PRR Scale Offset Hopper 3-pack (std O), *12*		200
_____**27077**	L&N Scale Offset Hopper "88494" (std O), *12–13*		70
27078	Frisco Scale 3-Bay Open Hopper "88299" (std O),		
_____	*12–14*		75
_____**27079**	NYC Boxcar, *09*		30
_____**27080**	Lionel Vision Boxcar, *14–15*		60
_____**27081**	BN PS-2 Hopper "424796" (std O), *12–13*		70
27082	Grand Trunk 4-Bay Covered Hopper "38111"		
_____	(std O), *12*		90
_____**27083**	RI PS-2 Hopper "500751" (std O), *12–13*		70
27084	Seaboard 8000-gallon 1-D Tank Car "27084"		
_____	(std O), *12*		70
_____**27085**	Wabash PS-2 Hopper "30425" (std O), *12–13*		70
_____**27086**	Grand Trunk 60' Boxcar "383575" (std O), *12, 14*		85
_____**27087**	CN 60' Boxcar "799424" (std O), *12, 14*		85
_____**27088**	MKT PS-5 Gondola "12447" (std O), *12–13*		65
_____**27089**	LIRR PS-5 Gondola "6053" (std O), *12*		65
_____**27090**	NP 8000-gallon 1-D Tank Car "27090" (std O), *12*		70
27091	WM Scale 3-Bay Open Hopper "85125" (std O),		
_____	*12*		80
_____**27092**	CSX Heritage 60' Boxcar "176740" (std O), *12*		85
_____**27093**	Boy Scouts PS-2 Hopper "2013" (std O), *13*		70
_____**27094**	BNSF PS-2 Hopper 2-pack (std O), *13–14*		130
_____**27095**	KCS PS-2 Hopper 2-pack (std O), *13*		130
_____**27096**	C&NW PS-2 Hopper 2-pack (std O), *13*		130
27099	North Pole Central PS-1 Boxcar "125025" (std O),		
_____	*13*		70
27100	C&NW PS-2CD 4427 Hopper "450669" (std O),		
_____	*04*		40
27101	Morton Salt PS-2CD 4427 Hopper "504" (std O),		
_____	*04*		43
_____**27102**	Pillsbury PS-2CD 4427 Hopper "3980" (std O), *04*		42
27103	Soo Line PS-2CD 4427 Hopper "70207" (std O),		
_____	*04*		49
_____**27104**	Wabash Cylindrical Hopper "33007" (std O), *03*		43
_____**27105**	PC Cylindrical Hopper "884312" (std O), *03*		42
_____**27113**	Govt. of Canada Cylindrical Hopper, *04–05*		60
_____**27114**	Canadian National Cylindrical Hopper, *04–05*		60
_____**27115**	D&H 3-bay ACF Hopper "3454" (std O), *05–06*		65
_____**27116**	NYC 3-bay ACF Hopper "886270" (std O), *05–06*		65
_____**27117**	DM&IR 3-bay ACF Hopper "5017" (std O), *05*		65
_____**27118**	WP 3-bay ACF Hopper "11774" (std O), *05–06*		65
_____**27129**	N&W 3-bay ACF Hopper "10717" (std O), *06*		70
_____**27130**	PRR 3-bay ACF Hopper "180658" (std O), *06*		70
_____**27131**	Conrail 3-bay ACF Hopper "473877" (std O), *06*		70
_____**27132**	UP 3-bay ACF Hopper "18137" (std O), *06*		70
_____**27133**	MILW PS-2CD Hopper "98606" (std O), *06*		70
_____**27134**	BNSF PS-2CD Hopper "414367" (std O), *06*		70
_____**27135**	N&W PS-2CD Hopper "71573" (std O), *06*		70
_____**27142**	CP Rail 3-bay Hopper, *06*		48

		Exc	Mint
27146	CP Soo 3-bay Hopper, *06*		48___
27165	C&O 3-bay Hopper "86912" (std O), *07*		70___
27166	Pennsylvania Power & Light 3-bay Hopper "347" (std O), *07*		70___
27167	Santa Fe 3-bay Hopper "178558" (std O), *07–08*		70___
27168	C&NW 3-bay Hopper "135000" (std O), *07*		70___
27169	CN Cylindrical Hopper "370708" (std O), *06*		65___
27172	IMC Canada Cylindrical Hopper "45726" (std O), *06*		65___
27177	Union Starch Cylindrical Hopper 3-pack (std O), *08*		210___
27186	PRR Cylindrical Hopper 3-pack (std O), *08*		210___
27187	TH&B Cylindrical Hopper 3-pack (std O), *08*		210___
27188	KCS 3-bay Covered Hopper 3-pack, *08*		225___
27189	BNSF 3-bay Aluminum Covered Hopper 3-pack, *08*		225___
27190	C&NW PS-2CD Covered Hopper 3-pack (std O), *08*		225___
27191	RI PS-2CD Covered Hopper 3-pack, *08*		225___
27192	NP PS-2CD Covered Hopper 3-pack (std O), *08*		225___
27203	NYC DD Boxcar "75509" (std O), *05*		63___
27204	Grand Trunk Western DD Boxcar "596377" (std O), *05*		63___
27205	D&RGW DD Boxcar "63798" (std O), *05*		40___
27206	UP PS 60' Boxcar "960342" (std O), *08*		75___
27207	IC PS 60' Boxcar "44295" (std O), *08*		75___
27208	ATSF PS 60' Boxcar "37287" (std O), *08*		75___
27209	D&RGW PS 60' Boxcar "63835" (std O), *08*		75___
27210	PRR PS-1 Boxcar "47009" (std O), *05*		60___
27211	MKT PS-1 Boxcar "948" (std O), *05*		60___
27212	Rutland PS-1 Boxcar "358" (std O), *05*		60___
27213	N&W DD Boxcar, *05*		35___
27214	Chessie System PS-1 Boxcar "23770" (std O), *06*		60___
27215	Rock Island PS-1 Boxcar "57607" (std O), *06*		60___
27216	Erie-Lack. PS-1 Boxcar "84433" (std O), *06*		60___
27217	Frisco PS-1 Boxcar "17826" (std O), *06*		19___
27218	Santa Fe DD Boxcar "9870" (std O), *06–07*		70___
27219	GN DD Boxcar "35449" (std O), *06–07*		70___
27220	L&N DD Boxcar "41237" (std O), *06–07*		70___
27221	CB&Q DD Boxcar "48500" (std O), *06–07*		70___
27224	CGW PS-1 Boxcar "5180" (std O), *06*		60___
27225	WP PS-1 Boxcar "19528" (std O), *06*		60___
27226	NH PS-1 Boxcar "32196" (std O), *06*		60___
27227	UP PS-1 Boxcar "100306" (std O), *06*		60___
27228	UP DD Boxcar "454400" (std O), *07*		70___
27229	Nickel Plate Road DD Boxcar "87100" (std O), *08*		70___
27230	LV DD Boxcar "8505" (std O), *08*		70___
27231	GN USRA Double-sheathed Boxcar (std O), *07*		65___
27232	UP USRA Double-sheathed Boxcar (std O), *07*		65___
27233	Cotton Belt USRA Double-sheathed Boxcar (std O), *07*		65___
27234	C&NW USRA Double-sheathed Boxcar (std O), *07*		65___
27235	Railbox Boxcar "10011" (std O), *07*		55___

		Exc	Mint
27239	SP DD Boxcar "232852" with auto rack (std 0), _08_		75
27240	Pere Marquette DD Boxcar with auto rack (std 0), _08_		75
27241	C&O PS-1 Boxcar "18719," _08_		60
27242	LV PS-1 Boxcar "62080," _08_		60
27243	SP PS-1 Boxcar "128131," _08_		60
27244	GN PS-1 Boxcar "39404," _08_		60
27246	SP Double-sheathed Boxcar "133" (std 0), _08_		70
27247	MP Double-sheathed Boxcar "45111" (std 0), _08_		70
27249	GN Express Boxcar "2500" (std 0), _08_		65
27250	CN Express Boxcar "11061" (std 0), _08–09_		65
27251	WP Express Boxcar "220116," _08–09_		65
27254	Western Pacific UP Heritage Boxcar (std 0), _09–11, 13_		85
27259	PRR ACF Stock Car "128988" (std 0), _10_		70
27260	ATSF Tool Car "190021" (std 0), _09–10_		80
27261	D&RGW Double-sheathed Boxcar "3282," _09_		80
27263	Polar Railroad PS-1 Boxcar, _09_		70
27264	C&O Double-sheathed Boxcar "3502," _10_		80
27265	Virginian PS-1 Boxcar "63300" (std 0), _10_		70
27266	PRR Express Boxcar "504141" (std 0), _10_		70
27267	SP UP Heritage 60' Boxcar "6991" (std 0), _10_		85
27270	B&O PS-1 Boxcar 2-pack (std 0), _10–11_		140
27273	Ann Arbor PS-1 Boxcar "1314" (std 0), _11_		70
27274	Polar Railroad Double-sheathed Boxcar "1201," _10_		70
27275	SP Overnight PS-1 Boxcar "97938" (std 0), _10_		70
27276	NKP Double-sheathed Boxcar "10580" (std 0), _10–11_		70
27277	WP Scale PS-1 Boxcar "1925" (std 0), _11_		70
27278	Cryo-Trans Trans-Mechanical Reefer (std 0), _10_		95
27282	UP DD Boxcar "163100" (std 0), _10_		70
27283	Postwar Scale Boxcar 2-pack, _10_		140
27286	Postwar Scale 6464 Boxcar 2-pack #2, _11–13_		140
27287	LV Boxcar and Caboose Set (std 0), _10–11_		160
27289	Jersey Central Boxcar and Caboose Set (std 0), _10–11_		160
27291	PRR Double-sheathed Boxcar "539335" (std 0), _10–11_		70
27294	ATSF 57' Mechanical Reefer "3006" (std 0), _10_		85
27296	Cryo-Trans 57' Mechanical Reefer (std 0), _11_		85
27299	WM Steel-sided Reefer (std 0), _11_		80
27300	Western Dairy General American Milk Car (std 0), _06_		65
27305	GN Steel-sided Reefer "70290" (std 0), _06_		65
27306	Santa Fe Steel-sided Reefer "3494" (std 0), _06_		42
27307	Pepper Packing Steel-sided Reefer "2330" (std 0), _06_		65
27327	BNSF Mechanical Reefer "798870" (std 0), _07_		70
27328	SP Fruit Express Reefer "456465" (std 0), _07–09_		70
27329	UP Fruit Express Reefer "55962" (std 0), _07_		70
27330	Great Northern WFE Reefer "8873" (std 0), _07–08_		70

		Exc	Mint
27331	Alderney Dairy General American Milk Car (std O), *07*		65___
27332	Freeport General American Milk Car (std O), *07*		65___
27345	Milwaukee Road 40' Steel-sided Reefer "5317" (std O), *12*		80___
27349	ADM Steel-sided Reefer "7019" (std O), *07*		65___
27350	National Car Steel-sided Reefer "2430" (std O), *07*		48___
27355	NYC Steel-sided Reefer "2570" (std O), *07–08*		65___
27358	Dubuque Steel-sided Reefer "63648" (std O), *07*		65___
27361	PFE Wood-sided Reefer "97680" (std O), *06*		65___
27364	Erie URTX Steel-sided Reefer (std O), *11*		80___
27365	Sheffield Farms Milk Car 2-pack (std O), *08*		140___
27368	CNJ 40' Steel-sided Reefer "1443" (std O), *12*		80___
27369	Borden's Milk Car 2-pack (std O), *08*		140___
27372	PFE Steel-sided Reefer 3-pack (std O), *08*		210___
27373	MILW Reefer 3-pack (std O), *08–09*		225___
27374	Alaska Reefer 3-pack (std O), *08–09*		225___
27375	NP Reefer 3-pack (std O), *08–09*		225___
27394	Detroit, Toledo & Ironton Steel-sided Reefer (std O), *09–10*		80___
27395	Amtrak ExpressTrak Baggage Car, *10*		75___
27396	C&NW UP Heritage Mechanical Reefer (std O), *10*		85___
27409	ATSF Water Tank Car "100844" (std O), *09–10*		70___
27410	30,000-gallon Ethanol Tank Car 3-pack, sound, *09*		270___
27411	30,000-gallon Ethanol Tank Car 3-pack, *09*		210___
27412	GATX TankTrain Car "53782" (std O), *10*		70___
27418	PRR NS Heritage Unibody Tank Car (std O), *10*		70___
27419	Pennsylvania Power & Light 3-bay Open Hopper, *08*		80___
27421	MoPac UP Heritage Cylindrical Hopper (std O), *09–11*		80___
27422	N&W 3-bay Open Hopper "1776" (std O), *09*		80___
27424	Penn Central PS-2 Hopper "440774" (std O), *10–11*		80___
27425	Saskatchewan Cylindrical Hopper "397015" (std O), *09*		80___
27426	Stourbridge Lion Anthracite Coal Car 2-pack, *09–10*		130___
27429	MKT UP Heritage PS2-CD Hopper (std O), *09*		80___
27431	CSX B&O Quad Hopper, *11*		50___
27432	UP 3-bay Open Hopper "78123" (std O), *10*		80___
27433	Conrail NS Heritage Cylindrical Hopper (std O), *10–11*		80___
27434	D&RGW UP Heritage PS2-CD Hopper (std O), *10*		80___
27435	Polar Railroad Tank Car, *09*		70___
27436	Alberta Cylindrical Hopper "396363" (std O), *10*		80___
27438	Virginian NS Heritage 3-bay Open Hopper (std O), *10*		80___
27439	NS Heritage Unibody Tank Car "14098" (std O), *10*		70___
27440	BN Cylindrical Hopper "458456" (std O), *10*		80___
27441	D&M PS-2 Hopper "6133" (std O), *11*		70___
27445	N&W NS Heritage PS-2CD Hopper (std O), *10*		80___

		Exc	Mint
____ 27446	Southern NS Heritage Cylindrical Hopper (std O), *10*		80
____ 27448	PRR NS Heritage 3-Bay Open Hopper (std O), *11*		80
27449	UP Boy Scouts 100th Anniversary Cylindrical Hopper (std O), *11*		80
____ 27450	NW NS Heritage 3-Bay Open Hopper (std O), *11*		80
27451	Conrail NS Heritage Unibody 1-D Tank Car (std O), *11*		70
27452	PRR NS Heritage PS-1 Boxcar "45540" (std O), *11*		70
____ 27453	NS Heritage PS-1 Boxcar "67850" (std O), *11*		70
____ 27454	CP Cylindrical Hopper (std O), *11*		80
____ 27455	Amtrak 57' Mechanical Reefer (std O), *11*		85
27456	Soo Line PS2 Covered Hopper "70702" (std O), *11*		70
____ 27457	NS 3-Bay Open Hopper "148028" (std O), *11*		80
____ 27458	UP Mechanical Reefer "457244" (std O), *11*		85
____ 27459	WP DD Boxcar "19404" (std O), *11*		70
27460	M&StL Double-sheathed Boxcar "26002" (std O), *11*		70
27461	UP ACF 4-Bay Covered Hopper "91341" (std O), *11*		85
27462	Chessie ACF 4-Bay Covered Hopper "601878" (std O), *11*		85
27463	PRR ACF 3-Bay Covered Hopper "259900" (std O), *11–12*		80
27464	BNSF ACF 3-Bay Covered Hopper "453403" (std O), *11*		80
____ 27465	CSX 89' Auto Rack Car "604540" (std O), *12–13*		150
____ 27466	UP 89' Auto Rack Car (std O), *12–13*		150
____ 27467	ATSF 89' Auto Rack Car (std O), *12–13*		150
____ 27468	Grand Truck 89' Auto Rack Car (std O), *12–13*		150
____ 27469	Frisco Cylindrical Hopper "81021" (std O), *11*		80
____ 27470	MKT Scale 1-D Tank Car (std O), *11*		70
____ 27471	DT&I 3-Bay Hopper "2070" (std O), *11*		80
____ 27472	CP Scale 1-D Tank Car "9943" (std O), *11*		70
____ 27473	Conrail 89' Auto Rack Car "456249" (std O), *12*		150
____ 27474	SP Cylindrical Hopper "491020" (std O), *11*		80
27475	Lionelville & Western Scale 1-D Tank Car "2747" (std O), *11*		80
____ 27476	U.S. Army Scale 1-D Tank Car (std O), *11*		70
____ 27477	D&RGW 3-Bay Hopper "14901" (std O), *11*		80
____ 27478	NYC 3-Bay Hopper "922158" (std O), *11*		80
27479	BN Scale 3-Bay Open Hopper "516400" (std O), *12*		80
____ 27480	NKP Scale Offset Hopper "33060" (std O), *12*		70
____ 27481	W&LE Scale Offset Hopper "62240" (std O), *12*		70
____ 27482	CP Scale Offset Hopper "354000" (std O), *12*		70
____ 27483	SP Unibody 1-D Tank Car "67200" (std O), *12*		70
____ 27484	D&H Unibody 1-D Tank Car "59" (std O), *12*		70
____ 27485	KCS Unibody 1-D Tank Car "996" (std O), *12*		70
27488	Clinchfield CSX Heritage 3-Bay Open Hopper (std O), *12*		80
27489	Chessie System CSX Heritage 3-Bay Open Hopper (std O), *12*		80

Exc Mint

		Exc	Mint
27490	ATSF 3-Bay Covered Hopper "314000" (std O), 12–13		85___
27491	GN 3-Bay Covered Hopper "171400" (std O), 12		85___
27492	CN 89' Auto Rack Car "710833" (std O), 12		150___
27493	CN PS-4 Flatcar with piggyback trailers (std O), 12		98___
27494	CN PS-4 Flatcar with piggyback trailers (std O), 12		98___
27495	CN PS-4 Flatcar with piggyback trailers (std O), 12		98___
27496	Polar PS-2 Covered Hopper "1245" (std O), 12, 14		70___
27497	UP Offset Hopper "74556" (std O), 12		80___
27498	DM&I 8000-gallon 1-D Tank Car "819" (std O), 12		70___
27499	Monon Scale PS-1 Boxcar "916" (std O), 12		70___
27510	WP PS-4 Flatcar "2001" (std O), 05–06		53___
27511	P&LE PS-4 Flatcar "1154" (std O), 05–06		35___
27512	Reading PS-4 Flatcar "9314" (std O), 05		53___
27513	UP 40' Flatcar "51219" (std O), 06		55___
27514	CP 40' Flatcar "307401" (std O), 06		55___
27515	Pennsylvania 40' Flatcar "473567" (std O), 06		55___
27516	N&W 40' Flatcar "32900" (std O), 06		55___
27517	NP PS-4 Flatcar "62829" with trailers (std O), 06		85___
27518	C&NW PS-4 Flatcar "44503" with trailers (std O), 06		85___
27519	UP PS-4 Flatcar "53007" with trailers (std O), 06		85___
27520	Coe Rail Husky Stack Car "5540" (std O), 06		85___
27521	Santa Fe Husky Stack Car "254220" (std O), 06		85___
27535	UP PS-4 Flatcar "53008" with trailers (std O), 07		65___
27536	UP PS-4 Flatcar "53009" with trailers (std O), 08		65___
27537	UP Flatcar with wood load, 06		39___
27541	NYC 40' Flatcar "496299" with load (std O), 07		63___
27542	NH 40' Flatcar "17808" with load (std O), 07–08		70___
27543	ATSF 40' Flatcar "191549" with load (std O), 07–08		70___
27544	GT 40' Flatcar "64301" with load (std O), 07–08		70___
27545	REA PS-4 Flatcar "81003" with trailers (std O), 07–08		85___
27546	Greenbrier Husky Stack Car "1993" (std O), 07		85___
27552	Arizona & California Husky Stack Car (std O), 07		85___
27562	NYC PS-4 Flatcar "506075" with trailers (std O), 07–08		85___
27563	Lackawanna PS-4 Flatcar "16540" with trailers (std O), 07		85___
27564	Milwaukee Road PS-4 Flatcar with trailers "64074" (std O), 07–08		85___
27583	UP 40' Flatcar "59292" with load (std O), 08		70___
27584	Reading Flatcar with covered load (std O), 08–09		70___
27585	B&M 40' Flatcar "33773" with stakes (std O), 08–09		65___
27586	Cass Scenic Skeleton Log Car 3-pack, 07		170___
27587	Birch Valley Lumber Skeleton Log Car 3-pack, 07		170___
27594	Wabash PS-4 Flatcar with stakes (std O), 08–09		65___
27600	RI Bay Window Caboose "17070" (std O), 07		90___

		Exc	Mint
27601	MILW Extended Vision Caboose "992300" (std 0), 07		90
___27603	MP UP Heritage Ca-4 Caboose "2891" (std 0), 08		95
___27604	UP Caboose "3881" (std 0), 08		90
27605	Pere Marquette Northeastern Caboose "A986" (std 0), 08		90
___27606	LL Northeastern Caboose "4679" (std 0), 08		90
___27607	Monongahela NS Heritage Caboose (std 0), 12		95
___27608	WM Caboose "1863" (std 0), 08		85
___27609	B&O Caboose "C-2445" (std 0), 07		90
___27612	WP Bay Window Caboose "446" (std 0), 08		90
___27615	NYC Bay Window Caboose "20383" (std 0), 07		90
___27617	D&H Bay Window Caboose "35725" (std 0), 08		90
27618	MKT UP Heritage Ca-4 Caboose "8891" (std 0), 08		95
___27619	WP UP Heritage Ca-4 Caboose "3891" (std 0), 08		95
___27623	N&W Northeastern Caboose "500837" (std 0), 09		90
___27624	D&RGW UP Heritage CA-4 Caboose (std 0), 09		95
___27625	C&NW UP Heritage CA-4 Caboose (std 0), 09		95
___27626	SP UP Heritage CA-4 Caboose (std 0), 09		95
27628	Wabash Northeastern Caboose "02222" (std 0), 09–10		90
___27629	C&O Northeastern Caboose (std 0), 10		90
___27630	Virginian NS Heritage CA-4 Caboose (std 0), 10		95
___27631	NS Heritage CA-4 Caboose (std 0), 10		95
___27633	UP CA-3 Caboose (std 0), 10		95
___27634	ATSF Extended Vision Caboose (std 0), 10		85
___27635	B&O I-12 Caboose (std 0), 10		85
___27636	NKP Northeastern Caboose (std 0), 10–11		85
27638	Southern NS Heritage CA-4 Caboose (std 0), 10–11		95
___27639	N&W NS Heritage CA-4 Caboose (std 0), 10		95
___27640	Clinchfield Northeastern CA-3 Caboose, 10–11		90
___27642	Virginian Scale Caboose with smoke, 10–13		90
27645	UP Boy Scouts 100th Anniversary Ca-3 Caboose (std 0), 11		95
___27648	PRR NS Heritage Ca-3 Caboose (std 0), 11		95
27649	Baldwin Locomotive Works I-12 Caboose "6000" (std 0), 12–13		85
27650	CSX Heritage Scale Bay Window Caboose "2510" (std 0), 12		90
___27651	B&O CSX Heritage I-12 Caboose (std 0), 11		90
27652	CSX Heritage Chessie System Scale Caboose (std 0), 12		90
27653	Family Lines CSX Heritage Ca-4 Caboose (std 0), 11		90
27654	CSX/Clinchfield Scale Bay-Window Caboose (std 0), 12		90
27655	WM CSX Heritage Extended Vision Caboose (std 0), 11		90
27658	Pennsylvania Power & Light Work Caboose (std 0), 11		80
___27659	Bethlehem Steel Work Caboose (std 0), 11		80
27660	UP George Bush Extended Vision Caboose (std 0), 11		90

Exc Mint

		Exc	Mint
27661	KCS Extended Vision Caboose (std O), *11*		90____
27662	GTW Northeastern Caboose (std O), *11*		90____
27663	IC Extended Vision Caboose (std O), *11*		90____
27664	Lionel & Western Northeastern Caboose (std O), *11–12*		90____
27665	BN Bicentennial Extended Vision Caboose (std O), *11*		90____
27666	NH Scale Northeastern Caboose "C-666" (std O), *12*		90____
27667	UP Scale Ca-4 Caboose "3857" (std O), *12–13*		95____
27668	UP Scale Ca-3 Caboose "3779" (std O), *12–13*		95____
27669	PC Scale Northeastern Caboose "18420" with smoke (std O), *12–13*		90____
27670	CP Scale Northeastern Caboose "400501" (std O), *12–13*		90____
27671	West Side Lumber Scale Work Caboose "8" (std O), *12*		80____
27672	Weyerhaeuser Timber Scale Work Caboose "12" (std O), *12–13*		80____
27673	NYC Scale Northeastern Caboose "20090" (std O), *12*		90____
27674	Elk River Lumber Work Caboose "6" (std O), *12, 14*		80____
27676	CN Wood-Sided Caboose (std O), *12*		90____
27677	UP Work Caboose "907306" (std O), *12*		80____
27678	ATSF Wood-Sided Caboose "1790" (std O), *12*		85____
27679	NP Wood-Sided Caboose "1282" (std O), *12*		85____
27680	GN Wood-Sided Caboose "X499" (std O), *12*		85____
27681	Southern NS Heritage Caboose (std O), *12*		95____
27682	Conrail NS Heritage Caboose (std O), *12*		95____
27683	Erie NS Heritage Caboose (std O), *12, 14–15*		95____
27684	Illinois Terminal NS Heritage Caboose (std O), *12, 14–15*		95____
27685	Central of Georgia NS Heritage Caboose (std O), *12*		95____
27686	LV NS Heritage Caboose (std O), *12*		95____
27687	Reading NS Heritage Caboose (std O), *13–15*		95____
27688	NYC NS Heritage Caboose (std O), *13*		95____
27689	Wabash NS Heritage Caboose (std O), *13–15*		95____
27690	Virginian NS Heritage Caboose (std O), *13*		95____
27691	PRR NS Heritage Caboose (std O), *12*		95____
27692	N&W NS Heritage Caboose (std O), *12*		95____
27693	CNJ NS Heritage Caboose (std O), *13–14*		95____
27694	NS Heritage Caboose (std O), *12*		95____
27695	DL&W NS Heritage Caboose (std O), *13–15*		95____
27696	Savannah & Atlanta NS Heritage Caboose (std O), *13–15*		95____
27697	Nickel Plate Road NS Heritage Caboose (std O), *12*		95____
27698	Interstate NS Heritage Caboose (std O), *12*		95____
27699	PC NS Heritage Caboose (std O), *13*		95____
27702	Maersk Husky Stack Car 2-pack (std O), *09*		225____
27705	ATSF Wedge Plow Flatcar "191369" (std O), *09*		90____
27706	ATSF Idler Flatcar "191852" with load (std O), *09*		75____
27707	UP Husky Stack Car 2-pack (std O), *09–10*		225____

Exc Mint

		Exc	Mint
____27710	No. 6464 Variation Boxcar 2-pack #2, *09*		110
____27767	Santa Fe Passenger 4-pack, *11–12*		240
____27771	Postwar "6572" REA Reefer, *11–13*		60
____27772	Santa Fe Baggage Car and Diner 2-pack, *11–12*		120
____27775	Postwar "2414" Santa Fe Blue-stripe Coach, *11–13*		60
____27776	No. 6464 Variation Boxcar 2-pack #3, *11*		105
____27779	Postwar Archive UP Caboose "8561," *11–12*		48
____27791	Archive 6464-50 M&StL Boxcar, *12*		55
____27792	Archive Pastel Freight Car 3-pack, *12*		170
____27800	B&M Gondola with coke containers, *09–11*		80
____27816	D&RGW Flatcar "22177" with pipes, *09–10*		80
____27820	Wabash PS-4 Flatcar with piggyback trailers (std 0), *09–10*		98
____27824	MILW 40' Flatcar with metal pipes (std 0), *10*		80
____27825	West Side Lumber Skeleton Log Car, *11*		70
____27826	CP Skeleton Log Car 2-pack (std 0), *10*		133
____27827	UP Bathtub Gondola "28081" (std 0), *10*		65
____27828	CN Bathtub Gondola "193140" (std 0), *10*		65
____27829	WM Skeleton Log Car 2-pack, *10*		133
____27834	Pere Marquette PS-5 Gondola "18400," *11*		70
____27835	P. Bunyan Lumber Skeleton Log Car, *11–12*		70
____27836	Elk River Lumber Skeleton Log Car "11203" (std 0), *11*		70
____27837	B&M PS-4 Flatcar with bulkheads (std 0), *10–11*		80
____27838	PRR PS-4 Flatcar with bulkheads (std 0), *10*		80
____27840	Polar Railroad PS-4 Flatcar with trailers, *10*		98
____27841	CSX Bathtub Gondola 2-pack (std 0), *11*		130
____27842	UP Scale Flatcar with bulkheads "15775" (std 0), *11*		70
____27843	WP Scale PS-5 Gondola "6774" (std 0), *11*		70
____27844	BNSF Bathtub Gondola 3-pack (std 0), *10*		200
____27848	Virginian NS Heritage 60' Boxcar (std 0), *11*		85
____27849	Southern NS Heritage 60' Boxcar (std 0), *11*		85
____27850	CSX 60' Boxcar "196911" (std 0), *11*		85
____27851	BNSF Bathtub Gondola 2-pack, *11*		130
____27854	B&O Double-sheathed Boxcar "196500" (std 0), *11*		70
____27855	NYC 60' DD Boxcar "53423" (std 0), *11*		85
____27856	KCS PS-1 Boxcar "18741" (std 0), *11*		70
____27857	PRR DD Boxcar "81919" (std 0), *11, 14*		75
____27858	MP DD Boxcar "90103" (std 0), *11*		70
____27860	Sugar Creek Lumber Skeleton Log Car "1749" (std 0), *11*		70
____27863	Merrill & Ring Lumber Skeleton Log Car, *11–12*		70
____27868	NS Bathtub Gondola 2-pack (std 0), *11*		130
____27871	NS 60' Boxcar "499646" (std 0), *11*		85
____27872	Polar Hot Cocoa Milk Car, *11, 13*		70
____27873	Polar Reindeer Stock Car, *11, 13*		70
____27874	Grove's Mortuary Double-sheathed Boxcar (std 0), *11*		70
____27875	NYC DD Boxcar "45395" (std 0), *11*		70
____27876	State of Maine PS-1 Boxcar "5141" (std 0), *11*		70
____27877	NH DD Boxcar "40510" (std 0), *11*		70

		Exc	Mint
27882	Southern ACF 40-ton Stock Car "45655" (std O), *11*		70____
27883	T&P ACF 40-ton Stock Car "24042" (std O), *11*		70____
27884	RI ACF 40-ton Stock Car "77601" (std O), *11*		70____
27885	ATSF ACF 40-ton Stock Car "60390" (std O), *11*		70____
27886	GN PS-1 Boxcar "11310" (std O), *11*		70____
27887	D&RGW PS-5 Gondola "56316" with covers (std O), *11*		65____
27888	LIRR 40' Flatcar with wheels (std O), *11*		70____
27889	Erie 40' Flatcar "6361" with wheels (std O), *11*		70____
27890	L&N 40' Flatcar "22269" with wheels (std O), *11*		70____
27891	NKP Heritage PS-4 Flatcar with trailers (std O), *11*		98____
27892	Conrail PS-5 Gondola "612690" with covers (std O), *11*		65____
27893	GTW PS-1 Boxcar "516650" (std O), *11*		70____
27894	C&O PS-5 Gondola "362600" with covers (std O), *11*		65____
27895	ATSF PS-4 Bulkhead Flatcar "90085" (std O), *11*		80____
27896	CP 40' Flatcar with pipe load (std O), *11*		80____
27899	UP Scale PS-1 Boxcar "196889" (std O), *12*		70____
27903	Sager Place Observation Car, *09*		65____
27912	Postwar "2445" Elizabeth Coach, *08*		60____
27917	Postwar "2550" Baggage-Mail Rail Diesel Car, nonpowered, *13–14*		70____
27928	UP Boy Scouts 100th Anniversary PS-1 Boxcar (std O), *11*		70____
27929	Postwar Nos. 2484/2485 UP Passenger Car 2-pack, *12–13*		120____
27935	Postwar "6820" Aerial Missile Transport Car, *13*		60____
27941	Postwar "3854" Merchandise Car, *12*		75____
27946	Postwar "6050-25" Christmas Savings Boxcar, *13–14*		55____
27947	Postwar "6473-25" Reindeer Transport Car, *13*		60____
27948	Postwar "6464-25" Great Northern Christmas Boxcar, *13*		60____
27949	Postwar "3854-25" PRR Christmas Merchandise Car, *13–14*		75____
27953	Reading PS-2 Hopper 2-pack (std O), *13–14*		140____
27962	L&N PS-2 Hopper 2-pack (std O), *13–14*		140____
27965	P&WV Offset Hopper 3-pack (std O), *13–15*		210____
27969	N&W Offset Hopper 3-pack (std O), *13–15*		210____
27973	C&O Offset Hopper 3-pack (std O), *13–15*		210____
27977	GN Offset Hopper 3-pack (std O), *13–15*		210____
27981	PRR USRA Double-sheathed Boxcar (std O), *13*		70____
27982	SP USRA Double-sheathed Boxcar (std O), *13–14*		80____
27983	UP USRA Double-sheathed Boxcar (std O), *13–14*		70____
27984	Procor 30,000-gallon 1-D Tank Car 3-pack (std O), *13*		240____
27988	UTLX 30,000-gallon 1-D Tank Car 3-pack (std O), *13*		240____
27992	ADM 30,000-gallon 1-D Tank Car 3-pack (std O), *13*		240____
27996	ACFX 30,000-gallon 1-D Tank Car 3-pack (std O), *13*		240____

Exc Mint

____	28000	C&NW 4-6-4 Hudson Locomotive "3005," *99*	205
____	28004	B&O 4-4-2 E6 Atlantic Locomotive, traditional, *99–00*	410
____	28005	PRR 4-4-2 E6 Atlantic Locomotive, traditional, *99–00*	345
____	28006	ATSF 4-4-2 E6 Atlantic Locomotive, traditional, *99–00*	285
____	28007	NYC 4-6-4 Hudson Locomotive "5406," *99*	380
____	28008	C&O 4-6-4 Hudson Locomotive "306," *99*	345
____	28009	Santa Fe 4-6-4 Hudson Locomotive "3463," *99*	330
____	28011	C&O 2-6-6-6 Allegheny Locomotive "1601," *99*	1800
____	28012	4-6-4 Commodore Vanderbilt Locomotive, red, *00 u*	1700
____	28013	NH 4-6-2 Pacific Locomotive "1335," *99*	325
____	28014	NYC 4-6-2 Pacific Locomotive "4930," *99*	305
____	28015	Santa Fe Pacific 4-6-2 Pacific Locomotive "3449," *99*	340
____	28016	Southern 4-6-2 Pacific Locomotive "1407," *99*	345
____	28017	Case Cutlery 4-6-2 Pacific Locomotive, *99 u*	313
____	28018	Reading 4-6-0 Camelback Locomotive "571," CC, *01*	495
____	28020	Lionel Lines 4-6-2 Pacific Locomotive "3344," *99*	250
____	28022	West Side Lumber Shay Locomotive "800," *99*	810
____	28023	PRR K4 4-6-2 Pacific Locomotive "3755," CC, *99*	375
____	28024	4-6-4 Commodore Vanderbilt Locomotive, blue, *00 u*	1663
____	28025	PRR K4 4-6-2 Pacific Locomotive, traditional, *99*	330
____	28026	LL 4-6-2 Pacific Locomotive, CC, *99*	325
____	28027	NYC 4-6-4 Hudson Locomotive "5413," *00*	590
____	28028	Virginian 2-6-6-6 Allegheny Locomotive "1601," *99*	1318
____	28029	UP 4-8-8-4 Big Boy Locomotive "4006," *99–00*	1500
____	28030	NYC 4-6-4 Hudson Locomotive "5450," gray, CC, *00*	315
____	28032	B&O 4-6-2 Pacific Locomotive, CC, *00*	315
____	28033	B&O 4-6-2 Pacific Locomotive, traditional, *00*	195
____	28034	UP 4-6-2 Pacific Locomotive, CC, *00*	310
____	28035	UP 4-6-2 Pacific Locomotive, traditional, *00*	210
____	28036	SP 2-8-0 Consolidation Locomotive "2685," CC, *00–01*	270
____	28037	SP 2-8-0 Consolidation Locomotive "2686," traditional, *00–01*	295
____	28038	UP 2-8-0 Consolidation Locomotive "324," CC, *00–01*	315
____	28039	UP 2-8-0 Consolidation Locomotive "326," traditional, *00–01*	240
____	28051	B&O 2-8-8-4 EM-1 Articulated Locomotive "7617," *00*	970
____	28052	N&W 2-6-6-4 Class A Locomotive "1218," *00*	870
____	28055	GN 4-6-4 Hudson Locomotive "1725," traditional, *00–01*	170
____	28057	Southern 4-8-2 Mountain Locomotive "1491," CC, *00*	690
____	28058	NH 4-8-2 Mountain Locomotive "3310," CC, *00*	670
____	28059	WP 4-8-2 Mountain Locomotive "179," CC, *00*	630

Exc Mint

28062	LL Gold-plated 700E J-1E 4-6-4 Hudson Locomotive, display case, *00*		1050____
28063	PRR T-1 4-4-4-4 Duplex Locomotive "5511," CC, *00*		910____
28064	UP Challenger Coal Tender "3985," CC, *00 u*	1350	1800____
28065	NYC Hudson 4-6-4 Locomotive "5412," RailSounds, *00*		290____
28066	B&O President Polk 4-6-2 Locomotive, CC, *01*		750____
28067	Erie 4-6-2 Locomotive "2934," CC, *01*		570____
28068	D&RGW 4-6-4 Hudson Locomotive, traditional, *01 u*		300____
28070	SP Daylight 4-4-2 Atlantic Locomotive "3000," CC, *01*		425____
28071	NP 4-4-2 Atlantic Locomotive "604," CC, *01*		415____
28072	NYC 4-6-4 Hudson J3a Locomotive "5444," CC, *01*		790____
28074	NP 2-8-4 Berkshire Locomotive "759," CC, *01*		640____
28075	C&O 2-6-6-2 Locomotive "1521," CC, *01*		930____
28076	NKP 2-6-6-2 Locomotive "921," CC, *01*		960____
28077	UP 4-6-6-4 Challenger Locomotive "3983," CC, *01*		680____
28078	PRR 2-10-4 J1a Locomotive "6496," CC, *01*		880____
28079	C&O 2-10-4 Class T Locomotive "3004," CC, *01*		882____
28080	NYC 0-8-0 Locomotive "7745," CC, *01–02*		540____
28081	C&O 0-8-0 Locomotive "75," CC, *01–02*		520____
28084	NYC Dreyfuss Hudson 4-6-4 Locomotive "5452," CC, *01–02*		790____
28085	N&W 2-8-8-2 Y6b Class Locomotive "2200," CC, *03*		1207____
28086	PRR H9 Consolidation Locomotive "1111," CC, *01*		480____
28087	UP Auxiliary Tender, yellow, CC, *01*		210____
28088	N&W Auxiliary Water Tender, CC, *01–02*		200____
28089	PRR 4-4-4-4 T-1 Duplex Locomotive "5511," 2-rail, *00*		1150____
28090	UP Challenger Oil Tender "3977," 2-rail, *00 u*		1800____
28098	NYC 4-6-0 10-wheel Locomotive "1916," CC, *01–02*		520____
28099	UP Challenger Oil Tender "3977," CC, *00 u*		1700____
28200	D&H U30C Diesel "702," CC (SSS), *02*		375____
28201	UP SD90MAC Diesel "8049," *03*		345____
28202	Conrail SD80MAC Diesel "7203," *03*		325____
28203	CSX SD80MAC Diesel "803," *03*		325____
28204	NS SD80MAC Diesel "7201," *03*		345____
28205	Chessie System SD9 Diesel "1833," CC, *03*		230____
28207	Erie-Lackawanna U33C Diesel "3304," CC, *02*		355____
28208	BN U33C Diesel "5734," CC, *02*		355____
28211	CP SD90MAC Diesel "9107," *03*		300____
28213	Amtrak GE Dash 8 Diesel "516," CC, *02*		300____
28214	BNSF GE Dash 8 Diesel "582," CC, *02*		325____
28215	B&O GP30 Diesel "6939," CC, *02*		315____
28216	Reading GP30 Diesel "5518," CC, *02*		315____
28217	Rio Grande GP30 Diesel "3013," CC, *02*		315____
28218	Lehigh Valley Alco C420 Switcher "407," CC, *04*		325____
28219	Seaboard Alco C420 Switcher "136," CC, *04*		300____

			Exc	Mint
___	28222	Santa Fe Dash 9 Diesel "605" CC, *05*		250
___	28223	BNSF SD70MAC Diesel "9433," CC, *05*		250
___	28224	Jersey Central SD40-2 Diesel "3067," CC, *04*		350
___	28225	SPSF SD40T-2 Diesel "8521," CC, *04–05*		430
___	28226	NS SD80MAC Diesel "7204," CC, *04–05*		430
___	28227	UP SD70MAC Diesel "4979," CC, *04*		375
___	28228	C&NW Dash 9-44CW Diesel "8669," CC, *03*		350
___	28229	SP Dash 9-44CW Diesel "8132," CC, *03*		350
___	28230	Amtrak Dash 8 Diesel "505," CC, *04*		295
___	28235	Great Northern U33C Diesel "2543," CC, *05*		455
___	28237	Reading U30C Diesel "6301," CC, *05*		455
___	28239	Union Pacific SD70 Diesel, TMCC, *04*		360
___	28241	C&NW U30C Diesel "935," CC, *06*		455
___	28242	SP U33C Diesel "8773," CC, *06*		475
___	28243	LIRR Alco C420 Hi-nose Switcher "206," CC, *06*		420
	28244	N&W Alco C420 Hi-nose Switcher "417," CC, *06–07*		420
	28245	Chessie System SD40T-2 Diesel "7617," RailSounds, *06*		265
	28246	Chessie System SD40T-2 Diesel "7618," nonpowered (std O), *06*		160
	28247	Rio Grande SD40T-2 Diesel "5348," RailSounds, *06*		265
	28248	Rio Grande SD40T-2 Diesel "5349," nonpowered (std O), *06*		160
	28250	N&W Alco C420 Hi-nose Switcher "416," nonpowered (std O), *06–07*		160
	28251	LIRR Alco C420 Hi-nose Switcher "206," nonpowered (std O), *06*		160
___	28252	SP U33C Diesel "8774," nonpowered (std O), *06*		160
	28253	C&NW U30C Diesel "936," nonpowered (std O), *06*		160
	28255	UP SD40T-2 Diesel "4551," traditional, CC, *07–08*		265
	28256	UP SD40T-2 Diesel "4596," nonpowered (std O), *07*		170
___	28257	NS SD40-2 Diesel "3340," CC, *06*		430
	28258	NS SD40-2 Diesel "3341," nonpowered (std O), *06*		170
___	28259	CN SD40-2 Diesel "5383," CC, *06*		430
	28260	CN SD40-2 Diesel "5384," nonpowered (std O), *06*		170
___	28261	UP (MP) SD70ACe Diesel "1982," CC, *07*		450
___	28262	UP (WP) SD70ACe Diesel "1983," CC, *07*		450
___	28263	UP (MKT) SD70ACe Diesel "1988," CC, *07*		450
	28264	UP "Building America" SD70ACe Diesel "8348," CC, *07*		450
___	28265	MILW U30C Diesel "5657," CC, *07*		455
	28266	MILW U30C Diesel "5657," nonpowered (std O), *07–08*		170
___	28267	Conrail U30C Diesel "6837," CC, *07*		455
	28268	Conrail U30C Diesel "6838," nonpowered (std O), *07–08*		170
___	28269	ATSF Dash 8-40BW Diesel "562," CC, *08*		500

		Exc	Mint
28270	ATSF Dash 8-40CW Diesel "563," nonpowered, *08*		220____
28272	"I Love USA" SD60 Diesel "1776," traditional, *06*		250____
28279	UP SD70ACe Diesel "1989," CC, *07*		450____
28280	UP (C&NW) SD70ACe Diesel "1995," CC, *07*		450____
28281	UP (SP) SD70ACe Diesel "1996," CC, *07*		450____
28283	UP "Building America" SD70AC3 Diesel, nonpowered (std O), *07*		170____
28284	Ferromex SD70ACe Diesel "4011," CC, *08*		495____
28287	KCS SD70ACe Diesel "4050," CC, *08*		495____
28292	Chessie System U30C Diesel "3312," CC, *02*		300____
28293	Santa Fe U28CG Diesel "354," CC, *02*		375____
28295	Conrail LionMaster SD80MAC Diesel, nonpowered, *08*		200____
28296	UP AC6000 Diesel "7526," CC, *08*		660____
28297	SP GP9 Diesel "446," CC, *10*		390____
28298	CSX AC6000 Diesel "608," CC, *08*		660____
28299	CSX AC6000 Diesel "609," nonpowered, *08*		220____
28300	NS Dash 9 Diesel "9607," nonpowered, *08*		220____
28302	BNSF SD70ACe Diesel "9380," CC, *08*		495____
28305	CSX AC6000 Diesel "610," nonpowered, RailSounds, *08*		430____
28306	GE ES44AC Evolution Hybrid Diesel "2010," CC, *09–10*		1000____
28307	Wabash Train Master Diesel "550," CC, *09–10*		495____
28311	UP DD35A Diesel, CC, *11*		600____
28312	BN SD60 Diesel "8301," CC, *09*		800____
28314	UP 3GS21B Genset Switcher "2701," CC, *10*		675____
28316	PRR NS Heritage SD70ACe Diesel "1854," CC, *10*		500____
28318	Conrail NS Heritage SD70ACe Diesel "1209," CC, *10*		500____
28320	CP Evolution Hybrid Diesel, *10*		875____
28323	NS Genset Switcher, CC, *11*		800____
28327	UP AC6000 Diesel "7050," CC, *10*		700____
28328	UPAC6000 Diesel "7055," nonpowered, CC, *10*		350____
28330	UP SD70ACe Diesel "8444," CC, *10*		500____
28331	CSX AC6000 Diesel "618," CC, *10*		700____
28333	Virginian NS Heritage SD70ACe Diesel, CC, *10*		500____
28334	NS Heritage SD70ACe Diesel "1982," CC, *10*		500____
28338	PRR NS Heritage SD70ACe Diesel, CC, *11*		500____
28339	ATSF AC6000 Diesel "9876," CC, *10*		550____
28340	WP GP7 Diesel "705," CC, *10*		450____
28343	Amtrak Dash 9 Diesel "519," CC, *10*		500____
28344	Southern NS Heritage SD70ACe Diesel, CC, *10*		500____
28345	N&W NS Heritage SD70ACe Diesel "247," CC, *10*		500____
28347	UP Boy Scouts 100th Anniversary ES44AC Diesel, CC, *11*		875____
28350	BNSF ES44AC Diesel, CC, *11*		850____
28351	KCS ES44AC Diesel "4655," CC, *11*		850____
28353	Erie GP7 Diesel, CC, *11*		450____
28354	CSX Genset Switcher "1303," CC, *11*		800____
28355	BNSF Genset Switcher "1249," CC, *11*		800____
28356	CSX SD60 Diesel, CC, *11*		500____
28357	CSX SD60 Diesel, CC, *11*		500____

		Exc	Mint
28358	Soo Line SD60 Diesel, CC, *11*		500
28359	Soo Line SD60 Diesel, CC, *11*		500
28360	WP GP7 Diesel "707," CC, *11*		450
28361	WM GP7 Diesel "21," CC, *11*		450
28362	WM GP7 Diesel "23," CC, *11*		450
28363	BN SD60 Diesel "8302," CC, *11*		500
28364	BNSF Dash-9 Diesel "4081," CC, *11*		500
28365	BNSF Dash-9 Diesel "5121," CC, *11*		500
28366	CN Dash-9 Diesel "2643," CC, *11*		500
28367	CN Dash-9 Diesel "2692," CC, *11*		500
28368	Amtrak Dash-9 Diesel, CC, *11*		500
28369	NYC DD35A Diesel "9950," CC, *11*		600
28370	UP DD35 Diesel "84," CC, *12*		600
28371	UP DD35A Diesel "72," CC, *11*		600
28372	NYC DD35A Diesel "9955," CC, *11*		600
28373	C&NW UP Heritage SD70ACe Diesel, CC, *11*		500
28374	SP UP Heritage SD70ACe Diesel, CC, *11*		500
28375	Katy UP Heritage SD70ACe Diesel, CC, *11*		500
28376	MoPac UP Heritage SD70ACe Diesel, CC, *11*		500
28377	Rio Grande UP Heritage SD70ACe Diesel, CC, *11*		500
28378	WP UP Heritage SD70ACe Diesel, CC, *11*		500
28380	NYC DD35A Diesel, nonpowered, *11*		440
28381	ATSF GP30 Diesel, CC, *11*		500
28382	U.S. Army Genset Switcher, CC, *11*		800
28383	Conrail Genset Switcher, CC, *11*		800
28384	CN Genset Switcher "7990," CC, *11–12*		800
28385	ATSF GP30 Diesel "1214," CC, *11*		500
28386	ATSF GP30 Diesel "2710," *11*		380
28387	ATSF GP30 Diesel "2715," nonpowered, *11*		240
28388	ICG GP30 Diesel "2268," CC, *11*		500
28389	ICG GP30 Diesel "2271," CC, *11*		500
28390	UP DD35 Diesel "79," nonpowered, *12*		440
28394	ICG GP30 Diesel "2277," *11*		380
28395	ICG GP30 Diesel "2279," nonpowered, *11*		240
28396	UP ES44AC Diesel "7454," CC, *11*		850
28397	UP ES44AC Diesel "7459," CC, *11*		850
28398	BNSF ES44AC Diesel "6436," CC, *11*		850
28399	KCS ES44AC Diesel "4682," CC, *11*		850
28400	Amtrak Rail Bonder, *05*		65
28403	Pennsylvania Ballast Tamper, traditional, *05–06*		105
28404	Maintenance Car, *05*		105
28405	Picatinny Arsenal Switcher, CC, *05*		290
28406	CSX Rail Bonder "92794," traditional, *05*		65
28407	UP Speeder, *05*		65
28408	CNJ Speeder "MW840," traditional, *06*		70
28409	Conrail Rail Bonder "X409," traditional, *06*		70
28411	U.S. Army Missile Launcher Locomotive, *06–07*		300
28412	Santa's Speeder, *06*		70
28413	Milwaukee Road Snowplow "X903," traditional, *06*		210
28414	Lionel Lines Burro Crane, traditional, *06*		160
28415	Third Avenue Trolley "1651," traditional, *06*		70

		Exc	Mint
28416	Hobo Handcar, traditional, *06*	70	____
28417	Christmas Rotary Snowplow, *06*	180	____
28418	Christmas Trolley, *06*	70	____
28419	Lionel Lines Speeder, *07–08*	70	____
28420	D&RGW Handcar, *07–08*	70	____
28421	Fort Collins Trolley, *07*	73	____
28422	PRR Burro Crane, *07–08*	160	____
28423	Alaska Rotary Snowplow, *06–07*	220	____
28424	Postwar "51" Navy Switcher, *07*	210	____
28425	Polar Express Elf Handcar, *06–16*	100	____
28427	Christmas Snowplow, *08–10*	210	____
28428	Halloween Handcar, *07*	70	____
28430	Wellspring Capital Management Trolley, *06*	85	____
28432	Bethlehem Steel Switcher, traditional, *07*	210	____
28434	Christmas Trolley, *07*	70	____
28438	Portland Birney Trolley, *08–09*	65	____
28440	PRR Inspection Vehicle, *08–09*	170	____
28441	Transylvania Trolley, *08*	75	____
28442	Postwar "50" Gang Car, *08*	120	____
28444	NH Handcar, *08–09*	75	____
28445	AEC Burro Crane Car	100	____
28446	Silver Bell Trolley, *09*	90	____
28447	4850TM Factory Trackmobile, CC, *10*	300	____
28448	CSX 4850TM Trackmobile, CC, *10*	300	____
28449	UP 4850TM Trackmobile, CC, *10*	300	____
28450	CP Rail Trackmobile, CC, *11*	300	____
28451	Christmas Track Cleaning Car, *10–13*	150	____
28452	MOW Early Era Inspection Vehicle, *10*	130	____
28453	PRR Early Era Inspection Vehicle, *10*	130	____
28454	CP Early Era Inspection Vehicle, *10*	130	____
28455	NYC Trackmobile, CC, *11–13*	300	____
28456	Coca-Cola Trolley, *10*	90	____
28457	B&M Rotary Snowplow "8457," *11*	250	____
28466	U.S. Army Trackmobile, CC, *11*	300	____
28467	PRR Trackmobile, CC, *11*	300	____
28468	Amtrak Trackmobile, CC, *11*	300	____
28469	BNSF Trackmobile, CC, *11*	300	____
28470	NYC Early Era Inspection Vehicle, *11*	130	____
28471	ATSF Early Era Inspection Vehicle, CC, *11*	130	____
28472	Southern Early Era Inspection Vehicle, *11*	130	____
28473	GN Early Era Inspection Vehicle, CC, *11*	130	____
28474	North Pole Central Elf Handcar, *11*	80	____
28475	UP Early Era Inspection Vehicle, *11*	130	____
28476	IC Early Era Inspection Vehicle, *11*	130	____
28478	Frisco Early Era Inspection Vehicle, CC, *11*	130	____
28479	Christmas Early Era Inspection Vehicle, *11*	130	____
28480	Grand Trunk Early Era Inspection Vehicle, CC, *11*	130	____
28500	Mopac GP20 Diesel "2274," *99–00*	205	____
28501	ATSF GP9 Diesel "2924," traditional, *99*	200	____
28502	ATSF GP9 Diesel "2925," CC, *99–00*	255	____
28503	ACL GP7 Diesel, CC, *00*	245	____
28504	ACL GP7 Diesel, traditional, *00*	170	____

Exc Mint

		Exc	Mint
___28505	Monon Alco C420 Switcher "505," CC, 00–01		230
28506	Monon Alco C420 Switcher "506," traditional, 00–01		170
___28507	NH Alco C420 Switcher "2556," CC, 00–01		275
28508	NH Alco C420 Switcher "2557," traditional, 00–01		290
___28509	FEC GP7 Diesel Set, 99		560
___28514	B&O GP9 Diesel "6590," 00		85
___28515	Lionel Service Station Alco C420 Switcher, CC, 00		205
___28516	Lehigh & Hudson River Alco C420 Diesel, 00		160
___28517	C&NW GP7 Diesel "1518," CC, 00–01		275
___28518	PRR EP-5 Electric Locomotive "2352," CC, 00		410
___28519	NP GP9 Diesel "2349," CC, 01		290
___28521	SP Alco RS-11 Switcher "5725," CC, 01–02		280
___28522	MP Alco RS-11 Switcher "4611," CC, 01–02		305
___28523	Soo SD40-2 Diesel "6622," CC, 01		375
___28524	Chessie SD40-2 Diesel "7616," CC, 01		355
___28527	AEC GP9 Diesel "2001," CC, 01		378
___28529	Norfolk Southern GP9 Diesel, CC, 02		200
___28530	NP Alco S4 Diesel "722," CC, 02		285
___28531	Santa Fe Alco S2 Switcher "2337," CC, 02		285
___28532	LV Alco S2 Switcher "150," CC, 02		280
___28533	Seaboard Air Line Alco S4 Diesel "1489," CC, 02		290
___28536	Rock Island GP7 Diesel "1274," CC, 02–03		230
___28538	WP Alco S2 Switcher "553," CC, 03		340
___28539	B&O Alco S2 Switcher "9045," CC, 03		320
___28540	UP SD40T-2 Diesel "4455," CC, 03		390
___28541	SP SD40T-2 Diesel "8239," CC, 03		400
___28542	Rio Grande SD40T-2 Diesel "5350," CC, 03		400
___28543	Ontario Northland RS3 Diesel "1308," 03		80
28544	Pennsylvania Alco RS-11 Switcher "8618," CC, 04		350
___28545	NP Alco RS-11 Switcher "900," CC, 03		325
___28548	Chessie System S4 Diesel "9009," CC, 05		400
28553	PRR Alco RS-11 Switcher "8620," traditional, 07–08		285
28554	Pennsylvania Alco RS-11 Switcher "8618," nonpowered, CC, 07		170
___28554	PRR RS-11 Diesel "8621," nonpowered, 08		170
28555	Alaska GP38-2 Diesel "2001," CC, 06		400
28556	Alaska GP38-2 Diesel "2002," nonpowered (std O), 06		160
___28557	CP GP30 Diesel "5000," CC, 06–07		400
28558	CP GP30 Diesel "5001," nonpowered (std O), 06–07		150
___28559	Chessie System GP30 Diesel "3044," CC, 06–07		400
28560	Chessie System GP30 Diesel "3045," nonpowered (std O), 06–07		150
___28561	NYC GP7 Diesel "5628," CC, 07–08		340
___28562	NYC GP7 Diesel "5629," nonpowered (std O), 07		170
___28563	GN GP7 Diesel "626," CC, 07		400
___28564	GN GP7 Diesel "627," nonpowered (std O), 07		170
___28565	RI GP7 Diesel "1265," CC, 07		400
___28566	RI GP7 Diesel "1266," nonpowered (std O), 07		170

		Exc	Mint
28567	UP GP7 Diesel "105," CC, *07*		400___
28568	UP GP7 Diesel "106," nonpowered (std O), *07*		170___
28570	D&RGW GP7 Diesel "5101," CC, *08*		440___
28573	PRR GP7 Diesel "8512," CC, *08*		440___
28578	D&H GP38-2 Diesel "7307," CC, *08*		440___
28587	PRR GP7 Diesel "8510," CC, *10*		450___
28592	N&W GP7 Diesel "2446," CC, *09*		500___
28594	White Pass & Yukon NW2 Diesel Switcher, traditional, *09–10*		300___
28595	ATSF SD40 Diesel "5004," CC, *09*		380___
28596	Erie GP7 Diesel "1210," CC, *11*		450___
28598	ATSF GP7 Diesel "2791," CC, *10*		450___
28599	Erie GP9 Diesel "1261," CC, *10*		390___
28612	WP 4-4-2 Atlantic Locomotive, traditional, *02*		80___
28613	Reading 0-6-0 Dockside Switcher "1251," traditional, *04*		100___
28615	B&O 4-6-4 Hudson Locomotive, traditional, *02*		225___
28616	Nickel Plate 2-8-4 Berkshire Locomotive, traditional, *02*		190___
28617	Southern 2-8-4 Berkshire Locomotive, traditional, *02*		235___
28624	Santa Fe 0-6-0 Dockside Switcher "2174," traditional, *04*		175___
28625	Wabash 4-4-2 Atlantic Locomotive "8625," traditional, *03*		85___
28626	PRR 4-6-4 Hudson Locomotive "626," traditional, *03*		175___
28627	C&O 2-8-4 Berkshire Locomotive "2755," traditional, *03*		200___
28628	L&N 2-8-4 Berkshire Locomotive "1970," traditional, *03*		200___
28633	JCPenney B&O 2-8-4 Berkshire Locomotive, *07*		135___
28636	D&RGW 4-4-2 Atlantic Locomotive "8636," traditional, *04*		95___
28637	UP 4-6-4 Hudson Locomotive "673," traditional, *04*		160___
28638	GN 2-8-4 Berkshire Locomotive "3414," traditional, *04*		200___
28639	NYC 2-8-4 Berkshire Locomotive "9401," traditional, *04*		200___
28646	North Pole Central 2-8-4 Berkshire "1900," traditional, *04*		230___
28649	Polar Express 2-8-4 Berkshire Locomotive, *03–10*		120___
28650	NYC 0-6-0 Dockside Switcher "X-8688," traditional, *05*		80___
28651	Bethlehem Steel 0-6-0 Dockside Switcher "72," traditional, *05*		80___
28652	LL 4-4-2 Locomotive "8652," traditional, *05*		105___
28655	Erie 2-8-4 Berkshire Locomotive "3338," traditional, *05*		240___
28656	PRR 2-8-4 Berkshire Locomotive "56," traditional, *05*		240___
28660	North Pole Central 0-6-0 Dockside Switcher "25," traditional, *05*		105___
28661	Santa Fe 0-4-0 Locomotive "2300" traditional, *05*		160___
28662	C&O 0-4-0 Locomotive "39," traditional, *05*		160___

		Exc	Mint
28674	C&O 0-6-0 Dockside Switcher "67," traditional, *06–07*		110
28675	SP 0-6-0 Dockside Switcher "675," traditional, *06–07*		110
28676	U.S. Steel 0-6-0 Dockside Switcher "76," traditional, *06–07*		110
28677	WM 4-4-2 Atlantic Locomotive "103," traditional, *06*		110
28678	Rio Grande 0-4-0 Locomotive "55," traditional, *06–07*		170
28679	U.S. Army Transportation Corps 0-4-0 Locomotive "40," traditional, *06*		170
28680	Reading 0-4-0 Locomotive "1152," traditional, *06*		170
28681	Virginian 2-8-4 Berkshire Locomotive "509," traditional, *06*		260
28683	B&O 2-8-2 Mikado Locomotive "1520," TrainSounds, *06–07*		260
28684	UP 2-8-2 Mikado Locomotive "2498," TrainSounds, *06–07*		260
28693	B&O 4-4-2 Locomotive "28," traditional, *05*		105
28694	NYC 4-4-2 Atlantic Locomotive "8637," traditional, *06*		100
28695	Halloween 0-6-0 Dockside Switcher "X-131," traditional, *06–07*		85
28699	Holiday 2-8-2 Mikado Locomotive "25," red, RailSounds, *08*		260
28700	CB&Q 0-8-0 Locomotive "543," RailSounds, *05*		650
28701	NP 0-8-0 Locomotive "1178," RailSounds, *05*		650
28702	Boston & Albany 0-8-0 Locomotive "53," RailSounds, *05*		650
28704	PRR 4-4-2 Atlantic Locomotive "68," CC, *05*		550
28706	PRR Reading Seashore 4-4-2 Atlantic Locomotive "6064," CC, *05*		550
28742	B&O 4-6-0 Camelback Locomotive "1630," CC, *03*		335
28743	B&O 4-6-0 Camelback Locomotive "1632," traditional, *03*		300
28744	D&H 4-6-0 Camelback Locomotive "548," CC, *03*		325
28745	D&H 4-6-0 Camelback Locomotive "555," traditional, *03*		300
28746	Erie 4-6-0 Camelback Locomotive "860," CC, *03*		375
28747	Erie 4-6-0 Camelback Locomotive "878," traditional, *03*		300
28748	Jersey Central 4-6-0 Camelback Locomotive "772," CC, *03*		300
28749	Jersey Central 4-6-0 Camelback Locomotive "773," traditional, *03*		300
28750	Lackawanna 4-6-0 Camelback Locomotive "690," CC, *03*		375
28751	Lackawanna 4-6-0 Camelback Locomotive "1031," traditional, *03*		300
28752	LIRR 4-6-0 Camelback Locomotive "126," CC, *03*		300
28753	LIRR 4-6-0 Camelback Locomotive "127," traditional, *03*		300
28754	NYO&W 4-6-0 Camelback Locomotive "249," CC, *03*		300

Exc Mint

28755	NYO&W 4-6-0 Camelback "253" Locomotive, traditional, *03*		300____
28756	PRR Reading Seashore 4-6-0 Camelback Locomotive "6000," CC, *03*		325____
28757	PRR Reading Seashore 4-6-0 Camelback Locomotive "6001," traditional, *03*		300____
28758	Susquehanna 4-6-0 Camelback Locomotive "30," CC, *03*		305____
28759	Susquehanna 4-6-0 Camelback Locomotive "36," traditional, *03*		300____
28800	N&W GP7 Diesel "507," *99–00*		80____
28801	Lionel Lines 44-ton Switcher, *99*		135____
28806	Jersey Central FM H16-44 Diesel "1516," CC, *01*		335____
28811	Santa Fe FM H16-44 Diesel "3003," CC, *01*		290____
28813	Milwaukee Road FM H16-44 Diesel "406," CC, *01*		280____
28815	B&O GP30 Diesel "6935," CC, *02*		295____
28817	Reading GP30 Diesel "5513," CC, *02*		310____
28819	Rio Grande GP30 Diesel "3013," CC, *02*		310____
28821	GT GP7 Diesel "4438," *01*		100____
28822	Southern RS3 Diesel "2127," *01*		70____
28823	Virginian Electric Locomotive "234," *01*		122____
28826	Pioneer Seed GP7 Diesel "2001," traditional, *00 u*		NRS____
28827	Chessie GP38 Diesel, traditional, *01*		100____
28830	Soo Line GP9 Diesel, traditional, *01 u*		NRS____
28831	Conrail U36B Diesel "2971," traditional, *02*		100____
28832	Santa Fe RS3 Diesel "2099," traditional, *02*		70____
28836	NYC FM H-16-44 Diesel "7000," CC, *02*		330____
28837	NH FM H-16-44 Diesel "591," CC, *02*		325____
28838	UP FM H-16-44 Diesel "1340," CC, *02*		325____
28839	Alaska GP 30 Diesel "2000," CC, *04*		315____
28840	Burlington GP30 Diesel "945," CC, *03*		325____
28841	Seaboard GP30 Diesel "1315," CC, *03*		220____
28842	C&O GP9 Diesel, horn, *04*		160____
28843	Southern GP38 Diesel, horn, *04*		140____
28845	Amtrak RS3 Diesel "106," *03*		70____
28846	Western Pacific U36B Diesel "3067," traditional, *04*		100____
28847	DM & IR GP38 Diesel "203," traditional, *04*		170____
28848	JCPenney Santa Fe GP38 Diesel, *04*		125____
28849	Western Maryland GP7 Diesel, horn, *04*		185____
28850	NYC GP30 Diesel "6115" CC, *04*		360____
28851	Pennsylvania RS3 Diesel, *04*		75____
28852	CSX U36B Diesel "1976," traditional, *05*		140____
28853	Santa Fe GP38 Diesel "2371," traditional, *05*		210____
28857	Alaska GP9 Diesel, *05*		125____
28859	Pennsylvania GP30 Diesel "2206," nonpowered, *06*		160____
28860	UP GP30 Diesel "844," CC, *06*		360____
28861	UP GP30 Diesel "845," nonpowered (std 0), *06*		150____
28862	CSX GP30 Diesel "4249," CC, *06*		400____
28863	CSX GP30 Diesel "4250," nonpowered (std 0), *06*		150____
28864	UP RS3 Diesel "1195," traditional, *06*		85____
28865	GN GP9 Diesel "688," traditional, *06*		210____

		Exc	Mint
28866	NYC GP20 Diesel "6110," traditional, *06*		140
28868	ATSF GP38 Diesel		140
28873	NYC RS3 Diesel "8226," traditional, *06*		85
28874	UP GP9 Diesel "178," traditional, *06–07*		210
28875	Santa Fe GP20 "1107," traditional, *06*		140
28876	GN FT Diesel "418," traditional, *07–08*		245
28879	UPS Centennial GP38 Diesel, traditional, *06*		210
28881	Conrail GP20 Diesel "2107," traditional, *07*		140
28882	Alaska RS3 Diesel "1079," traditional, *07*		85
28883	Diesel, *07–13*		120
28884	PRR GP38 Diesel "2389," traditional, *08–09*		210
28886	RI RS3 Diesel "492," traditional, *08*		95
28887	Southern RS3 Diesel "2028," traditional, *08*		95
28890	CN GP9 Diesel "4573," traditional, *08*		210
28897	Seaboard U36B Diesel "1762," traditional, *08*		140
28900	Iron 'Arry and Iron Bert 2-pack, *08–09*		240
28905	ATSF FT Diesel "160," nonpowered, *09–10*		120
29000	PRR Caleb Strong Madison Coach "2622," *99*		80
29001	PRR Villa Royal Madison Coach "2621," *99*		80
29002	PRR Philadelphia Madison Coach "2624," *99*	30	80
29003	PRR Madison Car 4-pack, *98*		220
29004	NYC Heavyweight Passenger Car 2-pack, *99*		170
29007	NYC Pullman Passenger Car 2-pack, *98 u*		95
29008	NYC Heavyweight Diner "383," *98*		95
29009	NYC Van Twiller Heavyweight Combination Car, *98*		95
29010	C&O Heavyweight Passenger Car 2-pack, *99*		150
29039	Lionel Lines Recovery Combination Car "9501," *99*		NRS
29041	Alaska Streamliner Car 4-pack, *99–00*		230
29042	Alaska Streamliner Baggage Car "6310," *99–00*		50
29043	Alaska Streamliner Coach "5408," *99–00*		65
29044	Alaska Streamliner Vista Dome Car "7014," *99–00*		65
29046	B&O Streamliner Car 4-pack, *99–00*		165
29047	B&O Streamliner Baggage Car, *99–00*		35
29048	B&O Streamliner Coach, *99–00*		50
29049	B&O Streamliner Vista Dome Car, *99–00*		50
29050	B&O Streamliner Observation Car, *99–00*		40
29051	ATSF Streamliner Car 4-pack, *99–00*		200
29052	ATSF Streamliner Baggage Car, *99–00*		40
29053	ATSF Streamliner Coach, *99–00*		60
29054	ATSF Streamliner Vista Dome Car, *99–00*		60
29055	ATSF Streamliner Observation Car, *99–00*		40
29056	NYC Streamliner Car 4-pack, *99–00*		180
29057	NYC Streamliner Baggage Car, *99–00*		40
29058	NYC Streamliner Coach, *99–00*		50
29059	NYC Streamliner Vista Dome Car, *99–00*		50
29060	NYC Streamliner Observation Car, *99–00*		45
29061	PRR Madison Passenger Car 4-pack, *99–00*		190
29062	PRR Indian Point Madison Baggage Car, *99–00*		50
29063	PRR Christopher Columbus Madison Coach, *99–00*		50

Exc Mint

		Exc	Mint
29064	PRR Andrew Jackson Madison Coach, *99–00*	50	___
29065	PRR Broussard Madison Observation Car, *99–00*	50	___
29066	CNJ Madison Passenger Car 4-pack, *99–00*	210	___
29067	CNJ Madison Baggage Car "420," *99–00*	50	___
29068	CNJ Beachcomber Madison Coach, *99–00*	50	___
29069	CNJ Echo Lake Madison Coach, *99–00*	50	___
29070	CNJ Madison Observation Car "1178," *99–00*	50	___
29071	NYC Baby Madison Car 4-pack, *00*	155	___
29072	NYC Baby Madison Baggage Car "1001," *00*	50	___
29073	NYC Baby Madison Coach "1005," *00*	50	___
29074	NYC Baby Madison Coach "1006," *00*	50	___
29075	NYC Detroit Baby Madison Observation Car "1019," *00*	40	___
29076	Southern Baby Madison Car 4-pack, *00*	155	___
29077	Southern Delaware Madison Baggage Car "702," *00*	30	___
29078	Southern North Carolina Madison Coach "800," *00*	50	___
29079	Southern Maryland Madison Coach "801," *00*	50	___
29080	Southern Madison Observation Car "1100," *00*	40	___
29081	ATSF Baby Madison Car 4-pack, *00*	160	___
29082	ATSF Baby Madison Baggage Car "1765," *00*	30	___
29083	ATSF Baby Madison Coach "3040," *00*	50	___
29084	ATSF Baby Madison Coach "1535," *00*	50	___
29085	ATSF Baby Madison Observation Car "10," *00*	45	___
29086	Madison Car 3-pack, *99*	280	___
29090	Lionel Liontech Madison Car "2656," *99*	75	___
29091	Lawrence Cowen Lionel Legends Madison Coach "2657," *99–00*	75	___
29105	PRR Trail Blazer Aluminum Passenger Car 4-pack, *04–05*	550	___
29108	Searchlight Car, *00*	30	___
29110	B&O Columbian Aluminum Passenger Car 4-pack, *04*	425	___
29115	SP Daylight Aluminum Passenger Car 4-pack, *04–05*	550	___
29122	Erie-Lack. F3 Diesel AB Passenger Set, *99*	840	___
29123	Erie-Lack. Aluminum Coach/Baggage Car "203," *99*	100	___
29124	Erie-Lack. Aluminum Coach/Diner "770," *99*	100	___
29125	Erie-Lack. Eleanor Lord Aluminum Coach, *99*	100	___
29126	Erie-Lack. Tavern Lounge Aluminum Observation Car "789," *99*	125	___
29127	ACL Aluminum Baggage Car "152," *99*	NRS	___
29128	ACL North Hampton Aluminum Coach, *99*	NRS	___
29129	Texas Special Passenger Car 4-pack, *99*	700	___
29130	Texas Special Edward Burleson Aluminum Coach "1200," *99*	115	___
29131	Texas Special David G. Burnett Aluminum Coach "1201," *99*	115	___
29132	Texas Special J. Pinckney Henderson Aluminum Coach "1202," *99*	115	___
29133	Texas Special Stephen F. Austin Aluminum Observation Car "1203," *99*	100	___

Exc Mint

29135	California Zephyr Silver Poplar Aluminum Vista Dome Car, *99*	150
29136	California Zephyr Silver Palm Aluminum Vista Dome Car, *99*	150
29137	California Zephyr Silver Tavern Aluminum Vista Dome Car, *99*	150
29138	California Zephyr Silver Planet Aluminum Vista Dome Car, *99*	150
29139	Kughn Lionel Legends Madison Car "2655," *99*	113
29140	NYC Castleton Bridge Aluminum Sleeper Car, *99*	120
29141	NYC Martin Van Buren Aluminum Combination Car, *99*	120
29142	CP Skyline Aluminum Vista Dome Car "596," *99*	125
29143	CP Banff Park Aluminum Observation Car, *99*	125
29144	Santa Fe El Capitan Aluminum Passenger Car 4-pack, *04*	400
29149	CB&Q California Zephyr Aluminum Passenger Car 2-pack, *03*	300
29152	Santa Fe Super Chief Aluminum Passenger Car 2-pack, *03*	190
29155	D&H Aluminum Passenger Car 2-pack, *03*	190
29158	Southern Aluminum Passenger Car 2-pack, *03*	205
29165	Amtrak Superliner Passenger Car 2-pack, Phase IV, *04*	195
29168	Amtrak Superliner Diner, StationSounds, Phase IV, *04*	200
29169	Alaska Superliner Passenger Car 2-pack, *04*	200
29172	Alaska Superliner Diner, StationSounds, *04*	200
29182	N&W Powhatan Arrow Aluminum Passenger Car 4-pack (std O), *05*	550
29187	N&W Powhatan Arrow Aluminum Passenger Car 2-pack (std O), *05*	290
29190	N&W Powhatan Arrow Aluminum Diner, StationSounds, *05*	290
29191	MILW Hiawatha Passenger Car 4-pack, *06*	370
29196	MILW Hiawatha Passenger Car 2-pack, *06*	190
29199	MILW Hiawatha Diner, StationSounds, *06*	190
29202	Santa Fe Map Boxcar "6464," *97 u*	53
29203	Maine Central Boxcar "6464-597," *97 u*	35
29205	Mickey Mouse Hi-Cube Boxcar "9555," *97*	65
29206	Vapor Records Boxcar #1, *97*	90
29209	Postwar "6464" Boxcar Series VII, 3 cars, *98*	87
29210	GN Boxcar "6464-450," *98*	33
29211	B&M Boxcar "6464-475," *98*	27
29212	Timken Boxcar "6464-500," *98*	28
29213	ATSF Grand Canyon Route 6464 Boxcar "6464-198," *98*	26
29214	Southern 6464 Boxcar "6464-298," *98*	27
29215	Canadian Pacific 6464 Boxcar "6464-398," *98*	26
29217	1997 Toy Fair Airex Boxcar, *97*	78
29218	Vapor Records Boxcar "6464-496," *97 u*	80
29220	Lionel Centennial Series Hi-Cube Boxcar Set, 4 cars, *97*	220
29221	Centennial Series Hi-Cube Boxcar "9697-1," *97*	58
29222	Centennial Series Hi-Cube Boxcar "9697-2," *97*	68

Exc Mint

Cat. No.	Description	Exc	Mint
29223	Centennial Series Hi-Cube Boxcar "9697-3," *97*		63___
29224	Centennial Series Hi-Cube Boxcar "9697-4," *97*		60___
29225	H.O.R.D.E. Music Festival Boxcar, *97*	48	65___
29229	Vapor Records Holiday Car, *98*		155___
29231	Halloween Animated Boxcar, *98*		42___
29233	Conrail PC Overstamped Boxcar "6464-598," *98*		38___
29234	Conrail Erie Overstamped Boxcar "6464-698," *98*		32___
29235	NYC Boxcar "6464-510," *99*		47___
29236	MKT Boxcar "6464-515," *99*		40___
29237	M&StL Boxcar "6464-525," *99*		25___
29247	Mainline Classic Street Lamps, 3 pieces, *08–16*		40___
29250	Phoebe Snow Boxcar "6464-199," *99*		41___
29251	BN Boxcar "6464-299," *99*		31___
29252	CP Boxcar "6464-399," *99*		33___
29253	B&M Boxcar "76032," *99*		50___
29254	B&M Boxcar "76033," *99*		50___
29255	B&M Boxcar "76034," *99*		50___
29256	B&M Boxcar "76035," *99*		50___
29257	Southern Boxcar "9464-199," *99*		38___
29258	Reading Boxcar "9464-299," *99*		36___
29259	NP Bicentennial Boxcar "9464-399," *99*		34___
29265	Maine Central Boxcar "8661," *99*		36___
29266	Frisco Boxcar "8722," *99*		36___
29267	No. 6464 Boxcar 3-pack, Series VIII, *99*		85___
29268	Rio Grande Boxcar "63067," *99*		40___
29271	Lionel Cola Tractor and Trailer, *98*		12___
29279	Conrail Jersey Central Overstamped Boxcar "6464-28X," *99*		40___
29280	Conrail LV Overstamped Boxcar "6464-31X," *99*		41___
29281	Conrail Overstamped Boxcar 2-pack, *99*		70___
29282	Postwar "6464" Boxcar 3-pack, *99*		130___
29283	NYC Boxcar, *99*		55___
29284	GN Boxcar, *99*		40___
29285	Seaboard Boxcar, *99*		36___
29286	Overstamped Boxcar 2-pack, *99*		65___
29287	NH PC Overstamped Boxcar "6464-29X," *99*	18	34___
29288	Conrail Reading Overstamped Boxcar "6464-32X," *99*		38___
29289	Postwar "6464" Series IX, 3 cars, *99–00*		70___
29290	D&RGW Boxcar "6464-650," *00*		41___
29291	ATSF Boxcar "6464-700," *00*		38___
29292	NH Boxcar "6464-725," *00*		39___
29293	NH Boxcar "6464-425," *99*		95___
29294	Hellgate Bridge Boxcar "1900-2000," *99 u*		38___
29295	PRR "Don't Stand Me Still" Boxcar "24018," *99–00*		65___
29296	PRR "Merchandise" Boxcar "29296," *99–00*		65___
29297	PRR "No Damage" Boxcar "47158," *99–00*		65___
29298	Lionel Boxcar "6464-2000," *00*		46___
29300	50th Anniversary Clear Shell Aquarium Car, *10*		85___
29301	Postwar "3662" Transparent Milk Car with platform, *11, 13*		155___
29302	Christmas Music Reefer, *10*		75___

			Exc	Mint
___	29303	North Pole Central Crane Car, *10–11*		65
	29305	UP Chisholm Trail Stock Car, Cattle Sounds, *11, 13*		200
___	29306	PRR Hi-Cube Lighted Garland Boxcar, *10–11*		70
___	29309	GN Pullman-Standard Diesel Freight Set, CC, *13*		830
	29310	Marine Science Deep Sea Exhibition Aquarium Car, *11*		75
___	29311	Strasburg Derrick Car, *11*		45
___	29312	Santa's Operating Boxcar, *11–12*		75
___	29314	SP DD Boxcar "214051" (std O), *13–14*		75
___	29317	CN DD Boxcar "214051" (std O), *13–14*		75
___	29320	CNJ DD Boxcar "214051" (std O), *13–14*		75
___	29321	Ice Skating Aquarium Car, *12*		80
___	29322	Koi Aquarium Car, *13–14*		80
___	29323	UP DD Boxcar "500019" (std O), *13–14*		75
___	29324	Walking Zombie Brakeman Car, *12*		80
___	29326	NP "Pig Palace" Operating Stock Car "84144," *12*		200
___	29327	Bethlehem Steel Operating Hopper "2025," *12*		60
___	29328	Beatles "Nothing is Real" Aquarium Car, *12–13*		85
___	29329	Peanuts Halloween Aquarium Car, *12–13*		85
___	29333	ATSF 89' Auto Carrier 2-pack (std O), *13–14, 16*		220
___	29338	BN 89' Auto Carrier 2-pack (std O), *13–14*		220
___	29344	C&NW DD Boxcar "57766" (std O), *13*		75
___	29345	ATSF 89' Auto Carrier (std O), *13–14*		110
___	29346	Soo Line 89' Auto Carrier 2-pack (std O), *13–16*		220
___	29349	SP 89' Auto Carrier 2-pack (std O), *13–16*		220
___	29364	NYC Water Level Steam Freight Set, CC, *12–13*		1600
___	29365	N&W Pocahontas Steam Passenger Set, CC, *12*		1950
___	29366	SP TankSet Diesel Set, CC, *12*		850
___	29372	BNSF 89' Auto Carrier "300267" (std O), *13*		110
___	29373	CN 89' Auto Carrier "710771" (std O), *13, 16*		110
___	29376	Conrail 89' Auto Carrier "964444" (std O), *13*		110
___	29377	CP 89' Auto Carrier 2-pack (std O), *13–14, 16*		220
___	29380	CSX 89' Auto Carrier "604544" (std O), *13*		110
___	29381	GTW 89' Auto Carrier "50450" (std O), *14–15*		110
___	29382	UP 89' Auto Carrier "604545" (std O), *13*		110
	29384	DL&W USRA Double-sheathed Boxcar "44153" (std O), *13*		70
	29385	ATSF USRA Double-sheathed Boxcar "39012" (std O), *13*		70
	29386	PRR PS-4 Flatcar with stakes "469614" (std O), *13*		70
___	29387	GN PS-4 Flatcar with stakes "629387" (std O), *13*		70
___	29400	Bethlehem Steel Slag Car 3-pack (std O), *03*		185
___	29404	Bethlehem Steel Hot Metal Car 3-pack (std O), *03*		210
___	29408	PRR Coil Car, *01*		40
___	29411	Sherwin-Williams Vat Car, *02*		35
___	29412	Tabasco Brand Vat Car, *02*		36
___	29413	Airex Boat Loader Car "29413," *02*		42
___	29414	PRR Evans Auto Loader "480123," *01*		56
___	29415	WM Skeleton Log Car 3-pack #2 (std O), *02*		90
	29419	West Side Lumber Skeleton Log Car 3-pack #2 (std O), *02*		90

		Exc	Mint
29423	Wellspring Capital Management Happy Holidays Vat Car, *03 u*		255___
29424	Meadow River Lumber Skeleton Log Car 3-pack (std O), *03*		90___
29429	Campbell's Soup Vat Car "29429," *03*		38___
29430	Meadow River Lumber Skeleton Log Car 3-pack #2 (std O), *03*		90___
29434	Weyerhauser Skeleton Log Car 3-pack, *05*		100___
29438	Trailer Train Flatcar with 2 UP trailers, *03*		60___
29439	Postwar "6414" Evans Auto Loader, *02*		43___
29441	UP Flatcar "53471" with grader, *02*		43___
29442	CSX Flatcar "600513" with backhoe, *02*		43___
29453	Elk River Lumber Skeleton Log Car 3-pack #2 (std O), *03*		90___
29457	NS Flatcar "157590" with Caterpillar loader, *03*		42___
29458	BNSF Flatcar "922268" with Caterpillar truck, *03*		44___
29459	Water Barrel Car "1878," Archive Collection, *03*		40___
29460	LL Flatcar "3460" with trailers, Archive Collection, *03*		39___
29461	Postwar "6500" Flatcar with red-and-white airplane, *03*		32___
29462	Postwar "6500" Flatcar with white-and-red airplane, *03*		31___
29463	Postwar "6414" Evans Auto Loader, *03*		30___
29464	U.S. Army Vat Car "29464," *04*		35___
29465	U.S. Steel Slag Car 3-pack (std O), *04–05*		160___
29469	U.S. Steel Hot Metal Car 3-pack (std O), *04–05*		190___
29473	Youngstown Sheet & Tube Slag Car 3-pack (std O), *03*		150___
29477	Youngstown Sheet & Tube Hot Metal Car 3-pack (std O), *03*		170___
29481	Cass Scenic Railroad Skeleton Log Car 3-pack (std O), *03*		80___
29487	Boat-loader with 4 boats, *04*		65___
29488	Cass Scenic Railroad Skeleton Log Car 3-pack #2 (std O), *04*		90___
29492	Pickering Lumber Skeleton Log Car 3-pack #1 (std O), *04*		100___
29496	Pickering Lumber Skeleton Log Car 3-pack #2 (std O), *04*		90___
29602	Celanese Chemicals 1-D Tank Car, *05*		45___
29603	Comet 1-D Tank Car, traditional, *05*		53___
29604	Meadow Brook Molasses 1-D Tank Car, traditional, *05*		53___
29606	Elvis Presley Gold Record Transport Car, *04*		120___
29607	Las Vegas Mint Car, traditional, *05*		58___
29609	Alien Suspension Car, *06*		60___
29610	Dixie Honey 1-D Tank Car, *06*		60___
29611	Sunoco 1-D Tank Car, *06*		60___
29612	Las Vegas Poker Chip Car, *06*		40___
29613	Postwar "6463" Rocket Fuel 2-D Tank Car, *06*		75___
29617	Cities Service Tank Car, *06–07*		48___
29618	Hooker Chemicals 3-D Tank Car, *07*		60___
29619	Grave's Formaldehyde 1-D Tank Car, *07*		60___
29622	Fort Knox Mint Car, lilac, Archive Collection, *07*		60___

		Exc	Mint
____29624	Monopoly Mint Car with money, *08*		65
29626	"Case Closed" Mint Car with shredded		
____	documents, *08*		109
____29628	Poinsettia Mint Car, *09*		70
____29629	AEC Glow-in-the-Dark Tank Car, *09–10*		60
____29633	Christmas Ornament Lighted Mint Car, *10*		70
____29634	Federal Reserve Bailout Mint Car, *10*		70
____29635	Monopoly "Go To Jail" Mint Car, *10*		70
____29636	Vampire Transport Mint Car, *10–11*		70
____29637	Candy Cane 2-D Tank Car, *10–11*		55
____29640	Coca-Cola Tank Car, *10*		62
____29642	Jolly Rancher 1-D Tank Car, *11*		55
____29643	Hershey's Syrup 1-D Tank Car, *11*		58
____29644	ATSF 1-D Tank Car, *11*		55
____29645	Atlantic City Casino Mint Car, *11*		70
____29646	Alaska Oil 2-D Tank Car, *11*		50
____29647	Gingerbread Man Mint Car, *11*		70
____29649	Lionel SP Smoke Pellets Mint Car, *12–13*		70
____29650	Cleveland Federal Reserve Mint Car, *11*		70
____29651	Richmond Federal Reserve Mint Car, *12*		70
____29654	Boston Federal Reserve Mint Car, *13*		70
____29655	PRR 16-wheel Flatcar with girders "469846," *12*		75
29656	ATSF 16-wheel Flatcar with transformer "90096,"		
____	*12*		75
____29671	Smoke Pellet Mint Car #2, *13–15*		70
____29694	Hershey's Mint Car, *14*		85
____29695	Trailer Set Maxi-Stack Pair "48," *13*		120
____29697	Santa's Flatcar with submarine, *13*		70
____29698	Tree Topper Star Transport Car, *13–14*		80
____29699	Silver and Gold Christmas Mint Car, *13–14*		70
____29703	PRR Porthole Caboose, *01*		45
____29708	C&O Bay Window Caboose "8315," *04*		45
____29709	Pennsylvania N5c Caboose "477938," *04*		40
____29711	Santa Fe Bay Window Caboose, *05*		60
____29712	Postwar "2420" Searchlight Caboose, *04*		50
____29718	N&W Work Caboose, *06*		48
____29719	Santa Fe Caboose "6427," Archive Collection, *06*		48
29726	Virginian Caboose "6427," Archive Collection,		
____	*06–07*		50
____29727	"I Love U.S.A." Bay Window Caboose "1985," *06*		60
____29729	Bethlehem Steel Searchlight Caboose, *06*		90
____29732	PRR Caboose "477871," *08*		45
29733	White Pass & Yukon Extended Vision Caboose,		
____	*09–10*		90
____29734	PRR NS Heritage CA-4 Caboose (std O), *10*		95
____29735	Conrail NS Heritage CA-4 Caboose (std O), *10*		95
____29737	ATSF Bay Window Caboose, traditional, *10–11*		70
____29739	B&M Transfer Caboose, *11*		50
____29765	TankSet Add-on 3-pack (std O), *12*		240
____29771	CN TankSet 2-pack (std O), *12*		160
____29774	GATX TankSet 2-pack (std O), *12*		160
____29777	Cibro TankSet 2-pack (std O), *12*		160
____29786	Bethlehem Steel PS-2 3-bay Hopper (std O), *13*		80

		Exc	Mint
29787	PRR PS-2 3-bay Hopper (std O), *13*	80	___
29791	Wizard of Oz Anniversary Boxcar, *13–15*	70	___
29792	Angela Trotta Thomas "Toyland Express" Boxcar, *13*	65	___
29793	Where the Wild Things Are Boxcar, *13–15*	70	___
29800	MOW Crane Car, TMCC, *04*	250	___
29804	UP Crane Car "JPX 250," CC, *05*	320	___
29805	Conrail Crane Car "50202," CC, *05*	320	___
29806	Weyerhaeuser Log Dump Car, *05*	75	___
29807	DM&IR Coal Dump Car, *05*	75	___
29808	Candy Cane Dump Car, *05*	55	___
29809	Dump Car with presents, *05*	60	___
29810	Operating Egg Nog Car with platform, *05*	140	___
29811	Merchant's Despatch Transit Hot Box Reefer "12425," *05*	85	___
29812	Santa Fe Hot Box Reefer "20699," *05*	90	___
29813	Santa Fe Boom Car "19144," Crane Sounds, *05*	210	___
29814	Pennsylvania Boom Car "491063," Crane Sounds, *05*	210	___
29815	NYC Boom Car "X923," Crane Sounds, *05*	210	___
29816	MOW Boom Car "X-816," Crane Sounds, *05*	210	___
29817	UP Boom Car "909438," Crane Sounds, *05*	210	___
29818	Conrail Boom Car, Crane Sounds, *05*	210	___
29821	Postwar "2460" Lionel Lines Crane Car, gray cab, *05*	43	___
29822	Postwar "773W" NYC Tender, whistle, *05*	48	___
29823	Postwar "3484" Pennsylvania Operating Boxcar, *05*	38	___
29827	Postwar "3419" Helicopter Launching Car, *06*	49	___
29828	Postwar "3666" Minuteman Car with cannon, *06*	85	___
29829	Postwar "6905" Radioactive Waste Car, *06*	85	___
29830	PFE Hot Box Reefer "5890" (std O), *06*	105	___
29831	Swift Hot Box Reefer "15342" (std O), *06*	150	___
29832	Chessie System Crane Car "940504," CC, *06*	320	___
29833	Chessie System Boom Car "940561," CC, *06*	210	___
29834	LL Bay Window Caboose "834," TrainSounds (std O), *06–07*	110	___
29835	SP Bay Window Caboose "4667," TrainSounds (std O), *06–07*	160	___
29839	Cherry Picker Car, *06*	63	___
29849	Lionel Lines Crane Car, silver cab, *06*	60	___
29850	N&W J Class Tender, air whistle, *06–07*	70	___
29853	Postwar "6651" Big John Cannon Car, *08*	75	___
29854	Satellite Launching Car, *07*	70	___
29855	Lionel Lines Operating Milk Car with platform, *07*	140	___
29856	Monon Operating Boxcar, *06–07*	65	___
29857	Lionel Lines Boom Car, *06–07*	55	___
29858	CP Rail Crane Car "414475," CC, *07*	320	___
29859	CP Rail Boom Car "412567," CC, *07*	210	___
29865	Southern Operating Barrel Car, *07–08*	75	___
29866	Pirates Aquarium Car, *07*	75	___
29867	NYC Jet Snow Blower "X27207," *07*	120	___
29868	Alaska Jet Snow Blower, *07*	120	___
29869	Bethlehem Steel Crane Car, *06*	60	___

			Exc	Mint
___	29870	MOW Jet Snow Blower "MWX-16," 07		120
___	29874	Peanuts Halloween Aquarium Car, 12		85
___	29877	Southern Crane Car "D76," CC, 08		350
___	29882	Witches Operating Brew Car, 08		150
___	29884	CNJ Twin Dump Car, 08		85
___	29885	BN Crane Car "S-104," CC, 10		340
___	29886	BN Boom Car "S-1040," CC, 10		220
	29888	Postwar "3494-625" Soo Lines Operating Boxcar, 08		70
	29893	PRR Operating Stock Car "129893," RailSounds, 09		150
___	29894	Christmas Chase Gondola, 09		65
___	29895	Christmas Operating Snow Globe Car, 10		75
___	29897	CSX Chessie System Research Car "3440," 11		65
___	29900	"I Love Wisconsin" Boxcar, 01		35
___	29901	"I Love Kentucky" Boxcar, 01		30
___	29902	"I Love Iowa" Boxcar, 01		31
___	29903	"I Love Missouri" Boxcar, 01		31
___	29904	2002 Toy Fair Boxcar, 02		22
___	29906	"I Love Connecticut" Boxcar, 02		33
___	29907	"I Love West Virginia" Boxcar, 02		33
___	29908	"I Love Delaware" Boxcar, 02		33
___	29909	"I Love Maryland" Boxcar, 02		65
___	29910	Toy Fair Centennial Boxcar, 03		40
___	29912	"I Love Alabama" Boxcar, 03		30
___	29913	"I Love Mississippi" Boxcar, 03		35
___	29914	"I Love Louisiana" Boxcar, 03		35
___	29915	"I Love Arkansas" Boxcar, 03		30
___	29918	2003 Toy Fair Boxcar, 03		48
___	29919	2004 Toy Fair Boxcar, 04		37
___	29920	"I Love North Dakota" Boxcar, 03		35
___	29921	"I Love South Dakota" Boxcar, 03		40
___	29922	"I Love Nebraska" Boxcar, 03		30
___	29923	"I Love Kansas" Boxcar, 03		30
___	29925	Toy Fair Polar Express Boxcar, 05		250
___	29927	"I Love Washington" Boxcar, 05		45
___	29928	"I Love Oregon" Boxcar, 05		40
___	29929	"I Love Idaho" Boxcar, 05		45
___	29930	"I Love Utah" Boxcar, 05		45
___	29932	"I Love Oklahoma" Boxcar, 06		45
___	29933	"I Love New Mexico" Boxcar, 06		45
___	29934	"I Love Hawaii" Boxcar, 06		45
___	29935	"I Love Alaska" Boxcar, 06		45
___	29936	"I Love Wyoming" Boxcar, 06		45
___	29937	2006 Toy Fair Boxcar, 06		38
___	29942	Santa Fe Railroad Art Boxcar, 06		50
___	29943	Texas Special Railroad Art Boxcar, 06		50
___	29944	1957 Lionel Art Boxcar, 06		50
___	29945	1947 Lionel Art Boxcar, 06		50
	29949	Weyerhaeuser Timber Skeleton Log Car 3-pack #2 (std O), 03		90
___	29950	1948 Lionel Art Boxcar, 08		50
___	29951	1954 Lionel Art Boxcar, 08		50

29952	GN Art Boxcar, *08*	50____
29953	SP Art Boxcar, *08*	50____
29954	Dealer Christmas Boxcar, *07*	75____
29955	Dealer Boxcar, *08*	75____
29958	Dealer Boxcar, *09*	50____
29959	1952 Lionel Art Boxcar, *09*	58____
29960	Rock Island Art Boxcar, *09–10*	58____
29961	Meet the Beatles Boxcar 2-pack, *10–14*	130____
29965	Lionel Art Boxcar 2-pack, *10–11*	116____
29968	Beatles "A Hard Day's Night" Boxcar, *11–14*	65____
29969	Beatles "Something New" Boxcar, *11–14*	65____
29973	NYC Pacemaker Boxcar "175005," *11*	60____
29974	SP Boxcar "128133," *11*	60____
29975	Holiday Boxcar, *11*	60____
29976	Holiday Boxcar, *12–13*	65____
29978	Railroad Museum of Pennsylvania Boxcar, *12*	65____
29979	Angela Trotta Thomas "Christmas Morning" Boxcar, *12–13*	60____
29980	Elvis Presley 35th Anniversary Boxcar, *12*	70____
29982	CV Milk Car "575" (std O), *16*	80____
29985	B&M Milk Car "1903" (std O), *16*	80____
29989	PFE Steel-sided Refrigerator Car 3-pack (std O), *14–15*	240____
29994	U.S. Army Boxcar, *13–15*	70____
29995	U.S. Navy Boxcar, *13–15*	70____
29996	U.S. Marines Boxcar, *13–15*	70____
29997	U.S. Air Force Boxcar, *13–15*	70____
29998	U.S. National Guard Boxcar, *13–16*	70____
29999	U.S. Coast Guard Boxcar, *13–16*	70____
30000	PRR Keystone Super Freight Steam Train, TMCC, *05*	450____
30001	Santa Fe El Capitan Passenger Set, TrainSounds, *05–10*	370____
30002	Neil Young's Greendale Diesel Freight Set, *04*	420____
30003	Pennsylvania Flyer Operating Freight Expansion Pack, *05*	99____
30004	Pennsylvania Flyer Passenger Expansion Pack, *05–08*	120____
30005	Disney Passenger Train, *05*	190____
30007	NYC Flyer Operating Freight Expansion Pack, *05*	99____
30008	NYC Flyer Passenger Expansion Pack, *05–08*	120____
30011	Holiday Expansion Pack, *05*	100____
30012	Thomas the Tank Engine Expansion Pack, *05–13, 16*	150____
30016	NYC Flyer Steam Freight Set, *06–08*	290____
30018	Pennsylvania Flyer Steam Freight Set, *06–07*	200____
30020	North Pole Central Christmas Steam Train, *06–07*	220____
30021	Cascade Range Steam Logging Train, *06–08*	190____
30022	Southwest Diesel Freight Set, TrainSounds, *06*	295____
30024	UP Fast Freight Steam Set, TrainSounds, *06–07*	340____
30025	Chesapeake Super Freight Steam Set, TMCC, *06–07*	475____
30026	CP Diesel Freight Set, TMCC, *06*	540____
30034	Great Western Train Set with Lincoln Logs, *07–09*	230____

		Exc	Mint
____30035	Sodor Freight Expansion Pack, *06–09*		120
____30036	Great Western Expansion Pack, *07–08*		120
30037	Pennsylvania Flyer Operating Freight Expansion Pack, *06–08*		120
30038	NYC Flyer Operating Freight Expansion Pack, *06–08*		120
30039	North Pole Central Passenger Expansion Pack, *06–11*		110
____30040	North Pole Central Freight Expansion Pack, *06–11*		110
____30041	Southwest Diesel Freight Expansion Pack, *06*		110
____30042	Cascade Range Expansion Pack, *06*		110
____30044	NYC Empire Builder Steam Freight Set, TMCC, *06*		2800
____30045	Alaska Steam Work Train, *07–09*		270
____30046	Alaska Work Train Expansion Pack, *07–08*		110
30047	Northwest Special Diesel Freight Set, TrainSounds, *07–08*		295
____30048	Northwest Special Freight Expansion Pack, *07–08*		110
____30049	D&RGW Fast Freight Set, TrainSounds, *08–09*		320
____30050	Pennsylvania Super Freight Set, CC, *08*		450
____30051	UP Diesel Freight Set, TMCC, *07*		500
____30056	Halloween Steam Freight Set, *07–10*		220
____30061	UPS Centennial Stream Freight Set, *07–08*		230
____30064	Pennsylvania Speeder Set, traditional, K-Line, *06*		75
____30065	Best Friend of Charleston Locomotive, *07*		425
30066/67	C&O Empire Builder Steam Freight Set, CC, *07–09*		2700
____30068	North Pole Central Christmas Freight Set, *08*		220
____30069	Thomas & Friends Passenger Train, *08–12*		170
____30070	Lionel Lines 4-4-2 Steam Freight Set, *07*		300
____30076	Disney Christmas Train, *07*		400
____30081	UP Merger Special GP38 Freight Set, *08*		300
____30082	UP Heritage Freight Car 3-pack, *08*		100
30084	British Great Western Shakespeare Express Passenger Train, *08*		300
____30085	MTA Metro-North M-7 Commuter Car Set, *07–08*		280
____30087	Alien Spaceship Recovery Freight Set, *08–09*		230
____30088	John Bull Passenger Train, *08*		430
____30089	Pennsylvania Flyer Freight Set, *08–10*		200
____30091	ATSF Steam Freight Set, *08–09*		270
____30094	Chicago & North Western Passenger Set, *08*		150
30096	Pennsylvania Keystone Special Steam Freight Set, *09*		260
____30103	NYC 0-8-0 Steam Freight Set, *09–10*		300
30108	American Fire and Rescue GP20 Freight Set, *09–10*		400
____30109	Nutcracker Route Christmas Train Set, *10–11*		270
____30111	Pullman Passenger Expansion Pack, *09–16*		155
____30112	Eastern Freight Expansion Pack, *09–16*		155
____30114	MTA LIRR M-7 Commuter Set, *09*		320
____30116	Lone Ranger Wild West Freight Set, *09–13*		400
____30118	A Christmas Story Steam Freight Set, *09–12*		330
____30120	Menards C&NW Steam Passenger Set, *09*		250
____30121	ATSF Baby Madison Car 3-pack, *10–11*		190
____30122	Wizard of Oz Steam Freight Set, *10–12*		310

MODERN ERA 1970-2017

		Exc	Mint
30123	Boy Scouts of America Steam Freight Set, *10*		310
30124	Thunder Valley Quarry Steam Freight Set, *10–11*		300
30125	Rio Grande Ski Train, TrainSounds, *10–11*		340
30126	Pennsylvania Flyer Steam Freight Set, *10*		230
30127	Scout Steam Freight Set, *10–12*		200
30128	Western Freight Expansion Pack, *10–12*		138
30131	Chessie System Merger Diesel Freight Set, *10*		300
30133	Strasburg Steam Passenger Set, *10–13*		330
30135	Scout Freight Expansion Pack, *11–15*		115
30136	Thunder Valley Quarry Freight Car Add-on 2-pack, *10–11*		110
30138	Chessie System Merger Freight Car Add-on 2-pack, *10–11*		120
30139	Santa Fe Flyer Steam Freight Set, *10*		270
30141	Sodor Tank and Wagon Expansion Pack, *10–16*		150
30142	Texas Special Freight Set, TrainSounds, *10–11*		700
30144	Operation Eagle Justice Diesel Freight Set, *10–11*		500
30145	Maple Leaf Diesel Freight Set, *10–11*		550
30146	Menards Soo Line Freight Set, *10*	175	275
30147	MTA Long Island M-7 Commuter Set, *11*		320
30153	CSX Diesel Freight Set, *11*		330
30154	BNSF Diesel Freight Set, *11*		340
30155	M&StL Diesel Freight Set, *11–12*		230
30156	NYC Flyer Freight Set, TrainSounds, *11*		300
30157	M&StL Flatcar and Erie-Lack. Gondola 2-pack, *11–15*		110
30158	Norfolk Southern GP38 Diesel Freight Train Set, *11*		320
30159	Wabash Blue Bird Passenger Set, *11–12*		360
30161	Boy Scouts Steam Freight Set, *11–13*		320
30162	Thomas & Friends Christmas Set, *13–15*		200
30164	Santa's Flyer Steam Freight Set, *11–13*		250
30165	Candy Cane Transit Commuter 2-pack, *11–13*		180
30166	Coca-Cola 125th Anniversary Steam Set, *11–12*		350
30167	SP Merger Steam Freight Train Set, *12*		400
30168	Rio Grande General Set, TrainSounds, *11–12*		300
30169	NJ Transit Train Set, *11*		350
30170	Sodor Freight 3-pack, *11–13*		100
30171	GG1 Electric Freight Train Set, *11–13*		550
30173	Santa Fe Flyer Freight Set, *11–12*		270
30174	Pennsylvania Flyer Freight Set, *11–13*		290
30178	ATSF Super Chief Diesel Passenger Train Set, *12–13*		400
30179	RI Rocket Diesel Freight Train Set, *12–13*		400
30180	Horseshoe Curve Steam Freight Train Set, *12–13*		440
30181	CP Diesel Passenger Set, RailSounds, *13, 15*		450
30183	Scout Remote Steam Freight Set, *13, 15*		220
30184	Polar Express Steam Freight Set, *13*		420
30185	NJ Transit Diesel MOW Train Set, *12–13*		350
30186	KCS Southern Belle Diesel Freight Train Set, *12–13*		350
30187	Titanic Centennial Diesel Freight Train Set, *12–13*		430
30188	UP Flyer Steam Freight Train Set, *12–13*		330

			Exc	Mint
____	30189	LIRR Diesel Passenger Train Set, *12–13*		330
____	30190	LionChief Thomas & Friends Set, *12–16*		200
____	30191	Sodor Work Set 3-pack, *12–15*		100
____	30193	Peanuts Christmas Steam Freight Set, *12–15*		370
____	30194	North Pole Express Steam Freight Set, *12–13*		290
____	30195	Grand Central Express Diesel Passenger Train Set, *12–14*		440
____	30196	Hershey's Steam Freight Train Set, *12–13*		312
____	30200	NYC Flyer Steam Freight Train Set, *12–13*		350
____	30205	Silver Bells Christmas Steam Freight Set, *513–14*		240
____	30206	Area 51 RS3 Diesel Freight Set, *13*		250
____	30207	Santa Fe RS3 Diesel Freight Set, *13*		200
____	30210	CP Rail Grain SetDiesel Freight Set, *13*		390
____	30211	BNSF Maxi Stack Diesel Freight Set, *13*		440
____	30213	Northeast NS Heritage Diesel Freight Set, *13*		410
____	30214	Peanuts Halloween Steam Freight Set, *13, 15–16*		320
____	30217	SP Black Widow Diesel Freight Set, *13, 15*		460
____	30218	Polar Express Steam Passenger Set, *13–16*		400
____	30219	Gingerbread Junction Steam Freight Set, *13–14*		290
____	30220	Polar Express 10th Anniversary Passenger Set, *13–14, 16*		500
____	30221	Diesel Remote Control Set, *13–16*		200
____	30222	Percy Remote Control Set, *13–15*		200
____	30223	James Remote Control Set, *13–15*		200
____	30224	Pennsylvania Limited Steam Passenger Set, *13*		340
____	30225	Medal of Honor Train, *13*		430
____	30226	NS Diesel Freight Set, RailSounds, *13*		410
____	30228	Chattanooga Express Steam Passenger Set, *13*		250
____	30233	Pennsylvania Flyer Remote Steam Freight Set, *13–16*		280
____	31569	Western & Atlantic Passenger Car 2-pack, *08*		100
____	31700	Postwar Girls Freight Set, *01*		570
____	31701	Postwar Boys Freight Set, *02*		345
____	31704	Alton Limited Steam Passenger Set, *02*		870
____	31705	50th Anniversary Hudson Passenger Set, *02*		910
____	31706	UP Burro Crane Set, *02*		210
____	31707	C&O Diesel Freight Set, *03*		280
____	31708	Postwar "1805" Marines Missile Launch Train, *03*		400
____	31710	BN Diesel Coal Train, RailSounds, *03*		690
____	31711	Postwar "1563W" Wabash Diesel Freight Set, RailSounds, *03*		570
____	31712	UP Alco PA Diesel Passenger Set, RailSounds, *03*		1495
____	31713	Southern Crescent Limited Steam Passenger Set, RailSounds, *03*		1195
____	31714	Amtrak Acela Diesel Passenger Set, RailSounds, *04–05*		2000
____	31715	Fire Rescue Steam Freight Set, *02*		296
____	31716	Fire Rescue Steam Freight Set, *03*		275
____	31717	CP Rail Snow Removal Train, *03*		255
____	31718	SP "Oil Can" Tank Train Freight Set, *03*		1600
____	31719	Western Maryland Fireball Diesel Freight Set, *04*		290
____	31720	FEC Champion Diesel Passenger Set, RailSounds, *04*		900

Exc Mint

No.	Description	Exc	Mint
31721	Postwar "13138" Majestic Electric Freight Set, RailSounds, *04*		580____
31724	Nabisco 3-car Passenger Set, *03*		110____
31727	Postwar "2291W" Rio Grande Diesel Freight Set, RailSounds, *04*		640____
31728	Elvis "He Dared to Rock" Steam Freight Set, *04*		325____
31730	Norman Rockwell Boxcar 4-pack, *05*		95____
31733	Jones & Laughlin Steel Slag Train, *05*		250____
31734	Chessie Steam Special Passenger Set, TMCC, *05*		405____
31735	Chessie Diesel Freight Set, TMCC, *05–06*		670____
31736	CP Diesel Grain Train, TMCC, *05*		700____
31737	Napa Valley Wine Train, TMCC, *05*		900____
31739	Postwar "13150" Hudson Steam Freight Set, Super O, *05*		940____
31740	Postwar "2519W" Virginian Diesel Freight Set, TMCC, *05–07*		620____
31742	Postwar "2544W" Santa Fe Super Chief Diesel Passenger Set, *05*		700____
31746	GN Mountain Mover Steam Freight Set, *12–13*		430____
31747	Pennsylvania Electric Ballast Train, TMCC, *06*		550____
31748	Santa Fe U28CG Diesel Freight Set (std O), TMCC, *06–07*		770____
31749	Pennsylvania Diesel Coal Train, TMCC, *06*		770____
31750	NYC Hotbox Reefer Steam Freight Set, TMCC, *06–07*		530____
31751	New York City Transit Authority R27 Subway Train, CC, *07*		700____
31752	B&O Diesel Freight Set, TMCC, *06–07*		740____
31753	GN Diesel Freight Set, TMCC, *06–08*		740____
31754	Postwar "2545WS" N&W Space Freight Set, TMCC, *06–07*		960____
31755	Texas Special Diesel Passenger Set, CC, *07–08*		1280____
31757	Postwar "2289WS" Berkshire Freight Set, CC, *07*		750____
31758	Postwar "2270W" Jersey Central Diesel Passenger Car Set, CC, *08*		750____
31760	CSX SD40-2 Diesel Husky Stack Car Set, CC, *07–08*		770____
31765	Postwar "11268" C&O Diesel Freight Set, *08*		580____
31767	Bethlehem Steel Rolling Stock Set, K-Line, *06*		100____
31768	B&O Rolling Stock Set, K-Line, *06*		100____
31772	Conrail LionMaster Diesel Freight Set, CC, *08–09*		535____
31773	NS Dash 9 Diesel TankTrain Set, CC, *08*		785____
31774	AEC Burro Crane Set, traditional, *09–11*		260____
31775	"1562" Burlington GP Passenger Set, *08*		470____
31776	"2219W" Lackawanna Train Master Freight Set, *08*		415____
31777	"2124W" GG1 Passenger Set, *08*		470____
31778	"1484WS" Steam Passenger Set, *08*		610____
31779	Amtrak HHP-8 Amfleet Passenger Set, CC, *09*		500____
31782	ATSF Crane Car and Boom Car, CC (std O), *09–10*		560____
31783	BNSF Ice Cold Express Diesel Freight Set, CC, *10*		1000____
31784	No. 1593 UP Work Train Set, *09*		470____
31787	CN SD70M-2 Diesel Coal Train, CC, *09*		800____
31790	PRR GG1 Passenger Set, *10*		500____

		Exc	Mint
____31791	NYC LionMaster Diesel Freight Set, CC, *10*		700
31793	White Pass & Yukon Freight Car Add-on 3-pack, *10–11, 13*		195
____31795	Pere Marquette Freight Car 3-pack (std O), *10–11*		210
____31796	Feather Route Freight Car 3-pack (std O), *10–11*		210
____31797	New York City Transit R16 Subway Set, CC, *10*		800
____31799	GN Empire Steam Freight Express Set, *10*		430
____31901	Christmas Steam Freight Set, *02*		145
____31902	PRR K4 Freight Set, *01–02*		580
____31904	C&O Steam Freight Set, RailSounds, *01*		400
____31905	NH Diesel Freight Set, CC, *01*		660
____31907	PRR Atlantic Freight Set, *01 u*		400
____31908	Reading Hobo Express Freight Set, *01 u*		365
____31909	Santa Fe Shell Tank Car Freight Set, *01 u*		320
____31910	Soo Line Diesel Freight Set, *01 u*		350
____31911	Snap-On Anniversary Steam Freight Set, *00 u*		600
____31913	PRR Flyer Steam Freight Set, *01*		145
____31914	NYC Flyer Steam Freight Set, RailSounds, *01–02*		170
____31915	Chessie GP38 Diesel Freight Set, *01–02*		155
____31916	Santa Fe Steam Freight Set, *01*		300
____31918	C&O Steam Freight Set, SignalSounds, *01*		315
____31919	T&P Steam Passenger Set, RailSounds, *01*		210
____31920	L.L. Bean Freight Set, *01 u*		250
____31922	Snap-On Tool Diesel Freight Set, *01 u*		352
____31923	PRR Flyer Freight Set, *01 u*		130
____31924	Union Pacific RS3 Diesel Freight Set, *02*		95
____31926	Area 51 FA Diesel Freight Set, *02*		160
____31928	Great Train Robbery Set, *02*		180
____31931	Ballyhoo Brothers Circus Train, *02*		190
____31932	NYC Limited Passenger Set, RailSounds, *02*		285
____31933	Santa Fe Steam Freight Set, RailSounds, *02*		320
31934 ____	Lionel 20th Century Express Steam Freight Set, *00 u*		285
____31936	Pennsylvania Flyer Steam Freight Set, *03–05*		190
____31938	Southern Diesel Freight Set, *03–04*		160
____31939	Great Train Robbery Steam Freight Set, *03*		185
____31940	NYC Flyer Steam Freight Set, RailSounds, *03*		225
____31941	Winter Wonderland Railroad Christmas Train, *03*		150
____31942	Norman Rockwell Christmas Train, *03*		330
31944 ____	NYC Limited Diesel Passenger Set, RailSounds, *03*		250
31945 ____	Santa Fe Steam Super Freight Set, RailSounds, *03*		350
____31946	Disney Christmas Steam Train, *04–05*		310
____31947	World of Disney Steam Freight Set, *03*		215
____31950	Kraft Holiday UP RS3 Diesel Freight Set, *02 u*		149
31952 ____	Great Northern Glacier Route Diesel Freight Set, *03–04*		110
____31953	"Riding the Rails" Hobo Train Set, *03–04*		225
____31956	Thomas the Tank Engine Set, *04–07*		195
____31958	Santa Fe Flyer Steam Freight Set, RailSounds, *04*		205
____31960	Polar Express Steam Passenger Set, *04–13*		420

Exc Mint

		Exc	Mint
31961	Bloomingdale's Pennsylvania Flyer Steam Freight Set, *02 u*		159____
31962	Nickel Plate Road Super Freight Set, RailSounds, *04*		350____
31963	Southern Pacific Overnight Steam Freight Set, *04*		340____
31966	Holiday Tradition Steam Freight Set, *04–05*		210____
31969	NYC Flyer Steam Freight Set, RailSounds, *04*		205____
31976	Yukon Special Diesel Freight Set, *05*		225____
31977	New York Central Flyer Steam Freight Set, *05*		250____
31985	Santa Fe Steam Fast Freight Set, TrainSounds, *05*		320____
31987	Mickey's Holiday Express Train, *04*		275____
31989	UP Overland Freight Express Set, *04*		880____
31990	Copper Range Steam Freight Mine Set, *05*		175____
31993	NS Black Diamond Diesel Freight Set, TMCC, *05*		500____
32900	DC Billboard, *99*		24____
32902	Construction Zone Signs, set of 6, *99–16*		10____
32904	Hellgate Bridge, *99*	235	415____
32905	Irvington Factory, *99–00*		295____
32910	Rotary Coal Tipple with bathtub gondola, *02*		442____
32919	Animated Maiden Rescue, *99*		65____
32920	Animated Pylon with airplane, *99*		130____
32921	Electric Coaling Station, *99–01*		125____
32922	Highway Barrels, set of 6, *99–16*		10____
32923	Accessory Transformer, *99–03, 06–16*		46____
32929	Icing Station with Santa, *99*		90____
32930	Power Supply Setwith ZW controller and 2 power supplies, *99–02, 06–09*	240	425____
32933	Christmas Stocking Hanger Set, 4-piece, *99–00*		50____
32934	Stocking Hanger, gondola, *99–00*		15____
32935	Stocking Hanger, boxcar, *99–00*		15____
32960	Hindenburger Cafe, *99*		195____
32961	Route 66 UFO Cafe, *99*		200____
32987	Hobo Campfire, *99–00*	25	45____
32988	Postwar "192" Railroad Control Tower, *99–00*		75____
32989	Postwar "464" Sawmill, *99–00*		75____
32990	Linex Oil Derrick, *99–00*		55____
32991	WLLC Radio Station, *99*		65____
32996	Postwar "362" Barrel Loader, *00*		125____
32997	Aluminum Rico Station, *00*		300____
32998	Hobby Shop, *99–00*		300____
32999	Hellgate Bridge, *99–00*		350____
33000	GP9 Diesel "3000," RailScope video camera system, *88–90*	125	170____
33002	RailScope Television Monitor, *88–90*	45	70____
34102	Amtrak Shelter, *04–08*		25____
34108	Lionelville Suburban House, *03*		20____
34109	Lionelville Large Suburban House, *03*		15____
34110	Lionelville Estate House, *03*		30____
34111	Lionelville Deluxe Fieldstone House, *03*		17____
34112	Lionelville Fieldstone House, *03*		17____
34113	Lionelville Large Suburban House, *03*		17____
34114	Late Illuminated Station and Terrace, red trim, *03*		475____

			Exc	Mint
	34117	Early Illuminated Station and Terrace, green trim, 03		475
	34120	TMCC Direct Lockon, 04–16		50
	34121	Lionelville Bungalow, 04		20
	34122	Lionelville Bungalow with garage, 04		20
	34123	Lionelville Bungalow with addition, 04		20
	34124	Lionelville Anastasia's Bakery, 04		20
	34125	Lionelville Cotton's Candy, 04		20
	34126	Lionelville Market, 04		20
	34127	Lionelville O'Grady's Tavern, 04		22
	34128	Lionelville Pharmacy, 04		15
	34129	Lionelville Kiddie City Toy Store, 04		20
	34130	Lionelville Jim's 5&10, 04		25
	34131	Lionelville Al's Hardware, 04		30
	34144	Santa Fe Scrap Yard, 05–06		80
	34145	New Haven Scrap Yard, 06		100
	34149	Sly Fox and the Hunter, 05–07		80
	34150	Reading Room, 05–06		70
	34158	Ring Toss Midway Game, 05–06		20
	34159	Camel Race Midway Game, 05–06		20
	34162	Operating Oil Pump, 04–09		53
	34163	Speeder Shed, 04–06		30
	34164	Nutcracker Operating Gateman, 05–08		80
	34190	Carousel, 04–06		165
	34191	Hobo Depot, 04–05		70
	34192	Operating Lumberjacks, 04–06		60
	34193	UPS Animated Billboard, 04		30
	34194	UPS Package Station, 05		120
	34195	UPS People Pack, 06–09, 11		27
	34210	TMCC Direct Lockon, 09		52
	34500	Rio Grande FT Diesel "5484," traditional, 06		245
	34501	Southern FT Diesel "4102," traditional, 06		400
	34504	B&O F3 Diesel A Unit "2368," nonpowered, 06–07		200
	34505	B&O E7 Diesel AA Set, CC, 07		700
	34508	PRR E7 Diesel AA Set, CC, 07		700
	34509	PRR E7 Diesel B Unit, nonpowered (std O), 07		170
	34510	PRR E7 Diesel B Unit, powered, CC, 07		300
	34511	NYC F7 Diesel ABA Set, CC, 07–08		900
	34512	NYC F7 Diesel B Unit "2439," powered, CC, 07–08		300
	34513	WP F7 Diesel ABA Set, CC, 07–08		900
	34514	WP F7 Diesel B Unit "918C," powered, CC, 07–08		300
	34515	NYC F7 Diesel Breakdown B Unit "2440," RailSounds, 07		270
	34518	PRR E7 Diesel Breakdown B Unit, RailSounds, 07		270
	34519	NYC Sharknose RF-16 Diesel AA Set, CC, 07–08		630
	34520	NYC Sharknose Diesel B Unit "3818," nonpowered (std O), 07–08		160
	34521	Santa Fe F3 Diesel A Unit "17," traditional, 07		265
	34522	Santa Fe F3 Diesel B Unit "17," nonpowered (std O), 07		150
	34544	ATSF F3 Diesel B Unit, CC, 08		270

Exc Mint

No.	Description	Exc	Mint
34545	D&RGW F3 Diesel B Unit, CC, *08*	270	
34546	Southern F3 Diesel B Unit, CC, *08*	270	
34547	Texas Special F3 Diesel B Unit, CC, *08*	270	
34559	Archive New Haven F3 Diesel AA Set, *10*	500	
34564	SP Alco PA Diesel AA Set, CC, *10–11*	750	
34567	SP Alco PB B Unit, CC, *10–11*	400	
34568	ATSF Alco PA AA Diesel Set, CC, *11*	750	
34569	ATSF Alco PB Diesel, CC, *11*	400	
34570	B&O FA Diesel AA Set, CC, *10*	650	
34573	Postwar Scale ATSF F3 AA Diesel Set, CC, *11*	700	
34576	Postwar Scale NYC F3 AA Diesel Set, CC, *11*	700	
34579	Postwar Scale ATSF F3 B Unit, CC, *11*	380	
34580	Postwar Scale NYC F3 B Unit, CC, *11*	380	
34581	Postwar "2331" Virginian Train Master Diesel, CC, *10*	495	
34582	Postwar "2373" CP F3 Diesel AA Set, CC, *10*	700	
34585	Postwar "2375" CP F3 B Unit, CC, *10*	380	
34586	Postwar "2378" MILW F3 Diesel AB Set, CC, *10*	700	
34589	Postwar "2377" MILW F3 A, powered, CC, *10*	425	
34594	UP Alco PA AA Diesel Set, CC, *11*	750	
34597	UP Alco PB Diesel, CC, *11*	400	
34600	SP GP30 Diesel "5010," CC, *11*	500	
34601	SP GP30 Diesel "5012," CC, *11*	500	
34602	SP GP30 Diesel "5014," *11*	380	
34603	SP GP30 Diesel "5017," nonpowered, *11*	240	
34604	Conrail GP30 Diesel "2178," CC, *11*	500	
34605	Conrail GP30 Diesel "2180," CC, *11*	500	
34606	Conrail GP30 Diesel "2182," *11*	380	
34607	Conrail GP30 Diesel "2185," nonpowered, *11*	240	
34608	Lionelville & Western GP30 Diesel "1100," CC, *11*	450	
34609	Lionelville & Western GP30 Diesel "1103," CC, *11*	450	
34610	Lionelville & Western GP30 Diesel "1107," *11*	330	
34611	Lionelville & Western GP30 Diesel "1112," nonpowered, *11*	190	
34612	NS SD70M-2 Diesel "2658," CC, *11*	550	
34613	NS SD70M-2 Diesel "2663," CC, *11*	550	
34614	CN SD70M-2 Diesel "8020," CC, *11*	550	
34615	CN SD70M-2 Diesel "8024," CC, *11*	550	
34616	FEC SD70M-2 Diesel "101," CC, *11*	550	
34617	FEC SD70M-2 Diesel "103," CC, *11*	550	
34618	George Bush SD70ACe Diesel "4141," CC, *11*	550	
34619	NH SD70ACe Diesel "8696," CC, *11*	550	
34620	NH SD70ACe Diesel "8699," CC, *11*	550	
34623	Texas Special SD70ACe Diesel "6340," CC, *11*	550	
34624	Texas Special SD70ACe Diesel "6344," CC, *11*	550	
34625	NP F3 AA Diesel Set, CC, *11*	700	
34628	NP F3 Diesel B Unit "6005C," CC, *11*	380	
34629	NP F3 Diesel B Unit "6006C," nonpowered, *11*	240	
34630	Frisco F3 AA Diesel Set, CC, *11*	700	
34633	Frisco F3 Diesel B Unit, CC, *11*	380	
34634	Frisco F3 Diesel B Unit, nonpowered, *11*	260	
34635	ATSF F3 AA Diesel Set, CC, *11*	700	
34638	ATSF F3 Diesel B Unit, CC, *11*	380	

		Exc	Mint
____34639	ATSF F3 Diesel B Unit, nonpowered, *11*		240
____34640	GTW F3 AA Diesel Set, CC, *11*		700
____34643	GTW F3 Diesel B Unit, CC, *11*		380
____34644	GTW F3 Diesel B Unit, nonpowered, *11*		260
____34645	CN F3 AA Diesel Set, CC, *11*		700
____34648	CN F3 Diesel B Unit, CC, *11*		380
____34649	CN F3 Diesel B Unit, nonpowered, *11*		260
____34650	MILW DD35A Diesel "1535," CC, *11*		600
____34651	MILW DD35A Diesel "1537," nonpowered, *11*		440
____34662	RI GP9 Diesel "1331," CC, *12–13*		480
____34663	RI GP9 Diesel "1327," CC, *12–13*		480
____34664	GN GP9 Diesel "688," CC, *12–13*		480
____34665	GN GP9 Diesel "695," CC, *12–13*		480
____34666	L&N GP9 Diesel "504," CC, *12–13*		480
____34667	L&N GP9 Diesel "525," CC, *12–13*		480
____34668	CN GP90 Diesel "4463," CC, *12*		480
____34669	CN GP90 Diesel "4455," CC, *12*		480
____34670	C&O GP9 Diesel "6240," CC, *12–13*		480
____34671	C&O GP9 Diesel "6243," CC, *12*		480
____34672	PRR Baldwin Centipede Diesel AA, CC, *12–13*		2200
____34673	UP Baldwin Centipede Diesel AA, CC, *12*		2200
34676	PRR Baldwin Centipede Diesel "5821," CC, *12–14*		1100
34677	Seaboard Baldwin Centipede Diesel "4503," CC, *12–14*		1100
34680	NdeM Baldwin Centipede Diesel "6402," CC, *12–14*		1100
____34681	UP GP9 Diesel "256," CC, *12*		480
____34682	UP GP9 Diesel "261," CC, *12*		480
____34683	PRR Baldwin Centipede Diesel AA, CC, *12–13*		2200
____34686	Baldwin Demonstrator Centipede AA, CC, *12*		2200
____34689	WM F7 AA Diesel Set, CC, *12–13*		730
____34692	WM F7 B Unit "410," CC, *12–13*		400
____34693	WM F7 B Unit, *12–13*		250
____34694	L&N F7 AA Diesel Set, CC, *12*		730
____34697	L&N F7 B Unit "900," CC, *12–13*		400
____34698	L&N F7 B Unit, *12–13*		250
____34701	PRR Baldwin RF-16 Diesel AA Set, CC, *12–14*		730
____34704	PRR Baldwin RF-16 Diesel B Unit, CC, *12–14*		400
34705	PRR Baldwin RF-16 Diesel B Unit, nonpowered, *12–14*		250
____34731	NH Alco RS-11 Diesel "1413," nonpowered, *12*		240
____34732	LV Alco RS-11 Diesel "7640," CC, *12*		480
____34733	LV Alco RS-11 Diesel "7642," CC, *12*		480
____34734	LV Alco RS-11 Diesel "7643," nonpowered, *12*		240
____34735	ATSF GP9 Diesel "726," CC, *12*		480
____34736	ATSF GP9 Diesel "741," CC, *12*		480
____34737	NP GP9 Diesel "202," CC, *12*		480
____34738	NP GP9 Diesel "317," CC, *12–13*		480
____34739	RI GP9 Diesel "1325," nonpowered, *12*		240
____34740	GN GP9 Diesel "668," nonpowered, *12*		240
____34741	L&N GP9 Diesel "531," nonpowered, *12*		240
____34742	CN GP90 Diesel "4527," nonpowered, *12*		240

Exc Mint

		Exc	Mint
34743	C&O GP9 Diesel "6249," nonpowered, *12*	240	___
34744	UP GP9 Diesel "268," nonpowered, *12*	240	___
34745	Monon Alco C-420 Diesel "509," CC, *12–13*	530	___
34746	Monon Alco C-420 Diesel "512," CC, *12–13*	530	___
34747	Monon Alco C-420 Diesel "514," nonpowered, *12–13*	260	___
34748	LV Alco C-420 Diesel "404," CC, *12*	530	___
34749	LV Alco C-420 Diesel "412," CC, *12*	530	___
34750	LV Alco C-420 Diesel "414," nonpowered, *12*	260	___
34754	Alaska Alco C-420 Diesel "1210," CC, *12*	530	___
34755	Alaska Alco C-420 Diesel "1214," CC, *12*	530	___
34756	Alaska Alco C-420 Diesel "1217," nonpowered, *12*	260	___
34757	Seaboard Alco C-420 Diesel "127," CC, *12–13*	530	___
34758	Seaboard Alco C-420 Diesel "129," CC, *12–13*	530	___
34759	Seaboard Alco C-420 Diesel "134," nonpowered, *12–13*	260	___
34760	NKP Alco C-420 Diesel "578," CC, *12–13*	530	___
34761	NKP Alco C-420 Diesel "575," CC, *12–13*	530	___
34762	NKP Alco C-420 Diesel "572," nonpowered, *12–13*	260	___
34763	CNJ Scale NW2 Diesel Switcher "1060," CC, *12*	470	___
34764	CNJ Scale NW2 Diesel Switcher "1061," CC, *12*	470	___
34765	KCS Scale NW2 Diesel Switcher "1221," CC, *12*	470	___
34766	KCS Scale NW2 Diesel Switcher "1224," CC, *12*	470	___
34767	L&N Scale NW2 Diesel Switcher "2203," CC, *12*	470	___
34768	L&N Scale NW2 Diesel Switcher "2206," CC, *12*	470	___
34769	MKT Scale NW2 Diesel Switcher "8," CC, *12*	470	___
34770	MKT Scale NW2 Diesel Switcher "12," CC, *12*	470	___
34771	Reading Scale NW2 Diesel Switcher "102," CC, *12*	470	___
34772	Reading Scale NW2 Diesel Switcher "104," CC, *12*	470	___
34773	PRR Scale NW2 Diesel Switcher "9163," CC, *12*	470	___
34774	PRR Scale NW2 Diesel Switcher "9171," CC, *12*	470	___
34775	N&W SD40-2 Diesel "6106," nonpowered, *12–13*	240	___
34776	N&W SD40-2 Diesel "6121," CC, *12–13*	530	___
34777	N&W SD40-2 Diesel "6109," CC, *12–14*	530	___
34778	CSX SD40-2 Diesel "8023," nonpowered, *12–13*	240	___
34779	CSX SD40-2 Diesel "8028," CC, *12–13*	530	___
34780	CSX SD40-2 Diesel "8033," CC, *12–13*	530	___
34781	BN SD40-2 Diesel "7140," nonpowered, *12–13*	240	___
34782	BN SD40-2 Diesel "7153," CC, *12–13*	530	___
34783	BN SD40-2 Diesel "7162," CC, *12–13*	530	___
34784	Frisco SD40-2 Diesel "957," CC, *12–13*	530	___
34785	Frisco SD40-2 Diesel "950," nonpowered, *12–13*	240	___
34786	Frisco SD40-2 Diesel "952," CC, *12–13*	530	___
34787	C&NW SD40-2 Diesel "6816," nonpowered, *12–13*	240	___
34788	C&NW SD40-2 Diesel "6820," CC, *12–13*	530	___
34789	C&NW SD40-2 Diesel "6832," CC, *12–13*	530	___
34790	MKT SD40-2 Diesel "602," nonpowered, *12–13*	240	___
34791	MKT SD40-2 Diesel "609," CC, *12–13*	530	___
34792	MKT SD40-2 Diesel "620," CC, *12–13*	530	___

			Exc	Mint
___	35100	NYC Vista Dome Car "7012," *07–09*		45
___	35101	NYC Baggage Car "5028," *07*		40
___	35102	Santa Fe El Capitan Streamliner Diner, *07*		65
	35124	Alton Limited Madison Passenger Car 4-pack, *08–10*		240
___	35128	ATSF El Capitan Baggage Car "2103," *08*		70
___	35129	ATSF El Capitan Vista Dome Car "3153," *08*		70
___	35130	Polar Express Disappearing Hobo Car, *08–14, 16*		75
	35133	MTA Metro-North M-7 Commuter Add-on 2-pack, *07–08*		85
___	35134	North Pole Central Vista Dome Car, *08*		45
___	35135	North Pole Central Diner, *08–10*		45
___	35167	PRR Diner "2044," *10*		52
___	35168	PRR Coach "4046," *09*		52
___	35173	North Pole Central Blitzen Coach, *09*		45
___	35174	MTA LIRR M-7 Add-on 2-pack, *09*		98
___	35184	Western & Atlantic Baggage Car, *09*		60
___	35185	Great Western Passenger Car 2-pack, *09*		100
___	35193	PRR Streamliner 4-pack, *10–11*		250
___	35200	Strasburg Observation Car, *10*		60
___	35205	D&RGW Pikes Peak Add-on Coach, *10–11*		70
___	35211	Strasburg Passenger Car Add-on 2-pack, *10*		100
___	35214	Rio Grande Winter Park Diner, *11*		70
___	35219	Hallow's Eve Express Passenger Car 2-pack, *11*		120
___	35229	Hogwarts Express Dementors Coach, *11–15*		60
___	35239	NJ Transit 2-pack Passenger Car Add-on, *11–14*		100
	35247	Grand Central Express Passenger Car 2-pack, *12–13*		140
___	35250	North Pole Coach 2-pack, *12–13*		120
	35256	Hallow's Eve Express Passenger Car 2-pack #2, *12*		120
___	35257	ATSF Vista Dome, *12*		70
___	35258	ATSF Baggage Car, *12–13*		70
___	35259	LIRR Passenger Car 2-pack, *12–15*		110
___	35281	ATSF Super Chief Diner "1495," *13*		70
___	35282	LIRR Jamaica Coach, *13–15*		60
___	35283	CP Baggage Car and Diner 2-pack, *13*		130
___	35286	Peanuts Coach 3-pack, *13*		165
	35290	Polar Express Passenger Car Add-on 2-pack, *13–14, 16*		150
___	35294	Polar Express Snow Tower, *13–14*		28
___	35295	Christmas Billboard Set, *13–14, 16*		13
	35403	NYC 20th Century Limited 18" Aluminum Passenger Car 4-pack (std O), *08*		625
	35408	NYC 20th Century Limited 18" Aluminum Passenger Car 2-pack (std O), *08*		325
	35411	NYC 20th Century Limited Diner, StationSounds (std O), *08*		325
___	35412	Lenny Dean Passenger Coach, *08*		100
___	35413	LL Streamliner Car 2-pack, *08*		270
___	35415	UP 18" Streamliner Car 4-pack (std O), *08*		625
___	35423	UP 18" Streamliner Car 2-pack (std O), *08*		325
___	35430	Amtrak Coach		45
___	35431	Amtrak Coach		45

		Exc	Mint
35432	Amtrak Coach		45____
35433	Amfleet Phase IVB Coach 2-pack (std O), *10*		140____
35445	SP Shasta Daylight 18" Passenger Car 4-pack (std O), *11*		640____
35446	SP Shasta Daylight 18" Passenger Car 2-pack (std O), *11*		320____
35454	Amfleet Cab Control End Car (std O), *10*		250____
35473	Amfleet Capstone Coach 3-pack (std O), *10*		180____
35481	NYC Add-on Passenger Car "M-498," *11*		120____
35490	Alaska Budd RDC Combination Car "702," nonpowered, *11*		130____
35497	RI Budd RDC Combination Car "751," nonpowered, *11*		130____
35498	RI Budd RDC Coach "750," nonpowered, *11*		130____
35499	Alaska Budd RDC Coach "712," nonpowered, *11*		130____
36000	Route 66 Flatcar with 2 red sedans, *98*		44____
36001	Route 66 Flatcar with 2 wagons, *98*		42____
36002	Pratt's Hollow Passenger Car 4-pack, *98*		445____
36006	Uranium Flatcar "6508," *98*		60____
36016	Flatcar with propellers, *98*		45____
36020	Flatcar "TT-6424" with auto frames, *99*		32____
36021	Alaska Flatcar "6424" with airplane, *99*		44____
36024	J.B. Hunt Flatcar "64245" with trailer, *99*		44____
36025	J.B. Hunt Flatcar "64246" with trailer, *99*		50____
36026	Flatcar with J.B. Hunt trailers 2-pack, *99*		85____
36027	Tredegar Iron Works Flatcar with cannon, *99*		45____
36028	Heavy Artillery Flatcar with cannon, *99*		45____
36029	SP Auto Carrier "516712," *99*		44____
36030	Troublesome Truck #1, *99*		35____
36031	Troublesome Truck #2, *99*		35____
36032	Christmas Gondola "6462" with presents, *99*		35____
36036	C&O Gondola, *99*		20____
36038	Construction Zone Gondola, *99 u*		NRS____
36040	Bethlehem Flatcar with block (SSS), *99*		75____
36041	Bethlehem Ore Car (SSS), *99*		40____
36043	Custom Consist Flatcar with pickup truck, *99*		40____
36044	Custom Consist Flatcar with dragster, *99*		40____
36045	Flatcar with dragster, *04*		30____
36046	Flatcar with custom truck, *04*		30____
36047	Construction Zone Gondola, *99 u*		NRS____
36048	Construction Zone Gondola, *99 u*		NRS____
36054	Archaeological Expedition Gondola with eggs, *00 u*		55____
36055	Flatcar with dragster, *01 u*		30____
36056	Flatcar with roadster, *01 u*		30____
36059	"Season's Greetings" Gondola, *99 u*		50____
36062	NYC 6462 Gondola, *99–00*		22____
36063	Conrail Gondola "604768," *99–00*		20____
36064	Billboard Flatcar "6424," *00*		41____
36065	Wabash Flatcar "25536" with trailer, *00*		35____
36066	Christmas Gondola with presents, *00*		32____
36067	King Auto Sales Flatcar "6424" with pink Cadillac, *00*		40____

		Exc	Mint
36068	Pine Peak Tree Transport Gondola, *00*		NRS
36079	Service Station Ltd. Flatcar with trailer, *00*		34
36082	Whirlpool Flatcar with trailer, *00 u*		NRS
36083	Santa Fe Gondola "168998," *01*		17
36084	Grand Trunk Western Coil Car, *00*		32
36085	FEC Coil Car, *00*		29
36086	SP Flatcar with trailer, *01*		35
36087	Flatcar "6424" with wooden whistle, *01*		25
36088	Allis Chalmers Condenser Car "6519," *00*		43
36089	Frisco Flatcar with airplane, *00*		35
36090	TT Flatcar "6424" with Pepsi truck, *01*		44
36091	Maersk Flatcar "250129" with die-cast tractors, *00*		55
36092	Maersk Flatcar "250130" with die-cast frames, *00*		55
36093	Soo TT Auto Carrier "906760," *00*		49
36094	PC F9 Well Car "768122," *01*		41
36095	Christmas Chase Gondola, *01*		37
36098	PRR Gondola "385186," *01*		20
36099	NYC Flatcar with stakes and bulkheads, *01*		25
36104	Area 51 3-D Tank Car, *07*		60
36108	Candy Cane 1-D Tank Car, *07*		60
36112	NP 3-D Tank Car, *08*		35
36113	IC 1-D Tank Car, *08*		35
36114	ART Wood-sided Reefer, *08*		35
36117	Lionel Lines 2-D Tank Car, *08*		50
36118	NYC Pastel Stock Car "63561," *08–09*		55
36128	Texas & Pacific 3-D Tank Car, *09*		40
36129	British Columbia 1-D Tank Car, *09*		40
36131	Lackawanna Wood-sided Reefer "7000," *09–10*		40
36145	Philadelphia Quartz 3-D Tank Car "606," *10*		40
36146	Cities Service 1-D Tank Car "11800," *10*		40
36149	Strasburg Wood-sided Reefer "105," *10*		55
36151	Grave's Blood Bank Tank Car, *10*		50
36156	Pennsylvania Power & Light 1-D Tank Car, *10*		40
36162	Diamond Chemicals 3-D Tank Car, *11*		40
36163	Celanese 2-D Tank Car, *11–12*		40
36166	Polar Express Reefer, *11–12*		55
36169	Coca-Cola 3-D Tank Car, *11*		55
36170	Partridge in a Pear Tree Reefer, *11–13*		55
36172	Bubble Yum 1-D Tank Car, *11*		55
36173	Santa's Flyer Hot Cocoa 3-D Tank Car, *11*		40
36176	C&O 1-D Tank Car, *13*		43
36177	WP 3-D Tank Car, *12*		40
36178	Frisco 2-D Tank Car, *12–13*		40
36182	Eggnog Unibody 1-D Tank Car, *12*		70
36191	GN Waffle-sided Boxcar, *13*		43
36195	PRR Flatcar with patrol helicopter, *13*		60
36200	Quaker Life Cereal Boxcar, *00*		480
36203	Whirlpool Boxcar, *00 u*		120
36205	eBay Boxcar, *00*		270
36206	REA Boxcar, *01*		25
36207	Vapor Records Christmas Boxcar, *01*		78

Exc Mint

		Exc	Mint
36208	Father's Day Boxcar, *00*		35____
36210	Burlington Hi-Cube Boxcar "19825," *01*		40____
36211	NP Hi-Cube Boxcar "659999," *01*		33____
36212	Lionel Employee Christmas Boxcar, *00 u*		410____
36213	Vapor Records Christmas Boxcar, *00*		45____
36215	Train Station 25th Anniversary Boxcar, *00 u*		48____
36218	Snap-On Boxcar, *00 u*		140____
36219	UP Boxcar "183518," *02*		78____
36220	Pioneer Seed Boxcar, *00 u*		NRS____
36221	PRR Boxcar "569356," *01*		20____
36222	NYC Boxcar "162440," *01*		20____
36223	Chessie System Boxcar, *01*		20____
36224	Santa Fe Boxcar "16263," *01*		20____
36225	C&O Boxcar "250549," *01*		20____
36226	E-Hobbies Boxcar, *01 u*		200____
36227	Monopoly Community Chest Boxcar, *00 u*		50____
36228	Lionel Visitor Center Boxcar, *01 u*		34____
36229	Island Trains 20th Anniversary Boxcar, *01 u*		29____
36232	Farmall Boxcar, *01 u*		NRS____
36236	TM Books "I Love Lionel" Boxcar "7474-1," *01 u*		43____
36238	Snap-On Tool Team ASE Racing Boxcar, *01 u*		NRS____
36239	L.L. Bean Boxcar, *01 u*		120____
36240	Do It Best Boxcar, *01 u*		100____
36242	Erie-Lackawanna Boxcar "73113," *02*		24____
36243	Christmas Boxcar "2002," *02*		31____
36244	Teddy Bear Centennial Boxcar, *02*		36____
36245	Lionel 20th Century Boxcar "1900-1925," *00 u*		30____
36246	Lionel 20th Century Boxcar "1926-1950," *00 u*		30____
36247	Lionel 20th Century Boxcar "1951-1975," *00 u*		30____
36248	Lionel 20th Century Boxcar "1976-2000," *00 u*		30____
36253	Christmas Boxcar (O), *03*		32____
36254	Goofy Hi-Cube Boxcar, *03*		37____
36255	Donald Duck Hi-Cube Boxcar, *03*		40____
36256	GN Boxcar "6341," *03*		23____
36261	PRR Boxcar, */03–05*		15____
36262	Southern Central of Georgia Boxcar, *03 04*		20____
36264	Santa Fe Boxcar "600196, *02*		18____
36265	Angela Trotta Thomas "Window Wishing" Boxcar, *02*		38____
36267	Mickey Mouse Hi-Cube Boxcar, *03*		50____
36270	Angela Trotta Thomas "Home for the Holidays" Boxcar, *02–03*		30____
36272	New Haven Boxcar "6501," *04*		20____
36273	Railbox Hi-Cube Boxcar "15000," *04*		21____
36275	Christmas Boxcar, *04*		35____
36276	Angela Trotta Thomas "Tis the Season" Boxcar, *04*		34____
36277	Pluto Hi-Cube Boxcar, *04–05*		50____
36278	Winnie the Pooh Hi-Cube Boxcar, *04–05*		50____
36281	B&O Boxcar, *04*		35____
36291	Simpsons Boxcar, *04–05*		44____
36294	UP Hi-Cube Boxcar, traditional, *05*		27____
36295	CN Boxcar, traditional, *05*		27____

		Exc	Mint
36296	2005 Holiday Boxcar, *05*		48
36297	Angela Trotta Thomas "Christmas Eve" Boxcar, *05*		48
36299	Hammacher Schlemmer Music Boxcar, *04*		65
36305	eBay Boxcar, *00 u*		120
36500	Western Pacific Caboose "36500," *04*		23
36501	D&RGW Caboose "36501," *04*		22
36502	Reading Caboose "36502," *04*		25
36515	North Pole Central Lines Caboose "36515," *04*		36
36519	Lionel Lines Caboose, *04*		22
36520	Santa Fe Caboose "36520," *04*		22
36525	CSX Work Caboose, lighted, *05*		35
36526	Pennsylvania Work Caboose, traditional, *05*		27
36527	Santa Fe Work Caboose, traditional, *05*		28
36528	Chesapeake & Ohio Work Caboose, traditional, *05*		40
36529	North Pole Central Work Caboose with presents, traditional, *05*		38
36530	Pennsylvania Caboose, traditional, *05*		33
36531	Erie Caboose "C150," traditional, *05*		33
36532	SP Caboose "1097," traditional, *05*		48
36533	Reading Caboose "92803," traditional, *05*		33
36534	NYC Center Cupola Caboose, traditional, *05*		40
36535	LL Center Cupola Caboose, traditional, *05*		28
36536	Southern Center Cupola Caboose, traditional, *05*		40
36544	Alaska Caboose, *05*		35
36547	Bethlehem Steel Transfer Caboose, traditional, *05*		40
36548	Transylvania RR Work Caboose, traditional, *05*		45
36550	Halloween Transfer Caboose, traditional, *06–07*		45
36551	Christmas Caboose, *06*		45
36552	U.S. Steel Work Caboose, traditional, *06–07*		45
36553	NYC Caboose, *08*		20
36554	SP Work Caboose, traditional, *06*		45
36555	Pennsylvania Transfer Caboose, *06*		45
36556	Lionel Lines Work Caboose, *06–07*		30
36557	Rio Grande Work Caboose, traditional, *06*		29
36558	Virginian Center Cupola Caboose "316," traditional, *06*		45
36559	WM Center Cupola Caboose "1863," traditional, *06*		45
36560	C&O Center Cupola Caboose "90876," traditional, *06*		45
36562	Army Transportation Work Caboose, traditional, *06*		45
36563	Reading Work Caboose, traditional, *06*		45
36565	UP SP-type Caboose, traditional, *06*		48
36566	NYC SP-type Caboose, traditional, *06*		48
36567	GN SP-type Caboose, traditional, *06*		48
36571	PRR Caboose, *08*		20
36580	B&O Center Cupola Caboose "C2047," traditional, *05*		40
36582	C&O Caboose, *05*		22
36583	Holiday Caboose, *07*		50
36587	SP Caboose "1121," *07–09*		40
36589	PRR Work Caboose, *07*		40

Exc Mint

		Exc	Mint
36590	UP Work Caboose, *07*		45____
36591	Southern Caboose "X99," *08*		45____
36592	Santa Fe Caboose "999471," *06*		48____
36593	NYC Caboose, *06*		48____
36601	UP Caboose, *06*		48____
36602	UPS Centennial Caboose, *06*		45____
36604	Pennsylvania Caboose, *06*		25____
36607	K-Line Caboose, *06*		40____
36611	Conrail Caboose "19674," *07*		40____
36612	Alaska Caboose "1080," *07*		40____
36613	NYC Caboose, *07*		30____
36622	C&O Caboose "C-1838," *08–09*		40____
36623	ATSF Caboose, *07–09*		40____
36624	Lionel Lines Caboose, *08–09*		40____
36625	B&M Caboose, *08*		50____
36626	Erie Caboose "C101," *08–09*		45____
36634	Holiday Porthole Caboose, green, *08*		50____
36646	Monopoly Caboose, *10*		48____
36647	Strasburg Caboose, *10*		48____
36649	Pennsylvania Power & Light Work Caboose, *10*		45____
36657	Western & Atlantic Caboose, *10–11*		48____
36659	PRR Illuminated Porthole Caboose, *11*		35____
36668	CSX Illuminated Square Window Caboose, *10*		35____
36672	NS Caboose, *11*		25____
36674	Polar Caboose, *11–12*		53____
36701	Baldwin Locomotive Works Operating Welding Car "36701," *02*		60____
36702	Bosco Operating Milk Car with platform, *02*		115____
36703	Circus Horse Car with corral, *06*		150____
36704	Animated Reindeer Stock Car and Corral, *02*		145____
36718	AEC Security Caboose, *02*		45____
36719	Lionel Lion Bobbing Head Car, *02*		20____
36720	Aladdin Aquarium Car, *03*		40____
36721	101 Dalmatians Animated Gondola, *03*		45____
36722	Peter Pan Bobbing Head Boxcar, *03*		45____
36726	Santa Fe Searchlight Car "36726," *03*		50____
36727	Weyerhaeuser Moe & Joe Flatcar, *03*		65____
36728	SP Walking Brakeman Boxcar 163143," *03*		42____
36729	Lionel Lines Animated Caboose, *04–05*		68____
36730	U.S. Army Missile Launch Sound Car "44," *03*		175____
36731	Motorized Aquarium Car "3435," *03*		83____
36732	C&NW Jumping Hobo Car, *03*		41____
36733	Christmas Music Boxcar, *03*		45____
36734	Santa Fe Operating Searchlight Car "20611," *02*		25____
36735	WP Ice Car "7045," *02*		55____
36736	D&RGW Stock Car "39268," RailSounds, *04*		45____
36738	T&P Poultry Dispatch Car "36738," *02*		50____
36739	Postwar "3461" Lionel Lines Log Dump Car, *03*		50____
36740	Postwar "3469" Lionel Lines Coal Dump Car, *03*		49____
36743	Santa Claus Bobbing Head Boxcar, *03*		40____
36744	Little Mermaid Aquarium Car, *03*		55____
36745	Toy Story Animated Gondola, *03*		70____

		Exc	Mint
36753	LFD Firecar with ladder, *02*		60
36757	Southern Searchlight Car, *03–04*		NRS
36758	Patriotic Lighted Boxcar, *02*		60
36760	B&O Sentinel Operating Brakeman Boxcar "3424," Archive Collection, *02*		65
36761	Wellspring Capital Management Lighted Boxcar, *02 u*		220
36764	West Side Lumber Log Dump Car "36764," *03*		55
36765	Alaska Coal Dump Car "401," *03*		50
36766	Erie Chase Gondola, *03*		50
36767	Santa's Radar Tracking Car, *03*		40
36769	Fourth of July Lighted Boxcar, *03*		70
36770	American Refrigerator Transit Ice Car "23701," *04*		42
36771	CN Barrel Car "74208," *04*		48
36772	Spokane, Portland & Seattle Log Dump Car "36772," *04*		46
36773	Jersey Central Coal Dump Car "92926," *04*		45
36774	PRR Moe & Joe Lumber Flatcar, *04*		50
36775	Santa Fe Animated Caboose "999010," *05*		75
36776	Santa Fe Walking Brakeman Car "19938," *04*		43
36778	C&O Searchlight Car "216614," *04*		30
36780	Sea-Monkeys Motorized Aquarium Car, *04*		45
36781	Finding Nemo Aquarium Car, *04*		50
36782	Goofy and Pete Jumping Boxcar, *05*		70
36783	Disney Operating Boxcar, *04–05*		65
36784	Monsters Inc. Bobbing Head Boxcar, *04*		40
36786	Postwar "3494-150" MP Operating Boxcar, *03*		40
36787	MOW Remote Control Searchlight Car, *04*		45
36788	Lionel Lines Tender, TrainSounds, *04*		75
36789	Railbox Boxcar, TrainSounds, *04–05*		105
36790	Christmas Music Boxcar, *04*		70
36793	Pennsylvania Derrick Car, *03*		22
36794	NYC Log Dump Car, *03*		25
36795	Southern Coal Dump Car, *03*		25
36796	GN Searchlight Car, *03*		24
36797	"Operation Iraqi Freedom" Minuteman Car, *03*		45
36803	Santa Animated Caboose, *06*		75
36804	Candy Cane Dump Car, *06*		80
36805	Reindeer Jumping Boxcar, *06*		70
36809	NYC Derrick Car, *07–08*		35
36810	PRR Searchlight Car, *07*		35
36811	UP Dump Coal Dump Car, *07*		35
36812	British Columbia Log Dump Car, *07–08*		35
36813	State of Maine Brakeman Car, *08*		80
36814	D&RGW Animated Caboose "01415," *07–09*		80
36815	Santa Fe Moe & Joe Flatcar, *07–08*		80
36816	Virginian Coal Dump Car, *08*		80
36818	U.S. Steel Searchlight Car, *07–08*		75
36821	"Naughty or Nice" Dump Car, *07*		80
36823	Halloween SpookySmoke Boxcar, *07*		115
36824	AlienSmoke Boxcar, *07*		110
36829	Alien Radioactive Car, *07*		70

		Exc	Mint
36830	Trick or Treat Aquarium Car, *07*	75	___
36831	MOW Welding Car, *07–08*	75	___
36833	Christmas Music Boxcar, *07*	65	___
36834	Santa Fe Transparent Instruction Car, *07–08*	65	___
36838	Lionel Power Co. Voltmeter Car, K-Line, *06*	75	___
36839	Operating Milk Car with platform, K-Line, *06*	140	___
36841	Visitor Center 15th Anniversary Lighted Boxcar, *06*	70	___
36847	Polar Express Tender, TrainSounds, *08–14*	130	___
36848	Candy Cane Dump Car, *07*	80	___
36849	Tell-Tale Reindeer Car, *07*	53	___
36850	Santa and Snowman Boxcar, *07*	75	___
36851	Generator Car with Christmas tree, *07*	75	___
36853	U.S. Army Exploding Boxcar, *08*	60	___
36855	GW Horse Car and Corral, *08*	160	___
36856	W&ARR Sheriff and Outlaw Car, *08*	75	___
36857	Bobbing Ghost Boxcar, *08*	65	___
36859	Lionel Lines Aquarium Car, *08*	80	___
36861	PRR Poultry Dispatch Car, *08–09*	80	___
36863	Alien Security Car, *08*	80	___
36864	Bethlehem Steel Searchlight Car, *08*	40	___
36866	WP Coal Dump Car "52369," *08*	40	___
36868	NH Barrel Ramp Car, *08*	40	___
36869	Bobbing Santa Boxcar, *08*	65	___
36870	Postwar "6812" Track Maintenance Car, *08*	65	___
36874	PRR Searchlight Car, *09*	35	___
36875	Polar Express Coach, sound, *08–14, 16*	132	___
36878	NYC Track Cleaning Car, *08*	150	___
36879	REA Ice Car "1221," *08*	65	___
36880	Koi Fish Aquarium Car, *10*	75	___
36881	Christmas Music Boxcar, *08*	70	___
36887	Great Western Animated Gondola, *08–09*	65	___
36888	Casper Aquarium Car, *09–10*	90	___
36889	PRR Barrel Ramp Car, *09–10*	46	___
36893	UP Transparent Instruction Car "195220," *09–10*	75	___
36896	Christmas Music Boxcar, *09*	80	___
36897	Pennsylvania Power & Light Coal Dump Car, *09–10*	46	___
36898	Wisconsin Central Log Dump Car, *09*	46	___
36900	Depressed Center Flatcar with backshop load, *99*	115	___
36913	Allied Chemical 1-D Tank Car 2-pack, *00*	150	___
36914	Allied Chemical 1-D Tank Car "68075," die-cast, white, *00*	90	___
36915	Allied Chemical 1-D Tank Car "68076," die-cast, white, *00*	90	___
36916	Allied Chemical 1-D Tank Car 2-pack, *00*	175	___
36917	Allied Chemical 1-D Tank Car "65124," die-cast, black, *00*	95	___
36918	Allied Chemical 1-D Tank Car "65125," die-cast, black, *00*	90	___
36927	B&O DC Hopper 6-pack, "435040-45," *01*	520	___
36935	Maersk Maxi-Stack Car 2-pack, "250131-32," *00*	135	___
36937	SP Maxi-Stack Car "513957," *02*	65	___

		Mint
____36998	Gingerbread Man Gateman, *12–13*	80
____37001	No. 3444 Erie Animated Gondola, *09*	70
____37002	Operating Plutonium Car 2-pack, *10–11*	140
____37003	PRR Jet Snow Blower "491252," *09–10*	138
____37004	Area 51 Searchlight Car, *09*	46
____37006	Lionel Flatcar with operating LCD billboard, *09*	180
____37009	Smoking Mount St. Helens Boxcar, *10–11*	125
____37010	Pennsylvania Power & Light Searchlight Car, *10*	46
____37011	B&M Operating Milk Car with platform, *10*	155
____37012	GN Jumping Hobo Boxcar, *10*	75
____37015	Jack-o-Lantern Flatcar, *11–13*	75
____37016	Radioactive Plutonium Flatcar, *11*	70
____37017	Plutonium Boom Car, *11*	70
____37022	ATSF Blinking Billboard, *12*	25
____37032	Postwar "3562" Operating Barrel Car, *11*	75
____37033	Casper Animated Gondola, *11*	70
____37035	Santa's Operating Snow Globe Car, *11*	75
____37036	Halloween Operating Globe Car, *11*	78
____37038	Halloween Searchlight Car, *12–13*	45
____37039	Minuteman Searchlight Car, *11*	45
____37040	UP Derrick Car, *11–12*	46
____37041	Pennsylvania Power & Light Coal Dump Car, *11*	80
____37042	IC Coal Dump Car, *11*	46
____37043	Seaboard Log Dump Car, *11*	46
____37044	CP Rail Log Dump Car, *11, 13*	80
____37045	Beatles Yellow Submarine Aquarium Car, *11*	85
____37047	Santa's Flyer Animated Gondola, *11*	55
____37053	EL Derrick Car, *12*	45
____37054	CSX Coal Dump Car, *12*	46
____37055	SP Log Dump Car, *12*	46
____37056	Zombie Aquarium Car, *12*	80
____37057	Bethlehem Steel Culvert Car, *12*	65
____37058	Ghost Globe Halloween Car, *12–15*	80
____37059	Christmas Snow Globe Car, *12*	85
____37060	LIRR Derrick Car, *13–14*	50
____37061	UP Railroad Speeder, CC, *12–14*	150
____37062	NS Railroad Speeder, CC, *12–14*	150
____37063	PRR Railroad Speeder, CC, *12–14, 16*	150
____37064	CSX Railroad Speeder, CC, *12–14*	150
____37065	BNSF Railroad Speeder, CC, *12–14*	150
____37066	MOW Railroad Speeder, CC, *12–14*	150
____37067	NYC Railroad Speeder, CC, *12–14*	150
____37068	CN Railroad Speeder, CC, *12–14*	150
____37069	Strasburg RR Crane Car, *12*	65
____37070	Gingerbread Man and Santa Animated Gondola, *12*	55
____37071	MOW Searchlight Car, *12*	46
____37073	U.S. Marine Corps Cannon Car, *12*	75
____37075	Boy Scouts of America Crane Car, *13*	75
____37076	Bethlehem Steel Coal Dump Car, *13*	50
____37078	RI Searchlight Car, *13*	50
____37079	Santa Fe Derrick Car, *13*	50

No.	Description	Exc	Mint
37081	Peanuts Pumpkin Jack-O-Lantern Car, *13*		85____
37082	Peanuts Animated Trick or Treat Chase Gondola, *14–16*		75____
37083	Strasburg Coal Dump Car, *13*		50____
37084	PRR Cop and Hobo Animated Gondola, *13*		65____
37085	BN Log Dump Car, *13*		50____
37086	Lionelville Aquarium Co. Aquarium Car, *13*		80____
37087	NH Walking Brakeman Car, *13–14*		75____
37089	Santa's List Snow Globe Car, *13*		90____
37090	Polar Express Searchlight Car, *13*		60____
37094	Wizard of Oz Aquarium Car, *13–15*		85____
37095	North Pole Sleigh Repair Welding Car, *13*		85____
37097	Where the Wild Things Are Aquarium Car, *13–15*		85____
37099	North Pole Central EV Caboose "2510" (std O), *13*		95____
37100	Barrel Loader Building, *12–14*		43____
37101	Smiley Water Tower, *12–14*		23____
37102	Watchman Shanty, *12–14*		30____
37103	031 Curved Track (FasTrack), *13–14, 16*		5____
37110	LionChief FasTrack Terminal, *14–16*		9____
37112	Helicopter 2-pack, *13–16*		35____
37115	Pedestrian Walkover, green, *16*		55____
37120	Railroad Crossing Signs, *13–16*		10____
37121	Christmas Station Platform, *13*		25____
37122	Santa Fe Blinking Billboard, *13*		25____
37123	Weyerhaeuser Timber Operating Sawmill, *12–13*		140____
37124	West Side Lumber Operating Sawmill, *12–13*		140____
37125	Legacy Writable Utility Mobile, *12–16*		20____
37127	Angela Trotta Thomas Gallery, *12*		75____
37129	Boy Scouts of America Girder Bridge, *13*		23____
37130	Boy Scouts of America Covered Bridge, *13*		60____
37139	Tis the Season Accessories, *12–13*		310____
37140	All Aboard Accessories, *12–13*		65____
37141	Rail Yard Accessories, *12–13*		277____
37142	Welcome Home Accessories, *12–13*		154____
37146	Legacy PowerMaster, *12–16*		100____
37147	CAB-1L/Base-1L Command Set, *12–16*		250____
37149	FasTrack Modular Layout Straight Section Kit, *13*		200____
37150	FasTrack Modular Layout Template, *13–16*		30____
37151	Christmas Classic Street Lamps, *14, 16*		40____
37152	Operating Coaling Station, *13–14*		180____
37153	FasTrack Modular Layout 45-Degree Reversible Corner Kit, *13*		225____
37154	FasTrack Modular Layout 45-Degree Corner Kit, *13*		225____
37155	CAB-1L Remote Controller, *12–16*		150____
37156	Base-1L, *12–16*		125____
37158	Hershey's Water Tower, *13*		30____
37159	Peanuts Figure Pack, *13–15*		30____
37160	Strasburg Girder Bridge, *13*		21____
37161	Container 4-pack, *13*		40____
37162	Lionelville Water Tower, *13*		25____
37163	LIRR Girder Bridge, *13*		21____
37164	NS Girder Bridge, *13*		21____

		Exc	Mint
____37165	CP Water Tower, *13*		25
____37166	Crossing Shanty, *13–14, 16*		25
____37167	Freight Platform, *13*		30
____37169	Peanuts Psychiatric Booth, *13–16*		40
____37172	Gooseneck Lamp 2-pack, *13–14, 15*		34
____37173	Globe Lamp 3-pack, *13–14, 16*		25
____37174	Classic Street Lamp 3-pack, black, *13–14, 16*		40
____37176	Santa Fe Shanty, *13*		25
37183	Polar Express 10th Anniversary Pewter Snowman		
____	and Children Figure Pack, *13–14,16*		37
____37184	Christmas Half Covered Bridge, *13*		43
____37185	Christmas Railroad Signs, *13–14, 16*		10
____37187	Kris Kringle's Kloseout Shop, *13*		50
____37191	LionChief 36-watt Power Supply, *14*		36
____37195	Grand Central Terminal 100th Anniversary, *13–15*		280
____37196	Christmas Extension Bridge, *13, 16*		15
____37197	North Pole Central Girder Bridge, *13–14, 16*		30
____37530	Santa Animated Caboose, *11*		80
____37807	Station Platform, *10–15*		23
____37808	Sunoco Spherical Oil Tank, *10–11*		100
____37810	Curved O Gauge Tunnel, *11–16*		65
____37813	Christmas Tractor and Trailer with trees, *10*		27
____37814	Christmas Crossing Shanty, *10–14*		30
____37816	Rockville Bridge, *11–12*		700
____37820	Lionel Auto Loader Cars 4-pack, *12–13, 16*		25
____37821	Smoke Fluid Loader, *11*		250
____37826	Classic Travel Billboard Set, *11–14*		13
____37827	Coca-Cola Covered Bridge, *11*		45
____37828	Vintage Boy Scouts Figure Pack, *11–14*		30
____37829	Polar Express Station Platform, *11–16*		45
____37831	NJ Transit Blinking Light Water Tower, *11–12*		30
____37834	Lionel Boat 4-pack, *11–16*		25
____37836	Monopoly Auto 4-pack, *12*		25
____37837	Polar Express Straight Tunnel, *12–14*		80
____37840	Santa Fe Diorama, *12–16*		34
____37841	Premium Smoke Fluid, *12–16*		7
____37842	CN Tractor with piggyback trailer, *12, 15*		90
____37846	PRR Tractor Trailer, *12*		90
____37847	SP Tractor Trailer, *12*		90
____37848	IC Tractor Trailer, *12*		90
____37849	ATSF Tractor Trailer, *12*		90
____37850	REA Tractor Trailer, *12*		90
____37851	Scale Telephone Poles, *12–16*		37
____37852	Christmas People Pack, *12–14, 16*		25
____37853	Alien Billboard, *13, 15*		13
____37854	Classic Christmas Billboard, *12*		11
____37855	Lionel Airplane 2-pack, *12–16*		37
____37900	Silver Truss Bridge, *11*		70
____37901	Lehigh Valley Tugboat, *10*		270
____37902	Illuminated Barge, *10*		180
____37903	Cell Tower, *10–16*		60
____37904	Boy Scouts Billboard Set, *10*		13

		Exc	Mint
37907	Christmas Street Lamps with wreaths, *10–14*	30	
37909	North Pole Central Jet Snowblower, *11–14*	138	
37910	Operating Lighthouse, *10*	180	
37911	D&RGW Blinking Light Water Tower, *10–11*	30	
37912	Lighted Coaling Tower, *10–15*	180	
37913	Hopper Shed, *10–15*	35	
37914	Work House, *10–16*	28	
37916	Beige Brick Suburban House, *10*	80	
37917	Red Brick Suburban House, *10*	80	
37919	Operating Sawmill, *10*	130	
37920	Bascule Bridge, *10*	350	
37921	ZW-L Transformer, *11–16*	675	
37923	Coca-Cola Blinking Light Water Tower, *11*	28	
37928	Passenger Station, sounds, *11*	90	
37929	Coca-Cola Diner, *11, 13*	75	
37930	Rotary Aircraft Beacon, *11–12*	81	
37933	MG Switch Tower, *11–13*	300	
37935	Operating Track Gang, *11*	100	
37939	Scale Telephone Poles, *11–16*	43	
37940	PRR Hobo Hotel, *12*	150	
37941	House Under Construction, *11*	90	
37942	Christmas Hobo Hotel, *12–13*	150	
37944	Weathered 50,000-gallon Water Tank, *11–12*	170	
37946	House Under Construction #2, *12–13*	90	
37947	GW-180 180-watt Transformer, *12–16*	280	
37948	Boy Scouts Flagpole with lights, *11*	30	
37951	Postwar "342" Culvert Loader, *11*	165	
37952	Postwar "345" Culvert Unloader, *11*	190	
37953	Jacobs Pharmacy, *11*	50	
37954	Halloween Station Platform, *11–13*	35	
37955	Sodor Station Platform, *11–15*	35	
37957	Deluxe Holiday House, *11*	85	
37958	SP Scrap Yard, *11–14*	110	
37959	Midway Basketball Shot Game, *11–13*	21	
37960	Burning Switch Tower, *11–13*	100	
37961	NYC Scrap Yard, *11–13*	110	
37962	NJ Transit Station Platform, *11*	37	
37964	Archive Operating Freight Terminal, *11–14*	150	
37965	Christmas Operating Freight Terminal, *11–14, 16*	150	
37966	Lionel Cylindrical Oil Tank, *11–16*	100	
37967	Boy Scouts Troop Cabin, *12–13*	80	
37971	Bethlehem Steel Culvert Loader, *11*	165	
37972	Bethlehem Steel Culvert Unloader, *11*	190	
37973	Coca-Cola Station Platform, *12*	37	
37975	PFE Operating Freight Terminal, *11–16*	150	
37977	Hooker Tank Car Accident, *11–16*	130	
37978	Deluxe Suburban House, *11–13*	80	
37979	Rotary Coal Tipple, *12*	540	
37980	Operating Coal Conveyor, *12*	90	
37984	Santa's Repair Work House, *12–14*	40	
37985	Operating Wind Turbine, *12–15*	75	
37986	NJ Transit Blinking Billboard, *12–13*	28	

		Exc	Mint
____37989	Sodor Train Shed, *12–16*		60
____37992	Coca-Cola Blinking Light Billboard, *10–11*		28
____37993	Snoopy and the Red Baron Animated Pylon, *12*		160
____37994	Deluxe Holiday House #2, *12–14*		120
____37995	Illuminated Scale Telephone Poles, *12–16*		50
____37996	Postwar 192 Control Tower, *12*		70
____37997	Christmas Lawn Figure Pack, *12–14, 16*		25
____37998	Halloween Haunted Passenger Station, *12–13, 15*		75
38004	Virginian 4-6-0 10-wheel Locomotive "203," CC, *01–02*		570
38005	Long Island 4-6-0 10-wheel Locomotive "138," CC, *01–02*		510
____38007	UP Auxiliary tender, black, CC, *01*		200
____38008	UP Auxiliary tender, gray, CC, *01*		205
38009	D&RGW 4-6-6-4 Challenger Locomotive "3803," CC, *01*		1550
38010	Clinchfield 4-6-6-4 Challenger Locomotive "673," CC, *01*		1400
38012	Wheeling & Lake Erie 2-6-6-2 Locomotive "8005," CC, *01*		610
38013	D&H 4-6-6-4 Challenger Locomotive "1527," CC, *01*		720
38014	D&RGW 4-6-6-4 Challenger Locomotive "3800," CC, *01*		710
____38015	NYC 4-6-4 Hudson Locomotive "773," CC, *01*		900
38016	Southern 0-8-0 Yard Goat Locomotive "6536," CC, *01–02, 05*		530
____38017	CN 2-6-0 Mogul Locomotive "86," CC, *03, 05*		600
____38018	Wabash 2-6-0 Mogul Locomotive "826," CC, *03*		485
38019	B&M 2-6-0 Mogul Locomotive "1455," CC, *03, 05*		600
38020	PRR 4-4-4-4 T1 Duplex Locomotive "5514," *02–03*		630
38021	WP 4-6-6-4 Challenger Locomotive "402," CC, *02*		650
38022	WM 4-6-6-4 Challenger Locomotive "1206," CC, *02*		690
38023	UP 4-6-6-4 Challenger Locomotive "3976," CC, *02*		620
38024	PRR 6-4-4-6 S-1 Duplex Locomotive "6100," TMCC, *03*		1000
38025	PRR 4-6-2 K4 Pacific Locomotive "1361," CC, *02*		950
38026	N&W 4-8-4 J Class Northern Locomotive "606," CC, *02*		1450
38027	Meadow River Lumber Heisler Geared Locomotive "6," CC, *03*		880
____38028	PRR 6-8-6 S2 Steam Turbine Locomotive, *01*		650
____38029	UP 4-12-2 Locomotive "9000," CC, *03*		570
____38030	Santa Fe 2-8-8-2 Locomotive "1795," CC, *03*		920
____38031	SP 2-8-8-4 AC-9 Locomotive "3809," CC, *04*		1100
____38032	Virginian 2-8-8-2 Locomotive "741," CC, *03*		928
____38036	Long Island 2-8-0 Consolidation Locomotive, *01*		500
38037	PRR Reading Seashore 2-8-0 Consolidation Locomotive "6072," CC, *01*		495
____38038	D&RGW Auxiliary Water Tender, *01*		230

Exc Mint

		Exc	Mint
38039	Clinchfield Auxiliary Water Tender, *01*	220	____
38040	LV 4-6-0 Camelback Locomotive, *01*	405	____
38042	C&NW 4-6-0 10-wheel Locomotive "361," CC, *02*	450	____
38043	Frisco 4-6-0 10-wheel Locomotive "719," CC, *02*	525	____
38044	PRR 4-6-2 K4 Pacific Locomotive "5385," CC, *02*	920	____
38045	NYC Hudson J-3a 4-6-4 Locomotive "5418," CC, *03*	495	____
38046	GN 0-8-0 Locomotive "815," CC, *02*	530	____
38047	N&W 0-8-0 Locomotive "266," CC, *02*	550	____
38048	NPR 0-8-0 Locomotive "303," CC, *02*	530	____
38049	N&W 2-6-6-4 Locomotive "1234," CC, *02*	690	____
38050	Nickel Plate 2-8-4 Berkshire Locomotive "779," CC, *03*	925	____
38051	Erie 2-8-4 Berkshire Locomotive "3315," CC, *03*	810	____
38052	Pere Marquette 2-8-4 Berkshire Locomotive "1225," CC, *03*	1000	____
38053	NYC 4-8-2 Mohawk L-2a Locomotive "2793," CC, *03*	915	____
38055	Santa Fe 4-8-4 Northern Locomotive "3751" CC, *04*	1100	____
38056	PRR 4-8-2 Mountain M1a Locomotive "6759," CC, *03*	850	____
38057	Weyerhaeuser Shay Locomotive, CC, *03*	1000	____
38058	C&O 2-8-8-2 H7 Locomotive "1580," CC, *04*	1200	____
38060	UP 2-8-8-2 H7 Locomotive "3590," CC, *04*	1200	____
38061	Cass Scenic Heisler Geared Locomotive "6," CC, *03*	940	____
38062	Lionel Lines 4-6-2 Pacific Locomotive "8062," CC, *02–03*	275	____
38065	UP 2-8-8-2 Mallet Locomotive "3672," CC, *02*	1002	____
38066	Elk River Shay Locomotive, CC, *03*	1000	____
38067	MILW 4-6-2 Pacific Locomotive "6316," CC, *03*	300	____
38068	WM 4-6-2 Pacific Locomotive "204," CC, *03*	300	____
38069	Erie Hudson Locomotive, whistle, *05*	150	____
38070	C&O 4-6-2 Pacific Locomotive "489," CC, *04*	300	____
38071	SP Cab Forward AC-12 Locomotive "4294," CC, *05*	1550	____
38075	UP 4-8-8-4 Big Boy Locomotive "4024," LionMaster, *03*	800	____
38076	C&O 2-8-4 Berkshire Locomotive "2699," CC, *04*	860	____
38077	Virginian 2-8-4 Berkshire Locomotive "508," CC, *04*	1000	____
38079	SP 4-8-4 Northern GS-2 Locomotive "4410" CC, *04*	980	____
38080	WP 4-8-4 Northern GS-64 Locomotive "485" CC, *04*	1000	____
38081	C&O 2-6-6-6 Allegheny Locomotive "1650," CC, *05–07*	1700	____
38082	Pennsylvania 2-8-8-2 Y3 Locomotive "374," CC, *04*	1000	____
38083	N&W 2-8-8-2 Y3 Locomotive "2009," CC, *04*	910	____
38085	NYC 4-6-4 Hudson J-3a Locomotive 5422," CC, *03*	495	____
38086	B&A 4-6-4 Hudson Locomotive "607," CC, *03*	495	____

		Exc	Mint
38087	Nickel Plate 2-8-4 Berkshire Locomotive, RailSounds, *05*		190
38088	NYC 2-6-0 Mogul Locomotive "1924," CC, *03, 05*		600
38089	Pennsylvania 4-6-2 Pacific Locomotive "3678," CC, *04*		300
38090	Clinchfield 4-6-6-4 Challenger Locomotive "672" CC, *04*		640
38091	NP 4-6-6-4 Challenger Locomotive "5121" CC, *04*		660
38092	Pickering Lumber Heisler Locomotive "5," CC, *04*		1000
38093	UP 4-6-6-4 Challenger Locomotive "3980," CC, *04*		700
38094	MILW Hiawatha 4-4-2 Atlantic Locomotive, CC, *06*		950
38095	N&W 4-8-4 J Class Locomotive "611," CC, *05–06*		1250
38100	Texas Special F3 Diesel AB Set, *99*		930
38103	Texas Special F3 Diesel "2245," *99*		510
38114	ATSF FT Diesel B Unit, *99–00*		170
38115	NYC FT Diesel B Unit "2403," nonpowered, *99–00*		130
38116	B&O FT Diesel B Unit, *99–00*		130
38144	C&O F3 Diesel AA Set "7019, 7021," *00*		700
38147	GN Alco FA2 AA Diesel Set, CC, *02*		405
38150	Platinum Ghost "2333," *99*		495
38153	"Spirit of the Century" F3 Diesel AA Set, *99*		800
38160	Pennsylvania Alco FB2 Diesel, *02*		125
38161	MKT Alco FB2 Diesel, *02*		125
38162	Burlington FT Diesel B Unit, *01*		NRS
38167	Burlington FT Diesel AA Set, *01*		225
38176	Pennsylvania Alco FA2 AA Diesel Set, CC, *02*		405
38182	MKT Alco FA2 AA Diesel Set, CC, *02*		360
38188	Southern F3 Diesel ABA Set, *00*		557
38194	GN Alco FB2 Diesel, *02*		125
38195	Santa Fe FT Diesel A Unit "170," *00*		125
38196	Santa Fe FT Diesel A Unit "171," *00*		175
38197	SP F3 Diesel ABA Set, *00*		640
38202	Wild West Handcar, *10*		75
38203	Holly Jolly Trolley 2-car Set, *10*		160
38204	ATSF FT B Unit, nonpowered, *10*		120
38210	PRR Alco Diesel AA Set, CC, *10*		400
38214	Rio Grande Ski Train FT B Unit, nonpowered, *11*		120
38215	ATSF FT Diesel "165," RailSounds, *10–11*		280
38216	Rio Grande Ski Train FT A Unit, nonpowered, *11*		120
38219	Texan FT B Unit Diesel, nonpowered, *11, 13–14*		120
38221	CNJ Alco AA Diesel Set, *11*		300
38224	Alaska Alco AA Diesel Set, *11*		300
38234	Classic PRR GG1 Electric Locomotive "4866," *12*		330
38235	Classic PC GG1 Electric Locomotive "4840," *12*		330
38240	Elf Gang Car, *12*		120
38241	MOW Gang Car, *12–13*		120
38300	Postwar "2331" Virginian Train Master Diesel, *08*		210
38303	Postwar "2340" GG1 Electric Locomotive, *08*		280
38305	Postwar "2338" Milwaukee Road GP7 Diesel, *08*		220

		Exc	Mint
38308	Postwar 2146WS Berkshire Passenger Set, *12*	460	
38310	"2185W" NYC F3 Diesel Freight Set, *09*	600	
38311	"2276W" B&O RDC Commuter Set, *09*	470	
38312	"2343" Santa Fe F3 Diesel AA Set, *09*	500	
38313	B&O Budd RDC 2-pack, *09*	350	
38323	Postwar "2348" M&StL GP9 Diesel, CC, *10*	390	
38324	Postwar 2507W NH F3 Diesel Freight Set, *10*	600	
38328	Postwar 1623W NP GP9 Diesel Freight Set, *10*	750	
38329	Postwar 2261W Freight Hauler Set, *10*	610	
38334	Postwar 11288 Orbitor Diesel Freight Set, *10*	500	
38338	Postwar 2129WS Berkshire Freight Set, *12*	550	
38339	Postwar 2505W Virginian Rectifier Freight Set, *10*	470	
38340	Postwar 1587S Girl's Steam Freight Set, *10*	580	
38342	Postwar 1619W Santa Fe Freight Set, *10–11*	470	
38348	Postwar "2339" Transparent Wabash GP7 Diesel, *11*	290	
38349	Postwar 12885-500 C&O GP7 Freight Set, *11–12*	600	
38351	Postwar Archive UP GP7 Diesel, *11*	290	
38353	Postwar X-628 Promotional U.S. Navy Diesel Freight Set, *12–14*	600	
38354	Postwar 1464W UP Anniversary Alco Diesel Passenger Set, *12–14*	460	
38357	Postwar 221 U.S. Marine Corps Alco Diesel A Unit, *12–14*	300	
38358	Postwar 2239 IC F3 Freight Set, *12–14*	600	
38365	Archive ATSF Black Bonnet F3 AA Diesel Set, *12–14*	500	
38368	Archive NYC Red Lightning F3 AA Diesel Set, *12–14*	500	
38371	Postwar 2031 RI Alco Diesel AA Set, *12–13*	400	
38374	Postwar 221 U.S. Marine Corps Alco Diesel B Unit, *12–14*	120	
38377	Postwar 2363T F3 A Unit, nonpowered, *12–14*	170	
38379	Archive ATSF Black Bonnet F3 B Unit, *12–14*	170	
38380	Archive NYC Red Lightning F3 B Unit, *12–14*	170	
38386	Postwar "2367" Wabash F3 Diesel AB Units, *12–14*	500	
38388	Postwar "2367" Wabash F3 Diesel A Unit, nonpowered, *12–14*	170	
38389	Postwar "2362" UP F3 Diesel AA Set, *14*	460	
38392	Postwar "2362" F3 Diesel B Unit, nonpowered, *14*	170	
38393	PRR Round-roof Boxcar "76648" (std O), *14*	80	
38401	NYC M-497 Jet-Powered Rail Car, *10*	300	
38402	Amtrak HHP-8 Electric Locomotive, RailSounds, *10*	400	
38403	B&O CSX Heritage AC6000 Diesel "6607," CC, *11*	550	
38404	B&O CSX Heritage AC6000 Diesel "7812," CC, *11*	550	
38405	Chessie System CSX Heritage AC6000 Diesel, CC, *11–14*	550	
38406	Chessie System CSX Heritage AC6000 Diesel, CC, *11–14*	550	
38407	WM CSX Heritage AC6000 Diesel "2652," CC, *11*	550	
38408	WM CSX Heritage AC6000 Diesel "2659," CC, *11*	550	

		Exc	Mint
_____	38409	Clinchfield CSX Heritage AC6000 Diesel, CC, *11–13*		550
_____	38410	Clinchfield CSX Heritage AC6000 Diesel, CC, *11–14*		550
_____	38411	Family Lines CSX Heritage AC6000 Diesel "4825," CC, *11*		550
_____	38412	Family Lines CSX Heritage AC6000 Diesel "4837," CC, *11*		550
_____	38413	CSX Heritage AC6000 Diesel "607," CC, *11–13*		550
_____	38414	CSX Heritage AC6000 Diesel "654," CC, *11–13*		550
_____	38415	PRR U28C Diesel "6531," CC, *11–12*		530
_____	38416	PRR U28C Diesel "6534," CC, *11–12*		530
_____	38417	BN Bicentennial U30C Diesel "1776," CC, *11*		530
_____	38418	BN Bicentennial U30C Diesel "1777," CC, *11*		530
_____	38419	UP U30C Diesel "2918," CC, *11–12*		530
_____	38420	UP U30C Diesel "2897," CC, *11–12*		530
_____	38421	NP U33C Diesel "3305," CC, *11–12*		530
_____	38422	NP U33C Diesel "3307," CC, *11–12*		530
_____	38423	Southern U30C Diesel "3801," CC, *11–12*		530
_____	38424	Southern U30C Diesel "3804," CC, *11–12*		530
_____	38425	RI Budd RDC Jet Car, *11*		330
_____	38428	Alaska Budd RDC Coach, *11*		300
_____	38429	NYC Budd RDC M-497 Jet Car, *11*		330
_____	38432	MKT H16-44 Diesel "1591," CC, *11*		500
_____	38433	MKT H16-44 Diesel "1731," CC, *11*		500
_____	38434	MKT H16-44 Diesel "1732," *11*		380
_____	38435	MKT H16-44 Diesel "1733," nonpowered, *11*		240
_____	38436	LIRR H-16-44 Diesel "1501," CC, *11*		500
_____	38437	LIRR H-16-44 Diesel "1504," CC, *11*		500
_____	38438	LIRR H-16-44 Diesel "1507," *11*		380
_____	38439	LIRR H-16-44 Diesel "1509," nonpowered, *11*		240
_____	38440	UP H-16-44 Diesel "1341," CC, *11*		500
_____	38441	UP H-16-44 Diesel "1342," CC, *11*		500
_____	38442	UP H-16-44 Diesel "1343," *11*		380
_____	38443	UP H-16-44 Diesel "1344," nonpowered, *11*		240
_____	38444	PRR H16-44 Diesel "8807," CC, *11*		500
_____	38445	PRR H16-44 Diesel "8810," CC, *11*		500
_____	38446	PRR H16-44 Diesel "8812," *11*		380
_____	38447	PRR H16-44 Diesel "8815," nonpowered, *11*		240
_____	38452	PC Alco RS-11 Diesel "7605," CC, *12*		480
_____	38453	PC Alco RS-11 Diesel "7608," CC, *12*		480
_____	38454	PRR Alco RS-11 Diesel "9622," CC, *12*		480
_____	38455	PC Alco RS-11 Diesel "7625," nonpowered, *12*		240
_____	38456	N&W Alco RS-11 Diesel "308," CC, *12–13*		480
_____	38457	N&W Alco RS-11 Diesel "318," CC, *12*		480
_____	38458	PRR Alco RS-11 Diesel "8631," CC, *12*		480
_____	38459	N&W Alco RS-11 Diesel "330," nonpowered, *12*		240
_____	38460	NKP Alco RS-11 Diesel "855," CC, *12*		480
_____	38461	NKP Alco RS-11 Diesel "859," CC, *12*		480
_____	38462	PRR Alco RS-11 Diesel "8639," nonpowered, *12*		240
_____	38463	NKP Alco RS-11 Diesel "863," nonpowered, *12*		240
_____	38464	Alaska Alco RS-11 Diesel "3602," CC, *12*		480
_____	38465	Alaska Alco RS-11 Diesel "3604," CC, *12*		480

Exc Mint

		Exc	Mint
38466	NH Alco RS-11 Diesel "1403," CC, *12*	480	____
38467	Alaska Alco RS-11 Diesel "3607," nonpowered, *12*	240	____
38468	Seaboard Alco RS-11 Diesel "101," CC, *12–13*	480	____
38469	Seaboard Alco RS-11 Diesel "102," CC, *12*	480	____
38470	NH Alco RS-11 Diesel "1405," CC, *12*	480	____
38471	Seaboard Alco RS-11 Diesel "104," nonpowered, *12*	240	____
38472	C&O Alco S2 Diesel Switcher "5001," CC, *11*	470	____
38473	C&O Alco S2 Diesel Switcher "5505," CC, *11*	480	____
38474	C&O Alco S2 Diesel Switcher "5020," *11*	360	____
38475	C&O Alco S2 Diesel Switcher "5027," nonpowered, *11*	220	____
38476	CN Alco S2 Diesel Switcher "7946," CC, *11*	480	____
38477	CN Alco S2 Diesel Switcher "7949," CC, *11*	480	____
38478	CN Alco S2 Diesel Switcher "7951," *11*	360	____
38479	CN Alco S2 Diesel Switcher "7954," *11*	360	____
38480	NYC Alco S2 Diesel Switcher "8504," CC, *11*	480	____
38481	NYC Alco S2 Diesel Switcher "8507," CC, *11*	480	____
38482	NYC Alco S2 Diesel Switcher "8514," *11*	360	____
38483	NYC Alco S2 Diesel Switcher "8521," nonpowered, *11*	220	____
38484	Southern Alco S2 Diesel Switcher "2209," CC, *11*	480	____
38485	Southern Alco S2 Diesel Switcher "2211," CC, *11*	480	____
38486	Southern Alco S2 Diesel Switcher "2215," *11*	360	____
38487	Southern Alco S2 Diesel Switcher "2218," nonpowered, *11*	220	____
38488	Mopac Alco S2 Diesel Switcher "9108," CC, *11*	480	____
38489	Mopac Alco S2 Diesel Switcher "9113," CC, *11*	480	____
38490	Mopac Alco S2 Diesel Switcher "9116," *11*	360	____
38491	Mopac Alco S2 Diesel Switcher "9131," nonpowered, *11*	220	____
38493	ATSF Early Era Inspection Vehicle, CC, *12*	150	____
38494	CP DD35 Diesel "9864," CC, *12*	600	____
38495	CP DD35 Diesel "9868," nonpowered, *12*	440	____
38496	SP DD35A Diesel "9903," CC, *11*	600	____
38497	SP DD35A Diesel "9914," nonpowered, *11*	440	____
38498	PRR DD35A Diesel "2380," CC, *11*	600	____
38499	PRR DD35A Diesel "2383," nonpowered, *11*	440	____
38505	CSX GP-38 Diesel, *11*	140	____
38521	PRR GG1 Electric "4839," *11*	330	____
38522	Amtrak GG1 Electric "926," *11*	330	____
38524	NYC GP35 Diesel "6131," CC, *12*	500	____
38525	NYC GP35 Diesel "6138," CC, *12*	500	____
38526	NYC GP35 Diesel "6147," nonpowered, *12*	260	____
38527	UP GP35 Diesel "742," CC, *12*	500	____
38528	UP GP35 Diesel "753," CC, *12*	500	____
38529	UP GP35 Diesel "760," nonpowered, *12*	260	____
38530	SP GP35 Diesel "7465," CC, *12*	500	____
38531	SP GP35 Diesel "7474," CC, *12*	500	____
38532	SP GP35 Diesel "7481," nonpowered, *12*	260	____
38533	CP GP35 Diesel "5014," CC, *12*	500	____
38534	CP GP35 Diesel "5018," CC, *12*	500	____

		Exc	Mint
___38535	CP GP35 Diesel "5023," nonpowered, *12*		260
___38536	PRR GP35 Diesel "2297," CC, *12*		500
___38537	PRR GP35 Diesel "2302," CC, *12*		500
___38538	PRR GP35 Diesel "2305," nonpowered, *12*		260
___38539	N&W Alco RS-11 Diesel "308," CC, *12*		480
___38539	Conrail GP35 Diesel "2297," CC, *12*		500
___38540	Conrail GP35 Diesel "2302," CC, *12*		500
___38541	Conrail GP35 Diesel "2305," nonpowered, *12*		260
___38542	Milwaukee Road GP35 Diesel "361," CC, *12*		500
___38543	Milwaukee Road GP35 Diesel "363," CC, *12*		500
38544 ___	Milwaukee Road GP35 Diesel "366," nonpowered, *12*		260
___38545	Pacific Harbor Line Genset Switcher "31," CC, *11*		800
___38546	KCS Genset Switcher "1404," CC, *11–12*		800
___38547	Santa Fe Genset Switcher "9910," CC, *11*		800
___38548	EL GP35 Diesel "2555," CC, *12*		500
___38549	EL GP35 Diesel "2558," CC, *12*		500
___38550	EL GP35 Diesel "2561," nonpowered, *12*		260
___38558	D&H Baldwin RF-16 Diesel AA Set, CC, *12*		730
___38561	D&H Baldwin RF-16 Diesel B Unit, CC, *12*		400
38562 ___	D&H Baldwin RF-16 Diesel B Unit, nonpowered, *12*		250
___38563	B&O Baldwin RF-16 Diesel AA Set, CC, *12–14*		730
___38566	B&O Baldwin RF-16 Diesel B Unit, CC, *12–14*		400
38567 ___	B&O Baldwin RF-16 Diesel B Unit, nonpowered, *12–14*		250
38568 ___	NYC Baldwin RF-16 Diesel AA Set "3806-3808," CC, *12–14*		730
___38571	NYC Baldwin RF-16 Diesel B Unit, CC, *12–14*		400
38572 ___	NYC Baldwin RF-16 Diesel B Unit, nonpowered, *12–14*		250
___38573	SP Baldwin RF-16 Diesel AA Set, CC, *12–14*		730
___38576	SP Baldwin RF-16 Diesel B Unit, CC, *12–14*		400
38577 ___	SP Baldwin RF-16 Diesel B Unit, nonpowered, *12–14*		250
___38579	ATSF GP9 Diesel "744," nonpowered, *12*		240
___38580	NP GP9 Diesel "324," nonpowered, *12*		240
___38581	CSX SD80MAC Diesel "809," CC, *12–13*		530
___38582	CSX SD80MAC Diesel "812," CC, *12*		530
___38583	CSX SD80MAC Diesel "804," nonpowered, *12*		260
___38584	NS SD80MAC Diesel "7207," CC, *12*		530
___38585	NS SD80MAC Diesel "7203," CC, *12*		530
___38586	NS SD80MAC Diesel "7209," nonpowered, *12*		260
___38587	Conrail SD80MAC Diesel "4126," CC, *12*		530
___38588	Conrail SD80MAC Diesel "4129," CC, *12*		530
38589 ___	Conrail SD80MAC Diesel "4103," nonpowered, *12*		260
38593 ___	UP NW2 Diesel Switcher Locomotive "1028," CC, *12*		470
38594 ___	UP NW2 Diesel Switcher Locomotive "1043," CC, *12*		470
___38595	CB&Q Scale NW2 Diesel Switcher "9227," CC, *12*		470
___38596	CB&Q Scale NW2 Diesel Switcher "9245," CC, *12*		470

		Exc	Mint
38597	CB&Q F3 AA Diesel Set "9962A-9962C," CC, *12–13*		730____
38600	UP 0-6-0 Dockside Switcher "87," traditional, *07–09*		110____
38601	Lionel Lines 0-6-0 Dockside Switcher, traditional, *07–09*		110____
38605	PRR 0-4-0 Locomotive "94," traditional, *07*		170____
38606	SP 0-4-0 Locomotive "71," traditional, *07–08*		170____
38607	Southern 2-8-4 Berkshire Locomotive "2718," RailSounds, *07–08*		175____
38608	LL 2-8-2 Mikado Locomotive "57," RailSounds, *07*		260____
38609	NYC 2-8-2 Mikado Locomotive "1843," CC, *07*		370____
38610	NKP 2-8-4 Berkshire Locomotive "779," CC, *07–08*		370____
38619	Santa Fe 4-6-2 Pacific Locomotive "2037," traditional, K-Line, *06*		260____
38620	B&O Porter Locomotive "16," traditional, K-Line, *06*		100____
38621	4-6-2 Pacific Locomotive, traditional, K-Line, *06*		260____
38626	Holiday 2-8-2 Mikado Locomotive "25," green, RailSounds, *08*		260____
38627	GN 4-4-2 Atlantic Locomotive "1702," traditional, *08–09*		110____
38630	U.S. Army 0-6-0 Dockside Switcher "486," traditional, *08–09*		110____
38634	NYC 4-6-4 Hudson Locomotive "5417," TrainSounds, *07*		200____
38635	C&O 4-6-4 Hudson Locomotive "309," TrainSounds, *08*		200____
38636	ATSF 4-6-4 Hudson Locomotive "3459," TrainSounds, *07*		200____
38637	LL 4-6-4 Hudson Locomotive "5242," TrainSounds, *08*		200____
38638	UP 4-6-2 Pacific Locomotive "2888," RailSounds, *08*		300____
38639	Erie 4-6-2 Pacific Locomotive "2939," RailSounds, *08*		300____
38640	Southern 4-6-2 Pacific Locomotive "1317," RailSounds, *08*		300____
38641	B&M 4-6-2 Pacific Locomotive "3713," RailSounds, *08*		300____
38642	PRR 4-6-2 Pacific Locomotive "5385," RailSounds, *08*		300____
38643	Alaska Mikado 2-8-2 Locomotive "701," CC, *08–09*		280____
38644	T&P Mikado 2-8-2 Locomotive "810," CC, *08–09*		400____
38649	Christmas 4-6-4 Hudson Locomotive, traditional, *08*		220____
38651	Lionel Lines 0-8-0 Locomotive "100," traditional, *08–09*		120____
38654	Bethlehem Steel 0-4-0 Locomotive, traditional, *08–09*		170____
38657	Alton Limited Pacific 4-6-2 Locomotive "659," traditional, *08*		300____
38658	W&ARR 4-4-0 General "1892," TrainSounds, *08–09*		165____

		Exc	Mint
38664	LL 4-4-2 Atlantic Locomotive "1058," traditional, _08–09_		110
38671	Santa Flyer 4-6-0 Locomotive, _09_		200
38677	Strasburg 0-6-0 Dockside Switcher "1252," _10_		130
38678	Monopoly Hudson Locomotive, TrainSounds, _10_		240
38679	ATSF 0-4-0 Switcher "1387," _10–11_		190
38684	Pennsylvania Power & Light Docksider Switcher, _10_		110
38687	Western & Atlantic 0-4-0 Locomotive "1897," _10–11_		190
38691	North Pole Central Santa Flyer "2," _10–11_		190
38692	Angela Trotta Thomas Signature Express, _10–11_		190
38700	CB&Q F3 B Unit "9962B," CC, _12–13_		400
38701	CB&Q F3 B Unit, _12–13_		250
38702	D&RGW F3 AA Diesel Set"5531-5533," CC, _12–14_		730
38705	D&RGW F3 B Unit "5532," CC, _12–14_		400
38706	D&RGW F3 B Unit, _12–14_		250
38707	WP F3 AB Diesel Set"803A-803B," CC, _12–14_		730
38710	WP F3 A Unit, nonpowered, _12–14_		380
38711	WP F3 B Unit "803C," CC, _12–14_		400
38712	Wabash F7 AA Diesel Set"1102A-1102C," CC, _12–13_		730
38715	Wabash F7 B Unit "1102B," CC, _12–13_		400
38716	Wabash F7 B Unit, _12–13_		250
38717	Milwaukee Road F7 AA Diesel SetCC, _12_		730
38720	Milwaukee Road F7 B Unit "109B," CC, _12_		400
38721	Milwaukee Road F7 B Unit, _12_		250
38722	Grand Trunk SD80MAC Diesel "9085," CC, _12_		530
38723	Grand Trunk SD80MAC Diesel "9088," CC, _12_		530
38724	Grand Trunk SD80MAC Diesel "9079," nonpowered, _12_		260
38725	CB&Q SD80MAC Diesel "9654," CC, _12_		530
38726	CB&Q SD80MAC Diesel "9651," CC, _12_		530
38727	CB&Q SD80MAC Diesel "9660," nonpowered, _12_		260
38728	PRR SD80MAC Diesel "9942," CC, _12_		530
38729	PRR SD80MAC Diesel "9945," CC, _12_		530
38730	PRR SD80MAC Diesel "9947," nonpowered, _12–13_		260
38731	Polar SD80MAC Diesel, CC, _12_		530
38732	CB&Q BNSF Heritage SD70ACe Diesel "1848," CC, _12–13_		530
38733	CB&Q BNSF Heritage SD70ACe Diesel "1852," CC, _12–13_		530
38734	CB&Q BNSF Heritage SD70ACe Diesel "1856," nonpowered, _12–13_		260
38735	ATSF BNSF Heritage SD70ACe Diesel "1996," CC, _12–13_		530
38736	ATSF BNSF Heritage SD70ACe Diesel "1997," CC, _12–13_		530
38737	ATSF BNSF Heritage SD70ACe Diesel "1999," nonpowered, _12–13_		260
38738	Frisco BNSF Heritage SD70ACe Diesel "1876," CC, _12–13_		530

		Exc	Mint
38739	Frisco BNSF Heritage SD70ACe Diesel "1896," CC, *12–14*		530____
38740	Frisco BNSF Heritage SD70ACe Diesel "1916," nonpowered, *12–13*		260____
38741	BN BNSF Heritage SD70ACe Diesel "1970," CC, *12–13*		530____
38742	BN BNSF Heritage SD70ACe Diesel "1975," CC, *12–13*		530____
38743	BN BNSF Heritage SD70ACe Diesel "1980," nonpowered, *12–13*		260____
38744	GN BNSF Heritage SD70ACe Diesel "1889," CC, *12–13*		530____
38745	GN BNSF Heritage SD70ACe Diesel "1891," CC, *12–13*		530____
38746	GN BNSF Heritage SD70ACe Diesel "1893," nonpowered, *12–13*		260____
38747	NP BNSF Heritage SD70ACe Diesel "1870," CC, *12–13*		530____
38748	NP BNSF Heritage SD70ACe Diesel "1872," CC, *12–13*		530____
38749	NP BNSF Heritage SD70ACe Diesel "1875," nonpowered, *12–13*		260____
38750	EMD Demonstrator SD70ACe Diesel "2012," CC, *12–13*		530____
38751	CNJ F3 AA Diesel Set, CC, *13–14*		730____
38752	Vision Centipede AA Pilot Diesels, CC, *13*		2200____
38754	C&NW F7 AA Diesel Set, CC, *13–14*		730____
38757	SP F7 AA Diesel Set, CC, *13–14*		730____
38760	CNJ F3 B Unit, CC, *13–14*		400____
38761	CNJ F3 B Unit, *13–14*		250____
38762	C&NW F7 B Unit "410," CC, *13–14*		400____
38763	C&NW F7 B Unit, *13–14*		250____
38764	SP F7 B Unit "8219," CC, *13*		400____
38765	SP F7 B Unit, *13*		250____
38768	N&W GP35 Diesel "1306," CC, *13–14*		500____
38769	N&W GP35 Diesel "1308," nonpowered, *13–14*		260____
38770	RI GP35 Diesel "307," CC, *13–14*		500____
38771	RI GP35 Diesel "309," CC, *13–14*		500____
38772	RI GP35 Diesel "323," nonpowered, *13–14*		260____
38773	WP GP35 Diesel "3002," CC, *13–14*		500____
38774	WP GP35 Diesel "3009," CC, *13–14*		500____
38775	WP GP35 Diesel "3014," nonpowered, *13–14*		260____
38778	C&NW LionChief RS3 Diesel "1621," *14–16*		330____
38779	NYC LionChief RS3 Diesel "8244," *14–16*		330____
38782	C&BQ GP35 Diesel "990," CC, *13*		500____
38783	C&BQ GP35 Diesel "996," nonpowered, *13*		500____
38784	CN GP35 Diesel "4000," CC, *13*		500____
38785	CN GP35 Diesel "4005," CC, *13*		500____
38786	CN GP35 Diesel "4001," nonpowered, *13*		260____
38787	D&RGW GP35 Diesel "3031," CC, *13*		500____
38788	D&RGW GP35 Diesel "3034," CC, *13*		500____
38789	D&RGW GP35 Diesel "3038," nonpowered, *13*		260____
38790	DT&I GP35 Diesel "351," CC, *13*		500____
38791	DT&I GP35 Diesel "353," CC, *13*		500____

		Mint
___38792	DT&I GP35 Diesel "355," nonpowered, *13*	260
___38794	GN GP35 Diesel "3018," CC, *13–14*	500
___38795	GN GP35 Diesel "3036," nonpowered, *13–14*	260
___38796	Chessie System GP35 Diesel "1125," CC, *13*	500
___38797	Chessie System GP35 Diesel "1128," CC, *13*	500
___38798	Chessie System GP35 Diesel "1113," nonpowered, *13*	260
___38799	N&W GP35 Diesel "1302," CC, *13–14*	500
___38800	B&M Early Era Inspection Vehicle, CC, *12*	150
___38801	KCS Trackmobile, CC, *12–13*	300
___38802	North Pole Central Trackmobile, CC, *12*	300
___38803	MOW Trackmobile, CC, *12*	300
___38804	LIRR Trackmobile, CC, *12*	300
___38805	Conrail Trackmobile, CC, *12*	300
___38806	NS Trackmobile, CC, *12*	300
___38807	NP Trackmobile, CC, *12–13*	300
___38808	Chessie System Trackmobile, CC, *12*	300
___38809	CN Trackmobile, CC, *12*	300
___38810	PRR Early Era Inspection Vehicle, CC, *12*	150
___38811	D&RGW Early Era Inspection Vehicle, CC, *12*	150
___38812	SP Early Era Inspection Vehicle, CC, *12–13*	150
___38813	C&O Early Era Inspection Vehicle, CC, *12–13*	150
___38814	Milwaukee Road Early Era Inspection Vehicle, CC, *12*	150
___38815	Transylvania Early Era Inspection Vehicle, CC, *12*	150
___38816	LionChief PRR RS3 Diesel "5620," *14–16*	330
___38819	LionChief D&RGW RS3 Diesel "5202," *14–16*	330
___38821	LionChief AT&SF GP7 Diesel "2656," *14–15*	330
___38824	LionChief NP GP7 Diesel "563," *14–15*	330
___38825	LionChief UP GP7 Diesel "121," *14–15*	330
___38827	LionChief CB&Q GP7 Diesel "1596," *14–15*	330
___38848	Christmas Pioneer Zephyr Set, CC, *13–14*	1100
___38853	Santa and Mrs. Claus Handcar, *13*	90
___38855	GN GP35 Diesel "2519," CC, *13–14*	500
___38856	CB&Q Mark Twain Zephyr, CC, *13–14*	1100
___38860	CB&Q Pioneer Zephyr, CC, *13–14*	1100
___38864	Lionel Lines Zephyr, CC, *13–14*	1100
___38865	L&N GP35 Diesel "1105," CC, *13*	500
___38866	L&N GP35 Diesel "1109," CC, *13*	500
___38867	L&N GP35 Diesel "1114," nonpowered, *13*	260
___38868	C&BQ GP35 Diesel "978," CC, *13*	500
___38874	B&O GP9 Diesel "6448," CC, *13–14*	480
___38875	B&O GP9 Diesel "6456," CC, *13–14*	480
___38876	B&O GP9 Diesel "6461," nonpowered, *13–14*	240
___38877	B&M GP9 Diesel "1705," CC, *13*	480
___38878	B&M GP9 Diesel "1714," CC, *13*	480
___38879	B&M GP9 Diesel "1722," nonpowered, *13*	240
___38883	C&NW GP9 Diesel "701," CC, *13*	480
___38884	C&NW GP9 Diesel "704," CC, *13*	480
___38885	C&NW GP9 Diesel "712," nonpowered, *13*	240
___38886	Erie GP9 Diesel "1260," CC, *13*	480
___38887	Erie GP9 Diesel "1263," CC, *13*	480
___38888	Erie GP9 Diesel "1265," nonpowered, *13*	240

		Exc	Mint
38889	Nickel Plate Road GP9 Diesel "514," CC, *13*	480	___
38890	Nickel Plate Road GP9 Diesel "452," CC, *13*	480	___
38891	Nickel Plate Road GP9 Diesel "457," nonpowered, *13*	240	___
38892	SP GP9 Diesel "3411," CC, *13*	480	___
38893	SP GP9 Diesel "3415," CC, *13*	480	___
38894	SP GP9 Diesel "3419," nonpowered, *13*	240	___
38895	Wabash GP9 Diesel "484," CC, *13*	480	___
38896	Wabash GP9 Diesel "488," CC, *13*	480	___
38897	Wabash GP9 Diesel "491," nonpowered, *13*	240	___
38918	Chessie System SD40-2 Diesel "7609," CC, *13*	530	___
38919	Chessie System SD40-2 Diesel "7611," CC, *13*	530	___
38920	Chessie System SD40-2 Diesel "7614," nonpowered, *13*	240	___
38921	SP SD40T-2 Diesel Locomotive "8322," CC, *13*	530	___
38922	SP SD40T-2 Diesel Locomotive "8326," CC, *13*	530	___
38923	SP SD40T-2 Diesel, nonpowered, *13*	260	___
38924	B&O SD40-2 Diesel "7602," CC, *13*	530	___
38925	B&O SD40-2 Diesel "7607," CC, *13*	530	___
38926	B&O SD40-2 Diesel "7611," nonpowered, *13*	240	___
38933	Conrail SD40-2 Diesel "6424," CC, *13*	530	___
38934	Conrail SD40-2 Diesel "6437," CC, *13*	530	___
38935	Conrail SD40-2 Diesel "6468," nonpowered, *13*	240	___
38936	UP SD40-2 Diesel "2929," CC, *13*	530	___
38937	UP SD40-2 Diesel "2932," CC, *13*	530	___
38938	UP SD40-2 Diesel "2947," nonpowered, *13*	240	___
38939	NS SD40-2 Diesel "3355," CC, *13*	530	___
38940	NS SD40-2 Diesel "3365," CC, *13*	530	___
38941	NS SD40-2 Diesel "3379," nonpowered, *13*	240	___
38942	Central of Georgia NS Heritage ES44AC Diesel, CC, *12*	550	___
38943	Central of Georgia NS Heritage ES44AC Diesel, CC, *12*	550	___
38944	Central of Georgia NS Heritage ES44AC Diesel, nonpowered, *12*	280	___
38945	Conrail NS Heritage ES44AC Diesel, CC, *12*	550	___
38946	Conrail NS Heritage ES44AC Diesel, CC, *12*	550	___
38947	Conrail NS Heritage ES44AC Diesel, nonpowered, *12*	280	___
38948	Interstate NS Heritage ES44AC Diesel Locomotive "8105," CC, *12*	550	___
38949	Interstate NS Heritage ES44AC Diesel, CC, *12*	550	___
38950	Interstate NS Heritage ES44AC Diesel, nonpowered, *12*	280	___
38951	LV NS Heritage ES44AC Diesel, CC, *12*	550	___
38952	LV NS Heritage ES44AC Diesel, CC, *12*	550	___
38953	LV NS Heritage ES44AC Diesel, nonpowered, *12*	280	___
38954	Nickel Plate Road NS Heritage ES44AC Diesel, CC, *12*	550	___
38955	Nickel Plate Road NS Heritage ES44AC Diesel, CC, *12*	550	___
38956	Nickel Plate Road NS Heritage ES44AC Diesel, nonpowered, *12*	280	___
38957	N&W NS Heritage ES44AC Diesel, CC, *12*	550	___

		Exc	Mint
____38958	N&W NS Heritage ES44AC Diesel, CC, *12*		550
38959	N&W NS Heritage ES44AC Diesel, nonpowered, *12*		280
____			
____38960	PRR NS Heritage ES44AC Diesel, CC, *12*		550
____38961	PRR NS Heritage ES44AC Diesel, CC, *12*		550
____38962	PRR NS Heritage ES44AC Diesel, nonpowered, *12*		280
____38963	Southern NS Heritage ES44AC Diesel, CC, *12*		550
____38964	Southern NS Heritage ES44AC Diesel, CC, *12*		550
38965	Southern NS Heritage ES44AC Diesel, nonpowered, *12*		280
____			
____38966	NS Heritage ES44AC Diesel, CC, *12*		550
____38967	NS Heritage ES44AC Diesel, CC, *12*		550
____38968	NS Heritage ES44AC Diesel, nonpowered, *12*		280
____38969	North Pole Central GP35 Diesel "2525," CC, *13*		500
____38970	North Pole Central GP35 Diesel "2512," CC, *13*		500
38971	North Pole Central GP35 Diesel "2513," nonpowered, *13*		260
____			
____38972	Reading GP35 Diesel "3625," CC, *13*		500
____38973	Reading GP35 Diesel "3630," CC, *13*		500
____38974	Reading GP35 Diesel "3633," nonpowered, *13*		260
____38975	AT&SF GP35 Diesel "3312," CC, *13*		500
____38976	AT&SF GP35 Diesel "3318," CC, *13*		500
____38977	AT&SF GP35 Diesel "3329," nonpowered, *13*		260
____38978	Alaska GP35 Diesel "2501," CC, *13*		500
____38979	Alaska GP35 Diesel "2503," CC, *13*		500
____38980	Alaska GP35 Diesel "2502," nonpowered, *13*		260
____38981	B&O GP35 Diesel "2506," CC, *13-14*		500
____38982	B&O GP35 Diesel "2511," CC, *13-14*		500
____38983	B&O GP35 Diesel "2517," nonpowered, *13-14*		260
____38984	C&O GP35 Diesel "3515," CC, *13-14*		500
____38985	C&O GP35 Diesel "3521," CC, *13-14*		500
____38986	C&O GP35 Diesel "3526," nonpowered, *13-14*		260
____38987	MP GP35 Diesel "603," CC, *13*		500
____38988	MP GP35 Diesel "607," CC, *13*		500
____38989	MP GP35 Diesel "611," nonpowered, *13*		260
____38990	GM&O GP35 Diesel "603," CC, *13-14*		500
____38991	GM&O GP35 Diesel "607," CC, *13-14*		500
____38992	GM&O GP35 Diesel "611," nonpowered, *13-14*		260
____38993	WM GP35 Diesel "3576," CC, *13*		500
____38994	WM GP35 Diesel "3578," CC, *13*		500
____38995	WM GP35 Diesel "3580," nonpowered, *13*		260
____38996	CSX GP35 Diesel "4355," CC, *13*		500
____38997	CSX GP35 Diesel "4363," CC, *13*		500
____38998	CSX GP35 Diesel "4390," nonpowered, *13*		260
____38999	NS GP35 Diesel "2916," CC, *13*		500
____39008	PRR Heavyweight Passenger Car 4-pack, *00*		225
39009	PRR Indian Rock Heavyweight Combination Car, *00*		50
____			
39010	PRR Andrew Carnegie Heavyweight Passenger Coach, *00*		60
____			
39011	PRR Solomon P. Chase Heavyweight Passenger Coach, *00*		60
____			
39012	PRR Skyline View Heavyweight Observation Car, *00*		50
____			

		Exc	Mint
39013	B&O Heavyweight Passenger Car 4-pack, *00*		400____
39016	B&O Heavyweight Passenger Car 4-pack, *00*		200____
39017	B&O Harper's Ferry Heavyweight Combination Car, *00*		50____
39018	B&O Youngstown Heavyweight Passenger Coach, *00*		50____
39019	B&O New Castle Heavyweight Passenger Coach, *00*		50____
39020	B&O Chicago Heavyweight Observation Car, *00*		50____
39028	LL Heavyweight Passenger Car 3-pack, *00*		195____
39029	LL Irvington Heavyweight Coach "2625," *00*		60____
39030	LL Madison Heavyweight Coach "2627," *00*		60____
39031	LL Manhattan Heavyweight Coach "2628," *00*		60____
39032	UP Madison Passenger Car 4-pack, *00*		275____
39038	SP Madison Baggage Car "6015," *01*		NRS____
39039	SP Madison Coach Car "1978," *01*		NRS____
39040	SP Madison Coach "1975," *01*		NRS____
39041	SP Madison Observation Car "2951," *01*		NRS____
39042	N&W Heavyweight Passenger Car 4-pack, *00*		325____
39047	B&O Heavyweight Passenger Car 2-pack, *01*		160____
39050	PRR Heavyweight Passenger Car 2-pack, *01*		215____
39053	Alaska Streamliner Car 2-pack, *01*		90____
39056	NYC Streamliner Car 2-pack, *01*		75____
39059	Santa Fe Streamliner Car 2-pack, *01*		100____
39062	B&O Streamliner Car 2-pack, *01*		75____
39065	PRR Streamliner Car 4-pack, *01*		165____
39082	Blue Comet Heavyweight Passenger Car 2-pack, *02*		325____
39085	"Freedom Train" Heavyweight Passenger Car 3-pack, *03*		260____
39092	PRR Streamliner Car 2-pack, *01*		70____
39099	Alton Limited Heavyweight Passenger Car 2-pack, *03*		230____
39100	William Penn Congressional Coach, *00*		115____
39101	Molly Pitcher Congressional Coach, *00*		100____
39102	Betsy Ross Congressional Vista Dome Car, *00*		100____
39103	Alexander Hamilton Congressional Observation Car, *00*		100____
39104	Phoebe Snow Car, StationSounds, *99*		255____
39105	Milwaukee Road Hiawatha Car, StationSounds, *99*		235____
39106	CP Aluminum Passenger Car 2-pack, *00*		185____
39107	CP Blair Manor Aluminum Passenger Coach "2553," *00*		115____
39108	CP Craig Manor Aluminum Passenger Coach "2554," *00*		110____
39109	"Spirit of the Century" Aluminum Passenger Car 4-pack, *99*		520____
39110	"Spirit of the Century" Full Vista Dome Car, *99–00*		100____
39111	"Spirit of the Century" Full Vista Dome Car, *99–00*		100____
39112	"Spirit of the Century" Full Vista Dome Car, *99–00*		100____

		Exc	Mint
39113	"Spirit of the Century" Skytop Observation Car, *99–00*		100
39118	Texas Special Garland Aluminum Passenger Coach "1203," StationSounds, *99–00*		220
39119	Southern Aluminum Passenger Car 4-pack, *00*		350
39120	Southern Grand Junction Aluminum Passenger/Baggage Car, *00*		280
39121	Southern Charlottesville Aluminum Passenger Coach "812," *00*		90
39122	Southern Roanoke Aluminum Passenger Coach "814," *00*		250
39123	Southern Memphis Aluminum Observation Car "1152," *00*		90
39124	Amtrak Superliner Aluminum Passenger Car 4-pack, *02*		405
39129	Santa Fe Superliner Aluminum Passenger Car 4-pack, *02*		305
39141	RI Aluminum Passenger Car 4-pack, *01*		400
39146	UP Aluminum Passenger Car 4-pack, *01*		285
39151	CP Aluminum Passenger Car 2-pack, *01*		315
39154	PRR Congressional Aluminum Passenger Car 2-pack, *02*		195
39155	PRR Congressional Baggage Car, *02*		105
39156	PRR Robert Morris Congressional Coach, *02*		100
39157	Southern Aluminum Passenger Car 2-pack, *01*		290
39160	KCS Aluminum Passenger Car 2-pack, *01*		260
39163	Erie-Lack. Aluminum Passenger Car 2-pack, *01*		230
39166	Texas Special Aluminum Passenger Car 2-pack, *01*	300	430
39169	ACL Aluminum Passenger Car 4-pack, *01*		360
39179	NP Aluminum Passenger Car 2-pack, *02*		305
39182	WP Aluminum Passenger Car 2-pack, *02*		280
39185	Rio Grande Aluminum Passenger Car 2-pack, *02*		290
39194	UP Aluminum Passenger Car 2-pack, *02*		220
39197	CP Aluminum Passenger Coach, StationSounds, *02*		225
39198	PRR Aluminum Passenger Coach, StationSounds, *02*		210
39200	Hellgate Bridge Boxcar #2 "1900-2000," *00 u*		55
39202	Lionel Centennial Boxcar "1900-2000," *00*		46
39203	Postwar "6464" Series X, 3 cars, *01*		115
39204	New Haven Boxcar "6464-725," *01*		44
39205	Alaska Boxcar "6464-825," *01*		55
39206	NYC Boxcar "6464-900," *01*		40
39207	UP Boxcar "508500," red, *00*		50
39208	UP Boxcar "903658," silver, *00*		42
39209	UP Boxcar "500200," yellow, *00*		40
39210	6530 Fire Fighting Car, *00*		37
39211	Postwar "6464" Boxcar 3-pack #2, *00*		85
39212	Postwar "6464" SP&S Boxcar, *00*		NRS
39213	Postwar "6464" Wabash Boxcar, *00*		NRS
39214	Postwar "6464" Kansas, Oklahoma & Gulf Boxcar, *00*		NRS
39216	PRR DD Boxcar "47211," *01*		46
39220	B&LE Heavyweight Boxcar "82101," *01*		41

Exc Mint

		Exc	Mint
39221	L&N Heavyweight Boxcar "109829," *01*	41	____
39222	Conrail Heavyweight Boxcar "269198," *01*	44	____
39223	Postwar "6464" Archive Boxcar Set, 3-pack, *02*	125	____
39227	Postwar "6468" Automobile Boxcar 3-pack, *01*	95	____
39229	B&O DD Boxcar, *01*	40	____
39236	WP Boxcar "6464-250," *01*	55	____
39238	Elvis Boxcar, *03*	36	____
39239	P&LE Boxcar "22300, *02*	35	____
39240	Pennsylvania Boxcar "118747," *02*	32	____
39241	PC Boxcar "252455," *02*	28	____
39242	Postwar "6464" Boxcar 3-pack #1, Archive Collection, *03–04*	80	____
39243	Soo Line Boxcar, Archive Collection	35	____
39247	NYC DD Boxcar "6468," *02–03*	32	____
39248	Lackawanna DD Boxcar with hobo, *03*	45	____
39250	Campbell's Kids Centennial Boxcar, *03–04*	40	____
39252	Lenny Dean 60th Anniversary Boxcar, *04*	38	____
39253	No. 6464 Boxcar 3-pack #2, Archive Collection, *04*	100	____
39257	WP Boxcar "6464-100," boys set add-on, *03*	50	____
39258	Elvis Presley "All Shook Up" Boxcar, *03–04*	40	____
39259	Buick Centennial Boxcar, *03*	35	____
39260	New Haven Boxcar, *04*	40	____
39262	Elvis Presley "Elvis Has Left the Building" Boxcar, *04*	38	____
39263	M&StL Boxcar, Postwar Celebration Series, *05*	35	____
39267	No. 6464 Boxcar 3-pack #3, Archive Collection, *05*	100	____
39271	State of Maine Boxcar, *04*	35	____
39273	No. 6464 Boxcar 3-pack #4, Archive Collection, *06*	100	____
39281	Florida State University Boxcar, *07*	45	____
39282	Purdue University Boxcar, *08*	50	____
39283	University of Virginia Boxcar, *08*	50	____
39284	Penn State University Boxcar, *06–07*	45	____
39285	U.S. Military Academy at West Point Boxcar, *08*	50	____
39286	University of Illinois Boxcar, *06–07*	45	____
39287	University of Alabama Boxcar, *06–07*	45	____
39289	University of Oklahoma Boxcar, *06–08*	50	____
39290	Postwar "6464" Boxcar 2-pack, rare variations, *08*	100	____
39291	University of Michigan Boxcar, *06–07*	45	____
39292	Monopoly Boxcar 3-pack, *08*	135	____
39296	UPS Centennial Boxcar #3, *08–09*	55	____
39297	Macy's Parade Boxcar, *07*	55	____
39298	Monopoly Boxcar 3-pack #2, *08*	145	____
39299	Lenny Dean Commemorative Boxcar, *08*	50	____
39302	University of Maryland Boxcar, *08*	50	____
39303	Villanova University Boxcar, *08*	50	____
39304	Auburn University Boxcar, *08*	50	____
39308	CP Rail "6565" Boxcar "58700," *08–10*	55	____
39309	Macy's Parade Boxcar, *08*	50	____
39310	Monopoly Boxcar 3-pack #3, *09–10*	165	____

		Exc	Mint
____39316	New Haven Automobile Boxcar, *09–10*		60
____39317	Wizard of Oz Boxcar #1, *09–10*		60
____39318	Wizard of Oz Boxcar #2, *09–10*		60
____39319	Boy Scouts "Scout Law" Add-on Boxcar, *10*		60
____39321	Lionel Art Boxcar 2-pack, *10*		116
____39325	Macy's Parade Boxcar, *09*		45
____39326	UPS Centennial Boxcar #4, *10–11*		60
____39328	Monopoly Boxcar 3-pack #4, *10–11*		190
____39332	Holiday Boxcar, *10*		60
____39334	Coca-Cola Christmas Boxcar, *10*		68
____39335	Thomas Kinkade Boxcar, *10, 12*		60
39336	Angela Trotta Thomas "My Turn Yet, Dad?" Boxcar, *10*		60
____39337	George Washington Boxcar, *11–12*		60
____39338	Abraham Lincoln Boxcar, *11–12*		60
____39339	Theodore Roosevelt Boxcar, *11–12*		60
____39340	Thomas Jefferson Boxcar, *11–12*		60
____39342	Strasburg Boxcar, *11*		55
____39343	New Jersey Central Boxcar, *10*		45
____39344	Monopoly Boxcar 3-pack #5, *11–12*		165
____39345	Monopoly Tennessee Avenue Boxcar, *11*		55
____39346	Monopoly Atlantic Avenue Boxcar, *11*		55
____39347	Monopoly Illinois Avenue Boxcar, *11*		55
____39348	Lionel NASCAR Collectables Boxcar, *11–12*		60
39350	Thomas Kinkade "All Aboard for Christmas" Boxcar, *12–13*		60
____39351	Peanuts Thanksgiving Boxcar, *12*		70
____39354	Monopoly North Carolina Avenue Boxcar, *12*		70
____39358	Boy Scouts "Prepared For Life" Boxcar, *12*		60
____39359	Thanksgiving Boxcar, *12*		60
____39360	Boy Scouts Cub Scout Boxcar, *12–13*		60
____39361	Coca-Cola Polar Bear Boxcar, *14*		70
____39362	Thomas Kinkade "Emerald City" Boxcar, *12–15*		75
____39363	Peanuts Halloween Boxcar, *12*		65
____39364	Christmas Boxcar, *13*		60
39376	Monopoly Boxcar 2-pack, States and Vermont Avenues, *13–15*		140
39379	Monopoly Boxcar 2-pack, Mediterranean and St. James Avenues, *13–15*		140
____39383	Prewar "2719" Boxcar, *13*		65
____39385	U.S. Navy 1-D Tank Car, *13–15*		70
____39386	U.S. Marines 1-D Tank Car, *13–15*		70
____39387	U.S. Air Force 1-D Tank Car, *13–15*		70
____39388	U.S. National Guard 1-D Tank Car, *13–16*		70
____39389	U.S. Coast Guard 1-D Tank Car, *13–16*		70
____39391	U.S. Army Flatcar, *13–16*		70
____39392	U.S. Navy Flatcar, *13–16*		70
____39393	U.S. Marines Flatcar, *13–16*		70
____39394	U.S. Air Force Flatcar, *13–16*		70
____39395	U.S. National Guard Flatcar, *13–16*		70
____39396	U.S. Coast Guard Flatcar, *13–16*		70
____39398	Santa's Flyer Reefer, *13*		43
____39399	U.S. Army 1-D Tank Car, *13–15*		70

		Exc	Mint
39400	Republic Steel Slag Car 3-pack (std O), *04*		100___
39404	Republic Steel Hot Metal Car 3-pack (std O), *04*		130___
39411	Jones & Laughline Hot Metal Car 3-pack (std O), *05*		190___
39423	Postwar "3460" LL Flatcar with trailers, *05*		45___
39424	U.S. Steel 16-wheel Flatcar with girders, *05*		70___
39425	Hood's Flatcar with milk container, traditional, *05*		55___
39426	Nestle Nesquik Flatcar with milk container, traditional, *05*		55___
39428	Bethlehem Steel Slag Car #4 (std O), *05*		60___
39429	Bethlehem Steel Hot Metal Car #8 (std O), *05*		70___
39430	Youngstown Sheet & Tube Slag Car #7 (std O), *05*		60___
39431	Youngstown Sheet & Tube Hot Metal Car #11 (std O), *05*		70___
39435	Postwar "6477" Flatcar with pipes, *06*		50___
39436	Postwar "6262" Wheel Car, *06*		50___
39437	Supplee Flatcar with milk container, *06*		60___
39439	6827 Flatcar with P&H power shovel, *04*		50___
39440	6828 Flatcar with P&H truck crane, *04*		50___
39443	U.S. Steel Slag Car 3-pack #2 (std O), *06*		170___
39447	Postwar "6561" LL Cable Reel Car, Archive Collection, *06–07*		55___
39450	Postwar "6414" Evans Auto Loader, Archive Collection, *06*		70___
39452	White Bros. Flatcar with milk container, *07*		60___
39457	Postwar "6175" Flatcar with rocket, *08*		55___
39458	Postwar "6844" Flatcar with missiles, *08*		55___
39463	Postwar "6430" Flatcar with trailers, *08*		55___
39468	Allis-Chalmers Car "52369," *08–09*		60___
39469	Christmas Egg Nog Barrel Car, *08*		50___
39470	UP Well Car "147128," *08*		65___
39471	Postwar "6264" Flatcar, *08*		60___
39472	ATSF Culvert Gondola, *08*		60___
39473	Play-Doh Vat Car, *08*		55___
39475	UPS Flatcar with trailer, *08*		65___
39476	Bethlehem Steel 16-wheel Flatcar, *08*		75___
39477	Christmas Flatcar with reindeer trailers, *08*		60___
39478	Postwar "6475" Pickles Vat Car, *08*		55___
39479	Postwar "6404" Flatcar with brown automobile, *08*		50___
39480	Western & Atlantic Cannon Flatcar, *09*		60___
39482	CSX WM Track Maintenance Car "6812," *11*		65___
39483	CSX P&LE Gondola "69812," *11*		65___
39484	Cocoa Marsh Vat Car, *10–12*		60___
39486	Deep Sea Challenger Submarine Car, *11*		60___
39488	Reese's Vat Car, *10*		60___
39490	Western & Atlantic Cannonball Flatcar, *10*		55___
39497	Christmas Reindeer Stock Car, *10–11*		60___
39498	CNJ Gondola with culvert pipes, *11*		55___
39499	Alaska Oil Barrel Ramp Car, *11*		50___
39502	Monongahela NS Heritage ES44AC Diesel, nonpowered, *13*		280___
39530	PRR 1955 Pickup Truck, CC, *13*		180___
39531	UP 1955 Pickup Truck, CC, *13*		180___

		Exc	Mint
____39532	ATSF 1955 Pickup Truck, CC, *13–14*		180
____39533	CP 1955 Pickup Truck, CC, *13–14*		180
____39534	D&RGW 1955 Pickup Truck, CC, *13*		180
____39535	GN 1955 Pickup Truck, CC, *13*		180
____39536	MKT 1955 Pickup Truck, CC, *13–14*		180
____39537	NYC 1955 Pickup Truck, CC, *13*		180
____39538	Nickel Plate Road 1955 Pickup Truck, CC, *13*		180
____39539	NP 1955 Pickup Truck, CC, *13–14*		180
____39540	Southern 1955 Pickup Truck, CC, *13*		180
____39541	SP 1955 Pickup Truck, CC, *13–14*		180
____39542	Weyerhaueser 1955 Pickup Truck, CC, *13–14*		180
____39543	Texas Special F3 B Unit, *13–14*		230
____39544	Texas Special F3 B Unit, CC, *13–14*		380
____39547	PRR F3 B Unit, *13–14*		230
____39548	PRR F3 B Unit, CC, *13–14*		380
____39554	NS GP35 Diesel "3918," CC, *13*		500
____39555	NS GP35 Diesel "2915," nonpowered, *13*		260
____39556	CP GP35 Diesel "5004," CC, *13–14*		500
____39557	CP GP35 Diesel "5007," CC, *13–14*		500
____39558	CP GP35 Diesel "5009," nonpowered, *13–14*		260
____39562	BN GP35 Diesel "2533," CC, *13–14*		500
____39563	BN GP35 Diesel "2509," CC, *13–14*		500
____39564	BN GP35 Diesel "2523," nonpowered, *13–14*		260
____39565	ATSF Dash-9 Diesel "612," CC, *13*		530
____39566	ATSF Dash-9 Diesel "623," CC, *13*		530
____39567	ATSF Dash-9 Diesel "631," nonpowered, *13*		260
____39568	BC Rail Dash-9 Diesel "4641," CC, *13*		530
____39569	BC Rail Dash-9 Diesel "4647," CC, *13*		530
____39570	BC Rail Dash-9 Diesel "4652," nonpowered, *13*		260
____39571	BNSF Dash-9 Diesel "4023," CC, *13*		530
____39572	BNSF Dash-9 Diesel "4037," CC, *13*		530
____39573	BNSF Dash-9 Diesel "4046," nonpowered, *13*		260
____39574	C&NW Dash-9 Diesel "8605," CC, *13*		530
____39575	C&NW Dash-9 Diesel "8610," CC, *13*		530
____39576	C&NW Dash-9 Diesel "8622," nonpowered, *13*		260
____39577	SP Dash-9 Diesel "8112," CC, *13*		530
____39578	SP Dash-9 Diesel "8123," CC, *13*		530
____39579	SP Dash-9 Diesel "8129," nonpowered, *13*		260
____39580	UP Dash-9 Diesel "9599," CC, *13*		530
____39581	UP Dash-9 Diesel "9714," CC, *13*		530
____39582	UP Dash-9 Diesel "9717," nonpowered, *13*		260
____39583	CSX Dash-9 Diesel "9036," CC, *13*		530
____39584	CSX Dash-9 Diesel "9048," CC, *13*		530
____39585	CSX Dash-9 Diesel "9051," nonpowered, *13*		260
____39586	NS Dash-9 Diesel "9310," CC, *13*		530
____39587	NS Dash-9 Diesel "9322," CC, *13*		530
____39588	NS Dash-9 Diesel "9334," nonpowered, *13*		260
____39589	CN Dash-9 Diesel "2534," CC, *13*		530
____39590	CN Dash-9 Diesel "2547," CC, *13*		530
____39591	CN Dash-9 Diesel "2570," nonpowered, *13*		260
____39592	CNJ NS Heritage SD70ACe Diesel "1071," CC, *13*		530
____39593	CNJ NS Heritage SD70ACe Diesel "1831," CC, *13*		530

Exc Mint

		Exc	Mint
39594	CNJ NS Heritage SD70ACe Diesel "1834," nonpowered, *13*	260	
39595	DL&W NS Heritage SD70ACe Diesel "1074," CC, *13*	530	
39596	DL&W NS Heritage SD70ACe Diesel "1853," CC, *13*	530	
39597	DL&W NS Heritage SD70ACe Diesel "1856," nonpowered, *13*	260	
39598	Monongahela NS Heritage ES44AC Diesel "8025," CC, *12*	550	
39599	Monongahela NS Heritage ES44AC Diesel "1901," CC, *12*	550	
39600	PRR E8 AA Diesel Set, CC, *13*	930	
39603	B&O E9 AA Diesel Set, CC, *13*	930	
39606	FEC E9 AA Diesel Set, CC, *13*	930	
39609	SP E9 AA Diesel Set, CC, *13*	930	
39612	SP E9 AA Diesel Set, CC, *13*	930	
39612	UP E9 AA Diesel Set, CC, *13*	930	
39615	CB&Q E9 AA Diesel Set, CC, *13*	930	
39618	MILW E9 AA Diesel Set, CC, *13*	930	
39621	KCS E9 AA Diesel Set, CC, *13*	930	
39624	Erie NS Heritage SD70ACe Diesel "1068," CC, *13*	530	
39625	Erie NS Heritage SD70ACe Diesel "1832," CC, *13*	530	
39626	Erie NS Heritage SD70ACe Diesel "1835," nonpowered, *13*	260	
39627	Illinois Terminal NS Heritage SD70ACe Diesel "1072," CC, *13*	530	
39628	Illinois Terminal NS Heritage SD70ACe Diesel "1896," CC, *13*	530	
39629	Illinois Terminal NS Heritage SD70ACe Diesel "1899," nonpowered, *13*	260	
39630	NYC NS Heritage SD70ACe Diesel "1066," CC, *13*	530	
39631	NYC NS Heritage SD70ACe Diesel "1831," CC, *13*	530	
39632	NYC NS Heritage SD70ACe Diesel "1834," nonpowered, *13*	260	
39633	Reading NS Heritage SD70ACe Diesel "1067," CC, *13*	530	
39634	Reading NS Heritage SD70ACe Diesel "1833," CC, *13*	530	
39635	Reading NS Heritage SD70ACe Diesel "1836," nonpowered, *13*	260	
39636	Savannah & Atlanta NS Heritage SD70ACe Diesel "1065," CC, *13*	530	
39637	Savannah & Atlanta NS Heritage SD70ACe Diesel "1915," CC, *13*	530	
39638	Savannah & Atlanta NS Heritage SD70ACe Diesel "1918," nonpowered, *13*	260	
39639	Virginian NS Heritage SD70ACe Diesel "1069," CC, *13*	530	
39640	Virginian NS Heritage SD70ACe Diesel "1907," CC, *13*	530	
39641	Virginian NS Heritage SD70ACe Diesel "1910," nonpowered, *13*	260	
39642	Wabash NS Heritage SD70ACe Diesel "1070," CC, *13*	530	

		Exc	Mint
39643	Wabash NS Heritage SD70ACe Diesel "1877," CC, *13*		530
39644	Wabash NS Heritage SD70ACe Diesel "1880," nonpowered, *13*		260
39645	PC NS Heritage SD70ACe Diesel "1073," CC, *13*		530
39646	PC NS Heritage SD70ACe Diesel "1968," CC, *13*		530
39647	PC NS Heritage SD70ACe Diesel "1971," nonpowered, *13*		260
51008	Burlington Pioneer Zephyr Diesel Passenger Set, RailSounds, *04*		875
51009	Prewar "269E" Steam Freight Set, TrainSounds, *06*		630
51010	Prewar "246E" Steam Passenger Set, TrainSounds, *07–08*		630
51012	Christmas Tinplate Freight Set, *08*		675
51014	Prewar "291W" Red Comet Passenger Car Set, *08*		675
51220	NYC Imperial Castle Passenger Coach, *93 u*		500
51221	NYC Niagara County Passenger Coach, *93 u*		500
51222	NYC Cascade Glory Passenger Coach, *93 u*		500
51223	NYC City of Detroit Passenger Coach, *93 u*		500
51224	NYC Imperial Falls Passenger Coach, *93 u*		500
51225	NYC Westchester County Passenger Coach, *93 u*		500
51226	NYC Cascade Grotto Passenger Coach, *93 u*		500
51227	NYC City of Indianapolis Passenger Coach, *93 u*		500
51228	NYC Manhattan Island Observation Car, *93 u*		500
51229	NYC Diner "680," *93 u*		500
51230	NYC Baggage Car "5017," *93 u*		500
51231	NYC Century Club Passenger Coach, *93 u*		500
51232	NYC Thousand Islands Observation Car, *93 u*		500
51233	NYC Diner "684," *93 u*		500
51234	NYC Baggage Car "5020," *93 u*		500
51235	NYC Century Tavern Passenger Coach, *93 u*		500
51236	NYC City of Toledo Passenger Coach, *93 u*		500
51237	NYC Imperial Mansion Passenger Coach, *93 u*		500
51238	NYC Imperial Palace Passenger Coach, *93 u*		500
51239	NYC Cascade Spirit Passenger Coach, *93 u*		500
51240	NYC Diner "681," *93 u*		500
51241	NYC City of Chicago Passenger Coach, *93 u*		500
51242	NYC Imperial Garden Passenger Coach, *93 u*		500
51243	NYC Imperial Fountain Passenger Coach, *93 u*		500
51244	NYC Cascade Valley Passenger Coach, *93 u*		500
51245	NYC Diner "685," *93 u*		500
51300	Shell Semi-Scale 1-D Tank Car "8124," *91*	50	135
51301	Lackawanna Semi-Scale Reefer "7000," *92*	119	161
51401	PRR Semi-Scale Boxcar "100800," *91*	84	128
51402	C&O Semi-Scale Stock Car "95250," *92*	98	138
51501	B&O Semi-Scale Hopper "532000," *91*	78	108
51502	LL Steel Die-cast Ore Car "6486-3" (SSS), *96*		80
51503	LL Steel Die-cast Ore Car "6486-1" (SSS), *96*		80
51504	LL Steel Die-cast Ore Car "6486-2" (SSS), *96*		70
51600	NYC Depressed Center Flatcar with transformer "6418," *96*		105
51701	NYC Semi-Scale Caboose "19400," *91*	84	123

Exc Mint

Number	Description	Exc	Mint
51702	PRR N-8 Caboose "478039," *91–92*	300	385
52054	Carail Boxcar, *94 u*		280
52066	Trainmaster Tractor and Trailer, *94 u*		110
52069	Carail Tractor and Trailer, *94 u*		70
52070	Knoebel's Boxcar #1, *95 u*		88
52075	United Auto Workers Boxcar, *95 u*		90
52082	Steamtown Lackawanna Boxcar, *95 u*		90
52132	Knoebel's Boxcar #2, *99 u*		90
52133	Knoebel's Boxcar #3, *98 u*		100
52134	Knoebel's Boxcar #4, *00 u*		95
52136A	Christmas Special Tractor and Trailer, *97*		NRS
52136B	Frisco Special Tractor and Trailer, *98*		NRS
52137	Red Wing Shoes Boot Oil Tank Car, *98*		65
52141	Zep Manufacturing Boxcar, *96*		95
52158	Monopoly Mint Car "M-0539," *98*		340
52159	Monopoly Depressed Center Flatcar with transformer, *98*		95
52160	Monopoly Water Works Tank Car, *98*		105
52161	Monopoly SP-type Caboose "M-1006," *98*		55
52168	Carail Flatcar with Trailer "17455," *99 u*		100
52169	Zep Manufacturing Flatcar with trailer "62734," *99 u*		80
52174	REA Baggage Car "0083," *00 u*		400
52181	Monopoly Set #2, 4-pack, *99*		295
52182	Monopoly Railroads Boxcar "M0636," *99 u*		78
52183	Monopoly Jail Car "M-1131," *99*		75
52184	Monopoly Free Parking Flatcar with 2 autos, *99*		60
52185	Monopoly Chance Gondola "M-0893," *99*		50
52187	Madison Hardware Flatcar with 2 trailers, *99*		98
52188	Carail Aquarium with 2 autos, 25th Anniversary, *99*		95
52189	Monopoly 4-6-4 Hudson Locomotive, *99*		550
52207	Lionel Lines SD40 Diesel, traditional, *00*		600
52208	Lionel Lines Extended Vision Caboose, *00 u*		200
52209	World's Fair Sleeper/Roomette Car "0183," *01 u*		170
52218	Monopoly 4-4-2 Steam Freight Set, *00 u*		388
52219	Monopoly 4-6-4 Hudson Locomotive, bronze, *00 u*		530
52224A	SP Flatcar with Navajo tractor and trailer, *01*		25
52224B	SP Flatcar with Trailer Flatcar Service tractor and trailer, *01*		25
52225	Monopoly 4-6-4 Hudson Locomotive, pewter, *01 u*		495
52231	British Columbia 1-D Tank Car, *00 u*		65
52235	World's Fair Vista Dome Car "0283," *02 u*		NRS
52249	Knoebel's Amusement Park 75th Anniversary Boxcar, *01 u*		89
52262	Plasticville Boxcar, *01 u*		120
52263	World's Fair Combination Car "0383," *02*		NRS
52282	Western Pacific Feather Boxcar, red, *03*		365
52315/20	PRR FM Diesel and Caboose, *04 u*		440
52330	B&O Museum Fundraiser Boxcar, *03 u*		100
52371	NYC Flatcar with tanker trailer, *05 u*		150

Exc Mint

			Exc	Mint
62162	Postwar "262" Automatic Crossing Gate and Signal, *99–14*			60
62180	Railroad Signs, set of 14, *99–04, 08–16*			10
62181	Telephone Pole Set, *99–04, 08–16*			10
62283	Die-cast Illuminated Bumpers, *99–16*			27
62709	Rico Station Kit, *99–00*			46
62716	Short Extension Bridge, *99–03, 07–16*			15
62900	Lockon, *99–13*			3
62901	Ives Track Clips, 12 pieces (027), *99–10, 13–16*			5
62905	Lockon with wires, *99–10, 13–14*			7
62909	Smoke Fluid, *99–12*			7
62927	Lubrication/Maintenance Set, *99–16*			25
62985	The Lionel Train Book, *99–03*			12
65014	Half Curved Track (027), *99–16*			1
65019	Half-Straight Track (027), *99–16*			1
65020	90-degree Crossover (027), *99–16*			11
65021	27" Manual Switch, left hand (027), *99–16*			17
65022	27" Manual Switch, right hand (027), *99–16*			18
65023	45-degree Crossover (027), *99–16*			11
65024	35" Straight Track (027), *99–16*			5
65033	27" Diameter Curved Track (027), *99–16*			2
65038	9" Straight Track (027), *99–16*			2
65041	Insulator Pins, dozen (027), *99–04, 06, 13–14*			3
65042	Steel Pins, dozen (027), *99–04, 06–09, 13–14*			3
65049	42" Diameter Curved Track (027), *99–16*			3
65113	54" Diameter Curved Track (027), *99–16*			3
65121	27" Path Remote Switch, left hand (027), *99–14*			43
65122	27" Path Remote Switch, right hand (027), *99–14*			43
65149	Uncoupling Track (027), *99–14*			12
65165	72" Path Remote Switch, right hand (O), *99–14*			125
65166	72" Path Remote Switch, left hand (O), *99–14*			125
65167	42" Remote Switch, right hand (027), *99–14*			25
65168	42" Remote Switch, left hand (027), *99–14*			25
65500	10" Straight Track (O), *99–16*			2
65501	31" Diameter Curved Track (O), *99–16*			2
65504	Half Curved Track (O), *99–16*			2
65505	Half Straight Track (O), *99–16*			2
65514	Half Curved Track (027), *99–03*			3
65523	40" Straight Track (O), *99–16*			7
65530	Remote Control Track (O), *99–16*			38
65540	90-degree Crossover (O), *99–14*			16
65543	Insulator Pins, dozen (O), *99–16*			3
65545	45-degree Crossover (O), *99–14*			27
65551	Steel Pins, dozen (O), *99–16*			3
65554	54" Diameter Curved Track (O), *99–16*			4
65572	72" Diameter Curved Track (O), *99–16*			5
81000	BNSF Waffle-sided Boxcar "496464," *14–15*			50
81001	SP&S Flatcar with bulkheads, *14–16*			50
81002	UP 3-D Tank Car, *14–15*			50
81003	CP Bilevel Auto Carrier, *14–16*			50
81004	B&O Depressed-Center Flatcar with transformer, *14–15*			50

Exc Mint

Number	Description	Exc	Mint
81005	Maine Central 2-bay Hopper "1005," 14–16	50	___
81006	PRR Hi-Cube Boxcar "31010," 14–16	50	___
81007	Seaboard Waffle-sided Boxcar "25335," 14–16	50	___
81008	Central of Georgia Boxcar "5818," 14–16	50	___
81009	Southern 2-D Tank Car "951005," 14–16	50	___
81010	FEC Gondola "6121" with reels, 14–16	50	___
81011	PFE Reefer "33280," 14–16	50	___
81012	T&P 1-D Tank Car, 14–16	50	___
81013	Frisco Boxcar "700117," 14–16	50	___
81014	D&RGW Ore Car "31101," 14–15	50	___
81015	B&M Reefer "1878," 14–16	50	___
81016	Coaling Station, 14, 16	110	___
81017	Barrel Loading Building, 14–16	43	___
81019	Short Tunnel, 14–16	45	___
81021	B&M Paul Revere GP9 Diesel Freight Set, 14–15	500	___
81023	Jersey Central Yard Boss 0-4-0 Steam Freight Set, 14–15	500	___
81024	Christmas Train Set, 02–04	150	___
81025	Lackawanna Pocono Berkshire Steam Freight Set, 14–15	480	___
81027	Thomas the Tank Engine Set, 01–04	120	___
81028	Marquette GP38 Diesel Freight Set, 14–15	430	___
81029	C&NW Windy City GP38 Diesel Freight Set, 14–15	400	___
81030	UP Gold Coast Flyer Steam Freight Set, 14–15	430	___
81031	Dinosaur LionChief Diesel Freight Set, 14–16	175	___
81038	MILW Heavy Mikado Locomotive "8693" CC, 15	1300	___
81063	Classic Automatic Gateman, 14–16	95	___
81064	Construction Zone Signs #2, 14–16	10	___
81066	Milwaukee Road Double-sheathed Boxcar "8775" (std O), 14	80	___
81067	Monopoly Aquarium Car, 14–15	85	___
81073	Monopoly Boxcar 2-pack, Ventnor and Indiana Avenues, 14–15	135	___
81076	Pennsylvania Salt 8,000-gallon 1-D Tank Car "4724" (std O), 14	73	___
81077	Pere Marquette 8,000-gallon 1-D Tank Car "71710" (std O), 14	73	___
81078	NYC 8,000-gallon 1-D Tank Car "107898" (std O), 14	73	___
81079	NKP 8,000-gallon 1-D Tank Car "50277" (std O), 14	73	___
81080	BN 8,000-gallon 1-D Tank Car "977100" (std O), 14	73	___
81081	Alaska Steel-sided Reefer "10806" (std O), 14	80	___
81090	NS Hi-Cube Boxcar 2-pack (std O), 14–15	190	___
81094	Conrail "Big Blue" High-Cube Boxcar Diesel Freight Set, CC, 14	970	___
81095	Conrail Hi-Cube Boxcar 2-pack (std O), 14–16	190	___
81101	Polar Express LionChief 10th Anniversary Steam Passenger Set, 14–15	430	___
81113	SP 50' DD Boxcar "214051" (std O), 14–15	75	___
81122	Christmas Inspection Truck, 15	180	___
81134	BN SD70MAC Diesel "9424," CC, 14	550	___
81135	BN SD70MAC Diesel "9431," CC, 14	550	___

		Exc	Mint
___81137	BNSF SD70MAC Diesel "9858," CC, *14*		550
___81138	BNSF SD70MAC Diesel "9860," CC, *14*		550
___81141	Conrail SD70MAC Diesel "4138," CC, *14*		550
___81142	PFE Steel-sided Reefers 3-pack (std O), *14*		300
___81144	CSX SD70MAC Diesel "781," CC, *14*		550
___81147	KCS SD7CMAC Diesel "3950," CC, *14*		550
___81148	KCS SD7CMAC Diesel "3953," CC, *14*		550
___81151	Alaska SD7CMAC Diesel "4002," CC, *14*		550
___81152	Alaska SD7CMAC Diesel "4005," CC, *14*		550
___81153	CSX SD70MAC Diesel "778," CC, *14*		550
___81154	UP ES44AC Diesel "7361," CC, *14*		550
___81155	UP ES44AC Diesel "7388," CC, *14*		550
___81160	CSX ES44AC Diesel "937," CC, *14*		550
___81161	CSX ES44AC Diesel "944," CC, *14*		550
___81169	Iowa Interstate ES44AC Diesel "504," CC, *14*		550
___81170	Iowa Interstate ES44AC Diesel "507," CC, *14*		550
___81171	Ferromex ES44AC Diesel "4617," CC, *14*		550
___81172	Ferromex ES44AC Diesel "4626," CC, *14*		550
___81176	CN ES44AC Diesel "2812," CC, *14*		550
___81177	CN ES44AC Diesel "2818," CC, *14*		550
___81179	2-8-2 Heavy Mikado Pilot Locomotive, CC, *14*		1300
___81180	2-8-2 Heavy Mikado Locomotive, CC, *15*		1300
81181	Southern 2-8-2 Heavy Mikado Locomotive "4866," CC, *15*		1300
81182	L&N 2-8-2 Heavy Mikado Locomotive "1757," CC, *14*		1300
81183	MP 2-8-2 Heavy Mikado Locomotive "1496," CC, *14*		1300
81184	P&WV 2-8-2 Heavy Mikado Locomotive "1152," CC, *14*		1300
81185	CNJ 2-8-2 Heavy Mikado Locomotive "845," CC, *14*		1300
81186	Frisco 2-8-2 Heavy Mikado Locomotive "4126," CC, *14*		1300
81187	C&IM 2-8-2 Heavy Mikado Locomotive "551," CC, *14*		1300
81188	NYC 2-8-2 Heavy Mikado Locomotive "9506," CC, *14*		1300
81189	CB&Q 2-8-2 Heavy Mikado Locomotive "5509," CC, *15*		1300
81190	WP 2-8-2 Heavy Mikado Locomotive "334," CC, *15*		1300
81191	Erie 2-8-2 Heavy Mikado Locomotive "3207," CC, *15*		1300
81192	GN 2-8-2 Heavy Mikado Locomotive "3148," CC, *14*		1300
81193	Wheeling & Lake Erie 2-8-2 Heavy Mikado Locomotive "6012," CC, *15*		1300
81194	NKP 2-8-2 Heavy Mikado Locomotive "689," CC, *15*		1300
___81195	PRR Boxcar, *14–15*		70
___81196	Timken Boxcar, *14–15*		70
___81197	Santa Fe Boxcar, *14–15*		70
___81198	GN Boxcar, *14–16*		70
___81199	PRR 1-D Tank Car, *14–15*		70

Exc Mint

		Exc	Mint
81200	Timken 1-D Tank Car, *14–16*	70	
81201	GN 1-D Tank Car, *14–16*	70	
81202	Santa Fe 1-D Tank Car, *14–15*	70	
81203	PRR Flatcar, *14–15*	70	
81204	Santa Fe Flatcar, *14–16*	70	
81205	Timken Flatcar, *14–16*	70	
81206	GN Flatcar, *14–16*	70	
81207	CP H-24-66 Train Master Diesel "8900," CC, *14*	550	
81208	CP H-24-66 Train Master Diesel "8903," CC, *14*	550	
81209	CNJ H-24-66 Train Master Diesel "2401," CC, *14*	550	
81210	CNJ H-24-66 Train Master Diesel "2406," CC, *14*	550	
81211	Reading H-24-66 Train Master Diesel "801," CC, *14*	550	
81212	Reading H-24-66 Train Master Diesel "804," CC, *14*	550	
81213	SP H-24-66 Train Master Diesel "4803," CC, *14*	550	
81214	SP H-24-66 Train Master Diesel "4809," CC, *14*	550	
81215	Southern H-24-66 Train Master Diesel "6300," CC, *14*	550	
81216	Southern H-24-66 Train Master Diesel "6303," CC, *14*	550	
81217	N&W H-24-66 Train Master Diesel "151," CC, *14*	550	
81218	N&W H-24-66 Train Master Diesel "164," CC, *14*	550	
81219	Santa Fe E8 Diesel AA Set"84/85," CC, *14*	930	
81222	PC E8 Diesel AA Set"4289/4325," CC, *14*	930	
81225	RI E8 Diesel AA Set"647/648," CC, *14*	930	
81228	C&O E8 Diesel AA Set"4027/4028," CC, *14*	930	
81231	Erie E8 Diesel AA Set"822/823," CC, *14*	930	
81234	MKT E8 Diesel AA Set"131/132," CC, *14*	930	
81237	SAL E8 Diesel AA Set"3051/3055," CC, *14*	930	
81240	Wabash E8 Diesel AA Set"1007/1011," CC, *14*	930	
81243	Pilot M1a 4-8-2 Locomotive, CC, *14*	1500	
81245	PRR M1a 4-8-2 Locomotive "6671," CC, *14*	1500	
81246	PRR M1a 4-8-2 Locomotive "6764," CC, *14*	1500	
81247	PRR M1a Coal Hauler Twin-hopper Steam Freight Set, CC, *14*	1800	
81248	10" Girder Bridge Track, *14–16*	25	
81249	Christmas Girder Bridge Track, *14, 16*	25	
81250	FasTrack O-96 Curve, *14*	7	
81251	FasTrack O-31 Manual Switch, right-hand, *14–16*	50	
81252	FasTrack O-31 Manual Switch, left-hand, *14–16*	50	
81253	FasTrack O-31 Remote Switch, right-hand, *14–16*	110	
81254	FasTrack O-31 Remote Switch, left-hand, *14–16*	110	
81256	Personalized Birthday Message Boxcar, *14–15*	85	
81257	Amtrak Water Tower, *14–16*	40	
81259	PRR Broadway Limited Steam Passenger Set, *14*	370	
81261	NYC Early Bird Special Steam Freight Set, *16*	380	
81262	UP LionChief Steam Freight Set, *15*	400	
81263	CNJ LionChief Diesel Passenger Set, *14–16*	390	
81264	Western Union Telegraph Steam Freight Set, *14–16*	390	
81266	Amtrak LionChief FT Diesel Passenger Set, *14–15*	460	
81269	PRR Allegheny Hauler Steam Freight Set, *16*	470	

____	81270	Bethlehem Steel LionChief Steam Work Train, *15*	340
	81279	Albert Hall LionChief European Steam Passenger	
____		Set, *14–15*	430
____	81280	Victorian Christmas Steam Passenger Set, *14*	400
	81284	Frosty the Snowman LionChief Steam Freight Set,	
____		*14–16*	320
____	81286	Lionel Junction "Little Steam" Freight Set, *14–15*	175
____	81287	Lionel Junction UP Steam Freight Set, *14–15*	175
____	81288	Pet Shop Diesel Freight Set, *14–16*	175
____	81290	Thomas Kinkade Holiday Covered Bridge, *14*	70
____	81292	Valley Central 1-D Tank Car "45003," *14–16*	45
____	81294	LCS Sensor Track, *13–16*	95
	81295	AT&SF LionChief 2-8-2 Locomotive "3158,"	
____		*14–16*	430
____	81296	GN LionChief 2-8-2 Locomotive "3123," *14–15*	430
____	81297	PRR LionChief 2-8-2 Locomotive "9633," *14–15*	430
____	82678	Angela Trotta Thomas Christmas Boxcar, *16*	85
	81299	Chessie System LionChief 2-8-2 Locomotive	
____		"2103," *14–15*	430
____	81301	NYC LionChief 4-6-4 Locomotive "5421," *14–15*	430
____	81302	C&O LionChief 4-6-4 Locomotive "308," *14–16*	430
____	81303	UP LionChief 4-6-4 Locomotive "674," *14–16*	430
____	81304	CN LionChief 4-6-4 Locomotive "5702," *14–16*	430
____	81307	B&O LionChief 4-6-2 Locomotive "5307," *14–15*	430
____	81308	CP LionChief 4-6-2 Locomotive "2469," *14–15*	430
____	81309	SP LionChief 4-6-2 Locomotive "3106," *14–15*	430
____	81311	Alaska LionChief 4-6-2 Locomotive "652," *14–15*	430
____	81313	FasTrack Power Lockon, *15–16*	23
____	81314	FasTrack Power Block Lockon, *15–16*	40
____	81315	Coaling Station, *15–16*	160
____	81316	Personalized Christmas Message Boxcar, *15*	80
____	81317	FasTrack Accessory Activator Track Pack, *15–16*	24
____	81325	LCS WiFi Module, *13–16*	180
____	81326	LCS Serial Converter #2, *14–16*	50
	81331	Iron Arry Locomotive with LionChief Remote,	
____		*14–15*	140
	81332	Iron Bert Locomotive with LionChief Remote,	
____		*14–15*	140
____	81373	Candy Cane Flatcar with bulkheads, *15*	60
	81395	Thomas Kinkade LionChief Christmas Passenger	
____		Set, *14–15*	380
____	81419	Alien Ooze 1-D Tank Car, *14–15*	65
____	81420	PRR Truss-rod Gondola with tarp, *14–16*	65
____	81422	NS Water Tower, *14*	31
____	81423	Sodor Coal and Scrap Cars 2-pack, *14–16*	70
____	81424	Sodor Crane Car and Work Caboose 2-pack, *14*	70
____	81425	Frosty the Snowman Passenger Station, *14*	65
____	81426	Frosty the Snowman Animated Gondola, *14*	75
____	81427	Frosty the Snowman Aquarium Car, *14*	85
____	81428	Frosty the Snowman Boxcar, *14*	65
____	81430	Lionelville Shanty, *14*	22
____	81432	PRR Girder Bridge, *14–15*	21
____	81433	PRR Crossing Shanty, *14*	22
____	81434	Pennsylvania Station Platform, *14–15*	23

		Exc	Mint
81435	N&W NS Heritage Quad Hopper with coal, *14–15*	60	___
81436	Intermodal Container 4-pack, *14*	43	___
81437	York Peppermint Patty Vat Car, *14–15*	70	___
81439	Halloween Pumpkinheads Handcar, *14–16*	90	___
81440	Western Union Handcar, *14–16*	100	___
81441	North Pole Central Snowplow, CC, *16*	280	___
81442	PRR Rotary Snowplow "1442," CC, *16*	280	___
81443	D&RGW Rotary Snowplow "443," CC, *16*	280	___
81444	PRR Tie-Jector, CC, *14–16*	200	___
81445	MOW Tie-Jector, CC, *14–16*	200	___
81446	Santa Fe Tie-Jector, CC, *14–16*	200	___
81447	NS Tie-Jector, CC, *14–16*	200	___
81448	Amtrak Tie-Jector, CC, *14–16*	200	___
81449	Zombie Motorized Trolley, *14*	100	___
81450	Polar Express Trolley, *14*	110	___
81451	St. Louis Motorized Trolley, *14*	100	___
81452	Neil Young Texas Special F3 AA Diesels, CC, *13–14*	650	___
81453	Neil Young PRR F3 AA Diesels, CC, *13–14*	650	___
81462	PRR Broadway Limited Add-on Baggage Car, *14–16*	70	___
81463	CNJ Water Tower, *14–16*	35	___
81464	CNJ Montclair Add-on Passenger Car, *14–16*	60	___
81465	SP Flatcar with piggyback trailers, *14–16*	75	___
81466	BN Maxi-Stack Pair, *14–16*	140	___
81469	GN Bilevel Stock Car "65385," *14–16*	65	___
81470	DC Comics Batman Phantom Train, *16*	400	___
81475	DC Comics Batman M7 LionChief Subway Set, *14–15*	370	___
81479	Batman Add-on M7 Subway Car 2-pack, *14–15*	140	___
81480	John Deere LionChief RS-3 Diesel Freight Set, *14–16*	320	___
81486	NYC Patrol Flatcar with helicopter, *14–15*	65	___
81487	Ronald Reagan Presidential Boxcar, *14–15*	70	___
81488	Andrew Jackson Presidential Boxcar, *14–16*	70	___
81489	Warren G. Harding Presidential Boxcar, *14–16*	70	___
81490	Dwight D. Eisenhower Presidential Boxcar, *14–16*	70	___
81491	Jersey Central Coal Dump Car, *14–15*	65	___
81492	Strasburg RR Searchlight Car, *14*	50	___
81493	U.S.A.F. Missile Carrying Car, *15–16*	65	___
81494	Santa's Sleigh Rocket Fuel Tank Car, *16*	65	___
81495	40-watt Power Supply, *15–16*	70	___
81499	LCS Power Supply with DB9 cable, *13–16*	37	___
81500	LCS Sensor Track 1' Cable, *13–16*	14	___
81501	LCS Sensor Track 3' Cable, *13–16*	15	___
81502	LCS Sensor Track 10' Cable, *13–16*	19	___
81503	LCS Sensor Track 20' Cable, *13–16*	19	___
81504	Ann Arbor FA-2 Diesel AA Set "53/53A," CC, *14*	750	___
81507	B&O FA-2 Diesel AA Set "817/827," CC, *14–15*	750	___
81510	Erie FA-2 Diesel AA Set "736A/736D," CC, *14–15*	750	___
81513	MKT FA-2 Diesel AA Set "331A/331C," CC, *14*	750	___
81516	NYC FA-2 Diesel AA Set "1075/1078," CC, *14–15*	750	___
81519	PRR FA-2 Diesel AA Set "9608/9609," CC, *14–15*	750	___

		Exc	Mint
____81522	Ann Arbor FB2 Diesel "53B," CC, *14*		450
____81523	B&O FB2 Diesel "817B," CC, *14–15*		450
____81524	Erie FB2 Diesel "736B," CC, *14–15*		450
____81525	MKT FB2 Diesel "331B," CC, *14*		450
____81526	NYC FB2 Diesel "3327," CC, *14–15*		450
____81527	PRR FB2 Diesel "9608B," CC, *14*		450
____81528	Ann Arbor FB2 Diesel, nonpowered, *14*		350
____81529	B&O FB2 Diesel, nonpowered, *14–15*		350
____81530	Erie FB2 Diesel, nonpowered, *14–15*		350
____81531	MKT FB2 Diesel, nonpowered, *14*		350
____81532	NYC FB2 Diesel, nonpowered, *14–15*		350
____81533	PRR FB2 Diesel, nonpowered, *14–15*		350
____81534	Christmas Toys Stock Car, *14*		70
____81545	Operation Eagle Missile Launcher Car, CC, *15*		350
____81546	Operation Eagle Sound Car, CC, *15*		240
____81568	4th of July Parade Boxcar, *14–16*		80
____81596	Weathered UP 4-12-2 Locomotive "9000," CC, *13*		1400
81597	Weathered B&O RF-16 Sharknose AA Diesels "855-857," CC, *13*		830
81600	Weathered PRR RF-16 Sharknose AA Diesels "2020A-2021A," CC, *13*		830
____81603	LionChief 72-watt Power Supply, *14–16*		55
____81605	Santa Fe PS-1 Boxcar 5-pack (std O), *14*		380
____81615	UP 1-D Tank Car, *14*		45
____81617	Pet Shop 1-D Tank Car, *14–16*		45
____81619	Reading PS-1 Boxcar "109448" (std O), *14*		80
____81620	Zombie Figure Pack, *14–15*		23
____81621	John Deere Billboard Set, *15*		25
____81622	John Deere Water Tower, *15*		40
____81625	Amtrak Add-on Baggage Car, *14–16*		85
____81626	Barrel Shed, *14–16*		35
____81627	Christmas Hopper Shed, *14, 16*		45
____81628	Grain Elevator, *15*		80
____81629	Lumber Shed Kit, *14–16*		35
____81635	Water Tower, *14*		35
____81639	LCS Accessory Switch Controller #2, *14–16*		120
____81640	LCS Block Power Controller #2, *14–16*		120
81644	Chessie System Baby Madison Passenger Car 3-pack, *14–16*		270
____81649	SP Baby Madison Passenger Car 3-pack, *14–16*		270
81654	Philadelphia Energy Solutions 1-D Tank Car "0765," *15–16*		60
____81662	FasTrack O-31 Quarter Curved Track, *14, 16*		5
81668	Philadelphia Energy Solutions 1-D Tank Car "0771," *15–16*		60
____81680	Dinosaur 1-D Tank Car, *14–16*		45
____81686	PRR GL-a 2-bay Hopper 3-pack (std O), *14*		220
____81687	LV GL-a 2-bay Hopper 2-pack (std O), *14–15*		146
____81688	CB&Q GL-a 2-bay Hopper 3-pack (std O), *14–16*		220
____81689	C&O GL-a 2-bay Hopper 3-pack (std O), *14–16*		220
____81693	Aerial Target Launcher, *15–16*		90
____81699	Polar Express Scale Twin Hopper, *15*		80
____81703	Santa Fe Hi-Cube Boxcar 2-pack (std O), *14–16*		190

		Exc	Mint
81704	Grand Trunk Hi-Cube Boxcar 2-pack (std O), *14–16*		190____
81705	Milwaukee Road Hi-Cube Boxcar 2-pack (std O), *14–16*		190____
81706	Frisco Hi-Cube Boxcar 2-pack (std O), *14–16*		190____
81707	NYC Hi-Cube Boxcar 2-pack (std O), *14–16*		190____
81708	Santa Fe Hi-Cube Boxcar "36715" (std O), *14–15*		95____
81710	Milwaukee Road Hi-Cube Boxcar "4980" (std O), *14–15*		95____
81711	Frisco Hi-Cube Boxcar "9125" (std O), *14–15*		95____
81712	NYC Hi-Cube Boxcar "67282" (std O), *14–15*		95____
81723	Postwar "3413" Mercury Capsule Launcher Car, *15*		80____
81725	UP Operating Merchandise Car, *14–15*		80____
81726	REA Operating Merchandise Car, *14–15*		80____
81729	Great Western Passenger Car Add-on 2-pack, *14*		130____
81733	Christmas Boxcar, *14*		65____
81734	FasTrack Oval Track and Power Pack, *14–16*		200____
81735	FasTrack Figure-8 Track and Power Pack, *14–16*		250____
81736	Classic Lionel Catalogs Billboard Pack, *14–15*		13____
81737	Passenger Station, *14–15*		60____
81738	Lionel Auto Loader Cars 4-pack, *14–15*		25____
81739	Santa Fe Baby Madison Passenger Car 3-pack, *14–16*		270____
81744	CP Baby Madison Passenger Car 3-pack, *14–16*		270____
81749	Pullman Baby Madison Passenger Car 3-pack, *14–16*		270____
81754	NYC Baby Madison Passenger Car 3-pack, *14–16*		270____
81759	NYC Coach/Diner 2-pack, *14–16*		180____
81760	NYC Coach/Baggage Car 2-pack, *14–16*		180____
81763	Pullman Baby Madison Passenger Car 3-pack, *14–16*		180____
81764	Pullman Coach/Baggage Car 2-pack, *14, 16*		180____
81768	Chessie System Coach/Diner 2-pack, *14–16*		180____
81769	Chessie System Coach/Baggage Car 2-pack, *14–16*		180____
81773	SP Coach/Diner 2-pack, *14–16*		180____
81774	SP Coach/Baggage Car 2-pack, *14–16*		180____
81778	Santa Fe Coach/Diner 2-pack, *14–16*		180____
81779	Santa Fe Coach/Baggage Car 2-pack, *14–16*		180____
81783	CP Coach/Diner 2-pack, *14–16*		180____
81784	CP Coach/Baggage Car 2-pack, *14–16*		180____
81789	NH GL-a 2-bay Hopper 2-pack (std O), *14–16*		146____
81793	Berwind GL-a 2-bay Hopper 3-pack (std O), *14–15*		220____
81800	Southern 18" Aluminum Observation/Coach Car, 2-pack (std O), *14*		320____
81801	Southern 18" Aluminum Combination/Vista Dome Car, 2-pack (std O), *14*		320____
81806	PRR N5b Caboose "477814" (std O), *14*		95____
81807	Conrail N5b Caboose "22882" (std O), *14–15*		95____
81808	PC N5b Caboose "22802" (std O), *14–16*		95____
81809	LIRR N5b Caboose "2" (std O), *14–15*		95____
81810	Lionel Lines N5b Caboose "1402" (std O), *14–16*		95____

		Exc	Mint
81811	Polar Express N5b Caboose, *16*		95
81812	RI 18" Aluminum Observation/Coach Car, 2-pack (std 0), *14*		320
81813	RI 18" Aluminum Combination/Vista Dome Car, 2-pack (std 0), *14*		320
81818	C&O 18" Aluminum Observation/Coach Car, 2-pack (std 0), *14*		320
81819	C&O 18" Aluminum Combination/Vista Dome Car, 2-pack (std 0), *14*		320
81824	P&WV GL-a 2-bay Hopper 2-pack (std 0), *14–16*		146
81827	PC Round-roof Boxcar "100104" (std 0), *14*		80
81828	GN Round-roof Boxcar "5885" (std 0), *14*		80
81829	WP Round-roof Boxcar "10211" (std 0), *14*		80
81830	MKT 18" Aluminum Observation/Coach Car, 2-pack (std 0), *14*		320
81831	MKT 18" Aluminum Baggage/Diner Car, 2-pack (std 0), *14*		320
81836	Erie Double-sheathed Boxcar "71107" (std 0), *14–15*		80
81837	Frisco Double-sheathed Boxcar "128528" (std 0), *14–15*		80
81838	CNJ Double-sheathed Boxcar "14014" (std 0), *14–15*		80
81839	Pacific Fright Express Steel-sided Reefer (std 0), *14*		80
81840	UP Ca-4 Caboose with smoke "3880" (std 0), *14*		90
81841	UP MOW Caboose "903224" (std 0), *14*		90
81842	Wabash 18" Aluminum Dome-Observation/Coach Car, 2-pack (std 0), *14*		320
81843	Wabash 18" Aluminum Combination/Vista Dome Car, 2-pack (std 0), *14*		320
81858	PRR GL-a 2-bay Hopper 3-pack (std 0), *14*		220
81862	FasTrack O-31 Curved Track 4-pack, *14, 16*		22
81866	RI 18" Aluminum Baggage/Diner Car, 2-pack (std 0), *14*		320
81869	C&O 18" Aluminum Baggage/Diner Car, 2-pack (std 0), *14*		320
81871	Loggers Figure Pack, *16*		30
81872	Wabash 18" Aluminum Baggage/Diner Car, 2-pack (std 0), *14*		320
81875	MKT 18" Aluminum Combination/Vista Dome Car, 2-pack (std 0), *14*		320
81878	Southern 18" Aluminum Baggage/Diner Car, 2-pack (std 0), *14*		320
81881	SP Crane Car, CC, *14–16*		500
81882	DT&I Crane Car, CC, *14–16*		500
81883	CSX Crane Car, CC, *14–16*		500
81884	Bethlehem Steel Crane Car, CC, *14*		500
81885	MOW Crane Car, CC, *14–16*		500
81886	SP Boom Car, RailSounds, CC, *14–16*		240
81887	DT&I Boom Car, RailSounds, CC, *14–16*		240
81888	CSX Boom Car, RailSounds, CC, *14–16*		240
81889	MOW Boom Car, RailSounds, CC, *14–16*		240
81890	Bethlehem Steel Boom Car, RailSounds, CC, *14*		240
81891	BNSF 52' Gondola "523300" with 3-piece covers (std 0), *14*		80

81892	Bethlehem Steel 52' Gondola "303022" with 3-piece covers (std O), *14*	80___
81893	GTW 52' Gondola "145391" with 3-piece covers (std O), *14*	80___
81894	CSX 52' Gondola "709190" with 3-piece covers (std O), *14*	80___
81895	North Pole Central 52' Gondola "128925" with 3-piece covers (std O), *14*	80___
81896	NYC PS-5 Flatcar "506266" with piggyback trailers (std O), *14*	100___
81897	Milwaukee Road PS-5 Flatcar "64660" with piggyback trailers (std O), *14*	100___
81898	Lionel PS-5 Flatcar with piggyback trailers (std O), *14*	100___
81899	CP PS-5 Flatcar "301000" with piggyback trailers (std O), *14*	100___
81900	UP PS-5 Flatcar "258255" with piggyback trailers (std O), *14*	100___
81901	NYC Tractor and Piggyback Trailer, *14*	90___
81902	Milwaukee Road Tractor and Piggyback Trailer, *14*	90___
81903	Lionel Tractor and Piggyback Trailer, *14*	90___
81904	CP Tractor and Piggyback Trailer, *14–15*	90___
81905	UP Tractor and Piggyback Trailer, *14*	90___
81908	PFE Steel-sided Reefers 3-pack (std O), *14*	240___
81912	New York Yankees Boxcar, *14*	70___
81913	St. Louis Cardinals Boxcar, *14*	70___
81914	Oakland Athletics Boxcar, *14*	70___
81915	San Francisco Giants Boxcar, *14*	70___
81916	Boston Red Sox Boxcar, *14*	70___
81917	Los Angeles Dodgers Boxcar, *14*	70___
81918	Cincinnati Reds Boxcar, *14*	70___
81919	San Diego Padres Boxcar, *14*	70___
81920	Detroit Tigers Boxcar, *14*	70___
81921	Atlanta Braves Boxcar, *14*	70___
81922	Baltimore Orioles Boxcar, *14*	70___
81923	Minnesota Twins Boxcar, *14*	70___
81924	Chicago White Sox Boxcar, *14*	70___
81925	Chicago Cubs Boxcar, *14*	70___
81926	Philadelphia Phillies Boxcar, *14*	70___
81927	Cleveland Indians Boxcar, *14*	70___
81928	New York Mets Boxcar, *14*	70___
81929	Toronto Blue Jays Boxcar, *14*	70___
81930	Miami Marlins Boxcar, *14*	70___
81931	Angels Baseball Boxcar, *14*	70___
81932	Pittsburgh Pirates Boxcar, *14*	70___
81933	Texas Rangers Boxcar, *14*	70___
81934	Milwaukee Brewers Boxcar, *14*	70___
81935	Houston Astros Boxcar, *14*	70___
81936	Colorado Rockies Boxcar, *14*	70___
81937	Tampa Bay Rays Boxcar, *14*	70___
81938	Seattle Mariners Boxcar, *14*	70___
81939	Washington Nationals Boxcar, *14*	70___
81940	Arizona Diamondbacks Boxcar, *14*	70___
81941	Kansas City Royals Boxcar, *14*	70___

		Exc	Mint
____81944	Rotary Beacon, yellow, *14–16*		85
____81945	Polar Express Scale Coach, *14*		210
____81946	FasTrack O-36 Remote Switch, right-hand, *14–16*		110
____81947	FasTrack O-36 Remote Switch, left-hand, *14–16*		110
____81948	FasTrack O-48 Remote Switch, right-hand, *14–16*		120
____81949	FasTrack O-48 Remote Switch, left-hand, *14–16*		120
____81950	FasTrack O-60 Remote Switch, right-hand, *14–16*		120
____81951	FasTrack O-60 Remote Switch, left-hand, *14–16*		120
____81952	FasTrack O-72 Remote Switch, right-hand, *14–16*		120
____81953	FasTrack O-72 Remote Switch, left-hand, *14–16*		120
____81954	FasTrack O-72 Remote Switch, wye, *14–16*		120
81968	Halloween Pacific Fright Express Caboose (std O), *14*		90
81969	PRR 18" Aluminum Parlor/Coach Car, 2-pack (std O), *14–15*		320
81972	B&O 18" Aluminum Baggage/Sleeper Car, 2-pack (std O), *14*		320
81975	SP 18" Aluminum Sleeper/Coach Car, 2-pack (std O), *14–15*		320
81978	UP 18" Aluminum Sleeper/Coach Car, 2-pack (std O), *14–15*		320
81981	KCS 18" Aluminum Sleeper/Coach Car, 2-pack (std O), *14*		320
81984	Postwar "1887" Christmas Flatcar with reindeer, *14*		70
____81985	Postwar "6428" Christmas Mail Car, *14*		60
____81986	Christmas Wish 1-D Tank Car, *14*		60
____81987	Angela Trotta Thomas "Santa's Letter" Boxcar, *14*		65
81988	Angela Trotta Thomas Christmas Billboard Pack, *14*		15
____81990	Christmas Gondola with reindeer feed vats, *14*		65
____81992	Santa Claus Bobbing Head Boxcar, *14*		65
81993	North Pole Central Santa Finder Searchlight Car, *14*		55
____81999	PRR Gondola with Christmas gifts and trees, *14*		65
____82000	PRR Christmas Crane Car, *14*		75
____82001	Merry & Bright Hot Cocoa Car, *14*		70
____82002	Old St. Nick Operating Billboard, *14, 16*		60
____82003	Christmas Blinking Water Tower, *14*		35
____82005	Christmas Wreath Clock Tower, *14, 16*		43
____82008	Bungalow House, *15–16*		80
____82009	Suburban House, *15–16*		80
____82010	Joe's Bait & Tackle Shop, *15–16*		65
____82011	Keystone Cafe, *15–16*		80
____82012	Single Floodlight Tower, *15–16*		75
____82013	Double Floodlight Tower, *15–16*		90
____82014	Postwar "192" Control Tower, *15–16*		100
____82015	Wind Turbine, *15–16*		80
____82016	Oil Pump, *15–16*		60
____82017	Lionel Art Operating Billboard, *15–16*		70
____82018	Track Gang, *15–16*		100
____82020	Burning Switch Tower, *15–16*		130
____82021	Bascule Bridge, *15*		450
____82022	Lionel Steel Gantry Crane, CC, *15–16*		400

Exc Mint

82023	Operating Sawmill, CC, *15–16*	350___
82024	Postwar "164" Log Loader, *15*	340___
82026	Postwar "497" Coaling Station, *15–16*	300___
82028	Postwar "352" Icing Station, *15–16*	150___
82029	Culvert Loader, CC, *15–16*	300___
82030	Culvert Unloader, CC, *15–16*	300___
82033	MOW B383, *16*	600___
82034	Loading Station, *16*	350___
82035	Work House, crane sounds, *16*	150___
82036	Luxury Diner, *15–16*	80___
82038	8" Female Pigtail Power Cable, *16*	10___
82039	36" Male Pigtail Power Cable, *16*	11___
82043	Plug-n-play Power Cable Extension, *16*	16___
82045	Plug-n-play Control Cable Extension, *16*	20___
82046	36" Power Tap Cable, *16*	16___
82047	Lionel Lines Log Dump Car, *15–16*	65___
82048	AT&SF Ice Car, *15–16*	75___
82049	Santa's Work Shoppe Log Dump Car, *16*	65___
82050	Santa's Work Shoppe Sawmill, *16*	240___
82051	North Pole Central Icing Station, *16*	150___
82052	PFE Ice Car, *15–16*	75___
82053	North Pole Central Icing Car, *16*	75___
82054	Weyerhaeuser Log Dump Car, *15–16*	65___
82055	Bethlehem Steel Trackside Crane, CC, *16*	600___
82064	Halloween Operating Billboard, *15–16*	80___
82066	PRR Log Dump Car, *15*	65___
82067	Lionel Lines Coal Dump Car, *15–16*	65___
82068	NS Coal Dump Car, *15*	65___
82069	Conrail Coal Dump Car, *15–16*	65___
82072	Philadelphia Quartz Hopper "755," *15–16*	50___
82073	CN Ore Car, *15–16*	50___
82074	SP 1-D Tank Car, *15–16*	50___
82075	NYC Waffle-sided Boxcar, *15–16*	50___
82076	Chessie System Gondola with containers, *16*	50___
82077	D&H Hi-Cube Boxcar, *16*	50___
82078	NP 1-D Tank Car, *16*	50___
82079	UP Wood-sided Reefer, *16*	50___
82080	C&NW 3-D Tank Car, *16*	50___
82081	CSX Auto Carrier, *16*	50___
82082	NS Flatcar with pipes, *16*	50___
82083	Central of Georgia Gondola with cable reels, *16*	50___
82084	Virginian Boxcar, *16*	50___
82085	AT&SF Waffle-sided Boxcar, *16*	50___
82086	MKT Reefer, *16*	50___
82087	WP Depressed Flatcar with Generator, *16*	50___
82088	Log Pack, *16*	10___
82091	PRR Tie Work Car "82091," *14–16*	75___
82092	MOW Tie Work Car "77," *14–16*	75___
82093	AT&SF Tie Work Car "82093," *14–16*	75___
82094	NS Tie Work Car "51," *14–16*	75___
82095	Amtrak Tie Work Car "67," *14–16*	75___
82096	Lionel Steel Culvert Gondola, *15–16*	65___

____	**82097**	Bucyrus-Erie Gantry Crane, CC, *15–16*	400
____	**82098**	Bucyrus-Erie Culvert Gondola, *15*	65
	82099	Zombie Apocalypse Survivors LionChief GP38 Diesel Freight Set, *15*	
____			440
____	**82100**	Polar Express Hero Boy's Home, *16*	90
	82101	Postwar "6512" Mercury Capsule Astronaut Car, *15–16*	
____			80
____	**82102**	Lumberjacks, *15–16*	65
____	**82103**	Playground Swing, *15–16*	75
____	**82104**	Playground Playtime, *15–16*	100
____	**82105**	Tire Swing, *15–16*	100
____	**82106**	Pony Ride, *15–16*	75
____	**82107**	Tug-of-War, *15–16*	65
____	**82108**	Hobo Campfire, *15*	100
____	**82110**	Extended Truss Bridge, *15–16*	300
	82111	Lionel Industrial Coal 2-bay Hopper "28111," *15–16*	
____			60
____	**82112**	B&M Alco S2 Diesel Switcher "1260," CC, *15*	650
____	**82113**	B&M Alco S2 Diesel Switcher "1263," CC, *15*	650
____	**82114**	CB&Q Alco S2 Diesel Switcher "9306," CC, *15*	650
____	**82115**	CB&Q Alco S2 Diesel Switcher "9308," CC, *15*	650
____	**82116**	CP Alco S2 Diesel Switcher "7020," CC, *15*	650
____	**82117**	CP Alco S2 Diesel Switcher "7024," CC, *15*	650
____	**82118**	GM&O Alco S2 Diesel Switcher "1001," CC, *15*	650
____	**82119**	GM&O Alco S2 Diesel Switcher "1007," CC, *15*	650
____	**82120**	GN Alco S2 Diesel Switcher "2," CC, *15*	650
____	**82121**	GN Alco S2 Diesel Switcher "5," CC, *15*	650
____	**82122**	PRR Alco S2 Diesel Switcher "5648," CC, *15*	650
____	**82123**	PRR Alco S2 Diesel Switcher "5652," CC, *15*	650
	82124	South Buffalo Alco S2 Diesel Switcher "102," CC, *15*	
____			650
	82125	South Buffalo Alco S2 Diesel Switcher "104," CC, *15*	
____			650
____	**82126**	UP Alco S2 Diesel Switcher "1111," CC, *15*	650
____	**82127**	UP Alco S2 Diesel Switcher "1138," CC, *15*	650
____	**82128**	C&O GP30 Diesel Locomotive "3011," CC, *15*	650
____	**82129**	C&O GP30 Diesel Locomotive "3018," CC, *15*	650
	82130	EMD Demonstrator GP30 Diesel Locomotive "1962," CC, *15*	
____			650
____	**82131**	TP&W GP30 Diesel Locomotive "700," CC, *15*	650
____	**82132**	PC GP30 Diesel Locomotive "2202," CC, *15*	650
____	**82133**	PC GP30 Diesel Locomotive "2246," CC, *15*	650
____	**82134**	GM&O GP30 Diesel Locomotive "501," CC, *15*	650
____	**82135**	GM&O GP30 Diesel Locomotive "521," CC, *15*	650
	82136	N&W GP30 Diesel Locomotive "522," black, CC, *15*	
____			650
	82137	N&W GP30 Diesel Locomotive "542," blue, CC, *15*	
____			650
____	**82138**	MILW GP30 Diesel Locomotive "344," CC, *15*	650
____	**82139**	MILW GP30 Diesel Locomotive "350," CC, *15*	650
____	**82140**	Southern GP30 Diesel Locomotive "2594," CC, *15*	650
____	**82141**	Southern GP30 Diesel Locomotive "2601," CC, *15*	650
____	**82142**	UP GP30 Diesel Locomotive "803" CC, *15*	650
____	**82143**	UP GP30 Diesel Locomotive "830," CC, *15*	650

Exc Mint

		Exc	Mint
82146	Soo Line PS-1 Boxcar "45025," *15*		80___
82147	N&W PS-1 Boxcar "44292," *15*		80___
82148	GB&W PS-1 Boxcar "777," *15*		80___
82150	Duluth, South Shore & Atlantic PS-1 Boxcar "15091," *15*		80___
82163	B&O LionChief NW2 Diesel Locomotive "9555," *15–16*		300___
82164	BN LionChief NW2 Diesel Locomotive "546," *15–16*		300___
82165	CB&Q LionChief NW2 Diesel Locomotive "9412A," *15–16*		300___
82166	Southern LionChief NW2 Diesel Locomotive "2401A," *15–16*		300___
82171	BNSF LionChief GP20 Diesel Locomotive "2050," *15–16*		340___
82172	NYC LionChief GP20 Diesel Locomotive "2102," *15–16*		340___
82173	NS LionChief GP20 Diesel Locomotive "10," *15–16*		340___
82174	NYS&W LionChief GP20 Diesel Locomotive "1800," *15–16*		340___
82175	Virginian LionChief Rectifier Locomotive "135," *15–16*		340___
82176	N&W LionChief Rectifier Locomotive "235," *15–16*		340___
82177	NH LionChief Rectifier Locomotive "306," *15–16*		340___
82178	Conrail LionChief Rectifier Locomotive "4605," *15–16*		340___
82179	PRR LionChief Rectifier Locomotive "4466," *15–16*		340___
82184	PRR B6sb 0-4-0 Locomotive "1670," CC, *15*		700___
82185	D&RGW Bicentennial Gondola with canisters, *16*		50___
82186	Patriot Chemicals 1-D Tank Car "2015," *15*		60___
82187	Bethlehem Steel Water Tower, *15*		35___
82188	Metro-North LionChief M7 Subway Set, *15*		350___
82196	Metro-North Add-on 2-pack, *15*		130___
82202	UP Big Boy Commemorative CA-4 Caboose, *15*		95___
82203	Remote Control Box, *15–16*		25___
82205	BNSF Golden Swoosh ES44AC Diesel Locomotive "7695," CC, *15*		650___
82206	N&W 2-6-6-4 Locomotive "1218," CC, *16*		1000___
82207	Iowa Interstate/Rock Island ES44AC Diesel Locomotive "513," CC, *15*		650___
82208	N&W 2-6-6-4 Locomotive "1212," CC, *16*		1000___
82209	NS ES44AC Diesel Locomotive "8056," CC, *15*		650___
82210	NS ES44AC Diesel Locomotive "8065," CC, *15*		650___
82213	KCS ES44AC Diesel Locomotive "4696," CC, *15*		650___
82214	KCS ES44AC Diesel Locomotive "4685," CC, *15*		650___
82215	AT&SF ES44AC Diesel Locomotive "440," CC, *15*		650___
82216	AT&SF ES44AC Diesel Locomotive "444," CC, *15*		650___
82218	FEC ES44AC Diesel Locomotive "802," CC, *15*		650___
82219	FEC ES44AC Diesel Locomotive "804," CC, *15*		650___
82220	SP Alco PA AA Diesel Locomotive Set "6006, 6015," CC, *15*		1000___

			Exc	Mint
	82223	D&RGW Alco PA AA Diesel Locomotive Set "6001, 6003," CC, *15*		1000
	82226	LV Alco PA AA Diesel Locomotive Set "601, 602," CC, *15*		1000
	82229	MP Alco PA AA Diesel Locomotive Set "8018, 8018," CC, *15*		1000
	82232	NKP Alco PA AA Diesel Locomotive Set "190, 189," CC, *15*		1000
	82235	PRR Alco PA AA Diesel Locomotive Set "5070A, 5071A," CC, *15*		1000
	82238	Southern Alco PA AA Diesel Locomotive Set "6900, 6901," CC, *15*		1000
	82241	Wabash Alco PA AA Diesel Locomotive Set "1020, 1020A," CC, *15*		1000
	82244	SP Alco PB Diesel Locomotive, CC, *15*		530
	82245	B&O 2-6-6-4 Locomotive "7620," CC, *16*		1000
	82246	D&RGW Alco PB Diesel Locomotive, CC, *15*		530
	82247	AT&SF 2-6-6-4 Locomotive "1798," CC, *16*		1000
	82248	LV Alco PB Diesel Locomotive, CC, *15*		530
	82249	Bethlehem Steel Boom Car, *15*		55
	82250	MP Alco PB Diesel Locomotive, CC, *15*		530
	82251	Zombie Animated Gondola, *15*		75
	82252	Nickel Plate Road Alco PB Diesel Locomotive, CC, *15*		530
	82253	John Deere 1-D Tank Car, *15*		65
	82254	PRR Alco PB Diesel Locomotive, CC, *15*		530
	82256	Southern Alco PB Diesel Locomotive, CC, *15*		530
	82258	Wabash Alco PB Diesel Locomotive, CC, *15*		530
	82263	PRR Scrapyard, *16*		130
	82265	MOW Welding Car, *15–16*		80
	82266	CN 4-6-0 Steam Locomotive "1158," CC, *15*		900
	82267	C&NW 4-6-0 Steam Locomotive "1385," CC, *15*		900
	82268	Frisco 4-6-0 Steam Locomotive "633," CC, *15*		900
	82269	NP 4-6-0 Steam Locomotive "1382," CC, *15*		900
	82270	SP 4-6-0 Steam Locomotive "2353," CC, *15*		900
	82271	NYC 4-6-0 Steam Locomotive "1258," CC, *15*		900
	82272	NH 4-6-0 Steam Locomotive "816," CC, *15*		900
	82273	ACL 4-6-0 Steam Locomotive "1031," CC, *15*		900
	82274	Chessie SD40 Diesel Locomotive "7500," CC, *15*		650
	82275	Chessie SD40 Diesel Locomotive "7593," CC, *15*		650
	82276	BN SD40 Diesel Locomotive "6314," CC, *15*		650
	82277	BN SD40 Diesel Locomotive "6320," CC, *15*		650
	82278	GT SD40 Diesel Locomotive "5922," CC, *15*		650
	82279	GT SD40 Diesel Locomotive "5927," CC, *15*		650
	82280	MP SD40 Diesel Locomotive "3007," CC, *15*		650
	82281	MP SD40 Diesel Locomotive "3014," CC, *15*		650
	82282	Conrail SD40 Diesel Locomotive "6308," CC, *15*		650
	82283	Conrail SD40 Diesel Locomotive "6350," CC, *15*		650
	82284	Conrail SD40 Diesel Locomotive "6300," CC, *15*		650
	82285	SP SD40 Diesel Locomotive "8402," CC, *15*		650
	82286	SP SD40 Diesel Locomotive "8451," CC, *15*		650
	82287	SP Daylight SD40 Diesel Locomotive "7342," CC, *15*		650

Exc Mint

		Exc	Mint
82288	Clinchfield SD40 Diesel Locomotive "3000," CC, *15*		650____
82289	Clinchfield SD40 Diesel Locomotive "3006," CC, *15*		650____
82290	AT&SF LionChief FT AA Diesel Locomotive Set "164, 164," *15–16*		500____
82293	ACL LionChief FT AA Diesel Locomotive Set "321, 322," *15–16*		500____
82296	Erie LionChief FT AA Diesel Locomotive Set "703, 703," *15–16*		500____
82299	D&RGW LionChief FT AA Diesel Locomotive Set "5471, 5474," *15–16*		500____
82302	AT&SF LionChief FT B Unit, *15–16*		280____
82303	ACL LionChief FT B Unit, *15–16*		280____
82304	Erie LionChief FT B Unit, *15–16*		280____
82305	D&RGW LionChief FT B Unit, *15–16*		280____
82307	PRR B6sb 0-4-0 Locomotive "5244," CC, *15*		700____
82308	PRR B6sb 0-4-0 Locomotive "3233," CC, *15*		700____
82309	PRR-Reading Seashore Lines B6sb 0-4-0 Locomotive "6096," CC, *15*		700____
82310	LIRR B6sb 0-4-0 Locomotive "2015," CC, *15*		700____
82311	Polar RR B6sb 0-4-0 Locomotive "2515," CC, *15*		700____
82312	UP ACF 40-ton Stock Car "48133," *15*		80____
82313	GN ACF 40-ton Stock Car "55989," *15*		80____
82314	MILW ACF 40-ton Stock Car "104954," *15*		80____
82315	NP ACF 40-ton Stock Car "84161," *15*		80____
82316	NKP ACF 40-ton Stock Car "42040," *15*		80____
82324	Chessie LionChief Diesel Freight Set, *15*		400____
82330	U.S.A.F. Minuteman Missile Launcher Car, CC, *15*		350____
82331	U.S.A.F. Missile Launch Sound Car, CC, *15*		240____
82333	Illuminated Hopper Shed, *15–16*		45____
82334	Ulysses S. Grant Presidential Boxcar, *15*		70____
82335	Franklin D. Roosevelt Presidential Boxcar, *15*		70____
82340	N&W Y6b 2-8-8-2 Steam Locomotive "2171," CC, *15*		2000____
82341	N&W Y6b 2-8-8-2 Steam Locomotive "2175," CC, *15*		2000____
82342	N&W Y6b 2-8-8-2 Steam Locomotive "2195," CC, *15*		2000____
82343	Lionel Steel Welding Car, *15*		80____
82344	WM Wood Chip Hopper "2945," *15–16*		65____
82349	Friday the 13th Jason Voorhees Boxcar, *16*		85____
82394	UP Auxiliary Water Tender "907853," CC, *15*		380____
82395	UP Auxiliary Water Tender "907856," CC, *15*		380____
82396	UP Commemorative Auxiliary Water Tender "809," CC, *15*		380____
82410	Virginian 2-bay Hopper "13168," *16*		60____
82411	N&W 2-bay Hopper "113733," *15–16*		60____
82412	Reading Birney Trolley, *15*		100____
82413	Lionel Transit Birney Trolley, *15*		100____
82414	CNJ LionChief 4-6-0 Camelback Locomotive "777," *15–16*		440____
82415	DL&W LionChief 4-6-0 Camelback Locomotive "1035," *15–16*		440____

		Exc	Mint
82416	LV LionChief 4-6-0 Camelback Locomotive "1602," *15–16*		440
82417	Philadelphia & Reading LionChief 4-6-0 Camelback Locomotive "675," *15–16*		440
82418	Erie LionChief 4-6-0 Camelback Locomotive "861," *15–16*		440
82419	UP 8-door Hi-Cube Boxcar, *16*		100
82420	SP 8-door Hi-Cube Boxcar, *16*		100
82421	B&O 8-door Hi-Cube Boxcar, *16*		100
82422	PRR 8-door Hi-Cube Boxcar, *16*		100
82423	C&NW 8-door Hi-Cube Boxcar, *16*		100
82424	Chessie 8-door Hi-Cube Boxcar, *16*		100
82425	PC 8-door Hi-Cube Boxcar, *16*		100
82426	RI 8-door Hi-Cube Boxcar, *16*		100
82427	Patriot LionChief U36B Diesel Freight Set, *15–16*		360
82436	Pennsylvania Keystone LionChief GP38 Diesel Freight Set, *15*		450
82453	Amtrak F40PH Diesel Phase II "200," CC, *16*		550
82454	Amtrak F40PH Diesel Phase II "207," CC, *16*		550
82455	Amtrak F40PH Diesel Phase III "364," CC, *16*		550
82456	Amtrak F40PH Diesel Phase III "388," CC, *16*		550
82460	CSX F40PH Diesel "9998," CC, *16*		550
82461	CSX F40PH Diesel "9999," CC, *16*		550
82473	N&W Early Era Inspection Vehicle, CC, *15*		200
82474	BN Early Era Inspection Vehicle, CC, *15*		200
82475	Bethlehem Steel Early Era Inspection Vehicle, CC, *15*		200
82476	NH Early Era Inspection Vehicle, CC, *15*		200
82477	Virginian Early Era Inspection Vehicle, CC, *15*		200
82478	Reading Early Era Inspection Vehicle, CC, *15*		200
82486	Weathered Virginian USRA Y-3 2-8-8-2 Locomotive "737," CC, *14*		1450
82487	Weathered AT&SF USRA Y-3 2-8-8-2 Locomotive "1797," CC, *14*		1450
82488	Weathered N&W USRA Y-3 2-8-8-2 Locomotive "2029," CC, *14*		1450
82489	MILW 18" Aluminum Coach/Dining Car 2-pack, *14*		320
82489	MILW Olympian 18" Aluminum Passenger Car 2-pack, *14–15*		320
82494	Turbo Missile Launch Flatcar, *15*		60
82495	D&RGW Scrapyard, *16*		130
82498	Polar Express Mail Car, *16*		70
82500	Polar Express Covered Bridge, *15*		70
82501	Providence & Worcester 89' Auto Carrier "190091," *15–16*		110
82502	C&NW 89' Auto Carrier "962255," *15–16*		110
82503	Chessie 89' Auto Carrier "255798," *15–16*		110
82504	TFM 89' Auto Carrier "987408," *15–16*		110
82505	BNSF 89' Auto Carrier "212878," *15–16*		110
82506	UP 89' Auto Carrier "992579," *15–16*		110
82508	NYC Milk Car "6589" (std O), *16*		80
82510	Polar Express Aquarium Car, *16*		85
82512	Polar Express Work Caboose with presents, *15*		85

		Exc	Mint
82514	Polar Express Reindeer Stock Car, *15*	90	___
82518	Moon Pie Boxcar, *15*	85	___
82528	NYC Empire State Express Steam Passenger Set, CC, *15*	1950	___
82534	NYC J3a 4-6-4 Hudson Locomotive "5429," tender, *15*	1500	___
82535	NYC J3a 4-6-4 Hudson Locomotive "5426," tender, *15*	1500	___
82536	NYC J3a 4-6-4 Hudson Locomotive "5429," tender, *15*	1500	___
82537	NYC J3a 4-6-4 Hudson Locomotive "5426," tender, *15*	1500	___
82543	Postwar "943" Exploding Ammunition Dump, *15–16*	50	___
82544	Missile Firing Range, *15–16*	65	___
82545	Santa's Helper Steam Freight Set, *16*	340	___
82550	Wabash 21" Streamlined Passenger Car 4-pack, *15*	600	___
82555	Wabash 21" Streamlined Passenger Car 2-pack, *15*	300	___
82558	Southern 21" Streamlined Passenger Car 4-pack, *15*	600	___
82563	Southern 21" Streamlined Passenger Car 4-pack, *15*	300	___
82566	RI 21" Streamlined Passenger Car 4-pack, *15*	600	___
82571	RI 21" Streamlined Passenger Car 4-pack, *15*	300	___
82574	Texas Special 21" Streamlined Passenger Car 4-pack, *15*	600	___
82579	Texas Special 21" Streamlined Passenger Car 4-pack, *15*	300	___
82582	C&O 21" Streamlined Passenger Car 4-pack, *15*	600	___
82587	C&O 21" Streamlined Passenger Car 4-pack, *15*	300	___
82590	Amtrak 21" Passenger Car 4-pack, *16*	600	___
82595	Amtrak 21" Passenger Car 2-pack, *16*	300	___
82598	NYC Empire State Passenger Car Add-on 2-pack, *15*	300	___
82611	PRR GL-a 2-bay Hopper 3-pack, *15*	220	___
82621	Buffalo Creek Flour PS-1 Boxcar "2366," *15*	80	___
82622	U.S. Army PS-1 Boxcar "26875, *15*	80	___
82623	West India Fruit & Steamship Co. PS-1 Boxcar "321," *15*	80	___
82624	Linde Air Products PS-1 Boxcar "3019," *15*	80	___
82625	Air Reduction Products PS-1 Boxcar "100," *15*	80	___
82629	PRR N5b Caboose "478883," *15–16*	95	___
82630	PRR N5b Caboose with trainphone antenna, *15–16*	95	___
82631	B&M N5b Caboose "C-16," *15–16*	95	___
82639	MILW Milk Car "370" (std O), *16*	80	___
82640	UTLX 30,000-Gallon 1-D Tank Car 3-pack, *15*	250	___
82644	Philadelphia Energy Solutions 1-D Tank Car 3-pack, *15*	250	___
82648	Midwest Ethanol Transport 1-D Tank Car 3-pack, *15*	250	___
82652	Global Ethanol Transport 1-D Tank Car 3-pack, *15*	250	___
82656	Conrail 60' Boxcar "216010," *15–16*	90	___

		Mint
___ 82657	WM 60' Boxcar "38020," *15–16*	90
___ 82658	BN 60' Boxcar "355145," *15–16*	90
___ 82659	RI 60' Boxcar "33825," *15–16*	90
___ 82660	N&W 60' Boxcar "600949," *15–16*	90
___ 82661	P&LE PS-5 Gondola and PS-4 Flatcar, *15–16*	175
___ 82664	B&LE PS-5 Gondola and PS-4 Flatcar, *15–16*	175
___ 82667	DT&I PS-5 Gondola and PS-4 Flatcar, *15–16*	175
___ 82670	Conrail PS-5 Gondola and PS-4 Flatcar, *15–16*	175
___ 82674	UP Bathtub Gondola 2-pack, *15*	140
___ 82677	Strasburg 3-D Tank Car, *16*	656
82683	Batman and Flash Justice League Boxcar 2-pack, *15–16*	170
82684	Superman and Green Lantern Justice League Boxcar 2-pack, *15–16*	170
___ 82685	New York Giants Cooperstown Boxcar, *15*	85
___ 82686	Washington Senators Cooperstown Boxcar, *15*	85
___ 82687	Detroit Tigers Cooperstown Boxcar, *15*	85
___ 82688	Pittsburgh Pirates Cooperstown Boxcar, *15*	85
___ 82689	Operation Eagle Missile Carrying Car, *15–16*	65
___ 82690	Coca-Cola Anniversary Bottle Boxcar, *15*	85
___ 82691	Christmas Boxcar, *15*	75
___ 82693	Santa's Helper Crane, *15*	85
82694	UP LionMaster 4-6-6-4 Challenger Locomotive "3985," CC, *15*	1000
82695	UP LionMaster 4-6-6-4 Challenger Locomotive "3977," CC, *15*	1000
82696	UP LionMaster 4-6-6-4 Challenger Locomotive "3989," CC, *15*	1000
82697	D&RGW LionMaster 4-6-6-4 Challenger Locomotive "3803," CC, *15*	1000
82698	WM LionMaster 4-6-6-4 Challenger Locomotive "1201," CC, *15*	1000
82699	Angela Trotta Thomas Lionelville Christmas Boxcar, *15*	75
___ 82701	Escaping Snowmen Handcar, *15*	90
82702	Ontario Northland PS-4 Flatcar with covered load, *15*	90
___ 82703	BN PS-4 Flatcar with covered load, *15*	90
___ 82704	D&RGW PS-4 Flatcar with covered load, *15*	90
___ 82705	Reading PS-4 Flatcar with covered load, *15*	90
___ 82706	Southern PS-4 Flatcar with covered load, *15*	90
___ 82708	Christmas Gingerbread Shanty, *16*	40
___ 82709	PRR Silver & Gold Ore Car 2-pack, *16*	130
___ 82710	PRR Ice Breaker Tunnel Car, *16*	65
___ 82711	Santa's Favorites Transparent Gift Car, *16*	85
___ 82713	Christmas Music Boxcar, *15*	80
___ 82716	Mickey's Holiday to Remember Freight Set, *16*	400
___ 82717	W. E. Disney Girder Bridge, *16*	33
___ 82718	Disney Villains Hi-Cube Boxcar 2-pack, *16*	160
___ 82721	Dumbo 75th Anniversary Boxcar, *16*	85
___ 82734	New York Yankees Cooperstown Boxcar, *15*	85
___ 82736	North Pole Central Water Tower, *15*	40
___ 82737	Coca-Cola Santa Boxcar, *15*	85
___ 82739	North Pole Central Boxcar, *16*	80

		Exc Mint
82740	Winter Wonderland Aquarium Car, *15*	95____
82741	Christmas Tinsel Vat Car, *16*	70____
82742	Candy Mountain Christmas Quad Hopper, *16*	65____
82743	Santa's Reindeer Station Platform, *15*	50____
82744	Santa Claus Automatic Gateman, *16*	100____
82745	Christmas Cocoa Barrel Shed, *15*	50____
82746	Christmas Floodlight Tower, *16*	75____
82747	Christmas Red Arch Under Bridge, *16*	30____
82748	Silver Bell Casting Co. Hopper, *15*	70____
82749	PRR GG1 Electric "4935," CC, *16*	1400____
82751	PRR GG1 Electric "4913," CC, *16*	1400____
82752	PRR GG1 Electric "4877," CC, *16*	1400____
82754	PC GG1 Electric "4828," CC, *16*	1400____
82755	Amtrak GG1 Electric "926," CC, *16*	1400____
82757	CP SD90MAC Diesel "9116," CC, *16*	650____
82758	CP SD90MAC Diesel "9130," CC, *16*	650____
82759	NS SD90MAC Diesel "7230," CC, *16*	650____
82760	NS SD90MAC Diesel "7245," CC, *16*	650____
82761	UP SD90MAC Diesel "8130," CC, *16*	650____
82762	UP SD90MAC Diesel "8133," CC, *16*	650____
82763	UP SD90MAC Diesel "8025," CC, *16*	650____
82764	UP SD90MAC Diesel "8055," CC, *16*	650____
82765	Indiana SD90MAC Diesel "9003," CC, *16*	650____
82766	Indiana SD90MAC Diesel "9006," CC, *16*	650____
82767	C&O 2-6-6-6 Locomotive "1601," CC, *16*	2200____
82768	C&O 2-6-6-6 Locomotive "1604," CC, *16*	2200____
82769	C&O 2-6-6-6 Locomotive "1608," CC, *16*	2200____
82770	Virginian 2-6-6-6 Locomotive "906," CC, *16*	2200____
82825	CP GP38 Diesel Locomotive "3019," *16*	340____
82826	CSX GP38 Diesel Locomotive "2145," *16*	340____
82827	SP GP38 Diesel Locomotive "4846," *16*	340____
82828	UP GP38 Diesel Locomotive "905," *16*	340____
82840	AT&SF PS-4 Flatcar with trailer (std O), *16*	110____
82841	E-L PS-4 Flatcar with trailer (std O), *16*	110____
82842	GN PS-4 Flatcar with trailer (std O), *16*	110____
82843	WM PS-4 Flatcar with trailer (std O), *16*	110____
82844	PRR PS-4 Flatcar with trailer (std O), *16*	110____
82845	B&O Truck with 40' trailer, *16*	90____
82846	MILW Truck with 40' trailer, *16*	90____
82847	MKT Truck with 40' trailer, *16*	110____
82848	Logging Disconnect with load, *16*	65____
82849	Logging Disconnect with load 2-pack, *16*	125____
82850	MILW 40' Flatcar with lumber (std O), *16*	90____
82851	NP 40' Flatcar with lumber (std O), *16*	90____
82852	Meadow River 40' Flatcar with lumber (std O), *16*	90____
82853	Pickering 40' Flatcar with lumber (std O), *16*	90____
82854	PRR 40' Flatcar with lumber (std O), *16*	90____
82855	ADM Unibody Tank Car "190516" (std O), *16*	75____
82856	GATX Unibody Tank Car "4415" (std O), *16*	75____
82857	AFPX Unibody Tank Car "413303" (std O), *16*	75____
82858	Shell Unibody Tank Car "82858" (std O), *16*	85____
82859	Engelhard Unibody Tank Car "24586" (std O), *16*	75____

		Exc	Mint
82860	PC PS-5 Gondola "557065" (std O), *16*		90
82861	E-L PS-5 Gondola "14552" (std O), *16*		90
82862	Frisco PS-5 Gondola "61442" (std O), *16*		90
82863	CB&Q PS-5 Gondola "82050" (std O), *16*		90
82864	NYC PS-5 Gondola "712603" (std O), *16*		90
82865	PRR N5b Caboose "5017" (std O), *16*		90
82866	PRR N5b Caboose "477746" (std O), *16*		90
82867	PRR N5b Caboose "477625" (std O), *16*		90
82868	NH N5 Caboose "C-507" (std O), *16*		90
82870	Loading Ramp, *16*		25
82872	Loader/Unloader Workers Figure Pack, *16*		30
82873	Loggers Cabin, sound, *16*		140
82874	Early Intermodal Work House, sound, *16*		130
82877	Thomas Kinkade Polar Express Boxcar, *16*		85
82879	Coca-Cola Christmas Boxcar, *16*		85
82884	Wabash 21" Streamlined Dining Car, StationSounds, *15*		300
82885	Southern 21" Streamlined Dining Car, StationSounds, *15*		300
82886	RI 21" Streamlined Dining Car, StationSounds, *15*		300
82887	Texas Special 21" Streamlined Dining Car, StationSounds, *15*		300
82888	C&O 21" Streamlined Dining Car, StationSounds, *15*		300
82889	Amtrak 21" Diner, StationSounds, *16*		300
82890	NYC Empire State Express Diner, StationSounds, *15*		300
82906	Pluto Walking Brakeman Car, *16*		100
82908	Mickey's Christmas Shanty, *16*		37
82913	Winnie the Pooh Boxcar, *16*		85
82914	Disney Aquarium Car, *16*		85
82942	James Monroe Presidential Boxcar, *16*		70
82943	John F. Kennedy Presidential Boxcar, *16*		70
82944	Herbert Hoover Presidential Boxcar, *16*		70
82945	James Madison Presidential Boxcar, *16*		70
82947	Wonder Woman/Green Arrow Boxcar 2-pack, *16*		170
82950	Aquaman/Martian Manhunter Boxcar 2-pack, *16*		170
82953	Joker/Lex Luthor Boxcar 2-pack, *16*		170
82954	Lionel Christmas Boxcar, *16*		65
82960	NYC 2-8-2 Steam Locomotive "1548," *16*		430
82961	UP 2-8-2 Steam Locomotive "2537," *16*		430
82962	Southern 2-8-2 Steam Locomotive "4501," *16*		430
82963	Rio Grande 2-8-2 Steam Locomotive "1208," *16*		430
82964	MILW 4-6-4 Steam Locomotive "125," *16*		430
82965	AT&SF 4-6-4 Steam Locomotive "3450," *16*		430
82966	DL&W 4-6-4 Steam Locomotive "1151," *16*		430
82967	CB&Q 4-6-4 Steam Locomotive "3007," *16*		430
82968	LL 4-6-2 Steam Locomotive "462," *16*		430
82969	WM 4-6-2 Steam Locomotive "202," *16*		430
82970	Reading & Northern 4-6-2 Locomotive "425," *16*		450
82971	C&NW 4-6-2 Steam Locomotive "600," *16*		300
82972	Lionel Junction PRR Diesel Freight Set, *16*		175
82973	PRR A5 0-4-0 Locomotive "3891," *16*		450

Exc Mint

		Exc	Mint
82974	SP A5 0-4-0 Locomotive "1040," *16*		450____
82975	B&O A5 0-4-0 Locomotive "317," *16*		450____
82984	NYC RS-3 Diesel Freight Set, *16*		260____
83002	Broadway Limited 21" StationSounds Diner 2-pack, *16*		300____
83003	PC 21" StationSounds Diner "4552," *16*		300____
83006	UP 21" Excursion Diner, *16*		300____
83007	Broadway Limited 21" Passenger Car 2-pack, *16*		300____
83010	PC 21" Passenger Car 2-pack, *16*		300____
83019	UP 21" Excursion Passenger Car 2-pack, *16*		600____
83022	Broadway Limited 21" Passenger Car 4-pack, *16*		600____
83027	PC 21" Passenger Car 4-pack, *16*		675____
83042	UP 21" Excursion Passenger Car 4-pack, *16*		675____
83063	AT&SF Super Chief Boxcar "143093," *16*		50____
83071	Universal Remote, *16*		50____
83080	Rio Grande 0-4-0 Switcher Freight Set, *16*		300____
83092	Steel City Switcher Freight Set, CC, *16*		1300____
83102	SP 21" Passenger Car 4-pack, *16*		600____
83107	SP 21" Passenger Car 2-pack, *16*		300____
83110	SP 21" StationSounds Diner "290," *16*		300____
83111	American Freedom Train 21" Passenger Car 4-pack, *16*		675____
83116	American Freedom Train 21" Passenger Car 2-pack, *16*		300____
83119	American Freedom Train 21" Crew Car, *16*		300____
83120	CSX 21" Passenger Car 4-pack, *16*		600____
83125	CSX 21" Passenger Car 2-pack, *16*		300____
83128	CSX 21" StationSounds Diner, *16*		300____
83147	Lighted Yard Tower, *16*		60____
83148	Christmas Express Boxcar, *16*		53____
83157	Smithsonian Air & Space Boxcar 2-pack, *16*		170____
83162	Nightmare on Elm Street Boxcar, *16*		85____
83163	Thomas Kinkade Christmas Boxcar, *16*		85____
83164	Frosty the Snowman 1-D Tank Car, *16*		65____
83165	PRR GG1 Electric "4899," CC, *16*		1400____
83166	PRR GG1 Electric "4800," CC, *16*		1400____
83167	Conrail Bicentennial GG1 Electric "4800," CC, *16*		1400____
83168	Iron Workers Figure Pack, *16*		30____
83169	NYC Flatcar with piggyback trailers, *16*		75____
83170	Steel Mill Structure, sound, *16*		130____
83171	MOW Workers Figure Pack, *16*		30____
83172	MOW Work Structure, sound, *16*		130____
83173	Single Signal Bridge, *16*		80____
83174	Double Signal Bridge, *16*		100____
83175	Christmas Music Boxcar, *16*		80____
83176	Lionel Lines Christmas Caboose, *16*		75____
83177	Angela Trotta Thomas Caboose, *16*		80____
83178	Coca-Cola Caboose, *16*		75____
83179	Conrail Caboose "23878," *16*		75____
83180	PRR Caboose "477100," *16*		75____
83181	AT&SF Caboose "999316," *16*		75____
83182	ACL Caboose "0634," *16*		75____
83183	Erie Caboose "C226," *16*		75____

		Exc	Mint
____ 83184	UP Caboose "25214," 16		75
____ 83185	Polar Express Elves Figure Set, 16		33
____ 83186	NYC Caboose "21777," 16		75
____ 83190	Moon Pie 1-D Tank Car, 16		75
____ 83191	Lionel Christmas 1-D Tank Car, 16		85
____ 83192	Smithsonian Dinosaur Aquarium Car, 16		85
____ 83193	SP GS-4 4-8-4 Locomotive "4449," CC, 16		1700
____ 83194	SP GS-4 4-8-4 Locomotive "4449," CC, 16		1700
____ 83195	SP GS-4 4-8-4 Locomotive "4443," CC, 16		1700
____ 83196	SP GS-4 4-8-4 Locomotive "4444," CC, 16		1700
83197	American Freedom Train GS-4 4-8-4 Locomotive, CC, 16		1700
____ 83198	Reading T1 4-8-4 Locomotive "2100," CC, 16		1700
____ 83199	Reading T1 4-8-4 Locomotive "2119," CC, 16		1700
____ 83200	Reading T1 4-8-4 Locomotive "2102," CC, 16		1700
____ 83201	Reading T1 4-8-4 Locomotive "2124," CC, 16		1700
83202	American Freedom Train T1 4-8-4 Locomotive, CC, 16		1700
____ 83203	Chessie T1 4-8-4 Locomotive "2101," CC, 16		1700
____ 83204	B&O 0-8-0 Locomotive "1695," CC, 16		900
____ 83205	GTW 0-8-0 Locomotive "8380," CC, 16		900
83206	Indiana Harbor Belt 0-8-0 Locomotive "312," CC, 16		900
____ 83208	Wabash 0-8-0 Locomotive "1526," CC, 16		900
____ 83209	Terminal Railroad 0-8-0 Locomotive, CC, 16		900
____ 83214	North Pole Central 4-6-2 Locomotive "1225," 16		430
____ 83215	Transformer 2-pack, 16		15
____ 83223	Steel I-Beam 12-pack, 16		15
____ 83230	Amtrak Metal Girder Bridge, 16		43
____ 83231	Polar Express Metal Girder Bridge, 16		37
____ 83232	Bethlehem Steel Metal Girder Bridge, 16		37
____ 83233	CSX Metal Girder Bridge, 16		37
____ 83234	John Deere Plastic Girder Bridge, 16		33
____ 83238	John Deere Flatcar with spreaders, 16		80
____ 83239	Polar Express Bells Mint Car, 16		80
____ 83240	Shell Operating Oil Derrick, 16		120
____ 83241	Shell Oil Storage Tank with Light, 16		85
____ 83242	Shell 1-D Tank Car, 16		75
____ 83243	Shell 3-D Tank Car, 16		75
____ 83246	Shell Boxcar, 16		85
____ 83247	Shell Billboard Pack, 16		25
____ 83248	"It's a Boy" Boxcar, 16		90
____ 83249	Polar Express Combination Car, 16		70
____ 83250	"It's a Girl" Boxcar, 16		90
____ 83251	Poultry Dispatch Sweep Car, 16		120
____ 83253	D&RGW Searchlight Car, 16		63
____ 83254	Western Union Animated Gondola, 16		70
____ 83256	GN Horse Transport, 16		80
____ 83257	Bobbing Werewolf Boxcar, 16		75
____ 83258	CP Boom Car, 16		63
____ 83266	Lionel Junction Santa Fe Steam Freight Set, 16		175
____ 83284	Peekaboo Reindeer Operating Boxcar, 16		75
____ 83286	John Deere Steam Freight Set, 16		400

Exc Mint

No.	Description	Exc	Mint
83291	Christmas Half-covered Bridge, *16*		70____
83292	Christmas Cookies & Candies Store, *16*		85____
83304	North Pole Elves Work Shanty, *16*		40____
83305	Illuminated Winter Covered Bridge, *16*		80____
83308	North Pole Central Tank Car "122416," *16*		75____
83311	Santa's Favorites Egg Nog Reefer, *16*		65____
83312	Santa's Cookies Vat Car, *16*		70____
83313	Reindeer Express Agency Flatcar with trailer, *16*		70____
83315	Christmas Toys Stock Car, *16*		70____
83316	Santa's Sleigh Aquarium Car, *16*		80____
83340	Boxcar Children Boxcar, *16*		85____
83347	ACL USRA Double-sheathed Boxcar, *16*		85____
83348	B&M USRA Double-sheathed Boxcar, *16*		85____
83349	RI USRA Double-sheathed Boxcar, *16*		85____
83350	Northwestern Pacific USRA Double-sheathed Boxcar, *16*		85____
83351	Wabash USRA Double-sheathed Boxcar, *16*		85____
83352	Polar Express USRA Double-sheathed Boxcar, *16*		95____
83353	D&RGW Flatcar with snowplow (std O), *16*		95____
83354	NYC Flatcar with snowplow (std O), *16*		95____
83355	UP Flatcar with snowplow (std O), *16*		95____
83356	MOW Flatcar with Snowplow (std O), *16*		95____
83357	Reading NE-style Caboose "92882" (std O), *16*		90____
83358	Reading NE-style Caboose "92902" (std O), *16*		90____
83359	Reading & Northern NE-style Caboose "92884" (std O), *16*		90____
83360	C&O NE-style Caboose "90352" (std O), *16*		90____
83361	N&W NE-style Caboose "500830" (std O), *16*		90____
83362	WM NE-style Caboose "1887" (std O), *16*		90____
83395	AC&Y H16-44 Diesel "201," CC, *16*		550____
83396	AC&Y H16-44 Diesel "202," CC, *16*		550____
83397	AT&SF H16-44 Diesel "2801," CC, *16*		550____
83398	AT&SF H16-44 Diesel "2807," CC, *16*		550____
83399	B&O H16-44 Diesel "6705," CC, *16*		550____
83400	B&O H16-44 Diesel "6708," CC, *16*		550____
83401	MILW H16-44 Diesel "402," CC, *16*		550____
83402	MILW H16-44 Diesel "404," CC, *16*		550____
83403	DL&W H16-44 Diesel "931," CC, *16*		550____
83404	DL&W H16-44 Diesel "934," CC, *16*		550____
83405	Southern H16-44 Diesel "6547," CC, *16*		550____
83406	Southern H16-44 Diesel "6550," CC, *16*		550____
83426	Johnstown Birney Trolley, *16*		100____
83434	Polar Express Passenger Station, *16*		90____
83437	Polar Express Conductor Announcement Car, *16*		110____
83444	Illuminated Station Platform, *16*		43____
83445	Smithsonian Old St. Nick Boxcar, *16*		85____
83455	Polar Express Operating Billboard, *16*		85____
83462	Bethlehem Steel Slag Car 3-pack, *16*		240____
83466	U.S. Steel Slag Car 3-pack (std O), *16*		240____
83470	Slag Car 3-pack (std O), *16*		240____
83474	Weathered Slag Car 3-pack (std O), *16*		240____
83478	Bethlehem Steel Hot Metal Car 2-pack, *16*		200____
83481	U.S. Steel Hot Metal Car 2-pack (std O), *16*		200____

Exc Mint

		Exc	Mint
____ 83484	Hot Metal Car 2-pack (std O), *16*		200
____ 83487	Weathered Hot Metal Car 2-pack (std O), *16*		200
____ 83490	Lighted Coaling Tower, *16*		80
____ 83491	Boston Red Sox Cooperstown Boxcar, *16*		85
____ 83492	St. Louis Cardinals Cooperstown Boxcar, *16*		85
____ 83493	Philadelphia Phillies Cooperstown Boxcar, *16*		85
____ 83494	Baltimore Orioles Cooperstown Boxcar, *16*		85
____ 83496	Station Platform, *16*		40
____ 83503	Thomas with remote, *16*		120
____ 83504	Birthday Thomas with remote, *16*		120
____ 83512	Thomas & Friends Christmas Freight Set, *16*		200
____ 83518	PRR Boxcar "83518" (std O), *16*		100
____ 83519	REA Reefer "7844" (std O), *16*		130
____ 83520	North Pole Central Flatcar with Snowplow, *16*		95
____ 83527	AT&SF PS-1 Boxcar "142501" (std O), *16*		130
____ 83528	BAR PS-1 Boxcar "5149" (std O), *16*		130
____ 83529	B&O PS-1 Boxcar "467931" (std O), *16*		130
____ 83530	BN PS-1 Boxcar "132909" (std O), *16*		130
____ 83531	C&NW PS-1 Boxcar "5" (std O), *16*		130
____ 83532	NYC PS-1 Boxcar "175001" (std O), *16*		130
____ 83533	PRR PS-1 Boxcar "47005" (std O), *16*		130
____ 83534	UP PS-1 Boxcar "196883" (std O), *16*		130
____ 83535	PRR GL-a 2-bay Hopper 3-pack #1 (std O), *16*		220
____ 83539	PRR GL-a 2-bay Hopper 3-pack #2 (std O), *16*		220
____ 83544	PRR N5b Caboose "477797" (std O), *16*		95
____ 83545	PFE Reefer 3-pack (std O), *16*		300
____ 83549	AT&SF Reefer 3-pack (std O), *16*		300
____ 83620	Hogwarts Express Passenger Set, *16*		400
____ 83624	UP Sherman Hill Scout RS-3 Freight Set, *16*		280
____ 83634	Keystone Smoke Fluid Loader, *16*		350
____ 83635	North American Smoke Fluid Loader, *16*		350
____ 83637	Mets-Phillies Mascot Aquarium Car, *16*		85
____ 83645	Polar Express Boxcar 2-pack, *16*		170
____ 83648	New York Yankees Subway Set, *16*		390
____ 83653	21" Passenger Car Figure Pack, *16*		30
____ 83655	Hamm's Heritage Beer Wood-sided Reefer, *16*		80
____ 83656	Coors Heritage Beer Wood-sided Reefer, *16*		80
____ 83657	Miller Heritage Beer Wood-sided Reefer, *16*		80
____ 83659	PRR Keystone Special Steam Freight Set, *16*		90
____ 83762	Personalized Christmas Boxcar, *16*		90
____ 83763	Personalized Holiday Boxcar, *16*		90
____ 83764	Happy Birthday Boxcar, *16*		90
____ 83765	Anniversary Boxcar, *16*		95
____ 83766	Personalized Polar Express Baggage Car, *16*		95
____ 99001	Mickey's Holiday Express Freight Set, *99 u*		168
____ 99002	Looney Tunes Square Window Caboose, *99 u*		NRS
____ 99006	Keebler Bulkhead Flatcar, *99 u*		NRS
____ 99007	Smuckers Fudge 1-D Tank Car, *99 u*		90
____ 99008	Mickey's Merry Christmas Boxcar, *99 u*		NRS
____ 99009	Mickey's Holiday Express Square Window Caboose, *99 u*		NRS
____ 99013	Case Cutlery Tank Car "1889," *00 u*		NRS

MODERN ERA 1970-2017

		Exc	Mint
99014	Case Cutlery Gondola "1889," *00 u*		NRS____
99015	Case Cutlery Boxcar "1889," *00 u*		NRS____
99018	Case Cutlery Rolling Stock 3-pack, *00 u*		210____
79C95204C	Sears Santa Fe Diesel Freight Set, *71 u*	150	165____
79C9715C	Sears 4-unit Diesel Freight Set, *75 u*	50	65____
79C9717C	Sears 7-unit Steam Freight Set, *75 u*	150	165____
79N95223C	Sears 6-unit Diesel Freight Set, *74 u*	150	165____
79N9552C	Sears 6-unit Steam Freight Set, *72 u*	150	165____
79N9553C	Sears 6-unit Diesel Freight Set, *72 u*	150	165____
79N96178C	Sears 4-unit Steam Freight Set, *74 u*	50	65____
79N97082C	Sears Steam Freight Set, *70 u*		NRS____
79N97101C	Sears 5-unit Steam Freight Set, *72 u*	150	165____
79N98765C	Sears Logging Empire Set, *78 u*	100	115____
T1428RRODTS	Tony Stewart NASCAR Steam Freight Set, *12–14*		300____
T1828RRMMKB	Kyle Busch NASCAR Steam Freight Set, *12–14*		300____
T2428RRDUJG	Jeff Gordon NASCAR Steam Freight Set, *12–14*		300____
T4828RRLOJJ	Jimmy Johnson NASCAR Steam Freight Set, *12–14*		300____
T4828RRLOJJ	Dale Earnhardt Jr. NASCAR Steam Freight Set, *12–14*		300____
TX328RRGMDE	Dale Earnhardt NASCAR Steam Freight Set, *12–14*		300____
UCS	Remote Control Track (O), *70*	4	7____

Unnumbered Items

	Exc	Mint
Amtrak Passenger Car Set, *89, 89 u*	640	770____
B&A Hudson and Standard O Car Set, *86 u*	1500	1700____
Baltimore & Ohio Set, *94, 96*		NRS____
Black Cave Flyer Playmat, *82*		8____
Blue Comet Set, *78–80, 87 u*	560	620____
Burlington Texas Zephyr Set, *80, 80 u*	980	1150____
C&NW Passenger Car Set, *93*	385	460____
Cannonball Freight Playmat, *81–82*		8____
Chesapeake & Ohio Set, *95–96*		NRS____
Chessie System Special Set, *80, 86 u*	560	620____
Chicago & Alton Limited Set, *81, 86 u*	560	620____
Commando Assault Train Playmat, *83–84*		8____
D&RGW California Zephyr Set, *92, 93*		900____
Erie Set (FF 7), *93*	385	460____
Erie-Lackawanna Passenger Car Set, *93, 94*	940	980____
Favorite Food Freight Set, *81–82*	248	338____
Frisco Set (FF 5), *91*	405	425____
The General Set, *77–80*	240	285____
GN Empire Builder Set, *92, 93*	620	730____
Great Northern Set (FARR 3), *81, 81 u*	620	690____
IC City of New Orleans Set, *85, 87, 93*	885	1045____
Illinois Central Set, *91–92, 95*	255	285____
Jersey Central Set, *86*	345	370____
Joshua Lionel Cowen Set, *80, 80 u, 82*	540	580____
L.A.S.E.R. Playmat, *81–82*		8____

	Exc	Mint
Lionel Lines Madison Car Set, *91, 93*	560	620
Lionel Lines Set, *82–84 u, 86, 86–87 u, 94–95*	530	620
Mickey Mouse Express Set, *77–78, 78 u*	1000	1693
Milwaukee Road Set (FF 2), *87, 90 u*	380	405
Mint Set, *79 u, 80–83, 84 u, 86 u, 87, 91 u, 93*	940	1073
Missouri Pacific Set, *95*		390
N&W Powhatan Arrow Passenger Car Set, *95*	370	445
N&W Powhatan Arrow Set, *81, 81 u, 82 u, 91 u*	1450	1700
New Haven Set, *94–95*		400
New York Central Set, *89, 91*	240	270
Nickel Plate Road Set (FF 6), *92*	385	460
Northern Pacific Set, *90–92*	190	250
NYC 20th Century Limited Set, *83, 83 u, 95*	980	1150
Pennsylvania Set, *79–80, 79–80 u, 81 u, 83 u*	1200	1350
Pennsylvania Set, *87–90, 95*	240	270
Pennsylvania Set (FARR 5), *84–85, 89 u*	600	660
Pere Marquette Set, *93*	720	770
Rock Island & Peoria Set, *80–82*	240	315
Rocky Mountain Platform, *83–84*		8
Santa Fe Super Chief Set, *91, 91 u, 92 u, 93, 95*	1400	1700
Santa Fe Set (FARR 1), *79, 79 u*	460	580
Southern Crescent Limited Set, *77–78, 87 u*	540	650
Southern Pacific Daylight Diesel Set, *82–83, 82–83 u, 90 u*	2150	2300
Southern Set (FARR 4), *83, 83 u*	620	690
SP Daylight Steam Set, *90, 92, 93*	790	940
Spirit of '76 Set, *74–76*	570	690
Station Platform, *83–84*		8
Toys "R" Us Thunderball Freight Set, *75 u*		NRS
Union Pacific Set, *94*	430	500
Union Pacific Set (FARR 2), *80, 80 u*	540	580
UP Overland Route Set, *84, 92 u*	770	840
Wabash Set (FF 1), *86, 87*	755	905
Western Maryland Set (FF 4), *89*	345	405

Section 4
LIONEL CORPORATION TINPLATE

		Retail
11-1001	No. 400E Locomotive, black, brass trim (std)	900____
11-1002	No. 400E Locomotive, gray, nickel trim (std)	900____
11-1003	No. 400E Locomotive, gray, brass trim (std)	900____
11-1005	No. 390 Locomotive, green	600____
11-1006	No. 400E Locomotive, crackele black, brass trim	900____
11-1008	No. 400E Lionel Lines Locomotive	900____
11-1009	No. 400E Locomotive, blue, brass trim	900____
11-1010	No. 385E Locomotive (std)	700____
11-1012	No. 1835E Locomotive, black, nickel trim	700____
11-1013	AF No. 4694 Warrior Passenger Set	1400____
11-1014	AF No. 4694 Iron Monarch Passenger Set	1250____
11-1015	No. 392E Locomotive, black, brass trim	800____
11-1016	No. 392E Locomotive, gray, nickel trim	800____
11-1017	No. 400E Locomotive, blue, nickel trim (std)	900____
11-1018	No. 7 Lionel Locomotive (std)	900____
11-1019	No. 6 Pennsylvania Locomotive (std)	900____
11-1020	American Flyer No. 4696 Locomotive	1000____
11-1021	No. 400E Presidential Locomotive (std)	1000____
11-1022	No. 400E Red Comet Locomotive (std)	1000____
11-1023	No. 400E Locomotive, blue, brass trim (std)	900____
11-1024	No. 400E Locomotive, black, brass trim (std)	900____
11-1025	No. 400E Lionel Lines Locomotive (std)	900____
11-1026	No. 400E Locomotive, pink (std)	1000____
11-1027	No. 400E Locomotive, state green (std)	1000____
11-1028	No. 400E Locomotive, black, brass trim (std)	1000____
11-1029	No. 6 NYC Locomotive (std)	900____
11-1030	No. 6 General Locomotive (std)	900____
11-1031	No. 6 Texas Locomotive (std)	950____
11-1038	No. 6 B&O Locomotive (std)	900____
11-1039	No. 6 Long Island Locomotive (std)	900____
11-1040	No. 6 Strasburg Locomotive (std)	900____
11-1041	No. 6 PRR Locomotive (std)	900____
11-1042	Great Northern Steam Locomotive (std)	1000____
11-1043	Lehigh Valley Steam Locomotive (std)	1000____
11-1045	PRR Steam Locomotive (std)	1000____
11-2003	No. 8E Electric Locomotive, olive green (std)	500____
11-2004	No. 8E Electric Locomotive, dark olive green (std)	500____
11-2005	No. 8E Electric Locomotive, orange (std)	500____
11-2006	No. 8E Electric Locomotive, red/cream (std)	500____
11-2007	American Flyer Presidential Passenger Set (std)	1800____
11-2008	AF No. 4689 Presidential Locomotive, blue (std)	800____
11-2009	Big Brute Electric Engine, zinc chromate	1500____
11-2010	Big Brute Electric Engine, green	1500____

____	11-2015	Super 381 Electric Engine, state green (std)	1300
____	11-2016	Super 381 MILW Electric Engine (std)	1300
____	11-2017	No. 408E Electric Locomotive (std)	900
____	11-2018	No. 408E Electric Locomotive, Mojave	900
____	11-2019	No. 408E Electric Locomotive, pink	900
____	11-2020	No. 9 Electric Locomotive, green	600
____	11-2021	No. 9 Electric Locomotive, orange	600
____	11-2022	No. 9 Electric Locomotive, gray, nickel trim	600
____	11-2023	No. 9 Electric Locomotive, dark green	600
____	11-2024	No. 8 Trolley (std)	530
____	11-2025	No. 9 Trolley (std)	650
____	11-2026	No. 8 Christmas Trolley (std)	570
____	11-2027	No. 381E Electric Locomotive, blue (std)	900
____	11-2028	No. 381E Electric Locomotive, brown (std)	900
____	11-2029	No. 381E Great Northern Electric Locomotive (std)	900
____	11-2031	No. 4689 President's Locomotive, red (std)	900
____	11-2033	Big Brute Electric Locomotive, brown (std)	1600
____	11-2034	Big Brute Electric Locomotive, orange (std)	1600
____	11-2038	Super 381 MILW Electric Locomotive (std)	1300
____	11-2039	Super 381 PRR Electric Locomotive (std)	1300
____	11-2040	Super 381 Electric Locomotive, two-tone brown (std)	1300
____	11-2041	Super 381 New Haven Electric Locomotive (std)	1300
____	11-5001	No. 384 Locomotive Passenger Set, black, brass trim	600
____	11-5002	No. 384 Locomotive Christmas Freight Set (std)	600
____	11-5003	No. 384 Locomotive LV Passenger Set (std)	600
____	11-5004	No. 384 Locomotive NYC Freight Set	600
____	11-5006	No. 384E Locomotive Girl's Passenger Set	600
____	11-5007	No. 386 Freight Set (std)	600
____	11-5008	No. 340E Coal Freight Set (std)	600
____	11-5009	No. 342E Baby State Passenger Set (std)	600
____	11-5010	No. 384E Blue Comet Passenger Set (std)	600
____	11-5011	No. 386 Christmas Freight Set (std)	600
____	11-5012	No. 342E Passenger Set (std)	600
____	11-5013	No. 318E Christmas Freight Set (std)	600
____	11-5014	No. 384E PRR Steam Passenger Set (std)	600
____	11-5501	No. 263E Steam Christmas Freight Set	600
____	11-5502	No. 263E Steam B&O Freight Set	600
____	11-5505	No. 249E Christmas Steam Passenger Set	500
____	11-5506	No. 299 Freight Set	450
____	11-5507	No. 269E Distant Control Freight Set	500
____	11-5508	Celebration Passenger Set	480
____	11-5509	No. 269E Christmas Distant Control Freight Set	500
____	11-5510	No. 269E Distant Control Freight Set	500
____	11-6001	No. 263E Locomotive, black, brass trim	430
____	11-6002	No. 263E Locomotive, blue	430

LIONEL CORPORATION TINPLATE

Retail

11-6003	No. 277W Remote Control Work Train	680____
11-6004	Blue Comet Distant Control Passenger Set	650____
11-6005	No. 275W Distant Control Freight Set	600____
11-6006	UP Streamliner Passenger Set, silver	800____
11-6007	UP Streamliner Passenger Set, yellow	800____
11-6008	No. 249E Steam Passenger Set, black, brass trim	600____
11-6009	No. 249E Steam Passenger Set, blue	600____
11-6010	No. 249E Steam Passenger Set, gray, nickel trim	600____
11-6012	No. 260E Locomotive, black, brass trim	430____
11-6013	No. 255E Locomotive, gray, nickel trim	430____
11-6014	No. 255E Lionel Lines Locomotive	430____
11-6015	No. 279E Distant Control Passenger Set	750____
11-6016	No. 295E Distant Control Passenger Set	750____
11-6017	Hiawatha Distance Control Streamliner Set	900____
11-6018	Hiawatha Passenger Train Set	900____
11-6019	Hiawatha Distance Control Freight Set	900____
11-6020	UP City of Denver Passenger Set, green	590____
11-6021	UP City of Denver Passenger Set, yellow/brown	700____
11-6022	No. 262E Locomotive, black, brass trim	300____
11-6023	No. 262E Locomotive, black, nickel trim	300____
11-6024	No. 260E Locomotive, black, brass trim	450____
11-6025	No. 214 Armored Motor Car Set	400____
11-6028	No. 256 Electric Locomotive, orange	450____
11-6029	No. 214 Armored Motor Car Set	400____
11-6030	No. 295E Distant Control Passenger Set	750____
11-6031	No. 279E NYC Distance Control Passenger Set	700____
11-6033	No. 265E Commodore Vanderbilt Locomotive	430____
11-6036	No. 263E Baby Blue Comet Locomotive	460____
11-6037	Girls Freight Set	830____
11-6038	No. 284E Distant Control Freight Set	700____
11-6039	No. 616 Flying Yankee Passenger Set, black/chrome	590____
11-6040	No. 616 Flying Yankee Passenger Set, red/chrome	590____
11-6041	No. 616 Flying Yankee Passenger Set, green/chrome	590____
11-6046	No. 279E Distant Control Passenger Set	700____
11-6047	No. 264 Red Comet Locomotive	460____
11-6048	No. 263E Baby Blue Comet Locomotive, brass trim	500____
11-6050	No. 256 New Haven Electric Locomotive	500____
11-6051	No. 256 Great Northern Electric Locomotive	500____
11-6052	No. 263E Locomotive, black, nickel trim	500____
11-6053	No. 263E Chessie Locomotive	500____
11-6054	No. 263E Southern Locomotive	500____
11-6055	Boys Freight Set	900____
11-6056	No. 261E LL Locomotive and Tender	350____
11-6057	No. 216E Locomotive and Tender	350____
11-6061	No. 256 MILW Electric Locomotive	500____
11-6062	No. 256 PRR Electric Locomotive	500____

____	**11-30004** No. 213 Cattle Car, cream/maroon (std)	130
____	**11-30005** No. 213 Cattle Car, terra-cotta/green (std)	130
____	**11-30006** No. 214 Boxcar, cream/orange (std)	130
____	**11-30007** No. 214 Boxcar, yellow/brown (std)	130
____	**11-30008** No. 214R Refrigerator Car, white/blue (std)	130
____	**11-30009** No. 215 Tank Car, silver, nickel trim (std)	130
____	**11-30010** No. 215 Tank Car, green, brass trim (std)	130
____	**11-30011** No. 215 Tank Car, white (std)	130
____	**11-30012** No. 216 Hopper Car, red (std)	130
____	**11-30013** No. 217 Caboose, orange/maroon (std)	140
____	**11-30014** No. 217 Caboose, red (std)	160
____	**11-30015** No. 513 Cattle Car, green/orange, brass trim (std)	100
____	**11-30016** No. 514 Boxcar, cream/orange (std)	100
____	**11-30017** No. 514R Refrigerator Car, ivory/peacock, brass trim (std)	100
____	**11-30018** No. 515 Tank Car, terra-cotta, brass trim (std)	100
____	**11-30019** No. 516 Hopper Car, red, brass trim (std)	120
____	**11-30020** No. 517 Caboose, pea green/red (std)	120
____	**11-30021** No. 212 Gondola, maroon (std)	110
____	**11-30022** No. 212 Gondola, pea green (std)	110
____	**11-30023** No. 513 Cattle Car, cream/maroon, nickel trim (std)	100
____	**11-30024** No. 514R Refrigerator Car, white/blue, nickel trim (std)	100
____	**11-30025** No. 515 Tank Car, silver, nickel trim (std)	100
____	**11-30026** No. 516 Hopper Car, red, nickel trim (std)	100
____	**11-30027** No. 517 Caboose, red, nickel trim (std)	120
____	**11-30028** No. 520 Floodlight Car, green, nickel trim (std)	130
____	**11-30029** No. 520 Floodlight Car, terra-cotta, brass trim (std)	130
____	**11-30030** No. 514R Christmas Refrigerator Car, (std)	100
____	**11-30031** No. 514 Christmas Boxcar (std)	100
____	**11-30032** No. 515 MTH/Lionel Tank Car (std)	100
____	**11-30033** No. 211 Flatcar, black, brass trim, with wood (std)	120
____	**11-30034** No. 211 Flatcar, black, nickel trim, with wood (std)	120
____	**11-30035** No. 218 Dump Car, Mojave, nickel trim (std)	140
____	**11-30036** No. 218 Dump Car, Mojave, brass trim (std)	140
____	**11-30037** No. 219 Crane Car, white (std)	200
____	**11-30038** No. 219 Crane Car, yellow, nickel trim (std)	200
____	**11-30039** No. 219 Crane Car, yellow (std)	380
____	**11-30042** No. 514 Boxcar, red/black (std)	100
____	**11-30043** No. 512 Gondola, peacock, brass trim (std)	80
____	**11-30044** No. 512 Gondola, green, nickel trim (std)	80
____	**11-30045** No. 514 Boxcar, yellow/brown (std)	100
____	**11-30046** No. 511 Flatcar, black, brass trim, with wood (std)	100
____	**11-30047** No. 511 Flatcar, black, nickel trim, with wood (std)	100
____	**11-30048** No. 216 Hopper Car, dark green (std)	130
____	**11-30050** No. 219 Crane Car, white, brass trim (std)	380
____	**11-30051** No. 514R NYC Refrigerator Car (std)	100
____	**11-30055** No. 212 Gondola, gray (std)	110

11-30056	No. 213 Cattle Car, Mojave/maroon (std)	130____
11-30057	No. 213 Cattle Car, terra-cotta/maroon (std)	130____
11-30058	No. 214 Boxcar, terra-cotta/black, brass trim (std)	130____
11-30059	No. 214R Refrigerator Car, white/peacock, brass trim (std)	130____
11-30060	No. 214R Refrigerator Car, ivory/peacock, brass trim (std)	130____
11-30061	No. 215 Tank Car, silver, brass trim (std)	130____
11-30062	No. 215 Tank Car, silver, nickel trim (std)	130____
11-30063	No. 217 Caboose, olive green (std)	140____
11-30064	No. 217 Lionel Lines Caboose (std)	140____
11-30065	No. 217 Caboose, pea green/red (std)	140____
11-30066	No. 217 Caboose, red/peacock (std)	160____
11-30067	No. 218 Dump Car, gray (std)	140____
11-30068	No. 218 Dump Car, pea green (std)	140____
11-30069	No. 218 Dump Car, peacock (std)	140____
11-30070	No. 219 Crane Car, peacock/dark green (std)	200____
11-30071	No. 219 Lionel Lines Crane Car (std)	380____
11-30072	No. 220 Floodlight Car, green, nickel trim (std)	140____
11-30073	No. 220 Floodlight Car, terra-cotta, brass trim (std)	140____
11-30074	No. 513 Cattle Car, orange/pea green (std)	100____
11-30075	No. 514 Christmas Boxcar (std)	100____
11-30076	No. 514R Refrigerator Car, ivory/blue (std)	100____
11-30077	No. 515 Tank Car, cream (std)	100____
11-30078	No. 515 Tank Car, ivory (std)	100____
11-30079	No. 515 Tank Car, orange (std)	100____
11-30080	No. 516 Christmas Hopper Car (std)	120____
11-30081	No. 516 Hopper Car, red (std)	120____
11-30082	No. 517 Caboose, red/black (std)	120____
11-30083	No. 520 Floodlight Car, green, nickel trim (std)	130____
11-30087	No. 516 Hopper Car, red, brass trim (std)	100____
11-30088	AF 4018 Automobile Car, white/blue	150____
11-30089	AF 4020 Stock Car, blue	150____
11-30090	AF 4006 Hopper Car, red	150____
11-30091	AF 4017 Sand Car, green	150____
11-30092	AF 4010 Tank Car, cream/blue	150____
11-30093	AF 4022 Machine Car, orange	110____
11-30094	AF 4021 Caboose, red	160____
11-30095	AF 4018 Automobile Car, orange/maroon	130____
11-30096	AF 4022 Machine Car, blue	110____
11-30097	AF 4022 Machine Car, orange/green	110____
11-30098	AF 4010 Tank Car, blue	130____
11-30099	AF 4017 Sand Car, maroon	130____
11-30100	AF 4006 Hopper Car, green	130____
11-30101	AF 4020 Stock Car, cream/maroon	130____
11-30102	AF 4021 Caboose, red/maroon	140____
11-30103	AF 4021 Caboose, cream/red	140____
11-30104	No. 215 Tank Car (std)	130____

____ **11-30105**	No. 214R Refrigerator Car (std)	130
____ **11-30107**	No. 214R Altoona 36 Lager Refrigerator Car (std)	130
____ **11-30108**	No. 214R Budweiser Refrigerator Car (std)	140
____ **11-30109**	No. 214R Burp-oh Beer Refrigerator Car (std)	130
____ **11-30110**	No. 214R Hood's Dairy Refrigerator Car (std)	130
____ **11-30111**	No. 214R Old Reading Refrigerator Car (std)	130
____ **11-30112**	No. 214R Palisades Park Refrigerator Car (std)	130
____ **11-30113**	No. 214 Circus Boxcar (std)	130
____ **11-30114**	No. 214 M&M's Christmas Boxcar (std)	140
____ **11-30115**	No. 215 Budweiser Tank Car (std)	140
____ **11-30116**	No. 215 Freedomland Tank Car (std)	130
____ **11-30117**	No. 215 Gulf Tank Car (std)	130
____ **11-30118**	No. 215 Tropicana Tank Car (std)	130
____ **11-30119**	No. 513 UP Cattle Car (std)	100
____ **11-30120**	No. 513 WM Cattle Car (std)	100
____ **11-30121**	No. 514 B&O Boxcar (std)	100
____ **11-30122**	No. 514 State of Maine Boxcar (std)	120
____ **11-30123**	No. 514R PFE Refrigerator Car (std)	100
____ **11-30124**	No. 514R Tropicana Refrigerator Car (std)	120
____ **11-30125**	No. 515 Anheuser Busch Tank Car (std)	110
____ **11-30126**	No. 515 Hooker Chemicals Tank Car (std)	100
____ **11-30127**	No. 516 Blue Coal Hopper Car (std)	100
____ **11-30128**	No. 516 Waddell Coal Hopper Car (std)	120
____ **11-30129**	No. 517 Pennsylvania Caboose (std)	120
____ **11-30130**	No. 517 Santa Fe Caboose (std)	140
____ **11-30131**	No. 215 Lionel Lines Tank Car (std)	130
____ **11-30134**	No. 515 Christmas Tank Car (std)	100
____ **11-30136**	No. 214 Christmas Boxcar (std)	150
____ **11-30137**	No. 214 UP Boxcar (std)	150
____ **11-30138**	No. 214R Horlacher's Brewing Refrigerator Car (std)	150
____ **11-30139**	No. 214R Coors Refrigerator Car (std)	140
____ **11-30140**	No. 215 Keystone Gasoline Tank Car (std)	150
____ **11-30141**	No. 215 Texaco Tank Car (std)	150
____ **11-30142**	No. 216 Peabody Hopper Car (std)	130
____ **11-30143**	No. 216 Pennsylvania Power & Light Hopper Car (std)	130
____ **11-30144**	No. 213 Cattle Car (std)	130
____ **11-30146**	No. 217 Jersey Central Caboose (std)	140
____ **11-30147**	No. 214 Jersey Central Boxcar (std)	130
____ **11-30148**	No. 214 U.S. Army Boxcar (std)	130
____ **11-30149**	No. 215 MTH/Lionel Tank Car	130
____ **11-30150**	No. 212 Lionel Lines Gondola (std)	130
____ **11-30151**	No. 212 Circus Gondola (std)	130
____ **11-30152**	No. 212 NYC Gondola (std)	130
____ **11-30153**	No. 214 MKT Boxcar (std)	150
____ **11-30154**	No. 214 NYC Boxcar (std)	150
____ **11-30155**	No. 215 C&O Tank Car (std)	150
____ **11-30156**	No. 215 Shell Tank Car (std)	150

11-30157	No. 216 Hopper Car, red, brass trim (std)	150____
11-30158	No. 216 LV Hopper Car (std)	150____
11-30159	No. 217 Pennsylvania Caboose (std)	160____
11-30160	No. 219 B&O Crane Car (std)	220____
11-30161	No. 219 Crane Car, ivory/red (std)	400____
11-30162	No. 219 Lionel Lines Crane Car (std)	220____
11-30163	No. 219 Crane Car, red/silver (std)	400____
11-30164	No. 514R Christmas Refrigerator Car (std)	120____
11-30168	No. 515 PRR Tank Car (std)	120____
11-30169	No. 515 Texaco Tank Car (std)	120____
11-30170	No. 515 Esso Tank Car (std)	120____
11-30180	No. 219 Crane Car, black/cream (std)	220____
11-30182	No. 217 NYC Illuminated Caboose (std)	160____
11-30185	No. 212 Gondola, pea green (std)	150____
11-30193	No. 514R Altoona Brewing Refrigerator Car (std)	120____
11-30194	No. 514R PFE Refrigerator Car (std)	120____
11-30195	No. 514R REA Refrigerator Car (std)	120____
11-30196	No. 514R Robin Hood Beer Refrigerator Car (std)	120____
11-30197	No. 514 UP Boxcar (std)	120____
11-30198	No. 514 Santa Fe Boxcar (std)	120____
11-30199	No. 514 PRR Boxcar (std)	120____
11-30200	No. 514 B&O Boxcar (std)	120____
11-30201	No. 215-3 Shell 3-D Tank Car (std)	150____
11-30202	No. 215-3 Mazda Lamps 3-D Tank Car (std)	150____
11-30203	No. 215-3 Celanese Chemicals 3-D Tank Car (std)	150____
11-30204	No. 215-3 Clark Oil 3-D Tank Car (std)	150____
11-30205	No. 215-2 Sterling Fuels 2-D Tank Car (std)	150____
11-30206	No. 215-2 Philadelphia Quartz 2-D Tank Car (std)	150____
11-30207	No. 215-2 Cook's Paints 2-D Tank Car (std)	150____
11-30208	No. 215-2 Hercules 2-D Tank Car (std)	150____
11-30209	No. 216-1 PRR Covered Hopper (std)	150____
11-30210	No. 216-1 P&LE Covered Hopper (std)	150____
11-30211	No. 216-1 Jack Frost Covered Hopper (std)	150____
11-30212	No. 216-1 GE Lamps Covered Hopper (std)	150____
11-30213	No. 212-1 PRR Covered Gondola Car (std)	150____
11-30214	No. 212-1 Covered Gondola Car (std)	150____
11-30215	No. 212-1 NYC Covered Gondola Car (std)	150____
11-30216	No. 212-1 GN Covered Gondola Car (std)	150____
11-30217	No. 211 Flatcar with wheel load (std)	150____
11-30218	No. 211 Altoona Shops Flatcar with wheel load (std)	150____
11-30219	No. 211 Baldwin Flatcar with wheel load (std)	150____
11-30220	No. 211 Lima Flatcar with wheel load (std)	150____
11-30221	No. 217-1 Chessie Bay Window Caboose (std)	160____
11-30222	No. 217-1 UP Bay Window Caboose (std)	160____
11-30223	No. 217-1 NYC Bay Window Caboose (std)	160____
11-30224	No. 217-1 Long Island Bay Window Caboose (std)	160____
11-30225	PRR Automobile Car (std)	150____

		Retail
____	**11-30227** Shell Tank Car (std)	150
____	**11-30230** Waddell Coal Hopper (std)	150
____	**11-30232** PRR Caboose (std)	160
____	**11-40001** Presidential Passenger Set, blue (std)	1200
____	**11-40002** No. 339 Pullman Car, green (std)	150
____	**11-40003** No. 332 Mail/Baggage Car, green (std)	150
____	**11-40004** No. 332 LV Ithaca Baggage Car	150
____	**11-40005** No. 339 LV Easton Passenger Coach	150
____	**11-40007** 300 Series 3-Car Passenger Set, blue/silver (std)	400
____	**11-40009** 3-Car State Passenger Set, green (std)	1200
____	**11-40010** Pennsylvania State Baggage Car, green (std)	400
____	**11-40011** Illinois State Coach, green (std)	400
____	**11-40012** Solarium State Car, green (std)	400
____	**11-40013** MILW 3-Car State Passenger Set (std)	1200
____	**11-40014** MILW State Baggage Car (std)	400
____	**11-40015** MILW State Passenger Coach (std)	400
____	**11-40016** MILW Solarium State Car (std)	400
____	**11-40017** 3-Car Showroom Passenger Set, green (std)	1500
____	**11-40018** Showroom Passenger Coach, green (std)	500
____	**11-40019** 3-Car Showroom Passenger Set, zinc chromate (std)	1500
____	**11-40020** Showroom Passenger Coach, zinc chromate (std)	500
____	**11-40021** 3-Car Blue Comet Passenger Set (std)	1100
____	**11-40022** No. 432 Olbers Blue Comet Baggage Car (std)	380
____	**11-40023** No. 419 Tuttle Blue Comet Passenger Coach (std)	380
____	**11-40024** No. 4343 Diner Car	180
____	**11-40025** 339 Series Passenger Car, pink	130
____	**11-40026** 332 Series Baggage Car, pink	130
____	**11-40027** 309 Series 3-Car State Passenger Set, brown (std)	1200
____	**11-40028** Pennsylvania State Baggage Car, brown (std)	400
____	**11-40029** Illinois State Passenger Coach, brown (std)	400
____	**11-40030** Solarium State Car, brown (std)	400
____	**11-40031** State 3-Car Passenger Set, blue (std)	1200
____	**11-40032** Pennsylvania State Baggage Car, blue (std)	400
____	**11-40033** Illinois State Passenger Coach, blue (std)	400
____	**11-40034** Solarium State Car, blue (std)	400
____	**11-40035** 309 Series 3-Car Passenger Set, blue (std)	400
____	**11-40036** 309 Series 3-Car Passenger Set, green (std)	400
____	**11-40037** 309 Series 3-Car Passenger Set, red (std)	400
____	**11-40038** No. 309 Passenger Coach (std)	140
____	**11-40039** No. 310 Baggage Car (std)	140
____	**11-40040** 3-Car Blue Comet Passenger Set, nickel trim (std)	1100
____	**11-40041** No. 432 Blue Comet Baggage Car, nickel trim (std)	380
____	**11-40042** No. 423 Blue Comet Passenger Coach, nickel trim (std)	380
____	**11-40043** 3-Car Stephen Girard Set, brass trim	600
____	**11-40044** No. 4427 Stephen Girard Baggage Car, brass trim	200
____	**11-40045** No. 427 Stephen Girard Passenger Coach, brass trim	200

LIONEL CORPORATION TINPLATE

Retail

11-40046	3-Car Stephen Girard Set, nickel trim	600____
11-40047	No. 4427 Stephen Girard Baggage Car, nickel trim	200____
11-40048	No. 427 Stephen Girard Passenger Coach, nickel trim	200____
11-40049	No. 418 3-Car Passenger Set, green, brass trim (std)	600____
11-40050	No. 418 Diner, green, brass trim (std)	200____
11-40051	No. 418 3-Car Passenger Set, orange, brass trim (std)	600____
11-40052	No. 418 Diner, orange brass trim (std)	200____
11-40053	No. 418 3-Car Passenger Set, Mojave, brass trim (std)	600____
11-40054	No. 418 Diner, Mojave, brass trim (std)	200____
11-40055	No. 418 3-Car Passenger Set, pink, brass trim (std)	600____
11-40056	No. 418 Diner, pink, brass trim (std)	200____
11-40057	Lionel 3-Car Pullman Passenger Set (std)	700____
11-40058	Pennsylvania 3-Car Pullman Passenger Set (std)	700____
11-40059	No. 332 Baggage Car (std)	140____
11-40060	No. 339 Passenger Coach (std)	140____
11-40061	Great Northern State 3-Car Passenger Set (std)	1200____
11-40062	Great Northern State Baggage Car (std)	430____
11-40063	Great Northern State Passenger Coach (std)	430____
11-40064	Great Northern State Solarium Car (std)	430____
11-40065	Presidential 3-Car Passenger Set (std)	1200____
11-40066	Presidential Baggage Car (std)	430____
11-40067	Presidential Passenger Coach (std)	430____
11-40068	Red Comet 3-Car Passenger Set (std)	1140____
11-40069	Red Comet Baggage Car (std)	400____
11-40070	Red Comet Passenger Coach (std)	400____
11-40072	President's Passenger Set, red (std)	1300____
11-40073	No. 310 Baggage Car (std)	140____
11-40074	No. 309 Passenger Coach (std)	140____
11-40076	Green Comet 3-Car Passenger Set (std)	1140____
11-40077	NYC 3-Car Passenger Set, brown (std)	700____
11-40078	General 3-Car Pullman Passenger Set (std)	700____
11-40079	Green Comet Baggage Car (std)	400____
11-40080	Green Comet Passenger Coach (std)	400____
11-40081	Showroom 3-Car Passenger Set, brown (std)	1600____
11-40082	Showroom Passenger Coach, brown (std)	540____
11-40083	Showroom 3-Car Passenger Set, orange (std)	1600____
11-40084	Showroom Passenger Coach, orange (std)	540____
11-40095	3-car B&O Pullman Passenger Set (std)	700____
11-40096	3-car Long Island Pullman Passenger Set (std)	700____
11-40097	3-car Strasburg Pullman Passenger Set (std)	700____
11-40098	3-car PRR Pullman Passenger Set (std)	700____
11-40099	3-car MILW State Passenger Set (std)	1200____
11-40100	MILW State Solarium Car (std)	400____
11-40101	MILW State Passenger Coach (std)	400____
11-40102	MILW State Baggage Car (std)	400____
11-40103	3-car PRR State Passenger Set (std)	1200____

		Retail
____ **11-40104**	PRR State Solarium Car (std)	400
____ **11-40105**	PRR State Passenger Coach (std)	400
____ **11-40106**	PRR State Baggage Car (std)	400
____ **11-40107**	3-car State Passenger Set, two-tone brown (std)	1200
____ **11-40108**	State Solarium Car, two-tone brown (std)	400
____ **11-40109**	State Passenger Coach, two-tone brown (std)	400
____ **11-40110**	State Baggage Car, two-tone brown (std)	400
____ **11-40111**	3-car Great Northern Presidential Set (std)	1200
____ **11-40112**	Great Northern Presidential Diner (std)	400
____ **11-40113**	3-car Lehigh Valley Presidential Set (std)	1200
____ **11-40114**	Lehigh Valley Presidential Diner (std)	400
____ **11-40115**	3-car New Haven State Passenger Set (std)	1200
____ **11-40116**	New Haven State Solarium Car (std)	400
____ **11-40117**	New Haven State Passenger Coach (std)	400
____ **11-40118**	New Haven State Baggage Car (std)	400
____ **11-60033**	No. 607 Christmas Coach Passenger	90
____ **11-70002**	No. 2814 Boxcar, cream/orange	80
____ **11-70003**	No. 2814R Refrigerator Car, white/brown	80
____ **11-70004**	No. 2814R Christmas Refrigerator Car	80
____ **11-70005**	No. 2814R Refrigerator Car, Ivory/peacock	80
____ **11-70006**	No. 2815 Tank Car, silver	90
____ **11-70007**	No. 2815 Tank Car, orange, nickel trim	80
____ **11-70008**	No. 2817 Caboose, red/green	90
____ **11-70009**	No. 2815 Christmas Tank Car	80
____ **11-70010**	No. 2813 Cattle Car, cream/maroon	80
____ **11-70011**	No. 2812 Gondola, apple green	80
____ **11-70012**	No. 2811 Flatcar, silver	70
____ **11-70013**	No. 2816 Hopper Car, red	90
____ **11-70014**	No. 2816 Hopper Car, olive green	80
____ **11-70015**	No. 2820 Floodlight Car, terra-cotta	90
____ **11-70016**	No. 2815 Sunoco Tank Car	80
____ **11-70017**	No. 2810 Crane Car, terra-cotta/maroon	180
____ **11-70018**	No. 2811 Flatcar, maroon	70
____ **11-70019**	No. 2814R MTH/Lionel Refrigerator Car	90
____ **11-70024**	No. 2814 Christmas Boxcar	80
____ **11-70025**	No. 2814 Boxcar, cream/orange	80
____ **11-70026**	No. 2814 Boxcar, orange/brown	80
____ **11-70027**	No. 2814 Boxcar, white brown	80
____ **11-70028**	No. 2816 Christmas Hopper Car	80
____ **11-70029**	No. 2817 Caboose, red/brown	90
____ **11-70030**	No. 2812 Gondola, dark orange	70
____ **11-70031**	No. 813 Cattle Car, brown	80
____ **11-70032**	No. 2816 Hopper Car, black	80
____ **11-70033**	No. 2820 Floodlight Car, light green	90
____ **11-70034**	No. 2814R Refrigerator Car, white/brown	80
____ **11-70035**	No. 2651 Flatcar, green	60
____ **11-70036**	No. 2652 Gondola, red	60

LIONEL CORPORATION TINPLATE

		Retail
11-70037	No. 2653 Hopper Car, black	60____
11-70038	No. 2654 Shell Tank Car, yellow	60____
11-70039	No. 2655 Boxcar, yellow/brown	60____
11-70040	No. 2656 Cattle Car, red/brown	60____
11-70041	No. 2657 Caboose, red/maroon	60____
11-70042	No. 659 Dump Car, green	60____
11-70043	No. 659 Dump Car, orange	60____
11-70045	No. 2814 Boxcar, yellow/brown	90____
11-70046	No. 2817 Caboose, red	100____
11-70047	No. 2814 Christmas Boxcar	80____
11-70048	No. 2815 Christmas Tank Car	90____
11-70049	No. 2814R Refrigerator Car, silver frame	90____
11-70050	No. 2814R Refrigerator Car, black frame	80____
11-70051	No. 2817 Caboose, red/maroon	90____
11-70052	No. 2654 Shell Tank Car, gray	60____
11-70053	No. 2654 Shell Tank Car, black	60____
11-70054	No. 2653 Hopper Car, green	60____
11-70055	No. 2653 Hopper Car, red	60____
11-70056	No. 2655 Boxcar, yellow/maroon	60____
11-70057	No. 2655 Boxcar, yellow/brown	60____
11-70058	No. 2656 Cattle Car, gray/red	60____
11-70059	No. 2656 Cattle Car, burnt orange	60____
11-70060	No. 659 Dump Car, blue	60____
11-70061	No. 900 Ammunition Car, gray	60____
11-70064	No. 2814R Hoods Dairy Refrigerator Car	80____
11-70065	No. 2814R Isaly's Refrigerator Car	80____
11-70066	No. 2814R Sheffield Farms Refrigerator Car	90____
11-70067	No. 2814R Palisades Park Refrigerator Car	80____
11-70068	No. 2654 UP Tank Car, yellow	60____
11-70069	No. 2654 M&M's Tank Car	70____
11-70070	No. 2654 Baker's Chocolate Tank Car	60____
11-70071	No. 2654 Budweiser Tank Car	70____
11-70072	No. 2655 Delaware & Hudson Boxcar	60____
11-70073	No. 2655 Railbox Boxcar	60____
11-70074	M&M's Christmas Boxcar	70____
11-70076	No. 2654 LL Tank Car, orange/blue	70____
11-70078	No. 900 Ammunition Car, green	60____
11-70079	No. 2820 LL Floodlight Car, black/orange	120____
11-70080	No. 2820 U.S. Army Air Corps Floodlight Car	120____
11-70081	No. 2810 Crane Car, yellow/red	180____
11-70082	No. 2810 Crane Car, white/red	180____
11-70083	No. 2660 Crane Car, cream/red	100____
11-70084	No. 2660 Crane Car, terra-cotta/maroon	100____
11-70085	No. 2660 Crane Car, yellow/red	100____
11-70086	No. 2660 Crane Car, peacock/dark green	100____
11-70087	No. 2813 LL Cattle Car, cream/tuscan	90____
11-70088	No. 2813 LL Cattle Car, terra cotta/pea green	90____

____ **11-70089**	No. 2810 B&O Crane Car	180
____ **11-70091**	No. 2815 LL Tank Car, cream, orange/blue	80
____ **11-70092**	No. 2810 Crane Car, blue	180
____ **11-70095**	No. 2820 LL Floodlight Car, black/peacock	120
____ **11-70096**	No. 2814 Southern Boxcar	90
____ **11-70097**	No. 2814 Chessie Boxcar	90
____ **11-70098**	No. 2814 Blue Comet Boxcar, nickel trim	90
____ **11-70099**	No. 2814 Blue Comet Boxcar, brass trim	90
____ **11-70102**	No. 2654 Mobilgas Tank Car	70
____ **11-70103**	No. 2654 Esso Tank Car	70
____ **11-70104**	No. 2653 Blue Coal Hopper	70
____ **11-70105**	No. 2653 Peabody Hopper	70
____ **11-70106**	No. 2655 Altoona Brewing Boxcar	70
____ **11-70107**	No. 2655 Hood's Grade A Milk Boxcar	70
____ **11-70108**	No. 2655 LL Boxcar	70
____ **11-70109**	No. 2657 LL Caboose, green/red	70
____ **11-70110**	No. 2657 LL Caboose, orange/red	70
____ **11-70113**	No. 2814 PRR Boxcar	90
____ **11-70114**	No. 2814 ATSF Grand Canyon Boxcar	90
____ **11-70115**	No. 2814 Long Island Boxcar	90
____ **11-70116**	No. 2814 Alaska Boxcar	90
____ **11-70117**	No. 2814R M. K. Goetz Brewing Refrigerator Car	90
____ **11-70118**	No. 2814R Gerber Refrigerator Car	90
____ **11-70119**	No. 2814R Roberts & Oake Meats Refrigerator Car	90
____ **11-70120**	No. 2814R Sullivan's Packing Refrigerator Car	90
____ **11-70121**	No. 2816 Western Maryland Coal Car	90
____ **11-70122**	No. 2816 P&LE Coal Car	90
____ **11-70123**	No. 2816 Waddell Mining Coal Car	90
____ **11-70124**	No. 2816 Blue Coal Car	90
____ **11-70125**	No. 2815 Clark Oil Tank Car	90
____ **11-70126**	No. 2815 Celanese Chemicals Tank Car	90
____ **11-70127**	No. 2815 Shell Tank Car	90
____ **11-70128**	No. 2815 Cook's Paints Tank Car	90
____ **11-70129**	No. 2817 C&O Caboose	100
____ **11-70130**	No. 2817 Long Island Caboose	100
____ **11-70131**	No. 2817 Southern Caboose	100
____ **11-70132**	No. 2817 Jersey Central Caboose	100
____ **11-70133**	No. 2814R Gerber Refrigerator Car	90
____ **11-70144**	No. 2815 Shell Tank Car	90
____ **11-70154**	No. 2814 ATSF Grand Canyon Boxcar	90
____ **11-80001**	2600 Series 4-Car Blue Comet Passenger Set	430
____ **11-80002**	UP Articulated Baggage Car, silver	150
____ **11-80003**	UP Articulated Baggage Car, yellow	150
____ **11-80004**	UP Articulated Coach, silver	150
____ **11-80005**	UP Articulated Coach, yellow	150
____ **11-80006**	No. 2613 Series Pullman Coach, blue	110
____ **11-80007**	2600 Series 3-Car Passenger Set, red	300

LIONEL CORPORATION TINPLATE

		Retail
11-80008	2600 Series 3-Car Passenger Set, green	300____
11-80009	Milwaukee Road Articulated Baggage Car	150____
11-80010	Milwaukee Road Articulated Coach	150____
11-80011	Articulated Streamliner Baggage Car	150____
11-80012	Articulated Streamliner Coach	150____
11-80013	No. 2613 Series Pullman Coach, red	100____
11-80014	No. 2613 Series Pullman Coach, green	100____
11-80015	No. 605 Christmas Baggage Car	90____
11-80016	710 Series 3-Car Passenger Set, blue	350____
11-80017	No. 710 Series Baggage Car, blue	120____
11-80018	No. 710 Series Passenger Coach, blue	120____
11-80019	710 Series 3-Car Passenger Set, orange	350____
11-80020	No. 710 Series Baggage Car, orange	120____
11-80021	No. 710 Series Passenger Coach, orange	120____
11-80022	710 Series 3-Car Passenger Set, red	350____
11-80023	No. 710 Series Baggage Car, red	120____
11-80024	No. 710 Series Passenger Coach, red	120____
11-80025	No. 1695 3-Car Passenger Set, blue/silver	350____
11-80026	No. 1685 Passenger Car, blue/silver	120____
11-80027	1695 Series 3-Car Passenger Set, red/maroon	380____
11-80028	No. 1695 Passenger Coach, red/maroon	130____
11-80029	City of Denver Coach, yellow/green	110____
11-80030	City of Denver Coach, green	110____
11-80031	No. 605 Baggage Car	90____
11-80032	No. 607 Passenger Coach	90____
11-80034	No. 2613 NYC Pullman Car, LCCA 2012 Convention	100____
11-80036	No. 605 Red Comet Baggage Car	90____
11-80039	600 Series 3-Car Red Comet Passenger Set	270____
11-80040	2600 Series 4-Car Blue Comet Passenger Set, brass trim	430____
11-80041	No. 2613 Pullman Coach, brass trim	110____
11-80042	Flying Yankee Chrome Coach	110____
11-80047	710 Series 3-Car NH Passenger Set	400____
11-80048	710 Series 3-Car GN Passenger Set	400____
11-80049	2600 Series 4-Car Chessie Passenger Set	430____
11-80050	2600 Series 4-Car Southern Passenger Set	430____
11-80051	No. 2613 Chessie Pullman Coach	110____
11-80052	No. 2613 Southern Pullman Coach	110____
11-80053	No. 710 NH Baggage Car	140____
11-80054	No. 710 NH Passenger Coach	140____
11-80055	No. 710 GN Baggage Car	140____
11-80056	No. 710 GN Passenger Coach	140____
11-80059	710 Series 3-car MILW Passenger Set	400____
11-80060	No. 713 MILW Baggage Car	140____
11-80061	No. 710 MILW Passenger Coach	140____
11-80062	710 Series 3-car PRR Passenger Set	400____
11-80063	No. 713 PRR Baggage Car	140____

____	**11-80064**	No. 710 PRR Passenger Coach	140
____	**11-90001**	No. 300 Hellgate Bridge, green/cream	500
____	**11-90002**	No. 300 Hellgate Bridge, silver/white	500
____	**11-90003**	No. 092 Signal Tower, cream/red	70
____	**11-90006**	No. 437 Switch Tower	280
____	**11-90007**	No. 155 Freight Shed	330
____	**11-90008**	No. 116 Passenger Station	400
____	**11-90009**	No. 438 Signal Tower	150
____	**11-90010**	No. 192 Villa Set	200
____	**11-90011**	No. 191 Villa	70
____	**11-90012**	No. 54 Street Lamp Set, green	45
____	**11-90013**	No. 54 Street Lamp Set, red	45
____	**11-90014**	No. 56 Gas Lamp Set, green	35
____	**11-90015**	No. 56 Gas Lamp Set, maroon	35
____	**11-90016**	No. 57 Corner Lamp Set, black	40
____	**11-90017**	No. 57 Corner Lamp Set, red	35
____	**11-90018**	No. 58 Lamp Set, single arc, cream	35
____	**11-90019**	No. 58 Lamp Set, single arc, dark green	35
____	**11-90020**	No. 59 Gooseneck Lamp Set, black	40
____	**11-90021**	No. 59 Gooseneck Lamp Set, maroon	40
____	**11-90022**	No. 1184 Bungalow (std)	200
____	**11-90023**	No. 1184 Bungalow (std)	200
____	**11-90024**	No. 1189 Villa (std)	300
____	**11-90025**	No. 1191 Villa (std)	300
____	**11-90026**	No.165 Magnetic Crane	300
____	**11-90027**	No. 441 Weighing Station (std)	380
____	**11-90028**	No. 69 Operating Warning Bell	50
____	**11-90029**	No. 78 Automatic Control Signal (std)	70
____	**11-90030**	No. 79 Flashing Railroad Signal	70
____	**11-90031**	No. 80 Operating Semaphore	70
____	**11-90032**	No. 63 Lamp Post Set, aluminum	50
____	**11-90033**	No. 87 Railroad Crossing Signal	50
____	**11-90034**	No. 92 Floodlight Tower Set	160
____	**11-90035**	No. 94 High Tension Tower Set	150
____	**11-90036**	No. Automatic Block Signal (std)	70
____	**11-90037**	No. 163 Freight Accessory Set, green cart	100
____	**11-90038**	No. 163 Freight Accessory Set, orange cart	100
____	**11-90039**	No. 208 Tools and Chest, dark gray	80
____	**11-90040**	No. 208 Tools and Chest, silver	80
____	**11-90041**	No. 550 Miniature Figures	100
____	**11-90042**	No. 64 Lamp Post Set, light green	30
____	**11-90043**	No. 85 Race Car Set	700
____	**11-90044**	Straight Race Car Track Section	20
____	**11-90045**	Inside Curve Race Car Track Section	20
____	**11-90046**	Outside Curve Race Car Track Section	20
____	**11-90047**	No. 55 Airplane & No. 49 Airport Set with mat	800
____	**11-90048**	No. 49 Airport Mat	60

LIONEL CORPORATION TINPLATE

Retail

11-90049	No. 90 Flagpole	50____
11-90050	No. 205 Merchandise Containers, 3 pieces (std)	130____
11-90052	No. 442 Diner	160____
11-90053	No. 43 Runabout Boat, red/white	450____
11-90054	No. 44 Speed Boat	450____
11-90055	No. 71 Telegraph Post Set, gray/red	80____
11-90056	Teardrop Lamp Set, pea green	20____
11-90057	No. 46 Crossing Gate	40____
11-90058	Small Oil Drum Set	20____
11-90060	No. 115 Passenger Station, beige/pea green	300____
11-90061	No. 115 Passenger Station, cream, orange/blue	300____
11-90062	No. 134 Lionel City Station with stop	330____
11-90063	No. 444 Roundhouse Section	500____
11-90064	No. 200 Turntable, red/black	200____
11-90065	No. 89 Flagpole, blue base (std)	50____
11-90066	No. 89 Flagpole, white base (std)	50____
11-90067	No. 89 American Flag Pole, white base (std)	50____
11-90068	Operating Industrial Crane	350____
11-90069	Operating Industrial Crane, TCA 2010 Convention	350____
11-90070	No. 552 Diner, orange/blue	200____
11-90071	No. 552 Diner, white/blue	200____
11-90072	No. 911 Country Estate, cream/red	140____
11-90073	No. 911 Country Estate, red/green	140____
11-90074	No. 912 Suburban Home, ivory/peacock	140____
11-90075	No. 912 Suburban Home, mustard/green	140____
11-90076	No. 913 Landscaped Bungalow, white/maroon	110____
11-90077	No. 913 Landscaped Bungalow, light green/peacock	110____
11-90078	AF No. 2050 Old Glory Flag Pole	100____
11-90079	No. 43 Runabout Boat, orange/blue	400____
11-90084	No. 57 Lamp Post Set, Lionel & American Flyer Aves.	40____
11-90085	No. 57 Lamp Post Set, orange, 21st St. & Fifth Ave.	40____
11-90086	AF No. 2013 Corner Lamp Set, yellow	40____
11-90089	No. 436 Power Station, cream	150____
11-90090	No. 436 Power Station, terra-cotta	150____
11-90094	No. 438 Signal Tower	160____
11-90095	No. 116 Passenger Station	400____
11-90096	No. 1184 Bungalow, gray/green	200____
11-90097	No. 1184 Bungalow, white/maroon	200____
11-90098	No. 1189 Villa (std)	300____
11-90099	No. 1191 Villa (std)	300____
11-90100	No. 442 Diner	160____
11-90101	No. 54 Lamp Post Set, pea green	45____
11-90102	No. 54 Lamp Post Set, state brown	45____
11-90103	No. 58 Lamp Post Set, peacock	35____
11-90104	No. 58 Lamp Post Set, orange	35____
11-90105	No. 59 Lamp Post Set, dark green	40____
11-90106	No. 59 Lamp Post Set, light green	40____

LIONEL CORPORATION TINPLATE

Retail

____ **11-90107**	No. 92 Floodlight Tower Set	170
____ **11-90108**	No. 79 Flashing Signal	70
____ **11-90109**	No. 69 Warning Signal	50
____ **11-90110**	No. 94 High Tension Tower Set	170
____ **11-90111**	No. 57 Corner Lamp Set, orange, Lionel	40
____ **11-90112**	No. 57 Corner Lamp Set, blue, Lionel	40
____ **11-90113**	No. 57 Corner Lamp Set, blue/yellow	40
____ **11-90114**	No. 152 Operating Crossing Gate	40
____ **11-90115**	No. 153 Operating Block Signal	40
____ **11-90116**	No. 154 Highway Flashing Signal	40
____ **11-90117**	No. 437 Switch Signal Tower, cream/orange	300
____ **11-90118**	No. 437 Switch Signal Tower, terra-cotta/green	300
____ **11-90119**	AF No. 4230 Roadside Flashing Signal	100
____ **11-90120**	No. 200 Turntable, gray/green	200
____ **11-90121**	No. 200 Turntable, orange/blue	200
____ **11-90122**	No. 437 Switch Tower	280
____ **11-90123**	No. 98 Coal Bunker	180
____ **11-99030**	No. 25 Illuminated Track Bumpers (std)	60

CLUB CARS AND SPECIAL PRODUCTION

Exc Mint

Artrain

		Exc	Mint	
9486	GTW "I Love Michigan" Boxcar, 87	155	305	___
17885	1-D Tank Car, 90	35	65	___
17891	GTW 20th Anniversary Boxcar, 91	40	75	___
19425	CSX Flatcar with "Art in Celebration" trailer, 96	40	80	___
52013	Norfolk Southern Flatcar with trailer, 92	115	230	___
52024	Conrail Auto Carrier, 93	45	90	___
52049	BN Gondola with coil covers, 94	30	55	___
52097	Chessie System Reefer, 95	20	35	___
52140	Union Pacific Bunk Car, 97	20	35	___
52165	SP Caboose "6256," 98	30	60	___
52197	Santa Fe GP38 Diesel, 99	125	245	___
52227	"Artistry in Space" Boxcar, 00	40	75	___
52255	30th Anniversary Flatcar with billboard, 01	50	100	___
52283	Paint Vat Car, 02	30	60	___
52331	Flatcar with "America's Railways" trailer, 03	75	150	___
52349	Hometown Art Museum Hopper, purple, 04	20	35	___
52350	"Native Views" 3-bay Hopper, 04	35	65	___
52411	"35 Years" 1-D Tank Car, 06	20	35	___

Carnegie Science Center

		Exc	Mint	
25085	Miniature Railroad & Village Boxcar, 09	25	50	___
26750	Great Miniature Railroad & Village Boxcar, 99	40	80	___
36202	Great Miniature Railroad 80th Anniversary Boxcar, 00	55	110	___
36234	Great Miniature Railroad & Village Boxcar, 01	25	50	___
52277	Carnegie Science Center 10th Anniversary Boxcar, 02	30	60	___
52332	Miniature Railroad & Village Boxcar, 03	30	60	___
52362	Miniature Railroad & Village 50th Anniversary Boxcar, 04	25	50	___
52399	MRR&V Express Boxcar, 05	25	50	___
52432	Miniature Railroad & Village Boxcar, 06	25	50	___
52510	Miniature Railroad & Village Caboose, 08	25	50	___

Chicagoland Railroad Club

		Exc	Mint	
52081	C&NW Boxcar "6464-555," 96	35	70	___
52101	BN Maxi-Stack Flatcar "64287" with containers, 97	40	80	___
52102	SF Extended Vision Caboose, red roof, 96	40	75	___
52103	SF Extended Vision Caboose, black roof, 96	40	75	___

CLUB CARS AND SPECIAL PRODUCTION

			Exc	Mint
____	52120	Shedd Aquarium Car "3435-557," *98*	50	100
____	52148	REA/Santa Fe Operating Boxcar, *99*	35	70
____	52170	SP Operating Boxcar "52170-561," *99*	35	65
____	52171	UP Operating Boxcar "52171-561," *99*	35	65
____	52178	Burlington Operating Boxcar "52178-559," *00*	35	70
____	52179	ACL Operating Boxcar "52179-560," *00*	40	75
____	52215	C&NW 3-bay Cylindrical Hopper, *01*	30	60
____	52216	C&NW Cylindrical Hopper, *02*	30	60
____	52223	REA/Santa Fe Centennial Operating Boxcar, *00*	35	65
____	52251	PRR Express Car, green, *01*	35	65
____	52259	MP GP20 Diesel, traditional, *01*	125	250
____	52292	PRR Express Car, tuscan red, *02*	25	50
____	52327	City of Los Angeles Express Car, *04*	35	65
____	52328	City of New Haven Express Car, *04*	30	55
____	52363	City of New Orleans Express Car, *04*	30	55
____	52364	City of New York Express Car, *04*	35	65
____	52388	Great Northern Tool Car, *06*	25	50
____	52389	Great Northern Crew Car, *06*	25	50
____	52390	Great Northern Welding Caboose, *06*	40	80
____	52391	Great Northern Racing Crew Car, *06*	25	50
____	52426	City of San Francisco Express Car, *07*	30	55
____	52427	Rock Island Rocket Express Car, *07*	30	55
____	52475	Western Pacific UP Heritage Boxcar, *07*	30	60

Classic Toy Trains

____	52126	MILW Boxcar "21027" with CTT Logo, *97*	25	50

Dept. 56

____	16270	Heritage Village Boxcar "9796," *96*	30	55
____	52096	Snow Village Boxcar "9756," *95*	45	85
____	52139	Square Window Caboose "6256," *97*	35	70
____	52157	Holly Brothers 3-D Tank Car, *98*	45	85
____	52175	4-6-4 Hudson Locomotive, CC, *99*	175	350
____	52199	4-bay Hopper "6756," *00*	30	55
____	52254	"Happy Holidays" Gondola, *01*	20	35

Eastwood Automobilia

____	16275	Radio Flyer Boxcar "16275," *96*	25	50
____	16757	Johnny Lightning Auto Carrier "3435," *96*	45	90
____	16985	Flatcar with 2 Ford vans, *97*	25	50
____	52044	Vat Car, *95*	15	30
____	52083	PRR Flatcar "21697" with tanker, *95*	20	40
____	52130	Flatcar with Hot Wheels tanker, *97*	30	60

Gadsden-Pacific Division
Toy Train Operating Museum

		Exc	Mint	
17872	Anaconda Ore Car, *88*	35	70	___
17878	Magma Ore Car, *89*	30	55	___
17881	Phelps Dodge Ore Car, *90*	20	40	___
17886	Cyprus Ore Car, *91*	15	30	___
19961	Inspiration Consolidated Copper Ore Car, *92*	15	30	___
52011	Tucson, Cornelia & Gila Bend Ore Car, *93*	15	30	___
52027	Pinto Valley Mine Ore Car, *94*	15	30	___
52071	Copper Basin Railway Ore Car, *95*	15	30	___
52089	SMARRCO Ore Car, *96*	10	25	___
52124	El Paso & Southwestern Ore Car, *97*	20	40	___
52164	SP Ore Car, *98*	20	35	___
52177	Arizona Southern Ore Car, *99*	20	35	___
52213	BHP Copper Ore Car, *00*	15	30	___
52248	Tombstone & Western Ore Car, *01*	20	40	___
52279	Dragoon & Northern Ore Car, *02*	25	50	___
52307	Twin Buttes Ore Car, *03*	20	35	___
52358	AJO & Southwestern Ore Car, *04*	25	45	___
52386	Ray & Gila Bend Ore Car, *05*	24	45	___
52421	Calabasas, Tuscon & Northwestern Ore Car, *06*	25	45	___
52473	Mascot & Western Ore Car, *07*	45	90	___
52524	Tucson, Globe & Northern Ore Car, *08*	20	40	___
52558	Port of Tucson Ore Car, *09*	25	45	___
52579	Rosemont Copper Ore Car, *10*	20	40	___
52588	ASARCO Ore Car, *11*	20	40	___
58513	Freeport-McMoRan Ore Car, *12*	20	40	___
58557	San Pedro & Southwestern Ore Car, *13*	20	40	___
58583	Arizona Eastern Ore Car, *14*	20	40	___

Houston Tinplate Operators Society

		Exc	Mint	
8900	Sam Houston Mint Car, *00*	60	120	___
8901	Miracle Petroleum 1-D Tank Car, *01*	50	100	___
8902	USS Houston Submarine Car, *02*	50	100	___
8903	Railway Express Boxcar, *03*	50	100	___
8904	Lone Star Bay Window Caboose, *04*	50	100	___
8999	Lone Star Aquarium Car, mermaid or trout, *99*	50	100	___

Inland Empire Train Collectors Association

		Exc	Mint
____ 1979	Boxcar, 79	5	15
____ 1980	SP-type Caboose, 80	5	15
____ 1981	Quad Hopper, 81	5	15
____ 1982	3-D Tank Car, 82	5	15
____ 1983	Reefer, 83	5	15
____ 1986	Bunk Car, 86	5	15
____ 7518	Carson City Mint Car, 84	25	45

Lionel Central Operating Lines

		Exc	Mint
____ 1981	Boxcar, 81	10	25
____ 1986	Work Caboose, shell only, 86	5	15
____ 5724	Pennsylvania Bunk Car, 84	20	40
____ 6508	Canadian Pacific Crane Car, 83	20	40
____ 6907	NYC Wood-sided Caboose, 97	25	50
____ 9184	Erie Bay Window Caboose, 82	10	20
____ 9475	D&H "I Love NY" Boxcar, 85	20	35
____ 16342	CSX Gondola with coil covers, 92	10	20
____ 17221	NYC Boxcar, 95	15	30

Lionel Collectors Association of Canada

		Exc	Mint
____ 5710	Canadian Pacific Reefer, 83	110	215
____ 5714	Michigan Central Reefer, 85	75	150
____ 6100	Ontario Northland Covered Quad Hopper, 82	125	250
____ 8103	Toronto, Hamilton & Buffalo Boxcar, 81	75	150
____ 8204	Algoma Central Boxcar, 82	75	150
____ 8507/08	Canadian National F3 Diesel AA, shells only, 85	200	400
____ 8912	Canada Southern Operating Hopper, 89	50	95
____ 9413	Napierville Junction Boxcar, 80	5	10
____ 9718	Canadian National Boxcar, 79	10	20
____ 17893	BAOC 1-D Tank Car "914," 91	60	120
____ 52004	Algoma Central Gondola "9215" with coil covers, 92	45	90
____ 52005	Canadian National F3 Diesel B Unit "9517," 93	15	30
____ 52006	Canadian Pacific Boxcar "930016" (std O), 93	55	110
____ 52115	Wabash Lake Railway 2-tier Auto Carrier "9519," 98		100
____ 52125	TH&B Gondola 2-pack, 99	45	90
____ 86009	Canadian National Bunk Car, 86	60	115
____ 87010	Canadian National Express Reefer, 87	60	115
____ 88011	Canadian National Caboose (std O), 88	250	500
____ 830005	Canadian National Boxcar, 83	150	300
____ 840006	Canadian Wheat Board Covered Quad Hopper, 84		165
____ 900013	Canadian National Flatcar with trailers, 90	115	225

Lionel Collectors Club of America

LCCA National Convention Cars

		Exc	Mint	
6112	Commonwealth Edison Quad Hopper with coal, 83	40	80	____
6323	Virginia Chemicals 1-D Tank Car, 86	35	65	____
6567	Illinois Central Gulf Crane Car "100408," 85	35	65	____
7403	LNAC Boxcar, 84	10	25	____
9118	Corning Covered Quad Hopper, 74	45	90	____
9155	Monsanto 1-D Tank Car, 75	25	45	____
9159UP	UP Reefer, 10	50	100	____
9212	Seaboard Coast Line Flatcar with trailers, 76	15	30	____
9259	Southern Bay Window Caboose, 77	20	40	____
9358	"Sands of Iowa" Covered Quad Hopper, 80	20	35	____
9435	Central of Georgia Boxcar, 81	15	30	____
9460	D&TS Automobile Boxcar, 82	20	35	____
9701	Baltimore & Ohio Automobile Boxcar, 72	85	170	____
9727	TA&G Boxcar, 73	70	135	____
9728	Union Pacific Stock Car, 78	10	25	____
9733	Airco Boxcar with tank car body, 79	25	50	____
17870	East Camden & Highland Boxcar (std O), 87	20	35	____
17873	Ashland Oil 3-D Tank Car, 88	35	70	____
17876	Columbia, Newberry & Laurens Boxcar (std O), 89	20	40	____
17880	D&RGW Wood-sided Caboose (std O), 90	30	55	____
17887	Conrail Flatcar with Armstrong Tile trailer (std O), 91	25	50	____
17888	Conrail Flatcar with Ford trailer (std O), 91	40	80	____
17892	Conrail Flatcar with Armstrong and Ford Trailers (std O), 91	70	140	____
17899	NASA Tank Car "190" (std O), 92	25	50	____
27019	Imco PS-2 Covered Hopper, 09	25	50	____
52023	D&TS 2-bay ACF Hopper "2601" (std O), 93	20	40	____
52038	Southern Hopper "360794" with coal (std O), 94	25	45	____
52074	Iowa Beef Packers Reefer "197095" (std O), 95	15	30	____
52090	Pere Marquette DD Boxcar "71996" (std O), 96	25	50	____
52110	CStPM&O Boxcar "71997" (std O), 97	25	50	____
52151	Amtrak Baggage Boxcar "71998" (std O), 98	35	65	____
52176	Fort Worth & Denver Boxcar "8277" (std O), 99	30	55	____
52195	Double-stack Car with 2 containers, 00	50	100	____
52244	Louisville & Nashville Horse Car "2001," 01	25	50	____
52266	PRR "Coal Goes To War" Hopper "707025," 02	45	85	____
52267	PRR "Coal Goes To War" Hopper "707026," 02	45	90	____
52299	Las Vegas Mint Car, 03	40	80	____
52343	MILW Milk Car, orange, 04	80	160	____
52344	MILW Milk Car, blue, 04	105	205	____

CLUB CARS AND SPECIAL PRODUCTION

		Exc	Mint
52393	MKT Speeder, yellow, nonpowered, *05*	10	20
52394	Frisco Speeder, red, powered, *05*	10	25
52395	Frisco Flatcar, silver, *05*	10	25
52396	Frisco Flatcar with 2 speeders, *05*	65	125
52412	UP Auxiliary Power Car, *06*	30	55
52455	C&NW/UP Tank Car, *07*	55	110
52491	PS-2 Covered Hopper 2-pack, *08*	70	140
52507	NYC Water Tower, *08*	45	85
52514	ATSF Mint Car with Gold, *09*	140	275
52543	BNSF Mechanical Reefer, *09*	70	140
52559	UP Cylindrical Hopper, *10*	50	100
52562	D&RGW Uranium Transport Mint Car, *10*	115	230
58254	Providence & Worcester Flatcar, *15*	50	130
58509	Norfolk Southern Camouflage PS-1 Boxcar, *12*	50	95
58560	Southern Tennessean Boxcar, *13*	45	90
58576	Monon Operating Boxcar, *14*	65	125
72511	Alamo Mint Car, *11*	75	150
75511	Federal Reserve Mint Car, *11*	100	200

LCCA Meet Specials

		Exc	Mint
1130	Tender, *76*	5	15
6014-900	Frisco Boxcar (027), *75*	15	30
6483	Jersey Central SP-type Caboose, *82*	15	30
9016	Chessie System Hopper (027), *79*	10	20
9036	Mobilgas 1-D Tank Car (027), *78*	10	20
9142	Republic Steel Gondola, green or blue, with canisters, *77*	10	25

Other LCCA Production

		Exc	Mint
4001	RJ Corman Boxcar, *99*	40	80
4002	RJ Corman Boxcar, *99*	20	40
6464-2002	Maddox Retirement Boxcar, *02*	50	100
8068	Rock Island GP20 Diesel, *80*	60	120
9739	D&RGW Boxcar, *78*	10	25
9771	Norfolk & Western Boxcar, *77*	15	30
14154	Water Tower with LCCA plaque, *04*	45	90
17174	Great Northern 3-bay Hopper, *03*	10	25
17234	Port Huron & Detroit Boxcar, *00*	25	45
17377	American Railway Express Reefer "302," *06*	25	50
17412	Gondola, blue, *02*	15	30
17895	LCCA Tractor, *91*	10	20
17896	Lancaster Lines Tractor, *91*	15	30
18090	D&RGW 4-6-2 Locomotive and Tender, *90*	155	305
18483	C&O Ballast Tamper, *07*	40	75
18490	UP Ballast Tamper, yellow, *06*	65	125
19998	"Seasons Greetings" Boxcar, *03*	20	40

CLUB CARS AND SPECIAL PRODUCTION

		Exc	Mint	
26023	Flatcar with bulldozer, *04*	30	55	___
26024	Flatcar with scraper, *04*	35	65	___
26049	Speedboat Willie Flatcar with boat, *05*	25	45	___
26132	UP 1-D Tank Car, *06*	15	30	___
26780	Operating Giraffe Car, green or pink, *05*	35	70	___
26791	UP Chase Gondola, red, *03*	15	30	___
26791	Rio Grande Chase Gondola, black, *06*	15	30	___
26795	Mrs. O'Leary's Dairy Farm Stock Car, *07*	50	100	___
26834	"La Cosa Nostra Railway" Operating Ice Car, *07*	40	75	___
29232	Lenny the Lion Hi-Cube, signed by Lenny Dean, *98*	35	65	___
52025	Madison Hardware Tractor and Trailer, *93*	10	20	___
52039	"Track 29" Bumper, *94*	10	25	___
52055	SOVEX Tractor and Trailer, *94*	10	20	___
52056	Southern Tractor and Trailer, *94*	15	25	___
52091	Lenox Tractor and Trailer, *95*	5	15	___
52092	Iowa Interstate Tractor and Trailer, *95*	10	20	___
52100	Grand Rapids Station Platform, *98*	10	25	___
52107	On-track Pickup, orange, *96*	25	50	___
52108	On-track Van, blue, *96*	20	35	___
52131	Beechcraft Airplane, blue, *97*	10	25	___
52138	Beechcraft Airplane, orange, *97*	10	25	___
52152	Ben Franklin and Liberty Bell Reefer, *98*	60	120	___
52153	6414 Auto Set, 4-pack, *98*	35	70	___
52206	SD40 Diesel and Extended Vision Caboose, *00*	325	650	___
52257	"Season's Greetings" Gondola, *01*	20	35	___
52273	Flatcar with submarine, *02*	110	220	___
52300	Halloween General Train, *04*	180	360	___
52348	Halloween General Sheriff and Outlaw Car, *04*	60	115	___
52405	Halloween General Add-on Cars, *06*	80	160	___
52406	Halloween General Cannon, *08*	70	135	___
52423	New Haven Alco Diesel Passenger Set, *09*	255	510	___
52468	Postwar "2434" Passenger Coach, *09*	40	75	___
52469	Postwar "2432" Passenger Coach, *09*	40	75	___
52540	Passenger Shelter, *09*	10	25	___
52581	Texas Special Milk Car, *10*	55	110	___
52582	Gondola with dinosaurs, *12*	25	45	___
58217	B&M Smoking Caboose, *15*		105	___
58224	Walking Brakeman Car, *15*		100	___
58249	Holiday Boxcar, *15*	20	80	___
58251	Maine Central Flatcar with trailers, *15*		100	___
58526	Texas Special Cow and Calf SW9 Switchers, *14*		375	___
58532	Lou Caponi Blue Coal Train, *14*	100	200	___
58549	Texas Special Diamonds Mint Car, *14*	40	75	___
58561	Southern Pelican Boxcar, *13*	35	70	___
58584	45th Anniversary Auto Rack Loader, *14*	60	120	___

Lionel Operating Train Society

LOTS National Convention Cars

			Exc	Mint
____	**303**	Stauffer Chemical 1-D Tank Car, *85*	105	210
____	**3764**	Kahn's Brine Tank Reefer, *81*	45	85
____	**6111**	L&N Covered Quad Hopper, *83*	20	40
____	**6211**	C&O Gondola with canisters, *86*	45	90
____	**9414**	Cotton Belt Boxcar, *80*	30	55
____	**16812**	Grand Trunk 2-bay ACF Hopper (std O), *96*	30	60
____	**16813**	Pennsylvania Power & Light Hopper with coal (std O), *97*	40	80
____	**17874**	Milwaukee Road Log Dump Car "59629," *88*	75	150
____	**17875**	Port Huron & Detroit Boxcar "1289," *89*	25	50
____	**17882**	B&O DD Boxcar "298011" with ETD, *90*	35	65
____	**17890**	CSX Auto Carrier "151161," *91*	40	80
____	**18890**	Union Pacific RS3 Diesel "8805," *89*	75	145
____	**19960**	Western Pacific Boxcar "1953" (std O), *92*	35	65
____	**38356**	Dow Chemical 3-D Tank Car, *87*	65	125
____	**52014**	BN TTUX Flatcar Set with N&W trailers, *93*	105	205
____	**52041**	BN TTUX Flatcar Set with Conrail trailers, *94*	45	85
____	**52067**	Burlington Operating Ice Car "50240," *95*	30	60
____	**52135**	ATSF Reefer "22739," *98*	30	55
____	**52162**	Gulf Mobile & Ohio DD Boxcar "24580," *99*	35	65
____	**52196**	CP Maxi-Stack Flatcar "524115" with 2 containers, *00*	50	95
____	**52234**	WM Well Car with transformer, *01*	30	60
____	**52261**	Schlitz Beer Reefer "92132," *02*	30	60
____	**52281**	PRR Operating Boxcar, *03*	30	55
____	**52342**	Southern Stock Car, sound, *04*	30	55
____	**52346**	D&H PS-2 Cement Hopper, *06*	35	65
____	**52347**	SF SD80 MAC Diesel, TMCC, *04*	175	350
____	**52380/81**	Virginian Coal Hopper, *05*	25	50
____	**52382**	SF Extended View Caboose, *05*	165	325
____	**52425**	SP&S Boxcar (std O), *07*	45	90
____	**52474**	NYC Evans Auto Loader with 4 Studebakers, *08*	40	80
____	**52550**	NC&StL Dixieland Boxcar, *09*	40	75
____	**52566**	NH State of Maine Boxcar, *10*	30	60
____	**52580**	Robin Hood Beer Double-sheathed Boxcar, *11*	40	80
	58223	Chicago Great Western Flatcar with Edelweiss Beer Trailers, *15*		75
____	**58508**	Genesee Beer & Ale Double-sheathed Boxcar, *11*	35	70
	58553	UP Maxi-Stack Car with WP feather containers, *13*	40	75
____	**58575**	H. J. Heinz Double-sheathed Boxcar, *14*	35	70
____	**80948**	Michigan Central Boxcar, *82*	115	230
____	**83862**	Cradle of Liberty Boxcar, *16*		75
____	**121315**	Pennsylvania Hi-Cube Boxcar, *84*	175	345

LOTS Meet Specials

		Exc	Mint	
52413	Saratoga Brewery Reefer, 06	30	60	____
52456	Alpenrose Dairy Milk Car, 07	50	95	____
52506	Studebaker Automobile Parts Boxcar, 08	40	75	____
52552	Radioactive Waste Removal Car, 09	45	85	____
58236	Tucker Automobile Parts Boxcar, 15		75	____

Other LOTS Production

		Exc	Mint	
1223	Seattle & North Coast Hi-Cube Boxcar, 86	100	200	____
52042	BN TTUX Flatcar "637500C" with CN trailer, 94	30	60	____
52048	Canadian National Tractor and Trailer "197993," 94	20	35	____
52129	Lighted Billboard with Angela Trotta Thomas art, 97	15	30	____
52217	LOTS/LCCA 2000 Convention Billboard, 00	5	10	____
52260	National Aquarium in Baltimore Car, 01	55	110	____
52280	"More Precious than Gold" Mint Car, 02	45	90	____
52309	Patriotic Tank Car, 03	35	70	____
52359	Silver Anniversary Ore Car "1979," 04	20	40	____
52360	Silver Anniversary Ore Car "2004," 04	20	40	____
52419	Touring Layout Aquarium Car, 05	45	90	____
52477	Santa Fe Warbonnet Boxcar, 07	40	75	____
52523	Santa Fe Flatcar with trailer and tractor, 08	45	90	____
52553	Tennessee Aquarium Car, 09	35	65	____
52567	Santa Fe ACF 2-bay Hopper, 10	30	60	____
52590	Santa Fe Warbonnet Mint Car, 11	40	75	____
58228	Burlington Zephyr Boxcar, 15		75	____
58535	Santa Fe ACF Transparent Boxcar, 12	40	75	____
58566	Virginia & Truckee Carson City Mint Car, 13	35	70	____
58593	Porter Locomotive Parts Boxcar, 14		70	____
58594/5	Santa Fe Crane and Work Caboose, 14		135	____

Lionel Century Club

		Exc	Mint	
14532	PRR Sharknose Diesel AA Set, LCC II, 00	350	690	____
18053	2-8-4 Berkshire Locomotive "726," 97	360	705	____
18057	6-8-6PRR S2 Steam Turbine Locomotive "671," 98	290	570	____
18058	4-6-4 Hudson Locomotive "773," 97	375	735	____
18068	Tender for PRR Steam Turbine Locomotive "773," 99	105	210	____
18135	NYC F3 Diesel AA Set, 99	325	650	____
18178	NYC F3 Diesel B Unit, 99	115	230	____
18314	PRR GG1 Electric "2332," 97	280	560	____
18340	FM Train Master Set, LCC II, 00	450	900	____
24510	PRR Sharknose Diesel B Unit, LCC II, 00	100	200	____

CLUB CARS AND SPECIAL PRODUCTION

		Exc	Mint
28069	NYC 4-8-6 Niagara Locomotive "6024," CC, LCC II, *00*	460	920
29173	Empire State Express Passenger Car 4-pack, LCC II, *02*	175	350
29178	Empire State Express Passenger Car 2-pack, LCC II, *02*	90	175
29181	Empire State Express Diner, LCC II, *02*	95	190
29204	Boxcar "1900-2000," *96*	165	330
29226	Berkshire Boxcar, *97*	75	145
29227	GG1 Boxcar, *98*	30	55
29228	PRR Turbine Boxcar "671," *99*	30	60
29248	F3 Boxcar "2333," *99*	35	65
31716	Niagara Milk Train Set, LCC II, *00*	150	300
31726	PRR Sharknose Coal Train Set, LCC II, *00*	90	180
31731	Train Master Freight Train Set, LCC II, *00*	90	180
38000	NYC 4-6-4 Hudson Empire State Locomotive, LCC II, *02*	495	990
39201	Hudson Boxcar "773," *00*	30	60
39215	Niagara Boxcar, LCC II, *01*	25	50
39217	Boxcar, LCC II, *00*	30	60
39218	Gold Boxcar, LCC II, *00*	45	85
39237	M-10000 Boxcar, LCC II, *00*	35	70
39246	PRR Sharknose Boxcar, LCC II, *00*	30	55
39265	Fairbanks-Morse Train Master Boxcar, LCC II, *00*	30	60
39266	Empire State Boxcar, LCC II, *00*	20	40
51007	UP M-10000 4-car Passenger Set, LCC II, *00*	485	970
51249	UP Overland Route Sleeper Car, LCC II, *02*	60	120

Lionel Railroader Club

		Exc	Mint
780	Boxcar, *82*	35	65
781	Flatcar with trailers, *83*	25	50
782	1-D Tank Car, *85*	25	45
784	Covered Quad Hopper, *84*	30	60
11183	Lincoln Funeral Train	400	800
11319	PRR Tuscan K4 Locomotive, CC	450	900
11320	PRR Tuscan K4 Locomotive	375	750
12875	Tractor and Trailer, *94*	10	20
12921	Illuminated Station Platform, *95*	10	20
14274	Water Tower, *07*	10	20
15034	50th Anniversary Mail Car, *10*	25	50
15035	Holiday Boxcar, *10*	25	50
16800	Ore Car, yellow, *86*	35	70
16801	Bunk Car, blue, *88*	20	35
16802	Tool Car, *89*	25	35
16803	Searchlight Car, *90*	10	25
16804	Bay Window Caboose, *91*	15	30

CLUB CARS AND SPECIAL PRODUCTION

		Exc	Mint	
16839	Covered Bridge, 11	25	50	____
18680	4-6-4 Hudson Locomotive, 00	150	300	____
18684	4-6-2 Pacific Locomotive, 99	110	220	____
18818	GP38-2 Diesel, 92	100	115	____
19399	Christmas Boxcar, 13	30	60	____
19437	Flatcar with trailer, 97	30	55	____
19473	Operating Log Dump Car "3351," 99	20	40	____
19685	Western Union Dining Car, 02	20	40	____
19695	Western Union 1-D Tank Car, 03	10	20	____
19774	Porthole Caboose, 99	25	50	____
19775	Stock Car, 99	25	50	____
19924	Boxcar, 93	10	20	____
19930	Quad Hopper with coal, 94	10	20	____
19935	1-D Tank Car, 95	10	25	____
19940	Vat Car, 96	15	30	____
19953	6464 Boxcar, 97	20	35	____
19965	Aquarium Car "3435," 99	30	55	____
19966	Gondola "9820" (std O), 98	15	30	____
19978	Gold Membership Boxcar, 99	25	45	____
19991	Gold Membership Boxcar, 00	35	65	____
19992	Western Union Tool Car "3550," 00	25	50	____
19993	Gold Membership Boxcar, 01	35	65	____
19994	Western Union Passenger Car "1307," 01	30	60	____
19995	25th Anniversary Boxcar (std O), 01	25	50	____
24217	Animated Billboard, 08	15	30	____
25073	Holiday Boxcar, 09	20	50	____
25631	Lincoln Train Passenger Car 2-pack	150	300	____
25635	Red Passenger Car 3-pack, 12	210	420	____
25635	Red Arrow Diner, 12	70	140	____
26089	Western Union Gondola with handcar, 05	35	65	____
26165	Western Union Reefer, 04	15	30	____
26382	Flatcar with tractor and tanker, 08	30	60	____
26413	Commemorative 4-bay Hopper, 08	35	70	____
26636	"6830" 50th Anniversary Flatcar with submarine, 11	30	55	____
26637	"6640" 50th Anniversary USMC Missile Launching Car, 11	35	65	____
27940	"6469" Liquified Gas Tank Car, 13	25	50	____
27943	"6416" Boat Loader, 13	25	50	____
27944	"3413" Mercury Capsule Launch Car, 13	30	60	____
27945	"6460-60" LV Covered Quad Hopper, 13	30	55	____
28062	4-6-4 Hudson Locomotive, 00	575	1150	____
28571	GP9 Diesel, CC, 07	125	250	____
28665	Western Union 2-8-4 Berkshire Locomotive "665," 05	90	175	____
29200	Lionel Boxcar "9700," 96	20	40	____

CLUB CARS AND SPECIAL PRODUCTION

			Exc	Mint
____	29313	"3409" 50th Anniversary Helicopter Car, *11*	35	70
____	29657	"6413" 50th Anniversary Mercury Capsule Car, *12*	30	55
____	29658	"6465" 50th Anniversary Cities Service 2-D Car, *12*	25	50
____	29931	Holiday Boxcar, *05*	10	25
____	29939	30th Anniversary Boxcar, *06*	25	50
____	29941	Holiday Boxcar, *06*	10	25
____	29946	Holiday Boxcar, *07*	20	35
____	29947	Commemorative Boxcar, *07*	15	30
____	29957	Holiday Boxcar, *08*	25	50
____	29977	Holiday Boxcar, *11*	30	60
____	36521	Western Union Searchlight Caboose, *05*	15	30
____	36769	4th of July Lighted Boxcar, *03*	35	70
____	37968	Clock Tower with wreath, *11*	25	45
____	39249	Holiday Boxcar, *03*	15	30
____	39264	Holiday Boxcar, *04*	25	50
____	39352	"6445" 50th Anniversary Fort Knox Mint Car, *12*	35	70
____	39353	50th Anniversary Santa Fe Boxcar, *11*	30	55
____	39496	"6475" 50th Anniversary Vat Car, *10*	30	60
____	58613	Holiday Boxcar, *14*	30	90
____	58632	1955 Maintenance of Way Truck, *13*	85	165
____	81116	Polar Express Operating Billboard, *14*	30	60
____	81117	Polar Express Flatcar with silver bell, *14*	25	45

Lionel Railroad Club Milwaukee

			Exc	Mint
____	52116	MILW Flatcar "194797," black, with tractor and trailer, *97*	40	75
____	52163	CMStP&P "Hiawatha" DD Automobile Boxcar, *98*	30	60
____	52180	MILW Flatcar "194799," tuscan, with trailer, *99*	40	75
____	52228	CMStP&P 1-D Water Tank Car "908309," *00*	25	50
____	52229	MILW 1-D Diesel Fuel Tank Car "907797," *00*	25	50
____	52230	1-D Tank Car 2-pack, *00*	70	140
____	52246	CMStP&P "Olympian" Boxcar "194701," *01*	35	65
____	52265	MILW/Zoological Society Aquarium Car "4701," orange, *02*	30	55
____	52278	MILW/Zoological Society Aquarium Car "4702," blue, *03*	50	95
____	52297	MILW Reefer "194703," yellow, *03*	35	65
____	52298	MILW Flatcar "194704" with orange trailer, *04*	60	115
____	52337	MILW/Zoological Society Motorized Aquarium Car, *04*	45	90
____	52368	MILW Flatcar "472004," black, *05*	35	65
____	52369	MILW Trailer Train Auto Carrier "194705," *05*	45	85
____	52370	CMStP&P Milk Car "364," tan, *05*	40	80
____	52387	CMStP&P Flatcar "194706," gray, *06*	25	50
____	52400	MILW PS-2 2-bay Hopper "99607," orange, *06*	45	85

CLUB CARS AND SPECIAL PRODUCTION

		Exc	Mint	
52401	MILW PS-2 2-bay Hopper "98809," yellow, 06	35	65	____
52402	CMStP&P URTX Operating Ice Car "4706," 06	45	85	____
52428	CMStP&P 0-4-0 Switcher and Caboose Set, 60th Anniversary, 06	140	275	____
52429	CMStP&P 0-4-0 Switcher, 06	100	200	____
52430	CMStP&P Offset Cupola Caboose, 06	35	70	____
52458	MILW Stock Car "102721" (std O), 07	35	65	____
52466	CMStP&P Stock Car "105254" (std O), 07	35	65	____
52551	MILW "Big M" DD Boxcar "200947," yellow, 09	30	60	____
52572	MILW Reiman Aquarium Car, 11	40	75	____
52599	MILW 2-bay ACF Hopper, 12	30	60	____
58263	Breast Cancer Awareness Boxcar, 16		80	____
58563	CMStP&P Round-Roof Boxcar, 13	35	70	____
58591	MILW Flatcar with auto frames, 14	30	60	____

Long Island Toy Train Locomotive Engineers

		Exc	Mint	
58520	Entenmann's Vat Car, 12	35	65	____
58556	Flatcar with U.S. Navy airplane, 13	35	70	____
58562	Entenmann's Quad Hopper, 14	40	75	____

Nassau Lionel Operating Engineers

		Exc	Mint	
8389	Long Island Boxcar, 89	50	100	____
8390	Long Island Covered Quad Hopper, 90	50	100	____
8391A	Long Island Bunk Car, 91	45	90	____
8391B	Long Island Tool Car, 91	45	90	____
8392	Long Island 1-D Tank Car, 92	55	105	____
52007	Long Island RS3 Diesel "1552," 93	125	250	____
52019	Long Island Boxcar, 93	35	65	____
52020	Long Island Bay Window Caboose, 93	50	95	____
52026	Long Island Flatcar "8394" with Grumman trailer, 94	235	465	____
52061	Long Island Stern's Pickle Products Vat Car "8395," 95	100	200	____
52072	Grumman Tractor, 94	40	75	____
52076	Long Island Observation Car "8396," 96	175	350	____
52112	Long Island Ronkonkoma Vista Dome Car "9783," 97	150	300	____
52122	Meenan Oil 1-D Tank Car "8397" (std O), 97	30	60	____
52123	Long Island Hicksville Diner Car "9883," 98	150	300	____
52144	Long Island Flatcar with Grumman van, 99	50	95	____
52145	Long Island Jamaica Passenger Coach, 99	150	300	____
52145	Long Island Penn Station Passenger Coach, 99	150	300	____
52166	Long Island Flatcar "8398" with Grumman trailer, 98	40	75	____
52186	Grucci Fireworks Boxcar, 00	35	70	____
52232	Central RR of Long Island Boxcar, 01	30	60	____

CLUB CARS AND SPECIAL PRODUCTION

			Exc	Mint
____	52256	New York & Atlantic Boxcar "8302," 02	30	60
____	52296	Long Island Flatcar with Republic tanker, 03	40	80
____	52329	New York & Atlantic Caboose, 04	40	80
____	52341	Long Island Flatcar with Pan Am trailer, 05	45	85
____	52365	Long Island Flatcar with Lilco transformer, 04	70	135
____	52420	Long Island 80th Anniversary Boxcar, 06	25	45
____	52480	Long Island Flatcar with pipes, 08	25	50
____	52489	Long Island Flatcar with P.C. Richard & Son trailer, 07	35	65
____	52555	Martha Clara Vineyards Vat Car, 09	30	60
____	52568	Flatcar with NY Islanders refrigerated trailer, 10	30	60
____	52586	Flatcar with Cradle of Aviation Museum trailer, 11	25	50
____	52592	Petland Discounts Aquarium Car, 11	35	70
____	58212	Cross Harbor Round-roof Boxcar, 15		65
____	58240	LIRR GLa Hopper, black, 16		80
____	58240	LIRR GLa Hopper, tuscan, 16		80
____	58500	Nassau County Firefighters Museum Tank Car, 12	30	55
____	58581	Long Island Double-sheathed Boxcar, 14		65
____	83131	Nathan's Famous Reefer, 13	40	75
____	83132	Nathan's Famous Reefer, 13	40	75
____	83163	Nathan's 100th Anniversary Reefer, 16		65

Railroad Museum of Long Island

____	52416	RMLI 15th Anniversary LIRR Boxcar, 05	85	170
____	52433	Atlantis Marine World Aquarium Car, 06	75	145
____	52453	North Fork Bank Mint Car, 07	45	90
____	52497	LIRR Flatcar with Entenmann's trailer and tractor, 08	55	110
____	52498	Boeing Fairchild Container Car, 10	40	75
____	52548	RMLI "Celebrating 175 Years of Railroading" Boxcar, 09	45	90
____	52557	Entenmann's Operating Boxcar, 10	45	90
____	52570	Riverhead Building Supply Boxcar, 11	30	60
____	52571	Riverhead Visitor's Center Boxcar, 11	30	60
____	52577	King Kullen Boxcar, 11	30	60
____	52595	J. P. Holland Submarine Car, 12	30	60
____	58227	World's Fair Crew Car, 15		75
____	58259	Steam Up LIRR 39 Boxcar, 16		85
____	58521	Wonder Bread PS-2 Covered Hopper, 12	30	60
____	58551	Flatcar with White Castle refrigerated trailer, 13	30	60
____	58554	RCA Operating Radar Car, 13	30	60
____	58555	Flatcar with produce trailers, 15		75
____	58579	World's Fair Exhibit Car, 14		80
____	58580	World's Fair Tool Car, 15		60

St. Louis Lionel Railroad Club

		Exc	Mint	
52099	MP Flatcar with St. Louis trailer, 96	35	65	___
52104	St. Louis tractor and trailer, 96	10	20	___
52117	Wabash Flatcar with REA tractor and trailer, 97	35	65	___
52136A	Christmas Tractor and Trailer, 97		NRS	___
52136B	Frisco Tractor and Trailer, 98		NRS	___
52147	Frisco Campbell TOFC Flatcar, 98	40	75	___
52150	Frisco Campbell TOFC Flatcar, 98	65	130	___
52167	ATSF Flatcar "831999" with Navajo trailer, 99	40	75	___
52190	IC Flatcar with trailers, 00	40	80	___
52222	Cotton Belt Flatcar with SP tractor and trailer, 01	25	50	___
52224A	SP Flatcar with Navajo tractor and trailer, 01	10	25	___
52224B	SP Flatcar with service tractor and trailer, 01	10	25	___
52258	UP Flatcar with UP tractor and trailer, 02	30	55	___
52290	UP Flatcar with tractor trailer, 03	40	75	___
52336	U.S. Army Flatcar with tanker truck, 04	65	125	___
52371	NYC Flatcar with Fire Company tanker truck, 05	70	145	___
52392	PRR Flatcar with Hood's Milk tanker truck, 06	50	100	___
52440	U.S.M.C. Flatcar with tractor and trailer, 07	70	135	___
52490	Silver Special Flatcar with USA tractor and trailer, 08	50	100	___
52513	Frisco Flatcar with U.S.A.F. trailer, 09	60	120	___

Train Collectors Association

TCA National Convention Cars

		Exc	Mint	
511	St. Louis Baggage Car, 81	20	40	___
2671-1968	TCA Tender, shell only, 68	30	55	___
5734	REA Reefer, 85	25	50	___
6315	Pittsburgh 1-D Tank Car, 72	30	60	___
6436-1969	Open Quad Hopper, red, 69	35	65	___
6464-1965	Pittsburgh Boxcar, blue, 65	125	210	___
6464-1970	Chicago Boxcar, 70	45	85	___
6464-1971	Disneyland Boxcar, 71	210	240	___
6517-1966	Bay Window Caboose, 66	150	250	___
6926	New Orleans Extended Vision Caboose, 86	20	40	___
7205	Denver Combination Car, 82	25	50	___
7206	Louisville Passenger Car, 83	30	55	___
7212	Pittsburgh Passenger Car, 84	25	50	___
7812	Houston Stock Car, 77	10	25	___
8476	4-6-4 Locomotive "5484," 85	155	310	___
9123	Dearborn 3-tier Auto Carrier, 73	20	35	___
9319	"Silver Jubilee" Mint Car, 79	65	130	___
9544	Chicago Observation Car, 80	25	50	___
9611	Boston Hi-Cube Boxcar, 78	10	25	___

CLUB CARS AND SPECIAL PRODUCTION

			Exc	Mint
____	9774	Orlando "Southern Belle" Boxcar, *75*	20	35
____	9779	Philadelphia Boxcar "9700-1976," *76*	20	35
____	9864	Seattle Reefer, *74*	25	50
____	11737	TCA 40th Anniversary F3 Diesel ABA Set, *93*	265	530
____	17879	Valley Forge Dining Car, *89*	30	60
____	17883	New Georgia Passenger Car, *90*	35	65
____	17898	Wabash Reefer "21596," *92*	25	45
____	19211	Vermont Railway Flatcars (2) with 4 trailers, *08*	80	160
____	52008	Bucyrus Erie Crane Car, *93*	25	50
____	52035	Yorkrail GP9 Diesel "1750," shell only, *94*	30	55
____	52036	TCA 40th Anniversary Bay Window Caboose, *94*	20	40
____	52037	Yorkrail GP9 Diesel "1754," *94*	75	150
____	52062	Skytop Observation Car, *95*	180	360
____	52085	Full Vista Dome Car, *96*	60	115
____	52106	City of Phoenix Diner, *97*	50	100
____	52142	Massachusetts Central Maxi-Stack Flatcar "5100-01," *98*	60	120
____	52143	City of Providence Passenger Car, *98*	70	140
____	52146	Ocean Spray Reefer, *98*	120	235
____	52155	City of San Francisco Baggage Car, *99*	70	140
____	52191	City of Grand Rapids Aluminum Passenger Car, *00*	70	135
____	52210	Rico Station, *00*	15	30
____	52220	City of Chattanooga Vista Dome Car, *01*	70	140
____	52221	Norfolk Southern Boxcar, *01*	25	50
____	52237	Lionel Gondola, yellow, *01*	55	110
____	52238	Lionel Gondola, red, *01*	55	110
____	52239	Lionel Gondola, silver, *01*	55	110
____	52240	Lionel Gondola 3-pack, *01*	55	110
____	52241	Lionel Gondola, black, *02*	5	15
____	52242	Lionel Gondola, blue, *02*	20	35
____	52250	City of Chicago Combination Car, *02*	65	130
____	52272	Lionel Gondola, gold, *02*	40	80
____	52276	California Gold Mint Car, *03*	35	65
____	52333	Harmony Dairy Milk Car, *04*	45	90
____	52338	Lionel 50th Anniversary Mint Car, *04*	40	75
____	52339	50th Anniversary Convention Banquet Car with coin, *04*	180	360
____	52340	Train Order Building, *04*	45	90
____	52373	Montana Rail Link 2-car Set, *05*	45	90
____	52374	Montana Rail Link 2-bay Hopper, *05*	25	50
____	52375	Montana Rail Link Flatcar with pulp-wood logs, *05*	25	50
____	52376	GN Reefer, *05*	30	60
____	52403	T&P Stock Car (std O), *06*	40	75
____	52414	Flatcar with 3 snowmobiles, *07*	40	80
____	52481	Ben & Jerry's Reefer, *08*	50	95

CLUB CARS AND SPECIAL PRODUCTION

		Exc	Mint	
52500	ATSF Grand Canyon Reefer, *09*	30	60	____
52508	Celebrate America Mint Car, *09*	50	95	____
58216	NYC Merchants Despatch Reefer, *15*		90	____
58258	Made in the USA Boxcar, *16*		80	____
58544	St. Louis Reefer, *13*	45	85	____
58547	Cotton Belt Blue Streak Merchandise Boxcar, *13*	35	75	____
58571	Bethlehem Steel PS-1 Boxcar, *14*	40	80	____
58572	Reading Philadelphia Mint Car, *14*	40	80	____

TCA Museum-Related and Other Cars

		Exc	Mint	
1018-1979	Mortgage Burning Hi-Cube Boxcar, *79*	20	35	____
5731	L&N Reefer, *90*	50	95	____
7780	TCA Museum Boxcar, *80*	10	25	____
7781	Hafner Boxcar, *81*	10	25	____
7782	Carlisle & Finch Boxcar, *82*	10	25	____
7783	Ives Boxcar, *83*	10	25	____
7784	Voltamp Boxcar, *84*	10	25	____
7785	Hoge Boxcar, *85*	10	25	____
9771	Norfolk & Western Boxcar, *77*	15	30	____
16811	Rutland Boxcar "5477096," *96*	20	35	____
52045	Pennsylvania Dutch Milk Car "61052," *94*	45	90	____
52051	Baltimore & Ohio Sentinel Boxcar "6464095," *95*	20	40	____
52052	TCA 40th Anniversary Boxcar, *94*	45	90	____
52063	NYC Pacemaker Boxcar "6464125," *95*	175	345	____
52064	Missouri Pacific Boxcar "6464150," *95*	185	370	____
52065	Pennsylvania Dutch Grain Operating Boxcar "9208," *96*	50	100	____
52118	Rio Grande Boxcar "5477097," *97*	30	55	____
52119	TCA Museum 20th Anniversary Boxcar, *97*	35	70	____
52128	Pennsylvania Dutch Pretzels Boxcar, *99*	40	80	____
52172	L&N "Share the Freedom" Boxcar "5477099," *99*	25	55	____
52198	Frisco Boxcar "5477000," *00*	25	45	____
52215	Museum Work Train Gondola with pipes, *03*	30	55	____
52226	Angela Trotta Thomas Boxcar "2000," *01*	50	100	____
52243	Museum Work Train 1-D Tank Car, *01*	25	50	____
52271	Museum Work Train Flatcar with wheel load, *02*	10	20	____
52289	National Toy Train Museum 25th Anniversary Bullion Car, *02*	40	75	____
52295	National Toy Train Museum Gondola with pipes, *03*	5	15	____
52310	Museum Work Train Boxcar, *04*	30	55	____
52311	50th Anniversary Golden Express Freight Set, *04*	200	450	____
52321	SP Trainmaster Locomotive, *04*	175	345	____
52372	Museum Work Train Baggage Car, *05*	35	70	____
52408	N&W Caboose, *06*	30	55	____
52409	Museum Work Train Idler Caboose, *06*	35	70	____
52437	Museum Work Train Crane Car, *07*	40	80	____

CLUB CARS AND SPECIAL PRODUCTION

			Exc	Mint

TCA Bicentennial Special Set

			Exc	Mint
____	1973	Bicentennial Observation Car, 76	25	50
____	1974	Bicentennial Passenger Car, 76	25	50
____	1975	Bicentennial Passenger Car, 76	25	50
____	1976	Bicentennial U36B Diesel, 76	85	165

Atlantic Division

____	1980	Atlantic Division Flatcar with trailers, 80	20	35
____	6101	Burlington Northern Covered Quad Hopper, 82	20	35
____	9186	Conrail N5c Caboose, 79	15	30
____	9193	Budweiser Vat Car, 84	55	110
____	9466	Wanamaker Boxcar, 83	70	135
____	9788	Lehigh Valley Boxcar, 78	10	25

Desert Division

____	52088	Desert Division 25th Anniversary On-track Step Van, 96	60	120
____	52105	Superstition Mountain Operating Gondola "61997," 97	40	80
____	52442	Verde Canyon Boxcar, 07	30	55
____	52443	Grand Canyon Boxcar, 07	30	55
____	58226	Cumbres & Toltec Boxcar, 16		80
____		Los Alamos Mint Car, 16		80

Dixie Division

____	27007/87	Dixie Division 20th Anniversary PS-1 Boxcar, 06	40	80
____	52127	Dixie Division 10th Anniversary Southern 3-bay Hopper, 98	35	70

Eastern Division

____	52059	Clinchfield Quad Hopper "16413" with coal, 94	55	110

Eastern Division: Washington, Baltimore & Annapolis Chapter

____	9412	Richmond, Fredericksburg & Potomac Boxcar, 79	10	25
____	9740	Chessie System Boxcar, 76	10	25
____	9771	Norfolk & Western Boxcar, 78	15	30
____	9783	B&O Time-Saver Boxcar, 77	15	30

Fort Pitt Division

____	1984-30X	Heinz Ketchup Boxcar, 84	250	500

Great Lakes Division

____	1983	Churchill Downs Boxcar, 83	100	200
____	1983	Churchill Downs Reefer, 83	125	250
____	9740	Chessie System Boxcar, 76	10	25

CLUB CARS AND SPECIAL PRODUCTION

Great Lakes Division: Detroit-Toledo Chapter

		Exc	Mint	
8957	Burlington Northern GP20 Diesel, *80*	115	230	____
8958	Burlington Northern GP20 Diesel Dummy Unit, *80*	75	150	____
9119	Detroit & Mackinac Covered Quad Hopper, *77*	10	20	____
9272	New Haven Bay Window Caboose, *79*	10	20	____
9401	Great Northern Boxcar, *78*	10	25	____
9730	CP Rail Boxcar, *76*	10	25	____
52000	Detroit-Toledo Division Flatcar with trailer, *92*	45	85	____

Great Lakes Division: Three Rivers Chapter

9113	Norfolk & Western Quad Hopper, *76*	15	30	____

Great Lakes Division: Western Michigan Chapter

9730	CP Rail Boxcar, *74*	10	25	____

Lake & Pines Division

52018	3-M Boxcar, *93*	225	450	____

Lone Star Division

7522	New Orleans Mint Car with coin, *86*	210	420	____
52093	Lone Star Division Boxcar "6464696," *96*	15	30	____
52585	Texas Special Mint Car, *11*	35	65	____
58512	SP Daylight Mint Car, *12*	35	65	____
58552	Texas Special Mint Car with silver bars, *12*	35	65	____

Lone Star Division: North Texas Chapter

9739	D&RGW Boxcar, *76*	10	20	____

METCA

10	Jersey Central F3 A Unit, shell only, *71*	10	25	____
9272	New Haven Bay Window Caboose, *79*	10	25	____
9754	New York Central Pacemaker Boxcar, *76*	15	30	____
52485	New York Central Mint Car with copper load, *08*	60	120	____
52486	Pennsylvania Mint Car, green, *09*	65	125	____
52487	Pennsylvania Mint Car, tuscan, *09*	65	125	____
52488	NYC Lightning Stripe Mint Car, *10*	30	60	____
52574	Fort Knox 50th Anniversary Mint Car, *11*	50	100	____
52583	B&O Capitol Dome Mint Car, *11*	50	100	____
52596	LIRR Mint Car, *12*	50	100	____
58174	Lehigh Valley Map Boxcar, *16*		80	____
58280	REA Christmas Boxcar, *16*		80	____
58523	Blue Comet Mint Car, *13*	35	70	____
58243	Entenmann's Gondola with load, *15*		70	____
58534	Jersey Central Mint Car, *13*	35	70	____
58569	Erie Lackawanna Mint Car, *14*	35	70	____

Midwest Division

			Exc	Mint
_____	4	C&NW F3 Diesel A Unit, shell only, *77*	40	80
_____	5	Midwest Division Covered Quad Hopper, *78*	25	45
_____	1287	C&NW Reefer, *84*		NRS
_____	7600	Frisco "Spirit of '76" N5c Caboose "00003," *76*	20	40
_____	9872	PFE Reefer "00006," *79*	205	410

Midwest Division: Museum Express

			Exc	Mint
_____	9264	ICG Covered Quad Hopper, *78*	10	25
_____	9289	C&NW N5c Caboose, *80*	25	45
_____	9785	Conrail Boxcar, *77*	20	35
_____	9786	C&NW Boxcar, *79*	10	20

NETCA

			Exc	Mint
_____	1203	Boston & Maine NW2 Diesel, shell only, *72*	35	65
_____	5710	Canadian Pacific Reefer, *82*	25	45
_____	5716	Vermont Central Reefer, *83*	15	30
_____	6124	Delaware & Hudson Covered Quad Hopper, *84*	15	30
_____	8051	Hood's Milk Boxcar, *86*	40	75
_____	9181	Boston & Maine N5c Caboose, *77*	20	35
_____	9400	Conrail Boxcar, tuscan or blue, *78*	10	25
_____	9415	Providence & Worcester Boxcar, *79*	20	35
_____	9423	NYNH&H Boxcar, *80*	15	30
_____	9445	Vermont Northern Boxcar, *81*	20	40
_____	9753	Maine Central Boxcar, *75*	20	35
_____	9768	Boston & Maine Boxcar, *76*	20	40
_____	9785	Conrail Boxcar, *78*	10	25
_____	16911	B&M Flatcar with trailer, *95*	75	150
_____	22677	B&M Baked Beans Boxcar, *10*	25	45
_____	52001	B&M Quad Hopper with coal, *92*	40	75
_____	52016	B&M Gondola with coil covers, *93*	35	65
_____	52043	L.L. Bean Boxcar, *94*	105	210
_____	52080	B&M Flatcar "91095" with trailer, *95*	110	215
_____	52111	Ben & Jerry's Flatcar with trailer, *96*	160	315
_____	52212	Berkshire Brewing Reefer, *00*	80	155
_____	52236	Moxie Boxcar, *01*	80	160
_____	52270	Jenney Manufacturing Tank Car, *02*	75	150
_____	52306	NH Flatcar with New England Transportation trailer, *03*	75	150
_____	52352	Poland Spring Boxcar, *04*	65	130
_____	52379	CP Rail with W.B. Mason trailer, *05*	40	75
_____	52383	Fisk Tire Boxcar, *05*	55	110
_____	52397	D&H Flatcar with Vermont Railway trailer, *06*	45	90
_____	52418	Indian Motocycle Boxcar, *06*	95	190
_____	52434	New England Central Flatcar with Cabot's trailer, *07*	50	95
_____	52448	Oilzum Tanker 2-car Set, *08*	55	105

CLUB CARS AND SPECIAL PRODUCTION

		Exc	Mint	
52457	Cape Cod Potato Chip Boxcar, 07	50	95	____
52484A	Cabot's Reefer, 08	125	250	____
52484B	Bay State Beer Reefer, 09	45	90	____
52589	B&M Flatcar with Howard Johnson trailer, 11	50	100	____
58522	Grafton & Upton Flatcar with Spag's trailer, 12	45	90	____

Ozark Division: Gateway Chapter

5700	Oppenheimer Reefer, 81	55	110	____
9068	Reading Bobber Caboose, 76	10	20	____
9601	Illinois Central Gulf Hi-Cube Boxcar, 77	10	20	____
9767	Railbox Boxcar, 78	10	20	____
52003	"Meet Me In St. Louis" Flatcar with trailer, 92	260	520	____

Pacific Northwest Division

52077	Great Northern Hi-Cube Boxcar "9695," 95	230	460	____

Rocky Mountain Division

1971-1976	Rocky Mountain Division Reefer, 76	40	75	____

Sacramento Sierra Chapter

6401	Virginian Bay Window Caboose, 84	20	35	____
9301	U.S. Mail Operating Boxcar, 76	20	40	____
9414	Cotton Belt Boxcar, 80	20	35	____
9427	Bay Line Boxcar, 81	15	30	____
9444	Louisiana Midland Boxcar, 82	20	35	____
9452	Western Pacific Boxcar, 83	20	35	____
9705	D&RGW Boxcar, 75	20	40	____
9723	Western Pacific Boxcar, 73	15	30	____
9726	Erie-Lackawanna Boxcar, 79	10	25	____
9730	CP Rail Boxcar, 77	15	30	____
9785	Conrail Boxcar, 78	10	20	____

Southern Division

1976	FEC F3 Diesel ABA, shells only, 76	140	275	____
1986	Southern Division Bunk Car, 86	15	30	____
6111	L&N Covered Quad Hopper, 83	10	20	____
9287	Southern N5c Caboose, 77	10	20	____
9352	Trailer Train Flatcar with circus trailers, 80	30	55	____
9403	Seaboard Coast Line Boxcar, 78	10	20	____
9405	Chattahoochie Boxcar, 79	10	20	____
9443	Florida East Coast Boxcar, 81	10	25	____
9471	ACL Boxcar, 84	10	25	____
9482	Norfolk & Southern Boxcar, 85	10	25	____
16606	Southern Searchlight Car, 88	10	25	____
19942	Southern Division 30th Anniversary Boxcar, 96	10	20	____

Western Division

			Exc	Mint
____	52275	Western Pacific Boxcar, *03*	55	105

Toy Train Operating Society

TTOS National Convention Cars

			Exc	Mint
____	1984	Sacramento Northern Boxcar, *84*	45	85
____	1985	Snowbird Covered Quad Hopper, *85*	30	55
____	6017	SP-type Caboose, blue, *68*	125	210
____	6017	SP-type Caboose, brown, *69*	200	300
____	6057	SP-type Caboose, orange, *69*	125	210
____	6076	Santa Fe Hopper (O27), *70*	45	85
____	6167-1967	Hopper, olive drab with gold lettering, *67*	45	85
____	6257	SP-type Caboose, red, *69*	125	210
____	6476-1	LV Hopper, gray, *69*	40	75
____	6582	Portland Flatcar with wood, *86*	30	55
____	9326	Burlington Northern Bay Window Caboose, *82*	10	25
____	9347	Niagara Falls 3-D Tank Car, *79*	25	45
____	9355	Delaware & Hudson Bay Window Caboose, *82*	25	50
____	9361	C&NW Bay Window Caboose, *82*	30	55
____	9382	Florida East Coast Bay Window Caboose, *82*	35	70
____	9512	Summerdale Junction Passenger Car, *74*	30	55
____	9520	Phoenix Combination Car, *75*	20	35
____	9526	Snowbird Observation Car, *76*	25	50
____	9535	Columbus Baggage Car, *77*	35	50
____	9678	Hollywood Hi-Cube Boxcar, *78*	15	30
____	9868	Oklahoma City Reefer, *80*	25	45
____	9883	Phoenix Reefer, *83*	25	50
____	17871	NYC Flatcar "81487" with Kodak and Xerox trailers, *87*	110	215
____	17877	MKT 1-D Tank Car "3739469," *89*	35	70
____	17884	Columbus & Dayton Terminal Boxcar (std O), *90*	20	40
____	17889	SP Flatcar "15791" (std O) with trailer, *91*	35	65
____	19963	Union Equity 3-bay ACF Hopper "86892" (std O), *92*	20	40
____	52010	Weyerhaeuser DD Boxcar "838593" (std O), *93*	20	40
____	52029	Ford 1-D Tank Car "12" (O27), *94*	20	40
____	52030	Ford Gondola "4023," *94*	15	30
____	52031	Ford Hopper "1458" (O27), *94*	20	35
____	52057	Western Pacific Boxcar "64641995," *95*	25	50
____	52087	New Mexico Central Boxcar "64641996," *96*	30	55
____	52114	NYC Flatcar with Gleason and SASIB trailers, *97*	30	60
____	52149	Conrail Flatcar with Blum coal shovel, *98*	30	60
____	52192	SP Crane and Gondola Set, *00*	40	75

CLUB CARS AND SPECIAL PRODUCTION

		Exc	Mint	
52193	SP Gondola "6060," 00	25	50	____
52194	SP Crane Car "7111," 00	20	35	____
52231	British Columbia 1-D Tank Car, 01	10	25	____
52253	San Pedro Boxcar, 02	20	35	____
52288	D&RGW Cookie Boxcar, 03	10	20	____
52293	D&RGW 1-D Tank Car, 03	20	40	____
52351	BNSF Icicle Reefer with ETD, 04	30	60	____
52378	Las Vegas & Tonopah Boxcar, 05	35	70	____
52410	SP Flatcar with 2 trailers, 06	35	70	____
52441	Pennsylvania Operating Hopper, 07	30	60	____
52445	Pennsylvania Boxcar, 07	35	70	____
52545	Erie "6464" Boxcar, 09	25	50	____
58257	50th Anniversary Mint Car, 16		65	____
58333	Sierra Railroad Sierra Beer Boxcar, 13	35	70	____
58535	Smokey Bear Gondola, 15		55	____

TTOS Division Cars

		Exc	Mint	
52009	Sacramento Valley Division WP Boxcar, 93	25	45	____
52040	Wolverine Division GTW Flatcar with tractor and trailer, 94	25	50	____
52058	Central California Division Santa Fe Boxcar, 95	20	40	____
52086	Canadian Division Pacific Great Eastern Boxcar, 96	25	50	____
52113	Northeastern Division Genesee & Wyoming 3-bay Hopper, 97	20	35	____
52264	New Mexico Division Durango & Silverton Operating Hopper, 02	30	55	____

Other TTOS Production

		Exc	Mint	
1983	Phoenix 3-D Tank Car, 83	50	100	____
17894	Southern Pacific Tractor, 91	10	20	____
27148	BNSF "4427" PS2 Hopper, 06	25	50	____
52021	Weyerhaeuser Tractor and Trailer, 93	15	30	____
52022	Union Pacific Boxcar, 93	200	400	____
52032	Ford 1-D Tank Car (027) with Kughn inscription, 94	50	95	____
52046	ACL Boxcar "16247," 94	55	110	____
52053	Carail Boxcar, 94	30	55	____
52068	Toy Train Parade Contadina Boxcar "16245," 94	30	55	____
52078	Southern Pacific SD9 Diesel "5366," 96	120	235	____
52079	Southern Pacific Bay Window Caboose, 96	30	55	____
52084	Union Pacific I-Beam Flatcar "16380" with load, 95	80	155	____
52384	Transparent Damage Control Boxcar, 03	35	70	____
52451	Pennsylvania "X2454" Boxcar, 07	90	175	____

CLUB CARS AND SPECIAL PRODUCTION

			Exc	Mint
	52505	Forest Service/Smokey Bear Flatcar with airplane, 08	25	45
	52525	SP "X6454" Boxcar, 08	25	50
	52526	SP "X6454" Boxcar, 08	45	90
	52547	C&NW Reefer, 09	45	85

TTOS Southwestern Division

			Exc	Mint
	19962	Southern Pacific 3-bay ACF Hopper "496035" (std O), 92	35	65
	52047	Cotton Belt Wood-sided Caboose (std O), smoke, 93–94	35	70
	52073	Pacific Fruit Express Reefer "459402" (std O), 95	30	65
	52098	National Bureau of Standards Boxcar (std O), 96	20	45
	52121	Mobilgas Tank Car "238" (std O), 97	40	75
	52154	Pacific Fruit Express Reefer "459403" (std O), 98	25	55
	52205	SP Overnight Merchandise Service Boxcar 5-pack, 00	95	185
	52287	Operating MX Missile Car, 02	30	55
	52385	Ward Kimball Boxcar, 05	30	55
	52431	Operating MX Missile Car, 06	30	60
	52476	Life Savers Tank Car, 07	45	85
	52515	Life Savers Wild Cherry Tank Car, 08	40	75
	52565	Life Savers Pep O Mint Tank Car, 09	30	60
	52569	Life Savers Butter Rum Tank Car, 10	30	60
	52591	Life Savers Wint O Green Tank Car, 11	30	60
	58208	Life Savers Peppermint Tank Car, 14		60
	58548	Life Savers Bay Window Caboose, 13	40	80

Virginia Train Collectors

			Exc	Mint
	7679	Boxcar, 79	5	15
	7681	N5c Caboose, 81	10	25
	7682	Covered Quad Hopper, 82	10	25
	7683	Virginia Fruit Express Reefer, 83	10	25
	7684	Vitraco 3-D Tank Car, 84	10	25
	7685	Boxcar, 85	10	25
	7686	GP7 Diesel, 86	50	100
	7692-1	Baggage Car (027), 92	25	45
	7692-2	Combination Car (027), 92	25	45
	7692-3	Dining Car (027), 92	25	45
	7692-4	Passenger Car (027), 92	25	45
	7692-5	Vista Dome Car (027), 92	25	45
	7692-6	Passenger Car (027), 92	25	45
	7692-7	Observation Car (027), 92	25	45
	7696	20th Anniversary Station, 96	35	65
	52060	Tender "7694" with whistle, 94	35	70

Section 6
BOXES

For more information on determining the condition of a box and a description of box types, see pages 8 and 9.

		Good (P-5)	Exc (P-7)
022	Switch Controller	1	7 ____
022	Remote Control Switches, pair (with both inserts)	6	18 ____
022	Remote Control Switches, pair (yellow, with both inserts)	10	27 ____
022A	Remote Control Switches, pair (with both inserts)	14	40 ____
25	Bumper	4	7 ____
26	Bumper	3	6 ____
30	Water Tower	19	46 ____
35	Boulevard Lamp	5	14 ____
37	Uncoupling Track Set	4	10 ____
38	Operating Water Tower	24	100 ____
40	Hookup Wire, 8 reels (dealer box)	33	145 ____
41	U.S. Army Switcher	10	61 ____
42	Manual Switches	5	20 ____
42	Picatinny Arsenal Switcher	25	71 ____
44	U.S. Army Mobile Launcher	38	98 ____
44	U.S. Army Mobile Launcher (with orange sleeve)	30	120 ____
45	U.S. Marines Mobile Launcher	45	120 ____
45/45N	Automatic Gateman	7	26 ____
48	Super O Insulated Straight Track, 6 pieces (dealer box)	15	48 ____
49	Super O Insulated Curved Track, 6 pieces (dealer box)	15	43 ____
50	Section Gang Car (early classic)	13	47 ____
50	Section Gang Car (brown corrugated)	5	20 ____
50	Section Gang Car (orange picture)	20	45 ____
51	Navy Yard Switcher	29	64 ____
52	Fire Car	36	81 ____
53	Rio Grande Snowplow	34	86 ____
54	Ballast Tamper	15	41 ____
55	PRR Tie-Jector Car	15	41 ____
56	Lamp Post	6	18 ____
56	M&StL Mine Transport	38	130 ____
57	AEC Switcher	77	249 ____
58	Lamp Post	8	24 ____
58	Great Northern Rotary Snow Blower	95	235 ____
59	Minuteman Switcher	90	265 ____

BOXES		Good (P-5)	Exc (P-7)
_____ 60	Lionelville Rapid Transit Trolley (classic)	13	43
_____ 60	Lionelville Rapid Transit Trolley (brown corrugated)	15	38
_____ 64	Street Lamp	2	17
_____ 65	Handcar	10	78
_____ 68	Executive Inspection Car	17	98
_____ 69	Maintenance Car	20	77
_____ 70	Yard Light	4	15
_____ 71	Lamp Post	3	9
_____ 75	Goose Neck Lamps	3	15
_____ 76	Boulevard Street Lamps	5	35
_____ 76	Boulevard Street Lamps (Hillside Checkerboard)	10	70
_____ 89	Flagpole	7	27
_____ 93	Water Tower	17	36
_____ 97	Coal Elevator	17	69
_____ 108	Trestle Set (ovestamped)	10	40
_____ 110	Graduated Trestle Set	1	7
_____ 111	Elevated Trestle Set	5	17
_____ 112	Remote Control Switches, pair (Super O)	10	25
_____ 112LH	Remote Control Super O Switch, left-hand	10	26
_____ 112RH	Remote Control Super O Switch, right-hand	8	21
_____ 114	Newsstand with horn	11	33
_____ 115	Passenger Station (113-1, Star Corp. stamped on box)	34	140
_____ 118	Newsstand with whistle	10	37
_____ 122	Lamp Assortment	35	100
_____ 123	Lamp Assortment	10	100
_____ 125	Whistle Shack	5	23
_____ 128	Animated Newsstand	18	37
_____ 132	Passenger Station	12	37
_____ 133	Passenger Station	10	30
_____ 138	Water Tower	5	40
_____ 140	Automatic Banjo Signal (classic)	3	12
_____ 142	Manual Switches, pair (Super O)	4	17
_____ 145	Automatic Gateman (brown corrugated)	6	22
_____ 145	Automatic Gateman (cellophane), 66	12	59
_____ 148	Dwarf Trackside Signal	5	22
_____ 150	Telegraph Pole Set	4	20
_____ 151	Automatic Semaphore	4	11
_____ 151	Automatic Semaphore (narrower box, earlier postwar)	22	48
_____ 151	Automatic Semaphore (blister pack enclosure)	20	75
_____ 152	Automatic Crossing Gate	3	15
_____ 153	Automatic Block Control Signal	7	22
_____ 154	Automatic Highway Signal (cellophane)	5	25

BOXES

		Good (P-5)	Exc (P-7)	
154	Automatic Highway Signal (all other boxes)	3	11	___
155	Blinking Light Signal	8	48	___
156	Station Platform	17	53	___
157	Station Platform	9	35	___
160	Unloading Bin	22	125	___
161	Mail Pickup Set (with liner)	10	45	___
163	Single Target Block Signal (white box)	20	65	___
164	Log Loader	25	62	___
167	Whistle Controller	5	15	___
175	Rocket Launcher	24	57	___
175-50	Dealer Display Box, 6 rockets	75	436	___
182	Magnetic Crane	20	69	___
192	Operating Control Tower	35	143	___
193	Industrial Water Tower	9	56	___
195	Floodlight Tower	5	25	___
195-75	Floodlight Extension, 8-bulb (classic)	4	54	___
195-75	Floodlight Extension, 8-bulb (white box)	6	60	___
197	Rotating Radar Antenna	8	50	___
197-15	Separate Sale Radar Head	30	115	___
199	Microwave Relay Tower	5	35	___
202	UP Alco Diesel A Unit	11	55	___
204	Santa Fe Alco AA Set (master carton)	89	215	___
204	Santa Fe Alco AA Set (P and T boxes)	19	82	___
204P	Santa Fe A Unit	20	50	___
204T	Santa Fe Diesel Dummy A Unit	23	53	___
208	Santa Fe Alco AA Set (master carton)	53	308	___
208	Santa Fe Alco AA Set (P and T boxes)	21	106	___
208P	Santa Fe Alco A Unit	18	35	___
208T	Santa Fe Alco Dummy A Unit	45	90	___
209	New Haven Alco AA Set (master carton)	70	343	___
209	New Haven Alco AA Set (P and T boxes)	50	321	___
209T	New Haven Diesel Dummy A Unit	45	135	___
210	Texas Special Alco AA Set (P and T boxes)	9	50	___
210P	Texas Special Alco A Unit	9	25	___
210T	Texas Special Alco Dummy A Unit	19	40	___
211	Texas Special Alco AA Set (P and T boxes)	29	144	___
211P	Texas Special Alco A Unit (brown corrugated)	20	70	___
212	USMC Alco Diesel A Unit	33	80	___
212T	USMC Diesel Dummy A Unit	136	459	___
214	Plate Girder Bridge (classic)	3	13	___
214	Plate Girder Bridge (Hillside orange picture)	9	34	___
216	Burlington Alco Diesel A Unit	15	60	___
217	B&M Alco AB Set (C and P boxes)	32	148	___
217P	B&M Alco A Unit	18	44	___
217-16	Sleeve for 217 and 218 outer boxes	40	85	___

BOXES

		Good (P-5)	Exc (P-7)
_____ 218	Santa Fe Alco AA Set (master carton)	19	110
_____ 218P	Santa Fe Alco Diesel A Unit	20	52
_____ 218T	Santa Fe Diesel Dummy A Unit	15	55
_____ 220	Santa Fe Alco AA Set (P and T boxes)	17	101
_____ 221	2-6-4 Locomotive	15	60
_____ 221T	Tender	10	20
_____ 221W	Whistling Tender	8	36
_____ 223P	Santa Fe Alco A Unit	15	60
_____ 224	2-6-2 Locomotive	17	52
_____ 224	U.S. Navy Alco AB Set (C and P boxes)	26	128
_____ 224P	U.S. Navy Alco A unit	45	275
_____ 225	C & O Alco Diesel A Unit	12	50
_____ 226	B&M Alco Diesel AB Set (C and P boxes)	24	100
_____ 226P	B&M Alco Diesel A Unit	8	47
_____ 228P	CN Alco Diesel A Unit	20	65
_____ 229C	M&StL Alco B Unit	8	35
_____ 229P	M&StL Alco A Unit (brown corrugated)	8	45
_____ 230P	C&O Alco A Unit	14	64
_____ 231P	Rock Island Alco A Unit	8	46
_____ 233	2-4-2 Scout Locomotive	10	40
_____ 234W	Whistle Tender	20	40
_____ 235	2-4-2 Scout Locomotive	26	89
_____ 237	2-4-2 Scout Locomotive	10	39
_____ 243	2-4-2 Scout Locomotive	10	33
_____ 243W	Tender	5	20
_____ 244T	Tender (overstamped 1625T box)	20	83
_____ 245	2-4-2 Scout Locomotive	15	75
_____ 246	2-4-2 Scout Locomotive	13	43
_____ 247	2-4-2 Scout Locomotive	13	35
_____ 247T	Tender	5	20
_____ 248	2-4-2 Scout Locomotive	9	35
_____ 249	2-4-2 Scout Locomotive	20	50
_____ 250	2-4-2 Scout Locomotive	10	30
_____ 250T	Tender	7	28
_____ 252	Crossing Gate	3	9
_____ 253	Block Control Signal	6	18
_____ 256	Illuminated Freight Station	13	40
_____ 257	Freight Station with diesel horn	10	32
_____ 260	Bumper (Hagerstown checkerboard)	6	26
_____ 260	Bumper (all other boxes)	3	6
_____ 262	Highway Crossing Gate	4	28
_____ 264	Operating Forklift Platform	24	72
_____ 282	Portal Gantry Crane	23	96
_____ 299	Code Transmitter Beacon Set	10	63
_____ 308	Railroad Sign Set	2	13

BOXES

		Good (P-5)	Exc (P-7)
309	Yard Sign Set	2	10 ____
310	Billboard Set	1	7 ____
313	Bascule Bridge	35	133 ____
314	Scale Model Girder Bridge	3	13 ____
315	Illuminated Trestle Bridge	29	110 ____
316	Trestle Bridge	5	15 ____
317	Trestle Bridge	9	32 ____
321	Trestle Bridge	5	14 ____
321-100	Trestle Bridge	7	20 ____
332	Arch-Under Trestle Bridge	4	17 ____
334	Operating Dispatching Board	10	40 ____
342	Culvert Loader	21	54 ____
345	Culvert Unloader	20	62 ____
350	Engine Transfer Table	10	58 ____
350-50	Transfer Table Extension	13	57 ____
352	Ice Depot	22	55 ____
353	Trackside Control Signal	3	15 ____
356	Operating Freight Station	8	39 ____
356-35	Baggage Trucks Set	10	46 ____
362	Barrel Loader	5	24 ____
362-78	Wooden Barrels	1	8 ____
364	Conveyor Lumber Loader	7	24 ____
365	Dispatching Station	13	42 ____
375	Turntable	36	93 ____
394	Rotary Beacon	8	25 ____
394-37	Rotating Beacon Cap	2	10 ____
395	Floodlight Tower	12	35 ____
397	Operating Coal Loader	7	43 ____
397	Operating Coal Loader (separate label on box)	10	35 ____
400	B&O Passenger Rail Diesel Car	31	57 ____
404	B&O Baggage-Mail Rail Diesel Car	39	97 ____
410	Billboard Blinker	3	10 ____
413	Countdown Control Panel	6	20 ____
415	Diesel Fueling Station	16	46 ____
419	Heliport Control Tower	22	133 ____
443	Missile Launching Platform	10	33 ____
445	Switch Tower	6	22 ____
448	Missile Firing Range Set	15	55 ____
450	Operating Signal Bridge	2	25 ____
452	Overhead Gantry Signal	5	33 ____
455	Operating Oil Derrick	17	74 ____
456	Coal Ramp	18	49 ____
460	Piggyback Transportation Set	16	40 ____
460-150	Two Trailers	71	224 ____
461	Platform with truck and trailer	10	50 ____

BOXES

		Good (P-5)	Exc (P-7)
_____ 462	Derrick Platform Set	55	188
_____ 464	Lumber Mill	5	46
_____ 465	Sound Dispatching Station	15	34
_____ 470	Missile Launching Platform	5	40
_____ 494	Rotary Beacon (classic)	5	24
_____ 497	Coaling Station	27	72
_____ 600	MKT NW2 Switcher	19	82
_____ 601	Seaboard NW2 Switcher	23	87
_____ 602	Seaboard NW2 Switcher	30	81
_____ 610	Erie NW2 Switcher	15	82
_____ 611	Jersey Central NW2 Switcher (overstamped 621 box)	50	124
_____ 613	UP NW2 Switcher	22	105
_____ 614	Alaska NW2 Switcher	29	124
_____ 616	Santa Fe NW2 Switcher	25	105
_____ 617	Santa Fe NW2 Switcher	30	133
_____ 621	Jersey Central NW2 Switcher	27	67
_____ 622	Santa Fe NW2 Switcher	44	100
_____ 623	Santa Fe NW2 Switcher	19	72
_____ 624	C&O NW2 Switcher	26	71
_____ 626	B&O GE 44-ton Switcher	42	150
_____ 628	Northern Pacific GE 44-ton Switcher	20	79
_____ 629	Burlington GE 44-ton Switcher	28	189
_____ 634	Santa Fe NW2 Switcher	26	130
_____ 637	2-6-4 Locomotive	14	59
_____ 637LTS	2-6-4 Locomotive and Tender (master carton)	40	188
_____ 646	4-6-4 Locomotive	29	65
_____ 665	4-6-4 Locomotive	19	52
_____ 671	6-8-6 Steam Turbine Locomotive	47	129
_____ 671-75	Smoke Lamp, 12 volt	3	10
_____ 671R	6-8-6 Steam Turbine Locomotive	37	165
_____ 671W	Whistle Tender	14	48
_____ 675	2-6-2 Locomotive (classic), *47–49*	20	75
_____ 675	2-6-2 Locomotive (brown corrugated), *52*	44	100
_____ 681	6-8-6 Steam Turbine Locomotive	25	119
_____ 681LTS	6-8-6 Steam Turbine Locomotive and Tender (master carton)	150	500
_____ 682	6-8-6 Steam Turbine Locomotive	58	139
_____ 682LTS	6-8-6 Steam Turbine Locomotive and Tender (master carton)	400	850
_____ 685	4-6-4 Hudson Locomotive	28	72
_____ 685LTS	4-6-4 Hudson Locomotive and Tender (master carton)	185	450
_____ 726	2-8-4 Berkshire Locomotive, *46*	63	184
_____ 726	2-8-4 Berkshire Locomotive (after 1946)	40	150
_____ 726RR	2-8-4 Berkshire Locomotive	23	67

BOXES

		Good (P-5)	Exc (P-7)
736	2-8-4 Berkshire Locomotive, *50*	47	106 ____
736	2-8-4 Berkshire Locomotive	28	77 ____
736X	2-8-4 Berkshire Locomotive	35	130 ____
736LTS	2-8-4 Berkshire Locomotive and Tender (master carton)	47	235 ____
736W	Pennsylvania Tender	10	65 ____
746	N&W 4-8-4 Locomotive	67	148 ____
746LTS	N&W 4-8-4 Locomotive and Tender (master carton)	90	389 ____
746W	N&W Whistle Tender	30	104 ____
746WX	N&W Whistle Tender, long stripe	60	135 ____
760	Curved Track	10	36 ____
773	4-6-4 Hudson Locomotive, *50*	109	286 ____
773	4-6-4 Hudson Locomotive, *64–66*	63	169 ____
773LTS	4-6-4 Hudson Locomotive and Tender (master carton), *50*	100	533 ____
773LTS	4-6-4 Hudson and Whistle Tender (master carton), *64–66*	65	334 ____
773W	NYC Tender	19	89 ____
810	Milwaukee Road Freight Set	75	450 ____
920-2	Tunnel Portals	7	20 ____
927	Lubricating Kit	2	9 ____
928	Maintenance and Lubricating Kit	5	25 ____
943	Ammo Dump	3	10 ____
951	Farm Set	15	45 ____
952	Figure Set	15	35 ____
953	Figure Set	10	50 ____
957	Figure Set	24	55 ____
959	Barn Set	16	52 ____
963	Frontier Set	15	50 ____
965	Farm Set	15	55 ____
966	Firehouse Set	15	55 ____
969	Construction Set	5	45 ____
970	Ticket Booth	7	35 ____
981	Freight Yard Set	12	35 ____
983	Farm Set	16	43 ____
984	Railroad Set	10	75 ____
986	Farm Set	18	115 ____
1000W	Steam Freight Set	49	95 ____
1001	Diesel Freight Set	20	65 ____
1001	2-4-2 Scout Locomotive	8	45 ____
1001T	Tender	6	12 ____
1002	Gondola	2	8 ____
X1004	PRR Baby Ruth Boxcar	2	8 ____
1005	Sunoco 1-D Tank Car	2	8 ____
1007	Sunoco 1-D Tank Car	2	8 ____

BOXES

			Good (P-5)	Exc (P-7)
____	1009	Manumatic Track Section	15	50
____	1025	Illuminated Bumper (027)	3	10
____	1032	Transformer, 75 watts	2	8
____	1033	Transformer, 90 watts	5	17
____	1034	Transformer, 75 watts	2	8
____	1041	Transformer, 60 watts	10	25
____	1043	Transformer, 50 watts	5	15
____	1041	Transformer, 50 watts	3	15
____	1043-500	Transformer, 90 watts, ivory	15	75
____	1044	Transformer, 90 watts	2	10
____	1045	Operating Watchman	5	26
____	1047	Operating Switchman	42	120
____	1060	2-4-2 Locomotive (brown corrugated)	24	112
____	1110	2-4-2 Locomotive	5	20
____	1112	Scout Set	8	25
____	1120	2-4-2 Scout Locomotive	5	20
____	1121	027 Remote Control Switches, pair	4	11
____	1121LH	027 Remote Control Switch, left-hand	5	18
____	1121RH	027 Remote Control Switch, right-hand	5	18
____	1122	027 Remote Control Switches, pair	5	14
____	1130	2-4-2 Locomotive	6	25
____	1130T	Tender (classic)	3	16
____	1130T	Tender (orange perforated)	23	47
____	1130T-500	Tender, pink, from Girls Set	27	180
____	1232	Transformer, 75 watts, made for export	4	15
____	1407B	Steam Switcher Work Set	45	310
____	1417WS	Steam Work Train Set	50	145
____	1423W	Steam Freight Set	28	129
____	1425B	Steam Switcher Freight Set	70	212
____	1429WS	Steam Freight Set	58	150
____	1432W	027 Steam Passenger Set	80	233
____	1447WS	Turbine Locomotive Set	33	150
____	1451WS	027 Steam Freight Set	50	110
____	1453WS	027 Steam Freight Set	28	83
____	1455WS	Steam Freight Set	25	70
____	1457B	Santa Fe Freight Set (marked "1457"), *49*	83	193
____	1457B	Santa Fe Freight Set, *50*	78	198
____	1459WS	Steam Freight Set	50	95
____	1464W	Union Pacific Diesel Passenger Set	125	367
____	1465	Steam Freight Set	23	76
____	1467W	Union Pacific Freight Set	33	144
____	1469WS	Steam Freight Set	25	70
____	1471	Steam Freight Set	25	70
____	1471WS	Steam Freight Set	20	53
____	1475	Steam Freight Set	15	40

BOXES		Good (P-5)	Exc (P-7)	
1479WS	Steam Freight Set	10	54	___
1481WS	Steam Freight Set	30	80	___
1483WS	Steam Freight Set	35	113	___
1485WS	Steam Freight Set	27	65	___
1500	Steam Freight Set	15	40	___
1502WS	Steam Freight Set	250	600	___
1503WS	Steam Freight Set	31	67	___
1505WS	Steam Freight Set	46	90	___
1507WS	Steam Freight Set	37	93	___
1511S	Steam Freight Set	25	60	___
1513S	Steam Freight Set	35	115	___
1515WS	Steam Freight Set	42	119	___
1517W	Texas Special Freight Set	35	181	___
1519WS	Steam Freight Set	50	170	___
1520W	Texas Special Passenger Set	195	675	___
1521WS	Steam Work Train Set	77	380	___
1523	Diesel Freight Set	65	155	___
1525	Diesel Freight Set	45	80	___
1527	027 Steam Work Train Set	40	175	___
1529	Pennsylvania Diesel Freight Set	88	250	___
1531W	Diesel Freight Set	30	82	___
1533WS	Steam Freight Set	35	65	___
1534W	Burlington Diesel Passenger Set	183	461	___
1535W	Diesel Freight Set	125	300	___
1537WS	Steam Freight Set	35	50	___
1538WS	Hudson Passenger Set	155	775	___
1539W	Santa Fe Diesel Freight Set	88	250	___
1542	Electric Freight Set	10	38	___
1543	Lehigh Valley Freight Set	9	41	___
1549	Steam Work Train Set	45	95	___
1551W	Diesel Freight Set	10	55	___
1553W	Diesel Freight Set	35	60	___
1555WS	027 Steam Freight Set	25	75	___
1557	Diesel Freight Set	30	88	___
1559W	MILW Diesel Freight Set	35	90	___
1569	UP Diesel Freight Set	35	55	___
1571	LV Diesel Freight Set	35	65	___
1573	Steam Freight Set	40	75	___
1578S	Steam Passenger Set	200	513	___
1581	Jersey Central Mixed Set	35	75	___
1583WS	Steam Freight Set	35	70	___
1587S	Girls Train Set	430	1263	___
1589WS	027 Steam Freight Set	45	180	___
1590	Steam Freight Set	33	60	___
1591	USMC Military Set	109	691	___

BOXES

			Good (P-5)	Exc (P-7)
____	1593	UP Diesel Work Train Set	35	80
____	1599W	Texas Special Freight Set	44	108
____	1600	Diesel Passenger Set	220	610
____	1601W	Wabash GP7 Diesel Set	43	310
____	1607WS	Steam Work Train Set	18	40
____	1608W	New Haven Passenger Set	76	559
____	1611	027 Alaska Diesel Freight Set	100	220
____	1612	027 General Set	40	125
____	1613S	Steam Freight Set	35	110
____	1615	B&M Diesel Freight Set	20	50
____	1615	0-4-0 Locomotive	15	46
____	1615LTS	0-4-0 Locomotive and Tender (master carton)	23	121
____	1615T	Tender	7	50
____	1619W	Santa Fe Diesel Freight Set	50	125
____	1621WS	027 Steam Freight Set	40	125
____	1623W	NP Diesel Freight Set	50	165
____	1625	0-4-0 Locomotive	23	109
____	1625T	Tender	13	108
____	1625WS	Steam Freight Set	41	140
____	1631WS	027 Steam Freight Set	25	75
____	1633	U.S. Navy Diesel Freight Set	120	353
____	1640-100	Presidential Kit	22	55
____	1643	C&O Diesel Freight Set	20	55
____	1648	Steam Freight Set	5	20
____	1650	Steam Military Set	43	85
____	1651	Passenger Train Set	40	95
____	1654	2-4-2 Locomotive	5	28
____	1655	2-4-2 Locomotive	10	40
____	1656	0-4-0 Locomotive	26	120
____	1656LTS	4-4-0 Locomotive and Tender (master carton)	50	225
____	1665	0-4-0 Locomotive	25	192
____	1666	2-6-2 Locomotive	20	45
____	1682T	Tender	5	18
____	1800	General Gift Pack	15	110
____	1809	Western Gift Pack	8	60
____	1862	4-4-0 Civil War General Locomotive	25	88
____	1862T	Tender	15	60
____	1865	Western & Atlantic Coach	8	46
____	1866	Western & Atlantic Mail-Baggage Car	10	45
____	1872	4-4-0 Civil War General Locomotive	35	100
____	1872LTS	4-4-0 Locomotive and Tender (master carton)	115	400
____	1872T	Tender	8	41
____	1875	Western & Atlantic Coach	38	176
____	1875W	Western & Atlantic Coach, whistle	15	91
____	1876	Western & Atlantic Baggage Car	13	70

BOXES

		Good (P-5)	Exc (P-7)	
1877	Flatcar with fence and horses	5	40	___
2001	Track Make-up Kit (O27)	800	2000	___
2002	Track Make-up Kit (O27)	700	1600	___
2016	2-6-4 Locomotive	4	30	___
2018	2-6-4 Locomotive	6	33	___
2020	6-8-6 Steam Turbine Locomotive	22	66	___
2020W	Tender	11	63	___
2023	Union Pacific Alco AA Set (master carton), *50*	35	97	___
2025	2-6-2 or 2-6-4 Locomotive	13	50	___
2026	2-6-2 or 2-6-4 Locomotive	10	60	___
2028	Pennsylvania GP7 Diesel	30	68	___
2029	2-6-4 Locomotive	12	53	___
2031	Rock Island Alco AA Set (master carton), *52*	70	144	___
2032	Erie Alco AA Set (master carton)	33	97	___
2033	Uinion Pacific Alco AA Set (master carton)	38	80	___
2034	2-4-2 Scout Locomotive	6	53	___
2035	2-6-4 Locomotive	19	85	___
2036	2-6-4 Locomotive	9	58	___
2036LTS	2-6-4 Locomotive and Tender (master carton)	450	1238	___
2037	2-6-4 Locomotive (brown corrugated)	9	33	___
2037-500	2-6-4 Locomotive, pink, from Girls Set	54	250	___
2046	4-6-4 Locomotive	29	72	___
2046LTS	4-6-4 Locomotive and Tender (master carton)	125	275	___
2046T	Lionel Lines Tender, for export	23	77	___
2046W	Lionel Lines Tender (early classic, with liner)	23	44	___
2046W	Lionel Lines Tender (marked "2046")	15	87	___
2046W-50	Pennsylvania Tender	10	49	___
2055	4-6-4 Locomotive	25	74	___
2055LTS	4-6-4 Locomotive and Tender (master carton)	55	269	___
2056	4-6-4 Locomotive	20	50	___
2065	4-6-4 Locomotive	15	44	___
2113WS	Steam Freight Set	21	213	___
2121WS	Steam Freight Set	45	255	___
2124W	GG1 Passenger Set	73	1785	___
2126WS	Steam Turbine Passenger Set	60	968	___
2139	GG1 Freight Set	113	1023	___
2140WS	Steam Turbine Passenger Set	60	848	___
2141WS	Steam Turbine Freight Set	55	180	___
2146W	Berkshire Passenger Set	75	255	___
2148WS	Hudson Passenger Set	232	2025	___
2149	Santa Fe Diesel Freight Set	105	435	___
2151W	F3 Freight Set	160	280	___
2153WS	Steam Freight Set	60	195	___
2155WS	Berkshire Freight Set	25	150	___
2159W	GG1 Freight Set	193	650	___

BOXES

		Good (P-5)	Exc (P-7)
_____ 2161W	Santa Fe Twin Diesel Freight Set	49	160
_____ 2163WS	Steam Freight Set	45	190
_____ 2167WS	Steam Freight Set	40	160
_____ 2175W	Santa Fe Diesel Freight Set	47	144
_____ 2177WS	Steam Freight Set	15	64
_____ 2183WS	Steam Freight Set	25	90
_____ 2187WS	Steam Freight Set	30	60
_____ 2190W	Santa Fe Diesel Passenger Set	30	80
_____ 2191W	Santa Fe Diesel Freight Set	35	150
_____ 2193W	NYC Diesel Freight Set	54	93
_____ 2201WS	Steam Freight Set	50	90
_____ 2203WS	Steam Freight Set	74	330
_____ 2205WS	Steam Freight Set	25	75
_____ 2207W	Santa Fe Diesel Freight Set	38	152
_____ 2209W	NYC Diesel Freight Set	40	80
_____ 2211WS	Steam Freight Set	30	75
_____ 2213WS	Steam Freight Set	35	70
_____ 2217WS	Steam Turbine Freight Set	87	173
_____ 2219WS	Diesel Freight Set	125	425
_____ 2221WS	Steam Freight Set	36	88
_____ 2222WS	Hudson Passenger Set	109	772
_____ 2223W	Lackawanna FM Freight Set	315	588
_____ 2225WS	Steam Freight Set	30	185
_____ 2226W	Tender	40	115
_____ 2226WX	Lionel Lines Tender	60	130
_____ 2227W	Santa Fe Diesel Freight Set	100	328
_____ 2234W	Santa Fe Passenger Set	67	365
_____ 2235W	Milwaukee Road Diesel Freight Set	60	175
_____ 2237WS	Steam Freight Set	60	170
_____ 2239W	Illinois Central Freight Set	150	375
_____ 2240	Wabash F3 AB Set (C and P boxes)	47	310
_____ 2240	Wabash F3 AB Set (master carton)	88	875
_____ 2240P	Wabash F3 A Unit	43	113
_____ 2242	New Haven F3 AB Set (C and P boxes)	60	575
_____ 2242	New Haven F3 AB Set (master carton)	300	1025
_____ 2242C	New Haven F3 B Unit	105	390
_____ 2242P	New Haven F3 A Unit	225	500
_____ 2243	Santa Fe F3 AB Set (C and P boxes)	24	105
_____ 2243	Santa Fe F3 AB Set (master carton)	50	126
_____ 2243P	Santa Fe F3 A Unit	31	110
_____ 2243W	Diesel Freight Set	30	85
_____ 2244W	Wabash Passenger Set	250	1053
_____ 2245	Texas Special F3 AB Set (C and P boxes)	33	255
_____ 2245	Texas Special F3 AB Set (master carton)	300	800
_____ 2245C	Texas Special F3 B Unit	40	122

BOXES

		Good (P-5)	Exc (P-7)	
2245P	Texas Special F3 A Unit	20	68	___
2247W	Wabash F3 Diesel Freight Set	80	280	___
2254W	Pennsylvania GG1 Passenger Set, *55*	203	1231	___
2255W	Diesel Work Train Set	34	169	___
2257	SP-type Caboose	4	16	___
2257WS	Steam Freight Set	28	93	___
2259W	New Haven Electric Freight Set	40	195	___
2263W	New Haven Freight Set	40	210	___
2265WS	Steam Freight Set	27	134	___
2267W	Diesel Freight Set	68	250	___
2269W	B&O Diesel Freight Set	95	712	___
2270W	Jersey Central Passenger Set	149	1095	___
2271W	Pennsylvania GG1 Freight Set	23	385	___
2273W	Milwaukee Road Diesel Freight Set	93	795	___
2274W	Pennsylvania Passenger Set	230	675	___
2276W	Budd Passenger Set	25	318	___
2277WS	Work Train Set	20	170	___
2283W	Steam Freight Set	20	125	___
2289WS	Berkshire Super O Freight Set	46	206	___
2291W	Rio Grande Diesel Freight Set	129	594	___
2292WS	Steam Passenger Set	83	979	___
2293W	Pennsylvania GG1 Freight Set	167	1035	___
2295WS	N&W Steam Freight Set	154	1038	___
2296W	Canadian Pacific Passenger Set	258	1629	___
2297WS	N&W Steam Freight Set	88	575	___
2321	Lackawanna FM Train Master Diesel	45	94	___
2322	Virginian FM Train Master Diesel	30	115	___
2328	Burlington GP7 Diesel	27	71	___
2329	Virginian Electric Locomotive	37	215	___
2330	Pennsylvania GG1 Electric Locomotive	47	274	___
2331	Virginian FM Train Master Diesel	34	115	___
2332	Pennsylvania GG1 Electric Locomotive	30	102	___
2332-275	Pennsylvania GG1 Electric Locomotive	100	278	___
2333	NYC F3 AA Set (master carton)	45	122	___
2333	NYC F3 AA Set (P and T boxes)	40	205	___
2333P	NYC F3 A Unit (brown corrugated)	20	75	___
2333	Santa Fe F3 AA Set (master carton)	65	185	___
2333	Santa Fe F3 AA Set (P and T boxes)	35	95	___
2333P	Santa Fe F3 A Unit	13	68	___
2337	Wabash GP7 Diesel, *58*	28	203	___
2338	MILW GP7 Diesel (classic)	13	77	___
2338	MILW GP7 Diesel (brown corrugated)	10	68	___
2338	MILW GP7 Diesel (brown corrugated marked "2338X")	29	103	___
2339	Wabash GP7 Diesel, *57*	21	137	___
2340-10	Pennsylvania GG1 Electric, tuscan	57	205	___

BOXES

			Good (P-5)	Exc (P-7)
____	2340-25	Pennsylvania GG1 Electric, green, gold stripes	31	135
____	2341	Jersey Central FM Train Master Diesel	192	881
____	2343	Santa Fe F3 AA Set (master carton)	54	114
____	2343	Santa Fe F3 AA Set (P and T boxes)	40	155
____	2343C	Santa Fe F3 B Unit	23	71
____	2343P	Santa Fe F3 A Unit	22	57
____	2343T	Santa Fe F3 Dummy Unit	25	60
____	2344	NYC F3 AA Set (master carton)	77	168
____	2344	NYC F3 AA Set (P and T boxes)	60	195
____	2344C	NYC F3 B Unit	37	75
____	2344P	NYC F3 A Unit	65	228
____	2344T	NYC F3 Dummy Unit	33	166
____	2345	Western Pacific F3 AA Set (master carton)	205	463
____	2345	Western Pacific F3 AA Set (P and T boxes, brown corrugated)	45	343
____	2345P	Western Pacific F3 A Unit	40	90
____	2345T	Western Pacific F3 Dummy A Unit	80	235
____	2346	B&M GP9 Diesel	29	132
____	2347	C&O GP9 Diesel	450	1200
____	2348	M&StL GP9 Diesel	37	190
____	2349	Northern Pacific GP9 Diesel	65	207
____	2349-12	Sleeve for 2349 and 2359 outer boxes	17	106
____	2350	New Haven EP-5 Electric Locomotive	36	120
____	2351	Milwaukee Road EP-5 Electric Locomotive	33	154
____	2352	Pennsylvania EP-5 Electric Locomotive	45	224
____	2353	Santa Fe F3 AA Set (master carton)	81	250
____	2353	Santa Fe F3 AA Set (P and T boxes)	40	138
____	2353P	Santa Fe F3 A Unit (brown corrugated)	28	55
____	2353T	Santa Fe F3 Dummy Unit	45	142
____	2354	NYC F3 AA Set (master carton)	31	185
____	2354P	NYC F3 A Unit (brown corrugated)	53	148
____	2354T	NYC F3 Dummy Unit	35	125
____	2355	Western Pacific F3 AA Set (master carton)	45	95
____	2355	Western Pacific F3 AA Set (P and T boxes)	55	358
____	2355P	Western Pacific F3 A Unit	60	180
____	2355T	Western Pacific F3 Dummy A Unit	25	60
____	2356	Southern F3 AA Set (master carton)	84	393
____	2356C	Southern F3 B Unit	47	292
____	2356P	Southern F3 A Unit	32	98
____	2356T	Southern F3 Dummy Unit	66	305
____	2357	SP-type Caboose	4	12
____	2358	Great Northern EP-5 Electric Locomotive	60	218
____	2359	Boston & Maine GP9 Diesel	18	105
____	2360-10	Pennsylvania GG1 Electric Locomotive, tuscan	76	200
____	2360-25	Pennsylvania GG1 Electric Locomotive, green	38	195
____	2363	Illinois Central F3 AB Set (master carton)	183	575

BOXES

		Good (P-5)	Exc (P-7)
2363	Illinois Central F3 AB Set (C and P boxes)	103	368 ___
2363C	Illinois Central F3 B Unit	35	60 ___
2363P	Illinois Central F3 A Unit	19	116 ___
2365	C&O GP7 Diesel	15	55 ___
2367C	Wabash F3 B Unit	22	455 ___
2367P	Wabash F3 A Unit	32	129 ___
2368	B&O F3 AB Set (master carton)	200	884 ___
2368C	B&O F3 B Unit	61	316 ___
2368P	B&O F3 A Unit	28	155 ___
2373	CP F3 AA Set (P and T boxes)	190	555 ___
2373P	CP F3 A Unit	55	160 ___
2373T	CP F3 Dummy A Unit	55	160 ___
2378	Milwaukee Road F3 AB Set (master carton)	169	834 ___
2378C	Milwaukee Road F3 B Unit	85	264 ___
2378P	Milwaukee Road F3 A Unit	73	212 ___
2379C	Rio Grande F3 B Unit	48	187 ___
2379P	Rio Grande F3 A Unit	67	162 ___
2383	Santa Fe F3 AA Units (master carton)	55	158 ___
2383P	Santa Fe F3 A Unit	17	68 ___
2383T	Santa Fe F3 Dummy Unit	23	80 ___
2400	Maplewood Pullman Car	14	69 ___
2401	Hillside Observation Car	20	54 ___
2402	Chatham Pullman Car	18	60 ___
2403B	Tender with bell	18	107 ___
2404	Santa Fe Vista Dome Car	21	59 ___
2405	Santa Fe Pullman Car	19	56 ___
2406	Santa Fe Observation Car	17	43 ___
2408	Santa Fe Vista Dome Car	15	48 ___
2409	Santa Fe Pullman Car	14	62 ___
2410	Santa Fe Observation Car	13	63 ___
2411	Lionel Lines Flatcar	15	41 ___
2412	Santa Fe Vista Dome Car	15	43 ___
2414	Santa Fe Pullman Car	13	43 ___
2416	Santa Fe Observation Car	10	40 ___
2419	DL&W Work Caboose	14	43 ___
2420	DL&W Work Caboose with searchlight	28	64 ___
2421	Maplewood Pullman Car	13	38 ___
2422	Chatham Pullman Car	17	39 ___
2423	Hillside Observation Car	12	36 ___
2426W	Hudson Tender (early classic)	64	251 ___
2426W	Hudson Tender (middle classic)	59	225 ___
2429	Livingston Pullman Car	19	72 ___
2430	Pullman Car, blue	12	36 ___
2431	Observation Car, blue	12	36 ___
2432	Clifton Vista Dome Car	12	35 ___

BOXES

		Good (P-5)	Exc (P-7)
____ 2434	Newark Pullman Car	13	43
____ 2435	Elizabeth Pullman Car	17	46
____ 2436	Mooseheart Observation Car	12	38
____ 2436	Mooseheart Observation Car (classic)	5	30
____ 2440	Pullman Car, green	8	30
____ 2441	Observation Car, green	8	30
____ 2442	Pullman Car, brown	8	30
____ 2442	Clifton Vista Dome Car	18	59
____ 2443	Observation Car, brown	9	30
____ 2444	Newark Pullman Car	15	49
____ 2445	Elizabeth Pullman Car	25	104
____ 2446	Summit Observation Car	15	46
____ 2452	Pennsylvania Gondola	9	24
____ 2452X	Pennsylvania Gondola	6	17
____ X2454	Pennsylvania Boxcar (marked "Box Car")	13	30
____ X2454	Pennsylvania Boxcar (marked "Merchandise Car")	17	66
____ 2456	Lehigh Valley Hopper	7	19
____ 2457	Pennsylvania N5-type Caboose	8	25
____ X2458	Pennsylvania Automobile Boxcar	12	41
____ 2460	Bucyrus Erie Crane Car (box with toy logo)	14	58
____ 2460	Bucyrus Erie Crane Car (box without toy logo)	20	68
____ 2461	Transformer Car	13	55
____ 2465	Sunoco 2-D Tank Car	3	12
____ 2466T	Tender	5	20
____ 2466W	Tender	17	37
____ 2466WX	Tender	12	40
____ 2472	PRR N5-type Caboose	3	13
____ 2481	Plainfield Pullman Car	35	175
____ 2482	Westfield Pullman Car	38	170
____ 2483	Livingston Observation Car	38	166
____ 2501W	M&StL Diesel Freight Set	18	248
____ 2503WS	Super O Steam Freight Set	30	70
____ 2505W	Super O Electric Freight Set	75	290
____ 2507W	New Haven Diesel Freight Set	28	541
____ 2509WS	Super O Steam Freight Set	18	238
____ 2511W	Pennsylvania Electric Work Set	45	248
____ 2513W	Virginian Rectifier Set	28	413
____ 2518W	Pennsylvania Electric Passenger Set	78	950
____ 2519W	Virginian Train Master Super O Freight Set	28	580
____ 2521	President McKinley Observation Car	19	68
____ 2521WS	Super O Steam Freight Set	25	110
____ 2522	President Harrison Vista Dome Car	19	108
____ 2523	President Garfield Pullman Car	28	75
____ 2523W	Santa Fe Super O Freight Set	25	308
____ 2525WS	Super O Steam Work Train Set	340	595

BOXES

		Good (P-5)	Exc (P-7)	
2526W	Santa Fe Passenger Set	33	705	
2527	Missile Launcher Set, yellow	28	87	
2528WS	Super O General Set	31	102	
2530	REA Baggage Car	17	89	
2530	REA Baggage Car (orange perforated)	118	411	
2531	Silver Dawn Observation Car	22	44	
2531WS	Super O Steam Freight Set	65	100	
2532	Silver Range Vista Dome Car	12	53	
2533	Silver Cloud Pullman Car	26	78	
2534	Silver Bluff Pullman Car	17	44	
2537W	New Haven Freight Set	39	535	
2541	Alexander Hamilton Observation Car	25	75	
2541W	Santa Fe Super O Freight Set	149	650	
2542	Betsy Ross Vista Dome Car	20	69	
2543	William Penn Pullman Car	16	80	
2543WS	Berkshire Freight Set	69	536	
2544	Molly Pitcher Pullman Car	25	80	
2544W	Santa Fe Passenger Set	73	1088	
2549W	Super O Military Set	20	65	
2550	B&O Baggage-Mail Rail Diesel Car	45	223	
2551	Banff Park Observation Car	28	103	
2551W	GN Electric Set	120	598	
2552	Skyline 500 Vista Dome Car	36	92	
2553	Blair Manor Pullman Car	64	173	
2553WS	Berkshire Freight Set	70	273	
2554	Craig Manor Pullman Car	78	196	
2555	Sunoco 1-D Tank Car	10	37	
2555	Sunoco 1-D Tank Car (overstamped 2755 box)	22	109	
2559	B&O Passenger Rail Diesel Car	31	107	
2560	Lionel Lines Crane Car	13	83	
2561	Vista Valley Observation Car	40	125	
2561	Vista Valley Observation Car (orange perforated)	88	173	
2562	Regal Pass Observation Car	30	125	
2562	Regal Pass Observation Car (orange perforated)	68	173	
2563	Indian Falls Pullman Car	38	110	
2572	Boston & Maine Military Set	27	155	
2574	Santa Fe Military Set	85	305	
2625	Irvington Pullman Car	28	134	
2627	Madison Pullman Car	28	140	
2628	Manhattan Pullman Car	34	119	
2671T	Pennsylvania Tender, for export	19	70	
2671W	Pennsylvania Tender	19	469	
2671WX	Lionel Lines Tender	19	57	
2755	Sunoco 1-D Tank Car	17	65	

			Good (P-5)	Exc (P-7)
BOXES				
____	**X2758**	PRR Automobile Boxcar	5	36
____	**2855**	Sunoco 1-D Tank Car	32	144
____	**3330**	Flatcar with submarine kit	14	75
____	**3330-100**	Operating Submarine Kit, separate sale	53	218
____	**3349**	Turbo Missile Launch Car	6	25
____	**3356**	Operating Horse Car and Corral Set (classic)	13	48
____	**3356**	Operating Horse Car and Corral Set (orange picture)	23	88
____	**3356-2**	Horse Car	77	467
____	**3356-100**	Black Horses (classic)	4	17
____	**3356-100**	Black Horses (white box)	8	23
____	**3356-150**	Horse Car Corral	75	825
____	**3357**	Hydraulic Maintenance Car	13	41
____	**3359**	Lionel Lines Twin-bin Coal Dump Car	12	45
____	**3360**	Operating Burro Crane	17	65
____	**3361**	Operating Log Dump Car	5	28
____	**3361X**	Operating Log Dump Car	5	28
____	**3362**	Helium Tank Unloading Car	15	41
____	**3362/3364**	Operating Unloading Car (Hagerstown checkerboard)	20	50
____	**3364**	Log Unloading Car	10	38
____	**3366**	Circus Car Corral Set	23	160
____	**3366-100**	White Horses	8	37
____	**3370**	W&A Outlaw Car	10	40
____	**3376**	Bronx Zoo Car	17	47
____	**3376-160**	Bronx Zoo Car, green	10	55
____	**3410**	Helicopter Car	20	95
____	**3413**	Mercury Capsule Car	10	63
____	**3419**	Helicopter Car	15	48
____	**3424**	Wabash Operating Boxcar	29	71
____	**3424-75**	Low Bridge Signal (marked "3424-75" or overstamped on 3424-100 box)	150	300
____	**3424-100**	Low Bridge Signal	5	18
____	**3428**	U.S. Mail Operating Boxcar	10	46
____	**3434**	Poultry Dispatch Car	17	60
____	**3435**	Traveling Aquarium Car	44	129
____	**3444**	Erie Operating Gondola	8	29
____	**3451**	Operating Log Dump Car	8	42
____	**3454**	PRR Operating Merchandise Car	42	156
____	**3456**	N&W Operating Hopper	23	63
____	**3459**	LL Operating Coal Dump Car (no toymaker's logo)	35	77
____	**3459**	LL Operating Coal Dump Car (toymaker's logo)	15	78
____	**3461**	LL Operating Log Car	10	25
____	**3461X**	Automatic Lumber Car	35	80
____	**3461X-25**	Lionel Lines Operating Log Car, green	7	25

BOXES

		Good (P-5)	Exc (P-7)
3462	Automatic Milk Car	15	53 ___
X3464	NYC Operating Boxcar	4	18 ___
3469	LL Operating Coal Dump Car	24	52 ___
3469X	LL Operating Coal Dump Car	8	20 ___
3470	Target Launching Car	17	44 ___
3472	Automatic Milk Car	15	40 ___
3474	Western Pacific Operating Boxcar	4	41 ___
3482	Automatic Milk Car	13	36 ___
3484	Pennsylvania Operating Boxcar	9	27 ___
3484-25	ATSF Operating Boxcar	7	33 ___
3494-1	NYC Operating Boxcar	17	44 ___
3494-150	Missouri Pacific Operating Boxcar	11	47 ___
3494-275	State of Maine Operating Boxcar	14	56 ___
3494-550	Monon Operating Boxcar	48	222 ___
3494-625	Soo Operating Boxcar	54	199 ___
3509	Satellite Launching Car	18	62 ___
3512	Fireman and Ladder Car	18	90 ___
3519	Satellite Launching Car	13	39 ___
3520	Searchlight Car	9	31 ___
3530	GM Generator Car	15	55 ___
3530-50	Searchlight with pole and base, separate sale	46	93 ___
3535	Security Car with searchlight	12	44 ___
3540	Operating Radar Car	23	75 ___
3545	Operating TV Monitor Car	21	75 ___
3559	Operating Coal Dump Car	10	40 ___
3562-1	ATSF Operating Barrel Car	31	136 ___
3562-25	ATSF Operating Barrel Car, gray	22	47 ___
3562-50	ATSF Operating Barrel Car, yellow	23	57 ___
3562-75	ATSF Operating Barrel Car, orange	28	57 ___
3619	Helicopter Reconnaissance Car	13	59 ___
3620	Searchlight Car	12	28 ___
3650	Extension Searchlight Car	8	31 ___
3656	Operating Cattle Car	15	36 ___
3656	Stockyard with cattle (set box with car box)	16	42 ___
3656-9	Cattle (marked "3656" on 4 sides, unnumbered tuck flaps)	8	19 ___
3656-9	Cattle (marked "3656" on 4 sides, "3656-44" on 1 tuck flap)	3	12 ___
3656-9	Cattle (marked "3656-34" on 4 sides, "3656-44" on 1 tuck flap)	3	10 ___
3656-9	Cattle (marked "3656" on 4 sides, "3656-44" on 1 tuck flap, OPS markings)	10	25 ___
3656-9	Cattle (unnumbered sides, marked "3656-44" on 1 tuck flap)	10	25 ___
3656-9	Cattle (unnumbered sides, marked "3656-34" on 1 tuck flap)	13	35 ___
3656-150	Corral Platform, separate sale	177	768 ___

BOXES

		Good (P-5)	Exc (P-7)
____ 3662	Automatic Milk Car (classic), *55*	18	58
____ 3662	Automatic Milk Car (orange picture), *64*	16	77
____ 3662	Automatic Milk Car (white box), *66*	20	88
____ 3665	Minuteman Operating Car	22	58
____ 3672	Bosco Operating Milk Car	36	149
____ 3830	Operating Submarine Car	17	52
____ 3854	Automatic Merchandise Car	73	400
____ 3927	Lionel Lines Track Cleaning Car	10	32
____ 4357	SP-type Caboose, electronic	25	107
____ 4452	PRR Gondola, electronic	18	125
____ 4454	Baby Ruth PRR Boxcar, electronic	20	79
____ 4457	PRR N5-type Caboose, tintype, electronic	20	93
____ 4671W	Tender	27	170
____ 5160	Viewing Stand	10	60
____ 5459	LL Coal Dump Car, electronic	15	127
____ 6001T	Tender	2	11
____ 6002	NYC Gondola	2	9
____ X6004	Baby Ruth PRR Boxcar	2	10
____ 6007	Lionel Lines SP-type Caboose	2	12
____ 6009	Remote Control Uncoupling Track	3	20
____ 6012	Gondola	2	9
____ 6014	Boxcar	2	17
____ 6014-60	Frisco Boxcar, white (middle classic)	20	27
____ 6014-60	Frisco Boxcar, white	8	24
____ 6014-85	Bosco or Frisco Boxcar, orange (classic)	8	37
____ 6014-100	Airex Boxcar, red	10	25
____ 6014-100	Airex Boxcar, red (orange perforated)	15	45
____ 6014-150	Wix Boxcar	25	214
____ 6014-335	Frisco Boxcar	7	25
____ 6014-410	Frisco Boxcar	18	90
____ 6015	Sunoco 1-D Tank Car	4	15
____ 6017	Lionel Lines SP-type Caboose	3	9
____ 6017-1	Caboose	16	37
____ 6017-50	U.S. Marine Corps SP-type Caboose (box marked "6017-60")	17	86
____ 6017-85	Lionel Lines SP-type Caboose, gray	9	30
____ 6017-100	B&M SP-type Caboose	18	64
____ 6017-185	ATSF SP-type Caboose	3	18
____ 6017-200	U.S. Navy SP-type Caboose	24	168
____ 6017-235	ATSF SP-type Caboose	8	30
____ 6019	Remote Control Track	2	9
____ 6020W	Tender	8	38
____ 6024	Nabisco Shredded Wheat Boxcar	5	21
____ 6024-60	RCA Whirlpool Boxcar	15	72
____ 6025	Gulf 1-D Tank Car (classic)	9	23
____ 6025-60	Gulf 1-D Tank Car	3	35

BOXES

		Good (P-5)	Exc (P-7)
6025-60	Gulf 1-D Tank Car (classic, overstamped 6024 box)	5	56 ____
6025-85	Gulf 1-D Tank Car (classic)	5	52 ____
6026T	Lionel Lines Tender	5	20 ____
6026W	Lionel Lines Tender	12	44 ____
6027	Alaska SP-type Caboose	43	283 ____
6029	Remote Control Uncoupling Track (classic)	2	14 ____
6029	Remote Control Uncoupling Track (orange picture)	9	35 ____
6032	Short Gondola	4	20 ____
X6034	Baby Ruth PRR Boxcar	2	13 ____
6035	Sunoco 1-D Tank Car	4	16 ____
6037	Lionel Lines SP-type Caboose	2	10 ____
6050	Lionel Savings Bank Boxcar	8	36 ____
6050-110	Swift Boxcar	7	28 ____
6057	Lionel Lines SP-type Caboose	4	31 ____
6059	M&StL SP-type Caboose	11	25 ____
6059-50	M&StL SP-type Caboose (Hagerstown checkerboard)	8	20 ____
6062	NYC Gondola	6	29 ____
6066T	Tender	7	17 ____
6110	2-4-2 Locomotive	4	20 ____
6111-75	Flatcar with logs	12	51 ____
6111-110	Flatcar	18	68 ____
6112-25	Canister Set	9	28 ____
6112-85	Short Gondola (marked "Canister Car")	4	23 ____
6112-135	Short Gondola (marked "Canister Car")	5	35 ____
6119	DL&W Work Caboose, red	5	26 ____
6119-25	DL&W Work Caboose, orange	7	25 ____
6119-50	DL&W Work Caboose, brown	10	29 ____
6119-75	DL&W Work Caboose	10	34 ____
6119-100	DL&W Work Caboose (classic)	10	42 ____
6119-100	DL&W Work Caboose (picture, perforated, or window)	10	42 ____
6121	Flatcar with pipes	14	64 ____
6121-60	Flatcar with pipes	14	79 ____
6121-85	Flatcar with pipes (classic)	15	140 ____
6130	ATSF Work Caboose (cellophane)	10	45 ____
6130	ATSF Work Caboose (Hagerstown checkerboard)	11	38 ____
6130	ATSF Work Caboose (all other boxes)	5	33 ____
6149	Remote Control Uncoupling Track, *64–69*	10	15 ____
6151	Flatcar with patrol truck	9	52 ____
6162-60	Alaska Gondola	13	100 ____
6162-110	NYC Gondola, blue (orange picture)	10	42 ____
6162-110	NYC Gondola, red, separate sale (orange picture with label)	21	92 ____

BOXES

		Good (P-5)	Exc (P-7)
6167-85	Union Pacific SP-type Caboose	25	95
6175	Flatcar with rocket	10	49
6220	Santa Fe NW2 Switcher	25	115
6250	Seaboard NW2 Switcher	33	135
6257	SP-type Caboose	5	13
6257X	SP-type Caboose	13	49
6257-25	SP-type Caboose	2	10
6257-50	SP-type Caboose	6	13
6262	Flatcar with wheel load	5	45
6264	Flatcar with lumber, separate sale	33	143
6311	Flatcar with pipes	11	62
6315	Gulf 1-D Chemical Tank Car (classic)	18	43
6315	Gulf 1-D Chemical Tank Car (Hagerstown checkerboard)	30	53
6315-60	Gulf 1-D Chemical Tank Car (orange picture)	5	25
6342	NYC Gondola	22	210
6343	Barrel Ramp Car	11	38
6346	Alcoa Quad Hopper	10	35
6356	NYC Stock Car	6	30
6357	SP-type Caboose (classic)	3	13
6357	SP-type Caboose (orange perforated, overstamped)	12	89
6357-50	ATSF SP-type Caboose	122	408
6361	Timber Transport Car	12	44
6361	Timber Transport Car (Hagerstown checkerboard)	16	64
6362	Truck Car	11	59
6376	LL Circus Stock Car	10	36
6401	Flatcar, gray	25	107
6403B	Tender with bell	21	63
6405	Flatcar with piggyback van	5	32
6407	Flatcar with rocket	150	310
6411	Flatcar with logs	5	37
6413	Mercury Capsule Carrying Car	15	58
6414	Evans Auto Loader (classic)	25	62
6414	Evans Auto Loader (orange picture)	35	117
6414	Evans Auto Loader (orange picture, overstamped 6416 box)	30	170
6414	Evans Auto Loader (orange perforated), *59*	18	112
6414	Evans Auto Loader (cellophane), *66*	25	113
6414-25	Four Automobiles	180	618
6414-85	Evans Auto Loader (orange picture)	196	495
6415	Sunoco 3-D Tank Car (classic)	8	23
6415	Sunoco 3-D Tank Car (orange picture)	20	40
6415	Sunoco 3-D Tank Car (cellophane)	31	87
6415	Sunoco 3-D Tank Car (Hillside checkerboard)	29	47

BOXES

		Good (P-5)	Exc (P-7)	
6415	Sunoco 3-D Tank Car (orange picture with label)	61	131	___
6416	Boat Transport Car	26	94	___
6417	PRR N5c Porthole Caboose	4	18	___
6417-1	PRR N5c Porthole Caboose, without "New York Zone"	9	37	___
6417-25	Lionel Lines N5c Porthole Caboose	8	31	___
6417-50	Lehigh Valley N5c Porthole Caboose	24	90	___
6418	Machinery Car	18	68	___
6419	DL&W Work Caboose	7	36	___
6419-25	DL&W Work Caboose	5	23	___
6419-50	DL&W Work Caboose	9	32	___
6419-100	N&W Work Caboose	35	71	___
6420	DL&W Work Caboose with searchlight	12	49	___
6424	Twin Auto Flatcar	23	45	___
6424-60	Twin Auto Flatcar	10	43	___
6424-85	Twin Auto Flatcar	10	71	___
6424-110	Twin Auto Flatcar	11	90	___
6425	Gulf 3-D Tank Car	14	30	___
6427	Lionel Lines N5c Porthole Caboose	7	26	___
6427-60	Virginian N5c Porthole Caboose	46	183	___
6427-500	PRR N5c Porthole Caboose, sky blue, from Girls Set	35	94	___
6428	U.S. Mail Boxcar	13	40	___
6429	DL&W Work Caboose	43	175	___
6430	Flatcar with trailers	15	33	___
6431	Flatcar with vans and tractor (cellophane), *66*	42	160	___
6434	Poultry Dispatch Stock Car	13	51	___
6436-1	Lehigh Valley Open Quad Hopper, black	10	34	___
6436-25	Lehigh Valley Open Quad Hopper, maroon	8	33	___
6436-110	Lehigh Valley Open Quad Hopper, red	8	30	___
6436-500	Lehigh Valley Open Quad Hopper, lilac, from Girls Set	34	118	___
6436-1969	TCA Hopper (Hagerstown checkered)	10	55	___
6437	PRR N5c Porthole Caboose	3	15	___
6440	Flatcar with vans	13	40	___
6440	Green Pullman Car	10	40	___
6441	Green Observation Car	10	38	___
6442	Brown Pullman Car	10	44	___
6443	Brown Observation Car	10	39	___
6445	Fort Knox Gold Reserve Car	20	50	___
6446	N&W Covered Quad Hopper	10	27	___
6446-25	N&W Covered Quad Hopper	11	36	___
6446-60	Lehigh Valley Covered Quad Hopper	93	362	___
6447	PRR N5c Porthole Caboose	48	228	___
6448	Exploding Target Range Boxcar	10	28	___

BOXES

			Good (P-5)	Exc (P-7)
____	6452	Pennsylvania Gondola	3	24
____	X6454	Santa Fe, NYC, or Baby Ruth Boxcar	5	27
____	X6454	PRR Boxcar	8	27
____	X6454	PRR Boxcar (classic, overstamped 3464 box)	9	39
____	X6454	SP Boxcar	7	28
____	X6454	Erie Boxcar	8	38
____	6456	Lehigh Valley Short Hopper	4	19
____	6456-25	LV Short Hopper ("25" rubber-stamped on end flaps)	9	39
____	6456-75	Lehigh Valley Short Hopper	28	156
____	6457	SP-type Caboose	4	16
____	6460	Bucyrus Erie Crane Car	11	48
____	6460-25	Bucyrus Erie Crane Car, red cab	12	50
____	6461	Transformer Car	7	29
____	6462	NYC Gondola, black	5	18
____	6462-25	NYC Gondola, green	6	17
____	6462-75	NYC Gondola, red	4	18
____	6462-125	NYC Gondola, red plastic	5	18
____	6462-500	NYC Gondola, pink, from Girls Set	34	122
____	6463	Rocket Fuel 2-D Tank Car	16	34
____	6464-1	Western Pacific Boxcar	14	66
____	6464-25	Great Northern Boxcar	13	40
____	6464-50	M&StL Boxcar	15	41
____	6464-50	M&StL Boxcar (overstamped with "S" and "Silver")	15	61
____	6464-75	Rock Island Boxcar	7	46
____	6464-100	Western Pacific Boxcar	33	67
____	6464-125	NYC Pacemaker Boxcar	14	58
____	6464-150	Missouri Pacific Boxcar	14	66
____	6464-175	Rock Island Boxcar	12	74
____	6464-200	Pennsylvania Boxcar	10	83
____	6464-200	Pennsylvania Boxcar (Hagerstown checkerboard)	15	40
____	6464-225	SP Boxcar	14	36
____	6464-250	Western Pacific Boxcar (orange picture with label)	38	142
____	6464-250	Western Pacific Blue Feather Boxcar (classic for 6464-100), *54*	93	425
____	6464-250	Western Pacific Boxcar (cellophane)	23	88
____	6464-275	State of Maine Boxcar	17	90
____	6464-300	Rutland Boxcar, *55*	27	108
____	6464-325	B&O Sentinel Boxcar	35	188
____	6464-350	MKT Boxcar	28	110
____	6464-375	Central of Georgia Boxcar	20	48
____	6464-400	B&O Time-Saver Boxcar	13	37
____	6464-425	New Haven Boxcar (classic)	9	40
____	6464-425	New Haven Boxcar (Hagerstown)	10	49

BOXES		Good (P-5)	Exc (P-7)
6464-450	Great Northern Boxcar	13	43 ____
6464-450	Great Northern Boxcar (cellophane)	15	66 ____
6464-475	B&M Boxcar	11	37 ____
6464-500	Timken Boxcar	18	76 ____
6464-510	NYC Pacemaker Boxcar	70	260 ____
6464-515	MKT Boxcar	75	260 ____
6464-525	M&StL Boxcar	12	37 ____
6464-650	D&RGW Boxcar (cellophane)	15	47 ____
6464-700	Santa Fe Boxcar	20	57 ____
6464-725	New Haven Boxcar (orange picture, "735" on box)	8	27 ____
6464-725	New Haven Boxcar (Hagerstown checkerboard)	21	67 ____
6464-825	Alaska Boxcar	56	222 ____
6464-900	NYC Boxcar	9	30 ____
6465	Gulf 2-D Tank Car, black (classic)	7	22 ____
6465	Sunoco 2-D Tank Car (classic, overstamped 2465 box)	2	21 ____
6465	Sunoco 2-D Tank Car (classic, overstamped 6555 box)	7	18 ____
6465	Sunoco 2-D Tank Car (orange picture, 6464-900 label)	10	84 ____
6465-60	Gulf 2-D Tank Car (classic)	5	26 ____
6465-60	Sunoco 2-D Tank Car (classic)	3	20 ____
6465-85	Lionel Lines 2-D Tank Car (orange perforated)	29	84 ____
6465-110	Cities Service 2-D Tank Car (orange perforated)	22	64 ____
6465-160	Lionel Lines Tank Car (orange picture)	58	170 ____
6466T	Lionel Lines Tender	7	17 ____
6466W	Lionel Lines Tender (with liner)	11	38 ____
6466WX	Lionel Lines Tender (with liner)	19	44 ____
6467	Miscellaneous Car	15	35 ____
6468	B&O Auto Boxcar, tuscan (marked "X")	49	108 ____
6468	B&O Auto Boxcar, blue	7	33 ____
6468-25	NH Auto Boxcar	14	49 ____
6469	Liquified Gas Tank Car	15	60 ____
6470	Explosives Boxcar	9	23 ____
6472	Refrigerator Car	7	21 ____
6473	Horse Transport Car	11	36 ____
6473	Horse Transport Car (end flaps half white, half orange)	35	130 ____
6475	Pickles Vat Car (orange picture)	22	67 ____
6476	Lehigh Valley Short Hopper	8	15 ____
6476	Lehigh Valley Short Hopper (orange perforated)	15	45 ____
6476-85	Lehigh Valley Short Hopper	16	68 ____
6476-135	Lehigh Valley Short Hopper	9	27 ____
6476-160	Lehigh Valley Short Hopper (Hagerstown checkerboard)	9	28 ____
6477	Miscellaneous Car with pipes	10	40 ____

BOXES

			Good (P-5)	Exc (P-7)
____	**6482**	Refrigerator Car	7	38
____	**6500**	Flatcar with Bonanza airplane	70	217
____	**6501**	Flatcar with jet boat	23	60
____	**6511**	Flatcar with pipes	11	29
____	**6512**	Cherry Picker Car	9	36
____	**6517**	Lionel Lines Bay Window Caboose	15	38
____	**6517-60**	Bay Window Caboose (TCA)	24	101
____	**6517-75**	Erie Bay Window Caboose	56	228
____	**6518**	Transformer Car	17	50
____	**6519**	Allis-Chalmers Flatcar (classic)	20	70
____	**6519**	Allis-Chalmers Flatcar (orange perforated)	27	78
____	**6520**	Searchlight Car	15	45
____	**6530**	Firefighting Instruction Car	10	70
____	**6536**	M&StL Open Quad Hopper	13	64
____	**6544**	Missile Firing Car	20	64
____	**6555**	Sunoco 1-D Tank Car	12	23
____	**6556**	MKT Stock Car	39	187
____	**6557**	SP-type Smoking Caboose	17	91
____	**6560**	Bucyrus Erie Crane Car (Hagerstown checkerboard)	15	55
____	**6560**	Bucyrus Erie Crane Car (all other boxes)	12	40
____	**6560-25**	Bucyrus Erie Crane Car, 8-wheel (with liner)	17	40
____	**6561**	Cable Car, 2 reels	9	35
____	**6562-1**	NYC Gondola, gray	7	23
____	**6562-25**	NYC Gondola, red	5	23
____	**6562-50**	NYC Gondola, black	7	25
____	**6572**	REA Reefer (classic)	7	54
____	**6572**	REA Reefer (orange picture)	10	29
____	**6636**	Alaska Open Quad Hopper	14	50
____	**6646**	Lionel Lines Stock Car	5	30
____	**6650**	IRBM Rocket Launcher	9	36
____	**6654W**	Whistle Tender	7	20
____	**6657**	Rio Grande SP-type Caboose	21	80
____	**6660**	Boom Car	8	56
____	**6670**	Derrick Car	17	58
____	**6672**	Santa Fe Refrigerator Car	7	25
____	**6736**	Detroit & Mackinac Open Quad Hopper	17	64
____	**6800**	Flatcar with airplane (classic)	17	82
____	**6800**	Flatcar with airplane (orange perforated)	15	87
____	**6800-60**	Airplane, separate sale	93	192
____	**6801**	Flatcar with brown and white boat	7	38
____	**6801-50**	Flatcar with yellow and white boat	10	52
____	**6801-60**	Boat, separate sale	30	92
____	**6801-75**	Flatcar with blue and white boat	11	38
____	**6802**	Flatcar with girders (late classic)	9	31
____	**6802**	Flatcar with girders (orange perforated)	31	65

BOXES

		Good (P-5)	Exc (P-7)
6803	Flatcar with USMC tank and sound truck	18	90 ___
6804	Flatcar with USMC trucks	20	88 ___
6805	Atomic Energy Disposal Flatcar	20	80 ___
6806	Flatcar with USMC trucks	24	94 ___
6807	Flatcar with boat	14	53 ___
6808	Flatcar with military units	15	40 ___
6809	Flatcar with USMC trucks	25	96 ___
6810	Flatcar with trailer	7	35 ___
6812	Track Maintenance Car	15	58 ___
6814	Rescue Caboose	18	75 ___
6816	Flatcar with Allis-Chalmers bulldozer	47	126 ___
6816-100	Allis-Chalmers bulldozer	125	450 ___
6817	Flatcar with Allis-Chalmers motor scraper	47	159 ___
6818	Flatcar with transformer	8	30 ___
6819	Flatcar with helicopter	7	30 ___
6820	Aerial Missile Transport Car with helicopter	96	281 ___
6821	Flatcar with crates	5	44 ___
6822	Searchlight Car	6	29 ___
6823	Flatcar with IRBM missiles	15	75 ___
6825	Flatcar with arch trestle bridge	7	26 ___
6826	Flatcar with Christmas trees	19	59 ___
6827	Flatcar with Harnischfeger power shovel	30	75 ___
6827-100	Harnischfeger Power Shovel	20	50 ___
6828	Flatcar with Harnischfeger crane (cellophane, no crane kit box)	30	114 ___
6828	Flatcar with Harnischfeger crane (orange picture, no crane kit box)	13	53 ___
6828	Harnischfeger Crane Kit, used with flatcar	12	97 ___
6828-100	Harnischfeger Crane, separate sale	46	186 ___
6830	Flatcar with submarine	24	51 ___
6844	Missile Carrying Car	16	62 ___
11001	Steam Freight Set (advance catalog 1962)	3	10 ___
11201	Steam Freight Set	20	65 ___
11222	027 Steam Freight Set	25	70 ___
11232	NH Diesel Freight Set	20	65 ___
11242	Steam Freight Set	30	70 ___
11268	Military Set	40	120 ___
11278	Steam Freight Set	25	55 ___
11288	Steam Freight Set	50	100 ___
11331	Steam Freight Set	15	40 ___
11415	Steam Freight Set (advance catalog 1963)	9	49 ___
11420	Steam Freight Set	10	30 ___
11450	Steam Freight Set	30	65 ___
11460	Steam Freight Set	10	30 ___
11490	Santa Fe Passenger Set	50	100 ___
11500	Steam Freight Set	50	110 ___

BOXES

		Good (P-5)	Exc (P-7)
_____ 11520	Steam Freight Set	40	90
_____ 11560	Texas Special Set	15	35
_____ 11590	Santa Fe Passenger Set	30	75
_____ 11710	Steam Freight Set	45	95
_____ 11750	Steam Freight Set	22	54
_____ 12710	Steam Freight Set	20	55
_____ 12730	Santa Fe Diesel Freight Set	75	185
_____ 12760	Berkshire Freight Set	175	400
_____ 12780	Santa Fe Passenger Set	200	575
_____ 12800	B&M Diesel Freight Set	25	75
_____ 12800X	B&M Diesel Freight Set	75	190
_____ 12820	Virginian Train Master Freight Set	88	270
_____ 13008	Super O Introductory Set	20	60
_____ 13018	Santa Fe Space-age Military Set	423	1068
_____ 13028	Super O Space Set	160	300
_____ 13048	Super O Steam Freight Set	65	140
_____ 13058	Santa Fe Space-age Military Set	150	400
_____ 13088	Santa Fe Passenger Set	523	1350
_____ 13098	Steam Freight Set	120	275
_____ 13118	Berkshire Freight Set	75	380
_____ 13128	Santa Fe Space-age Military Set	250	650
_____ 13150	Hudson Freight Set	335	900
_____ CO-1	Track Clips, 100	5	15
_____ ECU-1	Electronic Control Unit	15	70
_____ KW	Transformer, 190 watts	6	21
_____ KW	Transformer, 190 watts (yellow)	5	28
_____ LW	Transformer, 125 watts	8	18
_____ R	Transformer, 110 watts	10	20
_____ RCS	Remote Control Track	7	22
_____ RW	Transformer, 110 watts	6	17
_____ S	Transformer, 80 watts	4	12
_____ SW	Transformer, 130 watts	5	16
_____ TW	Transformer, 175 watts	3	18
_____ UCS	Remote Control Track (O)	1	7
_____ UTC	Lockon	10	20
_____ ZW	Transformer, 275 watts (classic)	13	43
_____ ZW	Transformer, 275 watts (orange, with inserts)	13	50
_____ ZW	Transformer, 275 watts (yellow, with inserts)	15	61

Exc

463W	Steam Freight Set, *45* (224, 2466W, 2458, 2452, 2555, 2457)	600___
1000W	027 Steam Freight Set, *55* (2016, 6026W, 6014, 6012, 6017)	250___
1001	027 Diesel Freight Set, *55* (610, 6012, 6014, 6017)	250___
1111	027 Scout Freight Set, *48* (1001, 1001T, 1002, 1005, 1007)	225___
1112	027 Scout Freight Set, *48* (1001 or 1101, 1001T, 1002, 1004, 1005, 1007)	250___
1113	027 Scout Freight Set, *50* (1120, 1001T, 1002, 1005, 1007)	115___
1115	027 Scout Freight Set, *49* (1110, 1001T, 1002, 1005, 1007)	190___
1117	027 Scout Freight Set, *49* (1110, 1001T, 1002, 1005, 1004, 1007)	150___
1119	027 Freight Scout Set, *51–52* (1110, 1001T, 1002, 1004, 1007)	160___
1400	027 Steam Passenger Set, *46* (221, 221T, two 2430, 2431)	600___
1400W	027 Steam Passenger Set, *46* (221, 221W, two 2430 2431)	720___
1401	027 Steam Freight Set, *46* (1654, 1654T, 2452X, 2465, 2472)	120___
1401W	027 Steam Freight Set, *46* (1654, 1654W, 2452X, 2465, 2472)	220___
1402	027 Steam Passenger Set, *46* (1666, 2466T, two 2440, 2441)	550___
1402W	027 Steam Passenger Set, *46* (1666, 2466W, two 2440, 2441)	550___
1403	027 Steam Freight Set, *46* (221, 221T, 2411, 2465, 2472)	400___
1403W	027 Steam Freight Set, *46* (221, 221W, 2411, 2465, 2472)	500___
1405	027 Steam Freight Set, *46* (1666, 2466T, 2452X, 2465, 2472)	145___
1405W	027 Steam Freight Set, *46* (1666, 2466W, 2452X, 2465, 2472)	281___
1407B	027 Steam Switcher Set, *46* (1665, 2403B, 2560, 2452X, 2419)	840___
1409	027 Steam Freight Set, *46* (1666, 2466T, 3559, 2465, 3454, 2472)	425___
1409W	027 Steam Freight Set, *46* (1666, 2466W, 3559, 2465, 3454, 2472)	445___
1411W	027 Steam Freight Set, *46* (1666, 2466WX, 2452X, 2465, 2454, 2472)	250___
1413WS	027 Steam Freight Set, *46* (2020, 2466WX, 2452X, 2465, 2454, 2472)	310___
1415WS	027 Steam Freight Set, *46* (2020, 2020W, 3459, 3454, 2465, 2472)	530___
1417WS	027 Steam Work Train Set, *46* (2020, 2020W, 2465, 3451, 2560, 2419)	700___

SETS

		Exc
1419WS	027 Steam Freight Set, *46* (2020, 2020W, 3459, 2452X, 2560, 2419, 97)	880
1421WS	027 Steam Freight Set, *46* (2020, 2020W, 3451, 2465, 3454, 2472, 164)	1100
1423W	027 Steam Freight Set, *48–49* (1655, 6654W, 6452, 6465, 6257)	253
1425B	027 Steam Switcher Freight Set, *48* (1656, 2403B, 6456, 6465, 6257X)	825
1425B	027 Steam Switcher Freight Set, *49* (1656, 6403B, 6456, 6465, 6257)	825
1426WS	027 Steam Passenger Set, *48–49* (2026, 6466WX, two 6440, 6441)	612
1427WS	027 Steam Freight Set, *48* (2026, 6466WX, 6454, 6465, 6257)	320
1429WS	027 Steam Freight Set, *48* (2026, 6466WX, 3451, 6454, 6465, 6257)	225
1430WS	027 Steam Passenger Set, *48–49* (2025, 6466WX, 2400, 2401, 2402)	800
1431	027 Steam Freight Set, *47* (1654, 1654T, 2452X, 2465, 2472)	255
1431W	027 Steam Freight Set, *47* (1654, 1654W, 2452X, 2465, 2472)	160
1432	027 Steam Passenger Set, *47* (221, 221T, two 2430, 2431)	850
1432W	027 Steam Passenger Set, *47* (221, 221W, two 2430 2431)	850
1433	027 Steam Freight Set, *47* (221, 221T, 2411, 2465, 2457)	560
1433W	027 Steam Freight Set, *47* (221, 221 W, 2411, 2465, 2457)	375
1434WS	027 Steam Passenger Set, *47* (2025, 2466WX, two 2440, 2441)	555
1435WS	027 Steam Freight Set, *47* (2025, 2466WX, 2452X, 2454, 2457)	230
1437WS	027 Steam Freight Set, *47* (2025, 2466WX, 2452X, 2465, 2454, 2472)	590
1439WS	027 Steam Freight Set, *47* (2025, 2466WX, 3559, 2465, 3454, 2457)	470
1441WS	027 Steam Work Train Set, *47* (2020, 2020W, 2560, 2461, 3451, 2419)	1225
1443WS	027 Steam Freight Set, *47* (2020, 2020W, 3459, 3462, 2465, 2457)	400
1445WS	027 Steam Freight Set, *48* (2025, 6466WX, 6454, 3559, 6465, 6357)	325
1447WS	027 Steam Work Train Set, *48* (2020, 6020W, 3451, 2461, 2460, 6419)	460
1447WS	027 Steam Work Train Set, *49* (2020, 6020W, 6461, 3461, 2460, 6419)	475
1449WS	027 Steam Freight Set, *48* (2020, 6020W, 3462, 3459, 6411, 6465, 6357)	430
1451WS	027 Steam Freight Set, *49* (2026, 6466WX, 6462, 3464, 6257)	232
1453WS	027 Steam Freight Set, *49* (2026, 6466WX, 3464, 6465, 3461, 6357)	325
1455WS	027 Steam Freight Set, *49* (2025, 6466WX, 6462, 6465, 3472, 6357)	351

SETS		Exc
1457B	027 Diesel Freight Set, *49–50* (6220, 3464, 6462, 6520, 6419)	540____
1459WS	027 Steam Freight Set, *49* (2020, 6020W, 6411, 3656, 6465, 3469, 6357)	1075____
1461S	027 Steam Freight Set, *50* (6110, 6001T, 6002, 6004, 6007)	175____
1463W	027 Steam Freight Set, *50* (2036, 6466W, 6462, 6465, 6257)	230____
1463WS	027 Freight Set, *51* (2026, 6466W, 6462, 6465, 6257)	158____
1464W	027 UP Diesel Passenger Set, *50* (2023 AA, 2481, 2482, 2483)	987____
1464W	027 UP Passenger Set, *51* (2023 AA, 2421, 2422, 2423)	865____
1464W	027 UP Passenger Set, *52–53* (2033 AA, 2421, 2422, 2423)	675____
1465	027 Steam Freight Set, *52* (2034, 6066T, 6032, 6035, 6037)	178____
1467W	027 UP Diesel Freight Set, *50–51* (2023 AA, 6656, 6465, 6456, 6357)	615____
1467W	027 Erie Diesel Freight Set, *52–53* (2032 AA, 6656, 6456, 6465, 6357)	683____
1469WS	027 Steam Freight Set, *50–51* (2035, 6466W, 6462, 6465, 6456, 6257)	227____
1471WS	027 Steam Freight Set, *50–51* (2035, 6466W, 3469, 6465, 6454, 3461, 6357)	459____
1473WS	027 Steam Freight Set, *50* (2046, 2046W, 3464, 6465, 6520, 6357)	558____
1475WS	027 Steam Freight Set, *50* (2046, 2046W, 3656, 3461, 6472, 3469, 6419)	615____
1477S	027 Steam Freight Set, *51–52* (2026, 6466T, 6012, 6014, 6017)	242____
1479WS	027 Steam Freight Set, *52* (2056, 2046W, 6462, 6465, 6456, 6257)	344____
1481WS	027 Steam Freight Set, *51* (2035, 6466W, 3464, 3472, 6465, 6462, 6357)	510____
1483WS	027 Steam Freight Set, *52* (2056, 2046W, 3472, 6462, 6465, 3474, 6357)	1010____
1484WS	027 Steam Passenger Set, *52* (2056, 2046W, 2421, 2422, 2423, 2429)	1270____
1485WS	027 Steam Freight Set, *52* (2025, 6466W, 6462, 6465, 6257)	176____
1500	027 Steam Freight Set, *53* (1130, 6066T, 6032, 6034, 6037)	172____
1500	027 Steam Freight Set, *54* (1130, 1130T, 6032, 6034, 6037)	125____
1501S	027 Steam Freight Set, *53* (2026, 6066T, 6032, 6035, 6037)	249____
1502WS	027 Steam Passenger Set, *53* (2055, 2046W, 2421, 2422, 2423)	750____
1503WS	027 Steam Freight Set, *53–54* (2055, 6026W, 6462, 6465, 6456, 6257)	314____
1505WS	027 Steam Freight Set, *53* (2046, 2046W, 6462, 6464-1, 6415, 6357)	418____
1507WS	027 Steam Freight Set, *53* (2046, 2046W, 6415, 6462, 3472, 6468, 6357)	450____

		Exc
1509WS	027 Steam Freight Set, *53* (2046, 2046W, 6456, 3520, 3469, 6460, 6419)	500
1511S	027 Steam Freight Set, *53* (2037, 6066T, 6032, 3474, 6035, 6037)	248
1513S	027 Steam Freight Set, *54–55* (2037, 6026T, 6012, 6014, 6015, 6017)	235
1515WS	027 Steam Freight Set, *54* (2065, 2046W, 6462, 6415, 6464-25, 6456-25, 6357)	345
1516WS	027 Passenger Set, *54* (2065, 2046W, 2434, 2432, 2436)	650
1517W	027 Diesel Freight Set, *54* (2245P/C AB, 6464-225, 6561, 6462-25, 6427)	1250
1519WS	027 Steam Freight Set, *54* (2065, 6026W, 6356, 6462-75, 3482, 3461-25, 6427)	550
1520W	027 Texas Special Passenger Set, *54* (2245P/C AB, 2432, 2435, 2436)	1700
1521WS	027 Steam Work Train Set, *54* (2065, 2046W, 3620, 6561, 6460, 3562, 6419)	700
1523	027 Diesel Work Train Set, *54* (6250, 6511, 6456-25, 6460-25, 6419-25)	613
1525	027 Diesel Freight Set, *55* (600, 6111, 6014, 6017)	164
1527	027 Steam Work Train Set, *55* (1615, 1615T, 6462-125, 6560, 6119)	500
1529	027 PRR Diesel Freight Set, *55* (2028, 6311, 6436, 6257)	650
1531W	027 Diesel Freight Set, *55* (2328, 6462-125, 6465, 6456 or 6456-25, 6257)	600
1533WS	027 Steam Freight Set, *55* (2055, 6026W, 3562-50, 6436, 6465, 6357)	465
1534W	027 Diesel Passenger Set, *55* (2328, 2432, 2434, 2436)	1000
1535W	027 Diesel Freight Set, *55* (2243P/2243C AB, 6462-125, 6436, 6464-50 or 6468X, 6257)	1650
1536W	027 Texas Special Passenger Set, *55* (2245P/C AB, two 2432, 2436)	1700
1537WS	027 Steam Freight Set, *55* (2065, 6026W, 3469, 6464-275, 3562-50, 6357)	500
1538WS	027 Steam Passenger Set, *55* (2065, 2046W, 2432, 2434, 2435, 2436)	900
1539W	027 Santa Fe Diesel Freight Set, *55* (2243P/C AB, 3620, 6446, 6561, 6560, 6419)	850
1541WS	027 Steam Freight Set, *55* (2065, 2046W, 3482, 6415, 3461-25, 3494-1, 6427)	600
1542	027 Electric Freight Set, *56* (520, 6014, 6012, 6017)	205
1543	027 Diesel Freight Set, *56* (627, 6121, 6112, 6017)	262
1545	027 Diesel Freight Set, *56* (628, 6424, 6014, 6025, 6257)	264
1547S	027 Steam Freight Set, *56* (2018, 6026T, 6121, 6112, 6014, 6257)	153
1549S	027 Diesel Work Train Set, *56* (1615, 1615T, 6262, 6560, 6119-25)	800

SETS

Exc

1551W	027 Diesel Freight Set, *56* (621, 6362, 6425, 6562-25, 6257)	408 ___
1552	027 Diesel Passenger Set, *56* (629, 2432, 2434, 2436)	840 ___
1553W	027 MILW Diesel Freight Set, *56* (2338, 6430, 6462-125, 6464-425, 6346, 6257)	700 ___
1555WS	027 Steam Freight Set, *56* (2018, 6026W, 3361, 6464-400, 6462-125, 6257)	280 ___
1557W	027 Diesel Work Train Set, *56* (621, 6436, 6511, 3620, 6560, 6119-25)	453 ___
1559W	027 MILW Diesel Freight Set, *56* (2338, 6414, 3562-50, 6362, 3494-275, 6357)	800 ___
1561WS	027 Steam Freight Set, *56* (2065, 6026W, 3424, 6262, 6562-25, 6430, 6257)	729 ___
1562W	027 Diesel Passenger Set, *56* (2328, two 2442, 2444, 2446)	2000 ___
1563W	027 Wabash Diesel Freight Set, *56* (2240P/C AB, 6467, 3562-50, 6414, 3620, 6357)	1570 ___
1565WS	027 Steam Freight Set, *56* (2065, 6026W, 3662, 3650, 6414, 6346, 6357)	535 ___
1567W	027 Santa Fe Diesel Freight Set, *56* (2243P/C AB, 3356, 3424, 6430, 6672, 6357)	1200 ___
1569	027 UP Diesel Freight Set, *57* (202, 6014, 6111, 6112, 6017)	220 ___
1571	027 LV Diesel Freight Set, *57* (625, 6424, 6476, 6121, 6112, 6017)	400 ___
1573	027 Steam Freight Set, *57* (250, 250T, 6112, 6025, 6476, 6464-425, 6017)	195 ___
1575	027 MP Diesel Freight Set, *57* (205P/T AA, 6121, 6112, 6111, 6560-25, 6119-100)	320 ___
1577S	027 Steam Freight Set, *57* (2018, 1130T, 6014, 6121, 6464-475, 6111, 6112, 6017)	237 ___
1578S	027 Steam Passenger Set, *57* (2018, 1130T, 2432, 2434, 2436)	500 ___
1579S	027 Steam Freight Set, *57* (2037, 1130T, 6476, 6121, 6468-25, 6111, 6112, 6025, 6017)	225 ___
1581	027 Jersey Central Diesel Freight Set, *57* (611, 6464-650, 6424, 6024, 6025, 6476, 6560-25, 6119-100)	540 ___
1583WS	027 Steam Freight Set, *57* (2037, 6026W, 6482, 6112, 6646, 6121, 6476, 6017)	300 ___
1585W	027 Seaboard Diesel Freight Set, *57* (602, 6014, 6111, 6464-525, 6025, 6121, 6112, 6476, 6024, 6017)	445 ___
1586	027 Santa Fe Diesel Passenger Set, *57* (204P/T AA, two 2432, 2436)	670 ___
1587S	027 Steam Freight Set (Girls Set), *57–58* (2037-500, 1130T-500, 6462-500, 6464-515, 6436-500, 6464-510, 6427-500)	2891 ___
1589WS	027 Steam Freight Set, *57* (2037, 6026W, 6424, 6464-450, 6025, 6024, 6111, 6112, 6017)	500 ___
1590	027 Steam Freight Set, *58* (249, 250T, 6014, 6151, 6112, 6017)	300 ___

1591	027 Military Set, *58*	
	(212, 6803, 6809, 6807, 6017-50)	843
1593	027 UP Diesel Work Set, *58*	
	(613, 6476, 6818, 6660, 6112, 6119-100)	650
1595	027 Military Set, *58*	
	(1625, 1625T, 6804, 6806, 6808, 6017-85)	2050
1597S	027 Steam Freight Set, *58*	
	(2018, 1130T, 6014, 6818, 6476, 6025, 6112, 6017)	320
1599	027 Texas Special Freight Set, *58*	
	(210P/T AA, 6801, 6014, 6424, 6112, 6465, 6017)	400
1600	027 Burlington Diesel Passenger Set, *58*	
	(216, 6572, 2432, 2436)	840
1601W	027 Wabash Diesel Freight Set, *58*	
	2337, 6800, 6464-425, 6801, 6810, 6017)	900
1603WS	027 Steam Freight Set, *58*	
	(2037, 6026W, 6424, 6014, 6818, 6112, 6017)	400
1605W	027 Santa Fe Diesel Freight Set, *58*	
	(208P/T AA, 6800, 6464-425, 6801, 6477, 6802, 6017)	900
1607WS	027 Steam Work Train Set, *58*	
	(2037, 6026W, 6465, 6818, 6464-425, 6660, 6112, 6119-100)	450
1608W	027 NH Diesel Passenger Set, *58*	
	(209P/T AA, two 2432, 2434, 2436)	1700
1609	027 Steam Freight Set, *59–60*	
	(246, 1130T, 6162-25, 6476, 6057)	147
1611	027 Alaska Diesel Freight Set, *59*	
	(614, 6825, 6162-60, 6465, 6027)	445
1612	027 General Set, *59–60*	
	(1862, 1862T, 1866, 1865)	290
1613S	027 B&O Steam Freight Set, *59*	
	(247, 247T, 6826, 6819, 6821, 6017)	345
1615	027 B&M Diesel Freight Set, *59*	
	(217P/C AB, 6800, 6464-475, 6812, 6825, 6017-100)	518
1617S	027 Steam Work Train Set, *59*	
	(2018, 1130T, 6816, 6536, 6812, 6670, 6119-100)	800
1619W	027 Santa Fe Diesel Freight Set, *59*	
	(218P/T AA, 6819, 6802, 6801, 6519, 6017-185)	450
1621WS	027 Steam Freight Set, *59*	
	(2037, 6026W, 6825, 6519, 6062, 6464-475, 6017)	325
1623W	027 NP Diesel Freight Set, *59*	
	(2349, 3512, 3435, 6424, 6062, 6017)	1600
1625WS	027 Steam Freight Set, *59*	
	(2037, 6026W, 6636, 3512, 6470, 6650, 6017)	400
1626W	027 Santa Fe Diesel Passenger Set, *59*	
	(208P/T AA, 3428, two 2412, 2416)	700
1627S	027 Steam Freight Set, *60*	
	(244, 244T, 6062, 6825, 6017)	186
1629	027 C&O Diesel Freight Set, *60*	
	(225, 6650, 6470, 6819, 6219)	295
1631WS	027 Steam Freight Set, *60*	
	(243, 243W, 6519, 6812, 6465, 6017)	293
1633	027 U.S. Navy Diesel Freight Set, *60*	
	(224P/C AB, 6544, 6830, 6820, 6017-200)	1185

SETS

		Exc
1635WS	027 Steam Freight Set, *60* (2037, 6026W or 243W, 6361, 6826, 6636, 6821, 6017)	460___
1637W	027 Santa Fe Diesel Freight Set, *60* (218P/T AA, 6475, 6175, 6464-475, 6801 or 6424-110, 6017-185)	585___
1639WS	027 Steam Freight Set, *60* (2037, 6026W or 243W, 6816, 6817, 6812, 6530, 6560, 6119-100)	1250___
1640W	027 Santa Fe Diesel Passenger Set, *60* (218P/T AA, 3428, two 2412, 2416, 1640-100)	750___
1641	027 Steam Freight Set, *61* (246, 244T, 3362, 6162, 6057)	150___
1642	027 Steam Freight Set, *61* (244, 1130T, 3376, 6405, 6119)	180___
1643	027 C&O Diesel Freight Set, *61* (230, 3509, 6050, 6175, 6058)	393___
1644	027 General Set, *61* (1862, 1862T, 3370, 1866, 1865)	420___
1645	027 Diesel Freight Set, *61* (229, 3410, 6465-110, 6825, 6059)	250___
1646	027 Steam Freight Set, *61* (233, 233W, 6162, 6343, 6476, 6017)	325___
1647	027 U.S. Marines Military Set, *61* (45, 3665, 3519, 6830, 6448, 6814)	850___
1648	027 Steam Freight Set, *61* (2037, 233W, 6062, 6465-110, 6519, 6476, 6017)	336___
1649	027 Santa Fe Diesel Freight Set, *61* (218P/C AB, 6343, 6445, 6475, 6405, 6017)	450___
1650	027 Steam Military Set, *61* (2037, 233W, 6544, 6470, 3330, 3419, 6017)	500___
1651	027 Santa Fe Diesel Passenger Set, *61* (218P/T or 220T AA, two 2412, 2414, 2416)	675___
1800	General Gift Pack, *59–60* (1862, 1862T, 1865, 1866, 1877, storybook)	365___
1805	027 Military Set (Land-Sea and Air Gift Pack), *60* (45, 3429, 3820, 6640, 6824)	1425___
1809	Western Gift Pack, *61* (244, 1130T, 3370, 3376, 1877, 6017)	300___
1810	Space Age Gift Pack, *61* (231, 3665, 3519, 3820, 6017)	1165___
2100	Steam Passenger Set, *46* (224, 2466T, two 2442, 2443)	550___
2100W	Steam Passenger Set, *46* (224, 2466W, two 2442, 2443)	754___
2101	Steam Freight Set, *46* (224, 2466T, 2555, 2452, 2457)	350___
2101W	Steam Freight Set, *46* (224, 2466W, 2555, 2452, 2457)	397___
2103W	Steam Freight Set, *46* (224, 2466W, 2458, 3559, 2555, 2457)	381___
2105WS	Steam Freight Set, *46* (671, 2466W, 2555, 2454, 2457)	425___
2110WS	Steam Passenger Set, *46* (671, 2466W, three 2625)	1875___

SETS

Exc

			Exc
	2111WS	Steam Freight Set, *46* (671, 2466W, 3459, 2411, 2460, 2420)	795
	2113WS	Steam Freight Set, *46* (726, 2426W, 2855, 3854, 2857)	1900
	2114WS	Steam Passenger Set, *46* (726, 2426W, three 2625)	2500
	2115WS	Steam Work Train Set, *46* (726, 2426W, 2458, 3451, 2460, 2420)	1500
	2120S	Steam Passenger Set, *47* (675, 2466T, two 2442, 2443)	500
	2120WS	Steam Passenger Set, *47* (675, 2466WX, two 2442, 2443)	500
	2121S	Steam Freight Set, *47* (675, 2466T, 2555, 2452, 2457)	400
	2121WS	Steam Freight Set, *47* (675, 2466WX, 2555, 2452, 2457)	388
	2123WS	Steam Freight Set, *47* (675, 2466WX, 2458, 3559, 2555, 2457)	450
	2124W	PRR Electric Passenger Set, *47* (2332 GG-1 green, 2625 Irvington, 2625 Madison, 2625 Manhattan)	3200
	2125WS	Steam Freight Set, *47* (671, 671W, 2411, 2454, 2452, 2457)	550
	2126WS	Steam Passenger Set, *47* (671, 671W, 2625 Irvington, 2625 Madison, 2625 Manhattan)	1950
	2127WS	Steam Work Train Set, *47* (671, 671W, 3459, 2461, 2460, 2420)	725
	2129WS	Steam Freight Set, *47* (726, 2426W, 3854, 2411, 2855, 2457)	2000
	2131WS	Steam Work Train Set, *47* (726, 2426W, 3462, 3451, 2460, 2420)	1200
	2133W	Diesel Freight Set, *48* (2333P/T AA, 2458, 3459, 2555, 2357)	1350
	2135WS	Steam Freight Set, *48* (675, 2466WX, 2456, 2411, 2357)	350
	2135WS	Steam Freight Set, *49* (675, 6466WX, 6456, 6411, 6457)	343
	2136WS	Steam Passenger Set, *48* (675, 2466WX, two 2442, 2443)	620
	2136WS	Steam Passenger Set, *49* (675, 6466WX, two 6442, 6443)	640
	2137WS	Steam Freight Set, *48* (675, 2466WX, 2458, 3459, 2456, 2357)	735
	2139W	PRR Electric Freight Set, *49* (2332, 6456, 3464, 3461, 6457)	1400
	2139W	PRR Electric Freight Set, *48* (2332, 2458, 3451, 2456, 2357)	1425
	2140WS	Steam Passenger Set, *48–49* (671, 2671W, 2400, 2401, 2402)	1250
	2141WS	Steam Freight Set, *48* (671, 2671W, 3451, 3462, 2456, 2357)	347
	2143WS	Steam Work Train Set, *48* (671, 2671W, 3459, 2461, 2460, 2420)	817
	2144W	PRR Electric Passenger Set, *48–49* (2332, 2625, 2627, 2628)	2065

SETS

		Exc
2145WS	Steam Freight Set, *48* (726, 2426W, 3462, 2411, 2460, 2357)	815 ___
2146WS	Steam Passenger Set, *48–49* (726, 2426W, 2625, 2627, 2628)	2000 ___
2147WS	Steam Freight Set, *49* (675, 6466WX, 3472, 6465, 3469, 6457)	400 ___
2148WS	Hudson Passenger Set, *50* (773, 2426W, 2625, 2627, 2628)	5550 ___
2149B	Diesel Work Train Set, *49* (622, 6520, 3469, 2460, 6419)	690 ___
2150WS	Steam Passenger Set, *50* (681, 2671W, 2421, 2422, 2423)	1000 ___
2151W	Diesel Freight Set, *49* (2333P/T AA, 3464, 6555, 3469, 6520, 6457)	900 ___
2153WS	Steam Work Train Set, *49* (671, 2671W, 3469, 6520, 2460, 6419)	620 ___
2155WS	Steam Freight Set, *49* (726, 2426W, 6411, 3656, 2460, 6457)	795 ___
2159W	Electric Freight Set, *50* (2330, 3464, 6462, 3461, 6456, 6457)	3000 ___
2161W	Santa Fe Diesel Freight Set, *50* (2343P/T AA, 3469, 3464, 3461, 6520, 6457)	1500 ___
2163WS	Steam Freight Set, *50* (736, 2671WX, 6472, 6462, 6555, 6457)	550 ___
2163WS	Steam Freight Set, *51* (736, 2671WX, 6472, 6462, 6465, 6457)	600 ___
2165WS	Steam Freight Set, *50* (736, 2671WX, 3472, 6456, 3461, 6457)	690 ___
2167WS	Steam Freight Set, *50–51* (681, 2671W, 6462, 3464, 6457)	545 ___
2169WS	Hudson Freight Set, *50* (773, 2426W, 3656, 6456, 3469, 6411, 6457)	3092 ___
2171W	NYC Diesel Freight Set, *50* (2344P/T AA, 3469, 3464, 3461, 6520, 6457)	1100 ___
2173WS	Steam Freight Set, *50* (681, 2671W, 3472, 6555, 3469, 6457)	545 ___
2173WS	Steam Freight Set, *51* (681, 2671W, 3472, 6465, 3469, 6457)	550 ___
2175W	Santa Fe Diesel Freight Set, *50* (2343P/T AA, 6456, 3464, 6555, 6462, 6457)	1100 ___
2175W	Santa Fe Diesel Freight Set, *51* (2343 AA, 6456, 3464, 6465, 6462, 6457)	1100 ___
2177WS	Steam Freight Set, *52* (675, 2046W, 6462, 6465, 6457)	225 ___
2179WS	Steam Freight Set, *52* (671, 2046WX, 3464, 6465, 6462, 6457)	330 ___
2183WS	Steam Freight Set, *52* (726, 2046W, 3464, 6462, 6465, 6457)	900 ___
2185W	NYC Diesel Freight Set, *50* (2344P/T AA, 6456, 3464, 6555, 6462, 6457)	1084 ___
2185W	NYC Diesel Freight Set, *51* (2344 AA, 6456, 3464, 6465, 6462, 6457)	800 ___
2187WS	Steam Freight Set, *52* (671, 2046WX, 6462, 3472, 3469, 6456, 6457)	650 ___
2189WS	Steam Freight Set, *52* (726, 2046W, 3520, 3656, 6462, 3461, 6457)	625 ___

SETS

		Exc
2190W	Santa Fe Diesel Passenger Set, *52* (2343P/T AA, 2531, 2532, 2533, 2534)	2000
2190W	Santa Fe Diesel Passenger Set, *53* (2353P/T AA, 2531, 2533, 2532, 2534)	1900
2191W	Santa Fe Diesel Freight Set, *52* (2343P/C/T ABA, 6462, 6656, 6456, 6457)	1350
2193W	NYC Diesel Freight Set, *52* (2344P/C/T ABA, 6462, 6656, 6456, 6457)	1040
2201WS	Steam Freight Set, *53* (685, 6026W, 6462, 6464-50, 6465, 6357)	355
2203WS	Steam Freight Set, *53* (681, 2046WX, 6415, 3520, 6464-25, 6417)	663
2205WS	Steam Freight Set, *53* (736, 2046W, 3484, 6415, 6468, 6456, 6417)	600
2207W	Santa Fe Diesel Freight Set, *53* (2353P/C/T ABA, 6462, 3484, 6415, 6417)	1248
2209W	NYC Diesel Freight Set, *53* (2354P/C/T ABA, 6462, 3484, 6415, 6417)	1200
2211WS	Steam Freight Set, *53* (681, 2046WX, 3656, 6464-75, 3461, 6417)	740
2213WS	Steam Freight Set, *53* (736, 2046W, 3461, 3520, 3469, 6460, 6419)	560
2217WS	Steam Freight Set, *54* (682, 2046WX, 6464-175, 3562-25, 6356, 6417)	1125
2219W	Diesel Freight Set, *54* (2321, 6456-25, 6464-50, 6462-25, 6415, 6417)	1535
2221WS	Steam Freight Set, *54* (646, 2046W, 6468, 3620, 3469, 6456-25, 6417-25)	600
2222WS	Steam Passenger Set, *54* (646, 2046W, 2530, 2531, 2532)	1800
2223W	Diesel Freight Set, *54* (2321, 6464-100, 3461-25, 3482, 6462-125, 6417-50)	1670
2225WS	Steam Work Train Set, *54* (736, 2046W, 3461-25, 3562 or 3562-25, 3620, 6460, 6419)	1018
2227W	Santa Fe Diesel Freight Set, *54* (2353P/T AA, 3562-25, 6356, 6456-75, 6468, 6417-25)	1950
2229W	NYC Freight Set, *54* (2354P/T AA, 3562-25, 6356, 6456-75, 6468, 6417-25)	1300
2231W	Southern Diesel Freight Set, *54* (2356P/C/T ABA, 6511, 6561, 3482, 6415, 6417-25)	2610
2234W	Santa Fe Diesel Passenger Set, *54* (2353P/T AA, 2530, 2531, 2532, 2533)	1046
2235W	MILW Diesel Freight Set, *55* (2338, 6436-25, 6362, 6560, 6419)	575
2237WS	Steam Freight Set, *55* (665, 6026W, 3562-50, 6464-275, 6415, 6417)	400
2239W	Illinois Central Diesel Freight Set, *55* (2363P/C AB, 6672, 6464-125, 6414, 6517)	1700
2241WS	Steam Freight Set, *55* (646, 2046W, 3359, 6446, 3620, 6417)	533
2243W	Diesel Freight Set, *55* (2321, 3662, 6511, 6462-125, 6464-300, 6417)	1400

SETS

2244W	Wabash Diesel Passenger Set, *55* (2367P/C AB, 2530, 2531, 2533)	3500 ___
2245WS	Steam Freight Set, *55* (682, 2046WX, 3562-25, 6436-25, 6561, 6560, 6419)	1152 ___
2247W	Wabash Diesel Freight Set, *55* (2367P/C AB, 6462-125, 3662, 6464-150, 3361, 6517)	2200 ___
2249WS	Steam Freight Set, *55* (736, 2046W, 6464-275, 6414, 3359, 3562-50, 6517)	800 ___
2251W	Diesel Freight Set, *55* (2331, 6464-275, 3562-50, 6414, 3359, 6517)	2000 ___
2253W	PRR Electric Freight Set, *55* (2340-25, 3361, 6464-300, 3620, 6414, 6417)	2700 ___
2254W	PRR Electric Passenger Set, *55* (2340, 2541, 2542, 2543, 2544)	5500 ___
2255W	Diesel Work Train Set, *56* (601, 3424, 6362, 6560, 6119-25)	725 ___
2257WS	Steam Freight Set, *56* (665, 2046W, 3361, 6346, 6467, 6462-125, 6427)	500 ___
2259W	NH Electric Freight Set, *56* (2350, 6464-425, 6430, 3650, 6511, 6427)	774 ___
2261WS	Steam Freight Set, *56* (646, 2046W, 3562-50, 6414, 6436-25, 6376, 6417)	570 ___
2263W	NH Electric Freight Set, *56* (2350, 3359, 6468-25, 6414, 3662, 6517)	1000 ___
2265WS	Steam Freight Set, *56* (736, 2046W, 3620, 3424, 6430, 6467, 6517)	675 ___
2267W	Diesel Freight Set, *56* (2331, 3562-50, 3359, 3361, 6560, 6419-50)	1700 ___
2269W	B&O Diesel Freight Set, *56* (2368P/C AB, 3356, 6518, 6315, 3361, 6517)	3200 ___
2270W	Jersey Central Diesel Passenger Set, *56* (2341, 2531, 2532, 2533)	5000 ___
2271W	PRR Electric Freight Set, *56* (2360-25, 3424, 3662, 6414, 6418, 6417)	2200 ___
2273W	MILW Diesel Freight Set, *56* (2378P/C AB, 342, 6342, 3562-50, 3662, 3359, 6517)	3500 ___
2274W	PRR Electric Passenger Set, *56* (2360, 2541, 2542, 2543, 2544)	3000 ___
2275W	Wabash Diesel Freight Set, *57* (2339, 3444, 6464-475, 6425, 6427)	790 ___
2276W	Budd RDC Set, *57* (404, two 2559)	2200 ___
2277WS	Steam Work Train Set, *57* (665, 2046W, 6446-25, 3650, 6560-25, 6119-75)	500 ___
2279W	NH Electric Freight Set, *57* (2350, 3424, 6464-425, 6424, 6477, 6427)	680 ___
2281W	Santa Fe Diesel Freight Set, *57* (2243P/C AB, 6464-150, 3361, 3562-75, 6560-25, 6119-75)	1052 ___
2283WS	Steam Freight Set, *57* (646, 2046W, 3424, 3361, 6464-525, 6562-50, 6357)	750 ___
2285W	Diesel Freight Set, *57* (2331, 6418, 6414, 6425, 3662, 6517)	2000 ___
2287W	MILW Electric Freight Set, *57* (2351, 342, 6342, 6464-500, 3650, 6315, 6427)	2000 ___

			Exc
2289WS	Super O Steam Freight Set, *57* (736, 2046W, 3359, 3494-275, 3361, 6430, 6427)		1184
2291W	Super O Rio Grande Diesel Freight Set, *57* (2379P/C AB, 3562-75, 3530, 3444, 6464-525, 6657)		1963
2292WS	Super O Steam Passenger Set, *57* (646, 2046W, 2530, 2531, 2532, 2533)		2000
2293W	Super O PRR Electric Freight Set, *57* (2360, 3662, 3650, 6414, 6518, 6417)		2900
2295WS	Super O Steam Freight Set, *57* (746, 746W, 342, 6342, 3530, 3361, 6560-25, 6419-100)		2288
2296W	Super O CP Diesel Passenger Set, *57* (2373P/T AA, 2551, 2552, 2553, 2554)		4670
2297WS	Super O Steam Freight Set, *57* (746, 746W, 264, 6264, 3356, 3662, 345, 6342, 6517)		2300
2501W	Super O Diesel Work Train Set, *58* (2348, 6464-525, 6802, 6560-25, 6119-100)		800
2502W	Super O Budd RDC Set, *58* (400, 2550, 2559)		2000
2503WS	Super O Steam Freight Set, *58* (665, 2046W, 3361, 6434, 6801, 6536, 6357)		550
2505W	Super O Electric Freight Set, *58* (2329, 6805, 6519, 6800, 6464-500, 6357)		1400
2507W	Super O Diesel Freight Set, *58* (2242P/C AB, 3444, 6464-425, 6424, 6468-25, 6357)		2000
2509WS	Super O Steam Freight Set, *58* (665, 2046W, 6414, 3650, 6464-475, 6805, 6357)		800
2511W	Super O Electric Work Set, *58* (2352, 3562-75, 3424, 3361, 6560-25, 6119-100)		1100
2513W	Super O Electric Freight Set, *58* (2329, 6556, 6425, 6414, 6434, 3359, 6427-60)		3000
2515WS	Super O Steam Freight Set, *58* (646, 2046W, 3662, 6424, 3444, 6800, 6427)		785
2517W	Super O Rio Grande Diesel Freight Set, *58* (2379P/C AB, 6519, 6805, 6434, 6800, 6657)		2550
2518W	Super O PRR Electric Passenger Set, *58* (2352, 2531, 2533, 2534)		1848
2519W	Super O Diesel Freight Set, *58* (2331, 6434, 3530, 6801, 6414, 6464-275, 6557)		1900
2521WS	Super O Steam Freight Set, *58* (746, 746W, 6805, 3361, 6430, 3356, 6424, 6557)		2000
2523W	Super O Santa Fe Diesel Freight Set, *58* (2383P/T AA, 264, 6264, 6434, 6800, 3662, 6517)		1300
2525WS	Super O Steam Work Train Set, *58* (746, 746W, 342, 345, 6519, 6518, 6560-25, 6419-100)		2300
2526W	Super O Santa Fe Diesel Passenger Set, *58* (2383P/T AA, 2530, 2531, two 2532)		1750
2527	Super O Missile Launcher Set, *59–60* (44, 3419, 6844, 6823, 6814, 943)		925
2528WS	Super O General Set, *59–61* (1872, 1872T, 1877, 1876, 1875W)		824
2529W	Super Electric Work Train Set, *59* (2329, 3512, 6819, 6812, 6560, 6119-25 or 6119-100)		1300

SETS		Exc
2531WS	Super O Steam Freight Set, *59* (637, 2046W, 3435, 6817, 6636, 6825, 6119-100)	1300____
2533W	Super O GN Electric Freight Set, *59* (2358, 6650, 6414, 3444, 6470, 6357)	1910____
2535WS	Super O Steam Freight Set, *59* (665, 2046W, 3434, 6823, 3672, 6812, 6357)	905____
2537W	Super O NH Diesel Freight Set, *59* (2242P/C AB, 3435, 3650, 6464-275, 6819, 6427)	2500____
2539WS	Super O Steam Freight Set, *59* (665, 2046W, 3361, 6464-825, 3512, 6812, 6357, 464)	1015____
2541W	Super O Santa Fe Diesel Freight Set, *59* (2383P/T AA, 3356, 3512, 6519, 6816, 6427)	2400____
2543WS	Super O Steam Freight Set, *59* (736, 2046W, 264, 6264, 3435, 6823, 6434, 6812, 6557)	1590____
2544W	Super O Santa Fe Diesel Passenger Set, *59–60* (2383P/T AA, 2530, 2561, 2562, 2563)	2500____
2545WS	Super O Military Set, *59* (746, 746W, 175, 6175, 6470, 3419, 6650, 3540, 6517)	3000____
2547WS	Super O Steam Freight Set, *60* (637, 2046W, 3330, 6475, 6361, 6357)	673____
2549W	Super O Military Set, *60* (2349, 3540, 6470, 6819, 6650, 3535)	1160____
2551W	Super O GN Electric Freight Set, *60* (2358, 6828, 3512, 6827, 6736, 6812, 6427)	2300____
2553WS	Super O Steam Freight Set, *60* (736, 2046W, 3830, 3435, 3419, 3672, 6357)	1613____
2555W	Super O Santa Fe Freight Set with matching HO Set, *60* (2383P/T AA, 3434, 3366, 6414, 6464-900, 6357-50)	10000____
2570	Super O Santa Fe Work Train Set, *61* (616, 6822, 6828, 6812, 6736, 6130)	800____
2571	Super O Steam Freight Set, *61* (637, 736W, 3419, 6445, 6361, 6119-100)	550____
2572	Super O B&M Diesel Freight Set, *61* (2359, 6544, 3830, 6448, 3519, 3535)	800____
2573	Super O Steam Freight Set, *61* (736, 736W, 3545, 6416, 6475, 6440, 6357)	1400____
2574	Super O Santa Fe Diesel Freight Set, *61* (2383P/T AA, 3665, 3419, 3830, 448, 6448, 6437)	1500____
2575	Super O PRR Electric Freight Set, *61* (2360, 6530, 6828, 6464-900, 6827, 6736, 6560, 6437)	2500____
2576	Super O Santa Fe Diesel Passenger Set, *61* (2383P/T AA, 2561, two 2562, 2563)	3030____
4109WS	Electronic Control Set, *46* (671R, 4424W, 4452, 4454, 5459, 4457)	1085____
4110WS	Electronic Control Set, *48–49* (671R, 4671W, 4452, 4454, 5459, 4357, 151, 97)	2500____
11201	027 Steam Freight Set, *62* (242, 1060T, 6042-75, 6502, 6047)	125____
11011	027 Diesel Freight Set, *62* (222, 3510, 6076, 6120)	147____
11212	027 Santa Fe Diesel Freight Set, *62* (633, 3349, 6825, 6057)	375____

			Exc
11222	027 Steam Freight Set, *62*		
___	(236, 1050T, 3357, 6343, 6119-100)		195
11232	027 NH Diesel Freight Set, *62*		
___	(232, 3410, 6062, 6413, 6057-50)		500
11242	027 Steam Freight Set, *62*		
___	(233, 233W, 6465-100, 6476, 6162, 6017)		177
11252	027 Texas Special Space Set, *62*		
___	211P/T AA, 3509, 6448, 3349, 6463, 6057)		500
11268	027 C&O Diesel Freight Set, *62*		
___	(2365, 3619, 3470, 3349, 6501, 6017)		1425
11278	027 Steam Freight Set, *62*		
___	(2037, 233W, 6473, 6162, 6050-110, 6825, 6017)		260
11288	027 Space Set, *62*		
___	(229P/C AB, 3413, 6512, 6413, 6463, 6059)		1215
11298	027 Steam Freight Set, *62*		
___	(2037, 233W, 6544, 3419, 6448, 3330, 6017)		500
11308	027 Santa Fe Diesel Passenger Set, *62*		
___	(218P/T AA, two 2412, 2414, 2416)		730
11311	027 Steam Freight Set, *63*		
___	(1062, 1061T, 6409-25, 6076-100, 6167-25)		100
11321	027 Rio Grande Diesel Freight Set, *63*		
___	(221, 3309, 6076-75, 6042-75, 6167-50)		300
11331	027 Steam Freight Set, *63*		
___	(242, 1060T, 6473, 6476-25, 6142, 6059-50)		100
11341	027 Santa Fe Diesel Freight Set, *63*		
___	(634, 3410, 6407, 6014-325, 6463, 6059-50)		950
11351	027 Steam Freight Set, *63*		
___	(237, 1060T, 6050-100, 6465-150, 6408, 6162, 6119-110)		190
11361	027 Texas Special Space Set, *63*		
___	(211P/T AA, 3665-100, 3413-150, 6470, 6413, 6257-100)		750
11375	027 Steam Freight Set, *63*		
___	(238, 234W, 6822-50, 6465-150, 6414-150, 6476-75, 6162, 6257-100)		700
11385	027 Santa Fe Space Set, *63*		
___	(223P/218C AB, 3619-100, 3470-100, 3349-100, 3830-75, 6407, 6257-100 or 6017-235)		2000
11395	027 Steam Freight Set, *63*		
___	(2037, 233W or 234W, 6464-725, 6469-50, 6536, 6440-50, 6560-50, 6119-100)		600
11405	027 Santa Fe Diesel Passenger Set, *63*		
___	(218P/T AA, two 2412, 2414, 2416)		750
11420	027 Steam Freight Set, *64*		
___	(1061, 1061T, 6042-250, 6167-25)		100
11430	027 Steam Freight, *64*		
___	(1062, 1061T, 6176, 6142, 6167-125)		116
11440	027 Rio Grande Diesel Freight Set, *64*		
___	(221, 3309, 6176-50, 6142-125, 6167-100)		200
11450	027 Steam Freight Set, *64*		
___	(242, 1060T, 6473, 6142-75, 6176-50, 6059-50)		197
11460	027 Steam Freight Set, *64*		
___	(238, 234W, 6014-335, 6465-150, 6142-100, 6176-75, 6119-100)		150
11470	027 Steam Freight Set, *64*		
___	(237, 1060T, 6014-335, 6465-150, 6142-100, 6176-75, 6119-100)		150

		Exc
SETS		
11480	027 Diesel Freight Set, *64* (213P/T AA, 6473, 6176-50, 6142-150, 6014-335, 6257-100 or 6059)	560____
11490	027 Diesel Passenger Set, *64–65* (212P/T AA, 2404, 2405, 2406)	360____
11500	027 Steam Freight Set, *64* (2029, 234W, 6465-150, 6402-50, 6176-75, 6014-335, 6257-100 or 6059)	275____
11500	027 Steam Freight Set, *65* (2029, 234W, 6465-150, 6402-50, 6076, 6014-335, 6257-100 or 6059)	275____
11500	027 Steam Freight Set, *66* (2029, 234W, 6465-150, 6402-50, 6176-75, 6014-335, 6059)	275____
11510	027 Steam Freight Set, *64* (2029, 1060T, 6465-150, 6402-50, 6176-75, 6014-335, 6257-100 or 6059)	300____
11520	027 Steam Freight Set, *65–66* (242, 1062T, 6176, 3362/64, 6142, 6059)	122____
11530	027 Santa Fe Diesel Freight, *65–66* (634, 6014, 6142, 6402, 6130)	150____
11540	027 Steam Freight Set, *65–66* (239, 242T, 6473, 6465, 6176, 6119-100)	155____
11550	027 Steam Freight Set, *65–66* (239, 234W, 6473, 6465, 6176, 6119)	165____
11560	027 Texas Special Freight Set, *65–66* (211P/T AA, 6473, 6076, 6142, 6465, 6059)	215____
11590	027 Santa Fe Diesel Passenger Set, *66* (212P/T AA, 2408, 2409, 2410)	651____
11600	027 Steam Freight Set, *68* (2029, 234W, 6014, 6476, 6315, 6560, 6130)	700____
11710	027 Steam Freight Set, *69* (1061, 1061T or 1062T, 6402, 6142, 6059)	170____
11720	Diesel Freight Set, *69* (2024, 6142, 6402, 6176, 6057)	239____
11730	027 UP Diesel Freight Set, *69* (645, 6402, 6014-85, 6176, 6142, 6167-85)	300____
11740	027 RI Diesel Freight Set, *69* (2041P/T AA, 6315, 6142, 6014-410, 6476, 6057)	300____
11750	027 Steam Freight Set, *69* (2029, 234T, 6014-85, 6476, 6473, 6315, 6130)	400____
11760	027 Steam Freight Set, *69* (2029, 234W, 6014-410, 6315, 6476, 3376, 6119)	355____
12502	Prairie-Rider Gift Pack, *62* (1862, 1862T, 3376, 1877 or 6473, 1866, 1865)	600____
12512	Enforcer Gift Pack, *62* (45, 3413, 3619, 3470, 3349, 6017)	1100____
12700	Steam Freight Set, *64* (736, 736W, 6464-725, 6162-100, 6414-75, 6476-125, 6437, no transformer)	1000____
12710	Steam Freight Set, *64–66* (736, 736W, 6464-725, 6162-100, 6414-75, 6476-125, 6437, LW transformer)	1150____
12720	Santa Fe Diesel Freight Set, *64* (2383P/T AA, 6464-725, 6162-100, 6414-75, 6476-125, 6437, no transformer)	1500____

			Exc
	12730	Santa Fe Diesel Freight Set, *64–66* (2383P/T AA, 6464-725, 6162-100, 6414-75, 6476-125, 6437, LW transformer)	1140
	12740	Santa Fe Diesel Freight Set, *64* (2383P/T AA, 3662, 6361, 6436-110, 6315-60, 6464-525, 6822, 6437)	1500
	12760	Steam Freight Set, *64* (736, 736W, 3662, 6361, 6436-110, 6315-60, 6464-525, 6822, 6437)	1100
	12780	Santa Fe Diesel Passenger, *64–66* (2383P/T AA, 2521, 2522, two 2523)	1853
	12800	B&M Diesel Freight Set, *65–66* (2346, 6428, 6436, 6464-475, 6415, 6017-100)	512
	12820	Diesel Freight Set, *65* (2322, 3662, 6822, 6361, 6464-725, 6436, 6315, 6437)	1525
	12840	Steam Freight Set, *66* (665, 736W, 6464-375, 6464-450, 6431, 6415, 6437)	925
	12850	Diesel Freight Set, *66* (2322, 3662, 6822, 6361, 6464-725, 6436, 6315, 6437)	1700
	13008	Super O Steam Freight Set, *62* (637, 736W, 3349, 6448, 6501, 6119-100)	500
	13018	Super O Santa Fe Diesel Freight Set, *62* (616, 6500, 6650, 3519, 6448, 6017-235)	1200
	13028	Super O Space Set, *62* (2359, 3665, 3349, 3820, 3470, 6017-100)	1000
	13036	Super O General Set, *62* (1872, 1872T, 6445, 3370, 1876, 1875W)	980
	13048	Super O Steam Freight Set, *62* (736, 736W, 6822, 6414, 6440, 6437)	720
	13058	Super O Space Set, *62* (2383P/T AA, 3619, 3413, 6512, 470, 6470, 6437)	1600
	13068	Super O PRR Electric Freight Set, *62* (2360, 6464-725, 6828, 6416, 6827, 6530, 6475, 6437)	3200
	13078	Super O PRR Electric Passenger Set, *62* (2360, 2521, two 2522, 2523)	3500
	13088	Super O Santa Fe Diesel Passenger Set, *62* (2383P/T AA, 2521, two 2522, 2523)	2500
	13098	Super O Steam Freight Set, *63* (637, 736W, 6469, 6464-900, 6414, 6446, 6447)	2000
	13108	Super O Santa Fe Space Set, *63* (617, 3665, 3419, 6448, 3830, 3470, 6119-100)	1000
	13118	Super O Steam Freight Set, *63* (736, 736W, 6446-60, 6827, 3362, 6315-60, 6560, 6429)	1500
	13128	Super O Santa Fe Space Set, *63* (2383P/T AA, 3619, 3413, 6512, 448, 6448, 64337)	1750
	13138	Super O PRR Electric Freight Set, *63* (2360, 6464-725, 6828, 6416, 6827, 6315-60, 6436-110, 6437)	3800
	13148	Super O Santa Fe Diesel Passenger Set, *63* (2383P/T AA, 2521, 2522, two 2523)	2500
	13150	Super O Hudson Steam Freight Set, *64* (773, 736W or 773W, 3434, 6361, 3662, 6415, 3356, 6436-110, 6437)	2500

ABBREVIATIONS

Descriptions

AAR	Association of American Railroads (truck type)
AEC	Atomic Energy Commission
AF	American Flyer
CC	Command Control
DD	Double-door
EMD	Electro-Motive Division
ETD	End-of-train device
FARR	Famous American Railroad Series
FF	Fallen Flag Series
FM	Fairbanks-Morse
GE	General Electric
LL	Lionel Lines
MOW	Maintenance-of-way
MU	Multiple unit (commuter cars)
O	Lionel gauge (1¼" between outside rails)
OO	Lionel gauge (¾" between outside rails)
PFE	Pacific Fruit Express
REA	Railway Express Agency
SSS	Service Station Special
std	Standard gauge (2⅛" between outside rails)
std O	Standard O (scale length and dimension)
TMCC	TrainMaster Command Control
USMC	United States Marine Corps
1-D	One dome
2-D	Two dome
3-D	Three dome

ABBREVIATIONS

Railroad names

ACL	Atlantic Coast Line
ATSF	Atchison, Topeka & Santa Fe
B&A	Boston & Albany
BAR	Bangor & Aroostook
B&LE	Bessemer & Lake Erie
B&M	Boston & Maine
BN	Burlington Northern
BNSF	Burlington Northern Santa Fe
B&O	Baltimore & Ohio
C&IM	Chicago & Illinois Midland
C&EI	Chicago & Eastern Illinois
CB&Q	Chicago, Burlington & Quincy
CMStP&P	Chicago, Milwaukee, St. Paul & Pacific
CN	Canadian National
CNJ	Central of New Jersey
C&IM	Chicago & Illinois Midland
C&NW	Chicago & North Western
C&O	Chesapeake & Ohio
CP	Canadian Pacific
D&H	Delaware & Hudson
DL&W	Delaware, Lackawanna & Western
DM&IR	Duluth, Missabe & Iron Range
D&RGW	Denver & Rio Grande Western
D&TS	Detroit & Toledo Shore Line
DT&I	Detroit, Toledo & Ironton
EJ&E	Elgin, Joliet & Eastern
Erie-Lack.	Erie-Lackawanna
FEC	Florida East Coast
GM&O	Gulf, Mobile & Ohio
GN	Great Northern
GTW	Grand Trunk Western
IC	Illinois Central
ICG	Illinois Central Gulf
KCS	Kansas City Southern
L&N	Louisville & Nashville
LIRR	Long Island Railroad
LNAC	Louisville, New Albany & Corydon

Build Your Toy Train Library

MAR '17

Track Plans for Lionel FasTrack

This one-stop resource for Lionel FasTrack includes 25 mostly small- and mid-sized plans collected from the pages of *Classic Toy Trains* magazine as well as new plans. Each plan includes a description, an illustration of the layout, and a list of FasTrack components. You'll also find essential track planning tips and learn how to adapt existing track plans to FasTrack.

10-8804 • $16.99

Greenberg's *Repair and Operating Manual for Lionel Trains, 1945–1969, Seventh Edition*

Get 1,000+ repair and maintenance tips for Lionel locomotives, operating cars, accessories, transformers, light bulbs, and switches. Provides technical advice as well as handy techniques submitted by toy train collectors and operators.

10-8160 • $24.95

American Flyer Pocket Price Guide 1946-2017

This essential pocket-sized guide provides accurate, current market values for American Flyer S gauge trains and accessories manufactured by A.C. Gilbert and Lionel. It also contains ready-to-run S gauge trains from contemporary manufacturers like American Models and MTH. This functional, easy-to-read volume is published every other year and is a valuable and reliable source of pricing information.

10-8617 • $15.99

Buy now from your local hobby shop!
Shop at KalmbachHobbyStore.com

KALMBACH BOOKS

P28140

Railroad names

LV	Lehigh Valley
MD&W	Minnesota, Dakota & Western
MKT	Missouri-Kansas-Texas
MN&S	Minneapolis, Northfield & Southern
MP	Missouri Pacific
MPA	Maryland & Pennsylvania
MILW	Milwaukee Road
I&StL	Minneapolis & St. Louis
&StL	Nashville, Chattanooga & St. Louis
deM	Nacionales de Mexico Railway
NH	New Haven
NKP	Nickel Plate Road
NP	Northern Pacific
NS	Norfolk Southern
&W	Norfolk & Western
YC	New York Central
&H	New York, New Haven & Hartford
&W	New York, Ontario & Western
PC	Penn Central
&E	Peoria & Eastern
LE	Pittsburgh & Lake Erie
RR	Pennsylvania Railroad
&P	Richmond, Fredericksburg & Potomac
RI	Rock Island
RCO	San Manuel Arizona Railroad Company
SP	Southern Pacific
SP&S	Spokane, Portland & Seattle
TA&G	Tennessee, Alabama & Georgia
TH&B	Toronto, Hamilton & Buffalo
T&P	Texas & Pacific
TP&W	Toledo, Peoria & Western
UP	Union Pacific
V&TRR	Virginia & Truckee Railroad
W&ARR	Western & Atlantic Railroad
WM	Western Maryland
WP	Western Pacific